OFFICE FOR
**NATIONAL
STATISTICS**

D1824994

Regional Trends 33

1998 edition

Editor :	John Pullinger
Associate Editor :	Alison Holding
Production team :	Jan Kiernan
	Martin Smith
	Mario Alemanno
	Nicola Amaranayake
	Eimear Schlindwein
	Max Bonini
	Betty Ankamah
Design & artwork :	Michelle Franco
Maps :	Alistair Dent
	Alan Smith

London: The Stationery Office

The *Regional Focus* series

Britain's countries and regions in the spotlight...

car ownership...crime...the economy...education...the environment...labour market...
population...transport...training...

Complementing the full regional overview provided each year by *Regional Trends*, there is now a
range of publications focusing on individual countries or regions of the UK.

The *Regional Focus* series presents regional, county and district-level data for the Government Office
Regions of England or the country in question. The series is produced by the Office for National
Statistics, the Welsh Office and the Northern Ireland Statistics and Research Agency.

Now available:

Focus on London 98
price £39.50 (*£29.50 to schools
and colleges*)
ISBN 0 11 621030 3
(published 1998)

Focus on Northern Ireland
price £30
ISBN 0 11 620772 8
(published 1997)

Focus on the South East
price £30 (*£19.50 to schools
and colleges*)
ISBN 0 11 620921 6
(published 1997)
(*covers the area of: Berkshire,
Buckinghamshire, East Sussex,
Hampshire, Isle of Wight, Kent,
Oxfordshire, Surrey and West Sussex*)

A Statistical Focus on Wales
price £10
ISBN 075 041 6815
(published 1996)

Due for publication in October 1998:

Focus on the East Midlands
price £19.95
ISBN 0 11 620718 3
(published 1995)
(*covers the area of: Derbyshire,
Leicestershire, Lincolnshire,
Northamptonshire and
Nottinghamshire*)

Focus on the South West

(*covering the area of: the former county of Avon,
Cornwall, Devon, Dorset, Gloucestershire, Somerset
and Wiltshire*)

All titles are available from:

**The Stationery Office
Publications Centre
PO Box 276
London SW8 5DT**

tel 0171 873 9090
fax 0171 873 8200

Contents

Contents

Regional Trends 33, © Crown copyright 1998

Contents

* Indicates related data available in the sub-regional tables in Chapters 14 to 17.

Symbols and
conventions

Reference years. Where a choice of years has to be made, the most recent year or a run of recent years is shown together with the past population census years (1991, 1981 etc) and sometimes the mid-points between census years (1986 etc). Other years may be added if they represent a peak or trough in the series.

Rounding of figures. In tables where figures have been rounded to the nearest final digit, there may be an apparent discrepancy between the sum of the constituent items and the total as shown.

Billion. This term is used to represent a thousand million.

Provisional and estimated data. Some data for the latest year (and occasionally for earlier years) are provisional or estimated. To keep footnotes to a minimum, these have not been indicated; source departments will be able to advise if revised data are available.

Survey data. Many of the tables and charts in *Regional Trends* present the results of household surveys which can be subject to large sampling error. Care should therefore be taken in drawing conclusions about regional differences.

Non-calendar years.
Financial year - eg 1 April 1996 - 31 March 1997 would be shown as 1996-97
Academic year - eg September 1996/July 1997 would be shown as 1996/97
Data covering more than one year - eg 1994, 1995 and 1996 would be shown as 1994-1996

Units. Figures are shown in italics when they represent percentages.

Symbols. The following symbols have been used throughout *Regional Trends*:
..	*not available*
.	*not applicable*
-	*negligible (less than half the final digit shown)*
0	*nil*

Introduction

Regional Trends provides a unique description of the regions of the United Kingdom. In 17 chapters it covers a wide range of demographic, social, industrial and economic statistics, taking a look at most aspects of life. The chapters fall broadly into four sections: regional profiles (Chapter 1), the European Union (Chapter 2), the main topic areas (Chapters 3 to 13) and sub-regional statistics (Chapters 14 to 17). To make it easy to understand the differences between regions, information is given in clear tables, maps and charts.

Regional statistics are essential for a wide range of people: for example, policy-makers and planners in both the public and private sectors; marketing professionals; researchers; students and teachers; journalists; and anyone with general regional interests. *Regional Trends* brings together data from diverse sources and, for some topics, is the only publication where data for the whole of the United Kingdom are available in one place. Indeed, wherever systems/data sources for the four countries of the United Kingdom are sufficiently comparable, figures have been aggregated to give a national average/total.

Recent changes in regional statistics

In 1994, Government Offices for the Regions of England were established based on the functions of the then four departments of Environment, Transport, Employment, and Trade and Industry. The Government Offices work in partnership with local people to maximise competitiveness, prosperity and quality of life in each region. Following public consultation, the decision was taken that with effect from April 1997 the Government Office Regions (GORs) would replace the Standard Statistical Regions as the primary classification for the presentation of English regional statistics. This is the second edition of *Regional Trends* to use the GOR classification, although there remain a few cases where the transition has not yet been made. A table showing the relationship between the GORs and the SSRs is included on page 12.

The effect of the change to the regional classification is that it has not always been possible to provide historic data for comparison/long-term trend analysis, although short-term trends are given where possible. The 1997 edition of *Regional Trends* provided the link year between the two classifications with most items being available for both GORs and SSRs – the GOR data in the published volume and the SSR data available from the Regional Reporting Branch at the address given overleaf.

Although Merseyside currently has its own Government Office, for statistical purposes it has not been adopted as a region in its own right because of the difficulties associated with obtaining the full range of data for a relatively small area, notably household surveys where the sample sizes are too small to provide reliable estimates. Wherever possible, however, figures for the two components of the North West and Merseyside region are given separately.

As last year, there are separate chapters for the presentation of the sub-regional statistics following the recent local government reorganisations in England, Wales and Scotland. Chapter 15 on Wales and Chapter 16 on Scotland present data for the Unitary Authorities (UAs) and the New Councils respectively which replaced the former two-tier systems on 1 April 1996. Chapter 17 on Northern Ireland continues to give figures at Board or district level as available.

The local government reorganisation in England has been more complex than in Wales and Scotland and has been introduced over a period of four years, 1995 to 1998. The first phase was in April 1995 when the Isle of Wight became a UA. In April 1996 three counties – Avon, Cleveland and Humberside – were abolished altogether in favour of UAs. In the case of Cleveland, the districts simply became UAs (one with a change of name), but in Avon and Humberside there were reductions in the number of UAs compared with the former districts. North Yorkshire was the one other county where local government was reorganised in April 1996: an extended York became a UA, while the rest of the county retained its two-tier system of local government administration – County Council and Local Authority Districts (LADs).

The third phase came into effect on 1 April 1997, with one or two LADs in each of Durham, Derbyshire, Leicestershire, Staffordshire, Bedfordshire, Buckinghamshire, East Sussex, Hampshire, Dorset and Wiltshire changing their status to become UAs. The final phase came into effect on 1 April 1998 and involved the counties of Berkshire, Cambridgeshire, Cheshire, Devon, Essex, Hereford and Worcester, Kent, Lancashire and Nottinghamshire. The tables in Chapter 14 give data for the local government structure in England as at 1 April 1997 and the maps in the regional profiles in Chapter 1 and on page 165 show the boundaries of the counties/ UAs as at that date.

A Gazetteer is available on request from the ONS Regional Reporting Branch. This has been prepared to assist users adapt to the GORs and the new structure of local government – notably in England where there is the mixture of UAs and two-tier systems. Although the local government structure in Northern Ireland has not been reorganised, the Gazetteer covers the United Kingdom for completeness. It lists every area in the old/new geographies (in alphabetical order of the old district geography within each of the four countries) giving its status and which (former/new) county, SSR and GOR it is in.

Regional boundaries

Apart from the GORs which are used as far as is possible throughout, there are a number of other regional classifications used in *Regional Trends 33*. Maps of these non-standard regions are given on pages 214 and 215 of the Notes and Definitions. Maps of the statistical regions of the United Kingdom and the sub-regions in each of the four countries are given in Chapters 1 and 14 to 17. The United Kingdom comprises Great Britain and Northern Ireland; Great Britain consists of England, Wales and Scotland. The Isle of Man and the Channel Isles are not part of the United Kingdom. The Scilly Isles are included as part of Cornwall throughout.

Coverage and definitions

Due to variations in coverage and definitions, some care may be needed when comparing data from more than one source. Readers should consult the Notes and Definitions towards the back of the book as well as reading the footnotes relevant to each table, map and chart for help in analysing trends or comparing different sources.

Sources

The source of the data is given at the foot of each table, map and chart. Much of the information included in the Population and Households and the Labour market chapters of *Regional Trends* can be found on NOMIS, the on-line database run by Durham University under contract to the Office for National Statistics (ONS). It contains government statistics down to the smallest available geographic area which may be unpublished elsewhere. The ONS' publication *Social Trends* (published by The Stationery Office) contains further details on many of the topics covered in this book, generally at national level only.

Regional and sub-regional statistics can be found in a range of other GSS publications, statistical bulletins and regular press releases. Details of these sources are contained in the ONS' *Guide to Official Statistics* (published by The Stationery Office). In late summer 1998, the ONS will launch *StatBase*, a database of information about sources of statistics together with some key social and economic statistics. *StatBase* will be accessible via the internet. Further information can be obtained from the *StatBase* helpline on 0171 533 5672.

Availability on electronic media

The complete set of data contained in this edition of *Regional Trends* is available on diskette. The data from the 1997 edition for the Standard Statistical Regions are also available. For more information, please contact the Regional Reporting Branch on the number below.

The first 30 editions of *Regional Trends* are available on CD-ROM, price £99 + VAT (£49 + VAT for public libraries and academia). To order a copy, please contact the ONS Sales Desk on 0171 533 5678.

From late summer 1998 onwards it will be possible to download some of the data from *Regional Trends 33* free of charge from the internet by accessing the Government Statistical Service website at www.statistics.gov.uk.

Contributors

The Editor and Associate Editor wish to thank all their colleagues in the ONS and the rest of the Government Statistical Service and all contributors in other organisations without whose help this publication would not be possible. A special thank you goes to Michelle Franco in onsdesign and to Alan Smith and Alistair Dent in the Geographic Information Systems Unit.

Regional Reporting Branch
Office for National Statistics
1 Drummond Gate
London
SW1V 2QQ

Telephone number for enquiries: 0171 533 5797/5801
FAX: 0171 533 5799
E-mail: jan.kiernan@ons.gov.uk

STANDARD STATISTICAL REGION	COUNTY#	GOVERNMENT OFFICE REGION
NORTH	Cleveland# Durham# Northumberland Tyne and Wear	NORTH EAST
	Cumbria	NORTH WEST
NORTH WEST	Cheshire# Greater Manchester Lancashire#	
	Merseyside	MERSEYSIDE
YORKSHIRE AND HUMBERSIDE	Humberside# North Yorkshire# South Yorkshire West Yorkshire	YORKSHIRE AND THE HUMBER
EAST MIDLANDS	Derbyshire# Leicestershire# Lincolnshire Northamptonshire Nottinghamshire#	EAST MIDLANDS
WEST MIDLANDS	Hereford and Worcester# Shropshire# Staffordshire# Warwickshire West Midlands	WEST MIDLANDS
EAST ANGLIA	Cambridgeshire# Norfolk Suffolk	EASTERN
	Bedfordshire# Essex# Hertfordshire	
	Greater London	LONDON
SOUTH EAST	Berkshire# Buckinghamshire# East Sussex# Hampshire# Isle of Wight# Kent# Oxfordshire Surrey West Sussex	SOUTH EAST
SOUTH WEST	Avon# Cornwall Devon# Dorset# Gloucestershire Somerset Wiltshire#	SOUTH WEST

Counties prior to local government reorganisation.

1 Regional profiles

Statistical Regions of the United Kingdom

SCOTLAND

NORTHERN IRELAND

NORTH EAST

NORTH WEST

YORKSHIRE AND THE HUMBER

MERSEYSIDE

EAST MIDLANDS

WEST MIDLANDS

WALES

EASTERN

LONDON

SOUTH WEST

SOUTH EAST

ENGLAND

——— Government Office Region boundary

North East

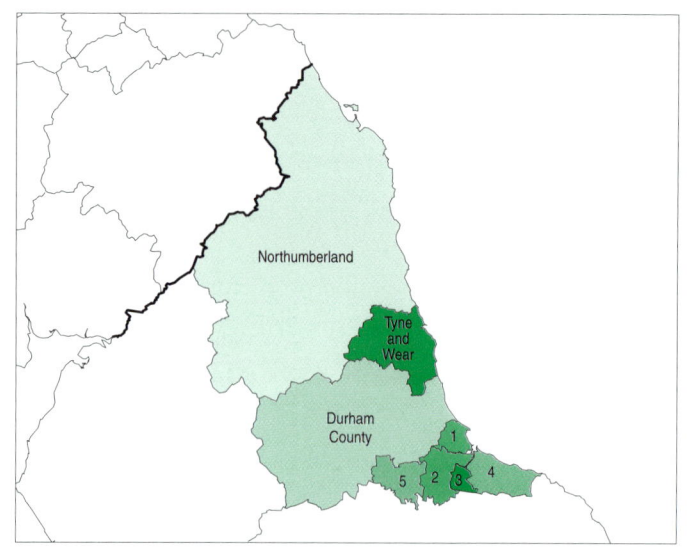

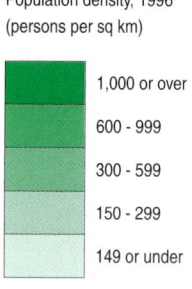

Population density, 1996
(persons per sq km)

	1,000 or over
	600 - 999
	300 - 599
	150 - 299
	149 or under

1 Hartlepool UA
2 Stockton-on-Tees UA
3 Middlesbrough UA
4 Redcar and Cleveland UA
5 Darlington UA

Population

The population of the North East fell marginally between 1991 and 1996 compared with growth of 2 per cent in the United Kingdom as a whole.

(Table 3.1)

Education

At 85 per cent in 1996/97, the North East has the highest proportion of three and four year olds in education.

(Table 4.4)

The North East has the poorest record of academic results among its 16 to 18 year olds, but the highest proportion of employers involved in Youth Training and National Vocational Qualifications.

(Tables 4.6 and 4.15)

Labour market

Nearly 40 per cent of men who worked part-time in the North East in Spring 1997 did so because they could not find a full-time job.

(Table 5.9)

The North East lost 38 days per 1,000 employees due to labour disputes in 1997, the highest of any region and nearly four times the national average.

(Table 5.13)

At Spring 1997 the North East had an ILO unemployment rate of nearly 10 per cent, the highest of any region.

(Table 5.21)

Housing

The average price of dwellings in the North East in the last quarter of 1997, at £55,000, was lower than in any other region of England and Wales except Merseyside.

(Table 6.11)

Health

Eighteen per cent of 16 to 29 year olds in the North East admitted in 1996 to having used a hallucinogenic drug in the previous year, the highest proportion in Great Britain.

(Chart 7.9)

Lifestyles

Seven in every ten households in the North East participated in the National Lottery, a higher proportion than in any other region.

(Table 8.17)

Crime

Recorded crime in the North East fell by 9 per cent between 1995 and 1996, the biggest fall of any region in England and Wales.

(Table 9.1)

Industry

On average, factories in the North East are bigger than in any other region.

(Table 13.4)

North West (GOR) and Merseyside

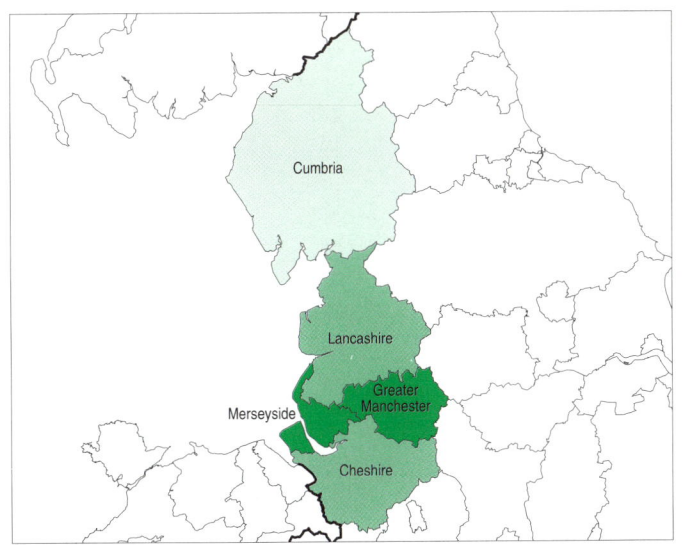

Population density, 1996
(persons per sq km)

1,000 or over

600 - 999

300 - 599

150 - 299

149 or under

Population

The population of Merseyside fell by 2 per cent between 1991 and 1996 compared with growth of nearly 1 per cent in North West and of nearly 2 per cent in the United Kingdom as a whole.

(Table 3.1)

Education and training

Female employees in Merseyside were more likely than those from any other region to have received job-related training in Spring 1997, but employers in the North West are the most likely to be involved in Investors in People.

(Tables 4.14 and 4.15)

Labour market

The economic activity rate among people of working age in the North West in Spring 1997 was 76 per cent compared with just over 71 per cent in Merseyside, the lowest rate of all the regions.

(Table 5.3)

Full-time male employees in the North West earned an average of £387 a week in April 1997, more than their counterparts in Merseyside at £382; for women, however, it was the reverse at £276 and £284 respectively.

(Table 5.17)

Housing

Over 40 per cent of households in the North West and Merseyside have secure windows and doors in their home, a higher proportion than in any other English region.

(Table 6.6)

Health

Higher rates of treated depression or anxiety are found in the North West than in any other NHS region in England or in Wales.

(Table 7.3)

Lifestyles

Nearly a quarter of households in the North West and Merseyside received Family Credit or Income Support in 1996-97.

(Table 8.7)

Crime

Recorded crime in Merseyside fell by 4 per cent between 1995 and 1996, double the fall in the North West.

(Table 9.1)

Transport

People living in the North West travel an average of nearly 6,600 miles per year, more than a third further than people living in Merseyside.

(Table 10.11)

Environment

Almost a half of the Merseyside region is Green Belt land compared with a sixth of the North West region.

(Table 11.15)

Industry

Over a fifth of gross value added in manufacturing in the North West and Merseyside was from factories of 1,000 or more employees, a higher proportion than in any other region.

(Table 13.6)

Yorkshire and the Humber

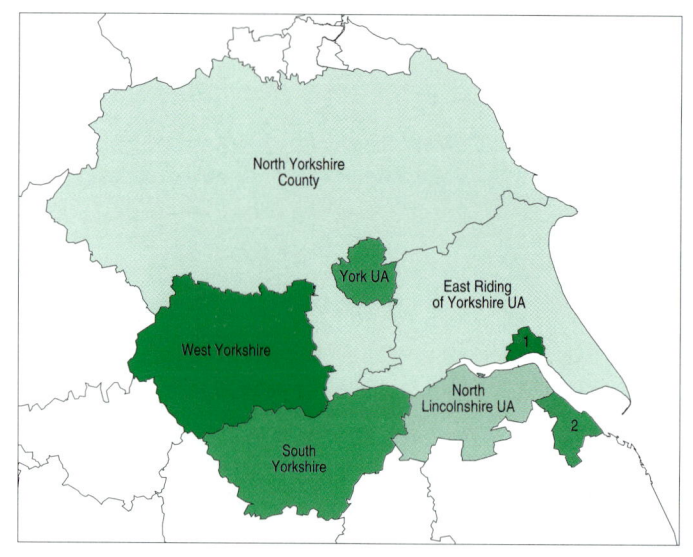

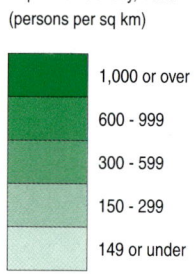

Population density, 1996
(persons per sq km)

- 1,000 or over
- 600 - 999
- 300 - 599
- 150 - 299
- 149 or under

1 Kingston-upon-Hull UA
2 North East Lincolnshire UA

Population

The population of the Yorkshire and Humber region grew by just over 1 per cent between 1991 and 1996 compared with growth of nearly 2 per cent in the United Kingdom as a whole.

(Table 3.1)

Education

The average A/AS level point score in 1995/96 was higher in Yorkshire and the Humber than in any other region in England and Wales.

(Table 4.6)

Labour market

Twenty-nine per cent of men in the Yorkshire and Humber region worked part-time in Spring 1997 because they could not find a full-time job, one of the highest proportions; for women working part-time, however, just over 8 per cent could not find a full-time job, one of the lowest proportions.

(Table 5.9)

Nearly 6 per cent of people in employment had a second job in the Yorkshire and Humber region in Spring 1997, a higher proportion than any other region except the South West.

(Table 5.11)

Housing

The average local authority rent in the Yorkshire and Humber region in April 1997 was £32 per week, the lowest in the United Kingdom.

(Table 6.9)

Health

More than two fifths of male smokers in the Yorkshire and Humber region smoke 20 or more cigarettes a day, one of the highest proportions in the United Kingdom.

(Table 7.7)

Lifestyles

Seventy seven per cent of households in Yorkshire and the Humber were in receipt of some form of Social Security Benefit in 1996-97.

(Table 8.7)

Crime

The Yorkshire and the Humber region had the highest recorded crime rate of all regions in England and Wales in 1996, and the joint lowest clear-up rate.

(Tables 9.1 and 9.3)

Transport

A higher proportion of people in the Yorkshire and the Humber region walk to work than in any other English region; however, on average they travel the shortest distance.

(Chart 10.9 and Table 10.10)

Environment

A fifth of the land of the Yorkshire and Humber region is designated as National Park.

(Table 11.15)

Agriculture

Almost a quarter of the total number of pigs in the United Kingdom were on agricultural holdings in the Yorkshire and Humber region.

(Table 13.20)

East Midlands

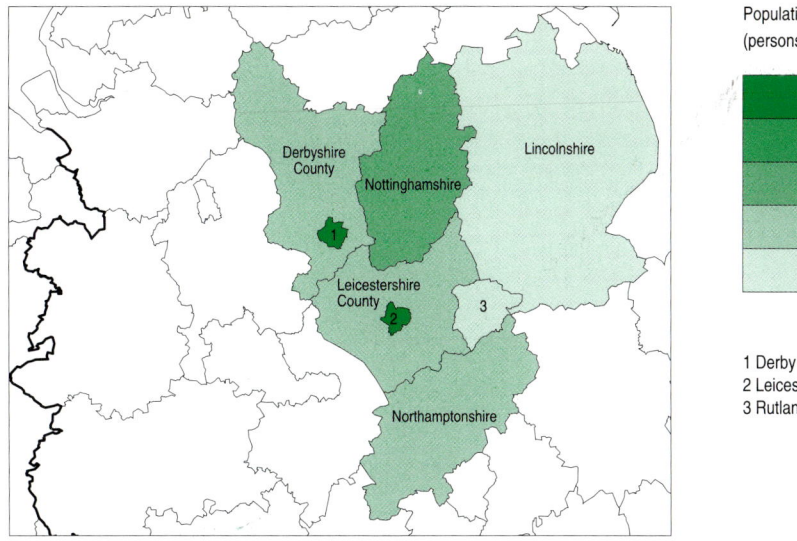

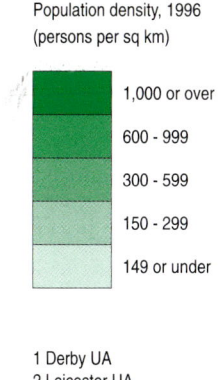

Population density, 1996
(persons per sq km)

	1,000 or over
	600 - 999
	300 - 599
	150 - 299
	149 or under

1 Derby UA
2 Leicester UA
3 Rutland UA

Population

The population of the East Midlands grew by nearly 3 per cent per cent between 1991 and 1996 compared with just under 2 per cent in the United Kingdom as a whole.

(Table 3.1)

Education

Two fifths of first degree graduates living in the East Midlands were known to be in permanent employment six months after graduating in 1996, a higher proportion than in any other region.

(Table 4.11)

Labour market

On average, women in the East Midlands work the longest paid hours for the lowest pay.

(Tables 5.17 and 14.5)

Housing

Just over seven in every ten dwellings in the East Midlands are owner occupied; one of the highest proportions in the United Kingdom.

(Table 6.3)

Householders in the East Midlands were more likely than those in any other region of England to have expressed some form of satisfaction with their accommodation in 1996-97.

(Table 6.8)

In the last quarter of 1997, detached and semi-detached houses in the East Midlands cost less, on average, than in any other English region.

(Table 6.11)

Health

Nine in every ten eligible women aged 25 to 64 in the Trent NHS region were screened for cervical cancer in the five years to 31 March 1997, a higher proportion than in any other region of England or in Wales.

(Table 7.12)

Lifestyles

People in the East Midlands on average use the most milk in the United Kingdom.

(Table 8.12)

Crime

Recorded sexual offences in the East Midlands fell by 7 per cent between 1995 and 1996, a bigger fall than in any other region in England and Wales, and the clear-up rate in 1996 was highest at 93 per cent.

(Tables 9.1 and 9.3)

People in the East Midlands travel less distance by public transport in a year than those in any other English region, but they walk further than those in any other region except in London.

(Table 10.11)

Gross domestic product

The East Midlands derived one of the highest proportions of its GDP from industry and one of the lowest shares from services.

(Map 13.1)

West Midlands

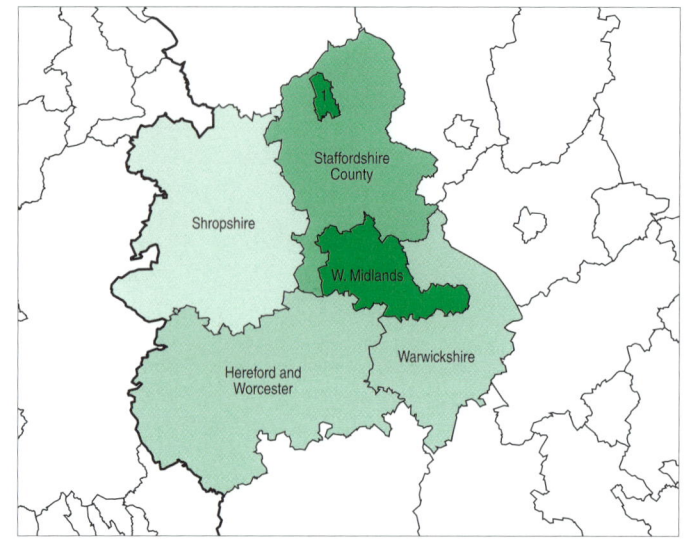

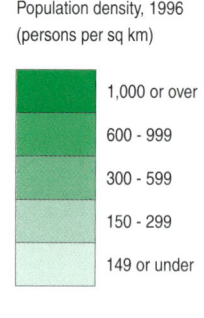

Population density, 1996
(persons per sq km)

■	1,000 or over
■	600 - 999
■	300 - 599
■	150 - 299
■	149 or under

1 Stoke-on-Trent UA

Population

The population of West Midlands rose by 1 per cent between 1991 and 1996 compared with an increase of nearly 2 per cent in the United Kingdom as a whole.

(Table 3.1)

Nine per cent of the population in the West Midlands is from an ethnic minority, the second highest proportion in Great Britain.

(Table 3.14)

Education and training

In 1997, nine out of every ten employers in the West Midlands had provided off-the-job training in the previous 12 months, the highest proportion of any region in Great Britain.

(Table 4.15)

Labour market

In 1996, almost 27 per cent of employees worked in manufacturing, a higher proportion than in any other region.

(Table 5.8)

The claimant count rate in January 1998 for local areas ranged from 3.2 per cent in Warwickshire to 6.5 per cent in the West Midlands metropolitan county.

(Map 5.24)

Health

The West Midlands had the highest infant mortality rate in 1996 at 6.8 deaths in the first year of life per 1,000 live births, compared with the UK average of 6.1.

(Table 7.2)

The West Midlands NHS region had the highest hospital throughput in 1996-97 of all the English regions in 1996-97, with nearly 43 cases treated per available bed.

(Table 7.16)

Lifestyles

Children in the West Midlands spent on average £7.60 per head per week in 1996-97, a lower amount than in any other region of Great Britain.

(Table 8.8)

Crime

The number of recorded sexual offences in the West Midlands fell by 4 per cent between 1995 and 1996, while the number of robberies rose by 4 per cent.

(Table 9.1)

Transport

One in six cars licensed to addresses in the West Midlands in 1996 was a company car, a higher proportion than in any other region.

(Table 10.1)

Industry

Manufacturing accounted for 30 per cent of gross domestic product in the West Midlands in 1996, the joint highest proportion of all the regions.

(Table 12.4)

Eastern

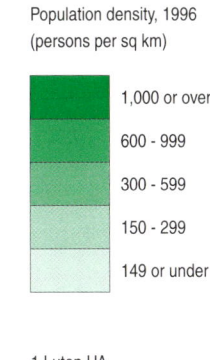

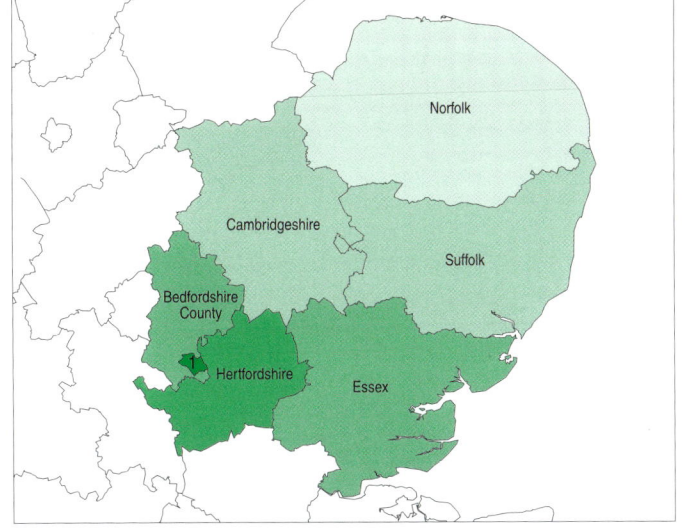

Population density, 1996
(persons per sq km)

▓	1,000 or over
▓	600 - 999
▓	300 - 599
▓	150 - 299
▓	149 or under

1 Luton UA

Population

Eastern region is one of the fastest growing regions with population growth of nearly 3 per cent between 1991 and 1996 compared with less than 2 per cent in the United Kingdom as a whole.

(Table 3.1)

Education

A little over 5 per cent of first degree graduates living in the Eastern region were believed to be unemployed six months after graduating in 1996, a lower proportion than in any other region.

(Table 4.11)

Labour market

The economic activity rate for men of working age in the Eastern region was over 87 per cent in Spring 1997, the second highest in the United Kingdom.

(Table 5.3)

Together with those in the South East (GOR), full-time employees in the Eastern region worked the longest hours in Spring 1997 (including unpaid overtime).

(Table 5.18)

Housing

In 1996, there were more new homes built per head of population in the Eastern region than in any other English region.

(Table 6.2)

Health

Seven per cent of 16 to 29 year olds in the Eastern region admitted in 1996 to having used a hallucinogenic drug in the previous year, the lowest proportion in Great Britain.

(Chart 7.9)

Social services

Two in 1,000 children under 18 were on child protection registers in the Eastern region in March 1996, the lowest rate in England, Wales or Northern Ireland.

(Table 7.22)

Lifestyles

Households in the Eastern region spent a higher proportion of their total expenditure on household goods and services in 1996-97 than those in any other region.

(Table 8.10)

Crime

The Eastern region had the lowest recorded crime rate in England and Wales in 1996 and the joint highest clear-up rate among the English regions.

(Tables 9.1 and 9.3)

Transport

People in Eastern region cycle an average of 69 miles per year, the furthest distance in Great Britain.

(Table 10.11)

Industry

Expenditure on Research and Development in the Eastern region in 1996 accounted for 3.5 per cent of gross domestic product, a higher proportion than in any other region.

(Table 13.8)

London

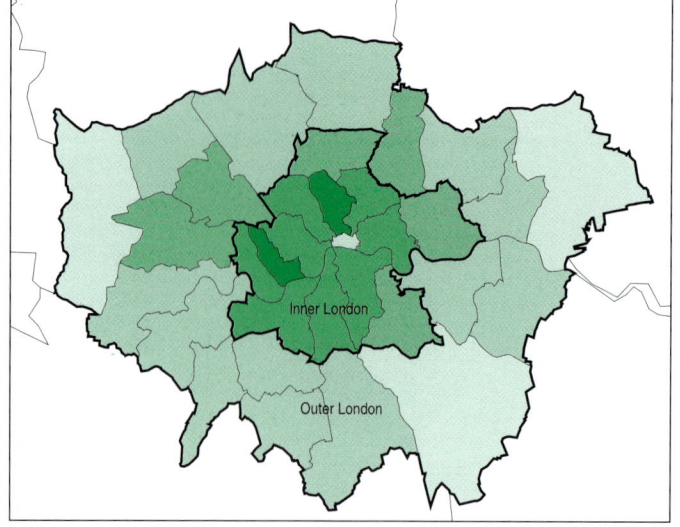

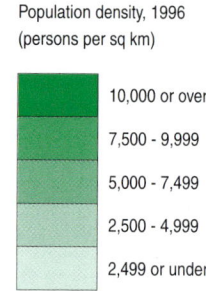

Population density, 1996
(persons per sq km)

	10,000 or over
	7,500 - 9,999
	5,000 - 7,499
	2,500 - 4,999
	2,499 or under

Population	London accounted for almost half the natural increase in the United Kingdom population between mid-1995 and mid-1996. *(Table 3.12)* Nearly half of the ethnic minority population of Great Britain lives in London, accounting for almost a quarter of the capital's population. *(Table 3.14)*
Education	London has the most highly qualified people of working age with almost 28 per cent possessing a higher education qualification in Spring 1997. *(Table 4.12)*
Labour market	London has the highest proportion of male employees in part-time employment and the lowest proportion of females. *(Table 5.9)* The average weekly wage for full-time employees in London in April 1997, at £480 per week, was almost £100 more than in any other region and £134 more than the national average. *(Table 14.5)*
Housing	Housing costs are much higher in London than elsewhere, but householders in the capital are less likely than those in any other region to be satisfied with their accommodation. *(Tables 6.8 - 6.11)*
Lifestyles	Nearly 4 per cent of people in London have a personal taxable income of £50,000 or more, while nearly a quarter of households receive Family Credit or Income Support. *(Tables 8.5 and 8.7)*
Crime	Recorded offences of violence against the person increased by 27 per cent in London between 1995 and 1996, the largest increase of any region in England and Wales. *(Table 9.1)*
Transport	Londoners walk further and travel further by public transport but drive fewer miles each year than people in any other region. *(Table 10.11)*
Environment	Almost a third of the total area of London is designated Green Belt land. *(Table 11.15)*
Industry	On average, factories in London are smaller than in any other region. *(Table 13.4)*

South East (GOR)

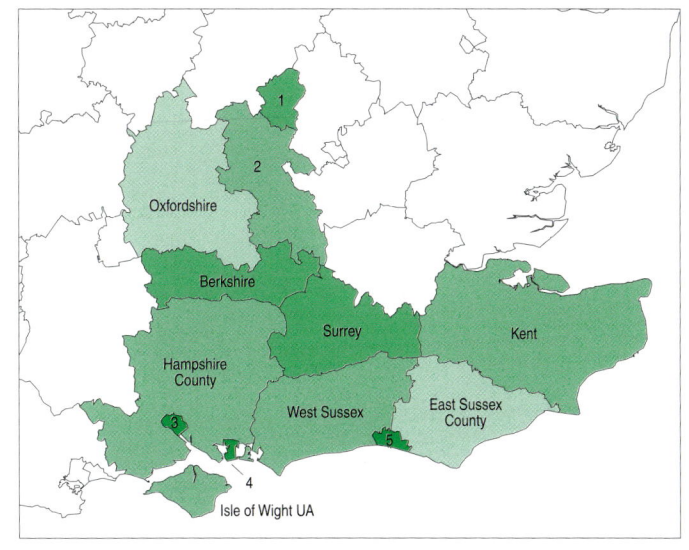

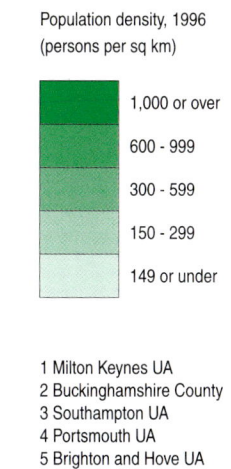

Population density, 1996
(persons per sq km)

- 1,000 or over
- 600 - 999
- 300 - 599
- 150 - 299
- 149 or under

1 Milton Keynes UA
2 Buckinghamshire County
3 Southampton UA
4 Portsmouth UA
5 Brighton and Hove UA

Population

The South East is one of the fastest growing regions with population growth of nearly 3 per cent between 1991 and 1996 compared with less than 2 per cent in the United Kingdom as a whole.

(Table 3.1)

Education and training

The South East has the lowest proportion of people of working age with no qualifications and one of the highest proportions qualified to at least A level or equivalent.

(Table 4.12)

In 1997, almost three-quarters of employers in the South East felt that the skill needs of their employees was increasing, the highest proportion of any region in Great Britain.

(Table 4.15)

Labour market

The South East has the highest economic activity rate for both males and females.

(Table 5.3)

The claimant count rate for local areas in January 1998 ranged from 1.6 per cent in Surrey to 10.3 per cent in the Isle of Wight.

(Map 5.24)

Housing

Nearly three quarters of dwellings in the South East are owner occupied, the highest proportion in the United Kingdom.

(Table 6.3)

Health

Less than one in five people in the South East reported having a limiting long-standing illness in 1996-97, a lower proportion than in any other region.

(Chart 7.4)

Lifestyles

In 1996-97, 14 per cent of households in the South East owned a Personal Equity Plan, 30 per cent stocks and shares and 36 per cent Premium Bonds, higher proportions than in any other region.

(Table 8.4)

Crime

Recorded crime in the South East fell by 2 per cent overall between 1995 and 1996 despite rises of 15 and 7 per cent respectively in recorded offences of violence against the person and robberies.

(Table 9.1)

Transport

A third of all households in the South East have two or more cars, the joint highest proportion of all the regions.

(Table 10.2)

Environment

Almost a third of the land in the South East is designated as Areas of Outstanding Natural beauty.

(Table 11.15)

South West

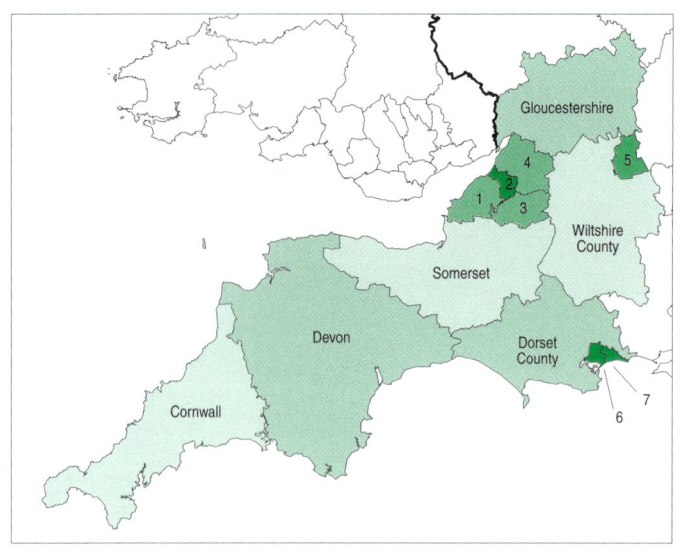

Population density, 1996
(persons per sq km)

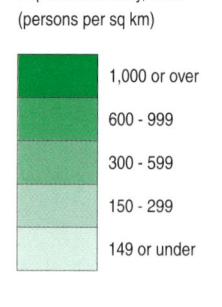

	1,000 or over
	600 - 999
	300 - 599
	150 - 299
	149 or under

1 North Somerset UA
2 City of Bristol UA
3 Bath and North East Somerset UA
4 South Gloucestershire UA
5 Swindon UA
6 Poole UA
7 Bournemouth UA

Population

Population growth in the South West has slowed in the 1990s compared with the 1980s; growth between 1991 and 1996 was only 1 percentage point more than the UK average.

(Table 3.1)

The South West has the oldest population: more than one person in five is a pensioner and more than one in 20 is aged 80 or over.

(Table 3.3)

Education and training

Almost half of pupils in their last year of compulsory schooling in the South West in 1995/96 achieved 5 or more GCSE Grades A*-C and only one in 20 achieved no graded result, together with the South East (GOR) the best record among the English regions.

(Table 4.6)

Labour market

Over 5 per cent of men and nearly 7 per cent of women in employment in the South West in Spring 1997, worked from home or in the same grounds or building as their home, the second highest and highest proportions respectively.

(Chart 5.10)

Almost 7 per cent of all people in employment in the South West had a second job in Spring 1997, a higher proportion than in any other region.

(Table 5.11)

Housing

Nearly seven in every ten households in the South West have double glazing and almost eight out of ten (in houses) have parking provision at the home, higher proportions than in any other region in England.

(Table 6.6)

Health

Allowing for the age structure of the population, the South and West NHS region has the lowest death rates of all regions.

(Table 7.14)

Lifestyles

Householders in the South West are more likely than those in any other region of England to be involved in voluntary work to improve their local area.

(Table 8.16)

Crime

The South West had the lowest number of offences recorded in which firearms were reported to have been used in both 1992 and 1996; however, the number more than doubled over the period.

(Table 9.4)

Transport

Relative to distances travelled, the South West had the lowest rate of fatal and serious road accidents in 1996 of all the regions in Great Britain.

(Table 10.6)

Environment

The South West has the highest projected rate of urban growth between 1991 and 2016, an estimated 18 per cent.

(Map 11.13)

Wales

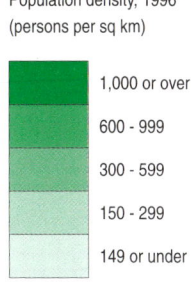

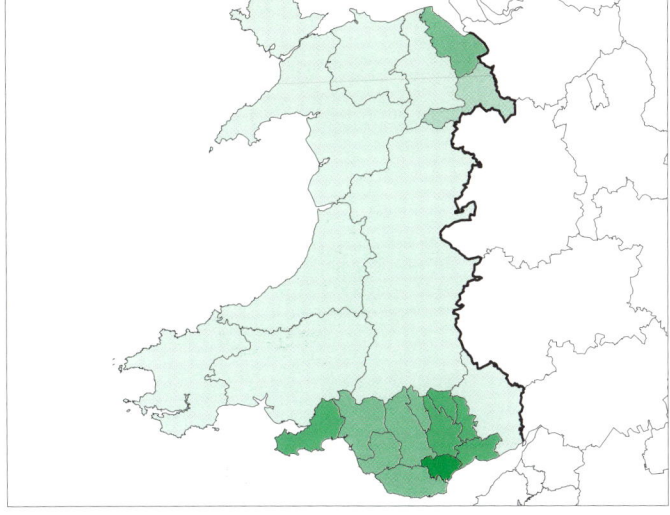

Population density, 1996
(persons per sq km)

- 1,000 or over
- 600 - 999
- 300 - 599
- 150 - 299
- 149 or under

NB: The map shows Unitary
Authorities in Wales
which came into effect
from 1 April 1996.
See map on page 198
for names.

Population	Wales has one of the highest proportions of people of pensionable age and the lowest proportion of 16 to 44 year olds. *(Table 3.3)*
Education	More than three quarters of three and four year olds in Wales were in education in 1996/97, one of the highest proportions in the United Kingdom. *(Table 4.4)*
Labour market	At 30 per cent, a higher proportion of female employees in Wales had a flexible working arrangement in Spring 1997 than in any other region; among men the proportion was 18 per cent, the same as the UK average. *(Table 5.12)* The ILO unemployment rate for 16 to 24 year olds in Wales in Spring 1997 was 18 per cent; only Merseyside and the North East had higher rates for this age group. *(Table 5.23)*
Housing	The average private sector rent in Wales in 1996-97 was lower than in any other region of Great Britain. *(Table 6.9)*
Health	The cost of prescribed drugs amounted to £100 per head in Wales in 1996-97, more than in any other region of the United Kingdom except Northern Ireland. *(Table 7.17)*
Lifestyles	A quarter of households in Wales were in receipt of Incapacity or a Disablement Benefit in 1996-97, a higher proportion than in any other region of Great Britain. *(Table 8.7)*
Crime	In 1996, the recorded crime rate for robberies in Wales was lower than in any English region and the clear-up rate was higher. *(Tables 9.1 and 9.3)*
Transport	People living in Wales, together with those in the South West, rely most on travel by car with 90 per cent of distance travelled per person per year by this form of transport. *(Table 10.11)*
Environment	A fifth of the land area of Wales is designated as National Park. *(Table 11.15)*
Industry	Wales had the highest level of gross value added per person employed in manufacturing in 1995 at £34,800. *(Table 13.5)*

Scotland

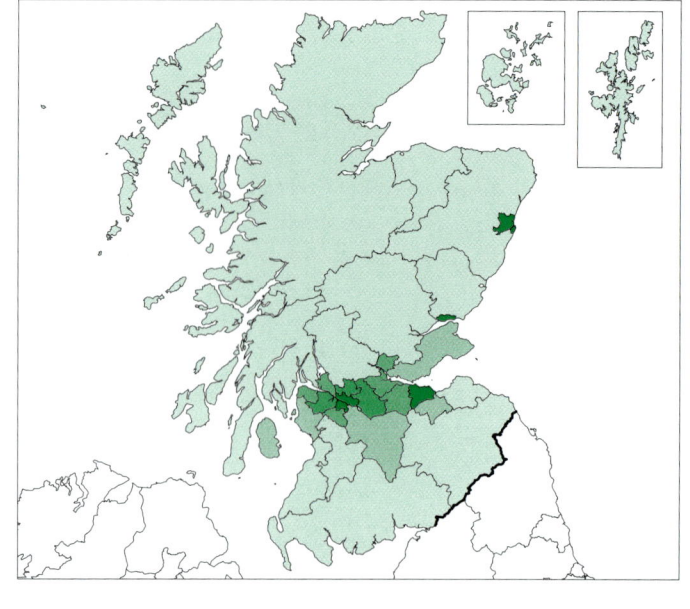

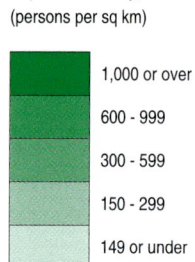

Population density, 1996
(persons per sq km)

■	1,000 or over
■	600 - 999
■	300 - 599
■	150 - 299
■	149 or under

NB: The map shows New Council Areas in Scotland which came into effect from 1 April 1996. See map on page 204 for names.

Population

Scotland is the most sparsely populated region in the United Kingdom, but Glasgow City is one of the most densely populated areas.

(Map 3.4 and Table 16.2)

Overall, Scotland has the lowest birth rate among women of child-bearing age.

(Table 3.8)

Over 30 per cent of households in Scotland consist of one person living alone, the second highest proportion after London.

(Table 3.19)

Education

Nearly 54 per cent of 16 year olds in Scotland achieved 5 or more SCE Standard Grades at level 1-3 in their last year of compulsory schooling and less than 4 per cent achieved no graded results, a better record than in any other region.

(Table 4.6)

Labour market

Scotland lost 26 days per 1,000 employees due to labour disputes in 1997, the highest rate of loss except for the North East.

(Table 5.13)

Housing

Nearly a third of all households in Scotland live in a purpose-built flat or maisonette, the same proportion as in London, but by far higher than any other region.

(Table 6.5)

Health

Allowing for the age structure of the population, Scotland has the highest death rates of all the regions from circulatory diseases, from cancer and from injuries and poisonings.

(Table 7.14)

Lifestyles

Just over a quarter of households in Scotland were in receipt of Housing Benefit in 1996-97.

(Table 8.7)

Transport

Total road casualties in Scotland in 1996 were 20 per cent lower than the average for 1981-1985, a greater reduction than in any other region.

(Table 10.7)

Environment

Scotland is the most heavily wooded region in the United Kingdom.

(Map 11.16)

Industry

Nearly 11 per cent of spending by UK tourists in 1996 was in Scotland, second only to the West Country.

(Table 13.14)

Northern Ireland

Population density, 1996
(persons per sq km)

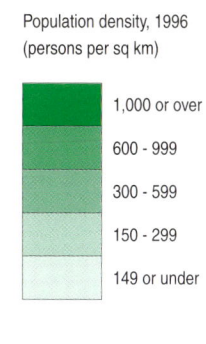

	1,000 or over
	600 - 999
	300 - 599
	150 - 299
	149 or under

Population

Northern Ireland is the fastest growing region with population growth of nearly 4 per cent between 1991 and 1996, more than double the growth in the United Kingdom as a whole.

(Table 3.1)

Education

Almost 36 per cent of pupils in Northern Ireland achieved 2 or more A levels (or equivalent) in 1995/96, the second highest proportion in the United Kingdom.

(Table 4.6)

Labour market

The claimant count rate in Northern Ireland in January 1998 ranged from 5.1 per cent in Ballymena to 13.0 per cent in Strabane.

(Map 5.24)

Nearly 19 per cent of people claiming unemployment-related benefits in January 1998 had been doing so for five years or longer, double the proportion in any other region.

(Table 5.25)

Housing

More new homes are being built in Northern Ireland per head of population than in any other region.

(Table 6.2)

A third of all households live in a detached house, a higher proportion than in any other region.

(Table 6.5)

Health

Northern Ireland has the highest proportion of tee-totallers, the lowest proportion of men drinking more than 21 units of alcohol per week, and the lowest proportion of women drinking more than 14 units per week.

(Table 7.8)

Lifestyles

On average over a fifth of the income of households in Northern Ireland comes from social security benefits, a higher proportion than in any other region.

(Table 8.1)

Households in Northern Ireland spend, on average, less on housing and more on food, on fuel, light and power and on clothing and footwear than those elsewhere in United Kingdom.

(Table 8.10)

Crime

The number of recorded crimes in Northern Ireland fell by 1 per cent between 1995 and 1996; just over a third were cleared up.

(Tables 9.1 and 9.3)

Transport

In 1997, nearly four fifths of people in Northern Ireland travelled to work by car or van, the highest proportion of any region.

(Table 10.10)

2 European Union regional statistics

Population

All regions of the United Kingdom had higher proportions of children aged under 15 than the EU average in 1995 but Northern Ireland had the third highest at nearly 24 per cent.

(Table 2.1)

The North West (SSR) with around 870 people per square kilometre, is one of the most densely populated regions in the European Union; only the major city regions of Brussels, île de France, Berlin, Bremen, Hamburg and Attiki have a greater density.

(Table 2.1)

Births

Northern Ireland had the second highest birth rate in the European Union in 1995 with 14.5 births per 1,000 population, nearly three times the rate in some German regions.

(Table 2.1)

Deaths

With 12.2 deaths per 1,000 population, Wales had one of the highest death rates of all the EU regions in 1995, a fifth higher than the EU average and about the same as the rate for Denmark.

(Table 2.1)

Dependency

In 1996, Scotland and every region of England had a lower dependency ratio of non-active to active people than the EU average; the South East (SSR) had the joint lowest.

(Table 2.2)

Transport

The North, Scotland and Northern Ireland had some of the lowest rates of private car ownership in the European Union in 1995.

(Table 2.2)

Labour market

The South East (SSR) had the third highest proportion of workers in the service sector of all the EU regions in 1996 at 77 per cent.

(Table 2.3)

In 1996, unemployment rates in East Anglia and the South West were amongst the lowest in the European Union.

(Table 2.3)

Gross domestic product

The South East (SSR) is the only region in the United Kingdom where GDP per head is above the EU average.

(Table 2.3)

Northern Ireland has the lowest GDP per head in the United Kingdom, but in 1995 nearly 30 per cent of EU regions had a lower per head figure than Northern Ireland.

(Table 2.3)

Agriculture

East Anglia has one of the highest proportions within the European Union of agricultural land used for arable purposes, while only Açores in Portugal has a lower proportion than Wales or Scotland.

(Table 2.4)

Wales had by far the highest density of sheep and lambs in the European Union in 1995, at over 4,000 animals per 1,000 hectares of utilised agricultural land.

(Table 2.4)

European Union Regions

NETHERLANDS
1 Noord-Nederland
2 Oost-Nederland
3 Zuid-Nederland
4 West-Nederland

BELGIUM
5 Vlaams Gewest
6 Région Wallonne
7 Bruxelles-Brussels

8 LUXEMBOURG

GERMANY
9 Saarland
10 Rheinland-Pfalz
11 Baden-Württemberg
12 Mecklenburg-Vorpommern
13 Hamburg
14 Schleswig-Holstein

non-EU countries

2.1 Population and vital statistics,1995

	Area (sq km)	Popu- lation (thousands)	Persons per sq km	Percentage of population		Births (per 1,000 population)	Deaths[1] (per 1,000 population)	Infant mortality (per 1,000 live births)
				Aged under 15	Aged 65 or over			
EUR 15	**3,192,279**	**372,100.3**	**117**	*17.6*	*15.4*	**10.8**	**10.0**	**5.6**
Austria	**83,859**	**8,046.5**	**96**	*17.6*	*15.1*	**11.0**	**10.1**	**5.4**
Ostösterreich	23,554	3,385.2	144	*16.2*	*16.4*	10.3	11.7	6.4
Südösterreich	25,921	1,767.3	68	*17.6*	*15.6*	10.4	9.8	2.8
Westösterreich	34,384	2,894.0	84	*19.2*	*13.1*	12.2	8.4	5.8
Belgium	**30,518**	**10,130.6**	**332**	*18.0*	*15.8*	**11.4**	**10.3**	**6.1**
Bruxelles-Brussels	161	951.6	5,896	*17.5*	*17.3*	..	11.9	..
Vlaams Gewest	13,512	5,866.1	434	*17.7*	*15.3*	..	9.5	..
Région Wallonne	16,844	3,312.9	197	*18.8*	*16.1*	..	11.2	..
Denmark	**43,080**	**5,227.9**	**121**	*17.3*	*15.3*	**13.4**	**12.1**	**5.1**
Finland	**338,147**	**5,107.8**	**15**	*19.1*	*14.1*	**12.4**	**9.7**	**3.9**
Manner-Suomi	336,595	5,082.6	15	*19.1*	*14.1*	12.3	9.6	3.9
Åland	1,552	25.2	16	*18.7*	*16.3*	11.9	11.9	10.0
France[2]	**543,965**	**58,139.1**	**107**	*19.6*	*15.0*	**12.5**	**9.1**	**4.1**
Île de France	12,012	11,009.1	916	*20.3*	*11.2*	14.8	7.0	3.9
Bassin Parisien	145,645	10,458.1	72	*20.3*	*15.2*	12.3	9.6	4.3
Nord-Pas-de-Calais	12,414	3,998.0	322	*22.6*	*12.9*	13.9	9.1	5.0
Est	48,030	5,130.1	107	*20.1*	*13.8*	12.4	8.8	4.1
Ouest	85,099	7,647.6	90	*19.2*	*16.6*	11.7	9.8	3.7
Sud-Ouest	103,599	6,089.5	59	*16.9*	*18.6*	10.4	10.7	4.6
Centre-Est	69,711	6,899.0	99	*19.6*	*14.6*	12.3	8.7	3.9
Méditerranée	67,455	6,907.6	102	*18.4*	*17.8*	11.7	10.2	3.8
Germany	**356,718**	**81,664.7**	**229**	*16.3*	*15.3*	**9.4**	**10.8**	**5.3**
Baden-Württemberg	35,751	10,295.2	288	*16.9*	*14.6*	10.9	9.5	4.7
Bayern	70,554	11,957.7	169	*16.5*	*15.3*	10.5	10.2	5.0
Berlin	889	3,471.0	3,904	*15.4*	*13.6*	8.2	11.3	5.6
Brandenburg	29,480	2,538.9	86	*17.7*	*13.0*	5.3	10.8	4.9
Bremen	404	679.9	1,682	*13.8*	*17.6*	9.4	12.4	5.6
Hamburg	755	1,707.3	2,260	*13.3*	*17.0*	9.3	11.9	4.8
Hessen	21,114	5,993.7	284	*15.4*	*15.6*	10.0	10.6	4.6
Mecklenburg-Vorpommern	23,171	1,828.2	79	*18.7*	*12.0*	5.4	10.6	4.5
Niedersachsen	47,348	7,745.9	164	*16.3*	*16.0*	10.5	11.2	5.7
Nordrhein-Westfalen	34,072	17,846.5	524	*16.2*	*15.7*	10.2	10.8	5.8
Rheinland-Pfalz	19,846	3,963.3	200	*16.5*	*16.2*	10.0	10.8	5.5
Saarland	2,570	1,083.7	422	*15.4*	*16.5*	9.0	11.6	6.4
Sachsen	18,412	4,575.4	249	*16.2*	*16.5*	5.2	12.6	5.7
Sachsen-Anhalt	20,446	2,750.4	135	*16.7*	*15.1*	5.3	12.2	6.2
Schleswig-Holstein	15,732	2,717.0	173	*15.6*	*15.9*	10.1	11.5	4.6
Thüringen	16,174	2,510.6	155	*17.1*	*14.7*	5.5	11.6	5.8
Greece	**131,626**	**10,454.0**	**79**	*17.1*	*15.4*	**9.7**	**9.6**	**8.1**
Voreia Ellada	56,457	3,373.2	60	*17.3*	*14.6*	10.0	9.5	8.2
Kentriki Ellada	53,902	2,609.1	48	*16.8*	*17.2*	8.0	9.8	8.3
Attiki	3,808	3,464.9	910	*16.6*	*14.4*	10.4	9.3	8.3
Nisia Aigaiou, Kriti	17,458	1,006.9	58	*18.7*	*16.7*	10.7	10.2	7.2
Ireland	**68,895**	**3,601.3**	**52**	*24.7*	*11.5*	**13.5**	**8.7**	**6.3**

2.1 *(continued)*

	Area (sq km)	Population (thousands)	Persons per sq km	Percentage of population		Births (per 1,000 population)	Deaths[1] (per 1,000 population)	Infant mortality (per 1,000 live births)
				Aged under 15	Aged 65 or over			
Italy	**301,316**	**57,300.8**	**190**	*15.1*	*16.4*	**9.2**	**9.7**	**6.1**
Nord Ovest	34,081	6,073.1	178	*11.6*	*19.8*	7.4	12.2	..
Lombardia	23,872	8,917.7	374	*13.1*	*15.8*	8.5	9.5	..
Nord Est	39,816	6,528.7	164	*13.3*	*17.0*	8.6	9.8	..
Emilia-Romagna	22,124	3,923.5	177	*10.9*	*20.9*	7.1	11.4	..
Centro	41,142	5,790.9	141	*12.2*	*20.4*	7.4	11.2	..
Lazio	17,227	5,197.7	302	*14.6*	*15.4*	8.9	9.1	..
Abruzzo-Molise	15,232	1,600.9	105	*15.7*	*18.1*	8.9	10.1	..
Campania	13,595	5,754.1	423	*20.7*	*12.1*	12.4	7.9	..
Sud	44,430	6,765.3	152	*19.0*	*13.9*	10.9	8.0	..
Sicilia	25,707	5,088.7	198	*19.3*	*14.5*	11.4	9.1	..
Sardegna	24,090	1,660.1	69	*16.6*	*13.5*	8.6	8.0	..
Luxembourg	**2,586**	**409.7**	**158**	*18.3*	*13.9*	**13.2**	**9.3**	**4.4**
Netherlands[3]	**41,029**	**15,459.0**	**377**	*18.4*	*13.2*	**12.3**	**8.8**	**5.5**
Noord-Nederland	11,388	1,624.9	143	*18.2*	*14.3*	11.8	9.6	6.3
Oost-Nederland	10,495	3,190.3	304	*19.5*	*12.8*	12.8	8.4	5.0
West-Nederland	11,854	7,228.6	610	*18.1*	*13.6*	12.4	9.0	5.6
Zuid-Nederland	7,292	3,415.2	468	*18.1*	*12.3*	11.9	8.3	5.4
Portugal	**91,906**	**9,916.5**	**108**	*18.0*	*14.4*	**10.8**	**10.5**	**7.5**
Continente	88,798	9,418.5	106	*17.7*	*14.6*	10.7	10.4	7.3
Açores	2,330	241.0	103	*24.5*	*12.2*	14.5	11.2	8.9
Madeira	779	256.9	330	*22.0*	*11.8*	12.1	10.1	10.6
Spain[4]	**504,790**	**39,209.7**	**78**	*16.9*	*15.1*	**9.2**	**8.7**	**5.6**
Noroeste	45,297	4,329.9	96	*14.7*	*17.8*	6.7	10.5	5.7
Noreste	70,366	4,044.9	57	*14.2*	*16.5*	7.8	9.1	5.9
Madrid	7,995	5,008.5	626	*16.3*	*13.3*	9.2	7.3	8.0
Centro	215,025	5,275.2	25	*16.5*	*18.4*	8.6	9.5	3.8
Este	60,249	10,696.2	178	*16.2*	*15.3*	9.2	9.0	4.6
Sur	98,616	8,305.7	84	*20.3*	*12.7*	9.9	8.1	7.0
Canarias	7,242	1,549.3	214	*19.6*	*10.4*	10.6	6.7	4.5
Sweden	**410,934**	**8,826.9**	**21**	*18.9*	*17.5*	**11.7**	**10.6**	**4.2**
United Kingdom[5]	**242,910**	**58,605.8**	**241**	*19.4*	*15.7*	**12.5**	**11.0**	**6.2**
North	15,415	3,095.4	201	*19.3*	*16.1*	11.6	11.8	6.7
Yorkshire & Humberside	15,411	5,029.5	326	*19.5*	*15.9*	12.5	11.1	6.9
East Midlands	15,627	4,123.9	264	*19.2*	*15.8*	12.0	10.7	5.7
East Anglia	12,570	2,123.0	169	*18.6*	*17.2*	11.7	10.9	5.5
South East (SSR)	27,224	17,988.7	661	*19.2*	*15.0*	13.3	10.2	5.7
South West	23,829	4,826.9	203	*18.2*	*18.6*	11.3	11.9	5.3
West Midlands	13,004	5,306.4	408	*19.8*	*15.5*	12.6	10.9	7.1
North West (SSR)	7,342	6,409.6	873	*20.1*	*15.6*	12.3	11.6	6.6
Wales	20,779	2,916.8	140	*19.4*	*17.3*	11.8	12.2	5.9
Scotland	78,133	5,136.6	66	*18.9*	*15.1*	11.7	11.8	6.2
Northern Ireland	13,576	1,649.0	122	*23.7*	*12.8*	14.5	9.3	7.1

1 Deaths are by date of occurrence and not by date of registration which is the definition used in Tables 3.7, 7.1, 7.14, 14.2, 15.2, 16.2 and 17.2.
2 The regional data are estimates.
3 Including 'centraal persoons register'.
4 The regional birth and death rates are estimates.
5 Standard Statistical Regions for the United Kingdom equal NUTS-1 regions for the European Union. See Notes and Definitions.

Source: Eurostat

2.2 Social statistics

	Dependency rate[1] 1996	Proportion of 16-18 year olds in education or training (percentages) 1995/96[2]	Causes of death 1994[3] (rate per 100,000 population)				Transport	
			Circulatory system	Cancer (all neoplasms)	All accidents	Motor vehicle accidents	Length of motorways (km) per 1,000 sq km 1995[4]	Private cars per 1,000 population 1995[5]
EUR 15	120	..	..	..	..	..	14	423
Austria	110	82	544	244	40	15	19	446
Ostösterreich	100	..	660	271	44	15	18	437
Südösterreich	120	..	516	250	37	15	21	467
Westösterreich	100	..	426	210	36	15	19	444
Belgium	140	97	399	270	42	18	55	422
Bruxelles-Brussels	150	..	409	302	44	12	68	452
Vlaams Gewest	140	..	386	263	38	17	61	430
Région Wallonne	150	..	419	273	48	23	49	398
Denmark	90	83	514	276	47	11	18	320
Finland	110	90	449	197	51	9	1	372
Manner-Suomi	110	90	449	197	51	9	..	371
Åland	120	81	450	307	36	8	..	508
France	120	91	301	247	53	15	15	422
Île de France	100	..	210	201	39	10	47	368
Bassin Parisien	120	..	312	260	59	18	15	433
Nord-Pas-de-Calais	150	..	304	258	46	10	44	353
Est	120	..	307	243	51	15	18	414
Ouest	130	..	318	263	57	15	8	451
Sud-Ouest	130	..	381	269	63	18	9	478
Centre-Est	120	..	291	238	56	14	19	445
Méditerranée	140	..	340	266	60	18	17	434
Germany	110	92	543	263	33	12	31	495
Baden-Württemberg	100	91	444	236	30	10	29	523
Bayern	100	91	508	248	33	14	31	525
Berlin	90	92	576	253	24	8	69	352
Brandenburg	90	91	583	245	54	25	26	474
Bremen	120	107	571	327	35	8	119	428
Hamburg	100	97	502	302	45	8	107	418
Hessen	110	93	479	270	37	10	45	535
Mecklenburg-Vorpommern	90	89	504	223	60	24	10	434
Niedersachsen	110	91	542	267	35	14	28	511
Nordrhein-Westfalen	130	95	553	281	21	8	63	492
Rheinland-Pfalz	110	87	558	267	23	12	41	531
Saarland	140	94	626	283	24	9	88	533
Sachsen	100	93	702	281	56	15	23	457
Sachsen-Anhalt	100	88	648	277	47	18	10	440
Schleswig-Holstein	100	92	580	273	32	10	28	513
Thüringen	90	88	650	237	34	15	15	464
Greece	140	69	460	202	36	19	2	211
Voreia Ellada	140	..	465	208	33	18	1	169
Kentriki Ellada	140	..	483	191	35	19	3	106
Attiki	150	..	428	209	40	21	18	343
Nisia Aigaiou, Kriti	130	..	496	189	34	17	-	168
Ireland	140	83	402	212	28	11	1	275

2.2 *(continued)*

	Dependency rate[1] 1996	Proportion of 16-18 year olds in education or training (percentages) 1995/96[2]	Causes of death 1994[3] (rate per 100,000 population)				Transport	
			Circulatory system	Cancer (all neoplasms)	All accidents	Motor vehicle accidents	Length of motorways (km) per 1,000 sq km 1995[4]	Private cars per 1,000 population 1995[5]
Italy	**150**	..	**422**	**264**	**38**	**14**	**21**	**526**
Nord Ovest	130	..	532	326	50	15	36	573
Lombardia	130	..	385	307	38	16	23	572
Nord Est	130	..	416	298	43	18	22	558
Emilia-Romagna	120	..	483	341	45	21	28	605
Centro	140	..	501	313	45	16	16	583
Lazio	150	..	373	250	39	14	28	580
Abruzzo-Molise	150	..	470	236	43	12	24	489
Campania	190	..	368	185	24	9	33	430
Sud	190	..	359	179	31	12	14	406
Sicilia	200	..	431	194	29	9	22	470
Sardegna	170	..	339	209	41	14	0	460
Luxembourg	**140**	..	**417**	**255**	**49**	**20**	**48**	**559**
Netherlands	**110**	*91*	**336**	**237**	**22**	**8**	**54**	**364**
Noord-Nederland	120	..	369	257	25	10	27	355
Oost-Nederland	110	..	333	229	23	10	56	365
West-Nederland	100	..	340	244	22	6	62	353
Zuid-Nederland	100	..	315	222	21	10	80	392
Portugal	**110**	*70*	**430**	**193**	**38**	**22**	**7**	**378**
Continente	100	*73*	430	194	38	22	8	398
Açores	150	..	509	208	30	13	0	..
Madeira	130	*21*	355	157	39	19	0	..
Spain	**140**	*74*	**342**	**212**	**32**	**15**	**13**	**351**
Noroeste	150	*79*	408	250	40	22	9	332
Noreste	140	*86*	326	231	32	16	14	327
Madrid	130	*82*	252	182	27	10	59	427
Centro	160	*73*	408	235	33	16	8	302
Este	130	*70*	352	222	35	16	26	392
Sur	160	*69*	331	183	26	15	13	298
Canarias	150	*71*	264	170	31	8	23	385
Sweden	**100**	*96*	**517**	**230**	**33**	**6**	**3**	**475**
United Kingdom[6]	**100**	*71*	**472**	**275**	**21**	**7**	**13**	**375**
North	110	*68*	523	306	22	7	10	307
Yorkshire & Humberside	110	*64*	478	279	19	7	20	333
East Midlands	100	*69*	459	268	23	8	12	357
East Anglia	100	*67*	463	274	25	9	2	418
South East (SSR)	90	*70*	418	254	17	5	33	391
South West	100	*68*	514	287	20	6	12	416
West Midlands	100	*76*	465	271	22	7	29	405
North West (SSR)	110	*69*	511	287	21	6	63	349
Wales	120	*64*	524	302	23	5	6	338
Scotland	100	*82*	529	300	28	7	4	315
Northern Ireland	130	*77*	427	223	26	10	8	317

1 Dependency rates are calculated as the number of non-active persons (total population *less* labour force) expressed as a percentage of those active.

2 Participation rates are calculated by dividing the number of pupils enrolled in a region by the resident population in that region. As some young people may be resident in one region and in education in another, this inter-regional movement may influence the results. Data for Belgium, and Portugal are for 1994/95. The UK data exclude Open University, independent and special schools in Wales, and Youth Training with employers, all of which are not available by region and age. For all countries, age is taken at 1 January except for the United Kingdom where it is on 31 August (ie the start of the academic year).

3 Unadjusted death rates using 1994 population estimates. 1990 for Belgium; 1993 for Denmark, Germany, Greece, Spain, France, Ireland, Italy, Luxembourg and Austria.

4 1994 for EUR15, Belgium, Germany, Spain, Ireland, Italy and the Netherlands.

5 1994 for EUR15 and Spain.

6 Standard Statistical Regions for the United Kingdom equal NUTS-1 regions for the European Union. See Notes and Definitions.

Source: Eurostat

2.3 Economic statistics

	Persons in employ-ment[1], 1996 (thousands)	Employment[1,2],1996 percentage in			Unem-ployment rate[1] (percent-ages) 1996	Long-term unemployed[1] as a percentage of the unem-ployed, 1996	Gross domestic product per head (PPS)[3] EUR 15=100 1995	Percentage of GDP (at factor cost)[4] in 1995 derived from		
		Agriculture	Industry	Services				Agriculture	Industry	Services
EUR 15	**149,147**	*5.0*	*29.7*	*64.9*	*10.9*	*..*	**100**	*..*	*..*	*..*
Austria	**3,617**	*7.4*	*30.3*	*62.3*	*4.5*	*30.1*	**111**	*..*	*..*	*..*
Ostösterreich	1,535	6.5	27.0	66.5	4.7	42.3	125	..	..	..
Südösterreich	752	9.9	30.4	59.7	5.5	30.3	89	..	..	..
Westösterreich	1,330	7.2	34.0	58.8	3.8	12.6	108	..	..	..
Belgium	**3,791**	*2.7*	*27.6*	*69.6*	*9.6*	*60.7*	**114**	*1.5*	*28.5*	*70.0*
Bruxelles-Brussels	323	0.3	14.6	85.1	14.1	61.8	172	0.0	14.4	85.6
Vlaams Gewest	2,338	3.1	30.8	66.1	7.1	57.0	117	1.7	32.4	65.9
Région Wallonne	1,130	2.8	24.7	72.5	12.9	64.3	91	1.9	27.5	70.6
Denmark	**2,623**	*3.9*	*26.4*	*69.6*	*7.4*	*24.4*	**113**	*4.1*	*27.6*	*68.3*
Finland	**2,064**	*7.8*	*26.8*	*64.3*	*15.7*	*..*	**96**	*6.0*	*34.2*	*59.8*
Manner-Suomi	2,051	7.8	26.8	64.3	15.8	..	96	6.0	34.4	59.7
Åland	13	16.0	23.5	54.6	4.7	..	120	8.5	17.2	74.3
France	**22,195**	*4.8*	*26.5*	*68.6*	*12.0*	*39.6*	**107**	*2.5*	*27.8*	*69.7*
Île de France	4,696	0.4	20.5	79.0	10.7	41.1	165	0.2	23.7	76.1
Bassin Parisien	3,897	6.2	30.5	63.2	12.6	39.6	95	4.2	33.2	62.6
Nord-Pas-de-Calais	1,244	3.0	31.2	65.7	16.8	44.6	89	1.3	31.1	67.6
Est	1,920	2.9	34.7	62.5	9.6	32.5	97	2.5	34.4	63.1
Ouest	2,948	8.9	28.2	62.8	10.8	39.8	89	5.1	27.6	67.3
Sud-Ouest	2,369	8.6	23.4	67.9	11.5	39.5	90	4.4	25.1	70.5
Centre-Est	2,841	4.8	30.2	65.0	10.7	38.2	99	2.3	32.8	64.9
Méditerranée	2,280	5.1	19.3	75.6	16.1	38.8	90	3.0	20.8	76.2
Germany	**35,634**	*2.9*	*35.3*	*61.8*	*8.8*	*46.2*	**110**	*1.4*	*32.6*	*66.0*
Baden-Württemberg	4,728	2.5	42.3	55.2	5.5	48.1	126	1.4	38.1	60.5
Bayern	5,689	4.0	37.5	58.6	5.3	41.2	126	1.6	32.9	65.6
Berlin	1,561	1.0	23.2	75.7	11.7	50.5	105	..	..	..
Brandenburg	1,087	4.7	34.4	60.9	15.3	50.2	66	..	..	..
Bremen	278	0.8	29.9	69.3	11.4	47.1	153	0.3	30.3	69.4
Hamburg	763	1.1	23.2	75.7	8.1	54.5	195	0.3	19.4	80.3
Hessen	2,664	2.0	32.4	65.6	6.5	53.4	150	0.8	26.5	72.7
Mecklenburg-Vorpommern	790	7.4	30.1	62.5	16.6	40.4	61	..	..	..
Niedersachsen	3,317	4.0	32.5	63.5	8.5	42.6	105	3.5	31.7	64.8
Nordrhein-Westfalen	7,272	1.9	36.4	61.7	8.4	40.4	113	0.8	35.0	64.2
Rheinland-Pfalz	1,699	3.1	36.4	60.5	6.4	53.0	98	1.9	34.9	63.1
Saarland	407	1.2	35.3	63.5	9.3	50.3	108	0.4	36.1	63.6
Sachsen	1,939	2.5	37.8	59.7	15.1	50.4	63	..	..	..
Sachsen-Anhalt	1,133	4.8	34.0	61.3	17.8	48.1	61	..	..	..
Schleswig-Holstein	1,235	3.9	27.3	68.8	6.6	49.4	106	2.8	27.5	69.8
Thüringen	1,071	3.6	36.9	59.5	15.8	45.4	60	..	..	..
Greece	**3,868**	*20.3*	*22.9*	*56.8*	*9.7*	*..*	**66**	*14.9*	*25.0*	*60.0*
Voreia Ellada	1,289	27.6	24.1	48.4	9.4	..	63	22.1	28.8	49.2
Kentriki Ellada	800	38.0	19.4	42.6	8.4	..	57	24.6	27.2	48.2
Attiki	1,401	1.1	25.6	73.3	11.9	..	74	2.2	24.9	72.9
Nisia Aigaiou, Kriti	378	29.0	16.0	55.0	4.4	..	68	23.5	14.1	62.3
Ireland	**1,308**	*11.2*	*27.2*	*61.2*	*11.8*	*..*	**93**	*8.6*	*36.7*	*54.7*

2.3 *(continued)*

	Persons in employ-ment[1], 1996 (thousands)	Employment[1,2],1996 percentage in			Unem-ployment rate[1] (percent-ages) 1996	Long-term unemployed[1] as a percentage of the unem-ployed, 1996	Gross domestic product per head (PPS)[3] EUR 15=100 1995	Percentage of GDP (at factor cost)[4] in 1995 derived from		
		Agriculture	Industry	Services				Agriculture	Industry	Services
Italy	**20,013**	**6.7**	**32.2**	**61.1**	**12.1**	**65.4**	**103**	**3.5**	**29.6**	**67.0**
Nord Ovest	2,359	4.8	36.0	59.3	8.6	67.2	119	2.7	32.6	64.6
Lombardia	3,658	2.9	42.4	54.7	6.3	56.2	133	1.8	38.3	59.9
Nord Est	2,681	5.6	37.9	56.5	5.3	39.0	125	3.6	32.8	63.7
Emilia-Romagna	1,679	7.3	34.6	58.2	5.3	35.1	132	4.1	33.2	62.7
Centro	2,221	4.9	35.5	59.6	8.1	56.1	108	3.1	30.9	66.0
Lazio	1,804	4.4	20.1	75.5	13.2	69.6	114	1.8	18.6	79.6
Abruzzo-Molise	556	10.2	32.2	57.6	11.5	64.3	88	5.1	29.4	65.5
Campania	1,475	9.5	22.3	68.1	25.5	77.6	66	4.0	20.4	75.7
Sud	1,830	13.2	23.6	63.2	20.2	66.0	67	7.4	21.1	71.5
Sicilia	1,269	12.5	18.9	68.6	24.0	70.5	67	6.2	20.0	73.8
Sardegna	482	12.0	24.1	63.9	21.8	72.0	75	5.1	24.0	71.0
Luxembourg	**165**	**2.6**	**22.9**	**74.3**	**3.2**	**28.5**	**168**	**1.3**	**23.9**	**74.8**
Netherlands	**6,932**	**3.6**	**21.8**	**68.9**	**6.2**	**46.4**	**107**	**3.3**	**27.1**	**69.6**
Noord-Nederland	679	5.1	24.2	64.5	8.3	45.8	105	4.5	38.2	57.4
Oost-Nederland	1,422	4.3	25.3	64.4	5.9	49.5	95	4.2	27.3	68.5
West-Nederland	3,278	2.8	17.3	74.4	6.2	45.6	116	2.8	21.2	76.1
Zuid-Nederland	1,553	3.8	27.2	63.2	5.8	45.6	103	3.6	32.1	64.3
Portugal	**4,431**	**12.2**	**31.3**	**56.5**	**7.4**	**49.2**	**70**	**4.1**	**33.5**	**62.5**
Continente	4,239	12.1	31.5	56.4	7.4	48.7	71	3.9	34.1	62.0
Açores	88	16.5	23.4	60.1	7.2	66.1	50	11.5	18.8	69.7
Madeira	105	12.3	29.3	58.4	5.5	59.6	52	4.3	19.4	76.3
Spain	**12,342**	**8.6**	**29.4**	**62.0**	**22.3**	**52.7**	**77**	**3.9**	**30.1**	**66.0**
Noroeste	1,368	21.4	27.2	51.5	20.4	56.2	65	6.1	32.2	61.7
Noreste	1,357	6.4	35.1	58.4	17.9	55.8	91	3.4	38.6	58.0
Madrid	1,713	1.0	26.0	73.0	20.6	60.2	96	0.2	24.8	75.0
Centro	1,543	14.3	29.4	56.3	22.2	47.3	65	8.7	31.4	60.0
Este	3,702	4.6	34.9	60.5	19.4	52.5	89	1.9	33.1	65.1
Sur	2,171	10.9	22.9	66.2	31.3	49.5	59	7.9	24.4	67.7
Canarias	489	8.3	19.2	72.5	21.7	53.5	75	2.6	16.1	81.3
Sweden	**3,988**	**3.3**	**25.8**	**70.8**	**10.0**	**..**	**101**	**2.5**	**30.1**	**66.5**
United Kingdom[5]	**26,177**	**2.0**	**27.3**	**70.3**	**8.3**	**38.4**	**96**	**1.9**	**29.2**	**68.9**
North	1,281	2.0	31.0	66.3	9.6	47.2	83	2.2	34.2	63.5
Yorkshire & Humberside	2,219	1.6	31.0	67.0	8.1	39.4	87	2.1	33.4	64.6
East Midlands	1,924	2.1	34.3	63.4	6.7	42.5	91	2.9	37.5	59.6
East Anglia	1,003	3.9	27.7	68.1	5.9	33.4	96	4.9	28.6	66.5
South East (SSR)	8,386	1.0	21.7	76.8	7.3	46.4	113	0.7	20.6	78.7
South West	2,213	3.8	24.1	71.6	6.5	35.5	93	3.7	27.6	68.7
West Midlands	2,344	2.0	34.9	62.8	7.5	42.9	89	2.2	36.6	61.2
North West (SSR)	2,724	1.0	29.6	68.8	7.9	37.9	86	1.0	32.9	66.1
Wales	1,194	3.1	31.1	65.5	8.0	36.5	80	2.3	33.7	63.9
Scotland	2,248	2.7	27.5	69.5	7.9	34.8	96	2.9	30.1	67.0
Northern Ireland	641	4.8	25.5	68.3	11.5	61.3	78	4.8	26.3	68.9

1 The interpretations of the ILO definitions of employment and unemployment differ slightly from those used in UK tables. See Notes and Definitions.
2 Where the percentages do not add up to 100 it is because activity has not been allocated to a particular branch.
3 Purchasing Power Standard; see Notes and Definitions.
4 Figures for Austria and France, 1994 at market prices; Germany, Greece and United Kingdom, 1994 at factor cost; Ireland, 1993 at factor cost; Portugal, 1995 at market prices.
5 Standard Statistical Regions for the United Kingdom equal NUTS-1 regions for the European Union. See Notes and Defintions.

Source: Eurostat

2.4 Agricultural statistics, 1995

	Agricultural land as a percentage of total land area[1]	Arable land as a percentage of agricul- tural land[1]	Average yield[2]		Livestock per 1,000 ha of utilised agricultural land			Economic value of farms (SGM)[4,5] EUR 15=100
			Wheat 100kg/ha	Barley 100kg/ha	All cattle	All sheep and lambs[3]	All pigs[3]	
EUR 15	*41.7*	*55.6*	54	40	629	703	865	100
Austria	*40.9*	*40.9*	51	47	678	106	1,081	70
Ostösterreich	49.5	74.3	51	47	504	55	1,046	88
Südösterreich	32.6	26.0	46	40	720	129	1,446	51
Westösterreich	41.3	22.4	53	48	796	135	894	68
Belgium	*44.7*	*68.7*	72	59	2,314	87	5,240	280
Bruxelles-Brussels	3.1	80.0	60	40	800	20	0	..
Vlaams Gewest	45.6	73.2	71	60	2,725	121	11,177	282
Région Wallonne	44.4	65.1	72	59	1,977	59	358	276
Denmark	*63.0*	*92.1*	76	55	771	28	3,944	340
Finland	*6.4*	*99.1*	38	34	546	53	645	102
Manner-Suomi	..	..	..	..	546	53	645	..
Åland	..	..	..	..	..	..	..	..
France	*54.8*	*60.2*	65	55	687	343	485	206
Île de France	49.3	95.5	70	57	..	..	..	512
Bassin Parisien	65.1	70.0	70	60	594	..	..	282
Nord-Pas-de-Calais	71.7	75.4	80	70	874	..	724	292
Est	47.1	51.2	62	55	829	..	..	183
Ouest	69.7	75.9	59	52	1,023	..	1,647	212
Sud-Ouest	49.2	54.2	53	43	640	846	..	147
Centre-Est	46.8	34.7	57	47	771	..	225	133
Méditerranée	33.9	22.7	37	38	..	..	..	190
Germany	*48.6*	*68.2*	69	56	916	138	1,369	184
Baden-Württemberg	41.3	56.9	55	46	948	197	1,473	102
Bayern	48.1	63.3	60	50	1,246	110	1,013	120
Berlin	2.5	71.6	..	..	535	668	891	224
Brandenburg	45.4	77.8	60	55	532	91	525	511
Bremen	23.3	19.0	..	..	1,445	32	276	..
Hamburg	19.5	43.9	83	67	618	102	211	..
Hessen	36.8	64.8	71	56	774	204	1,129	117
Mecklenburg-Vorpommern	57.4	78.9	68	65	477	52	393	871
Niedersachsen	57.3	65.4	80	59	1,111	87	2,488	253
Nordrhein-Westfalen	46.0	70.1	81	63	1,119	152	3,594	204
Rheinland-Pfalz	36.3	55.6	64	48	679	192	551	148
Saarland	28.5	52.9	58	48	845	255	338	137
Sachsen	49.0	79.1	62	55	714	142	624	521
Sachsen-Anhalt	56.6	86.1	72	68	391	119	615	856
Schleswig-Holstein	67.0	55.3	86	72	1,327	225	1,205	292
Thüringen	49.5	78.2	66	55	585	302	824	590
Greece	*30.0*	*57.6*	26	25	152	2,425	231	40
Voreia Ellada	33.7	82.3	27	28	233	1,714	178	48
Kentriki Ellada	26.5	41.5	27	25	79	2,860	325	37
Attiki	25.9	17.0	15	15	112	2,067	386	36
Nisia Aigaiou, Kriti	29.9	19.0	15	14	64	3,909	142	29
Ireland	*64.5*	*23.3*	82	61	1,442	1,232	341	107

2.4 *(continued)*

	Agricultural land as a percentage of total land area[1]	Arable land as a percentage of agricul-tural land[1]	Average yield[2]		Livestock per 1,000 ha of utilised agricultural land			Economic value of farms (SGM)[4,5] EUR 15=100
			Wheat 100kg/ha	Barley 100kg/ha	All cattle	All sheep and lambs[3]	All pigs[3]	
Italy	*58.3*	*51.3*	35	37	422	607	459	49
Nord Ovest	*44.9*	*44.9*	46	47	707	92	492	68
Lombardia	*50.1*	*66.8*	58	52	1,549	96	2,477	117
Nord Est	*44.1*	*46.5*	56	51	782	52	445	55
Emilia-Romagna	*62.8*	*72.1*	57	52	538	74	1,211	91
Centro	*52.0*	*64.8*	41	39	156	617	364	56
Lazio	*59.1*	*53.9*	33	31	334	1,277	149	37
Abruzzo-Molise	*59.1*	*52.3*	30	35	183	654	200	32
Campania	*63.8*	*49.4*	32	32	430	382	204	41
Sud	*69.9*	*47.9*	26	28	133	383	80	35
Sicilia	*77.5*	*52.0*	22	21	223	603	47	33
Sardegna	*69.7*	*21.1*	20	19	176	2,560	152	44
Luxembourg	*49.4*	*45.7*	57	50	1,605	52	537	198
Netherlands	*47.4*	*46.8*	93	57	2,361	849	7,303	518
Noord-Nederland	*48.3*	*44.1*	89	58	1,868	1,008	1,024	554
Oost-Nederland	*50.9*	*39.1*	93	56	3,258	585	8,669	412
West-Nederland	*40.5*	*50.1*	98	60	1,454	1,304	1,617	625
Zuid-Nederland	*52.2*	*58.1*	86	50	2,903	433	21,563	514
Portugal	*43.2*	*57.5*	14	10	333	863	605	36
Continente	*43.3*	*58.9*	14	10	290	888	610	37
Açores	*51.9*	*11.6*	..	..	1,653	33	339	32
Madeira	*10.3*	*50.0*	10	..	1,000	1,250	2,000	14
Spain	*51.1*	*54.5*	15	14	214	827	716	56
Noroeste	*30.4*	*39.6*	22	21	1,224	247	737	26
Noreste	*51.7*	*55.9*	21	19	159	1,109	947	71
Madrid	*47.9*	*50.5*	11	9	212	467	151	51
Centro	*58.1*	*62.4*	16	13	147	925	380	60
Este	*38.7*	*38.1*	31	24	324	876	2,685	50
Sur	*55.1*	*46.5*	7	4	102	581	531	69
Canarias	*16.6*	*50.6*	..	..	144	170	404	67
Sweden	*6.8*	*86.5*	59	40	581	151	756	152
United Kingdom[6]	*71.2*	*34.2*	77	57	687	1,693	432	343
North	*63.9*	*25.2*	84	63	893	3,315	182	298
Yorkshire & Humberside	*64.5*	*56.9*	81	62	654	1,762	1,886	413
East Midlands	*70.0*	*72.0*	79	58	582	1,000	501	547
East Anglia	*68.7*	*86.5*	79	59	228	343	1,745	766
South East (SSR)	*51.1*	*67.2*	73	57	522	1,046	489	617
South West	*69.8*	*41.2*	72	54	1,250	1,875	472	260
West Midlands	*66.9*	*52.2*	70	57	1,022	2,280	419	293
North West (SSR)	*57.2*	*30.8*	71	51	1,424	1,884	567	454
Wales	*77.9*	*12.8*	79	48	788	4,326	55	173
Scotland	*72.5*	*16.4*	83	57	379	1,140	99	241
Northern Ireland	*76.5*	*23.3*	78	52	1,529	1,608	509	130

1 1994 for Belgium and the Netherlands; 1988 for Italy.
2 1993 for Belgium; 1994 for Italy.
3 1994 for France.
4 The economic value of farms is measured in Standard Gross Margins (SGMs). See Notes and Definitions.
5 Vlaams Gewest includes Brussels. Berlin includes Bremen and Hamburg.
6 Standard Statistical Regions for the United Kingdom equal NUTS-1 regions for the European Union. See Notes and Definitions.

Source: Eurostat

2.5 Gross domestic product per head[1], 1995

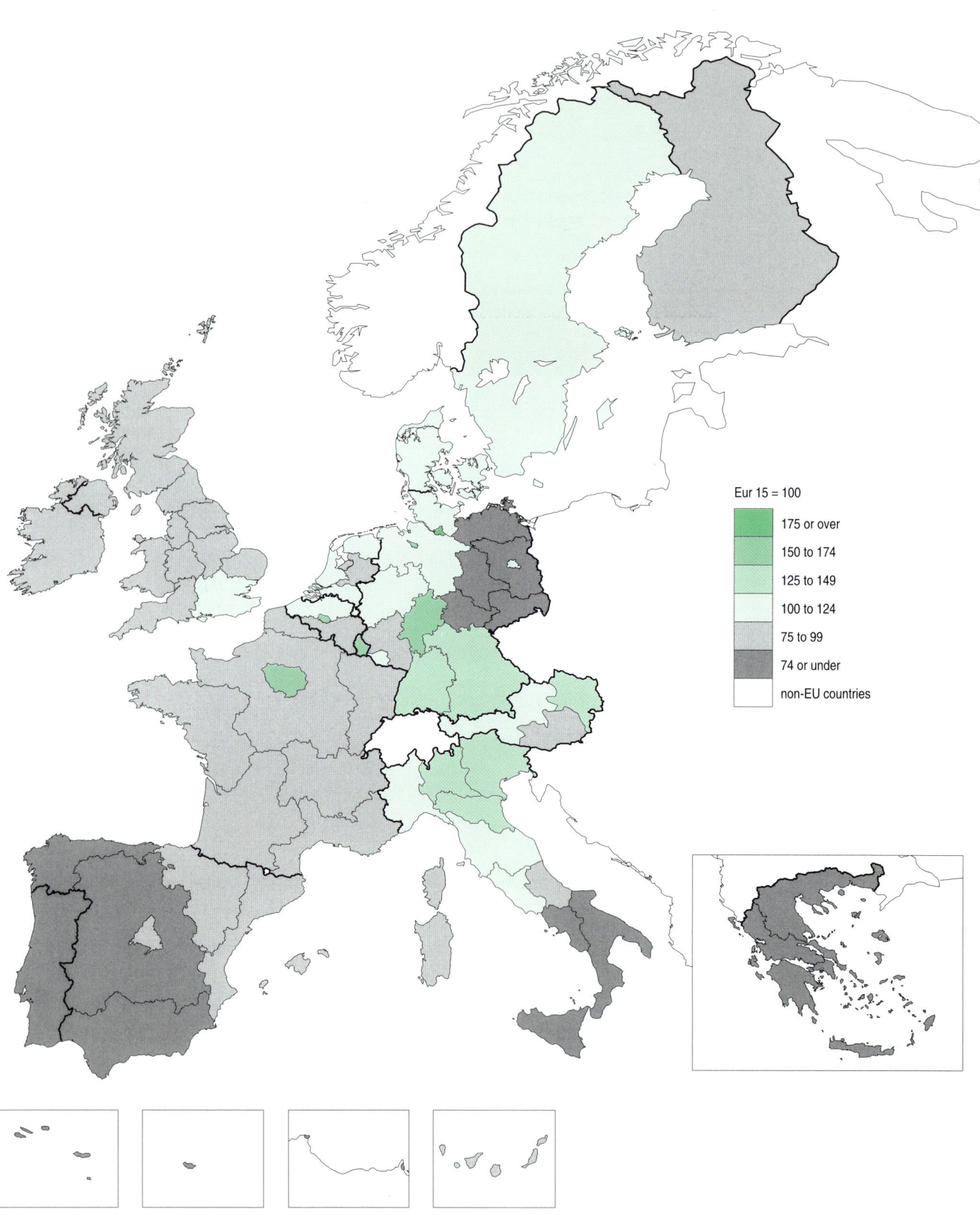

Eur 15 = 100

- 175 or over
- 150 to 174
- 125 to 149
- 100 to 124
- 75 to 99
- 74 or under
- non-EU countries

1 Purchasing Power Standard; see Notes and Definitions.

Source: Eurostat

3 Population and Households

Population change
Northern Ireland had the fastest growth in population between 1991 and 1996 at 4 per cent, more than double the UK average, while the population of Merseyside fell by 2 per cent over the period.

(Table 3.1)

The largest movement of people between regions is from London to the South East (GOR) with the second largest movement in the opposite direction.

(Table 3.11)

Age
Northern Ireland has the youngest population, with the highest proportion of children and the lowest proportion of pensioners of any region, while the South West has the oldest population with more than one in 20 aged 80 or over.

(Table 3.3)

Births
Scotland has the lowest birth rate and Northern Ireland the highest among all women of child-bearing age, but London has the highest rate among women aged 35 and over.

(Table 3.8)

Deaths
Allowing for the age structure of the population, Scotland has the highest death rate and the South West the lowest.

(Table 3.9)

Social class
London and the South East (GOR) have the highest proportions of working-age people in professional occupations, while the North East, Wales and Northern Ireland have the highest proportions in unskilled occupations.

(Table 3.13)

Ethnic minorities
One in four people living in London belongs to an ethnic minority group, compared with one in 100 in the North East, the South West, Wales and Scotland.

(Table 3.14)

Conceptions
The rate of under-age conceptions is highest in the North East and lowest in the South East (GOR) and the Eastern region.

(Table 3.15)

Cohabitation
Northern Ireland has the lowest proportion of non-married people aged between 18 and 49 who are cohabiting, while the South West, East Anglia and the South East (SSR) excluding London have the highest.

(Chart 3.17)

Households
A third of all households in London consists of one person compared with less than a quarter in Northern Ireland.

(Table 3.19)

Lone parents with dependent children account for one in ten households in Merseyside compared with one in 20 in the South West.

(Table 3.19)

Introduction

A full Census is conducted every ten years. Preparation for the next Census in 2001 is well under way: it began as early as 1993-94 with a development programme which is being taken forward by the Office for National Statistics, the General Register Office for Scotland and the Northern Ireland Statistics and Research Agency. A major Census test was conducted in 1997 and a full 'dress rehearsal' will be carried out in 1999. This extensive development programme is needed in order to identify, test, evaluate and develop all the procedures needed for 2001 as the decennial Census is the most valuable source of information about the characteristics of people in the United Kingdom, particularly for small areas.

A key use of the Census is as a benchmark for the population estimates: between Censuses the population figures are rolled forward using annual estimates of the components of population change (births, deaths, net migration and other changes). As the decade proceeds, problems with estimating migration in particular progressively affect these rolled-forward figures. Thus the Census is used as a base for both revising previous years' data and preparing estimates for the following decade.

Overall, the population of the United Kingdom increased by nearly 2 per cent between 1991 and 1996 to 58.8 million, although the population of Merseyside fell by 2 per cent over this period and there was a marginal decline in that of the North East. Northern Ireland had the fastest population growth, more than double the UK average (Table 3.1). The age structure of the population changed over this period as a result of variation in the number of births and in net migration and increases in life expectancy. The population of working age as a whole increased, but there was a substantial decline in the population aged 16-29 due to the low birth rates during the 1970s. Similarly, the number of people at the younger pensioner ages decreased as a result of low fertility in the 1930s. However, there was an increase in the population aged 75-84 because of the baby boom following the First World War, while the number of people aged 85 or over increased largely because of improvements in life expectancy.

There were 733 thousand live births in the United Kingdom in 1996 (Table 3.7), one thousand more than in 1995. The most noticeable change in fertility over the past 15 to 20 years has been a shift towards later child-bearing. Fertility amongst women in their twenties has been falling, while fertility for women in their thirties and, in most regions, their forties has been rising. This can be seen clearly in Table 3.8 which shows age-specific birth rates for 1981, 1991 and 1996. In every region except Northern Ireland, birth rates among women aged 35 or over were higher in 1996 than they had been in either 1991 or, in most cases 1981, while there have been significant reductions in all regions in the rates among women in their twenties compared with 1981. This pattern is most pronounced in London and the South East (GOR). The delaying of child-bearing is linked to the greater participation of females in both higher education and the labour force. However, over the period 1994 to 1996 under-age conceptions in Great Britain rose to their highest rate in more than a decade. Of these, just over half were terminated by abortion (Table 3.15). The rise in under-age pregnancies was partly blamed on a scare over the oral contraceptive pill in October 1995.

Another striking change in our society is the continuing rise in one-parent families. In addition, the number of dependent children per one-parent family has increased steadily: one-child families amongst one-parent families have fallen in relative numbers, while those with three and more children have grown. The highest prevalence of one-parent families with dependent children can be found in the regions of Merseyside, the North East and London (Table 3.19). Merseyside followed by the North East are the regions with the highest proportions of births outside marriage (Table 14.2).

3.1 Resident population[1]: by gender

Thousands and percentages

	Population (thousands)				Total population growth (percentages)		
	1971	1981	1991	1996	1971-1981	1981-1991	1991-1996
Males							
United Kingdom	27,167.3	27,409.2	28,245.6	28,855.6	0.9	3.1	2.2
North East	1,304.0	1,283.1	1,267.5	1,271.4	-1.6	-1.2	0.3
North West (GOR) & Merseyside	3,422.4	3,357.6	3,348.7	3,376.7	-1.9	-0.3	0.8
North West (GOR)	2,626.9	2,627.4	2,652.2	2,689.1	0.0	0.9	1.4
Merseyside	795.5	730.2	696.5	687.5	-8.2	-4.6	-1.3
Yorkshire and the Humber	2,384.9	2,395.0	2,441.7	2,479.8	0.4	2.0	1.6
East Midlands	1,797.8	1,894.8	1,989.6	2,047.7	5.4	5.0	2.9
West Midlands	2,542.4	2,555.6	2,596.3	2,627.7	0.5	1.6	1.2
Eastern	2,194.6	2,385.5	2,536.9	2,609.9	8.7	6.3	2.9
London	3,611.4	3,277.6	3,352.0	3,474.9	-9.2	2.3	3.7
South East (GOR)	3,321.1	3,528.6	3,759.8	3,874.8	6.2	6.6	3.1
South West	1,989.9	2,117.2	2,295.6	2,366.4	6.4	8.4	3.1
England	22,568.5	22,795.0	23,588.1	24,129.3	1.0	3.5	2.3
Wales	1,328.5	1,365.1	1,407.0	1,428.1	2.8	3.1	1.5
Scotland	2,515.7	2,494.9	2,469.5	2,485.8	-0.8	-1.0	0.7
Northern Ireland	754.6	754.2	780.9	812.5	-0.1	3.5	4.0
Females							
United Kingdom	28,760.7	28,943.0	29,562.3	29,945.8	0.6	2.1	1.3
North East	1,374.5	1,353.1	1,335.0	1,329.1	-1.6	-1.3	-0.4
North West (GOR) & Merseyside	3,685.4	3,582.7	3,536.7	3,514.6	-2.8	-1.3	-0.6
North West (GOR)	2,819.1	2,790.7	2,783.5	2,781.7	-1.0	-0.3	-0.1
Merseyside	866.3	792.0	753.1	732.9	-8.6	-4.9	-2.7
Yorkshire and the Humber	2,517.4	2,523.5	2,541.1	2,555.7	0.2	0.7	0.6
East Midlands	1,854.1	1,958.0	2,045.8	2,093.8	5.6	4.5	2.3
West Midlands	2,603.6	2,631.1	2,669.1	2,688.8	1.1	1.4	0.7
Eastern	2,259.7	2,468.5	2,613.0	2,682.7	9.2	5.9	2.7
London	3,918.0	3,528.0	3,538.0	3,599.3	-10.0	0.3	1.7
South East (GOR)	3,508.6	3,716.8	3,919.1	4,020.5	5.9	5.4	2.6
South West	2,121.9	2,264.1	2,422.1	2,475.2	6.7	7.0	2.2
England	23,843.2	24,025.8	24,619.9	24,959.8	0.8	2.5	1.4
Wales	1,411.8	1,448.4	1,484.5	1,493.0	2.6	2.5	0.6
Scotland	2,719.9	2,685.3	2,637.5	2,642.2	-1.3	-1.8	0.2
Northern Ireland	785.8	783.5	820.4	850.8	-0.3	4.7	3.7
All persons							
United Kingdom	55,928.0	56,352.2	57,807.9	58,801.5	0.8	2.6	1.7
North East	2,678.5	2,636.2	2,602.5	2,600.5	-1.6	-1.3	-0.1
North West (GOR) & Merseyside	7,107.8	6,940.3	6,885.4	6,891.3	-2.4	-0.8	0.1
North West (GOR)	5,446.0	5,418.1	5,435.7	5,470.8	-0.5	0.3	0.6
Merseyside	1,661.8	1,522.2	1,449.7	1,420.4	-8.4	-4.8	-2.0
Yorkshire and the Humber	4,902.3	4,918.4	4,982.8	5,035.5	0.3	1.3	1.1
East Midlands	3,651.9	3,852.8	4,035.4	4,141.5	5.5	4.7	2.6
West Midlands	5,146.0	5,186.6	5,265.5	5,316.6	0.8	1.5	1.0
Eastern	4,454.3	4,854.1	5,149.8	5,292.6	9.0	6.1	2.8
London	7,529.4	6,805.6	6,889.9	7,074.3	-9.6	1.2	2.7
South East (GOR)	6,829.7	7,245.4	7,678.9	7,895.3	6.1	6.0	2.8
South West	4,111.8	4,381.4	4,717.8	4,841.5	6.6	7.7	2.6
England	46,411.7	46,820.8	48,208.1	49,089.1	0.9	3.0	1.8
Wales	2,740.3	2,813.5	2,891.5	2,921.1	2.7	2.8	1.0
Scotland	5,235.6	5,180.2	5,107.0	5,128.0	-1.1	-1.4	0.4
Northern Ireland	1,540.4	1,537.7	1,601.4	1,663.3	-0.2	4.1	3.9

1 See Notes and Definitions.

Source: Office for National Statistics; General Register Office for Scotland; Northern Ireland Statistics and Research Agency

3.2 Population change, mid 1981-1996, and projected change, 1996-2011[1,2]

Population change mid 1981-1996

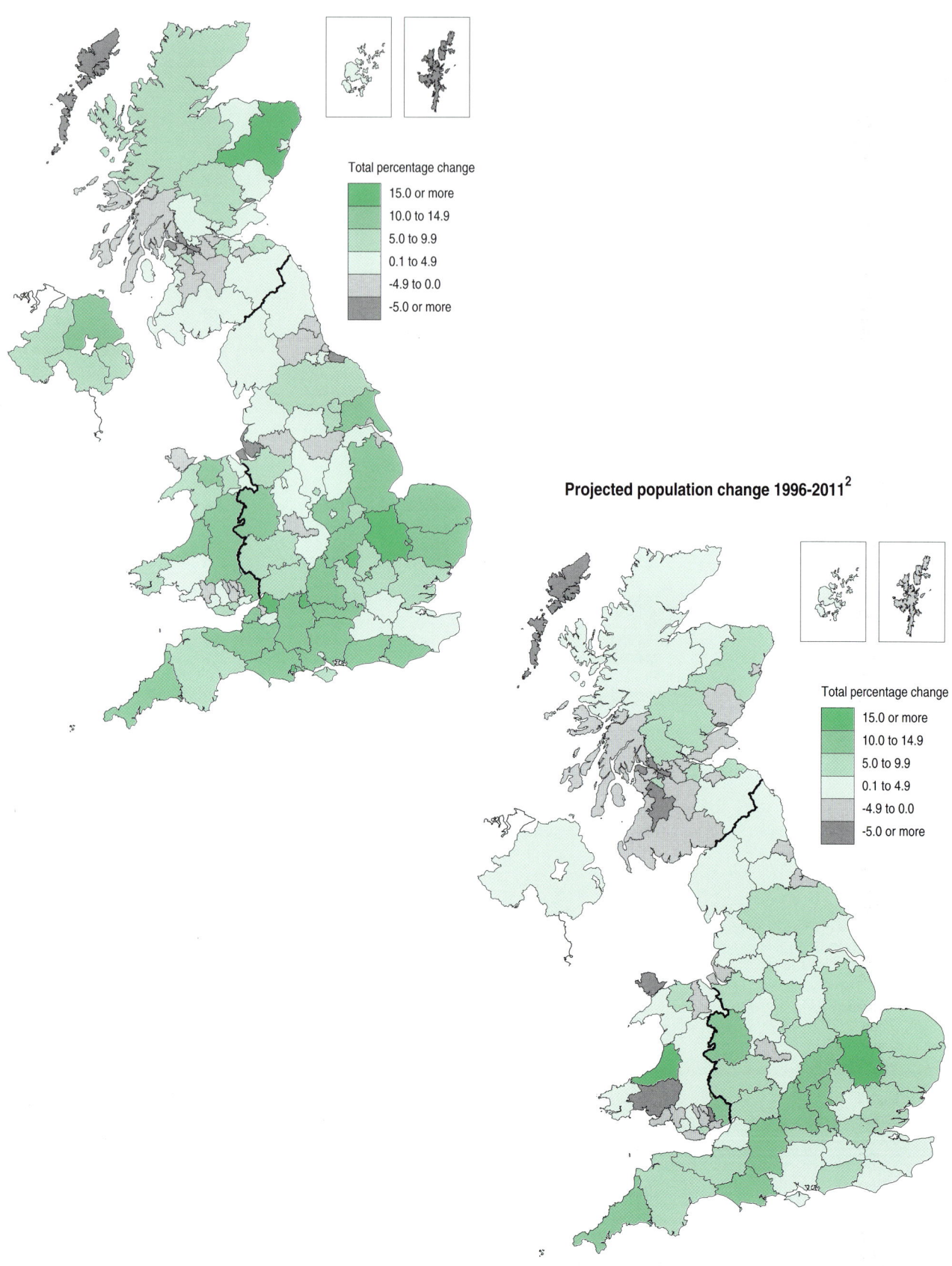

Total percentage change

- 15.0 or more
- 10.0 to 14.9
- 5.0 to 9.9
- 0.1 to 4.9
- -4.9 to 0.0
- -5.0 or more

Projected population change 1996-2011[2]

Total percentage change

- 15.0 or more
- 10.0 to 14.9
- 5.0 to 9.9
- 0.1 to 4.9
- -4.9 to 0.0
- -5.0 or more

1 See Notes and Definitions.
2 Mid-1996 estimates; 1993-based sub-national projections for England, 1994-based sub-national projections for Wales and 1996-based sub-national projections for Scotland; 1996-based national projection for Northern Ireland.

Source: Office for National Statistics; Welsh Office; General Register Office for Scotland; Northern Ireland Statistics and Research Agency

3.3 Resident population[1]: by age and gender, 1996

Thousands and percentages

	0-4	5-15	16-44	45-59	60-64	65-79	80 or over	All ages
Males (thousands)								
United Kingdom	1,929.3	4,276.0	12,257.7	5,269.8	1,354.6	3,042.5	725.8	28,855.6
North East	82.1	192.8	531.4	233.1	63.5	141.3	27.4	1,271.4
North West (GOR) & Merseyside	226.4	520.9	1,409.4	624.8	161.8	354.0	79.4	3,376.7
North West (GOR)	180.5	412.2	1,121.9	504.2	127.0	280.2	63.2	2,689.1
Merseyside	45.9	108.8	287.5	120.6	34.8	73.7	16.2	687.5
Yorkshire and the Humber	165.2	369.8	1,052.5	451.3	116.4	263.6	61.1	2,479.8
East Midlands	133.3	300.8	852.9	387.3	97.4	224.6	51.4	2,047.7
West Midlands	176.8	397.8	1,092.2	492.3	126.0	281.8	60.8	2,627.7
Eastern	172.3	377.5	1,088.0	492.5	124.5	284.3	70.8	2,609.9
London	259.5	486.5	1,648.8	559.8	142.2	299.9	78.3	3,474.9
South East (GOR)	253.5	562.6	1,626.7	731.1	180.5	409.4	110.9	3,874.8
South West	144.7	336.1	953.1	447.4	116.7	288.9	79.6	2,366.4
England	1,613.7	3,544.7	10,254.9	4,419.5	1,128.9	2,547.8	619.7	24,129.3
Wales	91.3	216.7	571.7	269.3	72.0	169.2	37.9	1,428.1
Scotland	160.4	365.6	1,080.0	450.1	120.9	254.8	54.1	2,485.8
Northern Ireland	63.9	149.0	351.1	130.9	32.9	70.7	14.1	812.5
Females (thousands)								
United Kingdom	1,834.1	4,058.8	11,840.5	5,312.2	1,417.7	3,839.6	1,643.0	29,945.8
North East	78.1	182.8	519.8	235.0	67.2	179.2	66.8	1,329.1
North West (GOR) & Merseyside	214.4	494.1	1,361.2	625.3	168.9	457.3	193.5	3,514.6
North West (GOR)	171.2	390.9	1,076.5	500.0	131.7	359.0	152.5	2,781.7
Merseyside	43.2	103.2	284.7	125.4	37.2	98.3	41.0	732.9
Yorkshire and the Humber	157.3	351.5	997.2	451.6	123.7	332.1	142.4	2,555.7
East Midlands	125.5	284.3	821.9	381.4	99.4	270.7	110.6	2,093.8
West Midlands	168.6	376.3	1,044.1	485.4	129.0	348.1	137.4	2,688.8
Eastern	164.9	359.4	1,045.6	492.5	127.5	345.2	147.7	2,682.7
London	245.2	464.5	1,609.3	578.3	143.9	378.0	180.1	3,599.3
South East (GOR)	240.8	531.7	1,562.9	734.8	187.1	518.1	245.2	4,020.5
South West	137.4	317.6	911.8	452.5	123.6	362.3	169.9	2,475.2
England	1,532.1	3,362.1	9,873.8	4,436.9	1,170.2	3,191.1	1,393.6	24,959.8
Wales	87.6	206.4	552.2	271.6	75.7	212.4	87.1	1,493.0
Scotland	153.5	348.5	1,065.7	468.6	135.3	341.6	129.0	2,642.2
Northern Ireland	61.0	141.8	348.8	135.1	36.5	94.5	33.2	850.8
All persons (percentages)								
United Kingdom	6.4	14.2	41.0	18.0	4.7	11.7	4.0	100.0
North East	6.2	14.4	40.4	18.0	5.0	12.3	3.6	100.0
North West (GOR) & Merseyside	6.4	14.7	40.2	18.1	4.8	11.8	4.0	100.0
North West (GOR)	6.4	14.7	40.2	18.4	4.7	11.7	3.9	100.0
Merseyside	6.3	14.9	40.3	17.3	5.1	12.1	4.0	100.0
Yorkshire and the Humber	6.4	14.3	40.7	17.9	4.8	11.8	4.0	100.0
East Midlands	6.2	14.1	40.4	18.6	4.8	12.0	3.9	100.0
West Midlands	6.5	14.6	40.2	18.4	4.8	11.8	3.7	100.0
Eastern	6.4	13.9	40.3	18.6	4.8	11.9	4.1	100.0
London	7.1	13.4	46.1	16.1	4.0	9.6	3.7	100.0
South East (GOR)	6.3	13.9	40.4	18.6	4.7	11.7	4.5	100.0
South West	5.8	13.5	38.5	18.6	5.0	13.5	5.2	100.0
England	6.4	14.1	41.0	18.0	4.7	11.7	4.1	100.0
Wales	6.1	14.5	38.5	18.5	5.1	13.1	4.3	100.0
Scotland	6.1	13.9	41.8	17.9	5.0	11.6	3.6	100.0
Northern Ireland	7.5	17.5	42.1	16.0	4.2	9.9	2.8	100.0

1 See Notes and Definitions.

Source: Office for National Statistics; General Register Office for Scotland; Northern Ireland Statistics and Research Agency

3.4 Population density[1], 1996

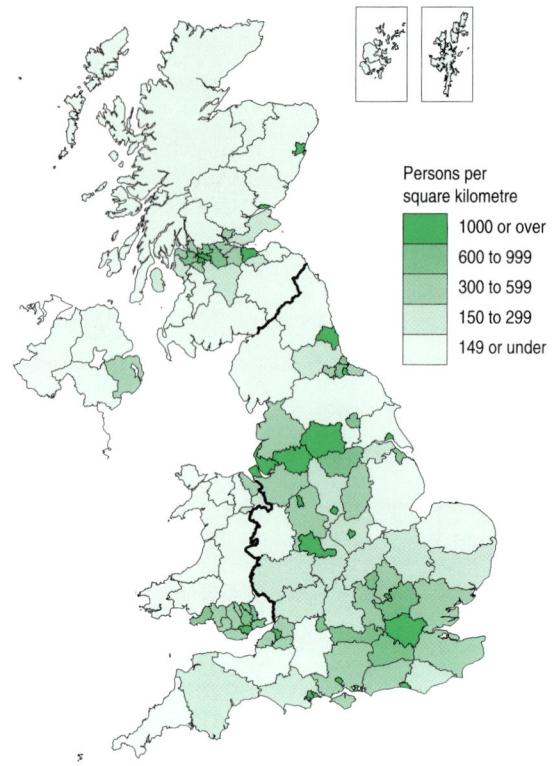

Persons per
square kilometre

- 1000 or over
- 600 to 999
- 300 to 599
- 150 to 299
- 149 or under

1 See Notes and Definitions.

*Source: Office for National Statistics; General Register Office for
Scotland; Northern Ireland Statistics and Research Agency*

3.5 Population under 16[1], 1996

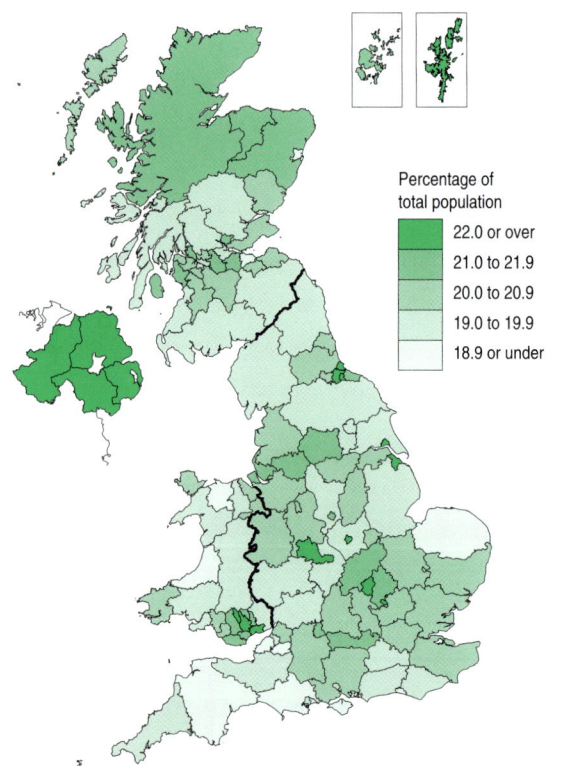

Percentage of
total population

- 22.0 or over
- 21.0 to 21.9
- 20.0 to 20.9
- 19.0 to 19.9
- 18.9 or under

1 See Notes and Definitions.

*Source: Office for National Statistics; General Register Office for
Scotland; Northern Ireland Statistics and Research Agency*

3.6 Population of retirement age[1], 1996

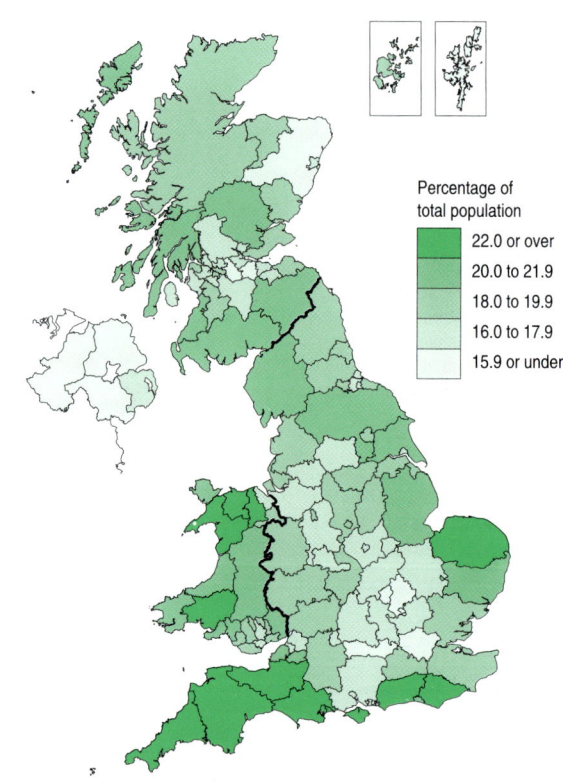

Percentage of
total population

- 22.0 or over
- 20.0 to 21.9
- 18.0 to 19.9
- 16.0 to 17.9
- 15.9 or under

1 Males aged 65 or over, females aged 60 or over. See Notes and Definitions.

*Source: Office for National Statistics; General Register Office for
Scotland; Northern Ireland Statistics and Research Agency*

3.7 Live births, deaths and natural change in population

Thousands and rates

	Thousands				Rates per 1,000 population			
	1981	1986	1991	1996	1981	1986	1991	1996
Live births[1]								
United Kingdom	730.8	755.0	792.5	733.4	13.0	13.3	13.7	12.5
North East	34.2	34.7	34.9	30.1	13.0	13.3	13.4	11.6
North West (GOR) & Merseyside	90.4	93.4	97.5	85.0	13.0	13.6	14.2	12.3
North West (GOR)	70.4	73.0	77.1	67.8	13.0	13.6	14.2	12.4
Merseyside	20.0	20.4	20.3	17.2	13.2	13.9	14.0	12.1
Yorkshire and the Humber	62.6	65.3	68.6	62.0	12.7	13.3	13.8	12.3
East Midlands	49.2	50.3	54.0	49.4	12.8	12.8	13.4	11.9
West Midlands	67.5	70.4	74.2	67.5	13.0	13.5	14.1	12.7
Eastern	62.6	64.4	68.4	64.6	12.9	12.8	13.3	12.2
London	92.4	97.7	105.8	105.4	13.6	14.4	15.4	14.9
South East (GOR)	89.0	92.9	99.8	95.3	12.3	12.4	13.0	12.1
South West	50.4	54.5	57.6	54.8	11.5	12.0	12.2	11.3
England	598.2	623.6	660.8	614.2	12.8	13.2	13.7	12.5
Wales	35.8	37.0	38.1	34.9	12.7	13.1	13.2	11.9
Scotland	69.1	65.8	67.0	59.3	13.3	12.8	13.1	11.6
Northern Ireland	27.3	28.2	26.3	24.6	17.8	18.0	16.4	14.8
Deaths[2]								
United Kingdom	658.0	660.7	646.2	638.9	11.7	11.6	11.2	10.9
North East	32.1	32.0	31.8	30.4	12.2	12.3	12.2	11.7
North West (GOR) & Merseyside	86.6	85.5	82.7	79.9	12.5	12.5	12.0	11.6
North West (GOR)	67.6	67.2	64.8	62.5	12.5	12.5	11.9	11.4
Merseyside	19.0	18.3	17.9	17.5	12.4	12.4	12.4	12.3
Yorkshire and the Humber	59.1	58.9	57.3	55.6	12.0	12.0	11.5	11.1
East Midlands	42.8	43.5	43.9	44.1	11.1	11.1	10.9	10.6
West Midlands	56.4	57.7	57.0	56.5	10.9	11.1	10.8	10.6
Eastern	50.7	52.4	53.3	54.1	10.4	10.5	10.3	10.2
London	77.6	73.9	68.9	65.7	11.4	10.9	10.0	9.3
South East (GOR)	81.3	84.2	83.0	84.0	11.2	11.2	10.8	10.6
South West	54.4	56.4	56.2	56.3	12.4	12.4	11.9	11.6
England	541.0	544.5	534.0	526.7	11.6	11.5	11.1	10.7
Wales	35.0	34.7	34.1	34.8	12.4	12.3	11.8	11.9
Scotland	63.8	63.5	61.0	60.7	12.3	12.4	12.0	11.8
Northern Ireland	16.3	16.1	15.1	15.2	10.6	10.3	9.4	9.1
Natural change								
United Kingdom	72.8	94.2	146.3	94.5	1.3	1.7	2.5	1.6
North East	2.1	2.7	3.1	-0.3	0.8	1.0	1.2	-0.1
North West (GOR) & Merseyside	3.8	7.9	14.8	5.1	0.5	1.2	2.2	0.7
North West (GOR)	2.8	5.7	12.3	5.3	0.5	1.1	2.3	1.0
Merseyside	1.0	2.2	2.4	-0.3	0.8	1.5	1.6	-0.2
Yorkshire and the Humber	3.5	6.4	11.3	6.4	0.7	1.3	2.3	1.2
East Midlands	6.4	6.8	10.1	5.3	1.7	1.7	2.5	1.3
West Midlands	11.1	12.7	17.2	11.0	2.1	2.4	3.3	2.1
Eastern	11.9	12.0	15.1	10.5	2.5	2.4	3.0	2.0
London	14.8	23.8	36.9	39.7	2.2	3.5	5.4	5.6
South East (GOR)	7.7	8.8	16.8	11.3	1.1	1.2	2.2	1.5
South West	-4.0	-1.9	1.4	-1.5	-0.9	-0.4	0.3	-0.3
England	57.2	79.1	126.8	87.6	1.2	1.7	2.6	1.8
Wales	0.8	2.3	4.0	0.1	0.3	0.8	1.4	-
Scotland	5.3	2.3	6.0	-1.4	1.0	0.5	1.1	-0.2
Northern Ireland	11.0	12.1	11.2	9.4	7.2	7.7	7.0	5.7

1 Births data for all countries and English regions are based on the mother's usual area of residence. UK figures include births registered in England and Wales to mothers usually resident outside England and Wales. Annual births data are given for year of occurrence in England and Wales, and for year of registration in Scotland and Northern Ireland. See Notes and Definitions.

2 UK figures include deaths registered in England and Wales to non-residents of England and Wales. These numbers are excluded from the data for the English regions, England and Wales.

Source: Office for National Statistics; General Register Office for Scotland; Northern Ireland Statistics and Research Agency

3.8 Age-specific birth rates

Rates

	Under 20	20-24	25-29	30-34	35-39	40 and over	All ages	TPFR[2]
	Live births per 1,000 women in age groups[1]							
1981								
United Kingdom	28	107	130	70	22	5	62	1.81
North East	34	114	128	60	18	4	62	1.79
North West (GOR) & Merseyside	35	114	130	65	21	5	63	1.85
North West (GOR)	35	115	132	64	20	5	63	1.86
Merseyside	36	109	124	70	23	5	64	1.83
Yorkshire and the Humber	31	117	128	59	18	6	62	1.80
East Midlands	30	113	127	63	19	4	61	1.79
West Midlands	32	108	133	69	20	7	62	1.84
Eastern	22	110	138	70	20	4	61	1.82
London	29	83	114	80	31	6	62	1.71
South East (GOR)	20	97	138	73	23	4	59	1.77
South West	24	103	131	63	18	3	57	1.71
England	28	104	129	69	22	5	61	1.78
Wales	30	121	127	67	21	6	63	1.86
Scotland	31	112	131	66	21	4	63	1.84
Northern Ireland	27	135	173	118	52	13	86	2.59
1991								
United Kingdom	33	89	120	87	32	5	64	1.82
North East	44	102	119	72	23	4	63	1.82
North West (GOR) & Merseyside	42	101	124	84	29	5	67	1.93
North West (GOR)	42	103	125	84	29	5	67	1.94
Merseyside	40	93	121	84	32	5	66	1.87
Yorkshire and the Humber	41	99	122	78	26	4	64	1.85
East Midlands	34	95	126	81	26	4	63	1.83
West Midlands	39	102	126	84	31	5	67	1.93
Eastern	24	86	129	91	31	5	62	1.83
London	29	69	97	96	47	10	64	1.74
South East (GOR)	23	78	122	95	35	5	61	1.80
South West	25	84	125	86	30	5	60	1.77
England	33	89	119	87	32	5	64	1.81
Wales	39	103	127	77	27	5	64	1.88
Scotland	33	82	117	78	27	4	60	1.69
Northern Ireland	29	98	148	107	47	10	76	2.17
1996								
United Kingdom	30	76	107	89	37	7	60	1.72
North East	41	83	106	73	26	5	56	1.67
North West (GOR) & Merseyside	36	85	108	83	33	6	61	1.76
North West (GOR)	36	87	109	83	32	6	61	1.77
Merseyside	36	79	106	82	34	6	59	1.71
Yorkshire and the Humber	36	88	113	79	30	6	60	1.76
East Midlands	31	78	110	82	31	6	58	1.69
West Midlands	33	90	113	85	35	7	63	1.82
Eastern	24	72	106	95	38	7	60	1.71
London	25	69	97	96	51	12	64	1.75
South East (GOR)	22	64	103	99	42	8	59	1.69
South West	24	71	110	91	36	7	58	1.70
England	29	77	106	89	38	7	60	1.73
Wales	38	92	116	82	31	6	61	1.82
Scotland	30	65	98	82	31	5	54	1.55
Northern Ireland	26	72	129	109	46	8	68	1.95

1 The rates for women aged under 20, 40 and over and all ages are based upon the population of women aged 15-19, 40-44 and 15-44 respectively.
2 The total period fertility rate (TPFR) is the average number of children which would be born to a woman if the current pattern of fertility persisted throughout her child-bearing years.

Source: Office for National Statistics; General Register Office for Scotland; Northern Ireland Statistics and Research Agency

3.9 Age-specific death rates: by gender, 1996

Rates and Standardised Mortality Ratios

	Deaths per 1,000 population for specific age groups											SMR[1] (UK = 100)
	Under 1[2]	1-4	5-14	15-24	25-34	35-44	45-54	55-64	65-74	75-84	85 and over	
Males												
United Kingdom	6.8	0.3	0.2	0.7	1.0	1.7	4.2	12.4	35.4	86.5	195.5	100
North East	7.8	0.3	0.2	0.7	0.9	1.7	4.7	14.8	41.1	96.7	202.8	113
North West (GOR) & Merseyside	6.7	0.3	0.2	0.8	1.1	1.8	4.7	14.2	38.9	93.2	197.2	108
North West (GOR)	6.7	0.3	0.1	0.8	1.0	1.8	4.6	13.7	38.0	92.5	196.0	107
Merseyside	6.4	0.2	0.2	0.7	1.2	1.9	5.3	16.0	42.5	96.3	202.1	116
Yorkshire and the Humber	7.3	0.5	0.2	0.7	0.9	1.5	4.0	12.3	36.8	89.0	190.8	101
East Midlands	7.3	0.4	0.2	0.7	1.0	1.5	3.6	11.4	34.3	87.1	198.2	98
West Midlands	7.9	0.3	0.1	0.6	0.8	1.6	4.1	12.1	36.3	87.7	197.1	101
Eastern	6.0	0.3	0.1	0.6	0.8	1.3	3.1	10.2	31.0	81.1	196.2	90
London	7.1	0.3	0.2	0.5	1.1	2.1	4.6	12.4	35.0	84.3	184.5	99
South East (GOR)	5.7	0.3	0.1	0.7	0.8	1.4	3.5	10.4	30.5	79.4	191.7	90
South West	6.5	0.2	0.1	0.8	0.9	1.5	3.4	10.2	30.1	77.5	190.0	89
England	6.8	0.3	0.2	0.7	0.9	1.6	4.0	11.9	34.5	85.1	193.2	98
Wales	6.0	0.4	0.1	0.9	1.0	1.7	4.2	12.8	36.2	88.7	190.6	102
Scotland	6.7	0.3	0.2	1.0	1.3	2.1	5.8	16.3	41.9	96.6	213.3	118
Northern Ireland	6.7	0.1	0.2	0.9	1.0	1.8	4.1	12.6	37.6	93.7	244.5	109
Females												
United Kingdom	5.4	0.2	0.1	0.3	0.5	1.1	2.7	7.3	21.2	56.8	153.7	100
North East	5.0	0.3	0.1	0.2	0.5	1.0	2.9	8.8	25.4	62.6	157.7	110
North West (GOR) & Merseyside	5.8	0.3	0.1	0.3	0.5	1.2	3.0	8.6	24.1	61.6	154.2	107
North West (GOR)	5.7	0.3	0.1	0.3	0.5	1.2	2.9	8.3	23.6	61.3	154.4	106
Merseyside	6.3	0.2	0.1	0.3	0.4	1.4	3.4	9.4	25.8	62.8	153.8	111
Yorkshire and the Humber	5.8	0.3	0.2	0.3	0.5	1.1	2.9	7.3	22.2	58.2	151.0	101
East Midlands	5.1	0.2	0.1	0.3	0.5	1.0	2.4	7.2	20.0	56.2	152.6	98
West Midlands	5.8	0.2	0.1	0.3	0.4	1.0	2.8	7.2	21.5	57.3	155.3	101
Eastern	4.8	0.3	0.1	0.3	0.4	0.9	2.4	6.0	18.1	53.5	152.9	93
London	5.6	0.2	0.1	0.3	0.5	1.1	2.6	7.2	20.6	54.8	141.2	95
South East (GOR)	4.8	0.3	0.1	0.3	0.4	0.9	2.2	5.9	18.4	53.2	156.0	94
South West	4.6	0.2	0.1	0.3	0.5	1.0	2.3	6.0	17.4	50.2	147.5	90
England	5.3	0.2	0.1	0.3	0.5	1.0	2.6	7.0	20.6	55.9	151.7	98
Wales	5.1	0.4	0.1	0.4	0.5	1.0	2.7	7.7	22.1	58.5	151.5	102
Scotland	5.5	0.2	0.2	0.4	0.5	1.2	3.6	9.3	25.0	63.1	172.2	115
Northern Ireland	4.8	0.2	0.1	0.2	0.5	0.9	2.9	7.8	21.7	59.1	175.2	107
All persons												
United Kingdom	6.1	0.3	0.1	0.5	0.7	1.4	3.4	9.8	27.7	68.1	164.4	100
North East	6.4	0.3	0.2	0.4	0.7	1.3	3.8	11.7	32.6	75.2	168.5	111
North West (GOR) & Merseyside	6.2	0.3	0.1	0.6	0.8	1.5	3.9	11.3	30.8	73.2	164.6	107
North West (GOR)	6.2	0.3	0.1	0.6	0.8	1.5	3.8	11.0	30.1	72.8	164.4	106
Merseyside	6.3	0.2	0.1	0.5	0.8	1.6	4.3	12.6	33.2	74.8	165.0	112
Yorkshire and the Humber	6.6	0.4	0.2	0.5	0.7	1.3	3.5	9.7	28.9	69.8	160.9	101
East Midlands	6.2	0.3	0.2	0.5	0.7	1.2	3.0	9.3	26.7	68.3	164.7	98
West Midlands	6.8	0.2	0.1	0.5	0.6	1.3	3.5	9.6	28.4	68.8	165.8	101
Eastern	5.4	0.3	0.1	0.5	0.6	1.1	2.7	8.1	24.1	64.4	164.6	92
London	6.4	0.3	0.1	0.4	0.8	1.6	3.6	9.8	27.2	65.8	152.2	97
South East (GOR)	5.3	0.3	0.1	0.5	0.6	1.1	2.9	8.1	23.9	63.2	165.3	92
South West	5.6	0.2	0.1	0.6	0.7	1.2	2.8	8.1	23.2	60.8	158.9	90
England	6.1	0.3	0.1	0.5	0.7	1.3	3.3	9.4	27.0	67.1	162.3	98
Wales	5.6	0.4	0.1	0.6	0.8	1.4	3.4	10.2	28.6	69.9	161.3	102
Scotland	6.2	0.3	0.2	0.7	0.9	1.7	4.7	12.6	32.4	75.3	182.3	116
Northern Ireland	5.8	0.2	0.1	0.6	0.8	1.4	3.5	10.1	28.7	71.9	192.0	107

1 Standardised Mortality Ratio is the ratio of observed deaths to those expected by applying a standard death ratio to the regional population. See Notes and Definitions.
2 Deaths of infants under 1 year of age per 1,000 live births.

Source: Office for National Statistics; General Register Office for Scotland; Northern Ireland Statistics and Research Agency

3.10 Migration

Thousands

	Inflow					Outflow				
	1981	1986	1991	1995	1996	1981	1986	1991	1995	1996
Inter-regional migration[1]										
North East	31	36	40	38	39	39	46	41	46	45
North West (GOR)	79	90	90	99	100	88	101	94	104	103
Merseyside	23	22	24	25	25	34	37	29	31	31
Yorkshire and the Humber	68	79	85	91	91	73	91	85	98	98
East Midlands	77	102	90	101	102	72	85	81	92	94
West Midlands	67	87	83	90	91	79	95	88	98	101
Eastern	121	145	122	135	139	104	128	113	119	121
London	155	183	149	171	168	187	232	202	208	213
South East (GOR)	202	243	198	219	228	166	204	185	196	199
South West	108	149	121	132	139	88	103	99	108	110
England	94	116	96	108	111	93	101	112	108	105
Wales	45	55	52	55	55	42	50	47	53	53
Scotland	47	44	56	49	47	48	58	47	52	54
Northern Ireland	7	9	13	14	11	10	15	9	12	12
International migration[2,3]										
United Kingdom	153	250	267	245	272	233	213	239	192	216
North East	4	9	7	2	3	14	7	4	3	4
North West (GOR) &										
Merseyside	15	26	14	17	17	24	17	19	20	18
North West (GOR)	12	23	13	14	15	18	14	14	17	16
Merseyside	3	3	1	3	2	6	3	5	3	2
Yorkshire and the Humber	9	13	20	13	13	14	14	14	12	9
East Midlands	5	9	12	10	14	10	5	7	10	9
West Midlands	11	11	14	16	24	13	8	18	9	17
Eastern	9	21	26	19	22	18	20	22	14	13
London	49	78	79	83	92	55	51	67	50	55
South East (GOR)	26	38	45	50	42	35	43	37	35	50
South West	10	18	18	15	17	13	16	19	19	14
England	138	223	233	224	245	196	182	207	172	189
Wales	3	8	8	8	7	11	6	6	5	6
Scotland	10	16	22	12	18	21	21	23	13	20
Northern Ireland	2	2	3	1	3	4	4	2	2	1

1 Based on patients re-registering with NHS doctors in other parts of the United Kingdom. See Notes and Definitions.

2 Subject to relatively large sampling errors where estimates are based on small numbers of contacts. See Notes and Definitions.

3 Figures for all years exclude migration to and from the Irish Republic. Data for the South East prior to 1988 include migration via the UK mainland between the Channel Islands and the Isle of Man and the rest of the world. Adjustment of the figures shown are required for 'visitor switchers' and migration to and from the Irish Republic. See Notes and Definitions.

Sources: National Health Service Central Register and International Passenger Survey, Office for National Statistics; General Register Office for Scotland; Northern Ireland Statistics and Research Agency

3.11 Inter-regional movements[1], 1996

Thousands

| | | | | | Region of origin | | | | | | | | |
Region of destination	United Kingdom	North East	North West (GOR)	Mersey-side	York-shire & the Humber	East Mid-lands	West Mid-lands	Eastern	London	South East (GOR)	South West	Wales	Scot-land	Nor-thern Ireland
United Kingdom	.	45	103	31	98	94	101	121	213	199	110	53	54	12
North East	39	.	5	1	8	3	2	3	4	5	2	1	4	-
North West (GOR)	100	6	.	11	16	9	11	6	9	10	7	7	7	1
Merseyside	25	1	9	.	2	1	2	1	2	2	1	2	1	-
Yorkshire and the Humber	91	10	16	3	.	15	8	8	8	10	6	3	5	1
East Midlands	102	4	9	1	18	.	15	15	10	15	7	3	4	1
West Midlands	91	3	11	2	8	13	.	8	9	14	12	8	3	1
Eastern	139	3	6	1	8	13	8	.	53	26	10	4	5	1
London	168	5	11	3	11	10	12	30	.	56	16	6	8	2
South East (GOR)	228	5	12	3	12	15	15	29	84	.	35	8	9	1
South West	139	3	9	2	7	9	16	13	21	43	.	10	5	1
Wales	55	1	9	2	3	3	9	3	5	8	9	.	2	-
Scotland	47	4	6	1	5	3	3	4	6	7	4	2	.	2
Northern Ireland	11	-	1	-	1	1	1	1	2	1	1	-	2	.

1 Based on patients re-registering with NHS doctors in other parts of the United Kingdom. See Notes and Definitions.

Source: Office for National Statistics; General Register Office for Scotland; Northern Ireland Statistics and Research Agency

3.12 Components of population change, mid-1995 to mid-1996[1]

Thousands

	Resident population mid-1995	Births	Deaths	Net natural change	Net migration and other changes	Total change	Resident population mid-1996
United Kingdom	58,605.8	722.9	645.5	77.3	118.3	195.7	58,801.5
North East	2,605.1	29.8	30.4	-0.5	-4.1	-4.6	2,600.5
North West (GOR) & Merseyside	6,899.9	83.1	81.0	2.1	-10.7	-8.6	6,891.3
North West (GOR)	5,472.7	66.1	63.4	2.7	-4.6	-1.9	5,470.8
Merseyside	1,427.2	16.9	17.6	-0.7	-6.1	-6.7	1,420.4
Yorkshire and the Humber	5,029.5	61.9	56.5	5.4	0.6	6.0	5,035.5
East Midlands	4,123.9	48.8	44.2	4.6	12.9	17.5	4,141.5
West Midlands	5,306.4	66.4	57.9	8.6	1.6	10.2	5,316.6
Eastern	5,257.4	64.0	54.7	9.3	26.0	35.2	5,292.6
London	7,007.1	104.0	67.0	37.0	30.2	67.2	7,074.3
South East (GOR)	7,847.2	94.6	85.1	9.5	38.6	48.1	7,895.3
South West	4,826.9	53.7	57.2	-3.5	18.2	14.7	4,841.5
England	48,903.4	606.3	533.9	72.4	113.3	185.6	49,089.1
Wales	2,916.8	34.0	35.2	-1.2	5.5	4.3	2,921.1
Scotland	5,136.6	58.9	61.2	-2.3	-6.3	-8.6	5,128.0
Northern Ireland	1,649.0	23.8	15.2	8.6	5.8	14.3	1,663.3

1 See Notes and Definitions.

Source: Office for National Statistics; General Register Office for Scotland; Northern Ireland Statistics and Research Agency

3.13 Social class[1] of working-age[2] population, Spring 1997

Percentages and thousands

	Social class							Total working age population (=100%) (thousands)
	Professional occupations (I)	Managerial and technical (II)	Skilled occupations non-manual (IIIN)	Skilled occupations manual (IIIM)	Partly skilled occupations (IV)	Unskilled occupations (V)	Other[3]	
United Kingdom	4.7	25.2	20.3	17.8	14.6	4.7	12.6	35,678
North East	3.6	19.9	19.4	19.6	15.5	6.4	15.5	1,570
North West (GOR) & Merseyside	3.4	23.5	19.9	19.6	15.0	4.9	13.7	4,167
North West (GOR)	3.5	23.7	20.0	19.9	15.2	4.9	12.8	3,335
Merseyside	2.7	22.7	19.6	18.4	14.1	5.0	17.4	832
Yorkshire and the Humber	3.9	22.6	19.4	19.7	16.2	5.3	12.9	3,057
East Midlands	4.2	23.7	19.5	20.1	17.1	5.0	10.4	2,538
West Midlands	3.7	23.6	18.7	20.3	16.4	4.6	12.7	3,218
Eastern	5.1	27.0	21.4	17.0	14.6	4.5	10.4	3,242
London	6.7	30.3	22.0	13.0	10.2	3.6	14.2	4,438
South East (GOR)	5.9	29.2	22.5	16.4	12.4	3.9	9.6	4,723
South West	5.1	25.6	19.6	17.8	16.2	4.7	11.1	2,866
England	4.8	25.8	20.5	17.8	14.4	4.6	12.1	29,818
Wales	4.4	21.9	18.1	17.5	17.7	5.9	14.6	1,729
Scotland	4.5	23.4	19.9	18.5	15.1	5.3	13.2	3,147
Northern Ireland	3.0	20.7	17.7	17.3	13.9	5.7	21.6	985

1 Based on occupation. See Notes and Definitions.
2 Males aged 16-64 and females aged 16-59.
3 Includes members of the armed forces, those who did not state their social class, and those whose previous occupation was more than eight years ago, or who had never had a job.

Source: Labour Force Survey, Office for National Statistics and Department of Economic Development, Northern Ireland

3.14 Resident population[1]: by ethnic group[2], 1996/97[3]

Percentages and thousands

	Ethnic minority population							
	Percentage in each group				Total (=100%) (thousands)	White population (thousands)	Total population (thousands)	Ethnic minority population as a percentage of total population
	Black	Indian	Pakistani/ Bangladeshi	Mixed/ other				
Great Britain	28	26	22	23	3,514	52,918	56,446	6
North East	..	..	55	31	30	2,551	2,581	1
North West (GOR) & Merseyside	13	22	44	21	300	6,538	6,838	4
North West (GOR)	14	23	47	16	271	5,155	5,427	5
Merseyside	..	..	..	72	28	1,383	1,412	2
Yorkshire and the Humber	11	20	53	16	263	4,730	4,993	5
East Midlands	18	53	11	18	206	3,910	4,116	5
West Midlands	22	35	28	15	452	4,812	5,265	9
Eastern	23	26	22	29	179	5,062	5,241	3
London	40	23	13	24	1,689	5,243	6,940	24
South East (GOR)	16	31	19	34	247	7,479	7,729	3
South West	29	17	10	44	57	4,720	4,778	1
England	29	26	22	23	3,423	45,045	48,481	7
Wales	..	16	33	39	37	2,858	2,896	1
Scotland	..	12	50	28	54	5,015	5,070	1

1 Population in private households, students in halls of residence and those in NHS accommodation. See Notes and Definitions.
2 For some ethnic origins in some regions, sample sizes are too small to provide a reliable estimate.
3 Four quarter average Autumn 1996 to Summer 1997.

Source: Labour Force Survey, Office for National Statistics

3.15 Under-age conceptions[1]: by age and outcome, 1994-1996[2]

Rates and numbers

	Leading to maternities					Leading to abortions				
	Rates[3] per 1,000 girls aged				Total under-age maternities 1994-1996 (numbers)	Rates[3] per 1,000 girls aged				Total under-age abortions 1994-1996 (numbers)
	13 or under	14	15	Under 16		13 or under	14	15	Under 16	
Usual residence of girls[4]										
Great Britain	0.5	2.5	9.8	4.3	13,171	0.8	3.6	9.1	4.5	13,972
North East	0.8	4.4	15.6	7.0	1,031	1.0	4.3	10.9	5.5	808
North West (GOR) &										
Merseyside	0.5	2.6	11.2	4.7	1,833	1.0	3.4	9.2	4.5	1,749
North West (GOR)	0.5	2.7	11.5	4.9	1,494	1.0	3.5	9.4	4.7	1,427
Merseyside	0.5	2.3	9.8	4.2	339	0.6	3.0	8.3	4.0	322
Yorkshire and the Humber	0.6	3.2	12.1	5.3	1,452	0.9	4.4	9.4	4.9	1,343
East Midlands	0.5	2.6	10.8	4.7	1,052	1.0	3.4	8.9	4.5	1,009
West Midlands	0.6	3.1	12.1	5.3	1,572	0.9	4.1	10.6	5.2	1,547
Eastern	0.3	1.5	6.7	2.8	814	0.6	2.8	7.3	3.6	1,024
London	0.7	2.4	8.5	3.9	1,345	1.1	4.1	10.9	5.3	1,851
South East (GOR)	0.3	1.6	6.5	2.8	1,191	0.5	3.0	7.4	3.6	1,542
South West	0.3	1.9	6.9	3.1	780	0.8	3.0	7.9	3.9	998
England	0.5	2.5	9.6	4.2	11,070	0.8	3.6	9.0	4.5	11,871
Wales	0.6	3.6	12.3	5.5	903	0.9	4.0	9.2	4.7	773
Scotland	0.4	2.4	9.7	4.2	1,198	0.6	3.6	9.7	4.6	1,328

1 Conception statistics are derived from numbers of registered births and registered abortions. They do not include spontaneous miscarriages and illegal abortions.

2 Three years' data combined.

3 The rates for girls aged 13 or under and under 16 are based on the population of girls aged 13 and 13 to 15.

4 Information about usual residence of girls undergoing abortions is known to be not wholly accurate. In particular, girls whose abortions take place in London but who live outside the region may report living within it.

Source: Office for National Statistics; General Register Office for Scotland

3.16 Marriages[1]

Thousands

	1976	1986	1996
United Kingdom	406.0	393.9	317.5
North East	20.1	17.6	12.4
North West (GOR) &			
Merseyside	50.3	46.3	34.1
North West (GOR)	38.9	37.1	28.1
Merseyside	11.4	9.1	6.0
Yorkshire and the Humber	36.3	35.2	26.3
East Midlands	26.7	27.4	22.2
West Midlands	36.6	35.2	27.3
Eastern	32.2	34.7	28.3
London	58.4	47.5	42.0
South East (GOR)	48.5	52.0	44.0
South West	30.1	32.5	27.6
England	339.0	328.4	264.2
Wales	19.5	19.5	14.8
Scotland	37.5	35.8	30.2
Northern Ireland	9.9	10.2	8.3

1 Marriages registered outside the United Kingdom are not included.

Source: Office for National Statistics; General Register Office for Scotland; Northern Ireland Statistics and Research Agency

3.17 Cohabitation amongst non-married people aged 18-49, 1994-1996[2]

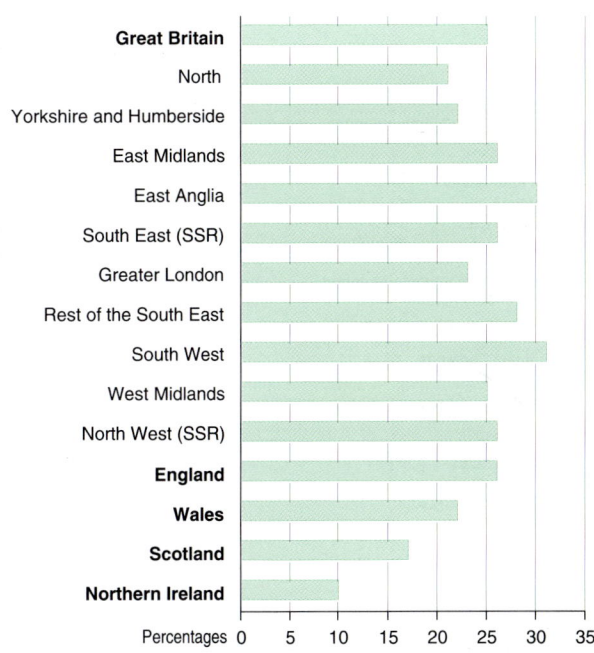

Source: General Household Survey, Office for National Statistics; Continuous Household Survey, Northern Ireland Statistics and Research Agency

3.18 Household numbers and projections[1]

Thousands

	1981	1991	1993	1995	1996	2001	2006	2011	2016
Great Britain	20,177	22,391	22,853	23,302	23,517	24,490	25,449	..	..
North East	977	1,047	1,065	1,076	1,081	1,119	1,153	1,185	1,213
North West (GOR) & Merseyside	2,550	2,721	2,764	2,801	2,817	2,911	3,005	3,105	3,203
North West (GOR)	2,003	2,156	2,194	2,228	2,243	2,319	2,399	2,484	2,568
Merseyside	547	564	570	573	574	592	606	620	635
Yorkshire and the Humber	1,827	1,992	2,033	2,063	2,077	2,156	2,231	2,307	2,380
East Midlands	1,409	1,596	1,637	1,674	1,691	1,775	1,855	1,935	2,014
West Midlands	1,861	2,042	2,081	2,115	2,132	2,199	2,267	2,338	2,410
Eastern	1,764	2,034	2,083	2,141	2,169	2,278	2,390	2,503	2,617
London	2,635	2,841	2,906	2,961	2,999	3,109	3,237	3,368	3,471
South East (GOR)	2,644	3,035	3,104	3,191	3,229	3,369	3,525	3,684	3,843
South West	1,638	1,902	1,947	1,995	2,012	2,129	2,235	2,342	2,448
England	17,306	19,211	19,619	20,017	20,207	21,046	21,897	22,769	23,598
Wales	1,017	1,128	1,148	1,166	1,174	1,211	1,248	1,287	1,318
Scotland	1,854	2,052	2,085	2,119	2,136	2,233	2,304	..	..

1 Projected from 1992-based estimates for England and 1994-based estimates for Wales and Scotland. See Notes and Definitions.

Source: Department of Environment, Transport and the Regions; Welsh Office; The Scottish Office Development Department

3.19 Households: by type, Spring 1997

Percentages and thousands

	Types of households (percentages)								Total house-holds (=100%) (thou-sands)
			Married couple			Lone parent			
	One person	Two or more un-related adults	With depen-dent children	With non-dependent children only	With no children	With depen-dent children	With non-dependent children only	Two or more families[1]	
United Kingdom	27.9	2.7	24.8	6.3	27.9	6.8	2.9	0.6	24,626
North East	28.3	2.1	23.7	7.8	26.3	8.2	3.3	..	1,111
North West (GOR) & Merseyside	27.1	2.4	24.6	6.6	27.2	8.0	3.4	0.8	2,887
North West (GOR)	27.5	2.3	24.7	6.4	27.5	7.4	3.3	0.8	2,307
Merseyside	25.6	2.9	23.9	7.0	25.7	10.5	3.8	..	580
Yorkshire and the Humber	27.0	2.5	24.8	6.0	29.2	6.9	2.7	0.9	2,145
East Midlands	25.6	2.4	26.1	7.2	29.6	6.1	2.6	..	1,728
West Midlands	26.5	2.1	25.5	6.9	27.8	7.0	3.2	1.0	2,167
Eastern	26.5	2.1	25.9	6.2	30.7	5.7	2.5	..	2,209
London	32.9	5.2	22.3	4.8	22.4	8.1	3.3	1.0	3,053
South East (GOR)	26.7	2.5	25.6	6.2	30.6	5.6	2.3	0.4	3,254
South West	27.3	2.6	24.5	5.6	31.9	5.3	2.4	..	2,059
England	27.7	2.8	24.7	6.2	28.3	6.8	2.9	0.6	20,614
Wales	27.8	1.8	24.1	6.6	28.8	7.6	2.7	..	1,228
Scotland	31.2	2.3	23.3	6.6	25.9	6.7	3.5	..	2,202
Northern Ireland	23.3	2.1	32.4	7.8	21.0	7.9	4.4	..	582

1 For some regions, sample sizes are too small to provide a reliable estimate.

Source: Labour Force Survey, Office for National Statistics and Department of Economic Development, Northern Ireland

4 Education and Training

Regional Trends 33, © Crown copyright 1998

Grant-maintained schools

Nearly two in every five secondary pupils in the Eastern region in 1996/97 were in grant-maintained schools compared with less than one in 100 in the North East and Scotland.

(Table 4.1)

Class sizes

Around a third of primary school classes in the North West (GOR), the Yorkshire and Humber region, the East Midlands and the South West contained more than 30 pupils in 1996/97 compared with a tenth in Northern Ireland.

(Table 4.2)

Under fives

In 1996/97, 85 per cent of the three and four year olds in the North East were in education, almost double the proportions in the South East (GOR) region and the South West, the regions with the lowest participation rates in England and Wales.

(Table 4.4)

Education and training after age 16

Sixteen year olds in Scotland were more likely than those elsewhere in Great Britain to be in full-time education or on a government-supported training scheme in 1995/96; among 17 year olds, the highest participation rate was in the South West.

(Table 4.5)

Examination results

In 1995/96, 35 per cent of 16 year olds in Scotland achieved SCE Standard Grades 1-3 in English, mathematics, a science subject and a modern language, compared with 20 per cent achieving equivalent GCSE Grades A*-C in the North East, the highest and lowest proportions in Great Britain.

(Table 4.7)

Higher education

Higher education students whose home is in the Eastern region are the least likely to study within their own region, while those in Scotland are the most likely.

(Table 4.9)

Qualifications

London and Scotland have the most highly qualified people of working age with more than 40 per cent qualified to at least A level standard or equivalent.

(Table 4.12)

Training

Male employees in London and female employees in Merseyside were the most likely to have received job-related training in Spring 1997, while employees in Northern Ireland were the least likely.

(Table 4.14)

Within Great Britain in 1997, over 70 per cent of employers in the North East, the Eastern region, London and the South East (GOR) felt that the skill needs of their employees were increasing, compared with 56 per cent in Merseyside.

(Table 4.15)

Employers in the North West (GOR) are the most likely within the GB regions to be involved with the Investors in People initiative, while those in the East Midlands, London and Scotland are the least likely.

(Table 4.15)

Learning activities

Excluding full-time students, adults in the Eastern region and the South East (GOR) were the most likely to have taken part in a recent learning activity in 1997, while those in the North West (GOR) and Merseyside and the North East were the least likely.

(Table 4.17)

Introduction

Education and training are no longer regarded as being relevant only to children and youngsters prior to starting work but are now considered an integral part of adult life. Education starts earlier and continues for longer than ever before: the emphasis is now on a lifetime of learning opportunities.

There are five stages of formal education: nursery, primary, secondary, further and higher. Schooling becomes compulsory at the age of five in England and Wales; in Scotland children generally commence primary school in the August prior to their fifth birthday while in Northern Ireland children who reach their fourth birthday on or before 1 July are required to start school in the following September. However, the educational value of attendance by even younger children has been increasingly recognised in recent years. Table 4.4 shows that the proportion of 3 and 4 year olds participating in education increased by 8 percentage points between 1990/91 and 1996/97 across the United Kingdom as a whole.

For a number of years now, close attention has been directed towards what happens to young people after completing their compulsory education at age 16 and in the preparation for their working life. The majority of young people continue on academic or vocational courses in school sixth forms or further education institutions or join government-supported training initiatives. Alternatively, they can seek work-based training through employment or, less satisfactorily, employment with little or no training. Table 4.5 shows the percentages of 16 and 17 year olds participating in education and/or government-supported training. In England and Wales the government-supported training initiatives aimed at young people are Modern Apprenticeships and National Traineeships, designed to lead to vocational qualifications.

The success of the UK economy rests to a large extent on the skills of the workforce. National Targets for Education and Training are now in place covering both Foundation learning by young people and Lifetime learning. They have been set using competence-based National Vocational Qualifications and their vocational and academic equivalents. Table 4.13 shows the proportions of people meeting the required qualification level for four of the targets. It should be noted that the data relate to the region in which the person is resident, and not where they obtained the qualifications. This can lead to some distortion of the regional picture of educational standards; this is particularly relevant in Northern Ireland, as many qualified young people leave home to enter higher education or seek employment in Great Britain. The National Targets are being reviewed and it is expected that new ones will be announced in Summer 1998. Measuring achievement against set targets is one way to gauge educational standards; another is to measure the proportion of the population who do not have any qualifications. Table 4.12 shows the population of working age by the highest qualification achieved. As the young increasingly gain more qualifications, so the percentage with no qualifications has fallen – the older age groups tend to have the highest percentage without any qualifications. Again the data relate to current region of residence, not where the qualifications were obtained.

Most employers invest in their workforce by providing training opportunities. Table 4.14 shows the proportions of employees receiving job-related training while Table 4.15 shows the proportion of employers providing off-the-job training. The most common types of off-the-job training provided were health and safety, induction, new technology and management. The table also shows the training initiatives employers had been involved in during the previous 12 months.

Table 4.17 shows the results of the National Adult Learning Survey. The survey found that nearly three quarters of adults in England and Wales had undertaken a learning activity of some kind in the three years prior to the survey (or since leaving full-time education, if that was more recent). The most common types of learning activity were training for a particular profession/ trade, keyboard/computing skills and leisure activities.

4.1 Pupils and teachers: by type of school, 1996/97[1]

		Public sector schools						
		Primary schools[2]		Secondary schools				
	Nursery schools	Total	Of which grant-maintained (percentages)	Total	Of which grant-maintained (percentages)	Non-maintained schools	All special schools	All schools
Pupils[3] (thousands)								
United Kingdom	61.5	5,184.9	2.6	3,711.2	16.5	595.2	114.3	9,667.0
North East	2.8	234.7	0.0	177.9	0.5	15.9	6.4	437.7
North West (GOR) & Merseyside	6.0	665.1	1.4	437.8	9.8	57.6	15.7	1,182.3
North West (GOR)	5.3	524.6	1.7	341.7	10.3	46.6	11.5	929.6
Merseyside	0.8	140.6	0.3	96.0	7.9	11.0	4.3	252.7
Yorkshire and the Humber	2.4	457.5	1.2	334.1	6.3	32.5	8.6	835.1
East Midlands	1.8	361.7	4.3	272.0	20.7	33.7	5.9	675.1
West Midlands	4.2	494.3	1.5	350.6	15.1	45.0	12.6	906.7
Eastern	2.5	434.6	7.4	348.2	38.3	58.5	9.3	853.2
London	5.6	597.8	3.6	375.1	31.5	115.5	12.3	1,106.2
South East (GOR)	2.8	637.0	4.2	454.8	25.7	136.0	17.6	1,248.2
South West	1.6	388.3	3.5	291.0	20.8	59.5	8.5	748.8
England	29.7	4,271.1	3.1	3,041.6	19.8	554.2	96.7	7,993.4
Wales	2.0	282.4	0.4	200.3	5.1	9.7	3.6	498.0
Scotland	25.5	441.7	0.1	316.6	0.2	30.3	9.2	823.3
Northern Ireland	4.2	189.6	.	152.7	.	0.9	4.7	352.2
Teachers[3] (thousands)								
United Kingdom	2.9	227.0	2.5	228.9	16.4	57.5	18.3	534.6
North East	0.1	9.9	0.0	10.4	0.5	1.3	0.9	22.6
North West (GOR) & Merseyside	0.3	27.9	1.4	26.3	9.8	4.8	2.6	61.9
North West (GOR)	0.3	21.9	1.7	20.5	10.3	4.0	1.9	48.4
Merseyside	-	6.0	0.3	5.9	8.0	0.9	0.7	13.5
Yorkshire and the Humber	0.1	19.0	1.3	19.4	6.3	2.8	1.4	42.7
East Midlands	0.1	14.8	4.3	16.0	21.6	3.2	1.0	35.1
West Midlands	0.2	20.9	1.5	20.8	15.4	4.3	1.8	48.0
Eastern	0.1	18.9	7.3	21.0	38.7	5.8	1.4	47.2
London	0.3	27.3	3.6	23.7	31.3	10.8	2.1	64.3
South East (GOR)	0.2	27.4	4.2	27.2	26.6	14.4	2.6	71.7
South West	0.1	16.4	3.4	17.0	21.0	6.2	1.2	40.8
England	1.6	182.4	3.1	181.7	20.3	53.7	15.0	434.3
Wales	0.1	12.5	0.4	12.4	5.2	0.9	0.5	26.5
Scotland	1.0	22.5	0.1	24.3	0.2	2.8	2.0	52.6
Northern Ireland	0.2	9.6	.	10.5	.	0.1	0.7	21.1
Pupils per teacher[3] (numbers)								
United Kingdom	21.3	22.8	23.3	16.2	16.4	10.3	6.2	18.1
North East	20.3	23.8	.	17.1	16.7	11.8	7.1	19.3
North West (GOR) & Merseyside	19.6	23.9	23.6	16.6	16.5	11.9	6.1	19.1
North West (GOR)	19.9	24.0	23.5	16.7	16.6	11.8	6.1	19.2
Merseyside	18.0	23.4	26.3	16.3	16.1	12.7	6.3	18.8
Yorkshire and the Humber	18.6	24.1	23.3	17.2	17.2	11.4	6.2	19.5
East Midlands	17.9	24.4	23.9	17.0	16.3	10.5	6.2	19.2
West Midlands	22.9	23.6	23.1	16.9	16.5	10.4	6.9	18.9
Eastern	18.8	23.0	23.4	16.6	16.4	10.1	6.7	18.1
London	16.9	21.9	22.1	15.9	16.0	10.7	5.7	17.2
South East (GOR)	16.3	23.2	23.4	16.7	16.2	9.5	6.7	17.4
South West	20.5	23.7	24.1	17.1	17.0	9.6	6.9	18.4
England	18.9	23.4	23.3	16.7	16.4	10.3	6.4	18.4
Wales	19.3	22.6	23.3	16.2	16.1	10.0	6.7	18.8
Scotland	24.7	19.6	23.1	13.0	12.1	11.0	4.6	15.7
Northern Ireland	23.4	19.8	.	14.5	.	8.5	6.4	16.7

1 See Notes and Definitions.
2 For Northern Ireland, figures include pupils and teachers in the preparatory departments of grammar schools.
3 Full-time equivalents.

Source: Department for Education and Employment; Welsh Office; The Scottish Office Education and Industry Department; Department of Education, Northern Ireland

4.2 Class sizes[1]

Numbers and percentages

	Primary				Secondary			
	Average class size[2] (numbers)		Proportion of classes with more than 30 pupils		Average class size[2] (numbers)		Proportion of classes with more than 30 pupils	
	1990/91	1996/97[3]	1990/91	1996/97[3]	1990/91	1996/97[3]	1990/91	1996/97
Great Britain	26.4	27.3	..	26.9	20.8	21.5	..	..
North East	26.5	27.3	19.8	25.6	21.2	22.4	5.5	7.1
North West (GOR) & Merseyside	27.5	28.2	29.0	33.8	20.7	22.0	5.2	7.5
North West (GOR)	27.8	28.3	31.9	35.8	20.7	22.2	5.3	7.8
Merseyside	26.4	27.3	18.9	26.6	20.8	21.3	4.9	6.4
Yorkshire and the Humber	26.4	28.2	18.9	32.2	20.9	22.1	4.8	6.4
East Midlands	26.5	28.0	20.3	32.8	20.7	21.9	4.0	5.6
West Midlands	26.9	27.6	22.3	28.3	20.8	22.1	6.2	8.1
Eastern	26.4	27.0	20.1	24.8	21.5	21.6	5.8	5.5
London	26.2	27.3	14.6	19.3	21.2	21.9	4.7	4.7
South East (GOR)	27.1	27.6	25.6	28.8	20.9	21.4	4.8	5.3
South West	26.7	27.6	24.3	32.2	21.3	21.2	5.5	7.3
England	26.8	27.7	22.1	28.6	21.0	21.9	5.1	6.3
Wales	24.8	25.9	17.3	22.9	21.0	20.6	..	..
Scotland	24.7	24.8	..	15.1	18.5	19.5	..	..
Northern Ireland[4]	25.8	24.1	20.1	9.6	..	..	..	..

1 Maintained schools only.
2 Includes classes where more than one teacher may be present, except in Wales.
3 Data for Scotland relate to 1995/96.
4 In Northern Ireland a class is defined as a group of pupils normally under the control of one teacher.

Source: Department for Education and Employment; Welsh Office; The Scottish Office Education and Industry Department; Department of Education, Northern Ireland

4.3 Distribution of pupils[1] in the public sector: by size of school, 1996/97

Percentages and thousands

	Maintained primary schools[2]					Maintained secondary schools				
	Number of pupils on the register				Total number of pupils (=100%) (thousands)	Number of pupils on the register				Total number of pupils (=100%) (thousands)
	100 or fewer	101-200	201-300	Over 300		600 or fewer	601-900	901-1,200	Over 1,200	
United Kingdom	4.9	16.1	33.8	45.2	5,353.7	13.6	29.1	32.1	25.2	3,711.2
North East	2.8	16.1	32.2	48.9	248.4	17.6	31.6	24.6	26.3	177.9
North West (GOR) & Merseyside	2.6	15.4	40.2	41.8	686.7	7.8	32.8	35.1	24.4	437.8
North West (GOR)	3.2	17.1	41.9	37.8	539.5	8.4	33.4	36.5	21.8	341.7
Merseyside	0.3	9.3	34.1	56.3	147.2	5.6	30.8	30.0	33.7	96.0
Yorkshire and the Humber	3.7	14.2	36.2	45.9	482.4	15.4	20.3	30.1	34.2	334.1
East Midlands	6.9	17.4	35.6	40.2	377.3	20.3	25.4	31.2	23.1	272.0
West Midlands	3.4	12.4	32.7	51.6	511.7	13.7	31.6	31.3	23.3	350.6
Eastern	6.0	19.6	41.7	32.7	448.4	18.1	29.6	30.6	21.7	348.2
London	0.2	5.2	30.5	64.1	624.7	6.6	28.8	39.2	25.5	375.1
South East (GOR)	4.3	17.3	33.6	44.8	653.4	11.8	30.0	30.6	27.7	454.8
South West	9.1	21.7	32.6	36.5	396.1	11.8	27.1	33.4	27.7	291.0
England	4.0	15.0	35.2	45.8	4,429.0	13.0	28.7	32.3	26.0	3,041.6
Wales	9.9	27.9	34.1	28.0	292.7	9.7	32.3	28.2	29.8	200.3
Scotland	8.1	18.2	27.4	46.3	441.7	12.6	30.5	36.7	20.2	316.6
Northern Ireland	11.0	19.3	16.1	53.5	190.2	32.0	30.4	24.1	13.4	152.7

1 Full-time and part-time (ie headcounts).
2 Includes 25 preparatory departments attached to grammar schools in Northern Ireland.

Source: Department for Education and Employment; Welsh Office; The Scottish Office Education and Industry Department; Department of Education, Northern Ireland

4.4 Children under five in education

Thousands and percentages

| | 1990/91 | | | | 1996/97 | | | |
| | Children under 5 in school (thousands) | Participation rates[1] (percentages) | | | Children under 5 in school (thousands) | Participation rates[1] (percentages) | | |
		Maintained nursery & primary schools	Independent and special schools	All schools		Maintained nursery & primary schools	Independent and special schools	All schools
United Kingdom	776.8	47	4	51	905.7	55	4	59
North East	53.4	76	3	78	56.5	84	2	85
North West (GOR) & Merseyside	119.9	61	3	64	127.4	66	3	69
North West (GOR)	91.2	59	3	62	98.6	64	3	66
Merseyside	28.7	70	3	73	28.8	74	3	77
Yorkshire and the Humber	81.4	60	2	62	94.4	68	3	71
East Midlands	55.4	49	4	53	62.1	54	3	58
West Midlands	83.0	55	4	59	93.1	62	4	66
Eastern	51.7	34	4	38	67.5	44	5	49
London	101.8	50	5	56	129.8	60	6	67
South East (GOR)	63.9	26	7	33	91.3	38	8	46
South West	44.0	34	5	38	51.6	39	5	44
England	654.5	48	4	52	773.7	56	5	60
Wales	52.7	68	1	69	56.3	74	1	76
Scotland[2]	45.2	33	1	34	51.1	37	1	39
Northern Ireland	24.5	46	1	46	24.5	47	1	48

1 Pupils under five in education as a percentage of the three and four year old population.
2 Excludes pupils aged four in primary schools.

Source: Department for Education and Employment; Welsh Office; The Scottish Office Education and Industry Department; Department of Education, Northern Ireland

4.5 16 and 17 year olds participating in education and government-supported training, 1995/96[1]

Percentages

| | 16 year olds | | | | | 17 year olds | | | | |
| | At school[1] | In further education[1,2] | | Government-supported training (GST) | All in full-time education and GST[3] | At school[1] | In further education[1,2] | | Government-supported training (GST) | All in full-time education and GST[3] |
		Full-time	Part-time				Full-time	Part-time		
Region of study										
United Kingdom	38.4	34.1	7.7	..	..	28.5	29.6	9.5	..	..
North East	24.3	37.8	7.6	19.0	80.0	18.0	30.6	10.2	18.8	66.4
North West (GOR) & Merseyside	24.0	42.3	8.0	14.5	78.9	19.5	34.7	9.8	15.5	68.0
North West (GOR)	19.6	46.4	8.3	14.3	78.2	16.8	37.9	10.3	15.0	68.0
Merseyside	38.0	29.1	7.0	15.4	81.0	28.0	24.3	8.3	17.0	68.1
Yorkshire and the Humber	29.9	35.6	8.5	13.7	77.4	22.4	29.0	9.7	15.3	65.2
East Midlands	35.6	30.8	7.7	12.4	77.5	27.4	27.4	8.8	14.6	67.9
West Midlands	30.1	38.2	7.8	12.9	79.7	24.1	33.1	9.7	12.7	68.6
Eastern	39.6	34.9	5.3	9.1	82.8	31.4	30.7	7.5	11.3	72.4
London	39.1	36.7	3.9	5.4	80.8	28.6	33.7	5.5	6.7	68.4
South East (GOR)	38.8	37.5	4.4	6.3	81.9	31.1	32.4	6.3	8.5	71.2
South West	38.8	36.8	6.0	9.8	84.0	31.1	31.5	7.5	11.7	73.2
England	33.8	37.1	6.4	10.8	80.4	26.4	31.8	8.1	12.2	69.2
Wales	37.1	32.0	6.1	11.7	80.8	28.0	27.2	8.1	14.5	69.7
Scotland	80.2	8.9	19.3	10.6	99.7	46.1	9.9	20.6	14.2	70.2
Northern Ireland	45.9	29.4	11.1	..	..	36.7	28.4	14.6	..	..

1 See Notes and Definitions.
2 Including sixth form colleges in England.
3 England figures exclude overlap between full-time education and government-supported training.

Source: Department for Education and Employment; Welsh Office; The Scottish Office Education and Industry Department; Department of Education, Northern Ireland

4.6 Examination achievements: by gender, 1995/96[1]

	Pupils in their last year of compulsory education[1]					Pupils/students in education[3] achieving 2 or more A levels/ 3 or more SCE Highers (percentages)	Average A/AS level point scores
	Percentage achieving GCSE or SCE Standard Grade				Total (=100%) (thousands)		
	5 or more grades A*-C	1-4 grades A*-C	Grades D-G only[2]	No graded results			
Males							
United Kingdom[4]	40.6	25.5	25.3	8.6	369.0	26.8	16.7
North East	33.6	23.4	31.8	11.2	17.0	19.2	15.6
North West (GOR) & Merseyside	38.8	23.9	27.6	9.7	43.8	25.1	17.9
North West (GOR)	40.1	23.9	27.4	8.6	34.6	25.3	17.9
Merseyside	34.2	23.7	28.3	13.8	9.1	24.3	18.0
Yorkshire and the Humber	34.7	22.1	31.9	11.3	32.0	22.0	18.4
East Midlands	38.3	24.3	28.9	8.5	26.3	25.5	16.5
West Midlands	37.2	24.4	28.8	9.6	34.5	25.1	16.8
Eastern	42.7	25.8	24.3	7.1	33.5	30.0	16.4
London	38.2	28.3	23.7	9.8	37.7	26.0	15.7
South East (GOR)	45.6	25.4	21.3	7.7	48.9	33.7	16.6
South West	44.6	25.3	23.4	6.7	29.6	29.9	16.5
England	39.9	24.9	26.3	8.9	303.3	27.0	16.7
Wales	36.8	23.9	26.7	12.6	19.1	23.9	15.1
Scotland	47.6	31.2	16.8	4.4	33.2	25.5	.
Northern Ireland	44.5	27.2	21.6	6.7	13.4	29.4	..
Females							
United Kingdom[4]	50.5	26.4	16.9	6.2	353.7	32.8	16.7
North East	42.7	25.5	22.5	9.3	16.5	24.8	15.9
North West (GOR) & Merseyside	48.2	25.5	19.0	7.3	42.7	29.8	17.7
North West (GOR)	49.7	25.4	18.5	6.5	33.7	30.4	17.9
Merseyside	42.8	26.0	20.8	10.3	9.0	27.4	17.0
Yorkshire and the Humber	43.4	25.5	22.5	8.6	30.5	27.0	18.1
East Midlands	47.5	26.6	19.7	6.3	25.3	30.6	16.6
West Midlands	46.3	27.4	19.5	6.8	32.7	31.5	16.7
Eastern	53.1	26.8	15.1	5.0	31.9	36.1	16.5
London	47.4	29.3	16.2	7.1	36.5	31.1	15.7
South East (GOR)	55.5	25.8	13.3	5.4	46.2	39.0	16.8
South West	55.3	25.7	14.4	4.6	28.4	36.6	17.0
England	49.4	26.5	17.5	6.6	290.7	32.4	16.8
Wales	46.7	24.7	19.7	8.9	18.1	30.2	15.4
Scotland	59.7	26.5	11.0	2.8	31.9	33.4	.
Northern Ireland	58.8	25.0	13.7	2.6	13.0	42.6	..
All pupils/students							
United Kingdom[4]	45.5	25.9	21.2	7.4	722.8	29.7	16.7
North East	38.1	24.5	27.2	10.3	33.5	21.9	15.7
North West (GOR) & Merseyside	43.5	24.7	23.3	8.5	86.5	27.4	17.8
North West (GOR)	44.8	24.6	23.0	7.6	68.4	27.8	17.9
Merseyside	38.5	24.9	24.6	12.1	18.1	25.8	17.5
Yorkshire and the Humber	39.0	23.8	27.3	10.0	62.5	24.4	18.2
East Midlands	42.8	25.4	24.4	7.4	51.6	27.9	16.5
West Midlands	41.6	25.9	24.3	8.3	67.2	28.2	16.8
Eastern	47.8	26.3	19.8	6.1	65.4	33.0	16.4
London	42.7	28.8	20.0	8.4	74.2	28.5	15.7
South East (GOR)	50.4	25.6	17.4	6.6	95.2	36.2	16.7
South West	49.8	25.5	19.0	5.7	58.0	33.1	16.7
England	44.5	25.7	22.0	7.8	594.0	29.6	16.8
Wales	41.6	24.3	23.3	10.8	37.2	27.0	15.3
Scotland	53.6	28.9	13.9	3.6	65.2	29.3	.
Northern Ireland	51.6	26.1	17.7	4.6	26.4	35.9	..

1 See Notes and Definitions.

2 No grades above D and at least one in the D-G range.

3 Pupils in schools and students in further education institutions aged 17-19 at the end of the academic year in England, Wales and Northern Ireland as a percentage of the 18 year old population. Pupils in Scotland generally sit Highers one year earlier and the figures tend to relate to the results of pupils in Years S5/S6 as a percentage of the 17 year old population.

4 England and Wales only for 'Average A/AS level point scores'.

Source: Department for Education and Employment; Welsh Office; The Scottish Office Education and Industry Department; Department of Education, Northern Ireland

4.7 Pupils[1] achieving GCSE grades A*- C[2]: by selected subjects and gender, 1995/96[3]

Percentages

| | English | Mathematics | Science | | | Any modern language[6] | French | Geography | History | Craft Design Technology | All core subjects[7] |
			Any science[4]	Single award[5]	Double award						
Males											
Great Britain	43.3	41.8	44.8	2.2	..	27.7	20.3	24.5	17.4	19.2	..
North East	36.2	34.8	37.0	0.7	28.7	20.1	14.8	21.4	15.4	15.6	16.1
North West (GOR) & Merseyside	41.7	39.8	42.0	1.4	32.3	27.3	20.1	24.4	17.6	15.6	21.0
North West (GOR)	42.4	41.2	43.5	1.4	34.6	28.2	20.4	25.3	17.9	16.1	21.7
Merseyside	38.9	34.2	36.3	1.4	23.7	24.0	19.1	20.9	16.3	14.0	18.4
Yorkshire and the Humber	36.2	36.1	38.9	0.9	31.7	24.0	16.8	22.9	15.8	17.6	17.9
East Midlands	40.6	39.7	43.0	1.4	37.6	23.3	17.2	23.8	15.5	18.8	18.6
West Midlands	39.5	38.3	40.6	1.0	33.3	25.1	18.3	23.9	16.6	17.9	19.0
Eastern	44.7	45.6	46.4	1.6	39.8	26.9	20.2	27.2	19.6	21.8	22.1
London	40.3	39.8	40.3	2.6	29.7	28.4	19.0	20.8	18.4	15.9	20.2
South East (GOR)	46.5	47.0	47.9	2.1	35.8	33.7	26.5	27.3	20.7	18.9	26.3
South West	46.0	46.4	48.9	1.3	40.1	31.2	23.6	26.9	18.5	24.3	24.9
England	41.8	41.4	43.2	1.5	34.4	27.5	20.2	24.5	17.9	18.5	21.2
Wales[8]	39.6	39.1	41.6	2.0	30.6	17.8	14.3	25.7	14.5	17.6	..
Scotland	59.5	47.5	61.1	8.1	.	35.4	24.5	23.2	14.7	27.2	29.2
Females											
Great Britain	60.9	42.9	46.1	2.9	..	43.1	32.3	22.8	22.0	16.0	..
North East	53.0	36.2	38.5	1.5	30.2	34.4	26.3	19.4	19.7	12.3	24.5
North West (GOR) & Merseyside	58.8	41.4	43.0	2.1	34.5	42.3	32.1	21.9	21.6	12.9	29.6
North West (GOR)	60.2	42.9	44.1	2.2	36.2	43.8	32.7	22.7	22.4	13.4	30.7
Merseyside	53.6	35.7	39.0	1.6	28.4	36.8	30.2	19.0	18.3	10.7	25.4
Yorkshire and the Humber	53.5	36.7	39.4	1.7	33.0	38.6	27.6	21.2	20.2	19.4	26.2
East Midlands	59.2	40.3	43.1	2.1	38.1	37.8	28.9	22.3	19.5	17.7	27.6
West Midlands	57.6	38.0	41.8	1.7	36.9	39.5	28.9	23.0	21.0	17.8	26.7
Eastern	63.4	47.0	47.2	2.6	40.8	42.7	32.6	24.8	24.9	20.9	32.1
London	55.9	40.4	41.6	3.9	34.1	41.8	28.2	20.1	21.9	15.1	27.9
South East (GOR)	64.2	47.9	49.0	3.0	39.7	48.8	38.2	26.6	24.2	15.7	35.4
South West	65.5	47.0	49.4	2.8	40.8	48.7	37.5	26.5	23.2	21.8	35.1
England	59.5	42.2	44.1	2.5	36.8	42.4	31.7	23.1	22.1	17.0	30.0
Wales[8]	57.9	41.6	42.6	3.3	32.8	32.6	27.4	21.8	20.7	15.0	..
Scotland	75.7	50.5	65.9	6.1	.	55.1	40.7	20.7	22.4	7.9	41.3
All pupils											
Great Britain	51.9	42.4	45.4	2.5	..	35.2	26.2	23.7	19.7	17.7	..
North East	44.4	35.5	37.7	1.1	29.4	27.2	20.4	20.4	17.5	14.0	20.3
North West (GOR) & Merseyside	50.1	40.6	42.5	1.7	33.4	34.7	26.1	23.2	19.5	14.3	25.2
North West (GOR)	51.2	42.1	43.8	1.8	35.4	35.9	26.4	24.0	20.1	14.8	26.1
Merseyside	46.2	35.0	37.7	1.5	26.0	30.3	24.6	20.0	17.3	12.4	21.8
Yorkshire and the Humber	44.6	36.4	39.2	1.3	32.3	31.2	22.1	22.1	18.0	18.5	22.0
East Midlands	49.7	40.0	43.0	1.8	37.9	30.4	22.9	23.1	17.5	18.3	23.0
West Midlands	48.3	38.1	41.2	1.3	35.0	32.1	23.4	23.5	18.7	17.8	22.7
Eastern	53.8	46.3	46.8	2.1	40.2	34.6	26.2	26.0	22.2	21.4	27.0
London	48.0	40.1	40.9	3.3	31.8	35.0	23.5	20.4	20.1	15.5	24.0
South East (GOR)	55.1	47.5	48.4	2.5	37.7	41.0	32.2	27.0	22.4	17.3	30.8
South West	55.5	46.7	49.1	2.0	40.4	39.8	30.4	26.7	20.8	23.1	29.9
England	50.4	41.8	43.7	2.0	35.6	34.8	25.9	23.9	19.9	17.7	25.5
Wales[8]	48.5	40.3	42.1	2.6	31.7	25.0	20.7	23.8	17.5	16.3	..
Scotland	67.5	49.0	63.5	7.1	.	45.1	32.4	22.0	18.5	17.8	35.1

1 Pupils in their last year of compulsory education.
2 SCE Standard Grade awards at levels 1-3 in Scotland.
3 See Notes and Definitions.
4 Includes double award, single award and individual science subjects. In Scotland, 'Any science' includes Biology, Chemistry, Physics or General Science Standard Grade. See Notes and Definitions.
5 General Science in Scotland.
6 Including French.
7 The core subjects of the National Curriculum applicable in England are English, mathematics and a science. Figures in this column also include a modern language. The National Curriculum does not apply in Scotland.
8 Welsh is included as a core subject in Welsh-speaking schools. In 1995/96, 6.4 per cent of pupils achieved GCSE grade A* to C in Welsh as a first language and a further 12.1 per cent in Welsh as a second language.

Source: Department for Education and Employment; Welsh Office; The Scottish Office Education and Industry Department

4.8 Home students in further education[1] in England: by level of course of study[2], 1995/96

Percentages and thousands

	Courses leading to NVQ/GNVQ or equivalent academic qualifications (percentages)						
	Level 1	Level 2	Level 3	Other recognised qualifications	All courses leading to recognised qualifications	Other courses (percentages)	Total FE students[1] in England (=100%) (thousands)
Region of domicile							
United Kingdom	14.5	24.4	36.0	19.4	94.4	5.6	1,936.5
North East	16.8	26.7	36.8	18.1	98.5	1.5	101.3
North West (GOR) & Merseyside	15.3	23.8	35.0	20.1	94.2	5.8	315.0
North West (GOR)	15.3	23.4	36.3	19.0	94.0	6.0	246.9
Merseyside	15.3	25.5	30.3	24.0	95.2	4.8	68.1
Yorkshire and the Humber	15.5	24.1	31.2	24.4	95.2	4.8	220.5
East Midlands	15.5	25.9	35.3	17.0	93.7	6.3	157.4
West Midlands	14.5	22.6	33.2	25.9	96.2	3.8	237.2
Eastern	13.1	26.0	39.2	15.8	94.0	6.0	175.4
London	13.6	24.2	36.6	20.1	94.4	5.6	209.9
South East (GOR)	12.6	25.9	41.6	14.4	94.5	5.5	251.3
South West	14.2	23.8	39.7	13.8	91.5	8.5	187.7
England	14.4	24.6	36.4	19.2	94.6	5.4	1,855.6
Wales	17.2	31.1	26.3	20.4	95.0	5.0	6.1
Scotland	31.0	7.5	25.4	26.4	90.4	9.6	1.8
Northern Ireland	15.8	7.3	23.7	50.3	97.2	2.8	0.4
Other[3]	15.2	21.3	28.3	26.2	91.0	9.0	72.6

1 Further education institutions only. See Notes and Definitions.
2 Highest level of qualification aimed for by students.
3 Includes Channel Islands, Isle of Man and home students whose region of domicile was unknown or unclassified.

Source: Department for Education and Employment

4.9 Home domiciled higher education students[1]: by region of study and domicile, 1996/97[2]

Percentages and thousands

	Region of study												All students (=100%) (thousands)
	North East	North West (GOR) & Merseyside	York-shire and the Humber	East Mid-lands	West Mid-lands	East-ern	London	South East (GOR)	South West	Wales	Scot-land	North-ern Ire-land	
Region of domicile													
United Kingdom[3]	4.6	11.0	9.3	7.0	8.8	5.7	14.7	11.7	6.5	5.2	12.9	2.6	1,629.8
North East	68.8	6.0	9.3	3.4	2.3	1.3	2.1	1.7	0.8	0.7	3.4	0.2	60.9
North West (GOR) & Merseyside	3.9	63.6	10.6	3.8	6.0	1.3	2.5	2.3	1.5	2.3	2.1	0.1	170.2
Yorkshire and the Humber	6.8	8.7	62.4	6.3	4.2	1.9	2.7	2.4	1.2	1.1	2.2	0.1	105.2
East Midlands	2.9	6.7	13.2	49.5	9.0	3.7	4.5	4.8	2.6	1.8	1.3	0.1	95.4
West Midlands	1.4	6.5	5.4	7.5	59.9	1.9	3.8	4.5	4.1	3.9	1.0	0.1	132.8
Eastern	2.0	4.0	5.7	8.6	4.9	41.5	15.3	10.6	4.0	1.8	1.4	0.1	122.6
London	0.8	2.5	2.2	2.6	2.8	5.0	66.8	12.1	2.6	1.1	1.2	0.1	216.1
South East (GOR)	1.6	3.4	3.8	5.0	4.7	4.3	16.0	50.0	6.8	2.7	1.6	0.1	204.2
South West	1.2	3.4	3.2	3.7	5.6	2.7	6.9	13.8	52.0	6.1	1.3	0.1	116.3
England[3]	5.5	13.0	11.3	8.5	10.7	7.0	18.0	14.2	7.8	2.4	1.7	0.1	1,295.7
Wales	0.7	6.8	2.6	2.8	4.4	1.5	3.3	4.5	5.5	67.0	0.8	-	77.6
Scotland	0.7	1.0	0.7	0.4	0.4	0.4	0.8	0.7	0.3	0.8	93.9	0.1	193.9
Northern Ireland	1.4	3.6	1.7	1.1	1.1	1.2	2.1	1.5	0.6	1.0	10.3	74.2	55.5

1 See Notes and Definitions. Open University students are excluded.
2 1995/96 for higher education students studying in further education institutions in England.
3 Includes higher education students whose region of domicile was unknown.

Source: Department for Education and Employment; Welsh Office; The Scottish Office Education and Industry Department; Department of Education, Northern Ireland

4.10 Local education authority expenditure[1], 1995-96

	Percentage of total LEA expenditure							Total expend-iture (=100%) (£ million)	Current expenditure per pupil[5] (£ per pupil)	
	Pre-primary & primary schools[2]	Secon-dary schools[2]	Special schools[2]	Contin-uing education	Admini-stration & inspec-tion[3]	Other educa-tional services[3,4]	Capital expend-iture		Nursery/ primary pupils	Second-ary pupils
United Kingdom	38.2	36.3	6.1	12.9	1.4	1.4	3.8	25,323.7	1,710	2,370
North East	39.4	38.4	5.4	13.6	0.6	-	2.7	1,301.5	1,600	2,160
North West (GOR) &										
Merseyside	39.4	35.6	6.8	14.1	0.7	-	3.4	2,833.3	1,590	2,250
North West (GOR)	39.6	35.2	6.5	14.3	0.5	-	3.9	2,169.8	1,590	2,230
Merseyside	38.9	36.8	7.7	13.4	1.2	-	2.0	663.5	1,560	2,300
Yorkshire and the Humber	39.5	38.5	4.7	14.0	0.3	0.1	2.9	2,114.1	1,650	2,210
East Midlands	38.6	40.0	5.3	13.1	0.5	-	2.5	1,666.5	1,620	2,280
West Midlands	40.1	36.9	6.4	13.2	0.7	-	2.7	2,261.3	1,670	2,260
Eastern	36.8	39.4	5.8	13.7	0.6	-	3.7	1,813.4	1,660	2,240
London	40.0	31.6	7.1	16.1	1.2	-	3.9	3,376.7	2,000	2,680
South East (GOR)	37.7	36.0	7.0	14.2	0.7	-	4.4	3,380.4	1,680	2,270
South West	36.9	37.2	6.3	15.1	0.5	-	4.1	1,841.4	1,600	2,240
England	38.8	36.5	6.3	14.3	0.7	-	3.5	20,588.7	1,690	2,290
Wales	35.8	35.3	3.8	12.0	3.6	5.0	4.6	1,364.6	1,680	2,310
Scotland	35.0	36.9	6.1	2.9	5.8	8.3	5.0	2,542.8	1,910	2,960
Northern Ireland	36.7	31.0	4.9	9.9	2.7	9.4	5.4	827.7	1,670	2,520

1 See Notes and Definitions.
2 Includes LEA expenditure on grant-maintained schools.
3 The bulk of expenditure on central services under these headings for England has been recharged to columns 1-4 along with transport of pupils for Wales.
4 Includes school catering services in Wales, Scotland and Northern Ireland.
5 These figures must be interpreted carefully in the light of different educational structures between regions.

Source: Department for Education and Employment

4.11 Destination of 1996 first degree graduates[1,2]

Percentages and thousands

	UK employment		Overseas employment[3]	Continuing education or training	Believed unemployed	Other destinations[4]	Unknown	All first degree graduates (=100%) (thousands)
	Permanent	Temporary						
Region of domicile								
United Kingdom	33.8	14.9	1.9	16.7	6.4	10.7	15.6	225.4
North East	29.7	20.3	2.1	16.3	6.4	11.0	14.2	11.1
North West (GOR) & Merseyside	31.7	18.6	1.8	17.2	7.6	10.1	12.9	24.4
Yorkshire and the Humber	35.8	15.6	2.4	15.7	6.6	9.9	13.9	23.2
East Midlands	40.2	10.0	1.4	15.3	5.8	10.7	16.5	17.6
West Midlands	31.2	17.4	1.7	15.9	5.4	11.1	17.3	19.1
Eastern	32.6	14.0	1.9	18.2	5.3	11.3	16.6	13.5
London	33.3	10.8	1.2	15.2	7.2	12.1	20.2	32.4
South East (GOR)	36.0	15.7	2.4	15.1	5.7	11.4	13.8	28.5
South West	38.2	16.3	2.1	13.7	6.5	8.2	15.0	14.5
England	34.4	15.1	1.8	15.8	6.4	10.8	15.8	184.3
Wales	32.5	13.9	1.9	21.7	6.6	10.9	12.5	12.6
Scotland	30.9	15.1	2.3	18.7	6.1	10.3	16.6	22.8
Northern Ireland	27.6	12.7	3.6	27.2	6.6	10.3	12.0	5.7

1 Destination six months after graduating in 1996.
2 Graduates from higher education institutions only.
3 Home students only.
4 Includes overseas graduates leaving the United Kingdom and graduates not available for employment.

Source: Department for Education and Employment

4.12 Population of working age[1]: by highest qualification[2], Spring 1997

Percentages and thousands

	Higher education	GCE A level or equivalent	Recog-nised trade appren-ticeship	GCSE grades A*-C or equivalent	Qualifi-cations at NVQ level 1 or below	Other qualifi-cations (level unknown)	No qualifi-cations	Total[3] (=100%) (thou-sands)
United Kingdom	20.5	13.6	9.9	22.4	6.7	8.3	18.7	35,678
North East	16.1	11.4	12.5	21.2	8.5	7.3	23.0	1,570
North West (GOR) & Merseyside	18.1	12.6	11.5	23.1	6.8	7.5	20.3	4,167
North West (GOR)	18.5	12.5	12.1	22.6	6.7	7.8	19.8	3,335
Merseyside	16.8	13.1	9.3	25.0	7.1	6.2	22.4	832
Yorkshire and the Humber	18.0	12.1	11.0	22.2	8.1	8.2	20.3	3,057
East Midlands	17.8	13.1	10.2	23.9	6.9	8.2	19.9	2,538
West Midlands	17.6	12.5	8.2	22.6	7.6	8.5	23.1	3,218
Eastern	18.6	14.2	9.7	25.7	6.8	8.1	17.0	3,242
London	27.5	12.8	6.1	19.3	4.5	13.9	15.8	4,438
South East (GOR)	23.3	15.3	8.8	24.5	6.3	7.4	14.4	4,723
South West	21.5	14.5	10.5	25.1	7.3	6.5	14.7	2,866
England	20.5	13.3	9.5	23.0	6.7	8.6	18.2	29,818
Wales	17.6	11.5	9.1	23.9	6.2	8.2	23.5	1,729
Scotland	22.4	18.1	12.9	16.9	5.0	7.2	17.5	3,147
Northern Ireland	17.4	10.6	13.4	17.8	10.5	3.4	26.9	985

1 Males aged 16-64 and females aged 16-59.
2 See Notes and Definitions. Data are not directly comparable with figures in earlier editions of *Regional Trends* which were based on the economically active and also used a slightly different classification.
3 Population in private households, students in halls of residence and those in NHS accommodation. Includes those who did not state their qualifications, but percentages are based on figures excluding them.

Source: Labour Force Survey, Office for National Statistics; Department of Economic Development, Northern Ireland

4.13 Progress towards achieving the National Targets for Education and Training[1,2], Spring 1997

Percentages

	Foundation learning[3]: percentage of the population		Lifetime learning: percentages of those in employment of working age[4]					
	Aged 19-21 qualified to at least NVQ level 2 or equivalent: all persons	Aged 21-23 qualified to at least NVQ level 3 or equivalent: all persons	Qualified to at least NVQ level 3 or equivalent			Qualified to at least NVQ level 4 or equivalent		
			Males	Females	All persons	Males	Females	All persons
United Kingdom	71	49	47	36	42	25	24	24
North East	69	46	44	32	39	20	21	20
North West (GOR) & Merseyside	69	49	46	34	41	22	22	22
Yorkshire and the Humber	69	47	45	34	40	22	22	22
East Midlands	72	48	44	31	38	21	19	20
West Midlands	66	45	41	33	38	20	22	21
Eastern	71	39	45	32	39	22	20	21
London	74	50	52	47	50	34	34	34
South East (GOR)	72	54	50	38	45	28	25	26
South West	78	50	47	36	42	25	24	24
England	71	48	47	36	42	25	24	24
Wales	67	44	45	31	39	23	21	22
Scotland	78	57	53	43	48	26	28	27
Northern Ireland	68	47	44	34	40	21	25	23

1 See Notes and Definitions for details of the targets.
2 The questions on qualifications in the Labour Force Survey were changed substantially in Spring 1996. Figures are therefore not directly comparable with those for earlier years.
3 The Foundation Learning Targets relate to 19 and 21 year olds, but data relate to 19-21 and 21-23 year olds respectively to increase the sample sizes.
4 Males aged 16-64 and females aged 16-59.

Source: Department for Education and Employment from the Labour Force Survey

4.14 Employees of working age[1] receiving job-related training[2]: by gender, Spring 1997

Percentages[3]

	Males				Females			
	On-the-job training only	Off-the-job training only	Both on and off-the-job training	Any job-related training	On-the-job training only	Off-the-job training only	Both on and off-the-job training	Any job-related training
United Kingdom	4.0	7.8	2.5	14.3	4.5	9.6	2.7	16.7
North East	4.0	7.3	3.2	14.6	4.4	9.6	3.1	17.1
North West (GOR) & Merseyside	3.4	7.7	2.7	13.7	5.3	9.3	2.8	17.4
North West (GOR)	3.5	7.7	2.7	13.9	5.2	9.1	2.8	17.1
Merseyside	..	7.6	..	12.8	5.8	10.0	..	18.7
Yorkshire and the Humber	4.7	7.6	2.4	14.8	4.7	9.4	3.0	17.2
East Midlands	4.0	6.5	2.3	12.9	4.5	8.5	2.6	15.6
West Midlands	3.5	7.0	2.2	12.7	4.7	8.9	2.5	16.1
Eastern	4.0	7.4	2.4	13.9	4.5	9.2	3.0	16.7
London	4.5	9.7	2.4	16.6	4.1	11.2	2.5	17.9
South East (GOR)	3.8	8.1	2.8	14.7	4.3	10.6	2.4	17.3
South West	4.5	7.9	2.4	14.8	4.6	10.3	3.2	18.1
England	4.0	7.8	2.5	14.4	4.6	9.8	2.7	17.1
Wales	3.7	7.1	2.0	12.7	3.4	9.1	2.2	14.7
Scotland	4.1	7.8	2.4	14.3	4.1	8.3	2.3	14.7
Northern Ireland	..	7.1	..	12.5	..	8.5	..	13.9

1 Males aged 16-64 and females aged 16-59.
2 Job-related education or training received in the four weeks before interview. In some cases sample sizes are too small to provide reliable estimates.
3 As a percentage of all employees of working age.

Source: Department for Education and Employment from the Labour Force Survey

4.15 Employers' provision of training, 1997

Percentages

	Proportion of employers:				Involved in the last 12 months with:				
	Reporting an increase in skill needs	With a training plan	With a training budget	Providing off-the-job training in the last 12 months	NVQs/SVQs	Youth Training	Investors in People	Modern Apprenticeship	Other nationally recognised vocational qualifications
Great Britain	69	65	63	82	52	16	32	15	17
North East	71	71	64	84	66	27	38	19	23
North West (GOR) & Merseyside	63	67	64	78	60	14	43	19	15
North West (GOR)	64	70	69	79	61	14	45	19	16
Merseyside	56	54	43	74	56	14	35	17	13
Yorkshire and the Humber	65	66	64	84	64	24	35	24	21
East Midlands	68	64	58	78	43	13	26	12	24
West Midlands	67	63	58	89	64	17	37	16	17
Eastern	72	65	63	83	56	13	27	12	19
London	72	61	65	82	36	13	26	10	15
South East (GOR)	74	67	69	82	48	16	32	17	15
South West	69	64	58	81	50	13	32	13	16
England	69	65	63	82	52	16	33	15	17
Wales	68	62	54	75	56	21	36	10	18
Scotland	66	69	65	78	50	17	26	13	14

Source: Skill Needs in Britain 1997, IFF Research Limited for the Department for Education and Employment

4.16 Average number of off-the-job training days per employee[1], 1997

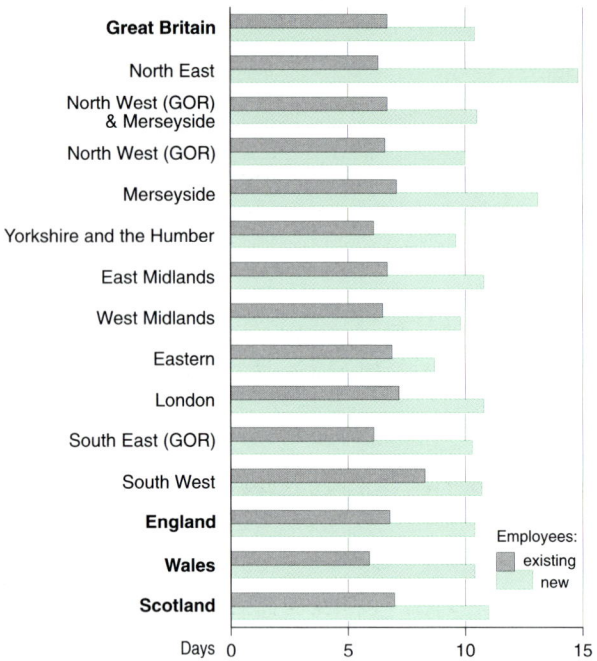

Days

1 Those who received training only.

Source: Skill Needs in Britain 1997, IFF Research Limited for the Department for Education and Employment

4.17 Recent learners[1]: by region, 1997

Percentages

	Vocational learners	Non-vocational learners	All learners
England and Wales	67	30	74
North East	57	25	64
North West (GOR) & Merseyside	64	22	70
Yorkshire and the Humber	67	31	74
East Midlands	65	24	71
West Midlands	64	32	74
Eastern	75	33	80
London	67	29	72
South East (GOR)	72	35	78
South West	65	30	73
England	67	30	74
Wales	58	34	71

1 Adults aged 16 to 69, excluding those still in full-time continuous education. See Notes and Definitions.

Source: National Adult Learning Survey 1997, Department for Education and Employment

4.18 Training for Work and Youth Training leavers[1], 1996-97

Percentages and thousands

	Training for Work						Youth Training					
	Status six months after leaving[2] (percentages)				Gained qualification[3] (percentages)	All leavers[4] (thousands)	Status six months after leaving[2] (percentages)				Gained qualification[3] (percentages)	All leavers[4] (thousands)
	In employment	In further education or training	Unemployed	Other			In employment	In further education or training	Unemployed	Other		
England and Wales	45	5	42	8	44	233.8	65	14	15	6	51	250.8
North East	42	4	46	7	46	19.9	55	16	24	6	50	18.9
North West (GOR) & Merseyside	44	5	43	8	43	41.8	64	14	16	5	51	46.1
North West (GOR)	45	5	42	8	43	25.4	67	13	15	5	53	33.0
Merseyside	43	6	44	8	43	16.4	56	18	20	6	46	13.0
Yorkshire and the Humber	41	5	45	8	41	25.7	61	15	18	5	48	27.5
East Midlands	48	4	40	8	41	18.1	67	13	13	6	51	22.3
West Midlands	44	6	42	9	46	26.0	69	12	13	6	55	26.4
Eastern	49	4	38	8	48	16.3	72	12	11	6	57	21.8
London	43	5	43	9	42	36.4	60	14	19	7	51	21.3
South East (GOR)	46	4	40	10	45	17.9	74	10	11	6	53	29.9
South West	46	4	40	9	45	18.6	68	14	12	5	52	21.2
England	44	5	42	8	44	220.7	66	13	15	6	52	235.4
Wales	48	5	39	8	45	13.1	59	15	20	7	42	15.4
Northern Ireland[1]	43	16	33	9	65	3.0	57	16	16	11	39	5.4

1 Schemes in Northern Ireland differ from those in England and Wales; see Notes and Definitions.
2 Status on completion of courses in Northern Ireland.
3 In Northern Ireland, full qualifications gained by completers expressed as a percentage of completers. Data are not comparable with previous editions of *Regional Trends*.
4 All those who left the programme during 1996-97 except in Northern Ireland where the figure covers completers of courses only and does not include early leavers.

Source: Department for Education and Employment; Training and Employment Agency, Northern Ireland

5 Labour market

Economic activity

Just over 82 per cent of people of working age in the South East (GOR) were economically active in Spring 1997 compared with around 71 per cent in Merseyside, the highest and lowest proportions.

(Table 5.3)

Twenty-six per cent of households in Merseyside in Spring 1997 with at least one member of working age contained no one in employment, more than double the proportion in the South East (GOR).

(Table 5.5)

Self-employed

Nearly four fifths of the self-employed in London are in service industries compared with a little over two-fifths in Northern Ireland.

(Table 5.7)

Jobs

Three in ten employee jobs in London are in financial and business services compared with around one in ten in Northern Ireland, Wales and the North East.

(Table 5.8)

Nearly 7 per cent of people in employment in the South West had a second job in Spring 1997, compared with less than 4 per cent in the North East and Scotland.

(Table 5.11)

Employees

More than half of females in employment in the South West worked part-time in Spring 1997 compared with a third in London; among men, however, London had the highest proportion at more than a tenth.

(Table 5.9)

Almost 40 per cent of men in the North East working part-time in Spring 1997 were doing so because they could not find a full-time job.

(Table 5.9)

Almost 30 per cent of female employees in the North East and Wales in Spring 1997 had some form of flexible working arrangement; the highest proportions for men were in the North East and Merseyside at 22 and 21 per cent respectively.

(Chart 5.12)

Earnings

In April 1997, average gross weekly earnings for full-time employees ranged from £541 in London to £356 in Northern Ireland for men and from £386 in London to £260 in the East Midlands for women.

(Tables 5.16 and 5.17)

Hours of work

Full-time employees in the Eastern region and in the South East (GOR) worked almost 45 hours a week, on average, in Spring 1997, two hours longer than employees in Northern Ireland.

(Table 5.18)

Unemployment

The ILO unemployment rate in the North East in Spring 1997 was 9.8 per cent, nearly double the rates in the South East (GOR) and the South West.

(Table 5.21)

Introduction

Interpretation of the labour market requires a number of different sources of data to be used. There are five main sources used in this chapter: the Labour Force Survey (LFS), the Annual Employment Survey (AES), the Northern Ireland Quarterly Employment Survey (QES), the New Earnings Survey and the claimant count. Problems can arise in drawing together data on the same subject from different sources. For example, the question in the LFS as to whether the respondent is employed produces a measure of employment based on the number of persons, whereas a question addressed to employers asking the number of people they employ, as in the AES and the QES, produces a measure of the number of jobs. Thus if someone has a second job they will be included twice. Details of all of the surveys can be found in the Notes and Definitions.

Unemployment is measured by the Labour Force Survey using the definition agreed by the International Labour Organisation (ILO). Counts of claimants of unemployment-related benefits are also published. There are advantages and disadvantages with both series (see Notes and Definitions), but they are complementary. The ILO unemployment rate is the number of people who are ILO unemployed as a proportion of the resident economically active population of the area concerned, while the claimant count rate is the number of people claiming unemployment-related benefits as a proportion of jobs in each area. This explains why the ILO unemployment rate for London, where inward commuting is an important feature of the local labour market, tends to be significantly higher than the equivalent claimant count rate (whereas the differential is much smaller for a region such as the South East where people commute out of the region into London). Trends in the two series appear in Tables 5.21 and 5.22.

In past editions of *Regional Trends*, economic activity rates (see Glossary) have been presented for all those aged 16 or over. In this edition, with the exception of Table 5.1, they are shown for those of working age only. By retaining rates for all those aged 16 or over in Table 5.1, it is possible to see the effect on regions which have a relatively high proportion of economically active pensioners within their population.

Table 5.5 looks at the economic activity of households with at least one member of working age. This includes households where at least one person of pensionable age lives with at least one person of working age. It also includes households made up entirely of students. In Spring 1997, 52 per cent of working-age households nationally contained only people in employment while 17 per cent contained no working members, including 9 per cent where at least one member was officially ILO unemployed. There was wide regional variation in the proportion of these 'workless' households, from 26 per cent in Merseyside and 22 per cent in the North East and Northern Ireland to 12 per cent in the South East and 14 per cent in the Eastern region and the South West.

The labour market has become more flexible in recent years. This edition of *Regional Trends* includes some new tables and charts which illustrate this flexibility. Table 5.9 looks at the reasons for working part-time. It shows clearly that gender differences are much more significant than those between regions, although there is a considerable difference between the North East and the South East (GOR) in the reasons for men working part-time. Chart 5.10 shows those usually working from home or in the same grounds or building as their home. It should be noted that although Northern Ireland has a much larger proportion of men working from home than the United Kingdom as a whole, this in part reflects the number of men living and working on farms. Table 5.11 shows that nationally around one in 20 people in employment has a second job, although this rises to one in 14 in the South West. This may reflect the varied job opportunities in the tourist industry which may need to be combined to create full-time employment. That more women than men have a second job is in part linked to the greater likelihood of women to work part time. Finally, Chart 5.12 shows employees with flexible working patterns.

Glossary of terms

Employees
(Labour Force Survey)

A household-based measure of persons aged 16 or over who regard themselves as paid employees. People with two or more jobs are counted only once.

Employee jobs
(employer surveys)

A measure, obtained from surveys of employers, of jobs held by civilians who are paid by an employer who runs a PAYE tax scheme. People with two or more jobs are counted in each job.

The self-employed

A household-based measure (from the LFS) of persons aged 16 or over who regard themselves as self-employed in their main job.

People on government-
supported training and
employment programmes
(Labour Force Survey)

A household-based measure of persons aged 16 or over participating in Youth Training, Training for Work and Community Action, together with those on similar programmes organised by a Training Enterprise Council (England and Wales), Local Enterprise Company (Scotland) or the Training and Employment Agency (Northern Ireland).

The labour force
in employment
(Labour Force Survey)

A household-based measure of employees, self-employed persons, participants in government-supported training and employment programmes, and persons doing unpaid work for a family business.

Workforce jobs

A measure of employee jobs (obtained from employer surveys), self-employment jobs, all HM Forces, and government-supported trainees (obtained from administrative returns).

The ILO unemployed

An International Labour Organisation (ILO) recommended measure used in household surveys such as the Labour Force Survey, which counts as unemployed those aged 16 or over who are without a job, are available to start work in the next two weeks and who have been seeking a job in the last four weeks, or were waiting to start a job already obtained in the next two weeks.

The claimant count

A count derived from administrative sources, of those people who are claiming unemployment-related benefits at Employment Service local offices (formerly Unemployment Benefit Offices).

The economically active/
the labour force

The **labour force in employment** *plus* the **ILO unemployed**.

The ILO unemployment rate

The percentage of the **economically active** who are **ILO unemployed**.

Claimant count rate

The percentage of **workforce jobs** *plus* the **claimant count** who are claiming unemployment-related benefits.

The economically inactive

Persons who are neither part of the labour force in employment nor ILO unemployed. For example, all people under 16, those retired or looking after a home, or those permanently unable to work.

The population of
working age

Males aged 16 to 64 years and females aged 16 to 59 years.

Economic activity rate

The percentage of the population in a given age group which is in the **labour force**.

Some of these terms are covered in more detail in the Notes and Definitions.

5.1 Economic activity[1], Spring 1997

Percentages and thousands

| | In employment | | | | | | | All aged | Economic activity | |
| | Employees | | | | ILO unem-ployed | Total econom-ically active | Econom-ically inactive | 16 or over[3] (=100%) (thousands) | rates (percentages) | |
	Full-time	Part-time	Self-employed	Total[2]					Males	Females
United Kingdom	37.4	12.7	7.3	58.1	4.4	62.6	37.4	45,898	71.7	53.9
North East	34.1	13.1	4.6	52.5	5.7	58.2	41.8	2,040	66.8	50.1
North West (GOR) &										
Merseyside	36.5	12.2	6.2	55.8	4.1	59.9	40.1	5,358	69.0	51.3
North West (GOR)	37.1	12.4	6.8	57.0	3.8	60.8	39.2	4,283	69.9	52.2
Merseyside	34.2	11.4	4.2	50.9	5.4	56.3	43.7	1,075	65.5	48.0
Yorkshire and the Humber	35.9	13.2	6.4	56.1	4.9	61.0	39.0	3,943	70.0	52.4
East Midlands	39.0	14.2	6.5	60.3	4.1	64.4	35.6	3,259	72.9	56.2
West Midlands	38.2	12.6	6.7	58.3	4.2	62.5	37.5	4,135	72.7	52.8
Eastern	39.3	12.7	8.2	60.9	3.8	64.7	35.3	4,164	74.1	55.6
London	39.7	10.6	7.9	58.7	5.9	64.6	35.4	5,478	74.1	55.7
South East (GOR)	38.8	13.7	9.1	62.1	3.4	65.6	34.4	6,141	74.9	56.7
South West	34.6	15.1	9.4	59.9	3.3	63.2	36.8	3,841	71.8	55.0
England	37.6	12.9	7.5	58.7	4.3	63.0	37.0	38,358	72.2	54.3
Wales	33.3	12.0	6.7	53.1	4.8	57.9	42.1	2,292	66.4	50.0
Scotland	38.1	11.9	5.7	56.6	5.3	61.8	38.2	4,026	70.6	53.8
Northern Ireland	35.8	9.7	7.2	55.1	4.5	59.5	40.5	1,222	69.9	49.9

1 See Notes and Definitions.
2 Includes those on government-supported employment and training schemes, and unpaid family workers.
3 Population in private households, student halls of residence and NHS accommodation.

Source: Labour Force Survey, Office for National Statistics and Department of Economic Development, Northern Ireland

5.2 Labour force[1]: by age, Spring 1997

Percentages and thousands

| | Percentage aged | | | | | All ages (=100%) (thousands) |
	16-24	25-34	35-44	Females 45-59, males 45-64	Females 60 or over, males 65 or over	
United Kingdom	15.7	26.7	24.0	30.7	2.9	28,716
North East	16.3	26.5	25.2	30.0	1.9	1,187
North West (GOR) & Merseyside	16.4	26.8	23.9	30.4	2.6	3,210
North West (GOR)	16.5	26.3	23.6	30.8	2.8	2,606
Merseyside	16.0	28.6	24.8	28.6	1.9	605
Yorkshire and the Humber	15.7	27.4	24.2	30.2	2.4	2,405
East Midlands	15.6	26.2	24.0	31.6	2.7	2,098
West Midlands	15.7	26.1	23.4	32.0	2.8	2,586
Eastern	15.4	25.3	24.1	32.4	2.9	2,694
London	14.7	31.7	24.2	26.7	2.6	3,539
South East (GOR)	15.2	25.3	23.3	32.6	3.5	4,026
South West	14.9	24.7	23.6	33.0	3.8	2,426
England	15.5	26.8	23.9	31.0	2.9	24,172
Wales	16.9	25.3	23.9	30.8	3.1	1,327
Scotland	16.8	26.5	24.9	29.1	2.7	2,490
Northern Ireland	17.9	28.2	23.7	27.5	2.8	727

1 See Notes and Definitions.

Source: Labour Force Survey, Office for National Statistics and Department of Economic Development, Northern Ireland

5.3 Labour force and economic activity rates[1]

Thousands and percentages

	Labour force (thousands)					Economic activity rates (percentages)				
	1993	1994	1995	1996	1997	1993	1994	1995	1996	1997
Males										
United Kingdom	16,021	15,996	15,981	15,992	16,023	85.6	85.2	84.7	84.6	84.4
North East	671	665	653	668	662	80.7	80.4	79.1	80.7	79.7
North West (GOR) &										
Merseyside	1,825	1,818	1,795	1,800	1,794	83.2	82.7	81.2	81.7	81.2
North West (GOR)	1,477	1,480	1,462	1,462	1,462	84.7	84.4	82.5	83.2	82.1
Merseyside	348	338	333	337	332	77.2	76.0	76.1	75.7	77.8
Yorkshire and the Humber	1,374	1,359	1,379	1,355	1,350	85.0	83.9	85.0	83.2	82.5
East Midlands	1,152	1,145	1,153	1,167	1,167	86.9	86.0	86.1	86.6	85.9
West Midlands	1,474	1,486	1,469	1,472	1,474	85.7	86.4	85.2	85.7	85.5
Eastern	1,514	1,514	1,543	1,526	1,517	89.7	88.9	89.6	88.3	87.4
London	1,978	1,950	1,950	1,948	1,969	85.9	84.3	84.1	83.9	84.6
South East (GOR)	2,217	2,212	2,216	2,232	2,238	88.9	88.7	88.6	88.7	88.3
South West	1,301	1,318	1,329	1,315	1,341	86.9	87.9	87.6	85.9	87.1
England	13,506	13,466	13,486	13,483	13,512	86.2	85.7	85.5	85.2	85.0
Wales	719	732	722	734	737	79.1	79.7	78.5	80.0	79.8
Scotland	1,390	1,400	1,371	1,369	1,364	84.1	84.7	83.0	82.6	82.4
Northern Ireland	406	399	403	406	411	82.0	79.5	79.5	79.9	79.5
Females										
United Kingdom	12,426	12,436	12,445	12,561	12,692	70.6	70.6	70.6	71.1	71.4
North East	530	519	511	518	525	67.5	66.3	66.5	66.7	68.0
North West (GOR) &										
Merseyside	1,430	1,426	1,395	1,425	1,416	69.8	69.5	67.9	69.4	68.2
North West (GOR)	1,147	1,160	1,131	1,148	1,144	70.8	71.1	69.7	70.7	69.2
Merseyside	283	266	263	276	273	65.6	62.9	60.8	64.4	64.4
Yorkshire and the Humber	1,072	1,060	1,055	1,064	1,055	71.7	70.7	70.8	71.5	70.3
East Midlands	899	882	896	913	931	73.0	71.8	72.4	73.4	74.5
West Midlands	1,104	1,118	1,110	1,115	1,112	69.6	70.8	70.1	70.3	69.9
Eastern	1,149	1,161	1,163	1,167	1,177	73.6	74.1	74.0	73.1	73.4
London	1,540	1,518	1,526	1,557	1,570	69.6	68.2	68.6	69.8	70.4
South East (GOR)	1,725	1,746	1,742	1,782	1,788	73.2	74.2	73.9	75.4	75.5
South West	1,040	1,040	1,045	1,050	1,085	74.0	74.4	74.0	73.7	75.2
England	10,489	10,468	10,444	10,590	10,660	71.4	71.3	71.0	71.7	71.8
Wales	559	566	583	569	590	65.8	65.9	68.3	66.9	68.4
Scotland	1,092	1,118	1,121	1,098	1,126	69.4	70.6	70.9	70.1	71.2
Northern Ireland	285	285	297	303	317	59.2	59.3	61.0	62.0	63.8
All persons										
United Kingdom	28,447	28,433	28,426	28,552	28,716	78.4	78.2	78.0	78.1	78.2
North East	1,200	1,184	1,165	1,186	1,187	74.4	73.7	73.1	74.0	74.1
North West (GOR) &										
Merseyside	3,255	3,243	3,190	3,224	3,210	76.8	76.4	74.8	75.8	75.0
North West (GOR)	2,624	2,639	2,593	2,610	2,606	78.1	78.1	76.4	77.3	76.0
Merseyside	631	604	597	614	605	71.6	69.7	68.6	70.2	71.3
Yorkshire and the Humber	2,446	2,419	2,434	2,419	2,405	78.7	77.6	78.3	77.7	76.7
East Midlands	2,051	2,026	2,048	2,081	2,098	80.3	79.3	79.6	80.3	80.5
West Midlands	2,578	2,604	2,579	2,587	2,586	78.1	79.1	78.0	78.4	78.1
Eastern	2,664	2,675	2,706	2,692	2,694	82.1	81.9	82.2	81.1	80.7
London	3,518	3,468	3,476	3,505	3,539	78.0	76.5	76.6	77.1	77.7
South East (GOR)	3,942	3,958	3,958	4,013	4,026	81.4	81.8	81.5	82.4	82.2
South West	2,341	2,358	2,374	2,366	2,426	80.8	81.5	81.1	80.1	81.5
England	23,996	23,934	23,930	24,073	24,172	79.2	78.9	78.6	78.8	78.7
Wales	1,279	1,298	1,304	1,303	1,327	72.8	73.1	73.6	73.8	74.4
Scotland	2,482	2,517	2,492	2,467	2,490	77.0	77.9	77.2	76.6	77.0
Northern Ireland	691	683	700	710	727	70.9	69.7	70.5	71.2	71.8

1 At Spring of each year. Based on the population of working age in private households, student halls of residence and NHS accommodation. See Notes and Definitions.

Source: Labour Force Survey, Office for National Statistics and Department of Economic Development, Northern Ireland

5.4 Labour force and economic activity projections[1,2]

Thousands and percentages

	Labour force (thousands)[3]				Economic activity rates (percentages)[4]					
	Males		Females		Males		Females		All persons	
	2001	2006	2001	2006	2001	2006	2001	2006	2001	2006
Standard Statistical Regions										
United Kingdom[2]	16,396	16,520	13,287	13,715	84.2	82.9	72.7	73.6	78.7	78.5
North	798	791	654	669	80.0	78.5	70.2	71.5	75.4	75.2
North West (SSR)	1,685	1,685	1,387	1,433	81.3	79.8	71.9	73.3	76.8	76.7
Yorkshire and Humberside	1,377	1,383	1,114	1,152	82.9	81.5	73.4	74.9	78.4	78.4
East Midlands	1,185	1,203	955	1,004	85.4	83.9	74.5	76.2	80.2	80.3
West Midlands	1,487	1,481	1,183	1,224	85.5	84.0	73.9	75.6	80.0	80.1
East Anglia	645	664	516	548	88.7	87.3	78.1	80.0	83.7	83.9
South East (SSR)	5,191	5,255	4,201	4,400	86.3	84.9	73.9	75.6	80.3	80.5
Greater London	1,991	2,022	1,600	1,686	83.8	82.6	69.8	71.4	77.0	77.2
Rest of South East	3,200	3,233	2,601	2,715	87.9	86.4	76.6	78.4	82.6	82.7
South West	1,381	1,412	1,124	1,181	87.2	85.7	77.1	78.9	82.4	82.5
England	13,751	13,874	11,134	11,610	84.9	83.5	73.9	75.5	79.7	79.8
Wales	737	737	599	620	78.4	77.0	68.2	69.6	73.6	73.5
Scotland	1,376	1,347	1,152	1,167	83.5	82.0	73.5	75.1	78.7	78.7
Northern Ireland	414	418	306	318	78.6	77.4	61.3	62.6	70.2	70.3

1 Based on the projected population living in households.
2 Projections are based on 1994 estimates of the labour force, except for figures relating to the United Kingdom which are based on 1997 estimates for Great Britain and 1994 estimates
  for Northern Ireland; therefore the country figures do not sum to those for the United Kingdom. See Notes and Definitions.
3 Includes all people aged 16 or over.
4 Relates to people of working age: 16-64 for males, 16-59 for females.

Source: Labour Force Survey, Office for National Statistics and Department of Economic Development, Northern Ireland

5.5 Economic activity of households with at least one member of working age[1,2], Spring 1997

Percentages and thousands

	Percentage of households where			All households with at least one member of working age (thousands)
	All members are in employment	At least one person is ILO unemployed	No one is in employment	
United Kingdom	52.3	9.4	17.3	18,225
North East	47.2	12.4	22.5	809
North West (GOR) & Merseyside	50.2	9.1	19.9	2,105
North West (GOR)	52.1	8.2	18.2	1,663
Merseyside	42.9	12.1	26.1	442
Yorkshire and the Humber	51.2	10.7	19.9	1,580
East Midlands	55.6	8.9	15.0	1,283
West Midlands	52.0	9.0	16.7	1,625
Eastern	56.5	8.1	13.8	1,615
London	49.2	11.3	18.8	2,302
South East (GOR)	57.0	7.4	12.4	2,421
South West	57.0	7.2	13.5	1,461
England	53.1	9.2	16.7	15,202
Wales	45.7	9.9	20.7	879
Scotland	51.1	10.6	20.5	1,663
Northern Ireland	44.5	10.6	22.0	481

1 Males aged 16-64 and females aged 16-59.
2 See Introduction.

Source: Labour Force Survey, Office for National Statistics and Department of Economic Development, Northern Ireland

5.6 Employee jobs and self-employment jobs[1]: by gender

Thousands

| | Employee jobs | | | | | | Self-employment jobs[2] | | | | | |
| | Males | | | Females | | | Males | | | Females | | |
	1995	1996	1997	1995	1996	1997	1995	1996	1997	1995	1996	1997
United Kingdom	11,158	11,284	11,568	10,855	11,230	11,361	2,519	2,534	2,459	811	839	871
North East	432	435	444	439	443	450	74	70	75	24	22	21
North West (GOR) & Merseyside	1,254	1,249	1,298	1,242	1,292	1,309	252	266	251	72	81	79
Yorkshire and the Humber	958	921	935	917	930	924	203	203	190	55	64	64
East Midlands	784	791	817	762	786	791	166	179	152	46	49	52
West Midlands	1,068	1,081	1,106	951	1,005	1,024	206	208	194	59	63	61
Eastern	965	971	995	926	954	970	270	258	259	87	83	94
London	1,646	1,684	1,706	1,547	1,587	1,615	307	329	305	110	116	128
South East (GOR)	1,435	1,528	1,566	1,426	1,535	1,559	407	411	407	137	136	146
South West	865	867	937	877	900	909	272	259	260	102	106	100
England	9,407	9,528	9,803	9,086	9,431	9,551	2,157	2,183	2,092	692	720	747
Wales	476	479	490	470	498	494	119	121	117	44	43	45
Scotland	987	991	984	1,012	1,010	1,023	173	164	183	63	64	63
Northern Ireland	288	286	291	288	291	294	71	66	66	12	12	16

1 At September each year. See Notes and Definitions.
2 With or without employees.

Source: Short-term Employment and Labour Force Surveys, Office for National Statistics;
Quarterly Employment and Labour Force Surveys, Department of Economic Development, Northern Ireland

5.7 Self-employment: by broad industry group[1], Spring 1997

Percentages and thousands

| | Agriculture & fishing | Industry | | | | Total self-employed[3] (=100%) (thousands) |
		Manufacturing	Construction	All industry[2]	Services	
United Kingdom	7.5	7.3	22.4	29.9	62.6	3,335
North East	..	..	21.6	28.9	67.5	95
North West (GOR) & Merseyside	6.7	6.4	23.6	30.1	63.1	335
North West (GOR)	7.7	7.1	22.3	29.5	62.8	290
Merseyside	..	..	32.4	34.0	65.2	45
Yorkshire and the Humber	6.0	8.4	23.1	31.6	62.5	252
East Midlands	6.5	8.0	23.3	31.6	61.9	211
West Midlands	7.9	8.2	24.2	32.6	59.6	277
Eastern	4.9	7.4	26.4	34.1	61.1	342
London	..	4.6	17.2	21.8	77.8	430
South East (GOR)	4.5	8.1	25.4	33.7	61.8	560
South West	12.0	9.9	21.4	31.8	56.3	361
England	5.7	7.5	23.0	30.7	63.6	2,863
Wales	18.7	7.4	19.4	26.8	54.5	153
Scotland	14.0	5.5	17.5	24.1	61.9	231
Northern Ireland	30.6	..	20.0	26.1	43.3	88

1 Based on SIC 1992. In some cases, sample sizes are too small to provide a reliable estimate.
2 Includes SIC groups C and E: Quarrying, Energy and Water.
3 Total includes those who did not state their industry and those whose workplace is outside the United Kingdom, but percentages are based on figures which exclude them.

Source: Labour Force Survey, Office for National Statistics and Department of Economic Development, Northern Ireland

5.8 Employee jobs: by industry and gender, September 1996[1]

Percentages and thousands

	Agriculture, hunting, forestry & fishing	Mining, quarrying, (inc oil & gas extraction)	Manufacturing	Electricity, gas, water	Construction	Distribution, hotels & catering, repairs
Males						
United Kingdom	2.1	0.8	26.0	1.0	6.1	19.9
North East	1.1	1.1	33.5	0.9	9.5	15.0
North West (GOR) & Merseyside	1.4	0.2	30.4	1.1	6.2	19.9
North West (GOR)	1.5	0.2	31.8	1.1	6.3	19.6
Merseyside	0.4	0.1	23.2	0.7	5.8	21.0
Yorkshire and the Humber	1.9	0.8	32.5	1.0	7.1	18.9
East Midlands	2.5	2.8	35.3	1.1	5.9	18.4
West Midlands	1.8	0.3	38.3	0.8	5.6	18.2
Eastern	3.2	0.4	26.1	0.9	5.5	21.2
London	0.1	0.2	10.8	0.4	4.3	20.6
South East (GOR)	2.3	0.3	20.5	1.0	5.1	22.6
South West	3.2	0.6	25.7	1.4	5.2	21.4
England	1.8	0.6	26.2	0.9	5.7	20.1
Wales	3.1	0.8	32.5	1.3	6.2	16.6
Scotland	2.8	2.2	21.9	1.4	9.9	19.7
Northern Ireland	5.8	0.6	24.6	1.4	7.1	18.4
Females						
United Kingdom	0.6	0.1	10.4	0.3	1.1	25.3
North East	0.4	0.1	11.7	0.4	1.2	25.5
North West (GOR) & Merseyside	0.4	-	11.3	0.3	1.3	25.6
North West (GOR)	0.5	-	11.9	0.4	1.3	26.0
Merseyside	0.1	-	8.5	0.1	0.9	23.8
Yorkshire and the Humber	0.5	0.1	12.3	0.3	1.3	26.7
East Midlands	0.7	0.7	17.0	0.3	1.2	24.3
West Midlands	0.6	-	14.5	0.3	1.0	25.0
Eastern	1.0	0.1	10.4	0.3	1.0	26.5
London	0.1	0.1	5.8	0.2	0.8	22.1
South East (GOR)	0.8	0.1	7.9	0.3	1.0	26.0
South West	1.1	-	8.6	0.4	0.9	27.9
England	0.6	0.1	10.4	0.3	1.1	25.3
Wales	1.0	0.1	11.4	0.3	1.3	24.3
Scotland	0.5	0.3	9.7	0.3	1.4	26.0
Northern Ireland	0.8	0.1	11.5	0.2	0.8	22.0
All persons						
United Kingdom	1.3	0.4	18.2	0.6	3.6	22.6
North East	0.7	0.6	22.5	0.6	5.3	20.3
North West (GOR) & Merseyside	0.9	0.1	20.7	0.7	3.7	22.8
North West (GOR)	1.0	0.1	21.8	0.8	3.8	22.9
Merseyside	0.2	-	15.3	0.4	3.2	22.5
Yorkshire and the Humber	1.2	0.4	22.4	0.6	4.2	22.8
East Midlands	1.6	1.8	26.3	0.7	3.6	21.3
West Midlands	1.2	0.2	26.8	0.6	3.4	21.5
Eastern	2.1	0.2	18.3	0.6	3.3	23.8
London	0.1	0.1	8.4	0.3	2.6	21.3
South East (GOR)	1.5	0.2	14.2	0.7	3.1	24.3
South West	2.1	0.3	17.0	0.9	3.0	24.7
England	1.2	0.4	18.3	0.6	3.4	22.7
Wales	2.0	0.4	21.8	0.8	3.7	20.6
Scotland	1.6	1.2	15.7	0.9	5.6	22.9
Northern Ireland	3.3	0.3	18.0	0.8	3.9	20.2

5.8 *(continued)*

Percentages and thousands

	Transport, storage & communication	Financial & business services	Public administration & defence	Education, social work & health services	Other	Whole economy (=100%) (thousands)
Males						
United Kingdom	8.7	15.9	6.3	9.2	4.1	11,308
North East	7.8	9.4	7.2	10.3	4.1	443
North West (GOR) & Merseyside	8.9	13.1	5.8	9.2	3.8	1,247
North West (GOR)	8.7	13.1	5.3	8.5	3.6	1,046
Merseyside	9.5	12.8	8.7	12.9	4.9	201
Yorkshire and the Humber	8.1	11.4	5.5	9.1	3.7	922
East Midlands	7.2	10.7	4.4	8.5	3.2	807
West Midlands	7.2	12.3	4.9	7.6	3.0	1,083
Eastern	9.6	16.0	4.8	8.5	3.7	972
London	11.7	30.5	7.2	8.2	5.8	1,682
South East (GOR)	9.1	19.9	6.3	9.3	3.6	1,533
South West	7.5	13.9	7.3	9.7	4.0	867
England	8.9	17.0	6.0	8.8	4.0	9,554
Wales	6.8	8.3	8.2	11.6	4.5	479
Scotland	8.0	12.0	7.1	10.6	4.4	988
Northern Ireland	6.0	7.2	12.5	11.6	4.8	286
Females						
United Kingdom	2.9	18.5	6.1	29.7	4.9	11,239
North East	2.5	13.3	8.7	31.0	5.3	449
North West (GOR) & Merseyside	2.7	15.6	6.2	32.0	4.6	1,291
North West (GOR)	2.7	15.5	5.8	31.5	4.4	1,061
Merseyside	2.5	16.2	7.9	34.3	5.7	230
Yorkshire and the Humber	2.6	16.2	5.9	29.2	4.8	930
East Midlands	2.4	14.4	4.8	29.5	4.6	791
West Midlands	2.5	17.3	5.3	28.9	4.6	1,005
Eastern	3.3	18.4	4.7	29.4	4.8	955
London	4.4	30.8	6.4	23.4	6.0	1,587
South East (GOR)	3.6	20.8	5.1	29.6	4.8	1,536
South West	2.3	17.1	6.1	30.9	4.6	900
England	3.1	19.5	5.8	28.9	4.9	9,444
Wales	1.6	12.0	9.0	33.8	5.1	498
Scotland	2.5	15.8	7.0	31.4	4.9	1,007
Northern Ireland	1.8	9.2	8.3	41.0	4.3	291
All persons						
United Kingdom	5.8	17.2	6.2	19.4	4.5	22,547
North East	5.1	11.4	8.0	20.7	4.7	892
North West (GOR) & Merseyside	5.7	14.4	6.0	20.8	4.2	2,538
North West (GOR)	5.7	14.3	5.6	20.1	4.0	2,107
Merseyside	5.8	14.6	8.3	24.3	5.3	431
Yorkshire and the Humber	5.3	13.8	5.7	19.2	4.3	1,852
East Midlands	4.8	12.5	4.6	18.9	3.9	1,598
West Midlands	4.9	14.7	5.1	17.8	3.8	2,088
Eastern	6.5	17.2	4.8	18.9	4.3	1,927
London	8.2	30.7	6.8	15.6	5.9	3,269
South East (GOR)	6.3	20.4	5.7	19.5	4.2	3,069
South West	4.9	15.5	6.7	20.5	4.3	1,767
England	6.0	18.2	5.9	18.8	4.5	18,999
Wales	4.2	10.2	8.6	22.9	4.8	977
Scotland	5.2	13.9	7.1	21.1	4.7	1,995
Northern Ireland	3.9	8.2	10.4	26.5	4.5	576

1 Based on SIC 1992. See Notes and Definitions.

Source: Annual Employment Survey, Office for National Statistics;
Quarterly Employment Survey, Department of Economic Development, Northern Ireland

5.9 Reasons given for working part-time[1], Spring 1997

Percentages and thousands

	Males					Females				
	Did not want a full-time job	Could not find a full-time job	Student or at school	All part-time workers[2,3] (=100%) (thousands)	Part-time workers as a percentage of all in employment[2]	Did not want a full-time job	Could not find a full-time job	Student or at school	All part-time workers[2,3] (=100%) (thousands)	Part-time workers as a percentage of all in employment[2]
United Kingdom	37.9	24.1	34.7	1,252	8.6	79.2	9.6	10.4	5,264	44.6
North East	27.1	39.8	30.5	52	9.0	79.3	10.3	9.4	233	48.3
North West (GOR) & Merseyside	36.6	26.6	32.9	129	7.9	78.1	12.1	9.5	583	44.1
Yorkshire and the Humber	34.9	29.1	33.6	102	8.4	82.2	8.3	8.6	465	47.5
East Midlands	39.0	21.9	36.9	78	7.3	81.6	8.4	9.4	426	48.8
West Midlands	39.6	20.2	37.6	104	7.7	81.1	9.1	9.2	473	45.8
Eastern	39.8	24.2	31.5	104	7.4	81.2	8.4	9.4	499	45.3
London	33.0	28.2	36.9	191	10.9	73.9	10.2	14.6	483	33.8
South East (GOR)	45.9	16.0	34.5	200	9.6	81.6	6.0	11.0	778	46.1
South West	39.8	24.7	32.5	125	10.1	78.5	10.4	10.4	533	52.0
England	38.2	24.4	34.4	1,085	8.8	79.8	9.1	10.3	4,474	45.0
Wales	34.5	22.0	35.3	51	7.9	77.0	11.7	10.1	249	46.2
Scotland	37.5	18.3	40.9	93	7.7	74.8	13.0	11.6	433	41.9
Northern Ireland[4]	..	..	..	23	6.3	76.1	13.3	9.8	107	37.3

1 Based on respondents' own definition of part-time.
2 Employees and the self-employed only.
3 Includes people who said they worked part-time because they were ill or disabled. Hence percentages shown do not add to 100 per cent.
4 For males, sample sizes are too small to provide reliable estimates.

Source: Labour Force Survey, Office for National Statistics and Department of Economic Development, Northern Ireland

5.10 Employees and self-employed working from home[1], Spring 1997

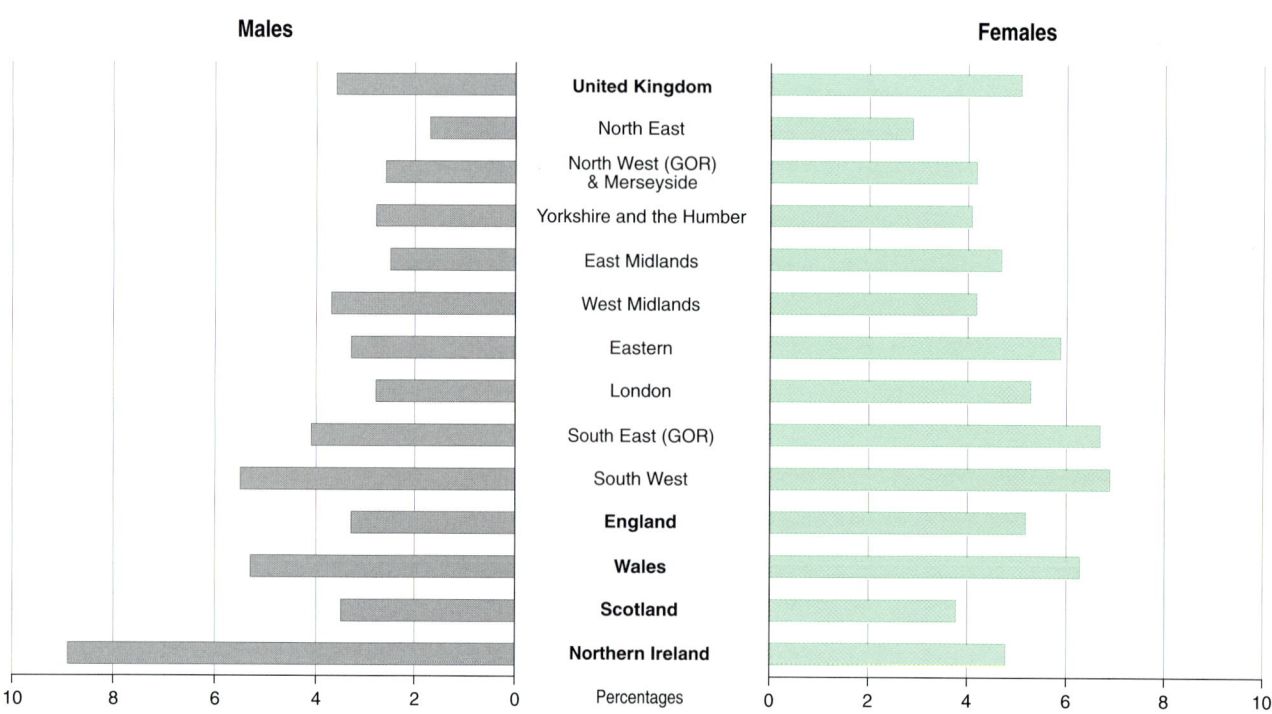

1 As a percentage of all employees and self-employed. Includes both those working at home or in the same grounds or buildings as their home.

Source: Labour Force Survey, Office for National Statistics and Department of Economic Development, Northern Ireland

5.11 Employees and self-employed people with a second job: by gender, Spring 1997

Thousands and percentages

	People with a second job (thousands)			As a percentage of all employees and self-employed		
	Males	Females	All persons	Males	Females	All persons
United Kingdom	551	703	1,254	3.8	6.0	4.8
North East	19	20	40	3.4	4.2	3.8
North West (GOR) & Merseyside	56	76	132	3.5	5.8	4.5
North West (GOR)	46	64	110	3.5	6.0	4.6
Merseyside	10	13	22	3.4	5.0	4.2
Yorkshire and the Humber	48	74	122	4.0	7.6	5.6
East Midlands	33	50	83	3.1	5.8	4.3
West Midlands	49	56	104	3.6	5.4	4.4
Eastern	52	66	117	3.7	6.0	4.7
London	56	72	129	3.2	5.1	4.0
South East (GOR)	87	107	193	4.1	6.3	5.1
South West	68	88	156	5.5	8.6	6.9
England	467	610	1,077	3.8	6.1	4.8
Wales	32	30	62	4.9	5.6	5.2
Scotland	39	49	88	3.2	4.8	3.9
Northern Ireland	13	14	27	3.9	4.8	4.3

Source: Labour Force Survey, Office for National Statistics and Department of Economic Development, Northern Ireland

5.12 Employees with flexible working patterns[1,2]: by gender, Spring 1997

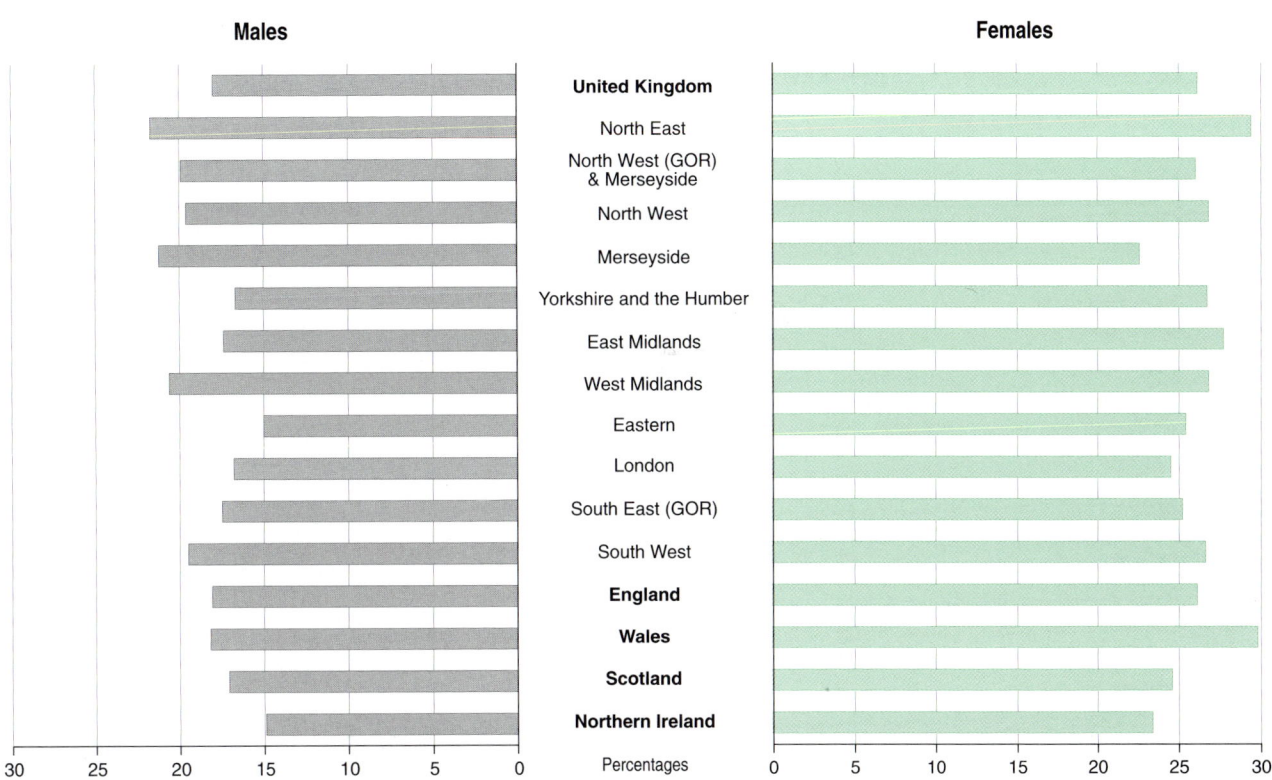

1 Includes those on flexi-time, annualised hours, term-time working, job sharing, nine day fortnight, four and a half day week and zero hours contract (not contracted to work a set number of hours but paid for the actual number of hours worked.
2 See Notes and Definitions.

Source: Labour Force Survey, Office for National Statistics and Department of Economic Development, Northern Ireland

5.13 Working days lost due to labour disputes[1]

	Days lost per 1,000 employees	
	1996	1997
United Kingdom	58	10
North East	89	38
North West (GOR) & Merseyside	54	7
North West (GOR)	53	4
Merseyside	61	22
Yorkshire and the Humber	47	7
East Midlands	44	3
West Midlands	56	7
Eastern	48	6
London	87	13
South East (GOR)	41	2
South West	54	-
England	59	9
Wales	62	3
Scotland	60	26
Northern Ireland	35	24

1 Regional rates are based on data for stoppages that exclude widespread disputes that cannot be allocated to a specific region. These are included in the United Kingdom strike rate only.

Source: Office for National Statistics

5.14 Employees absent due to sickness, Spring 1997[1]

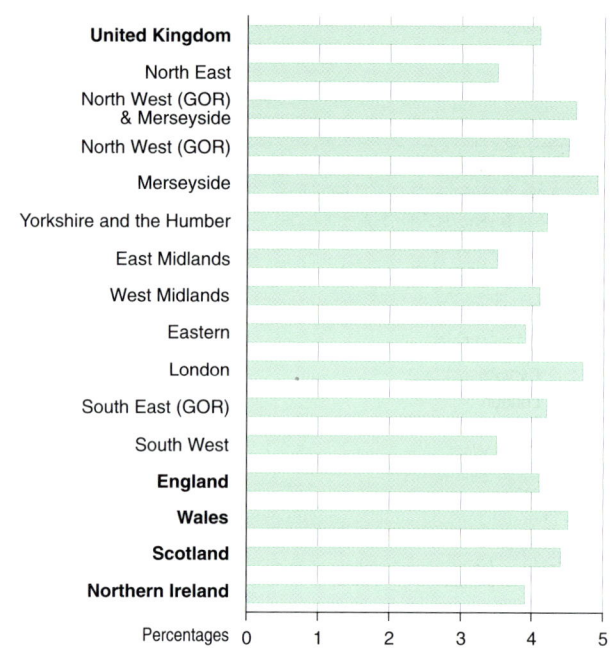

1 Percentages of employees absent from work due to illness or injury for at least one day in the week before interview. See Notes and Definitions.

Source: Labour Force Survey, Office for National Statistics and Department of Economic Development, Northern Ireland

5.15 Trade union membership, Autumn 1997

Percentages[1]

	Manual			Non-manual			
	Males	Females	All manual employees	Males	Females	All non-manual employees	All employees
United Kingdom	34.9	22.1	30.3	29.4	31.5	30.5	30.4
North East	46.7	34.0	42.2	37.9	38.9	38.5	40.2
North West (GOR) & Merseyside	41.4	27.8	36.6	34.9	39.2	37.3	37.0
North West (GOR)	40.5	25.9	35.5	33.2	37.7	35.7	35.6
Merseyside	45.8	36.4	42.3	42.7	45.0	44.1	43.3
Yorkshire and the Humber	35.6	24.8	31.7	35.6	33.7	34.5	33.3
East Midlands	32.9	21.8	28.9	27.0	32.1	29.8	29.4
West Midlands	38.7	23.1	33.3	30.5	30.1	30.3	31.6
Eastern	28.4	12.2	22.9	22.7	25.2	24.1	23.6
London	29.5	21.5	26.7	23.6	27.6	25.7	26.0
South East (GOR)	24.8	13.1	20.3	22.9	22.5	22.7	21.9
South West	28.2	12.3	22.0	29.5	30.4	30.0	26.7
England	33.6	20.4	28.8	27.9	29.9	29.0	29.0
Wales	48.5	31.7	42.2	40.0	44.3	42.5	42.4
Scotland	38.6	28.6	35.0	37.6	36.8	37.1	36.2
Northern Ireland	38.0	34.2	36.5	37.6	43.1	40.7	39.6

1 As a percentage of all employees in each region, excluding those who did not say whether or not they belonged to a trade union.

Source: Labour Force Survey, Office for National Statistics and Department of Economic Development, Northern Ireland

5.16 Average weekly earnings[1]: by industry[2] and gender, April 1997

£ per week

	Whole economy			Agriculture, forestry, fishing & hunting		Manufacturing	
	Males	Females	All persons	Males	Females	Males	Females
United Kingdom	407.3	296.2	366.3	279.4	218.6	390.8	257.2
North East	360.1	269.0	327.6	..	..	386.0	253.3
North West (GOR) & Merseyside	386.4	277.4	345.8	..	..	391.3	250.2
North West (GOR)	387.4	275.8	346.6	..	..	393.8	246.7
Merseyside	381.7	284.4	342.4	..		373.3	..
Yorkshire and the Humber	363.9	268.9	330.5	..	..	366.1	234.1
East Midlands	369.2	260.3	332.9	..	..	372.8	226.5
West Midlands	375.4	268.5	337.8	..	..	367.8	238.7
Eastern	399.5	295.9	362.4	277.1	..	410.3	279.6
London	541.3	386.3	480.1	..	..	497.5	368.6
South East (GOR)	428.3	306.5	382.5	294.0	..	429.2	284.0
South West	382.4	274.8	342.7	257.5	..	382.0	251.0
England	414.0	301.3	372.7	282.1	219.4	394.8	262.5
Wales	363.5	269.0	330.1	..	..	377.3	243.0
Scotland	378.0	272.4	336.8	277.0	..	380.4	233.9
Northern Ireland	355.9	265.2	319.7	179.9	..	314.0	205.1

	Mining, quarrying & electricity, gas, water		Construction		Distribution, hotels & catering, repairs		Transport, storage & communication	
	Males	Females	Males	Females	Males	Females	Males	Females
United Kingdom	484.1	352.2	371.7	269.1	345.6	239.7	385.3	305.8
North East	..	..	321.0	..	281.0	201.8	322.9	..
North West (GOR) & Merseyside	457.7	..	363.1	..	331.9	227.1	363.4	264.7
North West (GOR)	462.4	..	361.2	..	333.5	228.2	366.2	268.9
Merseyside	..		..	..	323.8	221.1	351.6	..
Yorkshire and the Humber	491.8	..	347.1	293.8	308.7	209.5	342.6	248.7
East Midlands	426.2	..	349.6	..	337.3	222.5	332.0	239.8
West Midlands	456.1	..	360.8	..	323.3	212.0	347.2	288.9
Eastern	470.8	..	382.3	232.1	359.0	253.4	385.1	293.2
London	601.1	..	479.6	..	415.6	307.0	486.7	388.6
South East (GOR)	539.3	..	400.1	..	384.1	265.8	403.6	327.5
South West	474.2	..	334.2	..	327.7	211.3	346.2	264.8
England	484.3	357.9	377.2	272.7	353.6	245.3	392.2	310.1
Wales	..	..	348.8	..	296.3	206.0	338.9	..
Scotland	521.9	..	354.2	..	297.8	210.1	341.2	284.6
Northern Ireland	429.2	..	320.5	..	291.0	197.0	341.5	254.7

	Financial & business services		Public administration & defence		Education, social work & health services		Other	
	Males	Females	Males	Females	Males	Females	Males	Females
United Kingdom	519.2	328.9	419.5	314.6	413.9	320.5	377.0	286.5
North East	365.8	266.0	402.2	298.7	376.2	298.3	..	..
North West (GOR) & Merseyside	447.5	283.4	403.0	318.2	415.2	309.8	..	269.0
North West (GOR)	448.0	279.6	411.4	322.0	415.0	310.7	334.6	278.6
Merseyside	445.3	298.6	379.9	311.2	415.9	306.5	..	..
Yorkshire and the Humber	411.9	271.3	391.2	304.5	386.2	312.8	..	229.0
East Midlands	400.0	270.3	386.9	290.8	404.8	300.3	..	..
West Midlands	447.5	276.4	411.6	294.6	416.9	305.5	..	..
Eastern	449.1	309.3	389.0	310.2	414.2	330.0	342.8	..
London	711.5	443.9	474.0	377.8	465.0	375.9	506.9	387.5
South East (GOR)	503.7	326.8	428.1	310.9	422.0	325.9	342.8	271.3
South West	449.7	291.7	390.3	282.5	414.2	309.5	330.2	..
England	530.5	336.5	420.3	322.0	417.9	323.1	386.1	292.8
Wales	393.3	267.0	384.2	292.9	390.1	299.5	..	..
Scotland	441.0	272.1	409.9	284.4	400.1	312.0	..	245.9
Northern Ireland	398.6	259.4	445.2	266.2	405.5	319.3	291.3	252.7

1 Average gross weekly earnings; data relate to full-time employees on adult rates whose pay for the survey pay-period was not affected by absence. See Notes and Definitions.
2 Based on SIC 1992.

Source: New Earnings Survey, Office for National Statistics and Department of Economic Development, Northern Ireland

5.17 Average weekly earnings and hours: by gender, April 1997[1]

| | | Average gross weekly earnings | | | | | | | | Percentage of employees who received overtime pay | Average weekly hours | |
| | Total (£) | Overtime pay (£) | PBR etc pay[2] (£) | Shift etc premium pay (£) | Percentage earning under | | | | | Total including overtime (hours) | Overtime (hours) |
					£200	£300	£400	£500			
All full-time male employees											
United Kingdom	407.3	27.7	19.3	6.9	10.6	37.4	61.6	77.7	35.4	41.8	3.1
North East	360.1	29.6	18.1	9.4	13.4	43.6	69.4	84.8	38.8	41.9	3.4
North West (GOR) & Merseyside	386.4	28.5	19.5	7.9	11.5	39.9	65.0	80.6	36.5	41.8	3.3
North West (GOR)	387.4	28.2	19.9	7.7	11.6	40.0	64.7	80.4	36.6	41.8	3.2
Merseyside	381.7	29.7	17.8	9.0	10.9	39.5	66.4	81.7	36.1	41.6	3.3
Yorkshire and the Humber	363.9	29.3	18.9	7.2	12.1	43.5	68.2	84.1	38.6	42.3	3.6
East Midlands	369.2	32.4	18.1	8.3	11.3	41.2	68.2	83.8	41.5	42.9	4.0
West Midlands	375.4	29.7	19.4	7.2	11.1	40.3	66.7	82.5	38.1	42.1	3.4
Eastern	399.5	29.2	17.2	6.7	8.9	36.0	61.2	77.6	37.0	42.4	3.3
London	541.3	22.3	27.5	5.1	5.6	23.3	43.7	61.3	26.1	40.4	2.2
South East (GOR)	428.3	25.2	18.9	5.4	9.2	33.0	56.9	73.2	32.3	41.6	2.8
South West	382.4	26.2	17.0	6.1	12.3	40.6	64.4	80.7	36.8	41.6	3.0
England	414.0	27.4	20.1	6.7	10.0	36.4	60.7	76.9	35.1	41.8	3.1
Wales	363.5	28.9	18.2	10.4	14.3	42.8	67.5	83.6	37.9	42.2	3.4
Scotland	378.0	29.1	15.4	7.1	11.7	42.1	66.2	80.9	36.8	41.9	3.3
Northern Ireland	355.9	30.5	10.7	5.2	18.8	48.1	67.7	82.3	37.0	41.7	3.3
Full-time manual male employees											
United Kingdom	313.1	45.1	16.6	11.0	15.2	53.2	80.6	92.5	54.4	45.1	5.5
North East	306.3	42.4	20.8	13.3	16.6	56.1	81.1	93.6	52.6	44.3	5.2
North West (GOR) & Merseyside	312.4	44.5	16.5	12.6	14.8	52.9	80.4	93.1	54.0	44.7	5.4
North West (GOR)	311.2	44.5	16.8	11.9	15.1	53.5	80.6	93.2	54.1	44.7	5.4
Merseyside	318.7	44.8	15.3	16.0	12.9	49.8	79.5	92.9	53.7	44.7	5.5
Yorkshire and the Humber	305.0	46.2	20.0	10.8	15.4	56.6	82.2	93.5	56.9	45.4	5.9
East Midlands	311.0	49.6	19.2	11.0	14.7	52.8	81.8	93.3	59.5	45.9	6.4
West Midlands	311.7	45.7	19.1	11.4	14.0	52.6	82.1	93.5	55.3	44.8	5.5
Eastern	320.0	48.6	15.4	9.5	12.3	50.5	79.6	91.9	58.2	45.7	5.8
London	351.0	46.2	15.0	9.8	11.2	41.7	70.6	86.2	48.7	45.3	5.2
South East (GOR)	320.5	46.0	12.7	9.4	14.2	50.7	79.2	91.6	53.6	45.4	5.4
South West	297.7	41.7	12.6	10.6	18.8	57.4	83.8	94.7	55.9	44.6	5.1
England	315.6	45.8	16.7	10.9	14.5	52.1	80.0	92.3	55.0	45.2	5.5
Wales	312.3	42.2	18.0	16.7	18.8	55.1	79.2	91.2	51.1	44.7	5.2
Scotland	303.3	42.1	16.7	10.0	15.8	57.8	83.5	93.6	51.4	44.7	5.1
Northern Ireland	269.2	37.4	11.7	8.2	28.4	68.7	89.5	97.1	50.2	44.3	5.0
Full-time non-manual male employees											
United Kingdom	482.2	13.9	21.5	3.6	6.9	24.8	46.6	65.9	20.4	39.1	1.3
North East	423.3	14.5	15.0	4.8	9.8	29.0	55.7	74.5	22.4	39.1	1.3
North West (GOR) & Merseyside	452.3	14.2	22.2	3.8	8.5	28.3	51.2	69.5	21.0	39.1	1.3
North West (GOR)	455.7	13.7	22.7	3.9	8.4	27.8	50.4	69.0	20.9	39.2	1.3
Merseyside	435.9	16.7	20.0	3.0	9.2	30.6	55.1	72.0	21.0	38.9	1.5
Yorkshire and the Humber	424.6	11.9	17.7	3.5	8.6	30.1	53.8	74.3	19.8	39.1	1.2
East Midlands	429.1	14.7	17.0	5.4	7.9	29.2	54.3	74.0	22.9	39.7	1.5
West Midlands	441.4	13.1	19.6	2.8	8.1	27.6	50.7	71.2	20.2	39.3	1.3
Eastern	463.6	13.5	18.7	4.4	6.1	24.2	46.3	66.1	19.8	39.6	1.3
London	614.0	13.1	32.3	3.3	3.5	16.2	33.4	51.8	17.5	38.5	1.1
South East (GOR)	494.1	12.5	22.7	3.0	6.2	22.3	43.3	61.9	19.3	39.3	1.2
South West	450.3	13.7	20.5	2.6	7.2	27.1	48.9	69.5	21.5	39.1	1.3
England	489.3	13.3	22.7	3.5	6.6	24.3	45.9	65.2	19.9	39.1	1.2
Wales	420.2	14.1	18.3	3.5	9.3	29.2	54.4	75.1	23.2	39.2	1.4
Scotland	449.8	16.7	14.2	4.4	7.7	27.0	49.6	68.8	22.7	39.2	1.6
Northern Ireland	431.3	24.5	9.8	2.6	10.5	30.2	48.8	69.4	25.5	39.5	1.9

Regional Trends 33, © Crown copyright 1998

5.17 *(continued)*

| | Average gross weekly earnings | | | | | | | | Percentage of employees who received overtime pay | Average weekly hours | |
| | Total (£) | of which | | | Percentage earning under | | | | | | |
		Overtime pay (£)	PBR etc pay[2] (£)	Shift etc premium pay (£)	£200	£300	£400	£500		Total including overtime (hours)	Overtime (hours)
All full-time female employees											
United Kingdom	296.2	7.3	9.2	3.4	26.7	61.4	80.6	92.4	18.9	37.6	0.9
North East	269.0	7.6	8.2	3.9	33.4	67.8	85.1	95.8	20.1	37.8	1.0
North West (GOR) & Merseyside	277.4	6.5	9.4	3.5	30.4	66.1	83.7	95.2	18.3	37.5	0.9
North West (GOR)	275.8	6.6	8.7	3.5	31.2	66.3	84.0	95.3	18.3	37.6	0.9
Merseyside	284.4	6.3	12.3	3.6	27.1	65.3	82.4	94.6	18.0	37.1	0.8
Yorkshire and the Humber	268.9	6.7	9.5	3.5	33.9	68.8	84.4	95.4	19.7	37.6	0.9
East Midlands	260.3	7.5	10.1	4.1	34.7	71.9	87.6	96.5	20.5	38.0	1.0
West Midlands	268.5	6.3	10.0	3.4	32.6	69.6	85.7	95.5	17.7	37.8	0.9
Eastern	295.9	7.9	7.8	3.4	24.3	62.1	81.3	92.6	19.5	37.7	0.9
London	386.3	8.2	13.6	2.4	10.0	37.0	64.1	81.6	17.2	37.3	0.8
South East (GOR)	306.5	8.1	9.2	3.0	21.4	59.0	79.6	91.4	20.0	38.0	1.0
South West	274.8	7.1	8.5	3.5	31.3	68.3	83.9	93.8	20.4	37.6	0.9
England	301.3	7.4	10.0	3.2	25.5	60.3	79.7	91.8	19.0	37.7	0.9
Wales	269.0	6.2	7.4	3.8	32.9	67.9	84.7	95.6	17.9	37.7	0.9
Scotland	272.4	7.8	4.8	4.6	31.4	66.6	86.2	95.5	19.1	37.5	1.0
Northern Ireland	265.2	6.1	4.1	4.0	37.7	68.7	83.1	95.9	16.1	37.5	0.8
Full-time manual female employees											
United Kingdom	200.2	13.2	9.8	5.8	59.1	90.2	97.8	99.5	29.5	40.2	2.0
North East	201.2	13.1	13.6	7.5	59.5	88.9	97.6	99.1	28.2	40.5	2.0
North West (GOR) & Merseyside	199.3	11.4	11.0	5.4	62.2	89.9	97.8	100.0	27.6	40.1	1.7
North West (GOR)	198.3	11.2	10.4	5.0	62.9	90.1	97.9	100.0	27.5	40.0	1.7
Merseyside	205.8	12.7	14.9	8.0	57.7	88.5	97.1	100.0	27.9	40.3	1.9
Yorkshire and the Humber	189.9	12.3	12.4	6.3	66.5	92.9	97.9	99.5	29.4	40.0	1.8
East Midlands	191.5	13.8	16.9	4.9	63.5	92.4	98.9	100.0	29.2	40.2	2.2
West Midlands	193.1	11.8	14.5	5.3	61.4	92.1	98.9	99.8	26.9	40.2	1.9
Eastern	207.2	16.1	5.6	5.5	53.6	89.4	96.2	98.7	32.7	40.5	2.3
London	232.6	17.4	4.7	4.9	40.7	81.5	95.0	98.4	33.0	40.9	2.5
South East (GOR)	215.7	15.4	6.0	7.0	51.2	86.2	96.9	99.4	32.9	40.5	2.1
South West	189.4	10.5	7.5	6.2	64.2	93.8	98.7	99.8	29.8	39.7	1.7
England	202.4	13.5	10.2	5.8	58.0	89.6	97.6	99.5	29.9	40.3	2.0
Wales	196.2	14.3	12.6	5.8	61.5	91.5	98.8	99.4	32.4	40.4	2.2
Scotland	193.9	12.5	5.7	6.8	61.3	92.0	98.4	99.8	27.1	40.0	1.9
Northern Ireland	173.3	8.4	10.3	3.6	74.5	97.7	99.5	100.0	25.1	39.5	1.5
Full-time non-manual female employees											
United Kingdom	316.9	6.1	9.1	2.9	19.8	55.2	76.9	90.9	16.6	37.1	0.7
North East	286.4	6.2	6.8	2.9	26.7	62.4	81.9	94.9	18.1	37.1	0.8
North West (GOR) & Merseyside	294.5	5.5	9.0	3.1	23.4	60.9	80.6	94.1	16.3	36.9	0.7
North West (GOR)	294.3	5.5	8.3	3.1	23.6	60.6	80.7	94.2	16.2	37.0	0.7
Merseyside	295.1	5.4	11.9	3.0	22.9	62.2	80.4	93.8	16.7	36.7	0.6
Yorkshire and the Humber	287.7	5.3	8.7	2.8	26.2	63.1	81.2	94.5	17.4	37.0	0.7
East Midlands	284.4	5.3	7.7	3.8	24.6	64.7	83.7	95.3	17.4	37.2	0.6
West Midlands	290.3	4.8	8.8	2.8	24.3	63.1	81.9	94.3	15.0	37.0	0.6
Eastern	313.2	6.3	8.2	3.0	18.6	56.8	78.4	91.3	17.0	37.2	0.7
London	402.7	7.2	14.6	2.1	6.7	32.3	60.8	79.8	15.5	36.9	0.6
South East (GOR)	323.0	6.8	9.8	2.2	16.0	54.1	76.5	90.0	17.7	37.5	0.8
South West	293.2	6.4	8.7	2.9	24.2	62.8	80.7	92.6	18.3	37.1	0.7
England	321.6	6.1	10.0	2.7	18.9	54.3	76.0	90.2	16.7	37.1	0.7
Wales	289.5	4.0	6.0	3.2	24.9	61.3	80.8	94.5	13.8	37.0	0.5
Scotland	293.9	6.5	4.5	4.0	23.2	59.7	82.8	94.3	16.9	36.8	0.7
Northern Ireland	286.1	5.6	2.6	4.1	29.4	62.1	79.3	94.9	14.1	37.1	0.7

1 Data relate to full-time employees on adult rates whose pay for the survey pay-period was not affected by absence. See Notes and Definitions.

2 PBR etc pay is payments-by-results, bonuses, commission and all other incentive payments *plus* profit-related payments.

Source: New Earnings Survey, Office for National Statistics and Department of Economic Development, Northern Ireland

5.18 Average weekly hours[1] of work of full-time employees: by occupational group, Spring 1997

Hours

	Man-agerial & admin-istrators	Professional, associate professional & technical	Clerical & secretarial	Craft & related	Personal & protective services	Sales	Plant & machine operative	Other[2]	All occu-pations[3]
United Kingdom	47.1	45.7	42.3	39.6	44.8	42.9	43.1	45.6	44.0
North East	46.2	45.9	42.3	39.4	44.9	42.6	43.1	44.7	43.7
North West (GOR) & Merseyside	46.5	45.1	41.2	39.5	44.4	42.4	43.4	44.7	43.4
North West (GOR)	46.7	44.9	41.1	39.6	44.3	42.3	43.1	45.0	43.5
Merseyside	45.7	45.8	41.2	38.7	45.0	42.6	44.5	43.4	43.1
Yorkshire and the Humber	47.1	46.4	41.7	39.7	45.2	41.8	42.8	46.0	44.2
East Midlands	47.8	46.2	42.1	39.6	44.6	42.8	43.6	45.5	44.3
West Midlands	47.3	46.6	41.4	39.4	44.4	42.2	43.0	44.5	43.9
Eastern	47.8	46.0	43.2	40.0	45.5	44.0	43.6	47.0	44.7
London	47.1	45.5	43.2	39.3	44.6	43.5	42.9	45.6	43.9
South East (GOR)	47.6	46.1	42.8	40.1	45.8	43.7	43.4	46.6	44.7
South West	47.2	46.1	42.3	40.0	45.0	41.4	42.6	45.7	44.1
England	47.3	45.9	42.4	39.7	44.9	42.8	43.2	45.5	44.1
Wales	46.8	44.5	41.8	39.4	44.4	43.1	43.1	45.5	43.8
Scotland	46.3	44.4	42.1	39.2	44.9	43.3	42.6	46.6	43.7
Northern Ireland	45.0	44.1	40.5	39.8	42.3	42.7	42.0	43.7	42.6

1 Includes paid and unpaid overtime and excludes meal breaks. The analysis also excludes those who did not state the number of hours they worked.
2 See Notes and Definitions.
3 Includes those whose workplace is outside the United Kingdom, and those who did not specify their occupation.

Source: Labour Force Survey, Office for National Statistics and Department of Economic Development, Northern Ireland

5.19 Vacancies[1] at jobcentres

Thousands

	1993	1994	1995	1996	1997
United Kingdom	127.8	158.0	181.9	226.1	283.4
North East	4.9	5.6	6.4	8.1	10.1
North West (GOR) & Merseyside	16.9	20.4	22.7	26.8	34.4
North West (GOR)	13.7	16.8	18.6	21.9	27.6
Merseyside	3.2	3.6	4.0	4.9	6.8
Yorkshire and the Humber	9.9	11.8	13.3	16.7	20.9
East Midlands	8.7	10.9	12.7	14.8	20.3
West Midlands	8.9	12.3	15.2	18.8	23.1
Eastern	10.2	13.0	14.7	17.7	23.5
London	10.0	13.2	16.3	28.8	35.1
South East (GOR)	15.3	20.7	22.7	28.2	34.4
South West	9.6	12.5	14.4	19.2	25.4
England	94.5	120.3	138.2	179.2	227.3
Wales	9.6	11.2	13.3	14.5	18.0
Scotland	18.5	19.9	23.1	25.5	31.4
Northern Ireland	5.2	6.5	7.4	7.0	6.8

1 Vacancies remaining unfilled, seasonally adjusted annual averages.
Source: Employment Service

5.20 Redundancies[1], Spring 1997

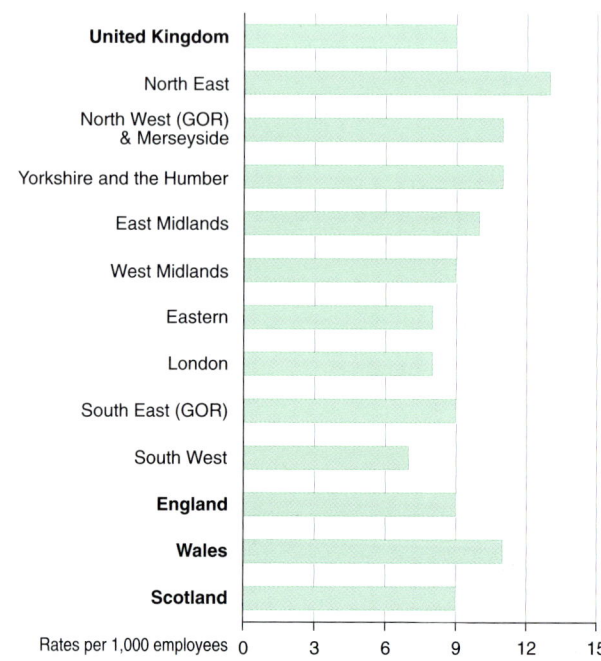

Rates per 1,000 employees

1 Relates to those made redundant in the three months prior to each interview. See Notes and Definitions. For Northern Ireland, the sample size is too small to provide a reliable estimate.
Source: Labour Force Survey, Office for National Statistics

5.21 ILO unemployment rates[1]

Percentages

	Spring quarter of each year				
	1993	1994	1995	1996	1997
United Kingdom	10.3	9.6	8.6	8.2	7.1
North East	12.0	12.5	11.4	10.8	9.8
North West (GOR) &					
Merseyside	10.8	10.3	9.0	8.4	6.9
North West (GOR)	9.8	9.5	8.3	7.3	6.3
Merseyside	15.4	13.6	11.7	13.3	9.6
Yorkshire and the Humber	10.0	9.9	8.7	8.1	8.1
East Midlands	9.1	8.3	7.5	7.4	6.3
West Midlands	11.8	10.0	9.0	9.2	6.8
Eastern	9.2	8.2	7.5	6.2	5.9
London	13.2	13.1	11.5	11.3	9.1
South East (GOR)	8.0	7.1	6.4	6.0	5.2
South West	9.2	7.5	7.8	6.3	5.2
England	10.3	9.5	8.6	8.1	6.9
Wales	9.6	9.3	8.8	8.3	8.4
Scotland	10.2	10.0	8.3	8.7	8.5
Northern Ireland	12.5	11.7	11.0	9.7	7.5

1 See Notes and Definitions.

Source: Labour Force Survey, Office for National Statistics and Department of Economic Development, Northern Ireland

5.22 Claimant count rates[1]

Percentages

	Seasonally adjusted annual averages				
	1993	1994	1995	1996	1997
United Kingdom	10.3	9.3	8.2	7.5	5.6
North East	12.9	12.4	11.5	10.5	8.4
North West (GOR) &					
Merseyside	10.6	9.9	8.6	7.9	6.1
North West (GOR)	9.5	8.7	7.5	6.8	5.1
Merseyside	15.1	14.9	13.6	12.9	10.6
Yorkshire and the Humber	10.2	9.6	8.7	8.0	6.3
East Midlands	9.5	8.7	7.6	6.8	5.0
West Midlands	10.8	9.9	8.3	7.4	5.6
Eastern	9.4	8.1	6.8	6.1	4.3
London	11.6	10.7	9.7	8.9	6.7
South East (GOR)	8.6	7.3	6.1	5.4	3.7
South West	9.5	8.1	7.0	6.2	4.4
England	10.2	9.2	8.1	7.3	5.4
Wales	10.3	9.3	8.7	8.2	6.4
Scotland	9.7	9.3	8.1	7.9	6.4
Northern Ireland	13.7	12.6	11.4	10.9	8.2

1 See Notes and Definitions.

Source: Office for National Statistics

5.23 ILO unemployment rates[1,2]: by age, 1996/97

Percentages and thousands

	Percentage of the economically active who are unemployed and aged				All ILO unemployed of working age (thousands)
	16-24	25-34	35-49	Males 50-64, females 50-59	
United Kingdom	14.8	7.3	5.4	6.0	2,126
North East	18.4	10.8	6.1	8.1	115
North West (GOR) & Merseyside	16.9	7.1	4.9	4.8	239
North West (GOR)	15.6	6.2	4.6	4.7	177
Merseyside	22.7	10.9	6.5	..	62
Yorkshire and the Humber	16.4	8.9	5.3	6.2	196
East Midlands	12.7	6.3	4.1	4.9	127
West Midlands	14.9	6.8	5.3	5.9	188
Eastern	12.9	5.3	4.8	5.6	169
London	17.3	10.0	7.9	8.5	351
South East (GOR)	11.4	4.3	3.9	4.9	212
South West	11.4	5.4	4.4	5.6	142
England	14.5	7.1	5.2	5.9	1,739
Wales	18.0	7.7	6.0	5.1	108
Scotland	16.2	8.8	6.4	6.7	215
Northern Ireland	11.7	8.1	8.2	9.0	64

1 Average of four quarters ending Summer 1997. See Notes and Definitions.
2 This table is on a different basis from those in previous editions of *Regional Trends* which showed the percentage of unemployed people within each age group.

Source: Labour Force Survey, Office for National Statistics and Department of Economic Development, Northern Ireland

5.24 Claimant count rate[1]: by sub-region[2], January 1998

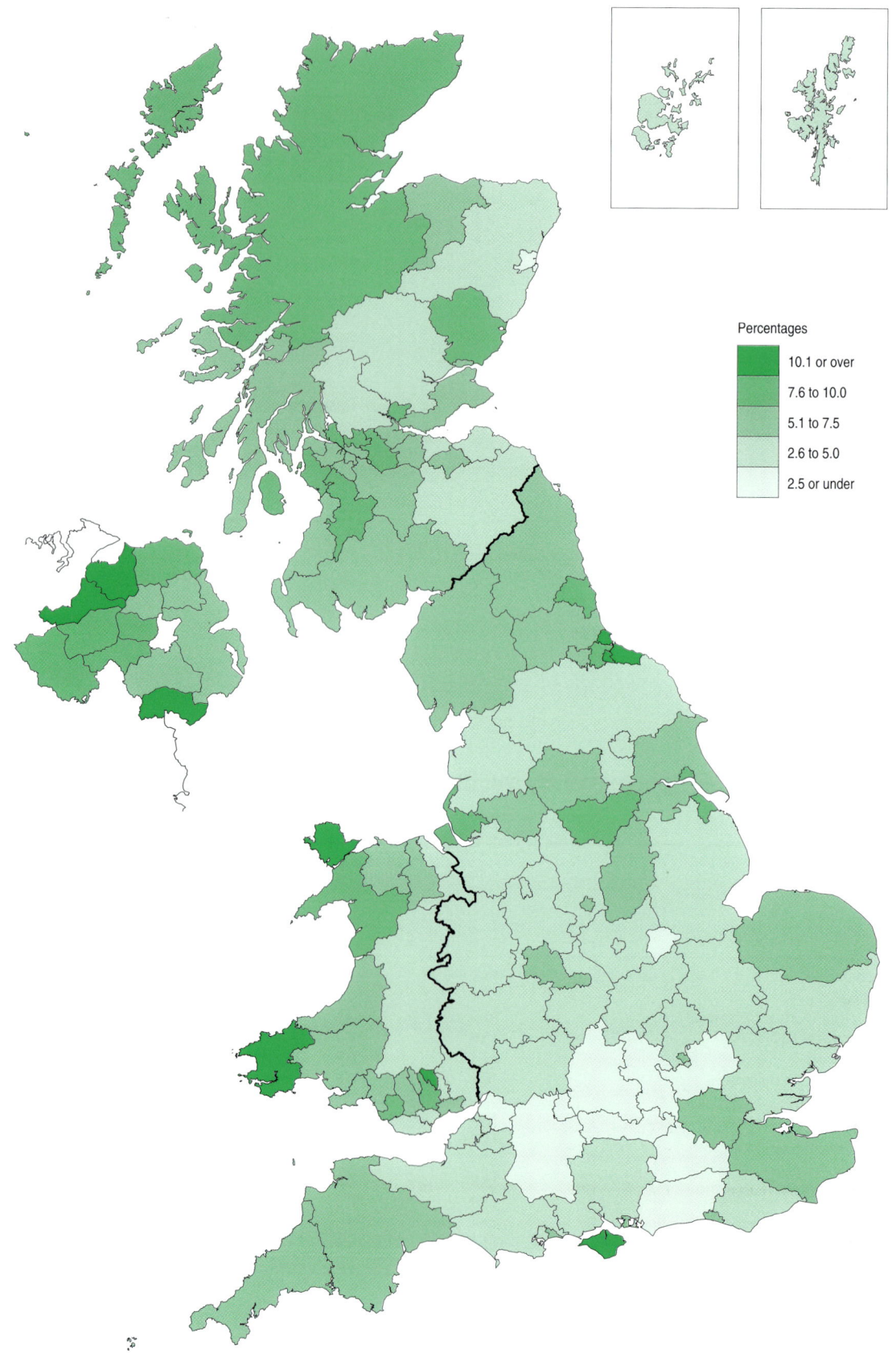

Percentages

■	10.1 or over
■	7.6 to 10.0
■	5.1 to 7.5
■	2.6 to 5.0
□	2.5 or under

1 The claimant count rate is the number of people claiming unemployment-related benefit as a proportion of jobs in each area. Not seasonally adjusted. See Notes and Definitions.
2 Travel-to-work areas for Northern Ireland.

Source: Office for National Statistics

Regional Trends 33, © Crown copyright 1998

5.25 Claimant count[1]: by duration and gender, January 1998

Percentages and thousands

	2 weeks or less	Over 2 and up to 8 weeks	Over 8 and up to 13 weeks	Over 13 and up to 26 weeks	Over 26 weeks up to 1 year	Over 1 and up to 2 years	Over 2 and up to 3 years	Over 3 and up to 5 years	Over 5 years	Total (=100%) (thousands)
Males										
United Kingdom	7.5	18.5	10.8	17.4	16.8	11.5	5.3	4.9	7.3	1,136.7
North East	6.7	18.9	10.4	17.2	16.6	11.1	5.1	5.5	8.5	75.8
North West (GOR) &										
Merseyside	7.9	19.7	11.3	17.4	16.4	11.3	4.7	4.3	7.0	142.6
North West (GOR)	9.0	22.0	12.4	17.9	15.9	10.2	3.9	3.5	5.2	97.4
Merseyside	5.7	14.7	8.9	16.3	17.5	13.8	6.3	5.9	10.9	45.1
Yorkshire and the Humber	7.2	19.3	11.0	17.8	17.6	11.6	5.0	4.1	6.4	114.1
East Midlands	8.9	21.8	11.9	17.1	15.8	10.9	4.4	3.6	5.6	67.8
West Midlands	6.8	17.4	10.2	17.1	18.1	11.8	5.2	4.7	8.5	99.9
Eastern	8.3	20.1	11.4	17.5	15.8	11.0	5.3	4.8	5.7	71.2
London	5.5	13.8	9.1	17.4	18.6	13.5	6.9	7.3	8.0	174.8
South East (GOR)	9.2	20.3	11.5	18.0	15.9	10.1	5.1	4.5	5.3	92.1
South West	9.2	21.1	12.2	18.5	14.6	10.2	4.9	4.1	5.2	72.5
England	7.5	18.6	10.8	17.5	16.9	11.5	5.3	5.0	6.9	910.7
Wales	7.7	18.9	11.8	18.4	16.6	11.5	5.4	3.9	5.7	59.6
Scotland	8.3	21.0	11.7	17.8	17.0	10.8	4.2	3.7	5.6	118.8
Northern Ireland	4.7	11.0	7.3	13.5	14.8	11.8	7.2	8.5	21.1	47.5
Females										
United Kingdom	10.7	20.0	12.3	20.5	16.4	9.7	3.8	3.2	3.4	342.6
North East	10.4	19.5	11.9	20.6	17.0	9.4	3.8	3.3	4.1	17.8
North West (GOR) &										
Merseyside	12.1	21.8	12.1	20.1	15.9	9.2	3.1	2.6	3.0	38.7
North West (GOR)	13.3	24.0	13.1	20.4	14.9	7.9	2.4	2.0	2.1	26.7
Merseyside	9.6	17.1	9.8	19.4	18.3	12.2	4.8	3.9	5.0	12.1
Yorkshire and the Humber	10.4	20.7	11.9	20.7	17.3	9.7	3.4	2.7	3.2	32.2
East Midlands	12.3	22.4	12.9	20.0	15.9	8.4	3.1	2.2	2.7	21.2
West Midlands	10.0	19.2	11.6	20.5	17.4	10.0	3.8	3.3	4.3	31.4
Eastern	12.3	20.3	12.9	20.5	15.1	9.1	3.6	3.3	2.9	23.7
London	7.2	15.6	10.7	21.6	18.9	12.5	5.3	4.7	3.5	61.9
South East (GOR)	12.6	21.3	12.8	20.1	15.0	8.6	3.8	3.1	2.8	28.6
South West	12.5	22.6	14.6	20.3	12.6	8.3	3.6	2.8	2.7	24.7
England	10.6	19.8	12.1	20.6	16.5	9.9	3.9	3.3	3.3	280.1
Wales	11.6	21.3	13.4	22.1	14.8	8.2	3.1	2.5	2.9	16.9
Scotland	12.0	22.8	13.7	19.2	16.1	8.4	2.8	2.2	2.7	33.4
Northern Ireland	8.0	15.9	9.9	20.2	15.9	10.1	5.3	5.6	9.0	12.2
All persons										
United Kingdom	8.2	18.9	11.1	18.2	16.7	11.0	5.0	4.5	6.4	1,479.3
North East	7.4	19.0	10.7	17.8	16.6	10.8	4.9	5.1	7.7	93.7
North West (GOR) &										
Merseyside	8.8	20.2	11.5	18.0	16.3	10.9	4.4	3.9	6.1	181.3
North West (GOR)	9.9	22.5	12.5	18.4	15.6	9.7	3.6	3.2	4.5	124.1
Merseyside	6.5	15.2	9.1	17.0	17.7	13.5	6.0	5.5	9.6	57.2
Yorkshire and the Humber	7.9	19.6	11.2	18.5	17.6	11.2	4.7	3.8	5.7	146.3
East Midlands	9.7	21.9	12.1	17.8	15.8	10.3	4.1	3.3	4.9	88.9
West Midlands	7.6	17.8	10.6	17.9	18.0	11.4	4.9	4.4	7.5	131.3
Eastern	9.3	20.2	11.8	18.3	15.6	10.5	4.9	4.4	5.0	94.8
London	6.0	14.3	9.5	18.5	18.6	13.2	6.5	6.6	6.8	236.6
South East (GOR)	10.0	20.6	11.8	18.5	15.7	9.8	4.8	4.2	4.7	120.7
South West	10.1	21.5	12.8	18.9	14.1	9.7	4.6	3.8	4.5	97.2
England	8.2	18.9	11.1	18.3	16.8	11.1	5.0	4.6	6.0	1,190.8
Wales	8.6	19.4	12.2	19.2	16.2	10.8	4.9	3.6	5.1	76.5
Scotland	9.1	21.4	12.1	18.1	16.8	10.3	3.9	3.3	4.9	152.2
Northern Ireland	5.4	12.0	7.9	14.9	15.0	11.4	6.8	7.9	18.6	59.8

1 Not seasonally adjusted. See Notes and Definitions.

Source: Office for National Statistics

5.26 Claimant count[1]: by age and gender, January 1998

Percentages and thousands

	Percentage aged						Total (=100%) (thousands)
	Under 20	20-29	30-39	40-49	50-59	60 or over	
Males							
United Kingdom	7.6	33.4	26.0	17.1	14.9	1.0	1,136.7
North East	9.2	32.5	24.8	17.6	15.1	0.8	75.8
North West (GOR) & Merseyside	8.8	35.9	25.4	16.0	13.1	0.9	142.6
North West (GOR)	8.7	36.0	24.9	16.0	13.4	1.0	97.4
Merseyside	8.9	35.7	26.4	15.9	12.4	0.6	45.1
Yorkshire and the Humber	8.4	34.7	24.6	16.4	14.8	1.0	114.1
East Midlands	7.9	34.6	24.1	16.7	15.5	1.2	67.8
West Midlands	7.9	33.9	25.3	16.8	15.1	1.1	99.9
Eastern	7.1	31.7	24.7	17.9	17.1	1.6	71.2
London	5.1	32.1	31.5	17.3	13.1	0.9	174.8
South East (GOR)	6.5	31.0	25.7	18.4	17.0	1.4	92.1
South West	7.5	32.5	24.4	17.6	16.9	1.1	72.5
England	7.4	33.3	26.2	17.1	14.9	1.1	910.7
Wales	9.3	34.9	24.3	16.3	14.6	0.7	59.6
Scotland	8.8	33.3	24.6	17.1	15.1	1.1	118.8
Northern Ireland	6.1	32.3	27.3	19.1	14.5	0.7	47.5
Females							
United Kingdom	14.1	33.9	17.4	17.2	17.4	-	342.6
North East	18.5	31.5	15.6	17.8	16.6	-	17.8
North West (GOR) & Merseyside	17.0	35.5	16.2	16.1	15.2	-	38.7
North West (GOR)	16.8	35.2	16.6	16.0	15.4	-	26.7
Merseyside	17.3	36.3	15.6	16.2	14.6	-	12.1
Yorkshire and the Humber	16.4	33.8	15.7	16.9	17.2	-	32.2
East Midlands	14.0	33.7	16.6	17.8	17.9	-	21.2
West Midlands	15.2	34.2	16.1	16.6	17.9	-	31.4
Eastern	12.9	31.2	16.4	18.8	20.6	-	23.7
London	9.9	37.5	21.7	16.1	14.7	0.1	61.9
South East (GOR)	11.9	31.4	17.4	18.8	20.4	-	28.6
South West	12.7	32.8	16.8	18.1	19.5	-	24.7
England	13.8	34.2	17.5	17.2	17.3	-	280.1
Wales	15.6	33.6	16.3	16.9	17.6	-	16.9
Scotland	15.6	30.9	17.4	18.0	18.0	-	33.4
Northern Ireland	13.9	37.0	15.7	16.3	17.1	-	12.2
All persons							
United Kingdom	9.1	33.5	24.0	17.2	15.5	0.8	1,479.3
North East	10.9	32.3	23.1	17.7	15.4	0.6	93.7
North West (GOR) & Merseyside	10.5	35.8	23.4	16.0	13.5	0.7	181.3
North West (GOR)	10.4	35.9	23.1	16.0	13.8	0.8	124.1
Merseyside	10.7	35.8	24.1	16.0	12.9	0.5	57.2
Yorkshire and the Humber	10.2	34.5	22.7	16.6	15.3	0.8	146.3
East Midlands	9.4	34.4	22.3	16.9	16.1	0.9	88.9
West Midlands	9.6	34.0	23.1	16.8	15.7	0.8	131.3
Eastern	8.6	31.6	22.6	18.1	18.0	1.2	94.8
London	6.3	33.5	28.9	17.0	13.6	0.7	236.6
South East (GOR)	7.8	31.1	23.7	18.5	17.8	1.1	120.7
South West	8.8	32.6	22.5	17.7	17.6	0.8	97.2
England	8.9	33.5	24.2	17.1	15.4	0.8	1,190.8
Wales	10.7	34.6	22.5	16.4	15.3	0.6	76.5
Scotland	10.3	32.7	23.0	17.3	15.8	0.9	152.2
Northern Ireland	7.7	33.2	25.0	18.6	15.0	0.5	59.8

1 Not seasonally adjusted. See Notes and Definitions.

Source: Office for National Statistics

6 Housing

Stock of dwellings

The stock of dwellings in Northern Ireland rose by 21 per cent between 1981 and 1996, almost three times the rate of growth in the North East.

(Table 6.1)

New homes

In 1996, private developers built more than three times as many homes per head of population in Northern Ireland as in London.

(Table 6.2)

Tenure

The rate of owner-occupation in Scotland rose by just over 13 per cent between 1991 and 1996, the highest increase.

(Table 6.3)

Age of dwellings

One in five dwellings in Wales was built before 1891 compared with around one in ten in the North East and the West Midlands.

(Table 6.4)

Amenities

More than three quarters of households living in houses in the South West and in the Eastern region have a parking provision at their home compared with just over half in London.

(Table 6.6)

Household mobility

Fifteen per cent of households in London in 1996-97 had been living at their current address for less than a year compared with 7 per cent in Northern Ireland.

(Table 6.7)

Satisfaction

Householders in the East Midlands, the Eastern region, and Scotland are the most likely to be satisfied with their accommodation and area, while those in London are least likely.

(Table 6.8)

Rents

Within Great Britain, private sector rents in 1996-97 were highest in London and lowest in Wales.

(Table 6.9)

House prices

The average price of dwellings in London for the last quarter of 1997, at £119,000, was more than double the price in the North East, Merseyside, the Yorkshire and Humber region and Wales.

(Table 6.11)

Council house sales

Local authorities in the South East (GOR) have sold or transferred more than half their housing stock since 1979, while those in the North West (GOR) and the Yorkshire and Humber region have reduced their stocks by just over a quarter.

(Table 6.13)

Homelessness

Mortgage arrears was the principal reason cited by 13 per cent of households accepted as homeless in the Eastern region in 1996, compared with only 1 per cent in Northern Ireland.

(Table 6.15)

Introduction

The first four tables in the chapter look at different aspects of the stock of dwellings. Changes in the stock are affected by a number of factors other than the building of new homes: some existing properties are converted – an important source of new homes in London and other urban areas – some are demolished either to make way for new development or because they are defective, some are closed as unfit for habitation and others that were previously closed are made fit again.

The biggest social change in housing during the 1980s was the growth in owner-occupation and the decline in public sector renting. This was in part due to the sale of dwellings by local authorities and new towns to sitting tenants (right-to buy-sales) and to others – for example to people who worked in the borough/district (Table 6.13). During the 1990s, the biggest change has been the growth in importance of housing associations as providers of social housing and the further decline in renting from local authorities. As can be seen from Table 6.2, the main responsibility for building new social housing in Great Britain has transferred from local authorities to housing associations. And in the last few years, Large Scale Voluntary Transfers – by which blocks of dwellings are transferred by local authorities or new towns to other landlords, usually a housing association registered with the Housing Corporation or Scottish Homes – have almost matched right-to-buy sales. Thus the stock of local authority housing has fallen significantly since the early 1980s; indeed some local authorities in England now have no housing stock at all.

Tables 6.9 to 6.12 examine various aspects of housing costs, either directly or indirectly. Housing costs are a sizeable proportion of a household's expenditure, although how sizeable varies quite widely by region: Table 8.10 in the Lifestyles chapter shows that the proportion ranges from 10 per cent in Northern Ireland to 18 per cent in both London and the South East, supporting the evidence of relative housing costs shown in Tables 6.9 to 6.11. Table 6.10 looks specifically at the housing costs of owner-occupiers. It should be noted that the table is on a different basis from that in last year's edition of *Regional Trends*. The figures for the individual categories of expenditure relate only to those who made a payment of that kind. However, total average costs relate to all owner-occupiers whether they own their home outright or with a mortgage. This means that the individual components do not add to the total.

For the first time, *Regional Trends* includes information from the Survey of English Housing and the Scottish House Condition Survey on householders' satisfaction with their accommodation and area (Table 6.8). Across England as a whole, 90 per cent of householders expressed some degree of satisfaction with their accommodation in 1996-97 with 57 per cent saying that they were very satisfied. In Scotland the corresponding proportions were 94 and 58 per cent respectively. Not surprisingly, the level of satisfaction varies by tenure and also by characteristics of the accommodation. Thus, 63 per cent of owner-occupiers in England said they were very satisfied with their accommodation compared with only 36 per cent of private renters in furnished accommodation.

Other characteristics found (in an earlier Survey of English Housing) to be independently associated with relatively low levels of satisfaction were living in a flat; living in property built before 1945; living in property valued in a low council tax band; and living in a deprived area. Personal characteristics associated with low levels of satisfaction were household heads who were not working and under retirement age; generally household heads aged under 30; and lone parents. Overall, householders in London were least likely to be very satisfied with their accommodation and also their area and while those in the South West and, for area, Scotland were the most likely.

6.1 Stock of dwellings[1]

	Thousands							Percentage increase	Rates per 1,000 population
	1981	1991	1992	1993	1994	1995	1996	1981-1996	1996
United Kingdom	21,586	23,711	23,881	24,062	24,252	24,426	24,607	14.0	418
North East	1,020	1,072	1,076	1,080	1,086	1,091	1,097	7.5	422
North West (GOR) & Merseyside	2,660	2,814	2,827	2,843	2,861	2,878	2,895	8.8	420
North West (GOR)	2,094	2,222	2,232	2,244	2,259	2,272	2,285	9.1	418
Merseyside	566	592	595	599	602	606	610	7.8	429
Yorkshire and the Humber	1,901	2,031	2,044	2,058	2,072	2,085	2,099	10.4	417
East Midlands	1,484	1,646	1,661	1,675	1,692	1,708	1,723	16.1	416
West Midlands	1,941	2,089	2,102	2,117	2,132	2,147	2,160	11.3	406
Eastern	1,859	2,108	2,132	2,155	2,177	2,200	2,222	19.5	420
London	2,682	2,928	2,945	2,962	2,980	2,997	3,011	12.3	426
South East (GOR)	2,750	3,117	3,142	3,166	3,194	3,219	3,245	18.0	411
South West	1,728	1,983	2,000	2,015	2,031	2,048	2,064	19.4	426
England	18,025	19,788	19,927	20,071	20,224	20,373	20,516	13.8	418
Wales	1,089	1,190	1,199	1,208	1,218	1,227	1,237	13.6	423
Scotland	1,970	2,160	2,175	2,193	2,210	2,229	2,246	14.0	438
Northern Ireland[2]	502	573	580	590	600	597	608	21.1	365

1 At 31 December each year. See Notes and Definitions.
2 Tenure data from 1995 are not directly comparable with previous years as they relate solely to properties liable for a rates charge.

Source: Department of the Environment, Transport and the Regions; Welsh Office;
The Scottish Office Development Department; Department of the Environment, Northern Ireland

6.2 New dwellings[1] completed: by sector

Thousands and rates per 1,000 population

	Private enterprise[2]				Housing associations				Local authorities, new towns and government departments[3]			
	Thousands		Rates		Thousands		Rates		Thousands		Rates	
	1991	1996	1991	1996	1991	1996	1991	1996	1991	1996	1991	1996
United Kingdom	159.1	153.5	2.8	2.6	20.8	32.5	0.4	0.6	11.2	1.4	0.2	-
North East	5.4	6.0	2.1	2.3	1.0	1.1	0.4	0.4	0.1	-	0.1	-
North West (GOR) & Merseyside	15.4	16.2	2.2	2.3	3.0	3.9	0.4	0.6	0.5	-	0.1	-
North West (GOR)	12.9	13.2	2.4	2.4	2.1	2.9	0.4	0.5	0.2	-	-	-
Merseyside	2.4	3.0	1.7	2.1	0.8	1.0	0.6	0.7	0.3	-	0.2	-
Yorkshire and the Humber	11.1	12.1	2.2	2.4	2.0	2.5	0.4	0.5	0.2	0.1	-	-
East Midlands	14.0	13.4	3.5	3.2	1.0	1.6	0.3	0.4	0.7	0.2	0.2	-
West Midlands	13.6	12.2	2.6	2.3	1.5	2.5	0.3	0.5	1.0	-	0.2	-
Eastern	18.9	18.2	3.8	3.5	0.6	3.3	0.1	0.6	1.5	0.1	0.3	-
London	12.8	8.6	1.9	1.2	2.7	5.0	0.4	0.7	0.7	-	0.1	-
South East (GOR)	23.0	21.1	3.0	2.7	2.3	4.0	0.3	0.5	2.3	-	0.3	-
South West	17.0	13.8	3.6	2.9	1.1	2.6	0.2	0.5	1.1	0.1	0.2	-
England	131.2	121.5	2.7	2.5	15.3	26.4	0.3	0.5	8.1	0.5	0.2	-
Wales	7.3	7.5	2.6	2.6	2.5	2.4	0.9	0.8	0.4	-	0.1	-
Scotland	15.5	17.8	3.0	3.5	2.3	2.7	0.4	0.5	1.7	-	0.3	-
Northern Ireland	5.2	6.7	3.2	4.0	0.8	1.0	0.5	0.6	1.0	0.9	0.6	0.5

1 Permanent dwellings only ie those with a life expectancy of 60 years or more. See Notes and Definitions.
2 Includes private landlords (persons or companies) and owner-occupiers.
3 Northern Ireland Housing Executive in Northern Ireland.

Source: Department of the Environment, Transport and the Regions; Welsh Office;
The Scottish Office Development Department; Department of the Environment, Northern Ireland

6.3 Tenure of dwellings[1]

Percentages

	Owner-occupied			Rented from local authority or New Town[2,3]			Rented from private owners or with job or business			Rented from housing association		
	1991	1993	1996	1991	1993	1996	1991	1993	1996	1991	1993	1996
Great Britain	66	67	67	21	20	19	10	10	10	3	4	5
North East	58	59	59	31	30	27	7	7	7	4	4	7
North West (GOR) & Merseyside	67	67	68	21	21	18	8	8	8	4	4	6
North West (GOR)	69	69	69	21	21	19	8	8	8	3	3	5
Merseyside	62	63	63	24	23	17	9	9	9	5	5	10
Yorkshire and the Humber	65	65	66	24	22	22	8	9	9	2	3	3
East Midlands	71	70	71	19	18	18	9	9	9	2	2	3
West Midlands	67	67	68	23	22	21	7	8	7	3	3	4
Eastern	71	71	71	17	16	15	10	10	10	3	4	4
London	57	57	57	24	22	21	12	14	15	5	6	7
South East (GOR)	74	74	74	12	11	11	11	11	11	3	4	4
South West	72	72	72	14	13	12	12	12	12	2	3	4
England	67	67	68	20	19	18	10	10	10	3	4	5
Wales	71	71	71	18	18	17	8	8	8	3	3	4
Scotland	52	56	59	38	34	30	7	7	7	3	3	4
Northern Ireland[4]	65	67	69	29	27	24	4	3	4	2	2	2

1 As at 31 December each year. See Notes and Definitions.
2 Including Scottish Homes, formerly the Scottish Special Housing Association.
3 Northern Ireland Housing Executive in Northern Ireland.
4 Changes in the method of data collection mean that the 1996 figures for Northern Ireland are not comparable with either the 1996 data for Great Britain or the Northern Ireland figures before 1995. The figures are based on occupied stock.

Source: Department of the Environment, Transport and the Regions; Welsh Office; The Scottish Office Development Department; Department of the Environment, Northern Ireland

6.4 Date of construction of dwellings, 1996[1]

Percentages

	Pre 1891	1891 -1918	1919 -1944	1945 -1970[2]	Post 1970[2]
England and Wales	14.3	12.1	19.5	31.2	22.9
North East	11.0	14.2	18.9	34.6	21.3
North West (GOR) & Merseyside	14.2	13.6	20.9	30.6	20.8
Yorkshire and the Humber	12.7	14.4	20.7	31.8	20.4
East Midlands	12.4	11.2	18.2	31.7	26.4
West Midlands	10.8	10.5	21.5	35.3	21.8
Eastern	14.2	8.1	15.7	33.5	28.5
London	17.7	17.0	27.7	22.0	15.6
South East (GOR)	11.4	8.8	17.5	36.0	26.3
South West	18.9	9.3	15.3	30.4	26.1
England	13.9	11.9	19.9	31.4	22.8
Wales	19.9	15.8	12.4	28.1	23.8
Northern Ireland	20.0		11.5	21.4	47.1

1 See Notes and Definitions.
2 Figures for Northern Ireland relate to 1945-1965 and post 1965.

Source: Department of the Environment, Transport and the Regions; Welsh Office; Department of the Environment, Northern Ireland

6.5 Households: by type of dwelling, 1996-97

Percentages

	Det-ached house	Semi-det-ached house	Terraced house	Purpose-built flat or mais-onette	Other[1]
United Kingdom	20	31	28	15	6
North East	14	39	32	13	1
North West (GOR) & Merseyside	14	38	35	10	4
Yorkshire and the Humber	17	40	30	10	3
East Midlands	31	38	21	7	2
West Midlands	22	38	26	12	2
Eastern	29	31	26	10	4
London	4	19	28	32	16
South East (GOR)	26	28	25	14	7
South West	29	28	25	11	7
England	20	32	28	14	6
Wales	23	34	30	9	4
Scotland	17	26	22	32	4
Northern Ireland	33	24	33	6	3

1 Includes converted flats which are particularly common in London.

Source: Survey of English Housing, Department of the Environment, Transport and the Regions; General Household Survey, Office for National Statistics; Continuous Household Survey, Northern Ireland Statistics and Research Agency

6.6 Households with different types of amenity

Percentages

	1991[1]					1996				
	Central heating	Double glazing	Secure windows and doors	Smoke detector(s)	Parking provision[2]	Central heating	Double glazing	Secure windows and doors	Smoke detector(s)	Parking provision[2]
North East	91.9	42.5	19.4	32.9	56.3	94.1	50.1	21.7	66.1	63.7
North West (GOR) & Merseyside	78.0	51.2	21.9	42.0	59.8	82.9	65.4	40.9	68.0	63.3
Yorkshire and the Humber	75.8	51.4	20.6	33.6	62.7	82.5	57.4	30.2	60.9	65.6
East Midlands	88.1	56.7	19.1	39.2	66.4	92.3	62.5	30.8	68.7	72.1
West Midlands	78.5	47.2	17.9	35.0	69.4	82.2	58.4	22.5	69.6	71.6
Eastern	91.0	56.7	17.4	44.7	74.7	92.3	65.7	22.5	73.5	75.9
London	83.8	50.0	35.3	33.6	51.2	87.5	50.7	34.8	56.9	52.9
South East (GOR)	86.2	58.6	26.3	49.4	72.0	91.6	59.6	32.9	70.0	73.0
South West	83.2	49.0	22.1	44.0	69.9	88.4	68.2	25.8	68.1	77.6
England	83.4	52.1	23.1	40.1	65.3	87.8	60.1	30.3	66.8	68.9
Wales[1]	..	49.8	..	55.8	..	..	..	..	..	..
Scotland	77.9	46.0	28.9	42.7	..	87.2	64.7	..	80.0	66.5
Northern Ireland	82.9	22.4	..	37.0	60.8	88.7	40.1	..	66.8	63.7

1 Data for Wales are for 1993.
2 Includes only facilities that are an integral part of the property, ie excludes street parking. Figures for England are based on households in houses only, excluding flats.

Source: National House Condition Surveys, Department of the Environment, Transport and the Regions, Welsh Office, Scottish Homes and Northern Ireland Housing Executive

6.7 Households: by length of time at current address, 1996-97

Percentages

	Under a year	1-4 years	5-9 years	10-19 years	20 or over
United Kingdom	11	24	19	46	
North East	10	22	19	22	26
North West (GOR) & Merseyside	11	23	18	22	25
North West (GOR)	11	23	19	23	23
Merseyside	11	21	17	20	31
Yorkshire and the Humber	10	25	19	23	23
East Midlands	8	24	18	23	26
West Midlands	9	20	18	23	29
Eastern	12	24	19	22	23
London	15	27	16	20	22
South East (GOR)	13	25	20	22	20
South West	11	27	21	22	20
England	11	24	19	22	23
Wales	9	25	16	23	27
Scotland	9	25	19	22	25
Northern Ireland	7	23	17	53	

Source: Survey of English Housing, Department of the Environment Transport and the Regions; General Household Survey, Office for National Statistics; Continuous Household Survey, Northern Ireland Statistics and Research Agency

6.8 Householders' satisfaction with their accommodation and area, 1996-97

Percentages

	Accommodation		Area	
	Very satisfied	Fairly satisfied	Very satisfied	Fairly satisfied
North East	60	31	49	35
North West (GOR) & Merseyside	56	33	48	34
Yorkshire and the Humber	56	34	52	32
East Midlands	60	32	55	33
West Midlands	59	32	52	32
Eastern	59	32	56	33
London	48	37	41	38
South East (GOR)	58	32	53	33
South West	61	30	59	31
England	57	33	51	34
Scotland	58	36	59	29

Source: Survey of English Housing, Department of the Environment, Transport and the Regions; Scottish House Condition Survey, Scottish Homes

6.9 Average weekly rents: by tenure, 1997[1]

£ per week

	Private sector average rent	Local authorities	Housing associations
Great Britain	80.0	39.9	45.2
North East	67.0	34.2	39.6
North West (GOR) & Merseyside	66.0	38.4	38.6
Yorkshire and the Humber	61.0	32.4	41.7
East Midlands	62.0	35.7	45.4
West Midlands	66.0	38.0	43.6
Eastern	75.0	42.7	46.8
London	124.0	54.2	53.1
South East (GOR)	87.0	47.0	51.6
South West	73.0	41.5	48.5
England	83.0	41.2	46.7
Wales	58.0	38.0	40.8
Scotland	63.0	33.6	32.9
Northern Ireland	..	34.4	..

1 See Notes and Definitions.

Source: Department of Social Security; Department of the Environment, Transport and the Regions; Welsh Office; The Scottish Office Development Department; Scottish Homes; Department of the Environment, Northern Ireland

6.10 Selected housing costs of owner occupiers, 1996-97[1,2]

£ per week

	Mortgage payments	Endowment policies	Structural insurance	Service payments	All owner-occupiers[3]
Great Britain	46	17	5	4	40
North East	35	14	4	2	34
North West (GOR) & Merseyside	38	14	4	1	32
Yorkshire and the Humber	38	14	4	2	31
East Midlands	37	15	4	5	33
West Midlands	40	15	4	3	35
Eastern	49	19	4	6	40
London	64	22	6	7	58
South East (GOR)	61	21	5	8	52
South West	45	19	4	5	38
England	47	17	5	4	41
Wales	35	14	4	2	26
Scotland	38	15	4	3	37
Northern Ireland	30	10	3	1	25

1 See Notes and Definitions.
2 Those who did not make any payments within each category are excluded. This table is therefore not comparable with data published in previous editions of *Regional Trends* which were based on all owner-occupiers.
3 Relates to both householders with a mortgage and those who owned their house outright.

Source: Family Resources Survey, Department of Social Security; Family Expenditure Survey, Northern Ireland Statistics and Research Agency

6.11 Average dwelling prices, 1997[1]

£ and percentages

	Average sale price (£)				All dwellings	
	Detached houses	Semi-detached houses	Terraced houses	Flats/ maisonettes	Average price, 1997	Percentage increase 1996-1997
England and Wales	119,951	69,439	60,496	73,292	79,732	9.2
North East	91,805	52,043	38,787	40,104	54,966	4.6
North West (GOR) & Merseyside	105,374	55,829	36,903	48,252	59,792	6.0
North West (GOR)	105,604	56,174	37,758	49,217	60,909	6.4
Merseyside	103,765	54,393	32,240	45,423	54,277	3.4
Yorkshire and the Humber	94,998	52,005	38,396	45,877	58,447	3.0
East Midlands	88,555	49,336	38,897	41,498	61,942	6.4
West Midlands	109,799	57,203	44,102	45,082	67,362	5.7
Eastern	120,934	71,816	60,049	49,056	80,911	10.9
London	237,019	136,148	121,117	101,068	118,862	13.0
South East (GOR)	161,017	88,084	70,355	55,907	97,739	11.0
South West	115,585	66,876	54,827	53,951	77,160	9.0
England	121,787	70,245	61,522	73,660	80,720	9.2
Wales	83,029	51,294	39,669	43,499	56,456	6.2

1 Excludes those bought at non-market prices. Averages are taken from the last quarter of each year. See Notes and Definitions.

Source: HM Land Registry

6.12 Mortgage advances, and income and age of borrowers[1], 1997

	First-time buyers				Previous owner-occupiers			
	Number of loans (thousands)	Average percentage of price advanced	Average recorded income[2] (£ per annum)	Average age of borrowers (years)	Number of loans (thousands)	Average percentage of price advanced	Average recorded income[2] (£ per annum)	Average age of borrowers (years)
United Kingdom	484	*88.4*	20,919	32	581	*64.6*	30,533	39
North East	20	*91.2*	16,698	32	19	*68.4*	24,994	39
North West (GOR) & Merseyside	50	*89.3*	18,348	31	52	*67.3*	27,846	39
North West (GOR)	41	*88.9*	18,447	31	44	*67.6*	28,108	39
Merseyside	9	*91.0*	17,886	32	8	*65.2*	26,363	41
Yorkshire and the Humber	38	*89.3*	18,151	31	39	*66.8*	26,728	39
East Midlands	36	*89.3*	18,906	31	40	*68.4*	27,205	39
West Midlands	39	*89.1*	18,763	31	45	*65.1*	27,595	38
Eastern	52	*87.5*	22,492	32	72	*64.7*	31,710	39
London	67	*88.0*	26,832	32	69	*62.4*	40,651	37
South East (GOR)	71	*88.2*	24,349	32	114	*63.4*	34,024	39
South West	42	*86.5*	19,995	32	65	*63.0*	26,836	41
England	415	*88.3*	21,427	31	515	*64.4*	31,089	39
Wales	22	*89.4*	17,929	32	22	*65.9*	25,519	39
Scotland	34	*89.6*	17,887	36	32	*66.6*	27,266	39
Northern Ireland	13	*87.3*	17,684	32	11	*63.1*	23,904	37

1 See Notes and Definitions.
2 The income of borrowers is the total recorded income taken into account when the mortgage is granted.

Source: Department of the Environment, Transport and the Regions

6.13 Sales and transfers of local authority dwellings[1]

Thousands and percentages

	April 1979 to March 1997				1996-97				Stock at 1 April 1997	Total sales and transfers April 1979 to March 1997 as a percentage of notional stock at 1 April 1979[4]
	Right-to-buy sales[2]	Large scale voluntary transfers[3]	Other sales and transfers	Total sales and transfers	Right-to-buy sales[2]	Large scale voluntary transfers	Other sales and transfers	Total sales and transfers		
United Kingdom	1,644	269	354	2,266	48	24	9	81	4,366	*34*
North East	109	0	6	115	3	0	-	3	298	*28*
North West (GOR) &										
Merseyside	149	8	39	196	3	0	2	5	523	*27*
North West (GOR)	112	8	23	143	2	0	1	3	407	*26*
Merseyside	37	0	16	53	1	0	1	2	116	*31*
Yorkshire and the Humber	135	8	14	157	3	0	1	4	441	*26*
East Midlands	119	0	15	134	3	0	-	3	294	*31*
West Midlands	152	32	24	208	5	16	-	21	410	*34*
Eastern	142	39	42	223	4	0	-	4	302	*42*
London	199	12	68	279	5	0	1	6	621	*31*
South East (GOR)	167	114	50	331	4	0	-	4	288	*53*
South West	114	31	18	163	3	5	-	8	224	*42*
England	1,286	244	276	1,806	33	21	4	58	3,401	*35*
Wales	97	1	6	104	2	0	0	2	204	*34*
Scotland	261	24	1	285	13	3	-	16	619	*32*
Northern Ireland[5]	.	.	71	71	.	.	5	5	142	*33*

1 Includes shared ownership deals and dwellings transferred to housing associations and private developers. Excludes New Towns. Figures for Scotland exclude sales by Scottish Homes.
2 Right-to-buy sales were introduced in Great Britain in October 1980. Figure for United Kingdom therefore relates to Great Britain.
3 Figure for United Kingdom relates to Great Britain. For Scotland includes large scale voluntary transfers and trickle transfers to housing associations.
4 Calculated as sales in the period April 1979 to March 1997 expressed as a percentage of stock at 1 April 1997 *plus* sales in the period April 1979 to March 1997.
5 The NI Housing Executive is responsible for public sector housing in Northern Ireland. Under the *Housing (NI) Order 1992* NIHE operates a voluntary house sales scheme which is comparable to the Right-to-buy schemes in Great Britain.

Source: Department of the Environment, Transport and the Regions; Welsh Office;
The Scottish Office Development Department; Department of the Environment, Northern Ireland

6.14 County Court actions for mortgage possessions[1]

Thousands

	1991			1995			1996			1997		
	Actions entered	Sus-pended orders	Orders made	Actions entered	Sus-pended orders	Orders made	Actions entered	Sus-pended orders	Orders made	Actions entered	Sus-pended orders	Orders made
England and Wales	186.6	69.1	73.9	84.2	44.6	30.4	79.8	43.4	27.8	67.0	34.8	22.5
North East	6.0	2.9	1.9	3.3	2.1	1.0	3.5	2.0	1.1	3.0	1.6	1.0
North West (GOR) & Merseyside	22.3	8.6	7.5	12.8	6.7	4.0	12.7	7.7	4.0	10.9	5.5	3.3
North West (GOR)	17.9	6.9	6.1	10.2	5.5	3.4	9.9	6.3	3.5	8.8	4.5	2.7
Merseyside	4.4	1.7	1.4	2.6	1.2	0.6	2.8	1.4	0.5	2.1	1.0	0.6
Yorkshire and the Humber	14.1	5.1	5.7	7.4	3.6	2.2	7.6	3.9	2.6	6.9	3.5	2.3
East Midlands	13.5	4.5	5.2	6.5	3.3	2.1	5.9	3.0	2.0	4.9	2.6	1.7
West Midlands	17.7	6.5	6.9	8.2	4.2	2.4	7.6	3.9	2.1	6.7	3.4	2.0
Eastern	18.6	6.0	8.4	8.5	4.3	3.4	8.3	4.0	3.4	6.7	3.0	2.5
London	35.3	13.1	14.4	12.1	6.7	6.0	11.4	6.4	4.8	9.2	4.7	3.4
South East (GOR)	32.2	13.2	13.2	13.0	7.6	5.3	11.6	6.6	4.0	9.1	5.4	3.1
South West	16.7	5.8	6.5	7.1	3.4	2.4	6.3	3.3	2.4	5.7	2.7	1.9
England	176.4	65.6	69.9	78.9	41.9	28.8	74.9	40.7	26.4	63.1	32.4	21.2
Wales	10.2	3.5	4.0	5.3	2.7	1.6	4.9	2.7	1.4	3.9	2.4	1.3
Northern Ireland[2]	3.1	..	..	1.2	..	..	1.2	..	..	1.2	..	..

1 Local authority and private. See Notes and Definitions.
2 Mortgage possession actions are heard in Chancery Division of Northern Ireland High Court.

Source: The Court Service; Northern Ireland Court Service

6.15 Households accepted as homeless: by reason[1], 1996

Percentages and numbers

	Reasons for homelessness						Total house-holds accepted as homeless (=100%) (numbers)
	No longer willing or able to remain with		Break-down of relation-ship with partner	Mort-gage arrears	Rent arrears or other reason for loss of rented or tie accomm-odation	Other reasons[2]	
	Parents	Relatives or friends					
England and Wales	17	12	24	7	23	17	126,159
North East	22	10	33	5	18	13	5,940
North West (GOR) & Merseyside	14	10	28	7	17	24	16,430
North West (GOR)	13	10	29	7	17	24	13,850
Merseyside	19	9	22	7	19	24	2,580
Yorkshire and the Humber	17	10	32	5	19	18	9,610
East Midlands	15	8	31	8	22	16	9,000
West Midlands	16	12	31	5	17	18	17,170
Eastern	18	9	21	13	29	10	8,680
London	19	20	16	4	22	20	26,020
South East (GOR)	18	10	16	10	32	14	14,290
South West	13	7	21	10	38	10	9,870
England	17	12	24	7	23	17	117,010
Wales	22	9	21	6	27	16	9,149
Scotland	32		32	3	14	19	17,200
Northern Ireland	28		18	1	10	43	4,785

1 See Notes and Definitions.
2 A large proportion of the Northern Ireland total is classified as 'Other reasons' due to differences in the definitions used.
3 In Scotland, the basis of these figures is households assessed by the local authorities as homeless or potentially homeless and in priority need, as defined in section 24 of the Housing (Scotland) Act 1987.

Source: Department of the Environment, Transport and the Regions; Welsh Office; The Scottish Office Development Department; Department of the Environment, Northern Ireland

7 Health

Infant deaths

The infant mortality rate in 1996 ranged from 5.3 deaths in the first year of life per 1,000 live births in the South East (GOR) to 6.8 in the West Midlands.

(Table 7.2)

Asthma

The prevalence of treated asthma is greatest among people living in Wales and in the Anglia and Oxford and the South and West NHS regions.

(Table 7.3)

Limiting long-standing illness

One in four people in Wales and in the North East reported having a limiting long-standing illness in 1996-97, compared with less than one in five in the South East.

(Chart 7.4)

Drug misuse

Twenty nine per cent of 16 to 29 year olds in London admitted in 1996 to illegal drug misuse in the previous year, more than double the proportion in Wales.

(Chart 7.9)

Breast cancer screening

Three in four women aged 50 to 64 in Northern Ireland were screened for breast cancer in the three years to 31 March 1997, compared with fewer than three in five in the North Thames NHS region.

(Table 7.12)

Cancer

The incidence of lung cancer is lowest in the East Anglian and the South Western RHAs and highest in Scotland for both males and females.

(Chart 7.13)

Death rates

Allowing for the age structure of the population, Northern Ireland had the highest death rates from respiratory diseases such as bronchitis for both males and females in 1996 while the South and West NHS region had the lowest.

(Table 7.14)

Hospital waiting lists

At the end of 1996-97, people living in the West Midlands NHS region had been waiting the shortest time on average for admission to hospital.

(Table 7.15)

Hospital activity

Within England, hospitals in the West Midlands, the North West and Trent NHS regions had the highest throughput per bed in 1996-97.

(Table 7.16)

Prescriptions

Nearly 13 prescription items were dispensed per person in Wales in 1996 compared with fewer than 9 in the Anglia and Oxford and the North and South Thames NHS regions.

(Table 7.17)

Residential care

One in five places available in residential homes in the Yorkshire and Humber region in March 1997 was for people with mental health problems compared with around one in 20 in the West Midlands, the Eastern region, Wales and Scotland.

(Table 7.20)

Introduction

T he regional breakdown within England of many of the tables in this chapter is the NHS Regional Office (NHSRO) areas, as administratively the NHS does not use the Government Office regions used throughout most of *Regional Trends.* On 1 April 1994 there was a reorganisation of the then 14 Regional Health Authorities (RHAs) to form eight. From 1 April 1996 the eight RHAs were replaced by NHSRO areas. Some of the statistics in this edition relate to the original 14 RHAs, but most relate to the NHSRO areas. Maps of these two structures are shown on page 214 of the Notes and Definitions. Due to differences in the collection of health statistics across the United Kingdom, it is not always possible to show national totals.

The contents of this chapter are a selection from the wide range of mortality, morbidity and health-related behaviour data available from administrative sources, for example registrations of births and deaths, hospital and general practice administration, or from household surveys. Surveys provide information about people who may not be in contact with health care services and can cover other inter-related factors such has lifestyle, housing conditions and local environment which can affect a person's health.

Items 7.1 to 7.5 cover the general health of the population. Table 7.3 shows the prevalence of selected medical conditions for which patients received treatment from their GP (consulted their GP in Scotland). Food is obviously a key element in people's health and Table 7.6 looks at nutritional intake. Tables 7.7 to 7.9 look at people's health-related behaviours - smoking, drinking alcohol and taking drugs.

The incidence of tuberculosis (TB) continues to be a public health problem, especially for inner city health authorities (the Inner London boroughs alone account for nearly 40 per cent of notified cases in England). Table 7.11 shows that notifications of TB in England have risen overall from their 1987 levels when they were at a low. Over half of cases in England are in the non-white ethnic population from areas of the world with a high prevalence of TB. Other high risk groups are older white people who were exposed to TB when they were younger, homeless people and people infected with HIV.

The national screening programmes for cervical and breast cancers in women continue to be key prevention measures carried out by the NHS. Table 7.12 examines the coverage of the target populations by the two programmes as at 31 March 1997. These target populations are women aged 25 to 64 in England and Northern Ireland, 20 to 64 in Wales, 20 to 59 in Scotland for cervical screening and those aged 50 to 64 for breast screening. Women in these age groups are routinely invited for screening at least every five years for cervical screening and every three years for breast screening. The figures do not include women in other age groups who have been screened. For breast screening, readers should note that figures in this edition of *Regional Trends* are on a different basis from those shown in previous editions which were based on uptake of the screening service (the number of women screened as a percentage of all invited for screening).

While about half of patients admitted to hospital are emergency cases, the rest are planned admissions for non-emergency operations. Table 7.15 shows the number of people waiting for admission to an NHS hospital either as a day case or as an ordinary admission on 31 March 1997. These waiting list figures relate to the region of residence of the patient, not the region in which the hospital is located. The table also shows the average time they had been waiting for admission. The median waiting time – that is the waiting time for the middle case of those admitted – is a better indicator than the mean of the length of time people can expect to be on the waiting list since it is generally unaffected by the minority of cases with abnormally long or short waiting times.

7.1 Population and vital statistics: NHS Regional Office areas, 1996

Thousands and rates

	Population aged (mid-year estimates) (thousands)					Vital statistics (rates)				
	0-15	16-64	65-84	85 or over	All ages	Live births[1]	Still births[2]	Deaths[3]	Perinatal mortality[4]	Infant mortality[5]
United Kingdom	12,098.3	37,452.4	8,183.6	1,067.2	58,801.5	60.1	5.5	10.9	8.7	6.1
Northern and Yorkshire	1,309.6	4,018.8	898.3	111.4	6,338.0	58.7	5.4	11.3	8.6	6.4
North West	1,400.8	4,170.7	915.6	118.0	6,605.1	60.7	5.5	11.6	8.7	6.4
Trent	1,038.5	3,257.3	735.7	89.7	5,121.2	58.5	5.4	10.9	8.7	6.3
West Midlands	1,119.5	3,369.0	741.6	86.5	5,316.6	62.7	6.1	10.6	10.2	6.8
Anglia and Oxford	1,113.3	3,456.4	699.1	92.1	5,360.9	59.2	4.9	9.6	7.7	5.8
North Thames	1,428.1	4,535.1	852.5	118.0	6,933.7	63.4	6.1	9.5	9.0	5.6
South Thames	1,354.4	4,352.9	964.0	147.8	6,819.1	60.8	5.3	10.9	8.6	6.1
South and West	1,288.6	4,124.0	1,032.3	149.5	6,594.4	58.4	4.6	11.3	7.5	5.5
England	10,052.7	31,284.2	6,839.1	913.1	49,089.1	60.4	5.4	10.7	8.6	6.1
Wales	602.0	1,812.4	450.2	56.4	2,921.1	61.1	4.9	11.9	7.5	5.6
Scotland	1,028.0	3,320.6	700.8	78.7	5,128.0	54.0	6.4	11.8	9.2	6.2
Northern Ireland	415.6	1,035.2	193.5	19.0	1,663.3	68.0	6.3	9.1	9.4	5.8

1 Per 1,000 women aged 15-44.
2 Per 1,000 live and still births. A still birth relates to a baby born dead after 24 completed weeks gestation or more.
3 Per 1,000 population.
4 Still births and deaths of infants under 1 week of age per 1,000 live and still births.
5 Deaths of infants under 1 year of age per 1,000 live births.

Source: Office for National Statistics; General Register Office for Scotland; Northern Ireland Statistics and Research Agency

7.2 Still births, perinatal mortality and infant mortality

Rates

	Still births[1]				Perinatal mortality[2]				Infant mortality[3]		
	1981	1993[4]	1993[4]	1996	1981	1993[4]	1993[4]	1996	1981	1993	1996
United Kingdom	6.6	4.4	5.7	5.5	12.0	7.6	9.0	8.7	11.2	6.3	6.1
North East	7.5	4.6	5.9	5.9	12.6	7.9	9.2	9.3	10.4	6.7	6.4
North West (GOR) & Merseyside	7.0	4.5	5.8	5.4	12.7	7.7	9.0	8.6	11.3	6.5	6.2
North West (GOR)	7.0	4.5	5.9	5.5	12.6	7.9	9.3	8.6	11.1	6.8	6.2
Merseyside	6.9	4.7	5.6	5.2	12.8	7.0	8.0	8.8	12.0	5.4	6.3
Yorkshire and the Humber	7.8	4.6	5.9	5.1	13.5	8.0	9.4	8.3	12.1	7.3	6.6
East Midlands	6.2	3.9	5.4	5.3	11.4	7.2	8.7	8.6	11.0	6.6	6.2
West Midlands	7.0	4.4	6.0	6.1	12.9	8.4	9.9	10.2	11.7	7.1	6.8
Eastern	5.5	3.9	5.2	4.6	10.0	6.8	8.1	7.5	9.7	5.4	5.4
London	6.3	4.9	6.1	6.3	10.3	8.2	9.5	9.6	10.7	6.4	6.4
South East (GOR)	5.8	4.0	5.4	5.1	10.5	7.0	8.3	7.6	10.3	5.3	5.3
South West	6.3	4.0	5.0	4.7	10.8	6.9	7.9	7.6	10.4	5.8	5.6
England	6.5	4.3	5.7	5.4	11.7	7.6	8.9	8.6	10.9	6.3	6.1
Wales	7.3	4.5	5.8	4.9	14.1	7.0	8.3	7.5	12.6	5.5	5.6
Scotland	6.3	4.8	6.4	6.4	11.6	8.0	9.6	9.2	11.3	6.5	6.2
Northern Ireland	8.7	4.1	5.2	6.3	15.3	7.7	8.8	9.4	13.2	7.1	5.8

1 Per 1,000 live and still births.
2 Still births and deaths of infants under 1 week of age per 1,000 live and still births.
3 Deaths of infants under 1 year of age per 1,000 live births.
4 On 1 October 1992, the legal definition of a still birth was altered from a baby born dead after 28 completed weeks gestation or more to one born dead after 24 weeks gestation or more. Figures are given on both the old and new definitions for continuity/comparison.

Source: Office for National Statistics; General Register Office for Scotland; Northern Ireland Statistics and Research Agency

7.3 Prevalence of selected medical conditions[1]: by gender, 1996

Rate per 1,000 patients[2]

	Males						Females					
	Coronary heart disease	Hyper-tension	Depress-ion/ anxiety	Insulin treated diabetes	Non-insulin treated diabetes	Asthma	Coronary heart disease	Hyper-tension	Depress-ion/ anxiety	Insulin treated diabetes	Non-insulin treated diabetes	Asthma
Treated medical conditions												
England and Wales[3]	34.7	48.1	36.2	5.1	9.6	66.8	20.8	52.5	81.9	4.3	7.0	68.6
Northern and Yorkshire	40.7	46.6	42.2	4.9	9.2	65.1	27.2	52.4	91.1	4.8	6.8	66.8
North West	41.3	49.4	44.4	5.1	9.4	68.4	25.6	52.2	94.9	4.3	6.8	68.2
Trent	37.0	48.3	36.2	5.1	9.4	67.4	23.5	53.3	83.1	4.4	7.1	70.9
West Midlands	32.9	49.6	32.0	5.5	10.0	63.6	19.7	53.9	78.1	4.5	7.9	64.5
Anglia and Oxford	30.1	47.3	34.9	4.8	8.9	70.4	16.8	52.7	80.7	4.8	6.7	72.5
North Thames	28.7	43.1	29.4	4.5	10.1	64.7	16.4	46.4	67.1	3.7	7.2	67.5
South Thames	29.7	48.0	31.4	5.2	9.0	62.1	16.7	52.9	72.4	4.0	6.4	65.2
South and West	32.3	48.2	38.3	5.3	10.1	69.7	17.6	53.5	85.1	4.1	7.1	71.2
England	34.3	47.8	36.2	5.1	9.5	66.4	20.6	52.3	81.8	4.3	7.0	68.2
Wales	39.6	52.2	36.9	6.1	10.2	72.3	23.7	54.8	83.3	4.6	7.5	72.5
Recorded medical conditions												
Scotland	43.8	59.9	58.9	11.1		33.2	29.3	74.5	133.5	8.9		35.4

1 Data are recorded in general practices. For England and Wales figures relate to treated medical conditions. For Scotland figures relate to recorded medical conditions; therefore data are not directly comparable with England and Wales. See Notes and Definitions.
2 All ages. Age-standardised using the European Standard Population.
3 Patients are allocated to regions according to the location of the practice at which they are registered.

Source: General Practice Research Database, Office for National Statistics; Continuous Morbidity Recording, Information and Statistics Division, NHS in Scotland

7.4 Consultations with an NHS GP and reports of limiting long-standing illness, 1996-97

Persons who consulted an NHS GP[1]

Persons who reported limiting long-standing illness[2]

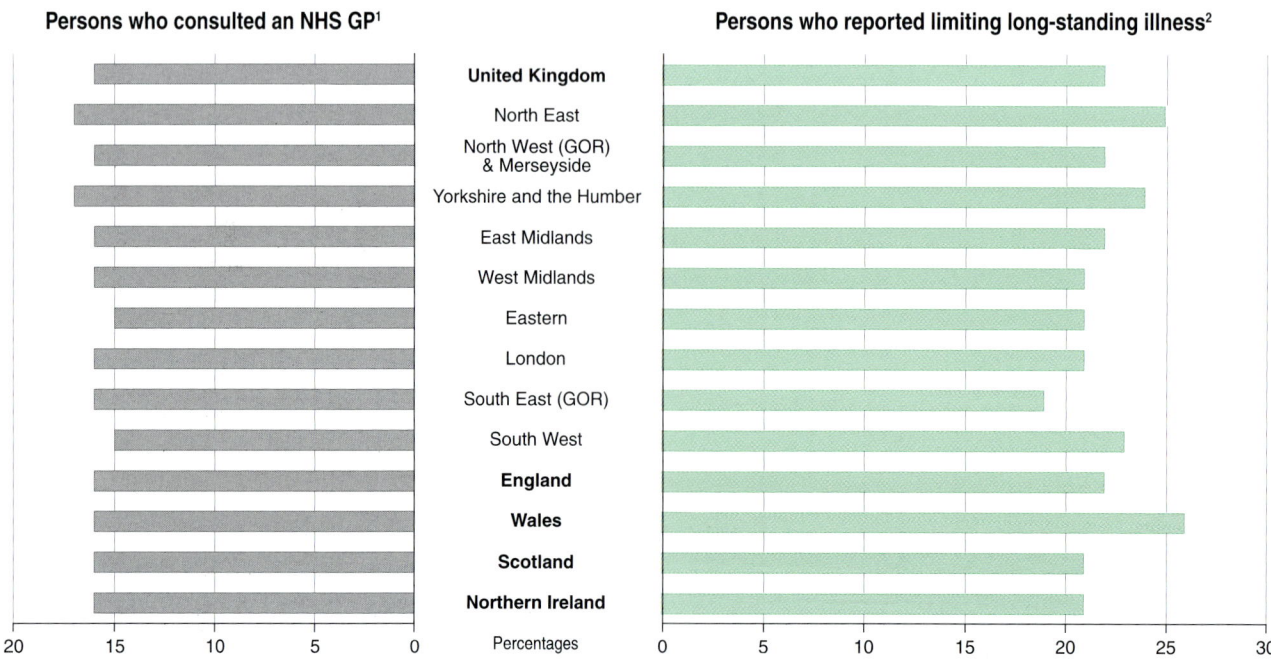

1 In the 14 days before interview.
2 See Notes and Definitions.

Source: General Household Survey, Office for National Statistics; Continuous Household Survey, Northern Ireland Statistics and Research Agency

7.5 GP patients referred to hospital out-patients[1]: by selected specialty and by gender, 1996

Rates per 1,000 patient years at risk[2]

	Males						Females					
	General medicine	General surgery	Ortho-paedic	Ophthal-mology	Ear, nose and throat	Psy-chiatry	General medicine	General surgery	Ortho-paedic	Ophthal-mology	Ear, nose and throat	Psy-chiatry
England and Wales[3]	16.9	28.0	18.3	10.5	16.0	6.3	18.0	28.7	18.5	12.3	15.4	7.4
Northern and Yorkshire	16.5	29.9	18.2	11.1	17.3	8.3	17.5	32.0	16.6	12.4	16.5	9.3
North West	20.1	30.5	20.5	11.6	17.5	6.8	20.7	30.3	20.6	14.1	16.4	6.7
Trent	16.7	28.8	20.4	11.2	16.1	6.4	17.5	28.2	19.5	12.1	16.5	6.8
West Midlands	17.1	28.0	19.1	9.6	15.5	6.3	19.0	29.3	20.0	11.6	15.6	7.8
Anglia and Oxford	15.4	26.6	16.6	9.8	14.5	4.7	15.9	26.2	17.6	11.2	14.1	6.2
North Thames	18.1	22.9	15.3	10.5	14.4	5.2	20.1	26.1	16.2	13.0	14.1	6.9
South Thames	16.9	27.8	17.5	9.8	16.7	6.2	19.1	31.0	18.1	12.0	15.1	7.5
South and West	14.9	28.3	17.8	10.0	15.7	6.3	15.1	25.8	18.5	12.6	14.8	8.3
England	17.0	28.0	18.3	10.4	16.0	6.3	18.1	28.7	18.5	12.3	15.4	7.4
Wales	16.0	28.2	18.2	11.1	16.2	6.1	17.4	29.0	18.6	12.0	15.8	7.6

1 Data are recorded in general practices. See Notes and Definitions.
2 All ages. Age-standardised using the European Standard Population.
3 Patients are allocated to regions according to the location of the practice at which they are registered.

Source: General Practice Research Database, Office for National Statistics

7.6 Contributions of selected foods to nutritional intakes (household food), 1995-1996[1]

	Percentage of fat and energy derived from										Total intake[2] per person per day		Per-centage of food energy derived from fat[2]
	Liquid & processed milk & cream		Meat & meat products		All fats		Fresh & processed fruit & vegetables		Cereals including bread		Fat (grams)	Energy (Kcal)	
	Fat	Energy	Fat	Energy	Fat	Energy	Fat	Energy	Fat	Energy			
Great Britain	10.9	10.3	22.5	14.5	30.2	12.1	7.6	14.9	16.2	34.2	80	1,810	39.8
North East	11.1	10.2	23.6	15.1	27.7	11.1	7.7	14.6	17.1	34.5	79	1,790	39.7
North West (GOR) & Merseyside	10.8	10.5	23.5	15.1	27.6	11.1	7.1	14.4	16.0	33.2	77	1,780	39.0
Yorkshire and the Humber	11.4	10.7	23.0	14.8	32.7	13.1	7.2	14.8	16.8	35.1	83	1,870	40.1
East Midlands	11.3	10.9	23.0	14.7	33.9	13.6	8.3	15.8	17.1	35.6	86	1,910	40.4
West Midlands	10.7	10.2	22.7	14.6	31.1	12.5	7.9	15.5	16.4	34.8	81	1,860	39.4
Eastern	10.9	10.3	23.4	15.0	31.2	12.6	7.6	15.4	16.3	32.8	82	1,830	40.3
London	10.5	9.6	18.7	12.1	30.6	12.2	6.8	13.8	14.6	37.1	74	1,770	37.7
South East (GOR)	10.8	10.3	21.5	13.8	29.5	11.9	8.0	15.0	16.6	33.4	80	1,800	40.2
South West	11.1	10.3	21.5	13.8	30.8	12.4	7.5	15.3	15.4	31.9	80	1,790	40.1
England	10.9	10.3	22.4	14.4	30.4	12.2	7.6	14.9	16.2	34.2	80	1,820	39.6
Wales	10.6	10.2	23.8	15.3	31.9	12.8	7.7	15.6	16.2	34.2	82	1,860	39.7
Scotland	11.1	10.3	22.7	14.6	27.3	11.0	7.4	13.7	16.4	33.3	77	1,750	39.7
Northern Ireland[3]	11.0	9.8	22.2	14.3	33.3	13.4	6.6	14.5	17.5	36.4	87	1,960	39.9

1 See Notes and Definitions.
2 Total intake from all household food, excluding household consumption of soft and alcoholic drinks and confectionery.
3 Figures relate to 1996 only.

Source: National Food Survey, Ministry of Agriculture, Fisheries and Food

7.7 Cigarette smoking among people aged 16 or over: by gender, 1996-97

Percentages and numbers

	Males					Females				
	Proportion who			Proportion of smokers smoking 20 or more daily	Smokers' average weekly con-sumption (numbers)	Proportion who			Proportion of smokers smoking 20 or more daily	Smokers' average weekly con-sumption (numbers)
	Have never smoked	Are ex-regular smokers	Smoke			Have never smoked	Are ex-regular smokers	Smoke		
United Kingdom	40	32	29	39	111	53	20	28	30	96
North East	43	28	29	42	114	49	18	33	36	108
North West (GOR) & Merseyside	44	26	30	41	114	52	18	30	30	98
Yorkshire and the Humber	36	34	30	43	117	54	21	25	39	101
East Midlands	42	34	25	43	116	52	21	27	31	94
West Midlands	40	32	28	36	106	54	18	28	35	99
Eastern	40	33	27	30	100	51	23	25	25	93
London	39	28	32	38	109	57	16	27	24	86
South East (GOR)	38	36	26	35	105	52	23	25	24	88
South West	39	34	28	35	109	54	21	26	29	91
England	40	32	28	38	109	53	20	27	29	95
Wales	39	33	28	34	108	55	18	27	33	94
Scotland	40	28	33	47	122	50	19	31	36	110
Northern Ireland	32	37	31	48	124	49	23	27	34	102

Source: General Household Survey, Office for National Statistics;
Continuous Household Survey, Northern Ireland Statistics and Research Agency

7.8 Alcohol consumption[1] among people aged 16 or over: by gender, 1996-97

Percentages and numbers

	Males					Females				
	Consumption levels (units per week)				Average weekly con-sumption (number of units)	Consumption levels (units per week)				Average weekly con-sumption (number of units)
	Non-drinker	Under 1-10	11-21	22 or more		Non-drinker	Under 1-7	8-14	15 or more	
United Kingdom	7	43	23	27	16	13	57	16	14	6
North East	9	34	24	33	19	17	55	15	13	6
North West (GOR) & Merseyside	7	40	22	31	19	11	54	17	18	8
Yorkshire and the Humber	7	41	23	30	17	12	55	18	15	7
East Midlands	6	43	25	26	15	10	59	19	12	6
West Midlands	9	39	24	28	16	16	55	16	12	6
Eastern	7	48	21	24	14	13	59	16	12	6
London	11	45	19	25	15	20	56	12	13	6
South East (GOR)	5	45	23	27	16	10	57	18	14	7
South West	6	46	24	25	15	9	60	17	13	6
England	7	43	23	27	16	13	57	16	14	6
Wales	6	50	19	25	15	13	56	15	16	5
Scotland	7	41	28	25	16	13	60	16	11	7
Northern Ireland	22	38	17	22	14	31	48	12	8	4

1 Comparative consumption levels are different for males and females. See Notes and Definitions.

Source: General Household Survey, Office for National Statistics;
Continuous Household Survey, Northern Ireland Statistics and Research Agency

7.9 Drug misuse among 16 to 29 year olds, 1995-96

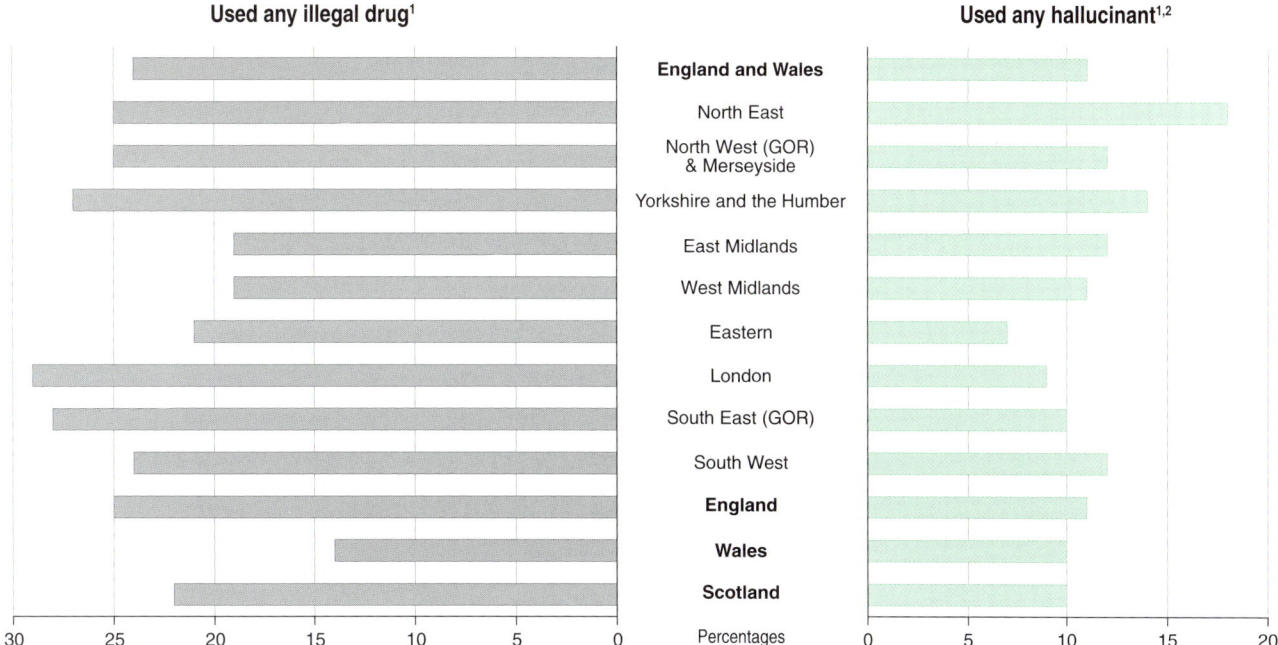

Used any illegal drug[1]

Used any hallucinant[1,2]

- England and Wales
- North East
- North West (GOR) & Merseyside
- Yorkshire and the Humber
- East Midlands
- West Midlands
- Eastern
- London
- South East (GOR)
- South West
- England
- Wales
- Scotland

Percentages

1 Interviews were conducted between January and April 1996, asking about drug use in the previous 12 months.
2 Amphetamine, LSD, magic mushrooms, ecstasy or poppers.

Source: British Crime Survey, Home Office;
Scottish Crime Survey, The Scottish Office Home Department

7.10 Exposure category of AIDS cases, cumulative totals to end-1997

Numbers

	Sexual intercourse			Injecting drug use			Other[3]/ undetermined		Total cases reported to 31 December 1997
	Between men[1]	Between men and women				Blood[2]			
		Males	Females	Males	Females		Males	Females	
Region of residence									
United Kingdom	10,126	1,164	1,096	648	277	730	238	144	14,423
Northern and Yorkshire	343	54	38	10	7	101	13	4	570
North West	589	54	37	36	13	89	15	8	841
Trent	262	55	33	25	10	37	9	7	438
West Midlands	243	32	28	6	5	59	9	3	385
Anglia and Oxford	403	65	49	54	15	63	10	2	661
North Thames	4,274	490	461	159	79	97	81	51	5,692
South Thames	2,865	251	316	103	37	109	67	50	3,798
South and West	552	65	42	18	11	72	11	7	778
England[4]	9,584	1,067	1,007	414	177	635	215	132	13,231
Wales	150	19	17	2	3	36	6	2	235
Scotland	349	74	65	231	96	50	16	10	891
Northern Ireland	43	4	7	1	1	9	1	0	66

1 Includes men who had also injected drugs.
2 Blood/blood factor and tissue recipients.
3 Includes mother to infant transmission.
4 Figures for England include some people living in London whose NHS region of residence was not known (London is split between the North and South Thames regions; see map on page 214).

Source: Public Health Laboratory Service, Communicable Disease Surveillance Centre;
Scottish Centre for Infection and Environmental Health

7.11 Notification rates of tuberculosis

Rates per 100,000 population

	1986	1987	1988	1989	1990	1991	1992	1993	1994	1995	1996
United Kingdom	12.1	10.1	10.1	10.6	10.2	10.5	11.1	11.3	10.7	10.5	10.6
Northern and Yorkshire	11.6	9.6	9.6	10.3	10.0	11.2	10.1	11.0	9.0	9.8	9.5
North West	14.3	10.7	11.0	10.5	11.3	10.1	11.6	12.0	10.0	9.6	8.8
Trent	11.7	10.8	11.1	10.1	9.3	9.3	8.7	10.5	9.2	10.2	10.6
West Midlands	16.5	12.7	12.8	16.1	13.9	15.6	16.5	14.9	13.8	12.3	12.3
Anglia and Oxford	6.2	6.8	7.0	6.7	6.1	6.2	7.0	6.6	5.9	6.7	6.2
North Thames	21.2	18.2	18.3	20.5	18.7	21.9	24.4	23.4	24.9	25.0	26.0
South Thames	9.8	8.2	8.4	8.6	9.7	8.9	9.3	10.4	10.3	9.5	10.4
South and West	4.6	4.2	4.7	4.2	3.6	3.5	3.8	4.2	4.2	4.2	4.0
England	12.1	10.2	10.4	10.9	10.4	10.9	11.6	11.8	11.1	11.1	11.2
Wales	8.8	8.2	7.0	7.3	6.7	5.7	6.9	6.8	6.2	6.2	5.5
Scotland	14.8	11.0	10.4	10.5	11.0	10.7	10.9	10.8	10.6	9.3	9.9
Northern Ireland	6.9	6.3	5.4	5.9	8.2	6.0	5.2	5.5	5.6	5.5	4.5

Source: Public Health Laboratory Service, Communicable Disease Surveillance Centre;
Scottish Centre for Infection and Environmental Health

7.12 Cervical and breast cancer: screening and age-adjusted death rates

	Cervical screening programme at 31 March 1997[1]							Breast screening programme at 31 March 1997					Age-adjusted death rates[6], 1996	
	Percentage of target population screened: women aged[2]					Total screened (thou-sands)	Per-centage recalled early[4]	Percentage of target population[5] screened: women aged				Total screened (thou-sands)	Cervical cancer	Breast cancer
	25-34[3]	35-44	45-54	55-64[3]	All aged 25-64[3]			50-54	55-59	60-64	All aged 50-64			
Northern and Yorkshire	86.0	89.2	88.8	81.8	86.8	1,333.2	3.2	56.9	74.8	72.2	67.3	350.1	6.7	56.9
North West	83.6	86.5	85.9	78.7	84.1	1,356.3	4.3	56.6	74.1	71.5	66.7	362.3	9.5	58.3
Trent	88.5	91.2	90.2	84.0	88.9	1,088.2	3.5	60.2	77.9	77.1	70.8	296.0	7.0	64.0
West Midlands	84.4	88.4	88.3	81.8	85.9	1,110.7	4.0	59.0	74.7	72.4	67.9	302.0	6.7	64.3
Anglia and Oxford	84.8	89.6	89.8	84.1	87.2	1,132.9	3.6	59.8	78.6	75.6	70.1	304.4	4.9	57.1
North Thames	74.4	79.8	81.4	78.2	77.9	1,497.2	3.9	48.0	63.4	62.4	57.0	310.4	5.8	60.6
South Thames	81.1	86.1	86.8	80.8	83.7	1,486.6	4.0	50.9	68.0	67.2	61.0	338.6	5.5	56.9
South and West	84.9	88.3	86.9	80.6	85.6	1,351.1	4.7	54.9	74.9	74.4	66.9	377.7	5.8	59.2
England	82.7	87.0	87.0	81.1	84.6	10,356.1	3.8	55.4	73.0	71.3	65.6	2,641.4	6.5	59.5
Wales	78.8	87.8	87.2	88.8	84.2	646.4	..	58.3	76.1	73.8	68.6	170.3	7.1	60.2
Scotland	81.1	89.5	89.4	82.8	85.3	955.0	..	71.0	70.3	66.3	69.3	309.5	6.8	59.9
Northern Ireland	..	..	..	..	..	..	..	75.3	76.4	71.9	74.6	90.9	7.8	56.3

1 For Scotland data relates to 31 December 1996.
2 For England the target population relates to women aged 25-64 years and for Wales figures relate to women aged 20-64 years screened in the previous 5 years. In Scotland figures relate to women aged 20-59 years, screened in the previous 5.5 years. Medically ineligible women (women who as a result of surgery etc do not require screening) in the target population are excluded from the figures; in Wales, all women classed as 'recall ceased' are excluded.
3 For Wales, the age groups are 20-34, 55-64 and 20-64 respectively. For Scotland, they are 20-34, 55-59 and 20-59 respectively.
4 Women whose screening test results are borderline or show mild dyskaryosis are recalled for a repeat smear in approximately 6 months instead of the routine 5 years; if the condition persists they are referred to a gynaecologist.
5 Percentage of the target population - women aged 50-64 years - screened in the previous 3 years. Medically ineligible women (women who as a result of surgery etc do not require screening) in the target population are excluded from the figures except in Scotland where they are included. See Notes and Definitions.
6 Deaths per 100,000 women aged 20 or over. Standardised to the mid-1991 United Kingdom population. See Notes and Definitions.

Source: Office for National Statistics; Department of Health; Welsh Office; General Register Office for Scotland;
Information and Statistics Division, NHS in Scotland; Northern Ireland Statistics and Research Agency;
Department of Health and Social Services, Northern Ireland

7.13 Cancer – directly age-standardised registration rates[1] for selected sites: by gender, 1992[2]

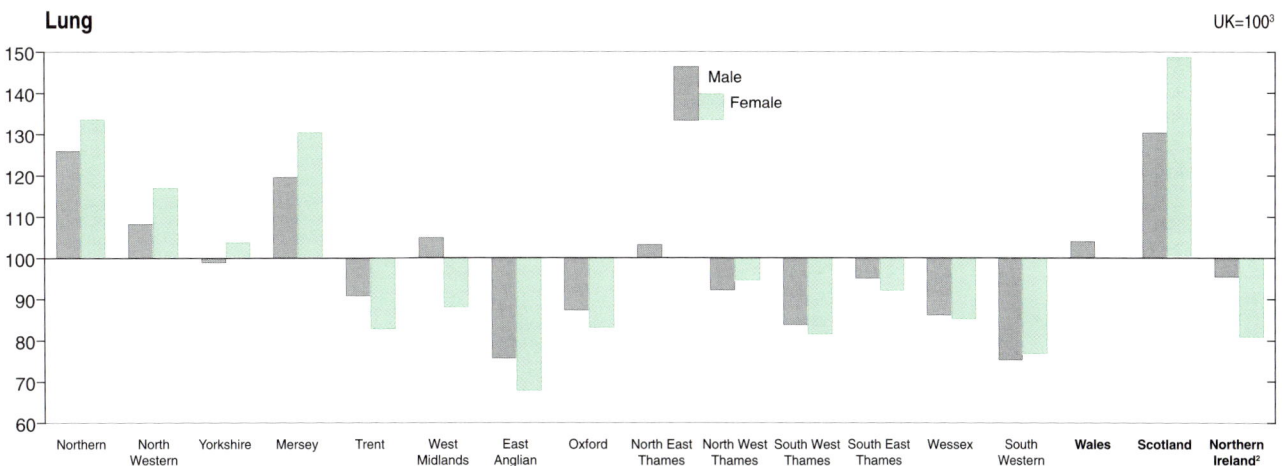

Lung
UK=100[3]

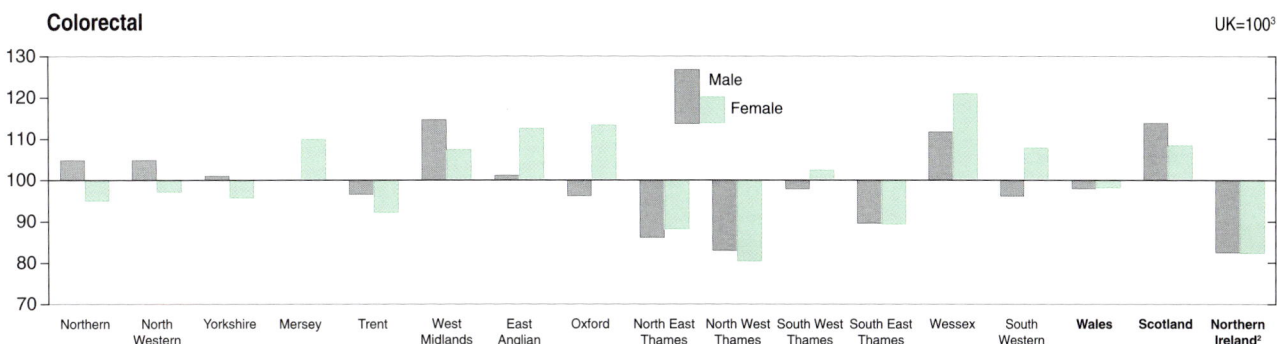

Colorectal
UK=100[3]

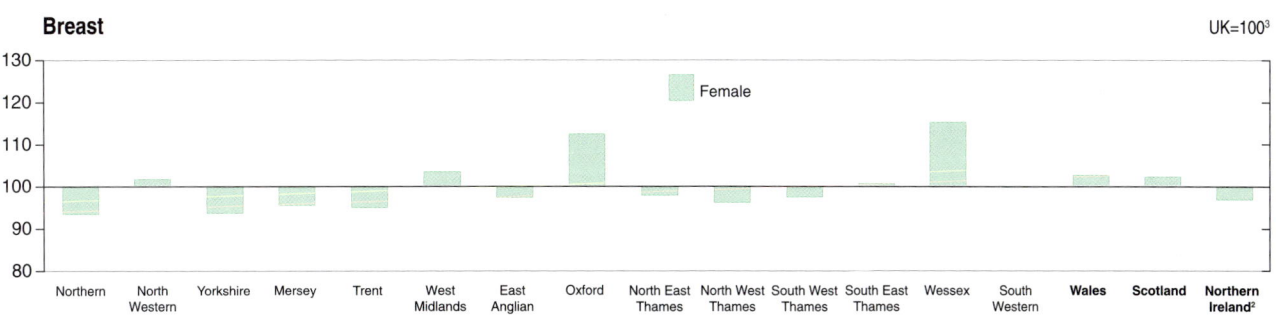

Breast
UK=100[3]

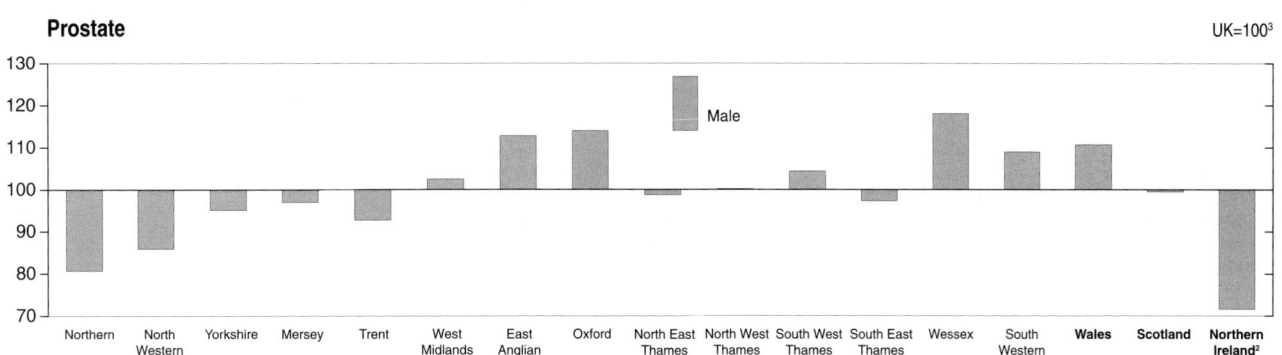

Prostate
UK=100[3]

1 Incidence has been directly age-standardised using the European Standard Population to take account of the differing age structures of population. See Notes and Definitions.
2 For Northern Ireland, 1991 numbers of new cases have been used to estimate 1992 incidence.
3 Regional registration rates as percentages of the United Kingdom rate; values for the United Kingdom rates are given in the Notes and Definitions.

Source: Office for National Statistics; Information and Statistics Division,
NHS in Scotland; Northern Ireland Cancer Registry

7.14 Age-adjusted mortality rates[1]: by cause[2] and gender, 1996

Rates per 100,000 population

	All circulatory diseases			All respiratory diseases			All injuries and poisonings				
	Total	Ischaemic heart disease	Cerebro-vascular disease	Total	Bronchitis and allied conditions	Cancer[3]	Total	Road traffic accidents	Suicides and open verdicts	All other causes	All causes[4]
Males											
United Kingdom	431	269	83	146	56	274	41	9	16	123	1,017
Northern and Yorkshire	454	291	91	153	61	297	43	10	17	120	1,067
North West	473	299	94	171	69	296	43	8	18	126	1,109
Trent	434	274	86	144	57	272	40	11	15	122	1,012
West Midlands	444	277	86	147	60	273	34	7	14	125	1,023
Anglia and Oxford	384	235	74	129	46	252	38	10	15	118	921
North Thames	398	250	69	154	54	258	36	6	14	125	971
South Thames	384	226	74	144	53	260	36	8	15	118	941
South and West	382	238	70	117	44	247	39	10	15	112	898
England	418	261	80	144	55	269	39	9	15	120	991
Wales	452	283	85	152	63	271	45	9	18	115	1,035
Scotland	519	325	109	149	58	317	60	10	25	155	1,200
Northern Ireland	478	309	91	190	65	283	53	11	15	105	1,109
Females											
United Kingdom	456	219	138	172	42	250	23	4	5	170	1,071
Northern and Yorkshire	481	243	143	182	52	262	23	4	5	174	1,122
North West	491	242	147	200	58	267	22	3	5	171	1,151
Trent	453	224	134	163	41	251	21	4	5	177	1,066
West Midlands	474	226	141	163	40	248	23	3	5	175	1,083
Anglia and Oxford	417	193	130	158	31	232	23	5	5	171	1,002
North Thames	403	194	115	183	40	240	20	3	5	166	1,012
South Thames	413	183	124	174	38	237	19	3	6	161	1,005
South and West	408	190	129	138	28	229	22	4	6	168	966
England	442	211	133	171	41	246	22	3	5	170	1,049
Wales	485	233	144	177	47	245	24	5	4	161	1,093
Scotland	556	266	177	167	49	288	38	4	8	180	1,229
Northern Ireland	521	269	160	231	40	243	27	4	3	127	1,150
All persons											
United Kingdom	446	245	111	161	49	263	32	6	11	147	1,049
Northern and Yorkshire	470	268	118	168	57	280	33	7	11	148	1,098
North West	483	270	121	186	64	281	32	5	11	149	1,131
Trent	448	251	111	156	50	264	30	7	10	150	1,048
West Midlands	462	253	114	156	50	262	28	5	9	151	1,060
Anglia and Oxford	406	218	103	146	40	245	31	7	10	146	973
North Thames	403	224	93	171	47	251	28	5	9	146	998
South Thames	400	205	100	160	46	249	27	6	10	140	977
South and West	399	216	100	129	37	240	31	7	11	141	939
England	433	237	107	159	49	259	30	6	10	146	1,026
Wales	471	259	116	166	55	259	35	7	11	139	1,069
Scotland	537	294	144	158	53	302	49	7	16	167	1,213
Northern Ireland	500	288	126	211	52	263	39	7	9	116	1,129

1 Rates standardised to the mid-1991 United Kingdom population for males and females separately. See Notes and Definitions.
2 Deaths at ages under 28 days occurring in England and Wales are not assigned an underlying cause.
3 Malignant neoplasms only.
4 Including deaths at ages under 28 days.

Source: Office for National Statistics; General Register Office for Scotland; Northern Ireland Statistics and Research Agency

7.15 NHS hospital waiting lists: by patients' region of residence, at 31 March 1997

	NHS hospital waiting lists[1]				Average numbers admitted from waiting list per month, 3 month average[2] (thousands)	Mean waiting time (months)[3]	Median waiting time (months)[3]
	Months waited (percentages)			Total waiting (=100%) (thousands)			
	Less than 6 months	6 months but less than 12	12 months or longer				
Patients' region of residence							
Northern and Yorkshire	*76.7*	*22.9*	*0.4*	137.7	40.2	3.9	2.9
North West	*75.2*	*22.8*	*2.0*	179.9	42.6	4.1	2.9
Trent	*70.8*	*23.6*	*5.6*	123.7	18.9	4.6	3.4
West Midlands	*85.9*	*13.7*	*0.5*	91.7	26.4	3.3	2.6
Anglia and Oxford	*74.6*	*23.0*	*2.4*	115.4	26.1	4.2	3.2
North Thames	*72.0*	*24.0*	*4.0*	166.6	37.3	4.5	3.4
South Thames	*70.6*	*26.1*	*3.3*	168.6	32.5	4.5	3.6
South and West	*78.0*	*19.6*	*2.5*	147.6	33.2	4.0	2.9
England	*74.9*	*22.4*	*2.7*	1,131.2	257.1	4.2	3.0
Wales	*90.1*		*9.9*	65.0	32.0	..	..
Scotland	*85.7*	*13.6*	*0.7*	84.6	39.4	3.0	1.9
Northern Ireland	*62.2*	*20.6*	*17.1*	45.8	12.5	..	..

1 The figures relate to people on the waiting lists on 31 March 1997 who were waiting for admission as either an in-patient or a day case and the length of time they had waited to date. Figures for Northern Ireland include all patients waiting for treatment at Northern Ireland Trusts including private patients and patients from outside Northern Ireland. Patients undergoing a series of repeat admissions and those who were temporarily suspended from the waiting list for medical or social reasons are excluded. There are differences between countries in the ways that waiting lists and waiting times are counted; comparisons between countries should be made with caution.
2 Figures relate to the three months ending 31 March 1997.
3 Average time patients had been waiting at 31 March 1997. The mean and median are different types of 'average'. See Introduction and Notes and Definitions.

Source: Department of Health; Welsh Office; Information and Statistics Division, NHS in Scotland;
Department of Health and Social Services, Northern Ireland

7.16 NHS hospital activity, 1996-97

	In-patients (all specialties)							Consultant out-patient attendances	
	Average daily available beds[1] per 1,000 population	Cases[2] treated per available bed[1]	Cases[2] treated per 1,000 population	Finished consultant episodes/ discharges and deaths[2] (thousands)	Average length of stay in hospital for non-psychiatric specialties[3] (mean)(days)	Day cases (thousands)	Total accident & emergency attend-ances (thousands)	Total (thousands)	Of which new (percentages)
United Kingdom	4.5	38.6	173	10,167	..	3,726	17,262	49,570	*27.6*
Northern and Yorkshire	4.5	38.4	183	1,163	6.3	423	1,882	5,472	*25.8*
North West	4.4	42.3	196	1,295	6.2	542	2,221	5,985	*26.4*
Trent	3.9	42.2	175	895	5.7	275	1,338	4,194	*29.0*
West Midlands	3.8	42.6	175	930	5.8	293	1,624	4,227	*27.0*
Anglia and Oxford	3.7	39.5	156	836	6.5	274	1,084	3,889	*29.8*
North Thames	4.4	34.1	162	1,124	7.0	420	2,070	6,787	*27.0*
South Thames	3.7	38.2	153	1,043	6.5	345	2,123	5,669	*27.8*
South and West	4.0	38.9	166	1,095	6.5	386	1,738	4,641	*29.7*
England	4.1	39.3	171	8,381	6.3	2,958	14,080	40,864	*27.6*
Wales	5.3	33.1	177	516	6.8	286	975	2,569	*26.0*
Scotland	7.7	24.4	189	969	8.2	384	1,551	4,721	*27.7*
Northern Ireland	5.7	31.7	181	300	7.3	98	656	1,416	*27.5*

1 Excluding cots for healthy new-born babies except in Northern Ireland.
2 Finished consultant episodes in England. Data for Wales relate to discharges and deaths. Data for Scotland relate to discharges and deaths and transfers to other specialties within hospital. Data for Northern Ireland relate to discharges and deaths and transfers to another hospital. Healthy new-born babies are included for Northern Ireland but excluded for the other countries. See Notes and Definitions.
3 Data for England are for 1995-96.

Source: Department of Health; Welsh Office; Information and Statistics Division, NHS in Scotland;
Department of Health and Social Services, Northern Ireland

7.17 Prescriptions dispensed, 1996[1]

	Prescription items dispensed (millions)[2]	Percentage of prescription items exempt from charge[3,4]	Percentage of prescriptions items[3,5] that were for		Number of prescription items per person	Average net ingredient cost[6]	
			Children	People aged 60 or over		£ per person	£ per pre-scription item
United Kingdom	597.3	86.5	..	..	10.2	84.5	8.3
Northern and Yorkshire	68.1	86.4	11.0	48.3	10.7	84.7	8.1
North West	76.7	87.1	10.9	47.4	11.6	91.6	7.9
Trent	53.9	86.0	10.5	50.1	10.5	83.6	7.9
West Midlands	53.8	86.6	12.5	45.9	10.1	80.8	8.0
Anglia and Oxford	47.2	82.2	11.7	48.0	8.8	76.7	8.7
North Thames	61.6	85.6	13.5	43.3	8.9	75.8	8.5
South Thames	60.9	84.8	11.2	50.5	8.9	79.0	8.8
South and West	62.8	84.7	9.6	53.3	9.5	80.7	8.5
England	484.9	85.6	11.3	48.3	9.9	81.7	8.3
Wales[1]	37.2	87.1	9.4	48.6	12.7	100.7	7.9
Scotland	54.6	90.1	..	..	10.6	94.4	8.9
Northern Ireland	20.6	94.7	..	..	12.4	108.5	8.8

1 For Wales data relate to 1996-97.
2 Figures relate to NHS prescription items dispensed by community pharmacists, appliance contractors and dispensing doctors, and prescriptions submitted by prescribing doctors for items personally administered.
3 For England figures relate to items dispensed by community pharmacists and appliance contractors only. Items dispensed by dispensing doctors and personal administration are not analysed into exempt, non-exempt or other categories and are therefore excluded. Personally administered items are free of charge.
4 Figures for the English regions, England and Wales exclude prescriptions for which prepayment certificates have been purchased. For Scotland and Northern Ireland they are included.
5 Items for children includes young adults aged 16 to 18 who are in full-time education. Data for Wales are calculated from a 5 per cent sample of prescriptions.
6 Net ingredient cost is the cost of medicines before any discounts and does not include any dispensing costs or fees.

Source: Department of Health; Welsh Office; Pharmacy Practice Division, NHS in Scotland;
Central Services Agency, Northern Ireland

7.18 NHS Hospital and Community Health Service staff: by type of staff[1], 30 September 1996

Percentages and thousands

	Direct care staff				Management and support staff			Total staff[1] (=100%) (thousands)
	Medical and dental[2]	Nursing, midwifery and health visiting[3]	Scientific, therapeutic and technical	All direct care staff	Adminis-tration[4] and estates	Other	All management and support staff[5]	
Northern and Yorkshire	7.4	46.9	12.2	66.4	20.6	13.0	33.6	105.5
North West	7.3	48.3	12.8	68.4	20.9	10.6	31.6	107.4
Trent	6.8	47.0	12.9	66.7	21.0	12.3	33.3	74.2
West Midlands	7.0	46.0	12.7	65.7	21.5	12.8	34.3	80.8
Anglia and Oxford	7.4	47.3	12.6	67.4	20.5	12.1	32.6	71.8
North Thames	9.1	46.3	13.5	68.9	23.1	7.9	31.1	107.7
South Thames	8.2	45.8	12.8	66.8	22.6	10.6	33.2	98.6
South and West	6.8	47.8	12.7	67.3	19.7	13.0	32.7	95.9
England[6]	7.4	46.2	13.0	66.5	21.9	11.6	33.5	763.8
Wales	6.4	46.1	12.1	64.6	20.6	14.7	35.4	53.5
Scotland	7.1	48.4	6.3	61.8	18.2	20.0	38.2	107.2
Northern Ireland	6.2	41.6	10.7	58.4	23.1	18.6	41.6	36.2

1 Directly employed whole-time equivalents. See Notes and Definitions.
2 Locums are included in the figures for England, but excluded for Wales, Scotland and Northern Ireland.
3 For England, Wales and Northern Ireland, the figures include nursing, midwifery and health visiting learners. For England and Wales, healthcare assistants are also included.
4 For Northern Ireland figure includes staff supporting Personal Social Services in Healthcare Facilities and Health and Social Services Boards.
5 For Northern Ireland, the figure is healthcare assistants.
6 The England totals include staff in special health authorities and other statutory authorities which are not assigned to a specific region.

Source: Department of Health; Welsh Office; Information and Statistics Division, NHS in Scotland;
Department of Health and Social Services, Northern Ireland

7.19 General practitioners[1], 1 October 1996

Numbers and percentages

| | General medical services | | | | | | General dental services[1] | | | |
	Number of practices	Number of general medical practitioners (GPs)[1]	Percentage who were female GPs	Average list size per GP	Number of practice staff[2] (whole-time equivalents)	Percentage who were direct care practice staff[2,3]	Number of dentists	Persons registered with a dentist as a percentage of the population[4]	Average list size	Number of opticians[5]
United Kingdom	10,947	33,227	30	1,827	69,428	17	19,720	55	1,630	..
Northern and Yorkshire	1,084	3,513	28	1,824	7,618	16	1,966	58	1,872	1,009
North West	1,341	3,540	29	1,925	7,824	15	2,190	60	1,795	993
Trent	885	2,718	27	1,891	6,152	17	1,428	57	2,054	867
West Midlands	1,046	2,823	26	1,927	6,306	18	1,495	55	1,939	807
Anglia and Oxford	775	2,970	29	1,830	6,459	18	1,663	50	1,614	990
North Thames	1,584	3,750	35	2,032	8,775	18	2,669	52	1,347	1,542
South Thames	1,277	3,640	32	1,957	8,069	17	2,661	50	1,289	1,381
South and West	1,009	3,901	29	1,706	8,115	18	2,264	55	1,608	1,128
England	8,999	26,855	30	1,885	59,318	17	16,336	55	1,640	6,939
Wales	532	1,736	25	1,724	3,860	17	900	55	1,782	522
Scotland	1,057	3,608	33	1,488	6,250	14	1,903	54	1,451	1,163
Northern Ireland	359	1,028	27	1,698	..	..	581	60	1,704	274

1 See Notes and Definitions. At 30 September 1996 for General Dental Practitioners. Dentists are assigned to the region where they carry out their main work.
2 Other than GPs. Figure for the United Kingdom relates to Great Britain as figures for Northern Ireland are not held centrally.
3 For Scotland, figure relates to practice nurses only.
4 Registrations at 30 September 1996 with dentists practising in each region.
5 Optometrists and Ophthalmic Medical Practioners contracted to perform NHS sight tests at 31 December (31 March 1997 for Optometrists in Scotland). As some practitioners have contracts in more than one region, the sum of the regions does not equal the England total. Similarly, as some practitioners have contracts in more than one country, it is not possible to calculate a United Kingdom figure.

Source: Department of Health; Welsh Office; Information and Statistics Division, NHS in Scotland; Central Services Agency, Northern Ireland

7.20 Places available in residential care homes[1]: by type of care home, at 31 March 1997

Percentages and thousands

| | Percentage of places available in | | | | Percentage of places available in homes for | | | | Total number of places available (=100%) |
| | | Registered homes | | | | | | | |
	Local authority homes[2]	Voluntary homes	Private homes	Independent small homes[3]	Elderly people	People with physical or sensory or learning disabilities	People with mental health problems	Other people	
Great Britain	21	20	54	..	72	17	10	1	380,202
North East	27	12	57	4	74	15	11	-	18,217
North West (GOR) & Merseyside	19	19	58	4	77	12	9	1	47,678
North West (GOR)	19	18	60	4	79	11	9	1	38,263
Merseyside	20	25	51	3	72	16	12	1	9,415
Yorkshire and the Humber	24	14	57	5	65	16	19	1	34,743
East Midlands	24	14	57	5	78	15	7	1	28,221
West Midlands	19	18	58	6	75	19	5	1	33,045
Eastern	23	21	52	3	77	16	6	-	32,913
London	27	35	33	5	63	18	17	2	30,062
South East (GOR)	14	19	61	6	65	20	14	1	65,577
South West	11	18	64	7	74	17	7	2	47,596
England	19	19	57	5	71	17	11	1	338,052
Wales	34	10	56	..	83	11	4	2	18,299
Scotland	38	40	21	..	70	20	5	5	23,851
Northern Ireland	37	27	37	..	74	18	9	..	6,734

1 The figures for England include residential places in homes registered as both residential and nursing. For Scotland figures relate to beds available.
2 For Northern Ireland figures relate to places available in statutory homes operated by the Health and Social Services Trusts.
3 Small homes have fewer than 4 places.

Source: Department of Health; Welsh Office; The Scottish Office Home Department; Department of Health and Social Services, Northern Ireland

7.21 Children looked after by local authorities, year ending 31 March 1996[1]

	Total children looked after per thousand resident population[2]			Manner of accommodation (percentages)			Number of children looked after[4] (=100%)
	Children admitted	Ceased to be looked after[3]	Looked after[4]	Foster homes	Community homes	Other	
North East	3.3	3.5	5.1	60	17	23	3,200
North West (GOR) & Merseyside	3.0	2.8	4.9	60	14	26	8,500
North West (GOR)	3.0	2.8	4.6	61	14	25	6,300
Merseyside	2.9	2.9	6.1	59	13	28	2,200
Yorkshire and the Humber	3.1	3.0	5.3	61	12	27	6,500
East Midlands	2.6	2.7	4.0	66	10	24	4,000
West Midlands	2.7	2.8	4.6	64	12	24	5,700
Eastern	2.4	2.5	3.6	69	7	24	4,600
London	3.2	3.1	5.7	66	8	26	8,700
South East (GOR)	2.4	2.3	3.8	67	10	23	5,300
South West	3.3	3.2	4.2	72	8	20	4,700
England	2.8	2.8	4.5	65	11	24	51,200
Wales	3.9	2.4	4.4	70	9	21	2,974
Northern Ireland	1.8	2.4	5.6	63	12	25	2,625

1 English regional figures are estimates which take account of missing or incomplete data. Estimated figures are rounded to the nearest hundred. For Wales, data for Cardiff, Powys and Torfaen are for 1995. For Scotland, comparable data are not available due to differences in legislation.
2 Rates are based on mid-1995 estimates of population aged under 18.
3 For Northern Ireland data refer to all discharges from care, not individual children discharged from care as some children may be admitted and discharged on more than one occasion.
4 At 31 March. For Northern Ireland data refer to children in care; they are therefore not strictly comparable with those for England and Wales.

Source: Department of Health; Welsh Office; Department of Health and Social Services, Northern Ireland

7.22 Children and young people on child protection registers: by age and category[1], at 31 March 1996

	Percentage aged					Number of children on registers[2] (=100%)	Rate per 10,000 children aged under 18	Percentage of children in each category of abuse[3]				
	Under 1	1-4	5-9	10-15	16 or over			Neglect	Physical injury	Sexual abuse	Emotional abuse	Other[4]
North East	8	28	34	27	3	2,221	37	34	32	23	16	7
North West (GOR) & Merseyside	10	32	32	24	2	4,305	26	38	40	22	9	3
Yorkshire and the Humber	8	31	31	27	3	4,938	42	32	40	27	11	3
East Midlands	11	32	29	26	2	3,160	33	27	39	33	12	-
West Midlands	9	33	30	25	2	3,073	24	35	38	27	14	1
Eastern	5	29	30	30	4	2,362	20	31	32	26	18	-
London	7	27	32	31	3	5,423	34	44	30	16	17	2
South East (GOR)	8	31	30	28	3	3,921	22	33	29	21	24	1
South West	7	32	30	27	2	2,948	28	29	35	27	19	1
England	8	31	31	27	3	32,351	29	35	35	24	15	2
Wales	9	36	28	23	5	1,649	24	32	41	18	18	0
Northern Ireland	7	30	31	27	4	1,551	33	28	10	11	10	44

1 Data for Scotland are not available in the same form; however, the total number of children on protection registers at 31 March 1996 was 2,479.
2 Includes a number of unborn children not included elsewhere in this table.
3 The total of the percentages will exceed 100 as children in mixed categories are counted more than once.
4 For England and Wales data relate to children or young people on the child protection registers who have not been allocated a specific category. For Northern Ireland data include the category 'Grave concern', which is no longer used in English and Welsh statistics.

Source: Department of Health; Welsh Office; Department of Health and Social Services, Northern Ireland

8 Lifestyles

Household income

Average gross weekly household income in 1996-97 was highest in the South East (GOR), at £483, and lowest in the North East, at £321.

(Tables 8.1 and 8.2)

People in the North East are the most likely to live in households in the bottom fifth of the income distribution, and the least likely to live in the top fifth, while the reverse is true for people in the South East.

(Table 8.3)

Savings

In 1996-97, 36 per cent of households in the South East (GOR) owned Premium Bonds, double the proportion in Scotland.

(Table 8.4)

Income tax

The average income tax payable by women in 1995-96 ranged from £1,470 in Wales to £2,710 in London, 15 and 19 per cent respectively of average total income.

(Chart 8.6)

Benefits

In 1996-97, one in four households in the North West and Merseyside, in London and in Wales receive either Family Credit or Income Support compared with one in eight in the South East (GOR).

(Table 8.7)

Household expenditure

Spending by children in 1996-97 ranged from £7.60 per head per week in the West Midlands to £11.20 in Scotland.

(Chart 8.8)

Charitable giving in 1996-97 ranged from an average of 50 pence per household per week in the North East to nearly £3.90 in Northern Ireland.

(Chart 8.9)

Households in Northern Ireland spent the most on fuel, light and power, on food and on clothing and footwear in 1996-97, those in the South East (GOR) the most on housing and on motoring and fares, and those in the Eastern region the most on household goods and services.

(Table 8.10)

Consumption

People in Wales and the North West (GOR) and Merseyside eat the most meat and meat products, those in Northern Ireland eat the most vegetables (including potatoes) and cereals (including bread), while those in London eat the most fruit.

(Table 8.12)

Consumer goods

Around a quarter of households in the South East (GOR) and the Eastern region owned a mobile phone in 1996-97 compared with about a tenth in Scotland, Wales, the North West and Merseyside, and the Yorkshire and Humber region.

(Table 8.13)

Leisure

In 1996-97 people in the Eastern region, the South East (GOR) and the South West were the most likely to spend some time gardening or carrying out DIY.

(Table 8.14)

National Lottery

Over 70 per cent of households in the North East participated in the National Lottery in 1996-97, compared with around 55 per cent in Northern Ireland and London.

(Table 8.17)

Introduction

T his chapter looks at the way we live. The first three tables show the source and distribution of household income. The chapter goes on to look at income tax payable, benefits, household expenditure, ownership of consumer durables, and some aspects of how we spend our leisure time.

Table 8.3 shows how the distribution of income in each region in 1995-96 compared with that of Great Britain as a whole. Individuals were ranked according to their household equivalised disposable income, that is after adjustment for the size and composition of the household (see Notes and Definitions). This adjustment provides an estimate of the standard of living of households and reflects the idea that a family of several people needs a higher income than a single individual for them to enjoy a comparable standard of living. It does not however, reflect regional differences in prices and incomes. Those who live in Wales and Scotland were over-represented in the bottom quintile on the before housing costs basis (25 and 22 per cent respectively) and under-represented in the top quintile (13 and 17 per cent respectively). After housing costs, however, there was a shift up the income distribution, with the proportion of those in Wales in the bottom quintile dropping to 23 per cent and in Scotland to 19 per cent. This is due to relative differences in housing costs.

Looking at the regions of England, before housing costs those in the north and central regions were over-represented in the lower two quintiles and under-represented in the top quintile. The reverse was generally true for the south of the country (although the South West was more concentrated in the middle three quintiles). However, after housing costs, the picture over England was more mixed and, particularly in London, the proportion in the bottom quintile was substantially higher reflecting the high cost of housing in the capital.

In 1995-96, the Family Expenditure Survey collected information on children's spending for the first time. The results showed that children aged between 7 and 15 across the United Kingdom spent an average £8.40 a week in that year. All spending by children was covered, including items bought with pocket money, expenditure on school dinners and fares to and from school. Food (including sweets, crisps, soft drinks, ice cream, and school meals bought by the child) was the largest item of expenditure by far (£3.20 on average). The other main items were leisure goods (including toys, CDs and sports goods) (£1.60) and clothing and footwear (£1.10). There were variations expenditure by age: 15 year olds spent, on average, over four times as much as 7 and 8 year olds – £16.80 per week compared with £3.80. Older children also spent their money differently compared with younger children: although food was the largest item of expenditure at all ages, among 13 to 15 year olds the second largest item was clothing and footwear while for 7 to 12 year olds it was leisure goods. Chart 8.8 shows the regional variation in children's weekly spending in 1996-97.

Table 8.14 shows the proportions of adults participating in selected leisure and sporting activities. Gardening and walking are the most popular physical activities, closely followed by DIY. Two thirds of adults take part in at least one sporting activity.

Another aspect of how we spend our leisure time is on voluntary work. Table 8.16 shows the proportions of householders who had been involved in some form of voluntary work to improve their local area or neighbourhood in the 12 months prior to the survey in 1996-97. This could include improving local people's quality of life for example being involved with cultural, sport or health activities, improving the local environment or tackling crime and improving community safety such as being involved with Neighbourhood Watch. The full definition can be found in the Notes and Definitions.

8.1   Household income: by source, 1996-97[1]

Percentages and £

	Percentage of average gross weekly household income						Average gross weekly household income[3] (=100%) (£)
	Wages and salaries	Self employ- ment	Invest- ments	Annuities and pensions[2]	Social security benefits[3]	Other income	
United Kingdom	64.6	9.4	4.5	6.5	13.6	1.3	396.9
North East	62.9	5.1	3.3	7.5	19.6	1.6	321.3
North West (GOR) & Merseyside	66.2	7.8	3.4	6.6	15.1	0.9	377.2
Yorkshire and the Humber	68.2	5.9	4.0	5.7	15.0	1.2	364.9
East Midlands	62.0	10.0	4.8	7.0	15.2	1.1	368.7
West Midlands	63.4	10.1	3.9	6.0	15.6	1.0	359.6
Eastern	68.2	9.8	3.6	5.6	11.3	1.5	427.2
London	66.2	10.7	4.5	6.0	11.1	1.4	454.5
South East (GOR)	65.7	9.7	6.4	6.9	9.6	1.8	482.8
South West	58.1	14.3	5.9	8.6	11.8	1.3	398.4
England	64.8	9.6	4.7	6.6	13.0	1.3	404.1
Wales	57.7	11.7	4.9	6.2	18.6	0.9	359.0
Scotland	66.0	7.8	2.7	5.7	16.1	1.7	367.4
Northern Ireland[4]	63.0	6.9	2.7	5.1	21.2	1.1	326.2

1 See Notes and Definitions.
2 Other than social security benefits.
3 Excluding Housing Benefit and Council Tax Benefit (rates rebate in Northern Ireland).
4 Northern Ireland data are obtained from an enhanced sample, but the United Kingdom figures are obtained from the main Family Expenditure Survey sample.

Source: Family Expenditure Survey, Office for National Statistics and Northern Ireland Statistics and Research Agency

8.2   Distribution of household income, 1996-97[1]

Percentages and £

	Percentage of households in each weekly income group								Average gross weekly income[2] (£)	
	Under £100	£100 but under £150	£150 but under £250	£250 but under £350	£350 but under £450	£450 but under £600	£600 but under £750	£750 or over	Per house- hold	Per person
United Kingdom	13.7	11.1	17.0	13.1	11.7	13.3	8.4	11.8	396.9	161.8
North East	19.5	16.1	14.0	15.8	6.7	11.9	8.5	7.6	321.3	136.6
North West (GOR) & Merseyside	14.6	10.2	18.5	13.4	10.1	14.3	8.3	10.6	377.2	152.3
Yorkshire and the Humber	14.3	12.3	17.1	12.7	13.6	11.8	9.2	9.2	364.9	147.1
East Midlands	12.8	11.6	20.7	12.8	11.2	14.7	6.4	9.7	368.7	150.1
West Midlands	16.1	9.7	18.2	14.0	11.6	14.2	7.6	8.7	359.6	146.1
Eastern	11.8	9.5	15.5	13.6	11.5	15.5	8.2	14.4	427.2	169.2
London	16.1	9.8	13.0	12.5	9.5	13.8	10.9	14.4	454.5	181.7
South East (GOR)	9.2	10.5	13.8	12.2	12.5	12.3	9.8	19.7	482.8	202.4
South West	10.1	11.3	16.3	13.1	16.3	16.6	7.7	8.6	398.4	163.2
England	13.4	10.9	16.3	13.2	11.7	13.9	8.6	12.1	404.1	164.7
Wales	16.4	11.3	21.5	14.1	7.1	11.6	8.8	9.3	359.0	150.6
Scotland	15.0	11.5	20.4	10.8	15.9	9.9	5.4	11.2	367.4	151.0
Northern Ireland[3]	15.1	13.9	18.9	15.0	12.2	10.8	7.4	6.5	326.2	123.6

1 See Notes and Definitions.
2 Excluding Housing Benefit and Council Tax Benefit (rates rebate in Northern Ireland).
3 Northern Ireland data are obtained from an enhanced sample, but the United Kingdom figures are obtained from the main Family Expenditure Survey sample.

Source: Family Expenditure Survey, Office for National Statistics and Northern Ireland Statistics and Research Agency

8.3 Income distribution of individuals, 1995-96[1]

Percentages

	Quintile groups of individuals ranked by net equivalised household income[2]				
	1	2	3	4	5
Great Britain	20	20	20	20	20
North East	26	24	22	16	12
North West (GOR) & Merseyside	21	22	19	22	16
Yorkshire and the Humber	23	21	21	19	16
East Midlands	21	21	22	19	16
West Midlands	22	21	21	19	17
Eastern	16	17	19	23	25
London	19	19	17	17	28
South East (GOR)	15	16	19	22	29
South West	19	22	21	20	19
England	19	20	20	20	21
Wales	25	22	21	19	13
Scotland	22	19	21	21	17

1 See Introduction to chapter and Notes and Definitions.
2 Income before housing costs.

Source: Department of Social Security from Households Below Average Income

8.4 Households[1] with different types of saving, 1996-97

Percentages[2]

	Accounts				Other savings					
	Current[3]	Post Office	TESSA	Other bank/ building society[4]	Gilts or unit trusts	Stocks & shares	National Savings	Save As You Earn	Premium Bonds	PEPs
Great Britain	81	13	13	63	7	20	9	2	27	10
North East	76	11	10	53	4	13	5	1	20	6
North West (GOR) & Merseyside	79	10	11	55	6	18	8	1	22	8
Yorkshire and the Humber	77	12	12	60	7	19	8	2	25	9
East Midlands	83	11	14	64	5	19	9	2	25	9
West Midlands	80	12	12	64	6	18	8	2	25	9
Eastern	88	15	16	70	7	24	12	2	34	12
London	79	11	12	61	6	20	8	2	26	9
South East (GOR)	89	16	16	74	9	30	13	3	36	14
South West	89	17	14	68	9	23	11	1	33	13
England	83	13	13	64	7	21	9	2	28	10
Wales	77	12	9	52	5	14	6	1	21	7
Scotland	69	9	9	57	6	16	6	1	18	8

1 Households in which at least one member has an account. See Notes and Definitions.
2 As a percentage of all households.
3 A current account may be either a bank or building society account.
4 All bank/building society accounts excluding current accounts and TESSAs.

Source: Family Resources Survey, Department of Social Security

8.5 Distribution of income liable to assessment for tax, 1995-96[1]

Percentages and thousands

	£3,525-£4,999	£5,000-£7,499	£7,500-£9,999	£10,000-£14,999	£15,000-£19,999	£20,000-£29,999	£30,000-£49,999	£50,000 and over	Individuals with incomes of £3,525 or more (=100%) (thousands)
			Percentage of individuals in each income range						
United Kingdom[2]	11.0	16.7	14.3	22.6	14.4	13.9	5.0	2.1	27,400
North East	13.7	18.6	15.5	23.2	13.3	11.5	3.1	1.1	1,150
North West (GOR) & Merseyside	10.7	18.7	15.7	22.1	14.4	13.4	3.6	1.4	3,030
Yorkshire and the Humber	12.4	17.3	14.4	24.5	13.5	12.7	3.8	1.4	2,280
East Midlands	12.1	17.2	14.9	23.0	14.7	12.8	3.9	1.4	1,990
West Midlands	10.8	16.6	15.8	23.9	14.4	12.7	4.2	1.6	2,500
Eastern	9.7	15.6	12.4	22.6	15.2	15.1	6.5	2.9	2,480
London	9.0	13.4	13.1	20.2	16.4	17.0	7.0	3.9	3,160
South East (GOR)	9.9	15.7	13.2	21.4	14.7	14.8	7.0	3.3	4,040
South West	11.7	17.0	16.6	22.5	13.9	12.4	4.4	1.5	2,340
England	11.0	16.4	14.4	22.4	14.6	13.9	5.1	2.2	23,000
Wales	15.3	18.0	15.6	22.3	11.8	12.9	3.1	1.0	1,290
Scotland	9.3	17.7	13.3	26.2	13.6	13.6	4.7	1.6	2,350
Northern Ireland	14.4	20.5	13.6	19.9	12.9	13.6	3.9	1.2	612

1 See Notes and Definitions.
2 Figures for United Kingdom include members of HM Forces and others who are liable to some UK tax but reside overseas on a long-term basis. In addition the United Kingdom total includes a very small number of individuals who could not be allocated to a region.

Source: Survey of Personal Incomes, Board of Inland Revenue

8.6 Average total income[1] and average income tax payable[2]: by gender, 1995-96[3]

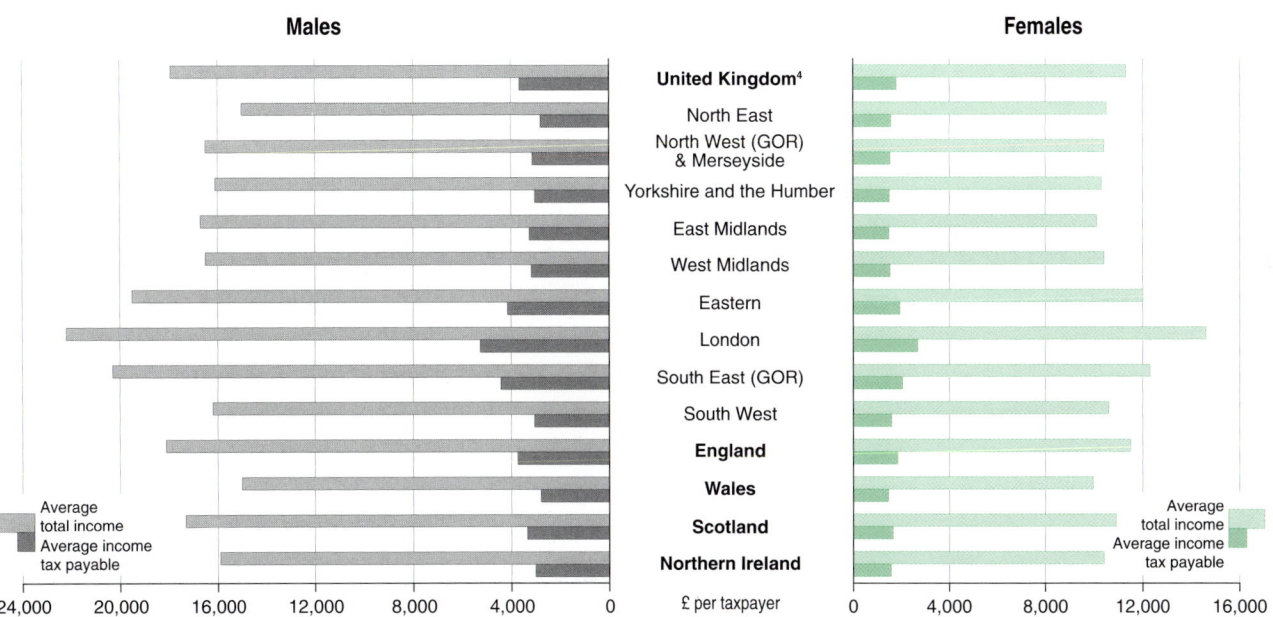

1 Figures are based on individuals with total income above the single person's allowance (£3,525 in 1995-96).
2 Figures relate to taxpayers only.
3 See Notes and Definitions.
4 Figures for United Kingdom include members of HM Forces and others who are liable to some UK tax but reside overseas on a long-term basis. In addition, the United Kingdom total includes a very small number of individuals who could not be allocated to a region.

Source: Survey of Personal Incomes, Board of Inland Revenue

8.7 Households in receipt of benefit[1]: by type of benefit, 1996-97

Percentages[2]

	Family Credit or Income Support	Housing Benefit	Council Tax Benefit	Unemployment Benefit/ Jobseeker's Allowance	Retirement Pension	Incapacity or Disablement Benefits[3]	Child Benefit or One-Parent Benefit	Any benefit
Great Britain	19	20	25	3	30	15	32	74
North East	23	27	32	4	28	21	34	80
North West (GOR) & Merseyside	24	22	32	3	31	20	32	77
Yorkshire and the Humber	22	21	28	3	32	16	33	77
East Midlands	17	16	22	3	29	15	33	73
West Midlands	20	18	25	2	30	15	33	74
Eastern	15	15	20	3	31	11	31	72
London	24	25	28	3	25	11	32	71
South East (GOR)	12	13	16	2	30	10	31	69
South West	16	15	20	3	34	13	29	72
England	19	19	24	3	30	14	32	74
Wales	25	24	31	2	33	25	32	81
Scotland	21	26	28	3	30	17	31	77

1 Households in which at least one member is currently in receipt of benefit. See Notes and Definitions.
2 As a percentage of all households.
3 Incapacity Benefit, Disability Living Allowance (Care and Mobility components), Severe Disablement Allowance, Industrial Injuries Disability Benefit, War Disablement Pension, War Widows Pension and Attendance Allowance.

Source: Family Resources Survey, Department of Social Security

8.8 Children's spending[1], 1996-97

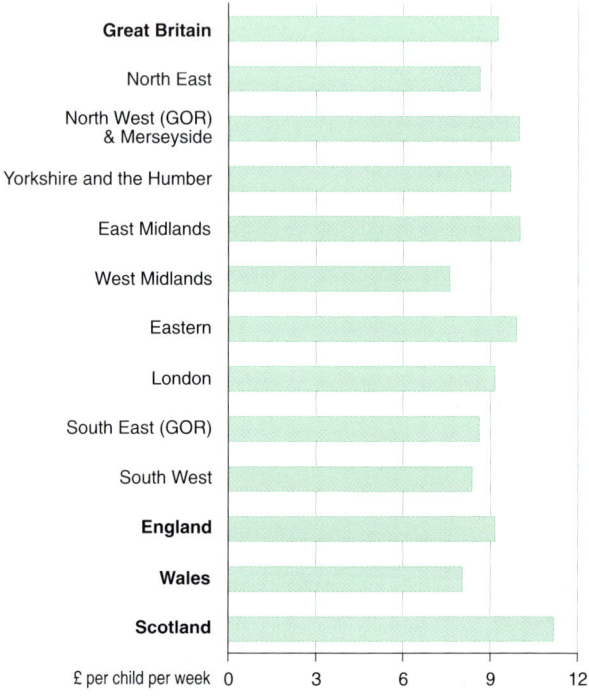

£ per child per week

1 See Introduction and Notes and Definitions.
Source: Family Expenditure Survey, Office for National Statistics

8.9 Charitable giving[1], 1996-97

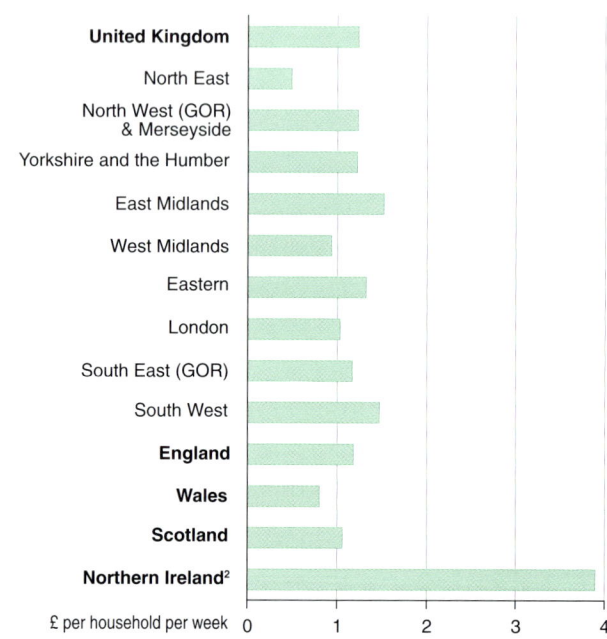

£ per household per week

1 See Notes and Definitions.
2 Northern Ireland data are obtained from an enhanced sample, but the United Kingdom figures are obtained from the main Family Expenditure Survey sample.
Source: Family Expenditure Survey, Office for National Statistics and Northern Ireland Statistics and Research Agency

8.10 Household expenditure: by commodity and service, 1996-97[1]

£ per week and percentages

	Housing	Fuel, light and power	Food	Alcohol and tobacco	Clothing and footwear	House-hold goods and services	Motoring and fares	Leisure goods and services	Miscellan-eous and personal goods and services	Average house-hold expend-iture	Average expend-iture per person
£ per week											
United Kingdom	49.1	13.3	55.1	18.5	18.3	43.1	48.7	49.1	13.8	309.1	126.0
North East	41.5	13.4	48.0	20.2	17.3	30.6	38.1	44.9	10.8	264.9	112.6
North West (GOR) & Merseyside	45.1	13.3	53.4	21.9	19.4	37.6	48.0	48.9	13.0	300.7	121.4
Yorkshire and the Humber	43.2	13.5	52.4	20.0	18.6	42.8	44.3	47.9	13.5	296.2	119.4
East Midlands	42.7	13.0	54.0	17.8	18.4	41.7	48.1	43.3	13.8	292.8	119.2
West Midlands	43.2	13.3	53.7	19.0	17.4	41.2	45.6	43.1	12.7	289.3	117.5
Eastern	55.8	13.2	58.5	16.3	20.6	51.1	52.3	57.0	16.7	341.4	135.3
London	61.7	12.6	57.9	16.6	19.9	48.5	47.0	57.6	16.2	337.9	135.1
South East (GOR)	63.2	13.0	58.0	17.2	17.7	48.9	59.3	57.5	16.3	351.0	147.2
South West	49.3	13.2	54.7	16.2	17.1	43.8	47.0	45.3	12.8	299.4	122.6
England	50.8	13.2	55.0	18.3	18.5	43.7	48.9	50.3	14.2	312.8	127.5
Wales	46.2	14.2	53.8	18.3	15.0	42.6	46.4	44.5	12.2	293.2	123.0
Scotland	39.3	14.1	56.1	20.1	17.1	39.1	48.9	41.7	11.2	287.6	118.2
Northern Ireland[2]	29.0	16.0	60.2	19.4	22.7	37.7	47.5	43.4	14.4	290.2	109.9
As a percentage of average weekly household expenditure											
United Kingdom	15.9	4.3	17.8	6.0	5.9	13.9	15.7	15.9	4.5	100.0	
North East	15.7	5.1	18.1	7.6	6.5	11.6	14.4	17.0	4.1	100.0	
North West (GOR) & Merseyside	15.0	4.4	17.8	7.3	6.5	12.5	16.0	16.3	4.3	100.0	
Yorkshire and the Humber	14.6	4.6	17.7	6.8	6.3	14.4	14.9	16.2	4.6	100.0	
East Midlands	14.6	4.4	18.4	6.1	6.3	14.2	16.4	14.8	4.7	100.0	
West Midlands	14.9	4.6	18.6	6.6	6.0	14.2	15.8	14.9	4.4	100.0	
Eastern	16.3	3.9	17.1	4.8	6.0	15.0	15.3	16.7	4.9	100.0	
London	18.3	3.7	17.1	4.9	5.9	14.3	13.9	17.1	4.8	100.0	
South East (GOR)	18.0	3.7	16.5	4.9	5.0	13.9	16.9	16.4	4.6	100.0	
South West	16.5	4.4	18.3	5.4	5.7	14.6	15.7	15.1	4.3	100.0	
England	16.2	4.2	17.6	5.9	5.9	14.0	15.6	16.1	4.5	100.0	
Wales	15.8	4.8	18.3	6.2	5.1	14.5	15.8	15.2	4.2	100.0	
Scotland	13.7	4.9	19.5	7.0	5.9	13.6	17.0	14.5	3.9	100.0	
Northern Ireland[2]	10.0	5.5	20.8	6.7	7.8	13.0	16.4	14.9	5.0	100.0	

1 See Notes and Definitions.
2 Northern Ireland data are obtained from an enhanced sample, but the United Kingdom figures are obtained from the main Family Expenditure Survey sample.

Source: Family Expenditure Survey, Office for National Statistics and Northern Ireland Statistics and Research Agency

8.11 Expenditure on selected foods bought for household consumption and expenditure on eating out: 1995-1996[1]

£ per person per week

	Liquid and processed milk and cream	Cheese	Uncooked carcass meat and poultry	Other meat and meat products	Fish	Vegetables and vegetable products[2]	Fresh and other fruit	Bread	Cereals other than bread	Drinks and confectionery	Total household food and drink	Eating out[3]
Great Britain	1.40	0.51	1.68	2.04	0.74	2.18	1.13	0.70	1.85	1.90	16.05	6.17
North East	1.35	0.41	1.54	2.03	0.73	2.07	0.94	0.77	1.88	1.80	15.29	6.19
North West (GOR) & Merseyside	1.46	0.45	1.72	1.03	0.73	2.04	1.00	0.74	1.81	1.99	15.95	6.90
Yorkshire and the Humber	1.41	0.47	1.58	1.94	0.71	2.05	0.97	0.72	1.81	1.55	15.02	5.25
East Midlands	1.43	0.54	1.64	2.07	0.70	2.22	1.12	0.67	1.93	2.02	16.24	6.46
West Midlands	1.36	0.55	1.73	1.97	0.73	2.20	1.06	0.70	1.76	1.87	15.84	5.51
Eastern	1.45	0.53	1.77	2.10	0.77	2.27	1.11	0.65	1.81	1.73	16.19	6.30
London	1.32	0.52	1.76	1.75	0.87	2.37	1.51	0.66	1.94	1.85	16.43	8.09
South East (GOR)	1.46	0.60	1.69	2.09	0.77	2.39	1.28	0.66	1.96	2.07	17.03	6.16
South West	1.41	0.53	1.60	1.83	0.68	2.14	1.21	0.64	1.73	1.71	15.52	5.29
England	1.41	0.52	1.68	2.00	0.75	2.21	1.15	0.69	1.85	1.87	16.04	6.29
Wales	1.39	0.49	1.73	2.12	0.69	2.20	1.12	0.73	1.73	1.84	15.97	6.12
Scotland	1.34	0.48	1.65	2.37	0.71	1.89	0.97	0.79	1.88	2.20	16.12	5.28
Northern Ireland[4]	1.46	0.37	2.16	2.20	0.61	2.06	0.95	1.04	2.16	1.51	16.53	..

1 See Notes and Definitions.
2 Including tomatoes, fresh potatoes and potato products.
3 Individual expenditure on all food and drink consumed outside the home and not obtained from household stocks, whether consumed by the purchaser or others or both. Expenditure which is to be reclaimed as business expenses is not included.
4 Figures relate to 1996 only.

Source: National Food Survey, Ministry of Agriculture, Fisheries and Food

8.12 Household consumption of selected foods, 1990-1991 and 1995-1996[1]

Kilograms per person per week[2]

	Liquid and processed milk and cream		Meat and meat products		Fish		Vegetables and vegetable products[3]		Fresh and other fruit		Cereals including bread	
	1990-1991	1995-1996	1990-1991	1995-1996	1990-1991	1995-1996	1990-1991	1995-1996	1990-1991	1995-1996	1990-1991	1995-1996
Great Britain	2.15	2.14	0.97	0.94	0.14	0.15	2.24	2.09	0.92	1.01	1.46	1.51
North East	2.08	2.08	1.02	0.97	0.15	0.15	2.44	2.07	0.83	0.86	1.56	1.54
North West (GOR) & Merseyside	2.11	2.23	0.98	1.00	0.14	0.15	2.23	2.03	0.81	0.92	1.42	1.51
Yorkshire and the Humber	2.13	2.19	0.97	0.96	0.16	0.15	2.21	2.15	0.85	0.93	1.46	1.57
East Midlands	2.35	2.26	0.91	0.95	0.13	0.14	2.26	2.20	0.95	1.07	1.42	1.58
West Midlands	2.02	2.11	0.99	0.96	0.13	0.15	2.33	2.22	0.70	0.98	1.52	1.56
Eastern	2.13	2.16	0.97	0.98	0.15	0.15	2.21	2.26	1.06	1.00	1.44	1.45
London	2.02	1.93	0.99	0.84	0.16	0.17	2.15	1.94	1.15	1.22	1.41	1.57
South East (GOR)	2.20	2.12	0.90	0.91	0.13	0.15	2.15	2.06	1.10	1.11	1.41	1.46
South West	2.25	2.13	0.96	0.90	0.12	0.13	2.45	2.15	0.98	1.08	1.46	1.40
England	2.13	2.14	0.97	0.94	0.14	0.15	2.26	2.11	0.95	1.03	1.45	1.51
Wales	2.29	2.16	1.02	1.02	0.14	0.14	2.41	2.20	0.74	1.00	1.52	1.53
Scotland	2.20	2.14	0.92	0.93	0.13	0.14	2.02	1.80	0.82	0.86	1.52	1.51
Northern Ireland[4]	..	2.11	..	0.99	..	0.13	..	2.42	..	0.70	..	1.79

1 See Notes and Definitions.
2 Except equivalent litres of milk and cream.
3 Including tomatoes, fresh potatoes and potato products.
4 Figures relate to 1996 only.

Source: National Food Survey, Ministry of Agriculture, Fisheries and Food

8.13 Households with selected durable goods, 1996-97[1]

Percentage of households in sample having

	Micro-wave oven	Wash-ing machine	Tumble drier	Dish-washer	Deep freezer[2]	Tele-phone	Mobile phone[3]	Video	Compact-disc player	Satellite dish	Home com-puter
United Kingdom	74	91	50	20	90	94	17	81	56	16	24
North East	78	92	47	14	90	90	11	82	54	18	20
North West (GOR) & Merseyside	73	89	48	15	89	92	12	79	53	19	20
Yorkshire and the Humber	74	92	48	15	89	92	12	78	49	18	22
East Midlands	76	92	53	18	90	94	15	81	56	17	23
West Midlands	74	90	53	19	89	93	15	81	54	15	23
Eastern	73	91	54	25	91	96	23	81	59	16	27
London	64	82	38	20	86	94	21	76	52	12	27
South East (GOR)	74	91	54	30	92	96	26	82	63	14	32
South West	72	90	50	23	90	95	17	80	56	14	26
England	73	90	49	21	90	94	18	80	56	16	25
Wales	76	88	47	15	88	89	11	78	48	20	17
Scotland	69	91	50	17	84	88	10	79	54	12	19
Northern Ireland	72	90	41	21	80	91	..	75	42	19	18

1 See Notes and Definitions.
2 Includes fridge-freezers.
3 Figure for the United Kingdom relates to Great Britain.

Source: Family Resources Survey, Department of Social Security;
Continuous Household Survey, Northern Ireland Statistics and Research Agency

8.14 Participation[1] in selected leisure and sporting activities, 1996-97

Percentages

	Watching television	Listening to music	Listening to radio	Reading books	Visiting friends	Gar-dening	DIY	Walk-ing[2]	Swim-ming	Cyc-ling	Keep fit	Any sport[3]
United Kingdom	99	77	88	65	96	48	42	44	15	11	12	64
North East	99	79	88	63	96	46	43	40	11	9	11	57
North West (GOR) & Merseyside	99	81	87	62	96	46	42	43	15	11	14	63
Yorkshire and the Humber	99	76	84	61	97	48	40	43	13	11	12	61
East Midlands	99	75	89	62	97	48	42	44	15	11	10	64
West Midlands	99	77	88	61	97	49	43	39	14	9	12	59
Eastern	99	79	90	66	96	55	46	43	17	17	12	67
London	98	78	89	69	95	40	39	43	14	8	14	62
South East (GOR)	99	80	90	70	97	56	46	48	16	14	13	67
South West	99	77	90	70	95	57	46	49	18	15	12	66
England	99	78	89	65	96	50	43	44	15	12	12	63
Wales	98	72	83	61	95	44	41	45	13	7	10	62
Scotland	99	76	86	67	97	38	38	50	15	8	12	66
Northern Ireland	96	60	80	61	89	38	32	43	11	6	9	59

1 By people aged 16 or over in the four weeks before interview.
2 Walks for pleasure of 2 miles or more.
3 At least one sports activity including walking.

Source: General Household Survey, Office for National Statistics;
Continuous Household Survey, Northern Ireland Statistics and Research Agency

8.15 Adults taking a holiday[1]: by region of domicile, 1997

Percentages

	Percentage of adults taking		
	A holiday abroad	A holiday in Great Britain	Any holiday
Standard Statistical Regions			
Great Britain	35	33	57
North	35	33	57
North West (SSR)	40	33	63
Yorkshire and Humberside	28	34	52
East Midlands	38	35	62
West Midlands	33	33	56
East Anglia	..	31	..
South East (SSR)	39	33	60
Greater London	39	25	53
Rest of South East	40	38	65
South West	33	31	56
England	35	33	58
Wales	35	32	57
Scotland	32	32	51

1 Defined as four or more nights away.

Source: British Tourist Authority

8.16 Participation in local voluntary work, 1996-97[1]

Percentages

	Still volunteering	No longer volunteering	Interested in volunteering	Not interested in volunteering
North East	8	1	32	59
North West (GOR) & Merseyside	11	2	36	52
Yorkshire and the Humber	8	1	30	61
East Midlands	10	2	39	49
West Midlands	11	2	35	53
Eastern	14	1	39	46
London	10	2	43	45
South East (GOR)	14	2	40	45
South West	16	2	40	43
England	11	2	37	50

1 Participation by householders in voluntary work to benefit their local area in the 12 months before interview. See Introduction and Notes and Definitions.

Source: Survey of English Housing, Department of the Environment, Transport and the Regions

8.17 Participation in the National Lottery, 1996-97[1]

Percentages and £

	Percentage of households participating	Average household expenditure[2] (£)
United Kingdom	64	3.1
North East	71	3.1
North West (GOR) & Merseyside	69	3.2
Yorkshire and the Humber	68	3.0
East Midlands	68	3.0
West Midlands	68	3.1
Eastern	65	3.2
London	56	3.2
South East (GOR)	60	3.1
South West	61	2.6
England	64	3.1
Wales	64	3.3
Scotland	63	3.0
Northern Ireland[3]	55	2.8

1 Participation in the Saturday Draw only, over the period April 1996 to March 1997.
2 Average weekly expenditure of participating households.
3 Northern Ireland data are obtained from an enhanced sample, but the United Kingdom figures are obtained from the main Family Expenditure Survey sample.

Source: Family Expenditure Survey, Office for National Statistics and Northern Ireland Statistics and Research Agency

8.18 The National Lottery grants: totals to end-1997

Numbers and £ million

	Number of grants awarded	Total value of grants (£ million)
United Kingdom[1]	26,498	4,661.6
North East	1,370	272.7
North West (GOR) & Merseyside	2,256	480.9
Yorkshire and the Humber	1,990	369.7
East Midlands	1,511	161.7
West Midlands	2,212	313.7
Eastern	1,544	250.8
London	2,735	976.8
South East (GOR)	2,594	385.1
South West	2,952	324.3
England[2]	19,396	3,570.5
Wales	2,142	251.5
Scotland	3,321	496.0
Northern Ireland	1,289	160.1

1 Includes 350 grants worth £183.4 million made UK-wide. A further 130 grants worth £25.0 million have been made overseas.
2 Includes 232 grants worth £34.8 million made England-wide.

Source: Department of Culture, Media and Sports

9 Crime and Justice

Crime rates

The Eastern region had the lowest recorded crime rate in England and Wales in 1996, nearly 40 per cent lower than the rate in the Yorkshire and Humber region, which was the highest.

(Table 9.1)

The fraud and forgery rate in London in 1996 was more than double that in any other region in England and Wales except Merseyside.

(Table 9.1)

Victims

Nearly two in every five households in the Yorkshire and Humber region suffered at least one crime against their property in 1995 compared with less than one in five in Scotland.

(Table 9.2)

Clear-ups

The police forces in the East Midlands and in Wales cleared up just over nine in every ten recorded sexual offences in 1996, nearly one and three quarter times the clear-up rate in London, which was the lowest.

(Table 9.3)

Firearms

The number of offences recorded in which firearms were reported to have been used more than doubled in Merseyside and the South West between 1992 and 1996, but halved in London and Northern Ireland.

(Table 9.4)

Drug seizures

The number of Class A drug seizures in London in 1996 was nearly 15 times higher than that in Northern Ireland, and twice that in the Yorkshire and Humber region, the region with the second highest number.

(Table 9.5)

Offenders

In 1996, offenders aged 18 or over either cautioned or found guilty were twice as likely to have been cautioned in London for offences of theft and handling stolen goods as those in Merseyside.

(Table 9.6)

Within England and Wales, the North East had proportionately the most offenders among their youngsters aged under 18 in 1996 and the South West the fewest; among adults, London had the most and again the South West the fewest.

(Table 9.7)

Sentences

Adult offenders found guilty of offences in the South West were the most likely to receive a fine in 1996, while those in Northern Ireland were the least likely.

(Table 9.8)

Courts in the South East (GOR) which imposed a custodial sentence on adult offenders in 1996 were more likely to impose a sentence of four years or over than elsewhere in the United Kingdom.

(Table 9.10)

Police assessment

In 1996, 85 per cent of adults in the Eastern region and the South East (GOR) said that their local police did 'a very or fairly good job' compared with 75 per cent or under in the North West (GOR) and Merseyside, Scotland and Northern Ireland.

(Table 9.12)

Introduction

Significant variations exist in the legal frameworks and crime recording systems in operation to deal with criminal activity in the United Kingdom and this results in a lack of comparability in the data from the three jurisdictions (England and Wales, Scotland and Northern Ireland). It has not therefore been possible to include figures for the United Kingdom in all tables and care should be taken in interpreting the information in this chapter. A map of the police force areas in England and Wales is included in the Notes and Definitions.

Crime affects not only the victims but also the families of offenders and society as a whole. Measuring the true extent of crime in the United Kingdom presents many problems. The two main measures of crime, each with its own particular strengths and weaknesses, do not comprehensively measure the scale of crime.

The first measure is the crime statistics recorded by the police (Table 9.1). An offence is only included when it is reported to the police and the police record it as such. The measure provides a full count of offences recorded by the police but as not all crimes are reported, the ability of this measure to reflect trends accurately can be affected by the changing patterns of reporting. For example, in recent years changes in the police treatment of, and their response to, women reporting sexual attacks has led to increases in the levels of recorded crime for such offences.

The other measure is the crime surveys: the British Crime Survey (which relates to England and Wales), the Scottish Crime Survey and the Northern Ireland Crime Survey. The strength of the surveys is that they provide a measure of crime which includes unreported offences and reported offences that were subsequently not recorded by the police. They also ask people about their experiences as victims and about their perceptions of crime and policing. The surveys count only those incidents that are technically criminal by applying a legal definition of crime, and do not simply accept the respondents' definitions of what happened. Nevertheless, as with crime statistics recorded by the police, the data in the surveys are limited; they cover only a selection of crime types and population, and like all surveys, the results are subject to sampling errors.

The majority of crimes recorded by the police are for offences against property. However, most media attention is attracted by the serious crimes of violence; these crimes are, in fact, comparatively rare and a higher proportion of them are cleared up (Tables 9.1 and 9.3).

Following identification of the alleged offender of a crime, the police have a number of choices. No further action may be taken when there is insufficient evidence to justify a prosecution. Where formal action is considered unnecessary, an informal warning may be given instead. When an offender admits guilt and there is sufficient evidence for a conviction but it is not in the public interest to start criminal proceedings, a formal caution may be given by, or on the instructions of, a senior police officer (cautioning is not applicable in Scotland). For more serious offences, pre-court alternatives may not be appropriate and a prosecution will be the likely outcome.

If convicted the court will decide upon the most appropriate sentence: again the sentencing options available to and used by the courts differ between the three jurisdictions. In making their decision, the courts will take account of the facts of the offence and the circumstances of the offender. Sentences range in severity from a discharge to immediate custody (Table 9.8).

Table 9.12 shows four out of five adults in the United Kingdom said in 1996 that they felt the police were doing a very or fairly good job. The sight of a uniformed police officer reassures a large proportion of the public, as well as making them feel that the levels of petty crime and anti-social behaviour are being reduced. However, time spent on the beat may do little to prevent the more serious crimes.

9.1 Notifiable offences recorded by the police[1]: by offence group, 1996 and percentage change, 1995-1996

Rates per 100,000 population and percentages

	Violence against the person	Sexual offences	Burglary	Robbery	Theft and handling stolen goods	Fraud and forgery	Criminal damage[2]	Other	Total
1996									
England & Wales	462	61	2,247	143	4,600	263	1,836	108	9,719
North East	384	49	2,999	88	4,935	187	2,774	104	11,520
North West (GOR) & Merseyside	422	55	2,430	153	4,632	241	2,126	120	10,179
North West (GOR)	382	53	2,526	139	4,536	225	2,189	118	10,167
Merseyside	577	62	2,063	209	5,002	300	1,885	127	10,227
Yorkshire and the Humber	422	62	3,481	107	5,512	226	2,076	125	12,012
East Midlands	573	62	2,488	89	4,685	254	1,976	95	10,222
West Midlands	379	45	2,619	173	4,701	212	1,798	84	10,011
Eastern	362	51	1,436	45	3,810	195	1,358	77	7,334
London	664	98	2,206	439	5,179	526	2,028	149	11,287
South East (GOR)	404	51	1,611	48	4,169	209	1,543	97	8,131
South West	432	57	1,874	68	4,278	218	1,256	83	8,266
England	457	61	2,275	150	4,643	266	1,837	106	9,795
Wales	543	58	1,777	30	3,885	207	1,815	128	8,442
Percentage change 1995-1996									
England & Wales	13	4	-6	9	-3	2	4	10	-1
North East	-7	5	-15	3	-9	-15	-5	3	-9
North West (GOR) & Merseyside	10	5	-6	10	-5	-3	4	-	-3
North West (GOR)	13	9	-4	10	-5	-4	4	5	-2
Merseyside	2	-4	-14	8	-4	1	5	-16	-4
Yorkshire and the Humber	-	3	-9	-	-4	-	2	20	-4
East Midlands	5	-7	-7	1	-3	2	-	8	-3
West Midlands	2	-4	-	4	-2	-8	7	22	-
Eastern	19	7	-6	13	-1	4	11	6	1
London	27	12	-4	11	-	18	3	20	2
South East (GOR)	15	-2	-7	7	-4	-5	6	6	-2
South West	11	-4	-5	22	-3	-6	7	-3	-1
England	12	3	-6	8	-3	2	4	10	-2
Wales	20	12	-8	9	-3	-	6	9	-1
Scotland[3]									
1996	318	71	1,257	102	4,022	428	1,736	880	8,813
Percentage change 1995-1996	3	12	-13	-1	-7	-1	3	-3	-5
Northern Ireland[3]									
1996	339	105	969	104	1,970	245	291	98	4,121
Percentage change 1995-1996	9	3	-3	12	-3	-17	27	-13	-1

1 See Notes and Definitions.
2 The Northern Ireland figures exclude criminal damage valued at under £200 in 1995 and 1996.
3 Figures for Scotland and Northern Ireland are not comparable with those for England and Wales, nor with each other, because of the differences in the legal systems, recording practices and classifications.

Source: Home Office; The Scottish Office Home Department; Royal Ulster Constabulary

9.2 Offences committed against households, 1995[1]

Rates and percentages

	Offences per 10,000 households[2]				Percentage of households[2] victimised at least once			
	Vandalism	Burglary[3]	Vehicle thefts[4]	All household offences[5]	Vandalism	Burglary[3]	Vehicle thefts[4]	All household offences[5]
England & Wales	1,614	829	2,747	5,864	10.2	6.3	19.5	32.4
North East	1,342	1,097	3,631	6,643	8.9	8.3	24.4	35.8
North West (GOR) & Merseyside	1,983	986	3,088	6,683	11.9	7.6	21.9	36.4
North West (GOR)	1,990	963	3,215	6,761	12.2	7.4	22.8	37.5
Merseyside	1,959	1,069	2,564	6,398	10.5	8.3	18.1	32.1
Yorkshire and the Humber	1,591	1,242	3,700	7,363	10.1	8.9	24.7	38.0
East Midlands	1,541	699	2,839	5,659	9.1	5.6	20.4	31.8
West Midlands	1,359	819	2,567	5,342	9.6	6.4	19.2	31.4
Eastern	1,424	627	1,877	4,842	9.9	4.5	13.6	28.5
London	1,474	919	3,017	5,652	9.8	7.2	20.2	31.9
South East (GOR)	1,898	611	2,390	5,589	11.7	4.2	17.7	30.7
South West	1,585	644	2,386	5,627	9.2	5.1	17.0	30.2
England	1,623	830	2,746	5,895	10.3	6.3	19.4	32.6
Wales	1,469	803	2,763	5,343	9.0	6.3	21.0	30.4
Scotland	1,105	386	1,657	3,211	6.4	3.0	12.6	18.6
Northern Ireland[1]	814	330	930	2,775	4.7	2.6	7.0	16.4

1 1993-94 for Northern Ireland. See Notes and Definitions.
2 The vehicle theft risks are based on vehicle-owning households only.
3 The term used in Scotland is housebreaking. The figures include attempts at burglary/housebreaking.
4 Comprises theft of vehicles, thefts from vehicles and associated attempts.
5 Comprises the three individual categories *plus* thefts of bicycles and other household thefts.

Source: British Crime Survey, Home Office; Scottish Crime Survey, The Scottish Office Home Department;
Northern Ireland Crime Survey, Northern Ireland Office

9.3 Notifiable offences cleared up by the police[1,2]: by offence group, 1996

Percentages

	Violence against the person	Sexual offences	Burglary	Robbery	Theft and handling stolen goods	Fraud and forgery	Criminal damage[3]	Other[4]	Total[3,4]
England & Wales	77	76	21	26	23	49	17	96	26
North East	73	79	17	30	24	50	21	100	25
North West (GOR) & Merseyside	74	83	17	23	23	60	18	98	25
North West (GOR)	78	82	15	23	22	61	19	99	24
Merseyside	66	84	27	24	27	60	15	97	29
Yorkshire and the Humber	80	83	18	35	21	47	15	103	23
East Midlands	84	93	23	33	27	48	20	100	30
West Midlands	78	77	24	22	24	39	16	95	26
Eastern	81	77	24	34	27	50	18	97	30
London	62	54	21	22	19	45	13	87	23
South East (GOR)	83	80	22	39	24	52	19	96	28
South West	84	83	20	27	21	54	21	97	26
England	76	75	21	25	23	49	17	96	26
Wales	86	92	31	52	35	53	23	101	37
Scotland[5]	79	81	18	29	27	77	21	98	37
Northern Ireland[5]	63	85	18	16	29	64	27	89	34

1 See Notes and Definitions.
2 Some offences cleared up in 1996 may have been initially recorded in an earlier year; hence figures can be higher than 100 per cent.
3 Figures for England and Wales exclude criminal damage valued at £20 or under. The Northern Ireland figure excludes criminal damage valued at under £200.
4 The Northern Ireland figure includes Offences against the State.
5 Figures for Scotland and Northern Ireland are not comparable with those for England and Wales, nor with each other, because of the differences in the legal systems, recording practices and classifications.

Source: Home Office; The Scottish Office Home Department; Royal Ulster Constabulary

9.4 Firearms

Numbers

	Offences recorded[1] by the police in which firearms were reported[2] to have been used					Operations in which firearms were issued to the police[3,4]				
	1992	1993	1994	1995	1996	1992	1993	1994-95[5]	1995-96[5]	1996-97[5]
United Kingdom	16,676	16,975	15,795	15,400	15,311	4,600	5,723	5,960	8,671	12,649
North East	742	687	767	723	681	375	455	800	1,050	2,517
North West (GOR) &										
Merseyside	1,671	2,118	2,044	2,308	2,426	234	284	420	922	1,578
North West (GOR)	1,210	1,488	1,397	1,465	1,333	177	210	304	642	907
Merseyside	461	630	647	843	1,093	57	74	116	280	671
Yorkshire and the Humber	1,948	2,146	2,264	2,270	2,175	487	616	427	1,026	1,128
East Midlands	1,078	1,044	970	1,014	1,187	109	230	283	346	470
West Midlands	1,328	1,372	1,394	1,510	1,570	266	339	237	420	730
Eastern	954	898	808	771	730	452	419	620	871	1,172
London	3,584	3,513	2,186	1,918	1,742	1,931	2,608	1,812	2,203	2,747
South East (GOR)	1,371	1,371	1,526	1,367	1,232	415	441	790	883	1,064
South West	263	416	569	588	608	139	157	284	511	575
England	12,939	13,565	12,528	12,469	12,351	4,408	5,549	5,673	8,232	11,981
Wales	366	386	449	635	662	44	76	151	244	398
Scotland	1,959	1,773	1,788	1,721	1,647	148	98	136	195	270
Northern Ireland	1,412	1,251	1,030	575	651	.	.	.	.	.

1 See Notes and Definitions.
2 'Alleged' in Scotland.
3 In England and Wales, police shots were fired in 12 operations in 1992, 5 in 1993, 6 in 1994-95 and 5 in both the years 1995-96 and 1996-97. In Scotland, police shots were fired in
   3 operations in each of the years 1992, 1993 and 1994, 4 in 1995-96 and 9 in 1996-97. In Northern Ireland, police officers are armed at all times.
4 Figures for the United Kingdom relate to Great Britain only.
5 In England and Wales the data collection changed from a calendar year to a financial year basis from 1 April 1994. In Scotland data collection changed to financial year basis from
   1 April 1995.

Source: Home Office; The Scottish Office Home Department; Royal Ulster Constabulary

9.5 Seizures of controlled drugs[1]: by type of drug, 1996

Number of seizures

	Class A drugs					Class B drugs			
	Heroin	Cocaine[2]	LSD	Ecstasy	All class A drugs[3]	Cannabis excluding plants	Cannabis plants	Ampheta -mines	All class B drugs[3]
United Kingdom[4]	9,819	4,093	1,133	6,173	21,916	87,026	4,814	18,207	104,085
North East	244	48	47	271	623	3,370	314	1,035	4,479
North West (GOR) & Merseyside	1,872	245	93	495	2,714	8,618	469	1,881	10,461
North West (GOR)	1,621	139	74	361	2,214	6,496	401	1,559	8,054
Merseyside	251	106	19	134	500	2,122	68	322	2,407
Yorkshire and the Humber	1,903	296	92	444	2,757	5,168	531	1,569	6,792
East Midlands	292	76	64	320	776	3,886	391	1,531	5,325
West Midlands	369	107	69	284	841	3,838	257	842	4,686
Eastern	427	136	68	424	1,099	5,558	507	1,349	6,933
London	1,839	2,056	222	1,402	5,684	21,962	518	3,380	24,960
South East (GOR)	554	185	92	482	1,341	7,168	463	1,757	8,721
South West	644	142	71	440	1,422	5,011	697	1,280	6,528
England	8,144	3,291	818	4,562	17,257	64,579	4,147	14,624	78,885
Wales	229	40	90	274	720	4,613	384	1,269	5,427
Scotland	1,197	115	131	855	2,389	9,668	247	2,035	11,326
Northern Ireland	9	12	57	333	387	971	22	91	1,062
British Transport Police[4]	101	27	5	15	157	537	11	39	563
Customs & Excise[4]	139	608	32	134	1,006	6,658	3	149	6,822

1 See Notes and Definitions.
2 Includes 'crack'.
3 Since a seizure may involve drugs other than those listed, figures for individual drugs cannot be added together to produce totals.
4 Figures for the British Transport Police and the Customs and Excise cannot be split by region or country, but are included in the UK totals.

Source: Home Office

9.6   Persons given a police caution[1]: by offence group and age, 1996

Percentages and thousands

	Those cautioned as a percentage of persons found guilty or cautioned for each offence category										All persons found guilty or cautioned (thousands)	
	Violence against the person	Sexual off-ences	Burglary	Robbery	Theft and handling stolen goods	Fraud and forgery	Criminal damage	Other indict-able off-ences	Total indict-able off-ences	Sum-mary off-ences[2]	Indictable offences	Summary offences[2]
Persons aged 10 - 17												
England & Wales	64	63	49	20	72	70	48	63	64	63	123.8	52.7
North East	64	63	46	16	71	73	47	65	64	64	11.6	5.8
North West (GOR) &												
Merseyside	58	51	48	20	70	66	36	56	61	66	19.2	10.2
North West (GOR)	58	47	49	20	72	68	33	57	63	65	15.6	7.6
Merseyside	58	64	45	20	57	58	69	54	54	66	3.6	2.6
Yorkshire and the Humber	65	53	43	19	66	64	25	57	58	59	12.1	4.8
East Midlands	65	81	45	21	73	65	38	64	65	60	9.5	4.3
West Midlands	65	69	50	26	71	67	33	57	63	65	13.9	4.9
Eastern	73	74	56	25	78	78	53	70	72	64	11.4	4.2
London	55	39	43	17	70	70	22	71	62	59	15.7	6.2
South East (GOR)	69	71	53	15	74	76	61	66	69	66	14.9	5.6
South West	71	77	55	32	75	69	74	64	70	59	7.4	2.6
England	64	64	48	20	72	70	46	63	65	63	115.5	48.8
Wales	59	50	52	19	70	68	60	63	64	64	8.3	4.0
Persons aged 18 or over												
England & Wales	33	25	8	1	32	28	13	38	31	12	356.2	528.6
North East	36	29	12	0	39	37	9	42	36	24	21.3	35.4
North West (GOR) &												
Merseyside	26	19	5	1	25	23	4	27	23	18	59.6	79.8
North West (GOR)	24	20	5	0	26	24	3	28	24	14	46.7	56.7
Merseyside	34	16	4	1	20	19	10	24	21	28	12.8	23.2
Yorkshire and the Humber	28	18	4	1	25	23	5	22	21	7	34.1	47.7
East Midlands	35	29	7	2	33	27	9	37	31	8	23.7	47.9
West Midlands	34	31	8	2	35	28	6	35	31	9	33.4	51.5
Eastern	44	24	13	3	36	25	12	39	34	8	27.7	44.4
London	43	30	11	2	41	37	8	53	43	12	70.4	94.2
South East (GOR)	35	25	8	1	30	24	22	33	29	10	39.3	45.0
South West	37	24	9	3	34	28	33	37	32	9	24.4	41.9
England	35	25	8	1	33	29	12	38	32	12	333.9	487.9
Wales	14	18	5	1	27	13	20	34	25	9	22.3	40.7

1 Persons committing an offence who on admission of guilt were given a formal oral caution by the police. See Notes and Definitions.
2 Excludes motoring offences for which written warnings were issued.

Source: Home Office

9.7 Persons found guilty or cautioned[1]: by type of offence and age, 1996

Rates per 100,000 population in the relevant age group

	Persons aged 10 - 17						Persons aged 18 or over					
	Violence against the person *plus* common assault[2]	Sexual off-ences	Burglary, robbery and theft[3]	Drugs off-ences	Other indict-able off-ences[4]	All indictable offences *plus* common assault[2]	Violence against the person *plus* common assault[2]	Sexual off-ences	Burglary, robbery and theft[3]	Drugs off-ences	Other indict-able off-ences[4]	All indictable offences *plus* common assault[2]
Males												
England & Wales	603	43	2,536	330	373	3,885	261	27	693	332	317	1,630
North East	911	46	4,868	472	526	6,824	329	30	908	317	328	1,914
North West (GOR) &												
Merseyside	698	44	2,795	401	438	4,376	293	33	925	367	430	2,048
North West (GOR)	698	43	2,919	345	429	4,434	300	34	929	342	413	2,017
Merseyside	700	48	2,329	611	473	4,160	268	31	911	464	496	2,170
Yorkshire and the Humber	586	46	2,622	226	336	3,816	257	28	722	257	339	1,604
East Midlands	742	59	2,436	235	282	3,753	297	31	608	231	236	1,403
West Midlands	602	56	2,704	277	406	4,046	241	28	623	256	337	1,486
Eastern	559	41	2,317	286	363	3,565	218	24	561	255	234	1,292
London	516	29	2,262	630	371	3,808	298	25	796	668	416	2,204
South East (GOR)	531	32	2,141	237	303	3,244	203	23	557	234	233	1,249
South West	421	37	1,641	162	290	2,551	220	22	553	216	207	1,218
England	599	42	2,514	330	363	3,849	258	27	692	329	313	1,619
Wales	670	52	2,885	327	534	4,467	320	32	716	388	371	1,827
Females												
England & Wales	196	1	849	35	72	1,153	36	-	174	38	51	299
North East	331	1	1,615	44	125	2,115	52	1	236	42	56	387
North West (GOR) &												
Merseyside	227	1	887	38	79	1,232	41	-	225	40	70	376
North West (GOR)	232	1	962	44	84	1,322	43	-	223	44	69	378
Merseyside	208	0	607	17	63	895	32	-	234	26	73	366
Yorkshire and the Humber	221	0	884	42	72	1,220	37	-	171	43	50	301
East Midlands	287	1	868	32	64	1,252	49	-	153	31	41	275
West Midlands	199	2	908	24	69	1,202	36	-	158	24	48	267
Eastern	201	3	884	39	75	1,202	32	-	151	37	34	255
London	103	1	703	45	58	910	34	-	216	55	76	382
South East (GOR)	147	0	697	27	60	931	26	-	125	29	34	213
South West	136	0	587	18	59	801	28	-	134	31	34	227
England	193	1	844	34	70	1,142	36	-	173	37	50	297
Wales	245	1	941	41	107	1,335	46	-	186	50	56	339
All persons												
England & Wales	405	22	1,716	187	227	2,557	145	13	425	180	179	944
North East	628	24	3,282	263	330	4,528	185	15	560	174	187	1,122
North West (GOR) &												
Merseyside	469	23	1,865	224	263	2,844	162	16	562	198	243	1,182
North West (GOR)	471	22	1,966	199	261	2,918	167	17	564	188	235	1,171
Merseyside	460	24	1,489	321	273	2,568	144	15	555	234	273	1,221
Yorkshire and the Humber	409	24	1,777	137	208	2,554	144	14	439	147	190	934
East Midlands	521	31	1,675	136	176	2,539	170	15	375	129	136	826
West Midlands	406	30	1,832	154	243	2,665	136	14	385	138	189	862
Eastern	384	22	1,617	165	223	2,411	123	12	351	143	131	760
London	315	15	1,503	345	219	2,398	162	12	496	352	241	1,262
South East (GOR)	345	17	1,442	135	185	2,124	111	11	334	128	130	714
South West	283	19	1,130	93	178	1,703	121	11	336	120	117	704
England	401	22	1,702	186	221	2,533	143	13	424	178	178	937
Wales	463	27	1,937	187	326	2,940	178	16	441	213	208	1,056

1 See Notes and Definitions.
2 Following the introduction of a charging standard on 31 August 1994, some people who would have been charged with an indictable offence are now charged with common assault, a summary offence. Common assaults have therefore been included for comparability with figures in previous editions of *Regional Trends*.
3 Includes handling stolen goods.
4 Includes criminal damage and fraud and forgery.

Source: Home Office

9.8 Persons aged 21 or over found guilty of offences[1,2]: by gender and type of sentence, 1996

| | Result as a percentage of number of persons sentenced | | | | | | Persons sentenced | |
	Absolute or condit-ional discharge	Fine	All community penalties	Fully sus-pended sentence[3]	Immed-iate custodial sentence[4]	Otherwise dealt with	Rates[5]	Numbers (=100%)
Males								
England & Wales	7	78	8	-	6	1	52	963,418
North East	10	71	10	-	7	1	44	40,252
North West (GOR) & Merseyside	8	77	7	-	7	1	67	161,295
North West (GOR)	8	77	7	-	7	1	69	132,513
Merseyside	7	77	8	-	8	1	59	28,782
Yorkshire and the Humber	8	73	10	-	7	2	50	88,899
East Midlands	6	77	8	-	6	1	48	71,272
West Midlands	6	80	8	-	6	1	51	96,248
Eastern	5	80	7	-	6	1	48	86,644
London	5	80	7	-	7	1	60	158,661
South East (GOR)	7	77	8	-	6	1	41	111,705
South West	7	81	7	-	5	1	50	86,565
England	7	78	8	-	6	1	52	901,541
Wales	7	79	7	-	6	1	60	61,877
Scotland[6]	8	74	6	.	11	1	54	96,531
Northern Ireland	6	70	2	9	7	6	37	19,606
Females								
England & Wales	8	85	5	-	2	1	12	235,054
North East	8	85	4	-	1	1	13	13,371
North West (GOR) & Merseyside	9	83	5	-	2	1	14	37,256
North West (GOR)	10	81	6	-	2	1	13	26,855
Merseyside	6	87	4	-	2	1	19	10,401
Yorkshire and the Humber	9	82	6	-	1	1	12	22,430
East Midlands	7	87	4	-	1	1	12	19,387
West Midlands	7	87	5	-	1	-	12	24,552
Eastern	7	86	5	-	1	1	10	19,378
London	6	85	5	-	2	1	13	38,542
South East (GOR)	9	82	6	-	2	1	8	22,821
South West	7	87	4	-	1	1	12	21,779
England	8	85	5	-	2	1	12	219,516
Wales	9	85	4	-	1	1	14	15,538
Scotland[6]	18	71	6	.	4	1	9	17,111
Northern Ireland	13	67	1	6	2	12	4	2,455

1 See Notes and Definitions.
2 The coverage of the table is all offences, including motoring offences. A defendant is recorded only once for each set of court proceedings, against the principal offence.
3 Fully suspended sentences are not available to courts in Scotland.
4 In Scotland includes custodial sentences imposed following a sentence deferred for good behaviour.
5 Rates per 1,000 population aged 21 or over.
6 To improve comparability, this table excludes breaches of probation and community service orders normally included in Scottish figures.

Source: Home Office; The Scottish Office Home Department; Royal Ulster Constabulary

9.9 Persons found guilty or cautioned: by police force area[1], 1996

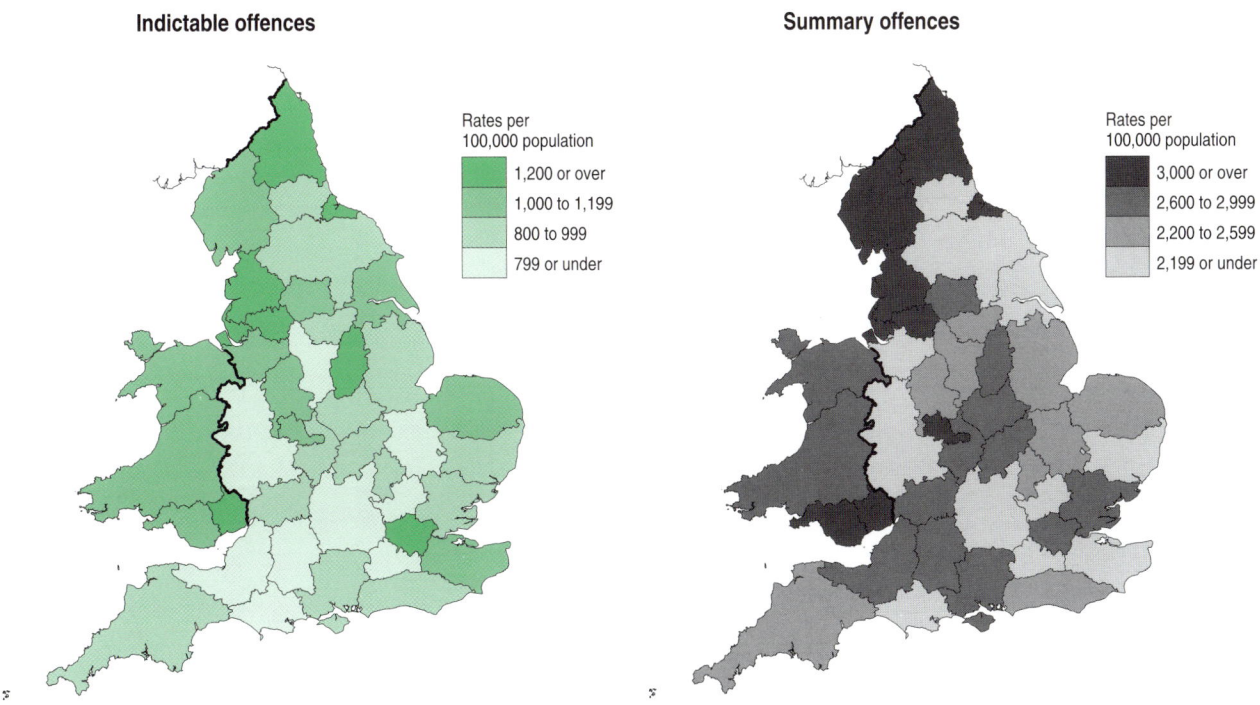

Indictable offences

Rates per 100,000 population

- 1,200 or over
- 1,000 to 1,199
- 800 to 999
- 799 or under

Summary offences

Rates per 100,000 population

- 3,000 or over
- 2,600 to 2,999
- 2,200 to 2,599
- 2,199 or under

1 Metropolitan Police Force area includes the City of London.

Source: Home Office

9.10 Persons aged 21 or over sentenced to immediate imprisonment: by gender and length of sentence imposed for principal[1] offence, 1996

Percentages and numbers

	Males				Females			
	Length of sentence (percentages)			Total sentenced to immediate imprisonment (=100%) (numbers)	Length of sentence (percentages)			Total sentenced to immediate imprisonment (=100%) (numbers)
	One year or less	Over one year but less than four years	Four years or over		One year or less	Over one year but less than four years	Four years or over	
United Kingdom	69	24	7	72,531	76	18	5	4,366
North East	59	31	10	2,896	73	22	5	146
North West (GOR) & Merseyside	66	27	7	10,923	76	20	4	792
North West (GOR)	66	27	7	8,700	74	21	5	608
Merseyside	66	26	8	2,223	82	17	2	184
Yorkshire and the Humber	64	28	8	6,339	75	20	5	318
East Midlands	68	26	6	4,439	71	25	4	199
West Midlands	65	28	8	5,745	66	28	6	248
Eastern	69	25	6	4,980	80	15	5	280
London	67	23	9	11,286	72	21	6	940
South East (GOR)	62	28	10	6,342	62	23	15	382
South West	67	27	6	3,968	77	19	3	176
England	66	26	8	56,918	73	21	6	3,481
Wales	64	30	6	3,450	75	24	2	153
Scotland[2]	87	9	5	10,758	94	4	1	692
Northern Ireland	75	16	9	1,405	95	5	0	40

1 Figures for Scotland are for the length of sentence in total given for all offences and not just for the principal offence. Figures on sentence lengths for principal offences only are not available for Scotland.
2 To improve comparability, this table excludes breaches of probation and community service orders normally included in Scottish figures.

Source: Home Office; The Scottish Office Home Department; Northern Ireland Office

9.11 Police manpower: by type, March 1997[1]

| | Police officers on ordinary duty[2] | | | | | Special constables and civilian staff (rates per 1,000 officers on ordinary duty) | | |
| | | Percentage of which | | | | | | |
	Number	Ethnic minorities	Women officers	Population per officer[3]	Officers per 100 sq km	Special con-stables[4]	Civilian staff	Traffic wardens (numbers)
United Kingdom[5]	151,245	1.7	14.5	389	62	153	393	4,806
North East	6,597	0.8	14.5	394	77	133	388	156
North West (GOR) & Merseyside	17,588	1.6	15.9	392	124	127	356	509
North West (GOR)	13,358	1.5	16.0	410	99	137	369	378
Merseyside	4,230	1.8	15.8	336	649	95	317	132
Yorkshire and the Humber	11,750	1.9	14.8	429	76	145	405	302
East Midlands	8,436	2.5	14.0	491	54	243	421	246
West Midlands	12,290	2.9	17.7	433	94	211	392	297
Eastern	9,727	1.1	15.6	521	51	226	435	353
London	27,536	3.1	14.6	275	1,370	65	503	1,383
South East (GOR)	15,111	1.1	15.5	505	80	174	423	421
South West	9,424	0.7	13.4	514	40	281	437	337
England	118,459	1.9	15.2	414	91	158	427	4,003
Wales	6,592	0.7	12.1	443	32	173	372	178
Scotland[6]	14,789	0.3	13.8	347	19	121	284	472
Northern Ireland[7]	11,405	..	9.5	146	81	126	203	153

1 Full-time equivalents as at 31 March 1997 for England and Wales and for Scotland. Actual numbers (whether full or part-time) as at 31 March 1997 for Northern Ireland.
2 Includes full-time Reserves in Northern Ireland.
3 Based on mid-1996 population estimates.
4 Part-time Reserves in Northern Ireland.
5 Great Britain for ethnic minorities.
6 For civilian staff and traffic wardens, part-time staff are counted as half full-time.
7 The figure for civilian staff relates to those who work to the Chief Constable and not to those who work to the Police Authority for Northern Ireland.

Source: Home Office; The Scottish Office Home Department; Royal Ulster Constabulary

9.12 Adults' assessment of the local police: by age, 1996[1]

Percentages

| | Percentage in each age group saying police do a very or fairly good job | | | |
	16-29[2]	30-59	60 or over	All aged 16 or over
United Kingdom	76	81	82	80
North East	..	77	87	77
North West (GOR) & Merseyside	72	75	78	75
Yorkshire and the Humber	76	77	83	78
East Midlands	..	82	83	82
West Midlands	71	81	83	79
Eastern	82	87	84	85
London	76	84	89	83
South East (GOR)	80	88	85	85
South West	85	82	83	83
England	77	82	84	81
Wales	..	76	75	77
Scotland	69	74	74	73
Northern Ireland	65	75	82	74

1 See Notes and Definitions.
2 For some regions, sample sizes are too small to provide a reliable estimate.

Source: British Crime Survey, Home Office; Scottish Crime Survey, The Scottish Office Home Department; Community Attitudes Survey, Northern Ireland Statistics and Research Agency

9.13 Feelings of insecurity: by gender, 1996[1]

Percentages

| | Percentage feeling 'very' or 'fairly' unsafe at night when: | | | |
| | Alone at home | | Walking alone[2] | |
	Males	Females	Males	Females
England & Wales	4	15	15	47
North East	5	17	15	51
North West (GOR) & Merseyside	4	18	17	51
Yorkshire and the Humber	4	16	14	49
East Midlands	5	16	14	45
West Midlands	8	19	18	49
Eastern	1	14	12	44
London	7	14	22	48
South East (GOR)	3	12	11	45
South West	4	15	13	40
England	5	15	15	47
Wales	4	20	13	45
Scotland	4	11	21	48
Northern Ireland[1]	2	11	13	40

1 1994-95 for Northern Ireland. See Notes and Definitions.
2 For Northern Ireland the question relates to fear of 'walking in the dark' (ie alone or with others); the figures also include those people who never go out.

Source: British Crime Survey, Home Office; Scottish Crime Survey, The Scottish Office Home Department; Northern Ireland Crime Survey, Northern Ireland Office

10 Transport

Cars

One in six cars licensed to addresses in the West Midlands in 1996 was a company car compared with one in 17 in the North East and Merseyside.

(Table 10.1)

Around four in every five households in the Eastern region, the South East (GOR) and the South West have at least one car compared with about three in five in the North East and London.

(Table 10.2)

On average, households in Scotland have the newest cars while those in Wales, the South West and London have the oldest.

(Table 10.3)

Traffic

The average daily traffic flow on major roads in London in 1996 was nearly five times greater than that on major roads in Scotland.

(Table 10.4)

Roads

Only 3 per cent of the total length of major roads in Wales and the North East is motorway, compared with 12 per cent in the North West and Merseyside.

(Table 10.5)

Accidents

In 1996, the fatal or serious accident rate per vehicle kilometre on major roads in London was more than twice that for any other region.

(Table 10.6)

One in five road casualties in London and Scotland in 1996 was a pedestrian compared with about one in ten in the Eastern region, the South East and Northern Ireland.

(Table 10.7)

Journeys

On average, people living in the Eastern region and the South East (GOR) travel the furthest to work, but Londoners take by far the longest time.

(Chart 10.9)

People living in London, Scotland and the North East travel, on average, more than 1,000 miles per year by public transport.

(Table 10.11)

People from Eastern region cycle more than five times further on average than those from Merseyside and Wales.

(Table 10.11)

Air travel

London Heathrow and Gatwick airports accounts for three fifths of all the air passenger traffic and three quarters of all freight handled at United Kingdom airports.

(Table 10.12)

Ports

Dover handled more than half of all the United Kingdom's international sea passengers during 1996.

(Table 10.13)

Introduction

Transport is an important factor in both the social and economic prosperity of a region. It affects us all in our daily life whether we are commuting to work or travelling on business or for leisure purposes, though for some people it is lack of transport that affects their daily life.

Table 10.1 presents the trend in the numbers of cars currently licensed and new registrations. There has been a steady increase in cars licensed in all regions. In recent years, most of the growth in car ownership has been in households acquiring second or even third cars. Increased car ownership and use have resulted in heavier volumes of traffic on our roads. Overall, road transport accounted for 94 per cent of all passenger traffic during 1996. However, as Table 10.4 shows, there are considerable regional differences in the volume of road traffic on our major roads.

Despite increased road traffic, the number of road accident deaths in Great Britain fell to 3.6 thousand in 1996, the lowest figure since records began 70 years ago. There are significant regional differences in accident and casualty rates (Tables 10.6 and 10.7). This disparity arises for a number of reasons. For example, figures are affected by the mix of pedestrian and vehicle traffic within a region. In Scotland, for instance, rates of pedestrian casualties are, on average, higher generally than elsewhere as lower car ownership means more people travelling on foot, especially in densely populated areas such as Glasgow. Other factors to bear in mind in interpreting accident and casualties statistics are the length of different types of road and the amount of traffic using those different road types. The evidence of the figures is that motorways are the safest roads on which to travel, despite the fact that average speeds are higher on motorways than on other roads.

The car is still the predominant method of travel to work for the majority of people in all the regions and its use is still increasing (Table 10.10): seven out of ten people across the United Kingdom go to work by car. However, in London, where the percentage travelling by rail is, not surprisingly, significantly higher than in any other region, the figure is less than five out of ten. One in eight people living in Scotland and the North East take a bus or coach to work, compared with only one in 25 in the Eastern region. In the South West, the Yorkshire and the Humber region and Scotland, people are more likely to walk to work than those in other regions.

Tables 10.12 and 10.13 show activity at major airports and seaports in the United Kingdom. Overall, international and domestic air passenger traffic rose by 84 and 72 per cent respectively between 1986 and 1996. The general growth in airport traffic is further reflected in the 5 per cent increase in aircraft movements and the 4 per cent rise in the volume of cargo handled between 1995 and 1996. Freight handled at seaports in the United Kingdom increased by 18 per cent in the ten years to 1996, while international sea passenger movements starting or ending in the United Kingdom rose by 38 per cent between 1986 and 1994 to 37.0 million. They fell back by 2.4 million in 1995 following the opening of the Channel Tunnel in May 1994, but the number rose again slightly in 1996 to 34.8 million. The majority of sea passengers travel between the United Kingdom and France, 25.5 million passengers in 1996.

The opening of the Channel Tunnel brought an important international link and opportunity for regeneration to the South East (GOR) region. Traffic through the Tunnel expanded rapidly with 1.2 million vehicles using Le Shuttle Tourist in 1995, 2.1 million in 1996 and 2.4 in 1997. The Eurostar trains carried 2.9 million passengers in 1995; by 1997 this had risen to 6.0 million. Altogether 14.6 million passengers and 2.9 million tonnes of rail freight passed through the Channel Tunnel in 1997.

10.1 Motor cars currently licensed and new registrations[1]

Thousands and percentages

	Currently licensed[2]				Percentage company cars 1996[4]	New registrations			Percentage company cars 1997[3,4]
	1993	1994	1995	1996		1995	1996	1997[3]	
United Kingdom	21,256	21,708	21,917	22,784	10	2,019	2,077	2,157	55
North East	747	756	765	783	6	68	74	76	35
North West (GOR) & Merseyside	2,360	2,407	2,426	2,501	12	227	235	255	52
North West (GOR)	1,957	1,999	2,017	2,076	13	193	199	217	56
Merseyside	403	408	409	426	6	34	36	37	23
Yorkshire and the Humber	1,632	1,656	1,674	1,708	9	131	138	151	45
East Midlands	1,423	1,451	1,464	1,609	10	140	140	152	62
West Midlands	2,067	2,116	2,146	2,183	16	266	275	292	68
Eastern	2,170	2,218	2,260	2,295	9	193	200	228	52
London	2,302	2,343	2,326	2,362	14	278	277	278	68
South East (GOR)	3,213	3,263	3,273	3,469	10	278	292	315	56
South West	1,948	1,980	1,997	2,109	10	121	130	132	50
England	17,862	18,191	18,330	19,018	11	1,702	1,762	1,873	57
Wales	974	982	986	1,067	7	68	73	76	40
Scotland	1,574	1,603	1,618	1,674	9	145	154	173	47
Northern Ireland	500	509	523	546	9	81	88	..	..

1 Figures for United Kingdom include motor vehicles where the country of the registered keeper is unknown.
2 At 31 December.
3 Figure for the United Kingdom relates to Great Britain.
4 Within the Private and light goods tax class only.

Source: Annual Vehicle Census/Vehicle Information Database, Department of the Environment,Transport and the Regions; Department of the Environment, Northern Ireland

10.2 Availability of cars[1], 1996-97

Percentages

	Percentage of households with			
	No car	One car	Two cars	Three or more cars
United Kingdom	30	46	21	4
North East	40	42	17	2
North West (GOR) & Merseyside	29	47	20	3
North West (GOR)	28	48	20	3
Merseyside	33	43	21	4
Yorkshire and the Humber	32	48	16	3
East Midlands	26	48	21	5
West Midlands	32	42	22	3
Eastern	22	46	27	5
London	38	44	15	3
South East (GOR)	23	44	27	6
South West	20	51	25	4
England	29	46	21	4
Wales	32	48	17	3
Scotland	36	46	15	3
Northern Ireland	30	47	19	4

1 Includes cars and light vans normally available to the household.
Source: General Household Survey, Office for National Statistics; Continuous Household Survey, Northern Ireland Statistics and Research Agency

10.3 Age of household cars, 1994-1996

Percentages

	Age of car[1]		
	Under 3 years old	3-6 years old	7 years or more
Great Britain	25	34	41
North East	31	36	33
North West (GOR) & Merseyside	29	33	38
North West (GOR)	31	33	36
Merseyside	20	35	45
Yorkshire and the Humber	27	37	35
East Midlands	27	33	41
West Midlands	26	35	40
Eastern	24	35	41
London	20	33	47
South East (GOR)	25	32	42
South West	20	31	49
England	25	33	42
Wales	18	39	43
Scotland	34	36	30

1 Age of main or only car or light van normally available to the household. See Notes and Definitions.
Source: National Travel Survey, Department of the Environment, Transport and the Regions

10.4 Average daily motor vehicle flows[1]: by major road class, 1996

Thousand vehicles per day

| | Motorway | Built-up major | | | Non built-up major | | | All major roads |
		Trunk	Principal	Total	Trunk	Principal	Total	
United Kingdom	59	19	15	16	16	8	10	15
North East	45	27	14	14	18	10	13	14
North West (GOR) & Merseyside	54	14	16	16	14	9	11	18
North West (GOR)	55	13	16	16	14	9	10	18
Merseyside	41	18	15	15	24	14	18	19
Yorkshire and the Humber	68	17	16	16	24	9	13	19
East Midlands	71	20	13	14	15	8	11	14
West Midlands	72	18	17	17	14	8	10	18
Eastern	78	16	14	14	25	11	17	20
London	93	43	22	25	63	23	52	29
South East (GOR)	75	17	16	16	27	13	16	23
South West	45	15	13	13	16	8	10	13
England	66	23	16	17	20	10	13	18
Wales	54	11	10	10	9	5	7	9
Scotland	35	15	11	12	8	3	4	6
Northern Ireland[2]	26	17	11	14	7	5	6	9

1 Annual average daily flow is the number of vehicles passing a point per year divided by 366. See Notes and Definitions.
2 Northern Ireland Primary Class 1 roads are shown as trunk roads. Non-primary Class 1 roads are shown as principal roads.

Source: Department of the Environment, Transport and the Regions; Department of the Environment, Northern Ireland

10.5 Road lengths and distribution of accidents on major roads

	1997					1996[1]				
	Share of total major road length (percentages)			All major roads (=100%) (kilometres)	All roads (kilometres)	Distribution of accidents (percentages)			Total accidents	
									On major roads (=100%) (numbers)	On all roads (numbers)[2]
	Motorway	Built-up 'A'	Non built-up 'A'			Motorway	Built-up 'A'	Non built-up 'A'		
United Kingdom	6.6	27.6	65.8	53,042	391,975	6.7	63.8	29.6	119,701	242,731
North East	3.1	27.5	69.3	1,840	15,902	2.1	56.4	41.5	3,583	8,690
North West (GOR) & Merseyside	12.2	38.8	49.0	4,757	34,376	9.6	71.9	18.4	15,443	31,381
North West (GOR)	12.2	35.5	52.3	4,258	29,901	10.5	68.5	21.0	12,415	24,788
Merseyside	12.4	66.9	20.7	499	4,475	6.1	86.1	7.8	3,028	6,593
Yorkshire and the Humber	8.8	35.8	55.4	3,687	29,541	7.0	63.9	29.1	9,141	20,843
East Midlands	4.5	23.0	72.5	4,186	29,367	5.8	49.6	44.6	7,909	16,123
West Midlands	9.6	30.7	59.7	3,895	30,690	8.9	63.3	27.9	9,927	20,796
Eastern	6.1	25.7	68.2	4,128	36,134	9.9	44.7	45.5	10,259	21,819
London	3.6	86.0	10.3	1,812	13,543	2.0	94.9	3.1	23,916	38,356
South East (GOR)	10.8	30.7	58.5	6,110	43,236	10.8	51.0	38.2	16,502	34,090
South West	5.8	22.1	72.1	5,335	48,590	5.8	47.4	46.8	8,010	17,497
England	7.9	32.2	59.9	35,748	281,379	7.0	65.6	27.5	104,690	209,595
Wales	3.0	24.4	72.6	4,392	34,230	5.0	46.8	48.2	4,356	10,288
Scotland	4.0	14.8	81.2	10,540	52,085	4.0	50.3	45.8	7,383	16,056
Northern Ireland[1]	4.7	22.5	72.8	2,361	24,281	4.1	59.3	36.6	3,272	6,792

1 Figures relating to distribution of accidents in Northern Ireland are for 1995.
2 Includes B,C and unclassified roads. See Notes and Definitions.

Source: Department of the Environment, Transport and the Regions; Department of the Environment, Northern Ireland; Royal Ulster Constabulary

10.6 Fatal and serious road accidents[1]

Numbers and rates

	Fatal and serious accidents on all roads						Fatal and serious accidents on major roads[2]			
	Numbers			Rates per 100,000 population			Numbers		Rates per 100 million vehicle kms	
	1981-1985 average[3]	1991	1996	1981-1985 average[3]	1991	1996	1991	1996	1991	1996
Great Britain	67,839	47,919	40,576	124	85	71	24,340	20,482	9.4	7.3
North East	2,255	1,769	1,382	86	68	53	734	610	8.3	6.2
North West (GOR) &										
Merseyside	6,178	4,914	4,660	90	71	68	2,506	2,284	8.4	7.3
North West (GOR)	5,079	3,901	3,911	94	72	71	2,030	1,955	7.7	7.1
Merseyside	1,099	1,013	749	73	70	53	476	329	14.4	9.4
Yorkshire and the Humber	5,714	4,352	3,512	117	87	70	2,084	1,598	10.1	6.2
East Midlands	5,334	3,451	3,377	138	86	82	1,796	1,726	9.3	7.8
West Midlands	6,525	4,447	3,941	126	84	74	2,055	1,876	8.5	7.3
Eastern	6,884	4,802	4,202	140	93	79	2,264	1,976	7.7	6.2
London	7,588	7,267	6,098	112	105	86	4,395	3,808	23.8	19.7
South East (GOR)	10,169	5,843	5,341	139	76	68	2,882	2,653	6.1	5.2
South West	6,697	3,793	2,682	158	80	55	1,833	1,277	7.1	5.1
England	57,344	40,638	35,195	123	84	72	20,549	17,808	9.2	7.4
Wales	3,083	2,112	1,758	107	73	60	1,139	878	8.9	5.9
Scotland	7,412	5,169	3,623	144	101	71	2,652	1,796	12.1	7.4
Northern Ireland	..	1,381	1,285	..	85	77	..	..	..	..

1 See Notes and Definitions.
2 Motorways, A(M) roads and A roads.
3 Used as a basis for the government targets for reducing road casualties in Great Britain, and fatal and serious road casualties in Northern Ireland, by a third by the year 2000.

Source: Department of the Environment, Transport and the Regions; Royal Ulster Constabulary

10.7 Road casualties[1]: by age and by type of road user, 1996

Percentages and numbers

	Percentage of all road casualties								All road casualties (=100%) (numbers)	Percentage change over 1981-85 average[4]
	Who were aged[2]			Type of road user						
	0 - 15	16 - 59	60 or over	Pedes-trians	Pedal cyclists	Motor cyclists	Car occupants[3]	Other road users		
United Kingdom	14.3	75.8	9.9	14.3	7.5	7.0	64.6	6.7	332,877	0.8
North East	17.6	72.4	10.0	18.1	6.5	3.1	64.1	8.3	12,351	11.2
North West (GOR) & Merseyside	15.9	75.0	9.1	15.0	7.0	4.2	67.2	6.7	44,817	23.5
North West (GOR)	15.8	75.2	9.0	14.8	7.2	4.4	67.0	6.6	35,166	21.0
Merseyside	16.5	74.3	9.2	15.5	6.1	3.3	68.2	7.0	9,651	33.6
Yorkshire and the Humber	15.9	74.1	10.0	15.4	7.2	5.8	64.4	7.1	28,892	11.5
East Midlands	14.2	76.2	9.6	12.0	8.1	7.1	66.6	6.3	22,845	-1.0
West Midlands	15.6	74.7	9.7	14.9	7.0	6.1	65.6	6.5	28,717	3.7
Eastern	12.3	78.1	9.6	9.4	8.3	7.6	68.7	6.0	30,370	0.3
London	11.7	79.3	8.9	20.2	9.5	12.9	49.8	7.6	45,457	-16.1
South East (GOR)	12.4	77.3	10.3	10.4	8.5	8.5	67.3	5.3	46,428	2.0
South West	12.5	75.6	11.9	11.5	7.6	8.6	67.0	5.4	23,876	-9.4
England	13.9	76.3	9.8	14.1	7.9	7.6	63.9	6.5	283,753	1.2
Wales	15.5	73.9	10.6	13.8	5.1	4.8	69.9	6.3	14,853	3.2
Scotland	17.6	70.6	11.7	19.9	6.0	3.9	62.1	8.1	21,696	-20.0
Northern Ireland	14.9	76.8	8.3	10.0	2.9	1.9	76.4	8.9	12,575	53.3

1 See Notes and Definitions.
2 Excludes age not reported.
3 Includes occupants of taxis and minibuses.
4 Used as a basis for the government targets for reducing road casualties in Great Britain, and fatal and serious road casualties in Northern Ireland, by a third by the year 2000.

Source: Department of the Environment, Transport and the Regions; Royal Ulster Constabulary

10.8 Journeys per person per year[1]: by journey purpose and by gender, 1994-1996[2]

Percentages and numbers

	Commuting	Business	Education	Shopping	Other personal business	Leisure	Average number of journeys (=100%)
Males							
Great Britain	18	5	6	18	20	31	1,084
North East	16	2	7	21	19	35	1,112
North West (GOR) & Merseyside	16	5	7	19	22	32	1,091
North West (GOR)	16	5	6	19	22	32	1,115
Merseyside	16	3	9	20	22	29	1,009
Yorkshire and the Humber	19	5	7	19	19	32	1,033
East Midlands	18	6	6	17	20	33	1,179
West Midlands	19	5	6	20	20	30	1,043
Eastern	20	7	6	18	18	31	1,138
London	16	6	9	18	23	29	1,051
South East (GOR)	18	6	6	18	21	31	1,100
South West	19	5	5	18	19	34	1,114
England	18	5	6	19	20	31	1,090
Wales	16	5	7	18	20	33	999
Scotland	18	6	6	19	20	31	1,067
Females							
Great Britain	12	2	6	24	25	31	1,033
North East	11	1	6	24	24	34	1,004
North West (GOR) & Merseyside	11	1	6	25	27	30	1,044
North West (GOR)	11	1	6	25	27	30	1,053
Merseyside	9	-	8	26	26	30	1,013
Yorkshire and the Humber	14	2	7	23	23	31	990
East Midlands	14	3	5	23	24	31	1,125
West Midlands	13	2	7	22	26	31	1,034
Eastern	14	2	6	23	27	29	1,055
London	12	2	7	24	27	28	984
South East (GOR)	12	2	6	23	26	31	1,102
South West	12	2	6	24	24	32	1,024
England	13	2	6	23	25	31	1,042
Wales	9	2	8	24	25	32	912
Scotland	14	1	8	24	22	30	1,021
All persons							
Great Britain	15	4	6	21	23	31	1,057
North East	13	2	7	22	22	34	1,055
North West (GOR) & Merseyside	13	3	7	22	24	31	1,067
North West (GOR)	14	3	6	22	25	31	1,083
Merseyside	12	2	9	23	24	30	1,011
Yorkshire and the Humber	17	3	7	21	21	32	1,011
East Midlands	16	4	5	20	22	32	1,150
West Midlands	16	3	6	21	23	30	1,038
Eastern	17	4	6	20	22	30	1,095
London	14	4	8	21	25	28	1,015
South East (GOR)	15	4	6	21	24	31	1,101
South West	16	4	5	21	21	33	1,068
England	15	4	6	21	23	31	1,065
Wales	13	3	8	21	23	33	952
Scotland	16	4	7	22	21	30	1,043

1 Within Great Britain only. Figures relate to region of residence of the traveller and include journeys undertaken outside of their region. They include journeys of less than one mile; these were excluded from the table in previous editions of *Regional Trends*.
2 See Notes and Definitions.

Source: National Travel Survey, Department of the Environment, Transport and the Regions

10.9 Travel to work: distance travelled and average time taken, 1994-1996[1]

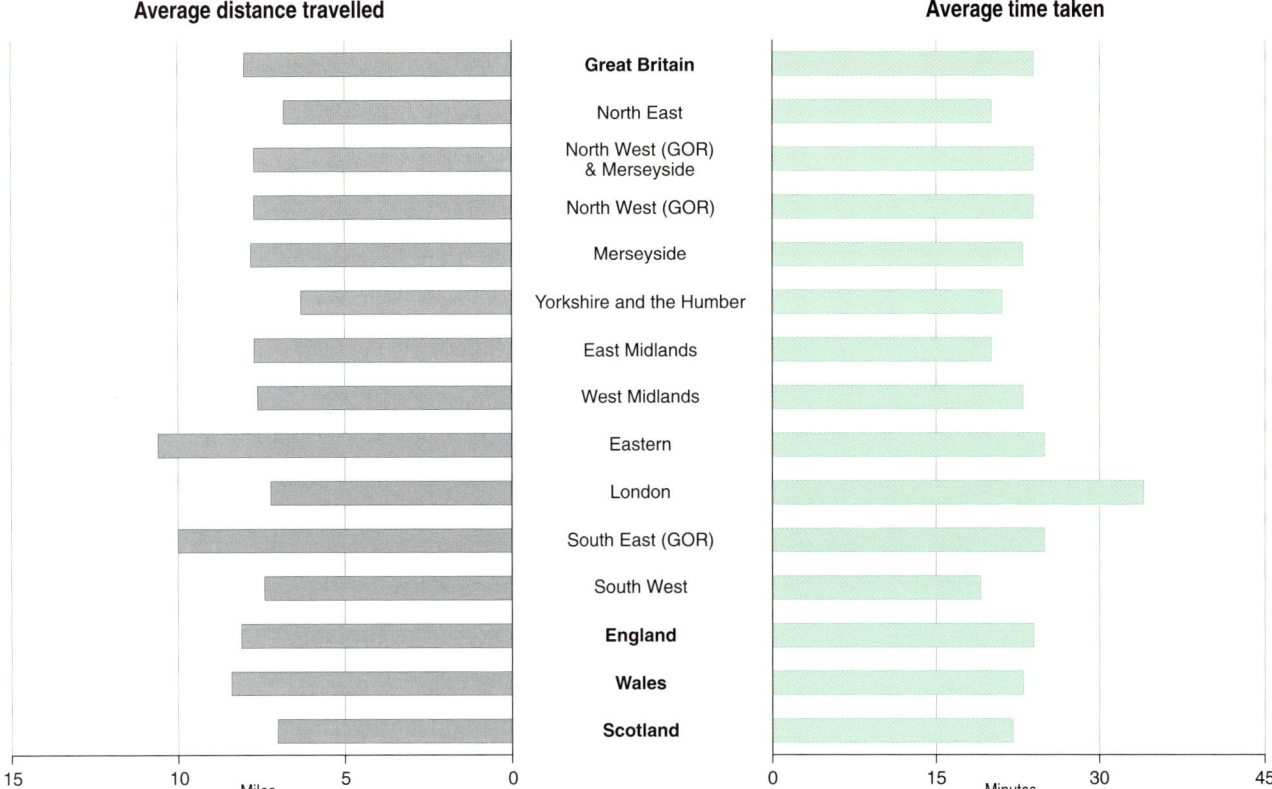

Average distance travelled   **Average time taken**

1 By region of residence. See Notes and Definitions.

Source: National Travel Survey, Department of the Environment, Transport and the Regions

10.10 Main method of travel to work, Autumn 1997[1]

Percentages

	Car, van, minibus, works van	Motorbike, moped, scooter[2]	Bicycle[2]	Bus, coach, private bus	Rail[2]	Other rail[2,3]	Foot	Other[2,4]
Region of residence								
United Kingdom	69.4	1.0	3.7	8.2	3.4	2.2	11.4	0.7
North East	69.3	..	2.5	13.0	..	..	12.1	1.0
North West (GOR) & Merseyside	73.7	0.8	3.4	8.2	1.7	0.4	11.1	0.6
North West (GOR)	75.1	0.8	3.5	7.2	1.1	0.5	11.3	0.6
Merseyside	67.7	..	3.1	12.7	4.3	..	10.4	..
Yorkshire and the Humber	69.2	0.8	3.9	10.8	1.2	..	13.2	0.7
East Midlands	73.6	1.0	5.0	7.1	0.7	..	12.0	..
West Midlands	74.9	0.8	3.0	8.9	1.1	..	10.7	0.5
Eastern	72.4	1.2	5.6	3.9	5.8	0.9	9.7	0.6
London	46.2	1.3	3.1	11.9	11.1	16.1	9.5	0.6
South East (GOR)	72.9	1.4	4.4	4.4	5.3	0.4	10.6	0.7
South West	73.6	1.8	4.5	5.2	0.9	..	13.1	0.7
England	69.0	1.1	4.0	7.8	3.8	2.6	11.1	0.6
Wales	76.7	..	2.1	6.6	1.1	..	11.8	..
Scotland	67.0	..	2.1	13.3	2.2	..	13.3	1.3
Northern Ireland	78.3	..	..	7.2	..	.	11.3	..

1 See Notes and Definitions to Labour market chapter. Analysis excludes those on government schemes, those who work from home or in the same grounds or building as their home, and those who work in different places using their home as a base.
2 For some regions, sample sizes are too small to provide a reliable estimate.
3 Underground, light railway and tram.
4 Includes taxi as main method.

Source: Labour Force Survey, Office for National Statistics and Department for Economic Development, Northern Ireland

10.11 Distance travelled per person per year[1]: by mode of transport, 1994-1996

Miles

	Walk	Pedal cycle	Cars and other private road vehicles	Public transport	All modes of transport
Great Britain	200	38	5,535	798	6,570
North East	209	37	4,151	1,075	5,472
North West (GOR) & Merseyside	204	29	5,259	667	6,159
North West (GOR)	204	34	5,692	647	6,577
Merseyside	204	13	3,810	736	4,763
Yorkshire and the Humber	204	39	5,067	682	5,991
East Midlands	223	49	6,451	491	7,214
West Midlands	167	23	5,504	648	6,342
Eastern	176	69	6,877	824	7,946
London	239	31	3,398	1,294	4,962
South East (GOR)	198	46	6,916	839	7,999
South West	188	56	6,464	512	7,220
England	201	41	5,597	791	6,631
Wales	162	13	5,332	423	5,930
Scotland	204	23	5,054	1,075	6,356

1 Within Great Britain only. Figures relate to region of residence of the traveller and include journeys undertaken outside of this region. They include journeys of less than one mile; these were excluded from the table in previous editions of *Regional Trends*.

Source: National Travel Survey, Department of the Environment, Transport and the Regions

10.12 Activity at major airports[1], 1996

Thousands and thousand tonnes

		Air passengers (thousands)[2]			Freight handled[3] (thousand tonnes)
		International			
	Domestic[3]	Scheduled	Non-scheduled	Total	
All UK airports[4]	30,553	74,766	30,673	135,998	1,783
Newcastle	813	414	1,206	2,433	1
Manchester	2,450	4,272	7,762	14,485	79
Leeds/Bradford	421	259	369	1,053	-
East Midlands	385	282	1,155	1,822	105
Birmingham	966	2,308	2,079	5,353	19
Luton	452	752	1,207	2,411	19
Stanstead	1,055	2,563	1,193	4,810	105
Heathrow	7,457	48,177	98	55,732	1,040
Gatwick	2,073	12,206	9,823	24,102	267
Bristol	274	277	844	1,394	-
Cardiff	93	167	750	1,010	1
Aberdeen	1,620	256	501	2,377	6
Edinburgh	2,992	538	279	3,810	7
Glasgow	3,040	699	1,734	5,472	12
Belfast City	1,348	10	3	1,361	1
Belfast International	1,675	76	600	2,351	27

1 Airports handling one million passengers or more in 1996.
2 Arrivals and departures.
3 Domestic traffic is counted at airports on arrival and departure.
4 Including airports handling fewer than one million passengers.

Source: Civil Aviation Authority

10.13 Activity at major seaports[1], 1996

Millions and million tonnes

	International sea passenger movements (millions)	Freight handled[3] (million tonnes)
All UK ports	34.8	551.2
All East coast ports	3.1	265.1
Sullom Voe	0.0	38.2
Forth	0.0	44.6
Tees and Hartlepool	0.0	44.6
Hull	1.0	9.7
Grimsby and Immingham	0.0	46.8
Harwich	1.7	3.5
All Thames and Kent ports	22.4	84.9
London	0.0	52.9
Ramsgate	2.7	3.7
Dover	18.8	13.2
All South coast ports	5.4	49.3
Portsmouth	3.0	4.4
Southampton	0.6	34.2
All West coast ports	3.9	131.6
Milford Haven	0.3	36.6
Holyhead	2.5	2.5
Liverpool	0.0	30.9
All Northern Ireland ports	0.0	20.3

1 Individual ports handling one million passengers or more in 1996 and/ or 25 million tonnes of freight.

Source: Department of the Environment, Transport and the Regions

11 Environment

Rainfall

In the 12 months to September 1997, the Northumbrian region was the only area to match its long-term average rainfall over both the winter and summer, while the Thames and Southern regions had the driest year overall compared with their long-term averages.

(Table 11.1)

Water consumption

Water consumption among unmetered households in 1996-97 ranged from 160 litres per head per day in the Southern Water and Sewage Company region to 132 in the Yorkshire region; among metered householders the range was from 151 in the Thames region to 109 in the North West.

(Table 11.2)

Water abstractions

The south and east of England relies more heavily on the abstraction of groundwaters for public water supply than the north and west of the country and Wales.

(Table 11.3)

Water pollution

Northern Ireland, Wales, the South West, Scotland and Southern region have the cleanest rivers and canals in terms of biological quality; in terms of chemical quality, Scotland and Wales have the cleanest rivers and canals.

(Table 11.4)

In 1997, all bathing waters in the Anglian and Thames coastal regions met the EU standards for cleanliness, but only half those in the North West region did so.

(Table 11.6)

Air pollution

Black smoke and sulphur dioxide concentrations have fallen considerably in most parts of the United Kingdom since the mid-1970s, but there are still significant local variations.

(Table 11.7)

The highest concentrations of ground-level ozone pollution tend to be across the South East (GOR) and the South West.

(Map 11.8)

Recycling

On average, households in the South West followed by those in the South East (SSR) provided the most waste for recycling in 1996-97 while those in the North and the North West (SSR) provided the least.

(Table 11.11)

Land

The South West has the highest projected rate of urban growth between 1991 and 2016 at 18 per cent, followed by the East Midlands and the Eastern region at around 15 per cent.

(Map 11.13)

Almost a third of the South East and South West regions are Areas of Outstanding Natural Beauty.

(Table 11.15)

Woodlands

Scotland, Wales, the South East and the North East have the highest woodland density.

(Map 11.16)

Introduction

P ublic awareness and interest in environmental issues remains high. In 1996, the Department of the Environment, Transport and the Regions' survey of public attitudes to the environment found that 88 per cent of adults in England and Wales were concerned about the environment.

Water resources, water use, water quality and the health of the aquatic environment are all affected by climatic conditions which vary from region to region and from year to year. Table 11.1 shows the winter and summer half year rainfall for the last three years. The very erratic rainfall patterns and well above average temperatures in recent years have resulted in large and protracted departures from seasonally normal river flows, groundwater levels and reservoir stocks. One consequence has been a greater emphasis on conserving water resources by promoting the efficient use of water.

Table 11.2 looks at estimated water consumption per head for households served by the ten water and sewerage companies of England and Wales and the average for the three Scottish Water Authorities. Among households with a meter, average consumption in 1996/97 was 11 per cent less than for unmetered households. The effect of metering is to increase the awareness of water usage and to offer incentives to customers to reduce bills by reducing demand. A significant number of metered households are customers who have opted for a meter because they expect to pay less for the volume of water they consume than they would otherwise pay on a rateable value basis. A number of companies have also introduced policies to compulsorily meter customers who use high amounts of water for non-domestic purposes, such as garden watering.

Water quality can be adversely affected by periods of low rainfall which lead to reduced river flows and more concentrated levels of pollution. Since 1990 the chemical quality of our rivers and canals has been monitored through a system called the General Quality Assessment Scheme. Between 1990 and 1996, there was an estimated net upgrading of almost 28 per cent in the overall water quality of the total length of rivers and canals in England and Wales. Table 11.4 examines the chemical and biological quality of rivers and canals.

As with water pollution, the effects of air pollutants have been a cause for concern for many years. For example, ground level ozone can damage crops and be detrimental to human health. Ozone occurs naturally but can increase through the reactions of sunlight on other pollutants (Map 11.8). Environmental damage can also be caused through the emission of gases such as sulphur dioxide and nitrogen dioxides from industrial manufacturing, which are a contributing factor towards 'acid rain'.

Waste disposal is another major environmental issue. Alternative methods of dealing with waste, for example through recycling materials, are becoming more popular. Table 11.11 shows the amount of materials recycled per household per year. Recycling constitutes only 7 per cent of all disposal of municipal solid waste; the majority is still disposed of through landfill sites.

National Parks, Areas of Outstanding Natural Beauty in England and Wales and Northern Ireland, Defined Heritage Coasts in England and Wales and National Scenic Areas in Scotland are the major areas designated by legislation to protect their landscape importance. Green Belts have been designated in England, Scotland and Northern Ireland to restrict the sprawl of built-up areas onto previously undeveloped land and to preserve the character of historic towns. The location of these and other protected areas are shown on Map 11.14. Table 11.15 also looks at these areas; altogether about 50 per cent of the land area of the United Kingdom is designated or protected by legislation. Other areas, such as National Nature Reserves, Special Protection Areas and Marine Nature Reserves, are protected for their value as wildlife habitats, in particular for endangered species.

11.1 Winter and summer half-year rainfall[1,2]

Percentages and millimetres

	Rainfall as a percentage of the 1961 - 1990 winter and summer rainfall averages						Rainfall average 1961 - 1990 (millimetres)	
	1994 - 1995		1995 - 1996		1996 - 1997			
	Winter	Summer	Winter	Summer	Winter	Summer	Winter	Summer
United Kingdom	132	73	86	76	102	98	609	471
North West	141	58	62	75	99	89	669	534
Northumbrian	127	69	92	73	100	100	456	397
Severn Trent	133	62	85	70	85	111	397	357
Yorkshire	132	60	72	72	93	103	441	380
Anglian	125	69	77	63	84	106	298	298
Thames	138	68	95	63	78	93	362	327
Southern	144	71	83	71	82	92	444	335
Wessex	147	78	110	81	88	110	477	361
South West	135	71	99	86	86	111	718	456
England	136	65	84	70	89	100	444	379
Wales[3]	137	64	83	83	90	101	796	560
Scotland	130	85	84	77	117	94	836	601
Northern Ireland	116	64	111	102	95	103	597	462

1 Winter rainfall is the October - March accumulation; summer rainfall is the April - September accumulation.
2 The regions of England shown in this table correspond to the original nine regions of the National Rivers Authority; the NRA became part of the Environment Agency upon its creation in April 1996. See Notes and Definitions.
3 The figures in this table relate to the country of Wales; in Tables 11.3-11.6 they relate to the Environment Agency Welsh Region.

Source: Meteorological Office; Institute of Hydrology

11.2 Estimated household water consumption

Litres per head per day

	Unmetered households[1]			Metered households		
	1994-95	1995-96	1996-97	1994-95	1995-96	1996-97
Water and sewage companies						
England and Wales[2]	145	154	149	130	134	132
North West	136	144	138	118	116	109
Northumbrian	139	149	144	115	130	122
Yorkshire	132	137	132	122	124	118
Severn Trent	128	140	137	130	133	130
Anglian	146	155	157	122	128	128
Thames	155	159	159	145	148	151
Southern	155	164	160	130	134	130
Wessex	144	150	145	138	120	124
South West	148	163	153	117	136	138
Welsh	142	150	146	117	127	136
Scotland[3]	152	153	154	..	..	..

1 Excluding underground supply pipe leakage.
2 Figures for England and Wales are industry averages; these include both the ten major water and sewerage companies and 18 smaller water companies.
3 Figures given are estimates taken from the forecast provided in the publication *Public Water Supply in Scotland an Assessment of Demands and Resources at 1994* produced by The Scottish Office Agriculture, Environment and Fisheries Department. They cover the North of Scotland, the East of Scotland and the West of Scotland Water Authorities.

Source: OFWAT; The Scottish Office Water Services Unit

11.3 Estimated abstractions from groundwaters: by purpose, 1996

Megalitres per day

	Public water supply	Spray irrigation	Agriculture (excluding spraying)	Electricity supply	Other industry	Mineral washing	Fish farming	Private water supply	Other	Total
Environment Agency Regions[1]										
North East	441	40	13	0	135	0	4	19	61	715
North West	262	2	5	0	94	27	3	0	1	392
Midlands	1,024	34	6	9	93	45	3	4	1	1,219
Anglian	735	68	16	0	149	69	2	31	2	1,072
Thames	1,378	8	6	0	128	48	35	22	0	1,625
Southern	1,056	10	9	0	137	18	190	3	0	1,422
South West	407	3	36	2	29	2	94	7	48	628
England	5,303	163	92	10	766	209	331	86	113	7,072
Wales[1]	113	2	6	3	28	0	2	1	0	155

1 The boundaries of the Environment Agency Regions are based on river catchment areas and not county borders. In particular, the figures shown for Wales are for the Environment Agency Welsh Region, the boundary of which does not coincide with the boundary of Wales. See map on page 214 and Notes and Definitions.

Source: Environment Agency

11.4 Rivers and canals: by biological[1] and chemical quality[2]

Percentages and kilometres

	Biological quality (percentages)				Total length surveyed (=100%) (kms) 1990	Total length surveyed (=100%) (kms) 1995	Chemical quality (percentages)				Total length surveyed (=100%) (kms) 1988-90	Total length surveyed (=100%) (kms) 1994-96
	1990[4]		1995				1988-90[5]		1994-96			
	Good/ Fair	Poor/ Bad	Good/ Fair	Poor/ Bad			Good/ Fair	Poor/ Bad	Good/ Fair	Poor/ Bad		
Environment Agency Regions3												
North East	83	17	86	14	4,130	5,460	82	18	86	14	4,240	6,410
North West	63	37	78	22	4,020	4,970	73	27	84	16	3,190	5,750
Midlands	82	18	92	8	3,810	5,840	80	20	89	11	5,700	6,720
Anglian	93	7	97	3	4,170	4,730	81	19	87	13	4,560	4,810
Thames	89	11	95	5	3,090	3,570	83	17	91	9	3,530	3,800
Southern	97	3	98	2	1,420	2,190	88	12	90	10	2,180	2,220
South West	96	4	99	1	5,550	5,940	94	6	96	4	6,720	6,070
England	86	14	92	8	26,190	32,690	84	16	89	11	30,130	35,760
Wales	97	3	99	1	3,810	4,860	96	4	98	2	4,020	5,040
Scotland	97	3	98	2	10,870	16,710	99	1	99	1	50,960	50,260
Northern Ireland	100	-	100	-	2,190	2,330	95	5	88	12	1,680	2,360

1 Classification based on the River Invertebrate Prediction and Classification System (RIVPACS). See Notes and Definitions.
2 Based on the chemical quality grade of the General Quality Assessment (GQA) scheme. See Notes and Definitions.
3 In England and Wales. The boundaries of the Environment Agency Regions are based on river catchment areas and not county borders. In particular, the figures shown for Wales are for the Environment Agency Welsh Region, the boundary of which does not coincide with the boundary of Wales. See map on page 214 and Notes and Definitions.
4 In Northern Ireland, 1991 survey.
5 In Northern Ireland, 1989-91 survey.

Source: Environment Agency; Department of the Environment, Northern Ireland

11.5 Water pollution incidents: by type, 1996[1]

Numbers

	Industrial		Sewage and water related[3]		Agricultural		Other		Total		Number of prose-cutions[4]
	All	Major[2]	All	Major[2]	All	Major[2]	All	Major[2]	All	Major[2]	
Environment Agency Regions[5]											
United Kingdom	5,239	122	5,970	46	2,991	123	10,891	183	25,091	474	270
North West	648	6	801	4	275	8	1,094	9	2,818	27	25
North East	424	8	722	5	166	0	831	5	2,143	18	14
Midlands	833	6	1,219	4	410	7	1,843	8	4,305	25	41
Anglian	405	4	461	6	200	2	1,351	19	2,417	31	19
Thames	372	3	471	1	93	1	1,023	4	1,959	9	16
Southern	212	4	298	7	95	2	584	2	1,189	15	4
South West	504	5	889	1	583	6	1,066	6	3,042	18	16
England	3,398	36	4,861	28	1,822	26	7,792	53	17,873	143	135
Wales[5]	627	6	738	3	289	2	631	2	2,285	13	4
Scotland	689	62	..	..	378	58	1,811	123	2,878	243	14
Northern Ireland	525	18	371	15	502	37	657	5	2,055	75	117

1 Data relate to substantiated reports of pollution only. Figures for Scotland relate to the financial year 1995-96.
2 Major incidents are those corresponding to Category 1 in the Environment Agency's pollution incidents classification scheme. For Scotland the term 'significant incidents' is used. See Notes and Definitions.
3 Not summarised separately for Scotland - included in other sectors.
4 For England and Wales, total prosecutions include cases concluded and prosecutions outstanding. Prosecutions concluded relate to cases which had been brought to court by 31 March 1997. In Scotland, this figure relates to legal proceedings resolved for 1996-97.
5 In England and Wales. The boundaries of the Environment Agency Regions are based on river catchment areas and not county borders. In particular, the figures shown for Wales are for the Environment Agency Welsh Region, the boundary of which does not coincide with the boundary of Wales. See map on page 214 and Notes and Definitions.
Source: Environment Agency; Scottish Environment Protection Agency; Department for the Environment, Northern Ireland

11.6 Bathing water – compliance with EC Bathing Water Directive[1] coliform standards[2]: by coastal region

Numbers and percentages

	Identified bathing waters (numbers)					Percentage complying during the bathing season[3]				
	1993	1994	1995	1996	1997	1993	1994	1995	1996	1997
Environment Agency Regions[4]										
United Kingdom	457	457	464	472	486	*80*	*82*	*89*	*90*	*88*
Northumbria & Yorkshire	56	56	56	56	56	*82*	*88*	*95*	*88*	*91*
North West	33	33	33	33	34	*39*	*73*	*45*	*61*	*50*
Anglian	33	33	34	35	35	*85*	*82*	*88*	*97*	*100*
Thames	3	3	3	3	3	*100*	*67*	*100*	*67*	*100*
Southern	67	67	67	69	75	*87*	*79*	*93*	*90*	*89*
South Western	175	175	176	180	180	*81*	*86*	*95*	*93*	*91*
England	367	367	369	376	383	*79*	*83*	*89*	*89*	*88*
Wales[4]	51	51	56	57	64	*82*	*76*	*88*	*91*	*94*
Scotland	23	23	23	23	23	*78*	*70*	*83*	*91*	*78*
Northern Ireland	16	16	16	16	16	*94*	*94*	*94*	*100*	*88*

1 76/160/EEC.
2 At least 95 per cent of samples must have counts not exceeding the mandatory limit values for total faecal coliforms.
3 The bathing season is from mid-May to end-September in England and Wales, but is shorter in Scotland and Northern Ireland.
4 In England and Wales. The boundaries of the Environment Agency Regions are based on river catchment areas and not county borders. In particular, the figures shown for Wales are for the Environment Agency Welsh Region, the boundary of which does not coincide with the boundary of Wales. See map on page 214 and Notes and Definitions.
Source: Environment Agency; Scottish Environment Protection Agency; Department of the Environment, Northern Ireland

11.7 Atmospheric pollution[1,2]

Micrograms per cubic metre and percentages

	Black smoke				Sulphur dioxide			
	Micrograms per cubic metre[3]			Percentage change 1976-77 to 1996-97	Micrograms per cubic metre			Percentage change 1976-77 to 1996-97
	1976-77	1986-87	1996-97		1976-77	1986-87	1996-97	
Newcastle	173	59	52	-70	252	111	73	-71
Manchester	296	81	55	-81	385	101	42	-89
Barnsley	367	158	74	-80	341	165	173	-49
Mansfield Woodhouse	275	139	66	-76	263	163	106	-60
Stoke-on-Trent	452	120	46	-90	334	147	91	-73
Norwich	121	53	45	-63	129	52	27	-79
Stepney	164	27	58	-65	328	186	77	-77
Slough	102	60	49	-52	171	84	30	-82
Gloucester	131	68	38	-71	248	94	38	-85
Cardiff	292	52	21	-93	190	62	49	-74
Glasgow	281	124	46	-84	345	147	54	-84
Belfast	629	195	68	-89	225	345	152	-32

1 One site chosen for each UK Statistical Region.
2 Figures shown are for 98th percentile daily mean concentration ie the level which is exceeded by the highest 2 per cent of daily mean concentrations during the year.
3 Measured in OECD units; measurements in British Standard units are equivalent to 0.85 x OECD units.

Source: National Environmental Technology Centre

11.8 Ground level ozone levels[1], 1990-1996

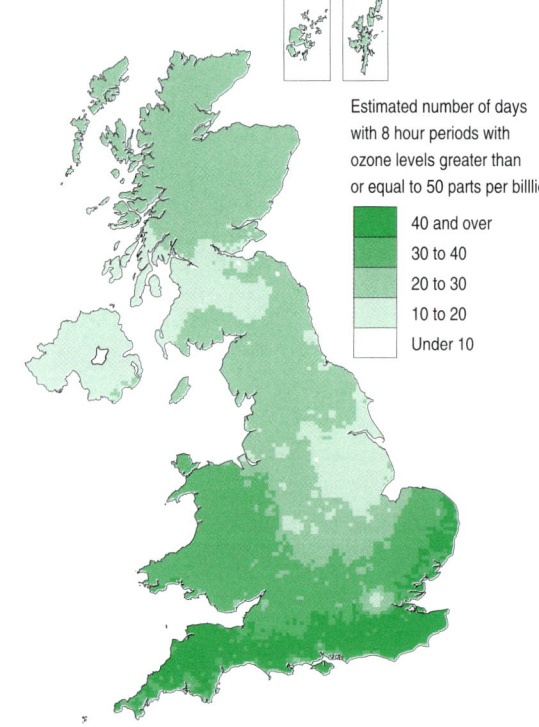

Estimated number of days with 8 hour periods with ozone levels greater than or equal to 50 parts per billlion

- 40 and over
- 30 to 40
- 20 to 30
- 10 to 20
- Under 10

1 See Notes and Definitions

Source: National Environmental Technology Centre

11.9 Outdoor gamma ray dose rates[1]

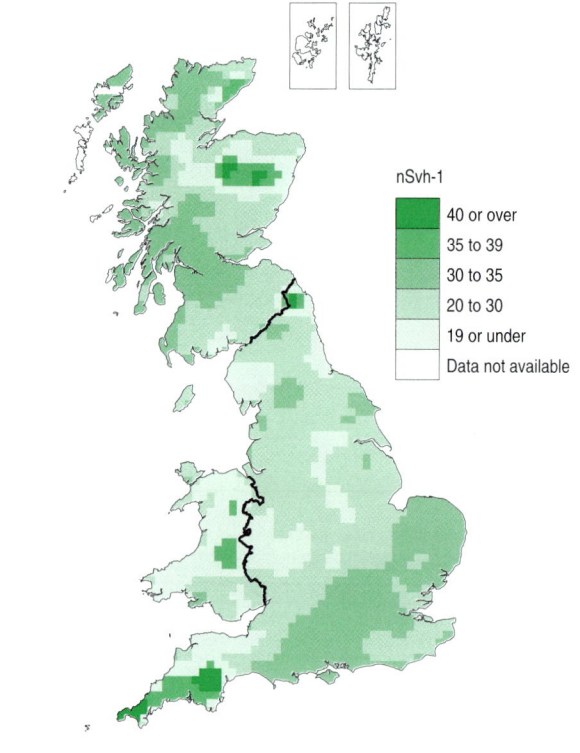

nSvh-1

- 40 or over
- 35 to 39
- 30 to 35
- 20 to 30
- 19 or under
- Data not available

1 See Notes and Definitions

Source: National Radiological Protection Board

11.10   Household waste, 1996-97[1]

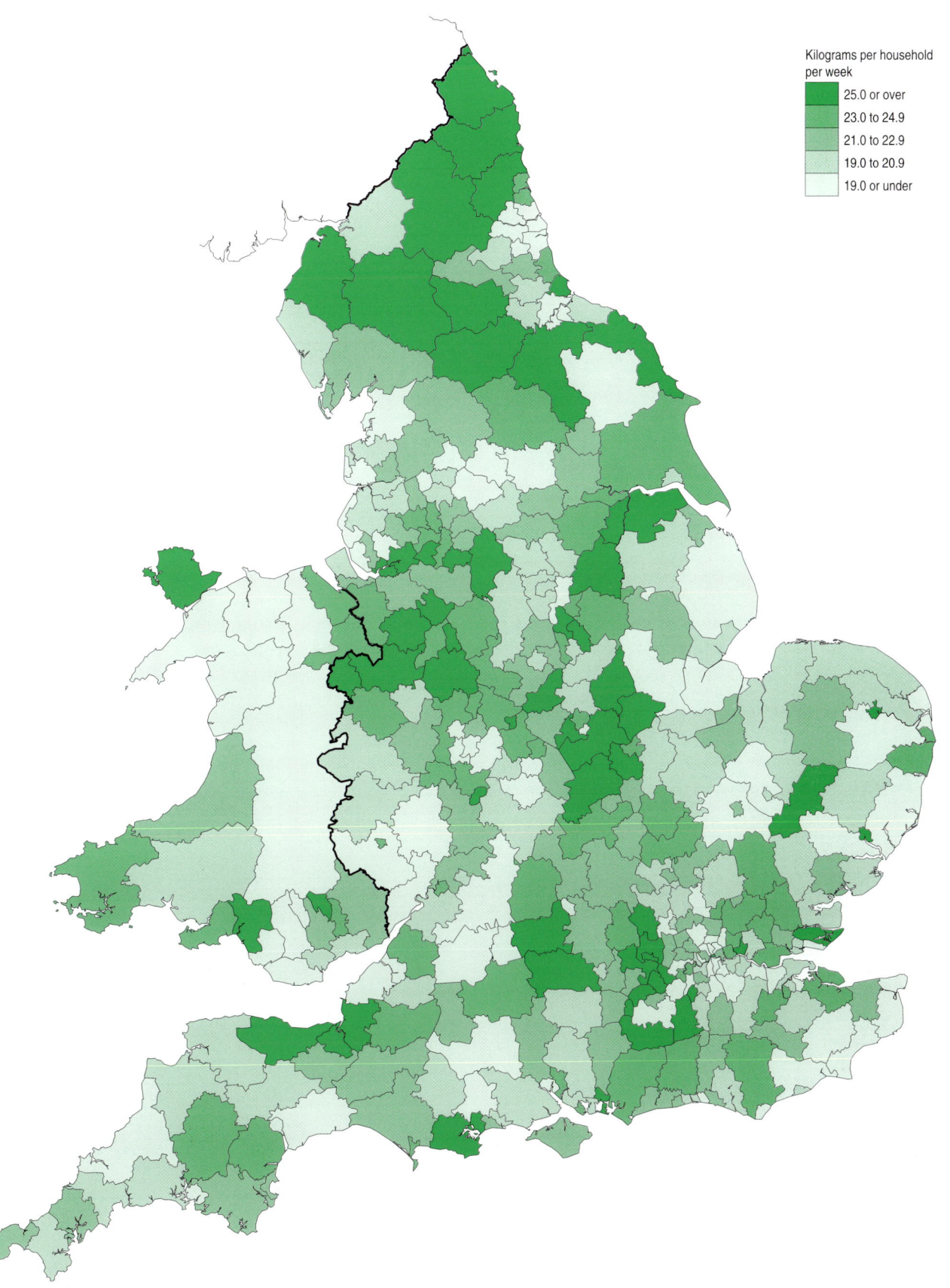

Kilograms per household per week

- 25.0 or over
- 23.0 to 24.9
- 21.0 to 22.9
- 19.0 to 20.9
- 19.0 or under

1 By local authority. See Notes and Definitions.

Source: Department of the Environment, Transport and the Regions; Welsh Office

11.11 Recycling of household waste[1], 1996-97

Kilogrammes per household per year

	Glass	Total paper and card	Total cans	Plastics	Textiles	Scrap metal/ white goods	Compost	Comingled collections	Other materials	Total
Standard Statistical Regions										
England and Wales	14.4	25.6	0.9	0.3	1.1	2.8	4.9	2.7	1.2	53.9
North	9.7	12.2	0.5	0.1	0.7	2.1	8.2	-	0.2	33.8
North West (SSR)	9.4	19.0	0.4	0.2	0.8	1.1	2.7	0.4	1.0	35.0
Yorkshire and Humberside	11.6	16.4	0.6	0.1	0.9	3.2	4.7	1.9	0.3	39.7
East Midlands	11.8	21.6	0.5	0.2	0.9	2.0	3.1	2.3	2.7	44.9
West Midlands	14.4	19.5	1.2	-	0.8	2.7	2.0	-	0.2	40.8
East Anglia	16.7	21.8	0.8	0.1	1.1	2.2	13.6	1.0	2.8	59.9
South East (SSR)	17.0	34.1	1.0	0.3	1.2	3.2	3.4	5.5	0.7	66.4
South West	18.7	30.3	1.5	0.7	1.4	3.0	10.6	2.2	2.4	70.7
Wales	11.2	22.1	0.6	0.1	1.5	7.7	4.4	-	0.2	47.8

1 Materials recycled by local authorities through civic amenity and bring/drop-off sites and kerbside collection schemes for household wastes.

Source: Department of the Environment, Transport and the Regions; Welsh Office

11.12 Previous use of land changing to urban use in 1992[1]

Hectares and percentages

	Land changing to urban uses		Percentage previously in rural use
	Total hectares	Hectares per 100,000 population[2]	
North East	865	33	*34*
North West (GOR) &			
Merseyside	1,970	29	*29*
North West (GOR)	1,585	29	*31*
Merseyside	385	27	*22*
Yorkshire and the Humber	1,590	32	*36*
East Midlands	1,430	35	*62*
West Midlands	1,400	26	*46*
Eastern	1,605	31	*46*
London	690	10	*9*
South East (GOR)	2,245	29	*47*
South West	1,200	25	*54*
England	12,995	27	*42*

1 The information relates only to map changes recorded by the Ordnance Survey between 1992 and 1996 for which the year of change is judged to be 1992. See Notes and Definitions.
2 Based on mid-1992 population estimates.

Source: Department of the Environment, Transport and the Regions

11.13 Projections of urban growth[1,2], 1991-2016

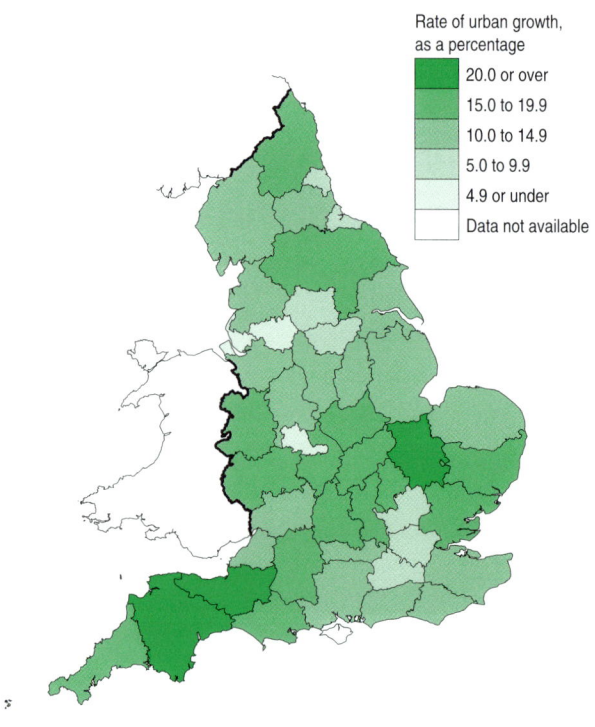

Rate of urban growth, as a percentage
- 20.0 or over
- 15.0 to 19.9
- 10.0 to 14.9
- 5.0 to 9.9
- 4.9 or under
- Data not available

1 Urban growth is the area projected to change net from rural uses to urban uses.
2 The area projected to change net from rural uses to urban uses expressed as a percentage of the area of land in urban uses, 1991.

Source: Department of the Environment, Transport and the Regions

11.14   Protected areas¹, as at 31 March 1997

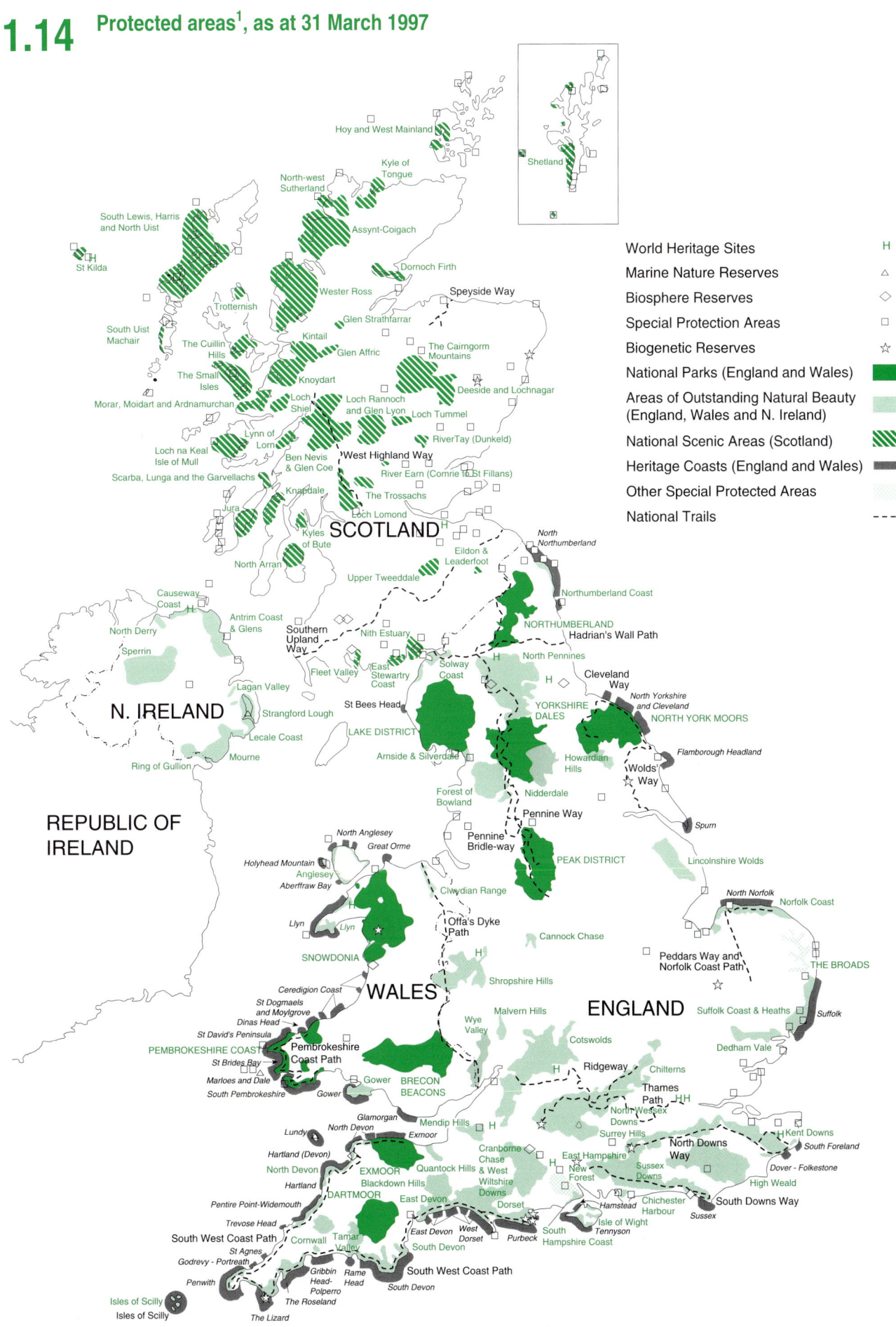

World Heritage Sites — H
Marine Nature Reserves — △
Biosphere Reserves — ◇
Special Protection Areas — ☐
Biogenetic Reserves — ☆
National Parks (England and Wales)
Areas of Outstanding Natural Beauty (England, Wales and N. Ireland)
National Scenic Areas (Scotland)
Heritage Coasts (England and Wales)
Other Special Protected Areas
National Trails — - - -

1. See Notes and Definitions.

Source: Countryside Commission; English Nature; Department of Culture, Media and Sport; Institute of Terrestial Ecology; Department of the Environment, Transport and the Regions; Countryside Council for Wales; Scottish Natural Heritage; Department of the Environment, Northern Ireland

11.15 Designated areas[1], 1997[2]

	National Parks		Areas of Outstanding Natural Beauty[3]		Green Belt land		Designated Heritage Coasts length (km)
	Area (sq km)	Percentage of total area in region	Area (sq km)	Percentage of total area in region	Area (sq km)	Percentage of total area in region	
North East	1,112	13	1,465	17	476	5	122
North West (GOR) & Merseyside	2,607	18	1,570	11	2,435	17	6
North West (GOR)	2,607	18	1,570	12	2,130	16	6
Merseyside	0	0	0	0	305	47	0
Yorkshire and the Humber	3,146	21	921	6	2,495	16	82
East Midlands	917	6	519	3	797	4	0
West Midlands	202	2	1,269	10	2,650	19	.
Eastern	303	2	1,122	6	2,312	1	121
London	0	0	..	..	451	29	.
South East (GOR)	0	0	6,406	31	3,613	19	72
South West	1,647	7	7,121	30	1,105	9	638
England	9,934	8	20,393	16	16,334	12	1,041
Wales	4,077	20	844	4	.	.	496
Scotland	.	.	10,020	13	1,550	2	.
Northern Ireland	.	.	2,850	20	2,266	16	.

1 See Notes and Definitions. Some areas may be in more than one category.
2 At 1 April 1998, except for Green Belt land which relates to 1 April 1997.
3 National Scenic Areas in Scotland. The South East includes London.

Source: Department of the Environment, Transport and the Regions

11.16 Proportion of land covered by trees, 1995[1]

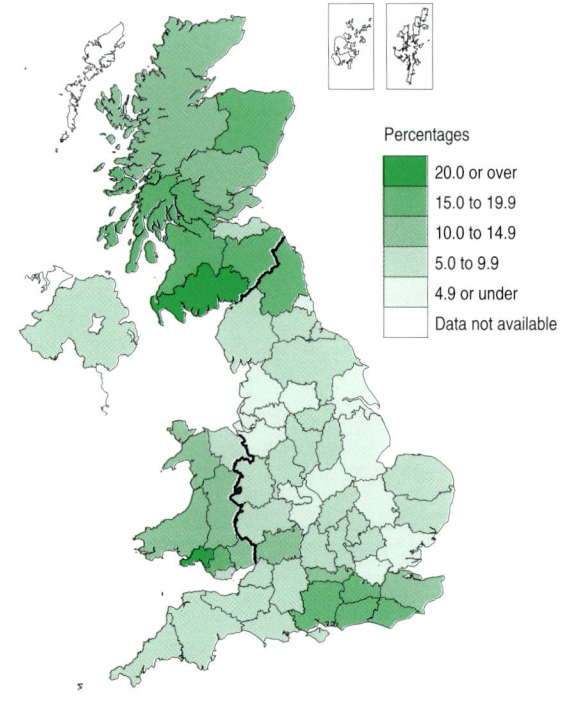

Percentages

- 20.0 or over
- 15.0 to 19.9
- 10.0 to 14.9
- 5.0 to 9.9
- 4.9 or under
- Data not available

1 Within Great Britain, figures are estimates projected from the 1980 Census of Woodland. For Northern Ireland, figure relates to 1992.
Source: The Forestry Commission; Department of the Environment, Northern Ireland

12 Regional accounts

Gross domestic product

London and the South East (GOR) together account for nearly a third of UK GDP.

(Table 12.1)

Only in London was GDP per head over £13,000 in 1996; it was lowest in Northern Ireland and Wales, at £8,700 and £8,900 respectively.

(Table 12.1)

GDP per head relative to the UK average has shown a general increase in the South East (GOR), Scotland and Northern Ireland since the late 1980s, while the North West (GOR) and Merseyside, the Yorkshire and Humber region, the East Midlands and Wales have all seen declines.

(Chart 12.2)

Income from employment was the source of 67 per cent of GDP in London and 65 per cent in the West Midlands and the Eastern region in 1996 compared with 60 per cent in the South West and 61 per cent in the East Midlands and Wales.

(Table 12.3)

Thirty per cent of GDP in the North and the West Midlands was derived from manufacturing compared with 12 per cent in London, the highest and lowest proportions.

(Table 12.4)

More than two fifths of London's GDP in 1996 was generated by financial and business services compared with less than a fifth in the North, Wales, Scotland and Northern Ireland.

(Table 12.4)

Household income/ disposable income

Households in Northern Ireland, Wales and the North East benefited most from the redistributive effects of the tax and benefit system in 1996, whilst those in London and the South East (GOR) contributed the most.

(Table 12.6)

Personal income/ disposable income

Personal income per head in 1996 was around 15 per cent below the UK average in Wales, Northern Ireland and the North East, while in London it was more than 27 per cent above the UK average.

(Table 12.7)

Personal disposable income per head in 1996 was highest in London, at around £11,500, followed by the South East (GOR) and the Eastern region, at £9,900, and lowest in Wales and the North East, at just under £7,900.

(Table 12.7)

Consumers' expenditure

The South East (GOR) had the highest consumers' expenditure per head in 1996, at nearly £9,400 per person in 1996, while Wales and Northern Ireland had the lowest, at around £7,400.

(Table 12.8)

Regional Trends 33, © Crown copyright 1998

Introduction

The regional accounts provide a breakdown of the main components of the national accounts into sub-national areas. The national accounts are published each year in the *ONS' Blue Book – United Kingdom National Accounts*. This chapter covers estimates for regions; county estimates of GDP and household income can be found in the sub-regional chapter for England. Estimates for Government Office Regions (GOR) are presented where possible throughout the chapter. Figures for GDP by industry groups and gross domestic fixed capital formation have not been calculated on this basis because they require data which is not yet available on the GOR classification. A detailed analysis of the figures can be found in a series of articles in the ONS' publication *Economic Trends* (most recently January and June 1998 editions).

Wales, Scotland, Northern Ireland and the regions of England differ in size, character, industrial structure and economic performance. The South East (GOR) has the largest population – nearly 8 million – and the largest GDP at nearly £97 billion in 1996. At the other extreme, Northern Ireland with a population of 1.7 million has a GDP of almost £14.5 billion. The wide variation in the size of the regions makes it difficult to compare the regions' economic performance using cash totals; comparisons are therefore usually made in terms of amounts per head of population. However, it is important to note that the growth in totals can differ from growth per head where the population has increased or decreased. Furthermore the level per head is determined both by the working population's incomes and by the proportion who do not work. In Northern Ireland, for example, households have a high proportion of children: a quarter of the population was aged under 16 in 1996 compared with about a fifth in most regions. This depresses income and expenditure per head in Northern Ireland relative to other regions. Ideally the age structure of the population should be taken into account when comparing figures on a per head basis.

UK GDP is defined as the sum of all incomes earned from productive activity in the United Kingdom. Regional GDP should thus be defined as the sum of incomes earned from productive activity in the region, so that the income of commuters should be included in the region where they work. However the estimates of regional GDP presented here are not compiled on this basis; they include regional estimates of income from employment on a residence basis, because this is the basis of the more reliable data source (the 1 per cent sample of Department of Social Security records). This has a significant effect on the estimates for London, for the South East (GOR) and for the Eastern region, but is assumed not to introduce any significant distortion for the other regions.

Estimates of GDP by region are at factor cost. They measure the income of factors of production and exclude taxes on expenditure such as VAT, but include subsidies. Regional accounts are only available in current prices which means that increases over time reflect inflation as well as real growth. Trends in totals per head cannot be analysed easily without deflating the data. However, there are no sub-national price indices, which could be used to remove the effect of inflation from the figures. Comparisons of trends can only therefore be based on either the difference between regional increases at current prices or on movements in levels relative to the UK average. Both approaches would be misleading if the rate of inflation in any region were different from the national average.

The regional accounts, although calculated as reliably as possible, cannot be regarded as accurate to the last digit shown. The are based partly on sample surveys and the quality of the results therefore varies according to sample size. This means that results for areas with smaller populations such as the Isle of Wight are likely to be less precise than those for more populous areas. An assessment of the quality of the regional and county estimates was published in *Economic Trends*, November 1990.

12.1 Gross domestic product[1]: current prices

	1986	1987	1988	1989	1990	1991	1992	1993	1994	1995	1996
£ million											
United Kingdom	328,272	360,675	401,428	441,759	478,886	496,253	518,132	547,870	580,135	608,090	642,916
North East	12,559	13,719	15,144	16,778	17,966	18,815	19,883	20,801	21,710	22,621	23,473
North West (GOR) &											
Merseyside	36,797	40,020	44,652	48,306	51,668	53,154	55,285	58,383	61,771	64,012	67,086
Yorkshire and the Humber	26,163	28,277	31,159	34,454	37,159	38,689	40,014	41,858	44,021	46,775	48,266
East Midlands	21,666	23,875	26,564	29,752	31,918	33,386	34,808	36,658	38,757	40,377	41,811
West Midlands	26,710	29,360	33,240	36,734	40,254	41,390	43,466	45,571	48,269	50,766	53,245
Eastern	30,966	33,880	38,477	42,829	46,198	47,616	49,803	52,011	55,334	57,695	61,684
London	47,111	52,143	58,187	64,182	69,737	72,479	75,778	81,454	84,686	87,517	93,450
South East (GOR)	45,798	50,641	58,233	64,185	70,017	72,412	74,888	79,682	85,360	89,217	96,821
South West	24,230	26,823	30,295	33,525	36,428	38,093	40,152	42,135	44,450	47,265	49,109
England	272,000	298,736	335,950	370,745	401,346	416,033	434,078	458,553	484,358	506,245	534,945
Wales	13,583	15,105	17,152	18,830	20,306	20,918	21,410	22,311	23,774	25,088	25,995
Scotland	27,263	29,785	32,975	36,253	40,231	42,231	44,589	46,840	49,720	52,518	54,430
Northern Ireland	6,999	7,536	8,369	9,232	10,166	11,098	11,660	12,434	13,091	13,890	14,470
United Kingdom *less* Continental											
Shelf and statistical discrepancy	319,845	351,162	394,447	435,060	472,048	490,281	511,738	540,138	570,943	597,741	629,841
Continental Shelf	8,426	9,511	6,981	6,698	6,839	5,971	6,394	7,731	9,191	10,348	13,670
Statistical discrepancy	-	-	-	-	-	-	-	-	-	-	-595
(income adjustment)											
As a percentage of											
United Kingdom *less* Continental											
Shelf and statistical discrepancy											
United Kingdom	100.0	100.0	100.0	100.0	100.0	100.0	100.0	100.0	100.0	100.0	100.0
North East	3.9	3.9	3.8	3.9	3.8	3.8	3.9	3.9	3.8	3.8	3.7
North West (GOR) &											
Merseyside	11.5	11.4	11.3	11.1	10.9	10.8	10.8	10.8	10.8	10.7	10.7
Yorkshire and the Humber	8.2	8.1	7.9	7.9	7.9	7.9	7.8	7.7	7.7	7.8	7.7
East Midlands	6.8	6.8	6.7	6.8	6.8	6.8	6.8	6.8	6.8	6.8	6.6
West Midlands	8.4	8.4	8.4	8.4	8.5	8.4	8.5	8.4	8.5	8.5	8.5
Eastern	9.7	9.6	9.8	9.8	9.8	9.7	9.7	9.6	9.7	9.7	9.8
London	14.7	14.8	14.8	14.8	14.8	14.8	14.8	15.1	14.8	14.6	14.8
South East (GOR)	14.3	14.4	14.8	14.8	14.8	14.8	14.6	14.8	15.0	14.9	15.4
South West	7.6	7.6	7.7	7.7	7.7	7.8	7.8	7.8	7.8	7.9	7.8
England	85.0	85.1	85.2	85.2	85.0	84.9	84.8	84.9	84.8	84.7	84.9
Wales	4.2	4.3	4.3	4.3	4.3	4.3	4.2	4.1	4.2	4.2	4.1
Scotland	8.5	8.5	8.4	8.3	8.5	8.6	8.7	8.7	8.7	8.8	8.6
Northern Ireland	2.2	2.1	2.1	2.1	2.2	2.3	2.3	2.3	2.3	2.3	2.3
£ per head											
United Kingdom *less* Continental											
Shelf and statistical discrepancy	5,626	6,160	6,901	7,585	8,201	8,481	8,822	9,282	9,777	10,199	10,711
North East	4,828	5,280	5,842	6,468	6,916	7,229	7,622	7,963	8,319	8,683	9,026
North West (GOR) &											
Merseyside	5,370	5,847	6,528	7,045	7,525	7,720	8,024	8,458	8,950	9,277	9,735
Yorkshire and the Humber	5,333	5,764	6,333	6,962	7,488	7,764	7,999	8,348	8,760	9,300	9,585
East Midlands	5,529	6,062	6,697	7,449	7,952	8,273	8,569	8,978	9,448	9,791	10,096
West Midlands	5,140	5,630	6,358	7,009	7,668	7,861	8,236	8,615	9,116	9,567	10,015
Eastern	6,179	6,714	7,577	8,412	9,035	9,246	9,623	10,015	10,594	10,974	11,655
London	6,925	7,667	8,594	9,440	10,177	10,520	10,975	11,749	12,154	12,490	13,210
South East (GOR)	6,112	6,722	7,678	8,437	9,162	9,430	9,711	10,299	10,966	11,369	12,263
South West	5,314	5,825	6,509	7,170	7,761	8,074	8,460	8,837	9,263	9,792	10,143
England	5,745	6,291	7,053	7,755	8,363	8,630	8,973	9,448	9,944	10,352	10,897
Wales	4,817	5,332	6,010	6,562	7,056	7,234	7,387	7,676	8,161	8,601	8,899
Scotland	5,324	5,826	6,473	7,113	7,885	8,269	8,724	9,148	9,688	10,224	10,614
Northern Ireland	4,467	4,784	5,303	5,832	6,396	6,930	7,205	7,620	7,974	8,423	8,700

1 See Notes and Definitions.

Source: Office for National Statistics

12.2 Gross domestic product per head

£ per head index, UK=100[1]

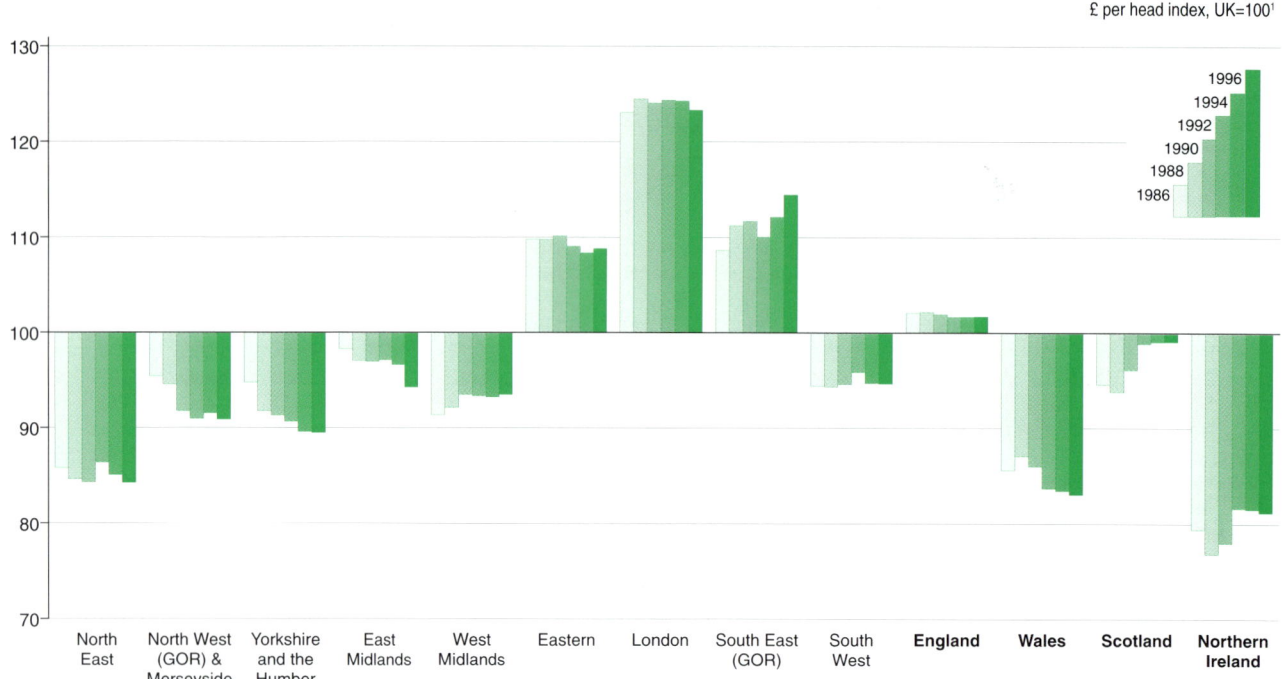

1 United Kingdom *less* Continental Shelf and statistical discrepancy.

Source: Office for National Statistics

12.3 Factor incomes in the gross domestic product[1]: current prices, 1996

£ million

	Income from employment	Income from self-employment and gross trading profits *less* stock appreciation	Rent[2]	Gross domestic product
United Kingdom	400,354	174,974	68,183	642,916
North East	15,036	6,043	2,394	23,473
North West (GOR) & Merseyside	42,015	17,996	7,076	67,086
Yorkshire and the Humber	30,206	12,969	5,092	48,266
East Midlands	25,693	11,767	4,351	41,811
West Midlands	34,483	13,658	5,105	53,245
Eastern	39,996	14,953	6,734	61,684
London	62,529	19,477	11,444	93,450
South East (GOR)	61,790	24,147	10,884	96,821
South West	29,440	13,623	6,045	49,109
England	341,188	134,631	59,126	534,945
Wales	15,895	7,579	2,521	25,995
Scotland	34,328	15,141	4,961	54,430
Northern Ireland	8,943	3,953	1,575	14,470
Continental Shelf	..	13,670	..	13,670
Statistical discrepancy (income adjustment)	..	..	..	-595

1 See Notes and Definitions.
2 Including imputed charges for consumption of non-trading capital.

Source: Office for National Statistics

12.4 Gross domestic product by industry groups[1,2]: current prices

£ million

Standard Statistical Regions	1991	1996	1991	1996	1991	1996	1991	1996
	North		North West (SSR)		Yorkshire and Humberside		East Midlands	
Agriculture, hunting, forestry and fishing	443	555	468	585	754	1,058	926	1,192
Mining, quarrying inc oil and gas extraction	551	358	132	99	904	492	1,030	258
Manufacturing	6,536	8,674	13,780	16,320	10,097	12,382	9,238	12,302
Electricity, gas, water	534	624	1,331	1,428	1,260	1,028	1,047	911
Construction	1,671	1,698	2,934	3,186	2,545	2,922	2,200	2,331
Distribution, hotels and catering; repairs	3,025	3,478	7,256	9,005	6,087	7,357	4,843	5,938
Transport, storage and communication	1,727	2,035	4,056	5,408	2,951	3,873	2,299	2,961
Financial & business services, etc[3]	4,164	5,272	10,105	13,982	6,982	10,284	6,286	8,595
Public administration and defence[4]	1,488	1,810	2,659	3,118	2,263	2,725	1,702	1,881
Education, social work and health services	2,920	4,019	5,970	8,523	4,788	6,346	3,651	5,164
Other services	782	1,024	1,710	2,171	1,289	1,673	968	1,274
Adjustment for financial services	-526	-633	-1,748	-2,180	-1,231	-1,875	-804	-995
Total	23,315	28,915	48,654	61,643	38,689	48,266	33,386	41,811

	1991	1996	1991	1996	1991	1996	1991	1996
	West Midlands		East Anglia		South East (SSR)		Greater London	
Agriculture, hunting, forestry and fishing	830	1,079	919	1,142	1,246	1,582	49	97
Mining, quarrying inc oil and gas extraction	363	193	106	145	439	648	177	185
Manufacturing	12,095	16,006	3,772	5,017	27,437	34,535	9,526	11,178
Electricity, gas, water	1,042	1,169	420	475	4,157	3,455	1,483	1,198
Construction	2,598	2,744	1,261	1,335	10,834	11,327	3,735	3,707
Distribution, hotels and catering; repairs	6,003	7,663	2,610	3,131	25,676	36,784	10,418	15,481
Transport, storage and communication	2,828	3,832	1,745	2,280	18,419	23,805	8,626	10,358
Financial & business services, etc[3]	8,455	11,491	3,775	5,045	57,050	79,366	27,903	38,476
Public administration and defence[4]	2,303	2,514	1,272	1,369	12,466	13,311	4,789	5,227
Education, social work and health services	4,807	6,610	1,929	2,934	18,901	27,146	7,909	10,909
Other services	1,316	1,768	646	844	7,595	10,516	3,748	5,319
Adjustment for financial services	-1,249	-1,823	-692	-825	-9,475	-13,413	-5,884	-8,685
Total	41,391	53,245	17,764	22,893	174,743	229,061	72,479	93,450

	1991	1996	1991	1996	1991	1996	1991	1996
	Rest of the South East		South West		England		Wales	
Agriculture, hunting, forestry and fishing	1,197	1,485	1,247	1,830	6,832	9,023	486	474
Mining, quarrying inc oil and gas extraction	263	463	381	672	3,908	2,865	225	224
Manufacturing	17,911	23,358	7,327	9,478	90,282	114,715	5,913	7,420
Electricity, gas, water	2,673	2,257	1,497	1,575	11,286	10,665	597	733
Construction	7,098	7,620	2,611	2,698	26,654	28,241	1,244	1,434
Distribution, hotels and catering; repairs	15,258	21,303	5,840	7,192	61,338	80,548	2,989	3,357
Transport, storage and communication	9,793	13,447	2,562	3,274	36,588	47,469	1,428	1,622
Financial & business services, etc[3]	29,147	40,889	8,652	12,411	105,469	146,445	3,400	4,528
Public administration and defence[4]	7,676	8,084	3,722	4,106	27,875	30,835	1,564	1,949
Education, social work and health services	10,992	16,237	4,515	6,304	47,481	67,046	2,859	4,025
Other services	3,847	5,197	1,326	1,777	15,633	21,047	693	912
Adjustment for financial services	-3,591	-4,728	-1,587	-2,210	-17,314	-23,953	-479	-682
Total	102,264	135,611	38,093	49,109	416,034	534,945	20,918	25,995

	1991	1996	1991	1996	1991	1996
	Scotland		Northern Ireland		United Kingdom[5]	
Agriculture, hunting, forestry and fishing	1,169	1,642	477	651	8,964	11,790
Mining, quarrying inc oil and gas extraction	1,048	1,220	51	88	5,232	4,398
Manufacturing	8,466	12,103	2,235	2,769	106,896	137,006
Electricity, gas, water	1,134	1,828	371	381	13,388	13,606
Construction	2,959	3,282	649	789	31,506	33,746
Distribution, hotels and catering; repairs	6,014	7,237	1,414	1,949	71,755	93,091
Transport, storage and communication	3,577	4,181	598	784	42,191	54,056
Financial & business services, etc[3]	8,291	10,780	1,653	2,530	118,813	164,282
Public administration and defence[4]	3,170	3,709	1,648	1,751	34,257	38,244
Education, social work and health services	6,217	8,250	1,814	2,555	58,371	81,876
Other services	1,629	2,160	432	594	18,387	24,713
Adjustment for financial services	-1,442	-1,962	-244	-370	-19,478	-26,968
Total	42,232	54,430	11,098	14,470	490,282	629,841

1 Gross domestic product is shown for each industry after deducting stock appreciation. See Notes and Definitions.
2 Based on SIC 1992.
3 Financial intermediation, real estate, renting, business activities, including rent on dwellings.
4 Public administration, national defence and compulsory social security.
5 The UK total excludes production from the Continental Shelf.

Source: Office for National Statistics

12.5 Gross domestic product per head: by county[1], 1995

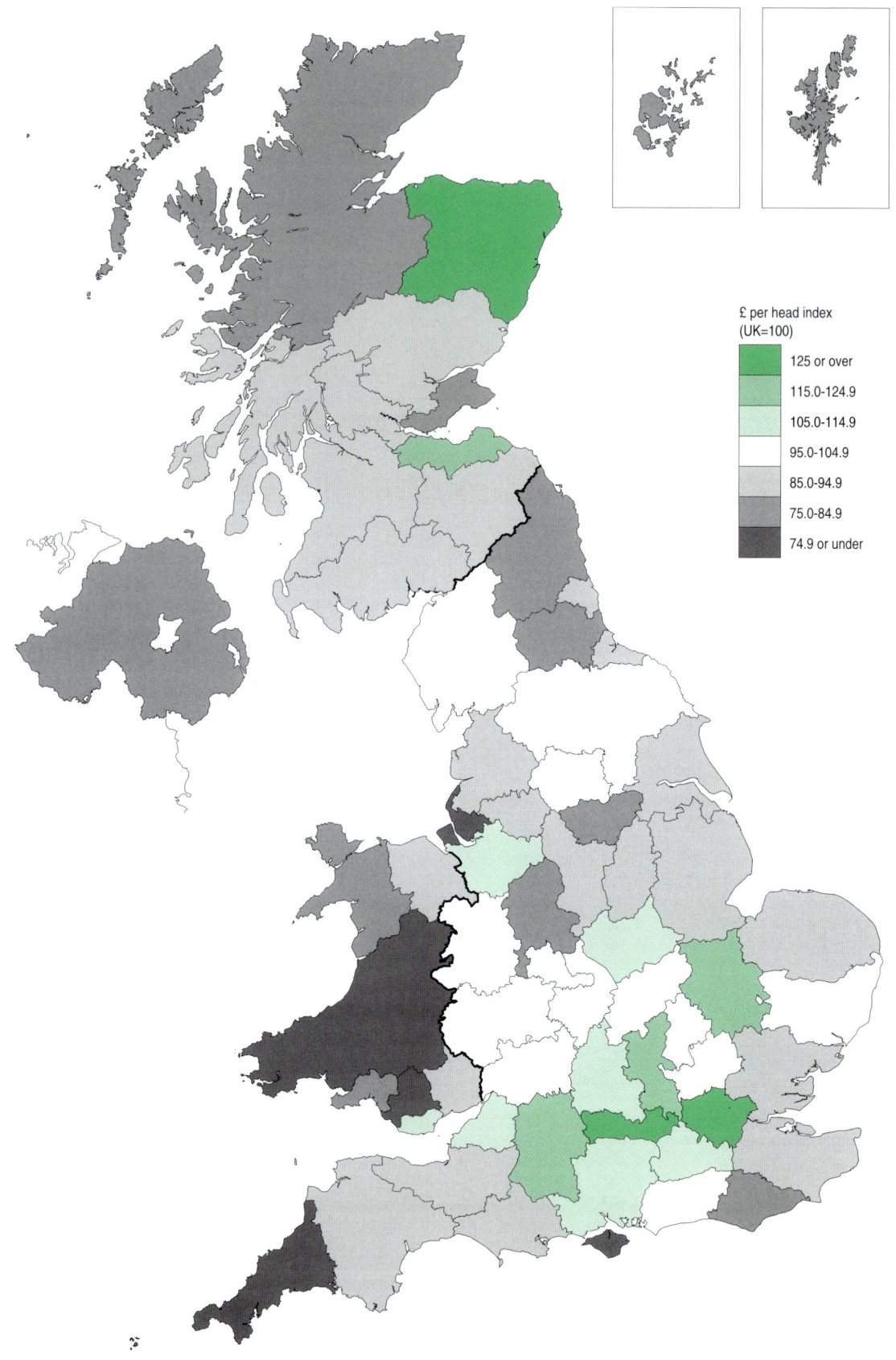

£ per head index
(UK=100)

- 125 or over
- 115.0-124.9
- 105.0-114.9
- 95.0-104.9
- 85.0-94.9
- 75.0-84.9
- 74.9 or under

1 Data are for counties in England and Wales and for local authority regions in Scotland prior to local government reorganisation.

Source: Office for National Statistics

12.6 Household income and disposable household income

	1986	1991	1992	1993	1994	1995	1996
Household income							
£ million							
United Kingdom	313,962	501,414	530,905	547,536	568,681	600,739	630,252
North East	12,703	19,840	21,156	21,725	22,079	23,106	24,070
North West (GOR) & Merseyside	35,222	55,184	58,158	59,499	61,437	64,248	67,091
Yorkshire and the Humber	25,499	39,810	42,316	43,573	45,173	47,413	49,248
East Midlands	20,924	33,223	34,940	36,388	38,132	40,063	41,339
West Midlands	25,733	42,260	44,857	45,942	47,954	50,846	53,177
Eastern	29,588	48,311	51,008	51,861	54,317	57,748	61,214
London	44,218	71,317	74,625	78,221	80,774	85,019	91,653
South East (GOR)	45,605	73,453	77,315	80,633	85,224	89,889	95,911
South West	26,297	41,044	43,721	44,752	46,078	49,465	50,543
England	265,790	424,441	448,097	462,594	481,169	507,797	534,246
Wales	13,455	22,072	23,476	23,770	24,797	26,379	27,212
Scotland	27,513	43,332	46,849	48,167	49,005	52,014	53,735
Northern Ireland	7,205	11,569	12,484	13,004	13,710	14,549	15,059
£ per head							
United Kingdom	5,523	8,674	9,153	9,409	9,739	10,251	10,718
North East	4,883	7,623	8,110	8,317	8,461	8,869	9,256
North West (GOR) & Merseyside	5,140	8,015	8,441	8,620	8,902	9,311	9,736
Yorkshire and the Humber	5,198	7,989	8,459	8,690	8,990	9,427	9,780
East Midlands	5,340	8,233	8,602	8,912	9,296	9,715	9,982
West Midlands	4,952	8,026	8,500	8,685	9,057	9,582	10,002
Eastern	5,904	9,381	9,856	9,986	10,400	10,984	11,566
London	6,499	10,351	10,808	11,282	11,593	12,133	12,956
South East (GOR)	6,087	9,565	10,025	10,422	10,948	11,455	12,148
South West	5,767	8,700	9,212	9,386	9,603	10,248	10,439
England	5,614	8,804	9,262	9,532	9,879	10,384	10,883
Wales	4,772	7,634	8,099	8,178	8,512	9,044	9,316
Scotland	5,372	8,485	9,166	9,407	9,548	10,126	10,479
Northern Ireland	4,598	7,224	7,714	7,969	8,351	8,823	9,054
Disposable household income							
£ per head							
United Kingdom	4,432	7,070	7,523	7,828	8,057	8,471	8,900
North East	4,000	6,421	6,863	7,101	7,178	7,492	7,861
North West (GOR) & Merseyside	4,133	6,652	7,084	7,304	7,477	7,818	8,216
Yorkshire and the Humber	4,222	6,650	7,085	7,334	7,553	7,913	8,248
East Midlands	4,272	6,790	7,153	7,468	7,713	8,040	8,319
West Midlands	3,994	6,631	7,069	7,305	7,570	7,989	8,399
Eastern	4,606	7,513	7,968	8,207	8,505	8,987	9,524
London	5,264	8,044	8,487	9,053	9,308	9,709	10,358
South East (GOR)	4,738	7,566	7,996	8,438	8,805	9,211	9,845
South West	4,686	7,199	7,676	7,912	8,085	8,636	8,828
England	4,493	7,139	7,575	7,897	8,143	8,548	9,001
Wales	3,923	6,448	6,890	7,019	7,266	7,718	7,998
Scotland	4,336	7,053	7,672	7,933	7,980	8,458	8,804
Northern Ireland	3,840	6,200	6,632	6,881	7,160	7,557	7,793
£ per head, United Kingdom = 100							
United Kingdom	100.0	100.0	100.0	100.0	100.0	100.0	100.0
North East	90.2	90.8	91.2	90.7	89.1	88.4	88.3
North West (GOR) & Merseyside	93.3	94.1	94.2	93.3	92.8	92.3	92.3
Yorkshire and the Humber	95.2	94.1	94.2	93.7	93.7	93.4	92.7
East Midlands	96.4	96.0	95.1	95.4	95.7	94.9	93.5
West Midlands	90.1	93.8	94.0	93.3	94.0	94.3	94.4
Eastern	103.9	106.3	105.9	104.8	105.6	106.1	107.0
London	118.8	113.8	112.8	115.7	115.5	114.6	116.4
South East (GOR)	106.9	107.0	106.3	107.8	109.3	108.7	110.6
South West	105.7	101.8	102.0	101.1	100.3	101.9	99.2
England	101.4	101.0	100.7	100.9	101.1	100.9	101.1
Wales	88.5	91.2	91.6	89.7	90.2	91.1	89.9
Scotland	97.8	99.8	102.0	101.3	99.0	99.8	98.9
Northern Ireland	86.6	87.7	88.2	87.9	88.9	89.2	87.6

Source: Office for National Statistics

12.7 Personal income and disposable personal income[1]

	1986	1991	1992	1993	1994	1995	1996
Personal income							
£ million							
United Kingdom	333,126	516,919	548,213	572,973	598,913	636,097	672,406
North East	13,449	20,516	21,788	22,513	22,994	24,190	25,280
North West (GOR) & Merseyside	37,556	56,832	59,906	62,121	64,580	67,645	71,079
Yorkshire and the Humber	27,174	41,117	43,543	45,376	47,250	49,949	52,079
East Midlands	22,285	34,154	35,695	37,698	39,655	42,066	43,519
West Midlands	27,849	44,373	47,088	48,569	50,782	53,909	56,722
Eastern	31,699	49,863	52,852	54,389	57,696	61,419	65,698
London	48,076	75,777	79,910	85,460	88,775	94,536	103,156
South East (GOR)	47,199	73,549	77,927	82,474	87,850	93,193	100,615
South West	26,981	40,872	43,909	45,396	46,883	50,766	52,352
England	282,268	437,054	462,619	483,995	506,465	537,673	570,500
Wales	14,108	22,308	23,588	24,190	25,445	27,078	28,004
Scotland	29,083	45,444	48,930	50,924	52,323	55,732	57,774
Northern Ireland	7,666	12,112	13,076	13,864	14,680	15,614	16,128
£ per head							
United Kingdom	5,860	8,942	9,451	9,846	10,256	10,854	11,435
North East	5,170	7,883	8,352	8,618	8,811	9,286	9,721
North West (GOR) & Merseyside	5,481	8,254	8,695	9,000	9,357	9,804	10,314
Yorkshire and the Humber	5,539	8,252	8,705	9,050	9,403	9,931	10,342
East Midlands	5,687	8,464	8,788	9,233	9,667	10,201	10,508
West Midlands	5,359	8,427	8,922	9,182	9,591	10,159	10,669
Eastern	6,325	9,682	10,212	10,473	11,046	11,682	12,413
London	7,067	10,998	11,573	12,327	12,741	13,491	14,582
South East (GOR)	6,300	9,578	10,105	10,660	11,286	11,876	12,744
South West	5,917	8,663	9,251	9,521	9,771	10,517	10,813
England	5,962	9,066	9,563	9,973	10,398	10,995	11,622
Wales	5,004	7,715	8,138	8,323	8,735	9,283	9,587
Scotland	5,679	8,898	9,573	9,946	10,195	10,850	11,266
Northern Ireland	4,893	7,563	8,080	8,496	8,942	9,469	9,696
Personal disposable income							
£ per head							
United Kingdom	4,648	7,031	7,509	7,892	8,173	8,624	9,144
North East	4,160	6,353	6,773	7,038	7,149	7,489	7,887
North West (GOR) & Merseyside	4,350	6,567	7,007	7,312	7,532	7,869	8,327
Yorkshire and the Humber	4,439	6,607	7,012	7,334	7,581	7,991	8,358
East Midlands	4,490	6,689	7,008	7,417	7,682	8,075	8,370
West Midlands	4,276	6,700	7,161	7,427	7,701	8,118	8,592
Eastern	4,911	7,492	8,000	8,301	8,722	9,202	9,866
London	5,681	8,389	8,947	9,699	10,020	10,566	11,466
South East (GOR)	4,848	7,267	7,762	8,283	8,714	9,143	9,929
South West	4,733	6,858	7,410	7,687	7,857	8,470	8,741
England	4,719	7,084	7,555	7,959	8,252	8,699	9,256
Wales	4,044	6,309	6,690	6,858	7,168	7,599	7,881
Scotland	4,520	7,143	7,747	8,056	8,193	8,701	9,102
Northern Ireland	4,028	6,385	6,839	7,208	7,537	7,960	8,181
£ per head, United Kingdom = 100							
United Kingdom	100.0	100.0	100.0	100.0	100.0	100.0	100.0
North East	89.5	90.4	90.2	89.2	87.5	86.8	86.3
North West (GOR) & Merseyside	93.6	93.4	93.3	92.7	92.2	91.2	91.1
Yorkshire and the Humber	95.5	94.0	93.4	92.9	92.8	92.7	91.4
East Midlands	96.6	95.1	93.3	94.0	94.0	93.6	91.5
West Midlands	92.0	95.3	95.4	94.1	94.2	94.1	94.0
Eastern	105.7	106.6	106.5	105.2	106.7	106.7	107.9
London	122.2	119.3	119.2	122.9	122.6	122.5	125.4
South East (GOR)	104.3	103.4	103.4	105.0	106.6	106.0	108.8
South West	101.8	97.5	98.7	97.4	96.1	98.2	95.6
England	101.5	100.8	100.6	100.9	101.0	100.9	101.2
Wales	87.0	89.7	89.1	86.9	87.7	88.1	86.2
Scotland	97.2	101.6	103.2	102.1	100.2	100.9	99.5
Northern Ireland	86.7	90.8	91.1	91.3	92.2	92.3	89.5

1 See Notes and Definitions.

Source: Office for National Statistics

12.8 Consumers' expenditure[1]

	Consumers' expenditure (£ million)			Regional shares of the UK (UK=100%) (percentages)			£ per head			£ per head index, UK=100		
	1994	1995	1996	1994	1995	1996	1994	1995	1996	1994	1995	1996
United Kingdom	427,395	446,169	473,509	*100.0*	*100.0*	*100.0*	7,319	7,613	8,053	100.0	100.0	100.0
North East	17,698	18,333	19,536	*4.1*	*4.1*	*4.1*	6,782	7,037	7,512	92.7	92.4	93.3
North West (GOR) &												
Merseyside	47,897	49,684	52,400	*11.2*	*11.1*	*11.1*	6,940	7,201	7,604	94.8	94.6	94.4
Yorkshire and the Humber	34,848	36,019	38,385	*8.2*	*8.1*	*8.1*	6,935	7,162	7,623	94.7	94.1	94.7
East Midlands	28,798	30,517	32,484	*6.7*	*6.8*	*6.9*	7,020	7,400	7,844	95.9	97.2	97.4
West Midlands	36,401	38,618	40,456	*8.5*	*8.7*	*8.5*	6,875	7,278	7,609	93.9	95.6	94.5
Eastern	36,440	38,854	41,698	*8.5*	*8.7*	*8.8*	6,977	7,390	7,879	95.3	97.1	97.8
London	60,326	61,131	63,386	*14.1*	*13.7*	*13.4*	8,658	8,724	8,960	118.3	114.6	111.3
South East (GOR)	66,173	69,038	74,092	*15.5*	*15.5*	*15.6*	8,501	8,798	9,384	116.1	115.6	116.5
South West	33,685	35,400	37,775	*7.9*	*7.9*	*8.0*	7,020	7,334	7,802	95.9	96.3	96.9
England	362,266	377,594	400,213	*84.8*	*84.6*	*84.5*	7,438	7,721	8,153	101.6	101.4	101.2
Wales	18,577	19,816	21,527	*4.3*	*4.4*	*4.5*	6,377	6,794	7,370	87.1	89.2	91.5
Scotland	36,115	37,354	39,446	*8.5*	*8.4*	*8.3*	7,037	7,272	7,692	96.1	95.5	95.5
Northern Ireland	10,437	11,405	12,323	*2.4*	*2.6*	*2.6*	6,357	6,916	7,409	86.9	90.8	92.0

1 See Notes and Definitions.

Source: Office for National Statistics

12.9 Consumers' expenditure[1]: by broad function, 1996

£ million

	Food, drink and tobacco	Clothing and footwear	Housing and fuel	House-hold goods and services	Vehicles, transport and commun-ications	Recreation	Other goods and services	Con-sumers' expend-iture in the UK[2]	Total con-sumers' expend-iture[3]
United Kingdom	91,851	27,434	90,764	29,945	81,470	42,727	99,858	464,049	473,509
North East	4,003	1,241	3,546	1,164	3,186	1,785	3,797	18,723	19,536
North West (GOR) &									
Merseyside	10,995	3,038	9,759	3,121	8,869	4,651	10,344	50,776	52,400
Yorkshire and the Humber	7,757	2,171	7,051	2,481	5,977	3,273	8,269	36,978	38,385
East Midlands	6,246	1,831	6,067	2,017	5,294	2,950	7,033	31,438	32,484
West Midlands	8,072	2,097	7,281	2,508	7,193	3,509	8,284	38,944	40,456
Eastern	8,095	2,205	8,939	2,453	6,390	3,918	8,386	40,386	41,698
London	11,197	4,534	13,204	4,295	11,526	5,676	15,651	66,084	63,386
South East (GOR)	12,579	3,919	14,332	4,927	14,110	7,001	15,494	72,362	74,092
South West	7,230	2,095	7,999	2,197	6,200	3,569	7,626	36,915	37,775
England	76,174	23,131	78,178	25,164	68,744	36,331	84,884	392,606	400,213
Wales	4,428	1,106	3,998	1,449	3,704	1,974	4,144	20,803	21,527
Scotland	8,680	2,350	6,521	2,495	6,980	3,448	8,348	38,822	39,446
Northern Ireland[4]	2,570	847	2,066	838	2,042	974	2,482	11,819	12,323

1 See Notes and Definitions.
2 Expenditure by UK households and foreign residents in the United Kingdom.
3 Expenditure by UK consumers, including private non-profit making bodies serving persons and UK households abroad but excluding expenditure in the United Kingdom by foreign residents.
4 Domestic rates which are levied in Northern Ireland are treated as part of consumers' expenditure. Council Tax levied in Great Britain is treated as a deduction from income, and is therefore not part of consumers' expenditure. These figures are therefore not comparable with those for the regions of Great Britain.

Source: Office for National Statistics

12.10 Gross domestic fixed capital formation: by selected industry groups[1], 1995

£ million

	Agriculture, hunting forestry and fishing	Energy, mining and water[2]	Manufacturing	Transport and com- munication[3]	Dwellings	Total of industries shown
Standard Statistical Regions						
United Kingdom	918	9,548	15,775	10,742	22,255	59,238
North	50	287	1,113	310	1,061	2,821
North West (SSR)	44	619	1,976	1,029	2,360	6,028
Yorkshire & Humberside	82	746	1,464	831	1,817	4,940
East Midlands	93	331	1,299	578	1,710	4,011
West Midlands	76	388	1,859	736	1,993	5,052
East Anglia	87	253	487	296	944	2,067
South East (SSR)	114	1,379	3,793	4,780	6,461	16,527
South West	128	376	1,028	736	1,921	4,189
England	674	4,379	13,019	9,297	18,267	45,636
Wales	76	402	988	357	1,077	2,900
Scotland	104	563	1,433	779	2,307	5,186
Northern Ireland	64	110	334	309	604	1,421
Continental Shelf[4]	.	4,094	.	.	.	4,094

1 Based on SIC 1992.
2 Includes extraction of mineral oil and natural gas, mining and quarrying, electricity, gas and water.
3 Excluding sea and air transport.
4 Oil and gas extraction only.

Source: Office for National Statistics

13 Industry and Agriculture

Gross domestic product

The North East, the East Midlands, Wales and the West Midlands derived the highest proportions of their GDP from industry in 1996 and the lowest shares from services.

(Map 13.1)

Northern Ireland followed by the South West derived a greater percentage of their GDP from agriculture in 1996 than any other region.

(Map 13.15)

Businesses

Over a third of business sites in London are in the financial and professional services sector while the figure for Northern Ireland is a tenth.

(Table 13.2)

The survival rates for businesses in Northern Ireland are higher than elsewhere in the United Kingdom.

(Table 13.12)

Manufacturing

The level of gross value added at basic prices in manufacturing in 1995 ranged from £34,800 per person employed in Wales and London to £26,000 in Northern Ireland.

(Table 13.5)

Research and Development

Expenditure on Research and Development in 1996 ranged from 3.5 per cent of GDP in the Eastern Region to less than 1 per cent in Wales and Northern Ireland.

(Table 13.8)

Assisted areas

Seventy per cent of expenditure on preferential assistance to industry in Great Britain in 1996-97 went to Assisted Areas in Wales and Scotland.

(Table 13.9)

Construction

New work accounted for 60 per cent of the value of construction contractors' output in Scotland in 1997, compared with less than 50 per cent in the South West.

(Table 13.13)

Tourism

Over half the spending by tourists from overseas was in London in 1996, while a sixth of spending by UK tourists was in the West Country.

(Table 13.14)

Farm type

Dairy farming is most prevalent in the North West, cereal farming in the Eastern region and mixed farming in the North East.

(Table 13.18)

Livestock

The South West and Scotland each account for just under 18 per cent of the cattle in the United Kingdom, the Yorkshire and Humber region accounts for 24 per cent of the pigs and Wales for 26 per cent of the sheep.

(Table 13.20)

Introduction

S ome of the tables in this chapter contain data on what is termed 'industry', while others cover manufacturing. 'Industry' includes manufacturing industries, mining and quarrying, construction, and the gas, water, and electricity utilities (see Notes and Definitions). The percentages of gross domestic product (GDP) derived from industry and services are shown in Map 13.1 and the corresponding percentage derived from agriculture in Map 13.15. Services far outweigh industry in their contribution to GDP. Agriculture, although smaller in its contribution to overall GDP, is more important in Northern Ireland, the South West and Scotland than in other regions. Data from the Inter-Departmental Business Register (IDBR) on the industrial classification of businesses (Table 13.2) also indicates this to be the case. This analysis, however, adds Wales to the list of regions where agriculture plays a more important role in the economy.

The IDBR is the Office for National Statistics' list of business units which combines information on VAT traders and PAYE employers. It covers 1.9 million enterprises in the United Kingdom which represent nearly 99 per cent of economic activity. Businesses generally register for VAT giving their head office address. Most businesses are single-site, but many have local units, that is individual factories or shops, spread across the region or in other regions. Presenting IDBR data on a local unit basis ensures that for businesses with many branches (for example a large chain of department stores) the data are included in the region where the branch is located. Although information from the IDBR is mostly presented at local unit level in *Regional Trends,* details for the agriculture industry are provided from this source at the enterprise level. Given that most farms are single-site businesses, however, it is believed that figures do not differ greatly from what they would be on a local unit basis. Figures from the UK Agricultural Departments are available at the individual holding (ie local unit) level.

Data on projects which have attracted inward investment appear in Table 13.7. They are based on information provided to the Invest in Britain Bureau (IBB) of the Department of Trade and Industry by the beneficiary companies at the time of the decision to invest. There is no obligation to notify the department, so the figures relate only to those projects where the IBB or its regional partners were involved or have come to their notice. They also take no account of subsequent developments: for example, if a company goes bankrupt several years later.

Some areas of Great Britain are classified as Development or Intermediate Assisted Areas and are thus eligible for assistance from the UK Government. Eligibility depends on various factors, the principal one being the level of unemployment. The Assisted Areas map, last revised in August 1993, was included in *Regional Trends 31.* Government expenditure on this assistance is shown in Table 13.9. Individual areas of the United Kingdom are also eligible for assistance from the European Union Structural Funds, allocated according to specific objectives. Details of these objectives can be found in the Notes and Definitions, while allocations from the Funds are given in Table 13.10.

Business survival rates are shown in Table 13.12. The longevity of new firms is an important feature of the business economy. The data show a gradual improvement in the survival rates of businesses after one year between 1992 and 1996 as the country recovered from the recession of the early 1990s. Northern Ireland consistently had the highest rates.

Although expenditure on Research and Development (R&D) does not lead directly to economic growth, it can lead to technological advances which in turn can contribute to the success of the economy. The level of R&D can be taken as an indicator of the growth potential of a region's economy. Expenditure on R&D in the South East (GOR) in 1996 was almost a quarter of total expenditure across the United Kingdom, but as a percentage of GDP it was highest in the Eastern region (Table 13.8).

13.1 Percentage of gross domestic product[1] derived from industry and services, 1996

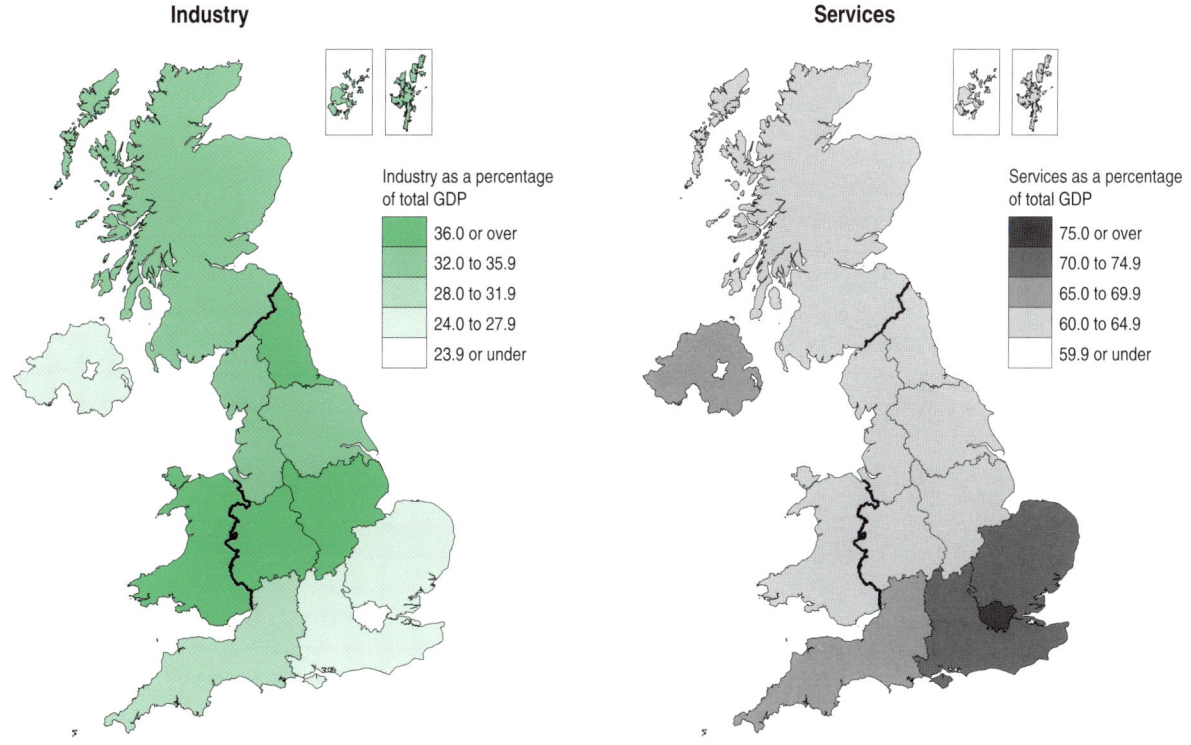

Industry

Industry as a percentage of total GDP

- 36.0 or over
- 32.0 to 35.9
- 28.0 to 31.9
- 24.0 to 27.9
- 23.9 or under

Services

Services as a percentage of total GDP

- 75.0 or over
- 70.0 to 74.9
- 65.0 to 69.9
- 60.0 to 64.9
- 59.9 or under

1 Factor cost at current prices. See Notes and Definitions.

Source: Office for National Statistics

13.2 Classification[1] of business sites[2], 1997[3]

Percentages and thousands

	Agriculture, hunting, forestry & fishing	Mining & quarrying, energy, water supply & manu-facturing	Con-struction	Distribution, hotels & catering; repairs	Transport & com-munication	Financial intermed-iation, real estate, renting & business activities	Education & health	Public admini-stration & other services	Total business sites (=100%) (thousands)
United Kingdom	7.8	9.0	8.6	30.8	4.3	22.9	6.5	10.0	2,407.7
North East	6.7	8.6	8.1	34.3	4.6	18.1	8.5	11.1	74.1
North West (GOR) & Merseyside	5.9	9.4	8.2	34.8	4.6	20.7	6.8	9.6	247.3
North West (GOR)	6.8	9.6	8.1	34.6	4.5	20.7	6.4	9.3	209.4
Merseyside	1.2	8.5	8.5	36.3	4.8	20.7	8.7	11.3	37.9
Yorkshire and the Humber	7.9	10.0	8.8	34.4	4.9	18.4	6.6	9.0	183.5
East Midlands	8.7	11.8	9.0	31.6	4.8	18.9	6.5	8.8	164.5
West Midlands	7.4	12.4	8.9	32.0	4.3	19.7	6.8	8.6	202.0
Eastern	7.3	9.4	10.4	28.4	4.9	24.0	5.7	9.8	228.5
London	0.3	7.7	5.8	28.3	4.1	35.2	5.6	12.9	356.0
South East (GOR)	4.3	8.5	9.6	28.2	4.0	28.7	6.3	10.3	349.9
South West	12.8	8.2	9.1	30.6	3.9	19.8	6.8	8.8	219.8
England	6.2	9.3	8.6	30.8	4.4	24.4	6.4	10.1	2,025.6
Wales	17.4	7.6	9.2	31.7	4.3	14.2	6.7	9.0	112.1
Scotland	12.7	7.0	8.0	32.6	4.2	18.2	6.9	10.5	193.9
Northern Ireland	25.7	6.7	9.1	27.3	3.5	9.9	9.4	8.3	76.0

1 Based on SIC 1992.
2 Registered for VAT and/or PAYE, local unit basis eg an individual factory or shop.
3 At April.

Source: Inter-Departmental Business Register, Office for National Statistics

13.3 Industry and services local units as a percentage of total local units, 1997[1]

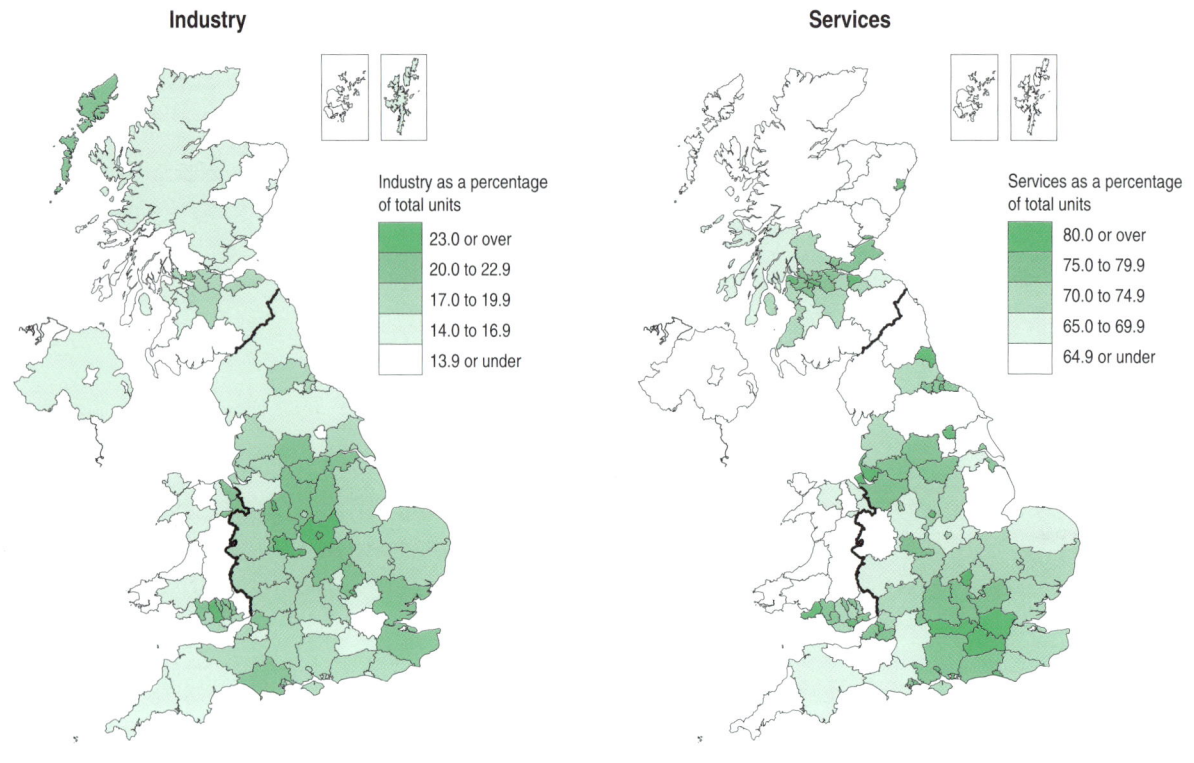

1 See Notes and Definitions.

Source: Inter-Departmental Business Register, Office for National Statistics

13.4 Manufacturing[1] industry business sites[2]: by employment sizeband[3], 1997[4]

Percentages and thousands

	\multicolumn{8}{c}{Percentage of manufacturing local units with an employment sizeband[3] of}	Total manu-facturing local units (=100%) (thousands)
	1-9	10-19	20-49	50-99	100-199	200-499	500-599	1,000 or over	
United Kingdom	72.5	11.7	8.5	3.4	2.2	1.4	0.3	0.1	208.8
North East	65.5	12.9	10.0	4.4	3.5	2.7	0.8	0.3	6.1
North West (GOR) & Merseyside	68.6	13.1	9.3	4.0	2.7	1.7	0.4	0.1	22.8
North West (GOR)	68.5	13.1	9.3	4.1	2.7	1.8	0.4	0.1	19.6
Merseyside	69.4	13.1	9.6	3.4	2.7	1.2	0.3	0.2	3.2
Yorkshire and the Humber	68.3	12.6	9.9	4.2	2.7	1.7	0.4	0.1	17.9
East Midlands	68.5	12.7	9.9	4.1	2.8	1.5	0.4	0.1	18.8
West Midlands	68.5	13.0	10.1	3.9	2.6	1.5	0.4	0.1	24.5
Eastern	75.1	10.8	7.9	3.0	1.9	1.1	0.3	0.1	20.8
London	81.2	10.0	5.5	1.7	0.9	0.6	0.1	-	26.8
South East (GOR)	77.1	10.1	7.0	2.8	1.7	1.0	0.2	0.1	28.7
South West	76.1	10.4	7.0	2.9	1.9	1.3	0.3	0.1	17.3
England	73.1	11.5	8.3	3.3	2.1	1.3	0.3	0.1	183.6
Wales	69.9	11.4	9.0	4.0	3.1	1.9	0.5	0.2	7.9
Scotland	66.6	13.1	10.5	4.4	2.8	1.8	0.5	0.2	12.4
Northern Ireland	69.1	13.0	9.6	3.7	2.4	1.7	0.3	0.2	4.8

1 Based on SIC 1992 Section D.
2 Registered for VAT and/or PAYE, local unit basis eg an individual factory.
3 Includes paid full and part-time employees and working proprietors.
4 At April.

Source: Inter-Departmental Business Register, Office for National Statistics

13.5 Turnover, expenditure and gross value added in manufacuring, 1995[1]

£ million and £ per person employed

	Total turnover (£ million)	Purchases of goods and services (£ million)	Wages and salaries		Net capital expenditure		Gross value added at basic prices	
			(£ million)	£ per person employed	(£ million)	£ per person employed	(£ million)	£ per person employed
United Kingdom	418,599	270,809	67,518	15,107	17,406	3,895	137,955	30,868
North East	19,256	12,728	2,836	14,935	888	4,675	6,336	33,370
North West (GOR) & Merseyside	56,511	36,830	9,047	15,429	2,576	4,393	18,879	32,195
North West (GOR)	47,720	30,601	7,765	15,269	2,228	4,381	16,333	32,119
Merseyside	8,791	6,229	1,283	16,471	348	4,470	2,546	32,689
Yorkshire and the Humber	36,837	25,185	6,414	14,427	1,567	3,523	12,477	28,063
East Midlands	34,325	21,123	6,212	13,843	1,358	3,026	12,132	27,038
West Midlands	47,302	31,143	8,710	14,500	1,967	3,274	16,167	26,913
Eastern	39,348	25,185	5,942	15,568	1,445	3,785	11,921	31,234
London	32,232	20,581	5,469	16,659	1,236	3,764	11,416	34,774
South East (GOR)	49,813	31,143	7,967	16,557	2,089	4,341	16,480	34,247
South West	28,046	17,873	4,861	14,927	1,149	3,528	9,498	29,163
England	343,670	221,792	57,458	15,172	14,273	3,769	115,305	30,447
Wales	26,790	17,873	3,308	15,074	1,114	5,076	7,638	34,800
Scotland	38,511	25,185	5,334	15,064	1,671	4,719	12,188	34,422
Northern Ireland	9,628	5,958	1,418	13,061	348	3,207	2,824	26,009

1 Based on SIC 1992 Section D. See Notes and Definitions.

Source: Annual Inquiry Into Production, Office for National Statistics

13.6 Gross value added in manufacturing: by size of local unit, 1995[1]

Percentages and £ million

	Percentage of gross value added by number employed[2]							Total (= 100%) (£ million)
	1-19	20-49	50-99	100-199	200-499	500-999	1,000 or over	
United Kingdom	14.2	10.9	10.8	13.5	20.3	14.0	16.3	137,955
North East	9.8	8.4	8.5	14.5	25.9	17.7	15.2	6,336
North West (GOR) & Merseyside	11.8	9.7	10.5	13.6	19.2	12.5	22.7	18,879
North West (GOR)	11.5	9.5	10.4	14.0	19.3	12.5	22.8	16,333
Merseyside	13.3	11.3	10.6	11.2	18.6	12.6	22.4	2,546
Yorkshire and the Humber	13.4	11.8	12.1	14.3	18.2	15.1	15.0	12,477
East Midlands	13.8	12.0	11.5	14.8	23.5	11.8	12.6	12,132
West Midlands	14.6	12.4	12.2	14.1	18.3	10.0	18.4	16,167
Eastern	16.3	12.2	11.7	13.6	20.3	14.9	11.0	11,921
London	21.5	12.4	10.8	11.8	16.7	8.8	17.9	11,416
South East (GOR)	16.2	10.9	10.6	12.3	20.9	13.9	15.1	16,480
South West	16.1	10.5	11.5	14.9	21.8	15.3	9.9	9,498
England	14.9	11.3	11.2	13.7	20.1	13.0	16.0	115,305
Wales	9.4	8.1	8.8	12.9	26.1	15.2	19.7	7,638
Scotland	10.9	9.4	9.3	12.0	18.2	22.9	17.2	12,188
Northern Ireland	16.4	11.8	9.9	13.5	20.8	13.1	14.5	2,824

1 Based on SIC 1992 Section D. See Notes and Definitions.
2 Average numbers employed during the year, including full and part-time employees and working proprietors.

Source: Annual Inquiry Into Production, Office for National Statistics

13.7 Direct inward investment[1]: project successes[2]

Numbers

	Manufacturing					Non-manufacturing				
	1991-92	1993-94	1994-95	1995-96	1996-97	1991-92	1993-94	1994-95	1995-96	1996-97
DTI Regions[3]										
United Kingdom	274	321	324	357	314	78	114	131	150	178
North East	28	35	31	49	36	11	5	10	13	9
North West	61	23	42	24	26	14	11	12	13	18
Yorkshire and the Humber	15	28	15	33	31	2	12	11	13	5
East Midlands	3	12	28	10	15	2	10	16	11	7
West Midlands	35	63	46	61	50	12	21	16	15	27
East	5	5	6	7	3	6	9	6	9	6
South East	17	10	17	26	16	12	10	23	47	69
South West	6	11	18	24	20	3	1	3	4	9
England	170	187	203	234	197	62	79	97	125	150
Wales	63	51	41	44	43	8	13	10	9	2
Scotland	31	65	63	57	53	7	22	18	15	23
Northern Ireland	10	18	17	22	21	1	0	6	1	3

1 See Introduction to chapter.
2 A project success is defined as a case where an overseas company specifies an interest and successfully completes investment in a UK company.
3 See map on page 215.

Source: Invest in Britain Bureau, Department of Trade and Industry

13.8 Expenditure on Research and Development, 1996

£ million and percentages

	R&D expenditure (£ million)			R&D expenditure as a percentage of regional GDP		
	Businesses	Government[1]	Higher education institutions	Businesses	Government[1]	Higher education institutions
United Kingdom	9,301	2,070	2,792	1.3	0.3	0.4
North East	187	18	95	0.7	0.1	0.3
North West (GOR) & Merseyside	1,064	87	227	1.4	0.1	0.3
North West (GOR)	929	75	166	1.3	0.1	0.2
Merseyside	135	12	61	1.5	0.1	0.7
Yorkshire and the Humber	275	59	216	0.5	0.1	0.4
East Midlands	710	69	146	1.4	0.1	0.3
West Midlands	628	188	154	1.0	0.3	0.2
Eastern	2,057	268	203	2.8	0.4	0.3
London	889	263	700	0.8	0.2	0.6
South East (GOR)	2,207	640	416	1.9	0.6	0.4
South West	726	260	124	1.3	0.5	0.2
England	8,743	1,852	2,282	1.4	0.3	0.4
Wales	117	32	105	0.4	0.1	0.3
Scotland	357	163	348	0.6	0.3	0.5
Northern Ireland	83	23	57	0.5	0.1	0.3

1 Figures include estimates of NHS and local authorities' R&D.

Source: Office for National Statistics

13.9 Government expenditure on regional preferential assistance to industry

£ million

	1988-89	1989-90	1990-91	1991-92	1992-93	1993-94	1994-95	1995-96	1996-97
DTI Regions[1]									
Great Britain[2]	615.7	539.3	497.3	427.8	364.0	394.4	368.9	343.0	371.3
North East	134.1	117.0	85.0	63.8	48.3	52.7	38.4	46.4	24.3
North West	82.3	74.3	57.5	49.5	36.8	40.3	32.4	24.3	23.2
of which									
Merseyside	.	.	.	.	.	.	15.0	13.0	9.0
Yorkshire & Humberside	50.2	32.4	29.4	18.2	13.7	35.6	23.0	19.7	11.1
East Midlands	8.8	9.5	5.5	2.6	1.2	1.9	5.2	7.3	10.5
West Midlands	26.2	19.9	18.0	8.7	10.8	14.4	14.7	14.2	25.5
East	.	.	.	.	.	.	0.7	2.1	1.5
South East	.	.	.	.	.	.	1.5	5.9	7.0
of which									
London	.	.	.	.	.	.	0.6	1.7	2.9
South West	14.7	10.7	9.0	8.3	8.2	9.5	9.4	7.7	7.4
Other[3]	.	.	.	.	.	.	.	.	0.2
England	316.3	263.8	204.4	151.1	119.0	154.4	125.3	127.6	110.7
Wales	148.2	131.7	133.7	153.9	140.6	118.8	109.2	98.0	132.4
Scotland	151.2	143.8	159.2	122.8	104.4	121.2	134.4	117.4	128.2
Northern Ireland	138.3	127.1	132.1	138.0	105.6	117.6	132.9	131.2	137.1

1 See map on page 215.
2 The system of assistance available in Northern Ireland is not comparable with that operating in Great Britain, and thus UK figures are not produced. See Notes and Definitions.
3 Includes payments for European Regional Incentives, General Consultancy Contracts & Regional Selective Assistance Repayments to the European Commission which are not included in data for the regions.

Source: Department of Trade and Industry; Department of Economic Development, Northern Ireland

13.10 Allocation of EU Structural Funds[1,2]

£ million, 1994 prices[2]

	Objective 1[3]			Objective 2[3]			Objective 5b[3]			Objectives 1,2 and 5b		
	1997	1998	1999	1997	1998	1999	1997	1998	1999	1997	1998	1999
United Kingdom	277	301	326	541	559	577	102	103	103	921	962	1,005
North East	.	.	.	77	80	82	4	4	4	81	83	86
North West (GOR) & Merseyside	96	104	113	93	97	100	4	4	4	193	204	216
North West (GOR)	.	.	.	93	97	100	4	4	4	97	100	103
Merseyside	96	104	113	.	.	.	.	.	.	96	104	113
Yorkshire and the Humber	.	.	.	79	82	84	6	6	6	85	88	90
East Midlands	.	.	.	22	22	23	8	8	8	29	30	31
West Midlands	.	.	.	96	99	102	5	5	6	101	104	108
Eastern	.	.	.	.	.	.	7	8	8	7	8	8
London	.	.	.	22	22	23	.	.	.	22	22	23
South East (GOR)	.	.	.	4	4	4	.	.	.	4	4	4
South West	.	.	.	8	8	8	27	27	28	35	36	36
England	96	104	113	400	413	426	61	61	62	557	579	601
Wales	.	.	.	46	48	49	23	23	23	69	71	72
Scotland	37	39	43	95	98	101	18	18	18	150	155	162
Northern Ireland	145	157	170	.	.	.	.	.	.	145	157	170

1 Only allocations resulting from the European Commission's Single Programming Documents are shown. Allocations resulting from Community Initiatives, the value of which is about 8 per cent of the total Objective 1, 2 and 5b allocations, are not included because not all of these can be allocated to the Government Office Regions in the table.
2 Allocations in ECUs have been converted to sterling using the exchange rate £1 = 1.45 ECU; see Notes and Definitions. In previous editions of *Regional Trends* these figures were presented in ECUs.
3 See Notes and Definitions.

Source: Department of Trade and Industry

13.11 Business registrations and deregistrations[1]

Thousands and percentages

	1995						1996					
	Re-gist-rations	De-regist-rations[2]	Net change	Re-gist-ration rates[3]	De-regist-ration rates[3]	End-year stock	Re-gist-rations	De-regist-rations	Net change	Re-gist-ration rates[3]	De-regist-ration rates[3]	End-year stock
United Kingdom	164.0	173.2	-9.3	10.2	10.8	1,600.1	168.2	157.0	11.2	10.5	9.8	1,611.3
North East	4.1	5.1	-1.0	9.4	11.6	42.5	4.1	4.3	-0.2	9.6	10.2	42.2
North West (GOR) & Merseyside	15.9	18.4	-2.5	10.0	11.5	157.4	16.5	16.2	0.3	10.5	10.3	157.7
North West (GOR)	13.5	15.5	-2.0	9.8	11.3	135.5	13.7	13.7	0.0	10.1	10.1	135.5
Merseyside	2.4	2.9	-0.5	10.9	13.0	21.9	2.8	2.5	0.3	12.7	11.4	22.2
Yorkshire and the Humber	11.1	13.2	-2.1	9.2	11.0	118.4	11.3	11.5	-0.2	9.6	9.7	118.2
East Midlands	10.7	11.4	-0.7	9.7	10.3	110.0	10.8	11.1	-0.3	9.9	10.1	109.7
West Midlands	13.3	14.7	-1.3	9.7	10.7	135.2	13.3	13.3	0.0	9.8	9.8	135.2
Eastern	16.0	16.5	-0.5	10.2	10.5	156.9	16.1	15.0	1.1	10.3	9.6	158.0
London	32.7	29.1	3.5	13.5	12.0	245.1	34.1	26.7	7.4	13.9	10.9	252.4
South East (GOR)	26.5	27.1	-0.6	11.0	11.2	240.4	27.1	24.8	2.3	11.3	10.3	242.7
South West	13.0	15.5	-2.6	8.6	10.3	147.6	13.8	13.8	0.1	9.4	9.3	147.6
England	143.2	151.0	-7.8	10.5	11.1	1,353.3	147.1	136.6	10.5	10.9	10.1	1,363.8
Wales	6.0	7.1	-1.2	7.8	9.2	76.1	6.1	6.5	-0.4	8.0	8.6	75.7
Scotland	11.2	12.0	-0.8	9.4	10.1	117.8	11.3	10.9	0.3	9.6	9.3	118.1
Northern Ireland	3.6	3.1	0.5	6.9	6.0	52.9	3.7	2.9	0.8	7.0	5.4	53.7

1 Enterprises registered for VAT. See Notes and Definitions.
2 Figures include an adjustment to allow for the change to the partial exemption rule.
3 Registrations and deregistrations during the year as a percentage of the stock figure at the end of the previous year.

Source: Department of Trade and Industry

13.12 Business survival rates

The percentage of businesses surviving the stated number of months after year of registration

	12 months				24 months			36 months	
	1992	1993	1994	1995	1992	1993	1994	1992	1993
United Kingdom	83.4	83.6	84.6	87.3	67.0	66.5	69.1	54.8	54.8
North East	83.4	81.7	81.7	84.3	66.7	63.6	64.5	52.3	51.5
North West (GOR) & Merseyside	81.5	82.3	82.6	85.7	64.5	64.3	66.4	51.6	52.3
North West (GOR)	81.6	82.4	82.8	85.8	64.9	64.7	66.8	52.2	52.9
Merseyside	80.3	81.6	81.8	85.3	63.2	62.7	64.6	51.1	49.6
Yorkshire and the Humber	83.0	83.6	83.4	86.3	67.4	66.0	67.1	54.1	53.3
East Midlands	84.3	84.9	84.5	85.9	68.9	67.7	68.3	56.5	55.5
West Midlands	82.8	82.6	83.4	85.0	66.3	65.9	68.1	54.6	54.1
Eastern	84.4	84.6	86.0	87.8	68.2	67.8	70.3	56.2	56.6
London	82.5	82.8	84.3	88.2	64.6	65.3	69.0	52.6	53.6
South East (GOR)	83.2	84.7	85.2	88.4	66.9	67.8	70.3	54.6	56.2
South West	84.6	84.5	85.6	91.9	68.6	67.6	70.2	56.9	55.7
England	83.3	83.6	84.4	87.2	66.8	66.4	68.8	54.6	54.6
Wales	84.5	82.8	85.4	87.4	68.2	65.5	70.7	56.2	54.4
Scotland	85.0	83.7	85.1	87.5	68.7	67.4	69.6	56.3	56.0
Northern Ireland	88.6	84.9	88.9	93.2	77.2	71.4	79.5	67.8	62.2

Source: Department of Trade and Industry

13.13 Construction: value at current prices of contractors' output[1]

£million and percentages

	Total work (£ million)						Of which new work (percentages)					
	1991	1993	1994	1995	1996	1997	1991	1993	1994	1995	1996	1997
Standard Statistical Regions												
Great Britain	47,389	42,797	45,870	48,942	51,969	55,191	*57.8*	*54.3*	*54.0*	*53.9*	*53.4*	*53.7*
North	2,058	1,863	2,139	2,186	2,506	2,601	*59.6*	*56.4*	*58.5*	*56.9*	*61.1*	*59.4*
North West (SSR)	4,273	4,117	4,576	5,072	5,412	5,577	*54.2*	*55.2*	*55.0*	*55.4*	*54.0*	*52.4*
Yorkshire & Humberside	3,673	3,468	3,703	3,862	4,324	4,576	*54.0*	*52.9*	*53.3*	*50.2*	*51.7*	*51.4*
East Midlands	3,060	3,019	3,301	3,446	3,827	4,252	*56.5*	*56.4*	*56.5*	*55.2*	*56.6*	*58.3*
West Midlands	3,937	3,716	4,039	4,157	4,399	4,813	*56.6*	*52.4*	*52.7*	*51.8*	*50.1*	*50.9*
East Anglia	1,895	1,786	1,977	2,064	2,021	2,137	*58.8*	*50.7*	*52.7*	*52.9*	*51.0*	*53.3*
South East (SSR)	18,576	14,970	15,598	16,690	17,965	19,094	*60.0*	*52.7*	*51.6*	*52.0*	*51.8*	*52.3*
Greater London	7,690	5,646	6,118	6,917	7,428	7,829	*65.0*	*55.0*	*55.8*	*57.8*	*59.2*	*58.7*
Rest of the South East	10,887	9,325	9,481	9,774	10,537	11,265	*56.4*	*51.2*	*48.8*	*47.8*	*46.6*	*47.9*
South West	3,846	3,781	4,055	4,317	4,193	4,427	*51.6*	*54.6*	*54.4*	*54.0*	*48.5*	*49.3*
England	41,319	36,720	39,389	41,794	44,647	47,476	*57.4*	*53.5*	*53.4*	*53.0*	*52.5*	*52.8*
Wales	1,959	1,826	2,172	2,377	2,331	2,533	*58.0*	*56.0*	*59.9*	*61.2*	*57.7*	*58.4*
Scotland	4,111	4,251	4,310	4,771	4,991	5,182	*61.2*	*60.5*	*57.1*	*58.5*	*59.6*	*60.1*

1 Output of contractors, including estimates of unrecorded output by small firms and self-employed workers, classified to construction in SIC 1992. For new work, figures relate to the region in which the site is located; for repair and maintenance, figures are for the region in which the reporting unit is based.

Source: Department of the Environment, Transport and the Regions

13.14 Tourism[1],1991 and 1996

Millions and £ million

	1991				1996			
	UK residents[2]		Overseas residents[3]		UK residents[2]		Overseas residents[3]	
	Number of tourists (millions)	Expenditure (£ million)	Number of tourists (millions)	Expenditure (£ million)	Number of tourists (millions)	Expenditure (£ million)	Number of tourists (millions)	Expenditure (£ million)
Tourist Board Regions								
United Kingdom	94.4	10,470	17.1	7,305	127.0	13,895	25.3	12,369
Northumbria	3.4	255	0.3	95	3.3	260	0.5	174
Cumbria	2.7	330	0.2	35	3.0	375	0.3	63
North West	8.3	770	1.0	246	10.6	1,020	1.3	429
Yorkshire	7.4	680	0.9	183	10.4	1,085	1.1	307
East of England	9.9	925	1.4	372	13.7	1,320	1.7	559
Heart of England	11.8	950	1.7	388	17.0	1,395	2.1	709
London	6.6	720	9.2	3,924	12.2	935	13.5	6,519
Southern	9.4	920	1.7	473	10.1	1,105	2.1	813
South East England	6.4	600	2.0	552	10.7	800	2.5	764
West Country	12.9	1,765	1.4	306	15.1	2,385	1.7	567
England	7.6	7,925	15.1	6,595	104.1	10,685	21.4	10,905
Wales	8.7	900	0.7	133	11.0	1,180	0.8	217
Scotland	8.2	1,190	1.6	501	10.5	1,495	2.0	923
Northern Ireland	1.4	145	0.1	26	1.4	205	0.1	51

1 Tourist Board Regions. See map on page 215.

2 The United Kingdom figures include the value of tourism in the Channel Islands, the Isle of Man, and a small amount where the region was unknown.

3 The England figures include the value of tourism in the Channel Islands, the Isle of Man, and a small amount where the region was unknown. The United Kingdom figures also include an amount which cannot be allocated to an individual country. The Northern Ireland figures include the value of tourism created by visitors from the Republic of Ireland.

Source: British Tourist Authority; International Passenger Survey, Office for National Statistics; Northern Ireland Tourist Board

13.15 Percentage of gross domestic product[1] derived from agriculture, 1996

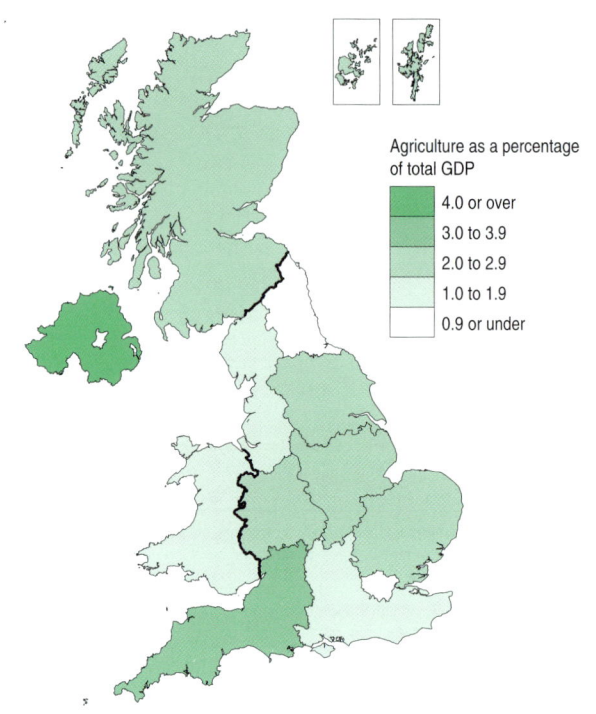

Agriculture as a percentage
of total GDP

- 4.0 or over
- 3.0 to 3.9
- 2.0 to 2.9
- 1.0 to 1.9
- 0.9 or under

1 Factor cost at current prices. See Notes and Definitions.
2 Based on SIC 1992. Gross domestic product for the agricultural industry includes income from related activities such as riding stables and bed and breakfast.

Source: Office for National Statistics

13.16 Agricultural legal units as a percentage of total legal units, 1997[1]

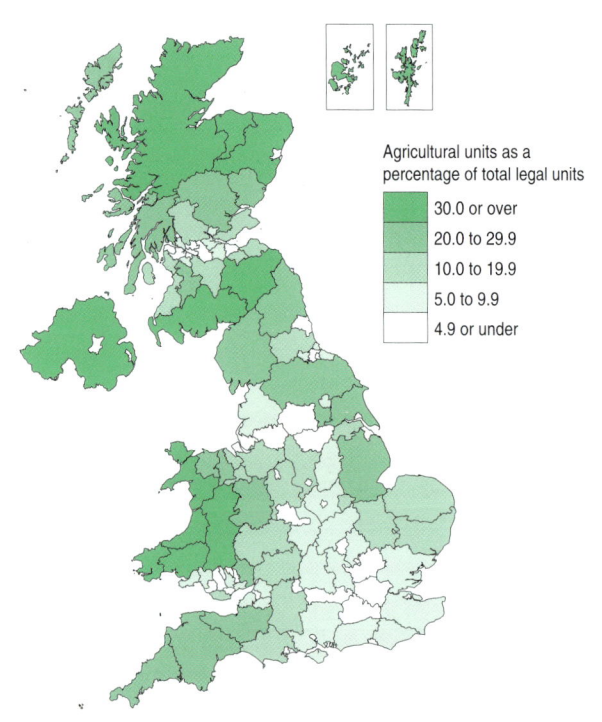

Agricultural units as a
percentage of total legal units

- 30.0 or over
- 20.0 to 29.9
- 10.0 to 19.9
- 5.0 to 9.9
- 4.9 or under

1 The figures include only those enterprises that are registered for VAT. Some smaller holdings will therefore not be included. See Notes and Definitions.

Source: Inter-Departmental Business Register, Office for National Statistics

13.17 Agricultural holdings[1]: by area of crops and grass, and by land use[2] June 1996

	None[3]	Under 10 hectares	10-49.9 hectares	50 hectares or over	Total holdings (=100%) (numbers)	Arable land[4]	Grass five years old and over (including sole right rough grazing)	Set-aside land	Other land on agricultural holdings including Woodland[5]	Total area on agricultural holdings (=100%) (thousand hectares)
United Kingdom	4.8	26.0	39.1	30.0	234,267	35.7	57.1	3.0	4.3	17,190
North East	4.1	20.0	29.7	46.2	5,200	32.7	61.0	3.0	3.3	580
North West (GOR) & Merseyside	4.6	26.0	41.0	28.4	17,533	22.9	73.5	0.8	2.8	898
Yorkshire and the Humber	4.4	25.7	35.5	34.4	16,093	53.4	38.7	4.7	3.2	1,096
East Midlands	3.2	24.3	36.4	36.0	16,052	66.1	24.3	6.3	3.3	1,230
West Midlands	4.0	27.9	38.2	29.9	18,847	49.9	42.2	3.7	4.3	956
Eastern	5.5	29.4	29.2	35.9	17,574	75.1	11.4	7.5	6.0	1,473
London	10.8	43.1	31.3	14.8	418	46.2	41.0	5.9	6.8	14
South East (GOR)	7.0	32.0	33.0	28.0	18,286	54.7	30.3	6.5	8.5	1,205
South West	3.5	28.0	39.8	28.8	35,634	39.6	52.6	2.9	4.9	1,812
England	4.5	27.5	36.4	31.6	145,637	51.0	39.6	4.6	4.8	9,347
Wales	5.1	22.6	44.8	27.5	28,090	14.0	81.8	0.4	3.8	1,509
Scotland	8.5	26.1	29.3	36.0	32,993	17.3	77.3	1.3	4.0	5,266
Northern Ireland	2.0	21.6	59.7	16.8	27,547	23.3	74.7	0.1	1.8	1,068

1 Figures exclude estimates for minor holdings which contribute less than 1 per cent of the total crops and grass area. See Notes and Definitions.
2 Figures include estimates for minor holdings except for Scotland and the regions of England. As a result the sum of the English regions is not equal to the national total.
3 These holdings consis only of rough grazing, woodland or other land.
4 Crops, bare fallow and all grass under five years old.
5 In Great Britain this includes farm roads, yards, buildings (except glasshouses), ponds and derelict land. In Northern Ireland it includes land under bog, water, roads, buildings etc
   and wasteland not used for agriculture.

Source: Ministry of Agriculture, Fisheries and Food; Welsh Office;
The Scottish Office Agriculture, Environment and Fisheries Department;
Department of Agriculture, Northern Ireland

13.18 Agricultural holdings: by farm type, 1996

Percentages and numbers

	Cereals	General cropping	Horti-culture	Pigs and poultry	Dairy	Cattle and sheep (LFA[1])	Cattle and sheep (Low-ground)	Mixed	Other	Total holdings (=100%) (numbers)
United Kingdom	10.5	6.8	4.1	2.7	13.0	21.2	17.0	6.9	17.8	234,267
North East	17.3	3.0	1.7	1.8	6.5	30.1	13.7	11.9	14.0	5,200
North West (GOR) & Merseyside	2.9	4.7	4.7	3.0	25.4	15.6	20.9	3.6	19.3	17,533
North West (GOR)	2.4	4.2	4.4	2.9	25.9	16.0	21.3	3.5	19.3	17,085
Merseyside	19.0	23.4	14.7	4.7	5.1	.	6.9	6.3	19.9	448
Yorkshire and the Humber	17.6	12.1	3.2	4.9	10.6	12.1	14.5	9.5	15.4	16,093
East Midlands	23.9	15.4	4.5	2.8	8.8	4.3	16.8	8.5	15.0	16,052
West Midlands	8.8	7.7	5.1	2.6	14.9	5.5	27.4	9.6	18.6	18,847
Eastern	29.2	24.6	9.0	5.0	1.5	.	8.1	6.6	16.0	17,574
London	11.0	5.5	22.2	4.5	4.1	.	12.2	5.0	35.4	418
South East (GOR)	16.6	4.4	10.9	3.1	5.6	.	24.9	8.4	26.1	18,286
South West	6.9	2.3	4.3	2.6	19.3	5.6	29.7	7.4	22.0	35,634
England	14.0	8.8	5.7	3.3	13.0	6.8	21.4	7.7	19.3	145,637
Wales	1.0	0.8	1.0	1.4	15.1	46.4	13.1	2.6	18.7	28,090
Scotland	10.5	7.2	1.7	1.5	6.2	38.3	3.8	8.0	22.8	32,993
Northern Ireland	1.8	1.8	1.4	2.2	19.4	50.9	13.9	5.2	3.5	27,547

1 Less Favoured Areas. See Notes and Definitions.

Source: Ministry of Agriculture, Fisheries and Food; Welsh Office;
The Scottish Office Agriculture, Environment and Fisheries Department;
Department of Agriculture for Northern Ireland

13.19 Areas and estimated yields of selected crops[1], 1991-1995[2] and 1996

Thousand hectares and tonnes per hectare

| | Areas (thousand hectares) | | | | | | Estimated yields (tonnes per hectare) | | | | | |
| | Wheat | | Barley | | Rape (for oilseed)[3] | | Wheat | | Barley | | Rape (for oilseed)[3] | |
	1991-1995	1996	1991-1995	1996	1991-1995	1996	1991-1995	1996	1991-1995	1996	1991-1995	1996
Standard Statistical Regions												
United Kingdom	1,895	1,976	1,230	1,267	399	356	7.3	8.1	5.5	6.1	2.8	3.5
North	71	77	64	63	22	20	7.7	8.6	5.7	7.0	..	..
North West (SSR)	23	25	26	25	4	3	6.9	7.6	5.2	6.0	..	..
Yorkshire and Humberside	244	254	129	129	46	40	7.7	8.5	6.0	7.1	..	..
East Midlands	368	385	114	114	80	75	7.4	8.2	5.7	6.5	..	..
West Midlands	145	156	86	85	24	21	6.9	8.3	5.4	6.6	..	..
East Anglia	322	336	151	152	38	33	7.5	7.9	5.7	5.5	..	..
South East (SSR)	418	433	160	165	98	87	7.0	8.0	5.7	6.1	..	..
South West	173	183	136	141	27	26	6.8	7.9	5.3	5.8	..	..
England	1,766	1,852	867	877	339	305	7.3	8.1	5.7	6.3	2.8	3.6
Wales	12	13	34	32	1	2	6.6	7.9	5.0	5.7	2.8	3.6
Scotland	111	104	294	324	58	49	7.7	8.3	5.2	6.0	2.7	3.0
Northern Ireland	7	7	36	33	1	-	6.9	7.7	4.5	5.4	2.5	2.9

1 Figures for England, Wales and Northern Ireland include estimates for minor holdings; figures for English regions exclude minor holdings hence their sum may be less than the England total. Figures for Scotland exclude minor holdings. See Notes and Definitions.

2 Five year average.

3 Excludes crops grown on Set-aside scheme land.

Source: Ministry of Agriculture, Fisheries and Food; Welsh Office;
The Scottish Office Agriculture, Environment and Fisheries Department;
Department of Agriculture for Northern Ireland

13.20 Livestock on agricultural holdings, June 1996[1]

Thousands

| | Cattle and calves | | | Sheep and lambs | Pigs |
	Total herd[2]	Dairy cows	Beef cows		
United Kingdom	12,023	2,587	1,859	41,813	7,512
North East	351	32	91	2,360	122
North West (GOR) & Merseyside	1,163	375	106	3,685	337
North West (GOR)	1,150	372	105	3,676	329
Merseyside	12	3	1	9	9
Yorkshire and the Humber	656	144	92	2,501	1,819
East Midlands	630	136	78	1,548	622
West Midlands	922	259	101	2,728	382
Eastern	292	52	49	447	1,618
London	7	2	1	3	9
South East (GOR)	627	151	82	1,708	565
South West	2,113	634	201	3,870	795
England	6,805	1,785	815	19,090	6,275
Wales	1,360	297	219	10,874	99
Scotland	2,099	224	510	9,096	573
Northern Ireland	1,759	281	315	2,753	565

1 Figures for England, Wales and Northern Ireland include minor holdings; figures for English regions exclude minor holdings and hence their sum may be less than the England total. Figures for Scotland exclude minor holdings. See Notes and Definitions.

2 Includes bulls, in-calf heifers and fattening cattle and calves.

Source: Ministry of Agriculture, Fisheries and Food; Welsh Office;
The Scottish Office Agriculture, Environment and Fisheries Department;
Department of Agriculture for Northern Ireland

Sub-regions of England

Government Office Regions, Counties and Unitary Authorities in England[1]

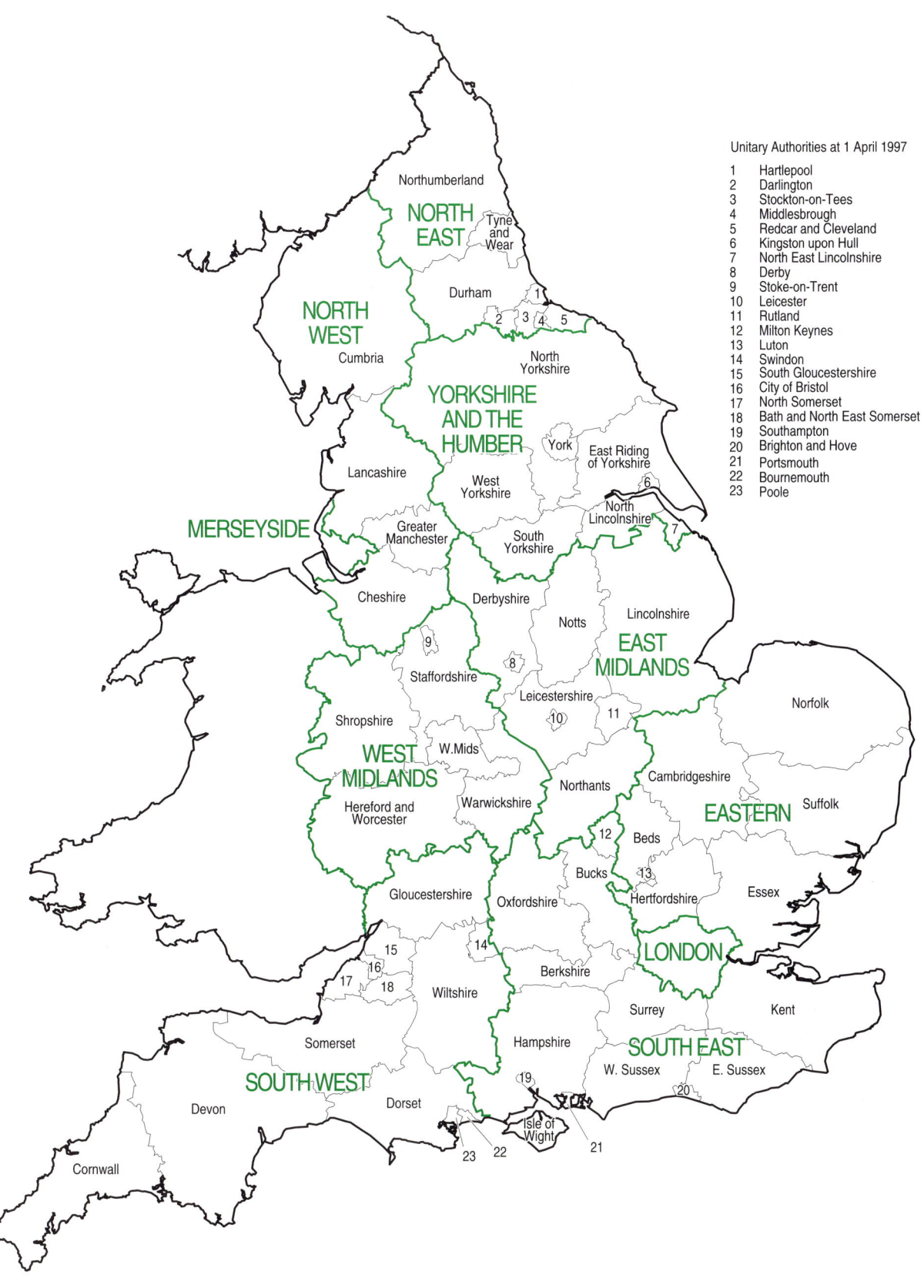

Unitary Authorities at 1 April 1997

1	Hartlepool
2	Darlington
3	Stockton-on-Tees
4	Middlesbrough
5	Redcar and Cleveland
6	Kingston upon Hull
7	North East Lincolnshire
8	Derby
9	Stoke-on-Trent
10	Leicester
11	Rutland
12	Milton Keynes
13	Luton
14	Swindon
15	South Gloucestershire
16	City of Bristol
17	North Somerset
18	Bath and North East Somerset
19	Southampton
20	Brighton and Hove
21	Portsmouth
22	Bournemouth
23	Poole

1 Local government structure as at 1 April 1997

14.1 Area and population: by local authority[1], 1996

	Area (sq km)	Persons per sq km	Population (thousands) Males	Population (thousands) Females	Population (thousands) Total	Total population percentage change 1981-1996	Total period fertility rate (TPFR)[2]	Standardised mortality ratio (UK=100) (SMR)[3]	Percentage of population aged Under 5	Percentage of population aged 5-15	Percentage of population aged 16 up to pension age[4]	Percentage of population aged Pension age[4] or over
UNITED KINGDOM	242,910	242	28,856	29,946	58,801	*4.3*	1.72	100	*6.4*	*14.2*	*61.3*	*18.1*
ENGLAND	130,422	376	24,129	24,960	49,089	*4.8*	1.73	98	*6.4*	*14.1*	*61.3*	*18.2*
NORTH EAST	8,592	303	1,271	1,329	2,600	*-1.4*	1.67	111	*6.2*	*14.4*	*60.9*	*18.5*
Hartlepool UA	94	973	45	47	92	*-2.9*	1.78	118	*6.7*	*15.4*	*60.0*	*17.9*
Middlesbrough UA	54	2,697	72	75	147	*-2.5*	1.78	108	*7.0*	*16.2*	*60.4*	*16.4*
Redcar & Cleveland UA	245	570	68	71	140	*-7.4*	1.90	109	*6.4*	*15.2*	*60.0*	*18.3*
Stockton-on-Tees UA	204	877	88	91	179	*2.9*	1.76	106	*6.6*	*15.8*	*61.3*	*16.3*
Former county of Cleveland	597	932	273	284	558	*-2.2*	1.80	109	*6.7*	*15.7*	*60.6*	*17.1*
Darlington UA	197	513	49	52	101	*2.7*	1.72	104	*6.4*	*14.3*	*60.1*	*19.1*
Durham County	2,232	227	249	258	507	*-1.2*	1.64	114	*6.0*	*14.1*	*61.4*	*18.5*
Chester-le-Street	68	830	28	28	56	*6.5*	1.55	120	*6.1*	*13.4*	*63.9*	*16.6*
Derwentside	271	324	43	45	88	*-0.7*	1.70	117	*6.0*	*13.9*	*60.7*	*19.4*
Durham	187	483	45	46	90	*2.6*	1.39	99	*5.2*	*13.6*	*64.7*	*16.5*
Easington	145	658	47	49	95	*-6.2*	1.90	125	*6.7*	*15.2*	*59.3*	*18.7*
Sedgefield	217	414	45	45	90	*-3.8*	1.82	115	*6.1*	*14.6*	*60.9*	*18.3*
Teesdale	840	29	12	12	24	*-1.5*	1.54	111	*5.5*	*12.1*	*60.0*	*22.4*
Wear Valley	505	125	31	33	63	*-1.3*	1.74	109	*5.7*	*14.1*	*59.6*	*20.5*
Former county of Durham	2,429	250	298	310	608	*-0.5*	1.66	112	*6.1*	*14.1*	*61.2*	*18.6*
Northumberland	5,026	61	150	157	307	*2.7*	1.66	111	*5.7*	*13.8*	*60.8*	*19.7*
Alnwick	1,079	29	15	16	31	*7.7*	1.71	95	*5.2*	*13.6*	*59.0*	*22.1*
Berwick-upon-Tweed	972	27	13	14	27	*1.7*	1.54	98	*4.8*	*12.4*	*58.1*	*24.6*
Blyth Valley	70	1,139	39	41	80	*2.8*	1.68	130	*6.2*	*14.3*	*63.6*	*15.9*
Castle Morpeth	619	80	24	26	50	*-0.6*	1.55	95	*4.8*	*13.5*	*60.8*	*20.8*
Tynedale	2,219	26	28	30	58	*7.2*	1.55	112	*5.5*	*14.2*	*59.6*	*20.6*
Wansbeck	67	932	30	32	62	*-0.6*	1.86	121	*6.3*	*13.7*	*60.5*	*19.5*
Tyne and Wear	540	2,086	550	578	1,127	*-2.4*	1.61	111	*6.1*	*14.2*	*60.9*	*18.9*
Gateshead	143	1,403	98	103	201	*-5.8*	1.62	114	*6.0*	*13.4*	*61.2*	*19.4*
Newcastle-upon-Tyne	112	2,526	139	143	282	*-0.6*	1.52	111	*6.1*	*13.5*	*62.5*	*17.8*
North Tyneside	84	2,314	93	101	194	*-2.5*	1.65	107	*5.9*	*13.7*	*59.7*	*20.8*
South Tyneside	64	2,440	76	80	156	*-3.6*	1.73	107	*6.1*	*14.9*	*58.6*	*20.4*
Sunderland	138	2,138	144	151	294	*-1.0*	1.68	114	*6.3*	*15.2*	*61.0*	*17.5*
NORTH WEST (GOR) & MERSEYSIDE	14,165	486	3,377	3,515	6,891	*-0.7*	1.76	107	*6.4*	*14.7*	*60.7*	*18.2*
NORTH WEST (GOR)	13,510	405	2,689	2,782	5,471	*1.0*	1.77	106	*6.4*	*14.7*	*60.9*	*18.0*
Cheshire	2,331	420	483	498	980	*5.1*	1.72	104	*6.2*	*14.4*	*61.6*	*17.7*
Chester	448	266	58	61	119	*2.0*	1.93	99	*5.9*	*13.7*	*60.7*	*19.7*
Congleton	211	410	43	44	87	*8.2*	1.65	91	*5.6*	*14.1*	*62.2*	*18.2*
Crewe and Nantwich	430	264	57	57	114	*15.3*	1.63	102	*6.5*	*14.1*	*62.1*	*17.3*
Ellesmere Port and Neston	87	930	39	41	81	*-2.3*	1.87	103	*6.3*	*15.0*	*60.9*	*17.9*
Halton	74	1,667	60	63	123	*-0.1*	1.74	125	*6.7*	*16.7*	*61.7*	*15.0*
Macclesfield	525	291	75	78	153	*1.8*	1.61	94	*5.6*	*13.2*	*61.3*	*19.9*
Vale Royal	380	303	57	58	115	*3.3*	1.80	105	*6.1*	*14.6*	*61.1*	*18.1*
Warrington	176	1,074	94	95	189	*11.3*	1.74	112	*6.6*	*14.4*	*62.7*	*16.3*
Cumbria	6,824	72	241	250	491	*2.0*	1.68	100	*5.8*	*13.5*	*60.2*	*20.4*
Allerdale	1,258	76	47	49	96	*-0.1*	1.68	101	*6.0*	*13.4*	*60.1*	*20.5*
Barrow-in-Furness	78	919	35	36	72	*-2.4*	1.78	107	*6.8*	*14.2*	*60.9*	*18.1*
Carlisle	1,040	99	50	53	103	*2.1*	1.73	106	*5.9*	*13.7*	*60.2*	*20.2*
Copeland	738	96	35	35	71	*-3.0*	1.72	110	*5.7*	*14.8*	*61.6*	*17.9*
Eden	2,156	23	24	25	49	*12.3*	1.67	98	*5.6*	*12.8*	*60.8*	*20.9*
South Lakeland	1,554	65	49	52	101	*6.3*	1.53	86	*5.2*	*12.4*	*58.6*	*23.8*
Greater Manchester	1,286	2,003	1,268	1,308	2,576	*-1.7*	1.78	110	*6.7*	*15.1*	*61.1*	*17.1*
Bolton	140	1,900	131	135	265	*1.2*	1.86	111	*6.6*	*15.1*	*61.1*	*17.1*
Bury	99	1,835	90	92	182	*3.0*	1.79	109	*6.3*	*14.7*	*62.1*	*16.9*
Manchester	116	3,710	213	218	431	*-6.9*	1.78	119	*7.6*	*16.2*	*60.5*	*15.7*
Oldham	141	1,561	108	112	220	*-0.5*	2.01	112	*7.1*	*15.7*	*60.6*	*16.6*
Rochdale	160	1,301	102	106	208	*-0.3*	1.99	114	*7.2*	*15.8*	*60.5*	*16.5*
Salford	97	2,368	114	116	229	*-7.2*	1.73	116	*6.7*	*14.4*	*60.3*	*18.6*
Stockport	126	2,311	141	150	291	*0.2*	1.64	92	*5.9*	*14.2*	*61.2*	*18.8*
Tameside	103	2,140	109	112	221	*1.0*	1.83	116	*6.7*	*15.0*	*61.2*	*17.1*
Trafford	106	2,074	107	112	219	*-1.2*	1.66	101	*6.2*	*14.4*	*61.0*	*18.4*
Wigan	199	1,558	153	156	310	*-0.2*	1.70	108	*6.3*	*14.4*	*63.0*	*16.3*

14.1 *(continued)*

	Area (sq km)	Persons per sq km	Population (thousands)			Total population percentage change 1981-1996	Total period fertility rate (TPFR)[2]	Standardised mortality ratio (UK=100) (SMR)[3]	Percentage of population aged			
			Males	Females	Total				Under 5	5-15	16 up to pension age[4]	Pension age[4] or over
Lancashire	3,070	464	698	727	1,425	2.8	1.80	104	6.3	14.6	60.0	19.1
Blackburn	137	1,018	69	71	139	-2.2	2.20	116	8.1	16.8	59.2	15.9
Blackpool	35	4,366	74	79	152	2.3	1.73	108	5.7	12.4	59.7	22.3
Burnley	111	817	44	46	90	-2.5	2.01	114	7.1	16.2	58.9	17.8
Chorley	203	476	48	49	97	4.8	1.71	102	6.0	14.5	63.1	16.4
Fylde	166	453	36	39	75	8.7	1.53	90	4.9	11.9	57.4	25.9
Hyndburn	73	1,094	39	40	80	0.5	2.14	114	7.4	15.4	59.4	17.8
Lancaster	576	238	67	70	137	9.3	1.68	100	5.7	13.8	60.1	20.4
Pendle	169	498	41	43	84	-2.3	2.05	107	6.9	16.0	59.0	18.1
Preston	142	947	67	68	135	6.7	1.83	107	6.9	14.9	61.4	16.8
Ribble Valley	584	90	26	26	53	-2.2	1.72	97	5.0	13.7	61.4	20.0
Rossendale	138	470	32	33	65	-0.1	1.75	107	6.7	15.1	61.1	17.2
South Ribble	113	912	50	53	103	6.4	1.55	99	5.9	14.8	62.0	17.3
West Lancashire	338	324	54	56	110	2.2	1.73	102	6.0	15.3	61.4	17.3
Wyre	284	368	50	55	104	5.0	1.77	94	5.2	13.4	56.3	25.1
MERSEYSIDE	655	2,168	688	733	1,420	-6.7	1.71	112	6.3	14.9	60.1	18.8
Knowsley	97	1,583	75	79	154	-11.5	1.97	127	7.3	17.1	59.5	16.1
Liverpool	113	4,148	228	240	468	-9.5	1.70	125	6.5	15.0	61.2	17.3
Sefton	153	1,895	138	151	290	-3.6	1.70	110	5.6	14.3	58.5	21.5
St Helens	133	1,346	88	91	179	-5.7	1.60	100	6.1	14.2	62.1	17.6
Wirral	159	2,074	158	172	329	-3.4	1.72	105	6.1	14.7	59.0	20.2
YORKSHIRE AND THE HUMBER	15,411	327	2,480	2,556	5,036	2.4	1.76	101	6.4	14.3	60.9	18.3
East Riding of Yorkshire UA	2,415	128	151	158	309	13.6	1.66	95	5.4	13.7	60.5	20.4
Kingston upon Hull UA	71	3,740	132	134	267	-2.5	1.79	108	6.9	15.2	60.6	17.3
North East Lincolnshire UA	192	830	78	81	159	-1.7	1.84	95	6.5	15.7	59.1	18.7
North Lincolnshire UA	833	183	75	77	153	1.1	1.76	98	6.1	14.5	60.4	18.9
Former county of Humberside	3,511	252	436	450	887	3.4	1.74	99	6.2	14.6	60.3	18.9
York UA	271	644	85	90	175	5.9	1.55	90	5.6	13.3	61.6	19.4
North Yorkshire County	8,038	70	272	287	560	9.4	1.72	94	5.7	13.5	59.9	20.9
Craven	1,179	44	25	27	51	7.2	1.77	93	5.5	13.9	57.0	23.5
Hambleton	1,311	65	42	43	85	12.8	1.65	89	5.9	13.6	61.5	19.1
Harrogate	1,305	113	70	77	148	7.9	1.59	100	5.8	13.3	61.0	19.9
Richmondshire	1,319	36	24	23	47	8.7	1.99	96	6.4	13.4	62.7	17.4
Ryedale	1,506	33	25	25	49	12.4	1.80	87	5.0	13.1	57.4	24.5
Scarborough	817	133	52	57	108	5.8	1.73	93	5.4	13.2	57.0	24.4
Selby	601	119	35	36	71	14.4	1.92	93	6.1	14.3	61.9	17.8
Former county of North Yorkshire	8,309	89	358	377	735	8.5	1.68	93	5.7	13.5	60.3	20.5
South Yorkshire	1,559	837	646	659	1,305	-0.9	1.72	105	6.4	13.9	61.2	18.4
Barnsley	328	692	112	116	227	0.6	1.81	111	6.5	14.1	61.0	18.4
Doncaster	581	502	144	148	292	0.3	1.84	113	6.6	15.0	60.3	18.2
Rotherham	283	904	126	129	255	1.1	1.82	105	6.6	14.6	61.3	17.5
Sheffield	367	1,444	264	267	530	-3.2	1.60	100	6.2	13.0	61.8	19.1
West Yorkshire	2,034	1,037	1,040	1,069	2,109	2.1	1.81	103	6.7	14.7	61.3	17.2
Bradford	366	1,320	238	245	483	4.0	2.07	103	7.5	16.1	59.8	16.6
Calderdale	363	531	94	99	193	-	1.90	106	6.7	14.4	60.9	17.9
Kirklees	410	949	191	198	389	3.1	1.89	104	6.8	14.8	61.3	17.1
Leeds	562	1,294	359	368	727	1.3	1.63	100	6.3	13.9	62.1	17.6
Wakefield	333	953	157	160	317	1.0	1.77	107	6.5	14.5	62.0	17.0
EAST MIDLANDS	15,627	265	2,048	2,094	4,141	7.5	1.69	98	6.2	14.1	61.4	18.3
Derby UA	78	2,995	116	118	234	7.5	1.69	98	6.8	14.4	60.8	18.0
Derbyshire County	2,551	286	361	367	728	4.5	1.70	101	6.0	13.4	61.6	18.9
Amber Valley	265	435	57	58	115	5.3	1.67	100	5.5	13.0	62.0	19.5
Bolsover	160	443	35	36	71	-0.1	1.73	106	6.4	13.0	60.4	20.2
Chesterfield	66	1,525	50	51	101	2.8	1.65	110	6.1	13.1	61.4	19.5
Derbyshire Dales	795	88	34	35	70	2.7	1.67	88	5.2	12.7	60.7	21.4
Erewash	109	977	53	54	107	3.1	1.82	99	6.6	13.9	61.2	18.3
High Peak	540	163	44	45	88	7.0	1.73	108	6.3	14.7	62.2	16.8
North East Derbyshire	277	358	49	50	99	3.0	1.67	102	5.7	13.2	61.6	19.4
South Derbyshire	338	230	39	39	78	13.6	1.63	97	5.9	13.9	63.5	16.6
Former county of Derbyshire	2,629	366	477	485	962	5.2	1.70	100	6.2	13.7	61.4	18.7

14.1 *(continued)*

	Area (sq km)	Persons per sq km	Population (thousands) Males	Females	Total	Total population percentage change 1981-1996	Total period fertility rate (TPFR)[2]	Standardised mortality ratio (UK=100) (SMR)[3]	Percentage of population aged Under 5	5-15	16 up to pension age[4]	Pension age[4] or over
Leicester UA	73	4,021	146	148	295	4.2	1.80	108	7.5	15.8	60.7	16.1
Rutland UA	394	90	17	18	35	7.1	1.26	88	5.5	14.6	62.5	17.4
Leicestershire County	2,084	287	297	300	597	10.1	1.65	95	6.0	14.0	62.6	17.5
Blaby	130	656	43	43	86	10.9	1.74	85	6.5	13.9	63.4	16.3
Charnwood	279	558	78	78	156	11.1	1.55	83	5.7	14.0	63.2	17.2
Harborough	593	124	37	37	74	20.0	1.73	86	6.1	14.6	62.1	17.2
Hinckley and Bosworth	297	329	49	49	98	11.1	1.62	90	6.0	13.6	62.5	17.9
Melton	481	97	23	23	47	6.9	1.88	102	6.4	13.7	62.0	18.0
North West Leicestershire	279	302	42	42	84	6.5	1.60	96	5.8	14.1	62.1	18.0
Oadby and Wigston	24	2,275	26	27	53	0.8	1.80	91	5.7	14.0	61.6	18.7
Former county of Leicestershire	2,551	364	461	466	927	8.0	1.69	95	6.4	14.6	62.0	17.0
Lincolnshire	5,921	104	301	315	616	11.4	1.68	98	5.7	13.4	59.3	21.5
Boston	362	150	27	28	54	3.1	1.60	101	5.5	13.0	59.2	22.4
East Lindsey	1,760	70	59	64	123	16.7	1.68	96	5.2	12.6	56.5	25.7
Lincoln	36	2,340	41	43	83	9.1	1.79	100	6.7	13.8	61.0	18.5
North Kesteven	922	94	43	44	87	8.0	1.61	94	5.9	13.0	59.6	21.5
South Holland	742	96	35	36	71	14.6	1.67	104	5.0	12.4	59.0	23.7
South Kesteven	943	127	58	62	120	21.9	1.57	94	6.1	14.6	61.1	18.2
West Lindsey	1,156	67	38	39	77	-0.7	1.91	102	5.6	14.5	59.4	20.5
Northamptonshire	2,367	255	299	305	604	13.5	1.74	100	6.6	15.0	62.0	16.4
Corby	80	649	26	26	52	-0.8	1.81	104	6.8	16.3	60.6	16.3
Daventry	666	98	33	33	65	12.5	1.74	100	6.4	14.4	63.0	16.2
East Northamptonshire	510	139	35	36	71	13.5	1.66	103	6.1	14.7	61.6	17.5
Kettering	233	346	40	41	81	13.0	1.72	104	6.6	14.1	61.7	17.5
Northampton	81	2,382	95	98	192	21.1	1.78	101	6.9	15.2	62.4	15.5
South Northamptonshire	634	118	38	37	75	16.5	1.54	94	6.2	15.3	62.6	16.0
Wellingborough	163	416	33	34	68	4.9	1.92	88	6.6	14.8	61.2	17.4
Nottinghamshire	2,160	478	510	522	1,032	3.8	1.68	99	6.3	14.1	61.5	18.1
Ashfield	110	988	54	55	109	1.7	1.86	104	6.2	13.8	61.7	18.3
Bassetlaw	637	167	53	54	106	3.3	1.81	101	6.1	13.6	61.8	18.5
Broxtowe	81	1,375	55	56	111	6.7	1.50	87	5.7	13.4	62.8	18.2
Gedling	120	935	55	57	112	3.7	1.70	93	5.8	13.5	62.1	18.6
Mansfield	77	1,318	50	51	101	1.4	1.80	105	6.3	14.9	60.6	18.1
Newark and Sherwood	651	160	52	53	104	3.7	1.79	107	5.9	14.1	61.0	19.0
Nottingham	75	3,806	140	144	284	2.1	1.61	102	7.1	14.8	61.0	17.2
Rushcliffe	409	253	51	52	104	11.2	1.55	90	5.5	13.6	62.2	18.7
WEST MIDLANDS	13,004	409	2,628	2,689	5,317	2.5	1.82	101	6.5	14.6	60.9	18.0
Hereford and Worcester	3,923	178	343	354	697	9.5	1.74	96	6.0	13.9	60.8	19.3
Bromsgrove	220	388	42	44	85	-3.4	1.65	99	5.6	13.0	61.8	19.6
Hereford	20	2,403	24	25	49	1.9	1.98	101	6.6	14.5	58.8	20.1
Leominster	933	45	20	21	42	10.3	1.86	97	5.6	12.9	58.0	23.5
Malvern Hills	899	102	45	47	91	7.2	1.73	95	5.1	13.7	58.1	23.2
Redditch	54	1,423	38	39	77	14.0	1.93	91	6.9	15.9	63.2	14.0
South Herefordshire	904	61	27	28	56	18.9	1.66	91	5.9	14.3	58.5	21.3
Worcester	33	2,773	46	47	92	19.6	1.68	88	6.8	13.6	62.8	16.8
Wychavon	664	163	53	55	108	14.7	1.71	95	5.7	13.4	60.9	20.0
Wyre Forest	195	495	48	49	97	5.5	1.67	103	5.8	14.0	62.4	17.9
Shropshire	3,488	121	209	213	421	10.6	1.82	95	6.2	14.3	61.1	18.4
Bridgnorth	633	80	26	25	51	0.7	1.67	94	5.2	13.2	62.6	19.0
North Shropshire	679	80	27	27	54	5.5	2.04	89	5.8	13.3	59.4	21.5
Oswestry	256	135	17	18	35	9.7	1.67	101	5.7	13.7	59.7	21.0
Shrewsbury and Atcham	602	161	48	49	97	10.6	1.56	94	6.0	14.2	60.4	19.3
South Shropshire	1,027	39	20	20	40	18.4	1.76	91	5.0	13.3	58.2	23.5
The Wrekin	290	497	72	73	144	14.9	2.02	101	7.2	15.5	62.8	14.4

Regional Trends 33, © Crown copyright 1998

14.1 (continued)

	Area (sq km)	Persons per sq km	Population (thousands)			Total population percentage change 1981-1996	Total period fertility rate (TPFR)[2]	Standardised mortality ratio (UK=100) (SMR)[3]	Percentage of population aged			
			Males	Females	Total				Under 5	5-15	16 up to pension age[4]	Pension age[4] or over
Stoke-on-Trent UA	93	2,744	126	128	254	0.8	1.68	108	6.4	14.3	61.2	18.2
Staffordshire County	2,623	306	398	403	801	4.5	1.70	101	5.9	14.3	62.5	17.3
Cannock Chase	79	1,151	46	45	91	6.6	1.96	111	6.6	14.8	63.7	14.9
East Staffordshire	390	257	50	50	100	4.2	1.70	106	6.6	14.5	60.5	18.5
Lichfield	329	283	46	47	93	4.7	1.72	101	5.8	13.3	64.2	16.8
Newcastle-under-Lyme	211	580	60	62	122	1.4	1.72	101	5.5	14.1	60.8	19.5
South Staffordshire	408	253	51	52	103	6.0	1.53	92	5.2	14.1	63.3	17.4
Stafford	599	208	62	63	125	6.2	1.58	97	5.7	13.8	62.3	18.2
Staffordshire Moorlands	576	164	47	47	94	-1.5	1.58	102	5.1	13.6	62.3	19.0
Tamworth	31	2,346	36	36	72	10.9	1.83	107	6.9	16.8	64.3	12.0
Former county of Staffordshire	2,715	389	525	531	1,056	3.6	1.69	103	6.0	14.3	62.2	17.5
Warwickshire	1,979	253	247	253	501	4.9	1.68	99	5.9	13.8	62.1	18.2
North Warwickshire	285	215	31	31	61	2.4	1.69	106	6.3	14.2	62.8	16.8
Nuneaton and Bedworth	79	1,498	59	59	118	3.9	1.86	105	6.4	15.1	62.2	16.4
Rugby	356	245	43	44	87	-0.5	1.75	92	6.4	14.1	61.5	18.1
Stratford-on-Avon	977	114	54	57	111	10.4	1.61	94	5.2	12.5	62.1	20.2
Warwick	282	434	60	62	123	6.4	1.54	100	5.6	13.3	62.1	19.1
West Midlands (Met. County)	899	2,940	1,304	1,338	2,642	-1.1	1.90	103	7.0	15.0	60.2	17.7
Birmingham	265	3,844	504	516	1,021	-	1.99	107	7.5	15.7	59.9	16.8
Coventry	97	3,176	152	155	307	-4.0	1.83	104	6.9	15.2	60.1	17.8
Dudley	98	3,187	155	157	312	3.8	1.78	98	6.4	13.6	61.6	18.4
Sandwell	86	3,412	143	149	292	-5.7	1.96	111	6.9	14.8	59.6	18.7
Solihull	179	1,142	100	104	204	2.9	1.69	87	6.0	14.3	61.5	18.2
Walsall	106	2,483	130	132	263	-1.9	1.92	100	6.7	14.8	60.5	17.9
Wolverhampton	69	3,554	120	124	244	-4.7	1.94	104	6.9	14.9	59.4	18.8
EASTERN	19,120	277	2,610	2,683	5,293	9.0	1.71	92	6.4	13.9	61.3	18.4
Luton UA	43	4,186	91	90	181	10.1	2.06	100	8.2	16.4	62.1	13.3
Bedfordshire County	1,192	308	183	185	367	6.4	1.71	95	6.6	14.4	63.2	15.8
Mid Bedfordshire	503	237	59	60	119	13.9	1.51	86	6.8	14.2	64.2	14.7
Bedford	477	288	68	69	137	3.0	1.92	102	6.3	14.1	62.3	17.3
South Bedfordshire	213	521	55	56	111	3.4	1.67	96	6.7	14.8	63.2	15.2
Former county of Bedfordshire	1,236	444	274	275	549	7.6	1.83	96	7.1	15.1	62.8	15.0
Cambridgeshire	3,400	207	349	354	703	19.3	1.58	93	6.4	14.0	63.2	16.4
Cambridge	41	2,867	58	58	117	15.6	1.04	83	5.3	10.8	68.3	15.6
East Cambridgeshire	655	103	34	34	68	25.1	1.53	92	5.9	14.0	61.5	18.6
Fenland	546	145	39	40	79	19.1	2.02	104	6.3	13.0	59.0	21.6
Huntingdonshire	923	165	75	77	153	22.3	1.60	93	6.9	14.9	64.1	14.1
Peterborough	333	477	79	79	159	18.3	1.91	102	7.2	15.5	61.7	15.6
South Cambridgeshire	902	142	63	65	128	17.9	1.63	86	6.0	14.4	63.0	16.6
Essex	3,675	432	778	808	1,586	7.0	1.71	95	6.3	13.7	61.2	18.7
Basildon	110	1,484	80	83	163	7.1	1.98	97	7.0	15.0	61.2	16.9
Braintree	612	206	63	64	126	12.1	1.71	95	6.3	14.1	62.7	16.9
Brentwood	149	482	35	37	72	-1.0	1.45	106	5.7	12.8	62.0	19.4
Castle Point	45	1,886	42	43	85	-2.2	1.64	97	5.6	13.6	62.8	18.0
Chelmsford	342	458	77	79	157	12.2	1.54	81	6.1	14.2	63.4	16.2
Colchester	334	462	76	78	154	11.5	1.60	91	6.4	13.5	63.4	16.7
Epping Forest	340	351	58	61	120	2.3	1.71	97	6.2	12.6	61.8	19.3
Harlow	30	2,437	36	37	73	-7.8	1.90	101	6.8	14.5	60.8	17.9
Maldon	360	152	27	27	55	13.1	1.97	95	6.1	14.5	61.5	18.0
Rochford	169	451	37	39	76	3.8	1.73	85	5.9	13.8	60.7	19.5
Southend-on-Sea	42	4,126	83	89	172	9.3	1.62	100	6.3	13.0	59.5	21.2
Tendring	337	392	63	69	132	15.3	1.71	94	5.4	12.1	52.9	29.5
Thurrock	164	807	66	66	132	3.8	1.90	108	7.4	14.6	63.0	15.0
Uttlesford	641	107	34	35	69	9.3	1.60	92	6.2	14.4	62.6	16.9

14.1 *(continued)*

	Area (sq km)	Persons per sq km	Population (thousands)			Total population percentage change 1981-1996	Total period fertility rate (TPFR)[2]	Standardised mortality ratio (UK=100) (SMR)[3]	Percentage of population aged			
			Males	Females	Total				Under 5	5-15	16 up to pension age[4]	Pension age[4] or over
Hertfordshire	1,639	620	502	514	1,016	5.0	1.75	89	6.7	14.1	62.0	17.2
Broxbourne	52	1,566	40	41	82	2.4	1.73	92	6.3	13.9	63.1	16.7
Dacorum	212	634	66	68	135	3.0	1.80	85	6.7	14.6	61.5	17.2
East Hertfordshire	477	259	62	62	124	12.8	1.75	88	6.5	13.6	64.5	15.4
Hertsmere	98	970	46	49	95	7.1	1.74	92	6.7	14.3	59.8	19.1
North Hertfordshire	375	306	57	58	115	5.8	1.72	90	6.5	14.0	61.4	18.2
St Albans	161	808	64	66	130	4.0	1.83	85	6.5	13.1	63.4	17.0
Stevenage	26	2,956	38	39	77	2.8	1.88	87	7.8	16.4	60.5	15.4
Three Rivers	89	952	42	43	85	4.3	1.64	79	5.8	13.6	61.6	19.1
Watford	21	3,684	39	40	79	5.8	1.70	107	7.7	14.0	63.8	14.5
Welwyn Hatfield	127	748	47	49	95	1.4	1.67	89	6.7	14.2	59.9	19.3
Norfolk	5,372	145	381	396	777	10.5	1.67	89	5.7	13.0	59.1	22.2
Breckland	1,305	87	56	58	114	17.5	1.68	85	6.0	13.4	58.7	22.0
Broadland	552	206	56	58	114	16.1	1.48	100	5.6	13.0	60.5	21.0
Great Yarmouth	174	514	43	46	89	9.7	1.83	96	6.2	13.7	58.0	22.1
Kings Lynn and West Norfolk	1,429	92	65	67	131	7.5	1.76	89	5.8	12.9	57.7	23.5
North Norfolk	965	100	47	50	97	16.3	1.72	83	5.0	12.2	55.5	27.3
Norwich	39	3,234	62	64	126	0.1	1.52	88	6.1	12.8	62.1	19.0
South Norfolk	908	117	52	54	106	11.1	1.74	84	5.3	12.8	60.5	21.4
Suffolk	3,798	174	326	336	662	10.0	1.68	91	6.2	14.2	59.5	20.1
Babergh	595	133	39	40	79	6.6	1.91	91	5.1	14.1	60.3	20.5
Forest Heath	374	184	34	34	69	30.3	1.38	101	7.9	17.5	61.5	13.1
Ipswich	39	2,883	56	58	114	-5.4	1.86	96	6.8	14.3	59.1	19.7
Mid Suffolk	871	92	40	40	80	13.7	1.95	80	5.9	13.9	59.8	20.4
St Edmundsbury	657	142	46	47	94	7.4	1.63	94	6.1	13.0	62.4	18.5
Suffolk Coastal	892	133	58	60	119	22.5	1.43	86	5.9	14.5	58.4	21.2
Waveney	370	291	52	56	108	7.7	1.80	95	5.9	13.2	56.3	24.5
LONDON	1,578	4,482	3,475	3,599	7,074	3.9	1.75	97	7.1	13.4	64.2	15.3
Barking and Dagenham	34	4,504	75	79	154	1.4	2.11	111	7.9	15.3	58.0	18.8
Barnet	89	3,569	156	163	319	8.2	1.60	92	6.7	13.5	63.3	16.5
Bexley	61	3,617	107	112	219	1.0	1.76	93	6.6	14.3	61.6	17.6
Brent	44	5,603	124	124	248	-2.6	1.91	98	7.6	14.0	65.1	13.3
Bromley	152	1,948	143	152	296	-1.0	1.74	87	6.2	12.6	61.7	19.5
Camden	22	8,707	92	97	189	5.6	1.53	91	6.3	10.9	68.1	14.8
City of London	3	1,893	3	2	5	-4.1	1.81	72	5.0	7.0	66.6	21.4
City of Westminster	22	9,468	101	103	204	8.4	1.24	85	5.3	9.1	70.2	15.3
Croydon	87	3,853	164	170	334	4.0	1.71	98	7.0	14.1	64.0	14.9
Ealing	55	5,358	148	149	297	5.3	1.72	99	7.3	13.5	65.4	13.8
Enfield	81	3,236	129	133	263	0.6	1.97	94	7.5	13.7	62.1	16.6
Greenwich	48	4,448	103	109	212	-1.6	1.92	108	7.4	15.5	61.2	15.9
Hackney	20	9,940	96	98	194	4.7	2.24	100	8.5	15.2	63.7	12.5
Hammersmith and Fulham	16	9,703	75	82	157	3.6	1.39	106	6.6	10.3	69.9	13.2
Haringey	30	7,137	107	109	216	4.3	1.83	103	7.6	13.2	66.8	12.5
Harrow	51	4,146	104	107	211	5.9	1.68	85	6.6	14.1	63.2	16.1
Havering	118	1,961	113	118	231	-4.7	1.64	102	5.8	13.6	61.3	19.3
Hillingdon	110	2,246	123	125	248	6.2	1.71	93	6.8	13.6	63.5	16.1
Hounslow	58	3,570	103	103	206	1.0	1.94	96	7.3	13.9	64.3	14.5
Islington	15	11,825	86	90	176	6.0	1.51	102	7.1	13.0	66.1	13.8
Kensington and Chelsea	12	13,320	77	82	159	13.5	1.29	85	5.7	9.8	70.8	13.8
Kingston upon Thames	38	3,778	70	72	142	5.6	1.62	92	6.2	12.6	64.6	16.6
Lambeth	27	9,706	130	135	265	4.7	1.71	104	7.7	13.5	66.2	12.6
Lewisham	35	6,953	116	125	241	2.1	1.74	109	7.6	14.0	63.5	14.9
Merton	38	4,807	90	93	182	8.7	1.68	91	7.0	12.7	64.8	15.5
Newham	36	6,295	115	114	229	7.5	2.66	109	9.7	17.6	60.6	12.1
Redbridge	56	4,083	113	117	231	0.6	1.80	91	6.8	14.2	62.2	16.8
Richmond-upon-Thames	55	3,255	87	93	180	11.2	1.55	84	6.2	11.7	65.2	16.9
Southwark	29	7,993	113	117	230	5.3	1.99	106	8.4	14.0	63.3	14.3
Sutton	43	4,046	85	90	176	3.2	1.66	91	7.0	13.5	62.3	17.3
Tower Hamlets	20	8,949	89	88	177	21.6	2.36	116	8.8	17.2	60.3	13.6
Waltham Forest	40	5,555	108	112	220	1.2	1.96	97	8.0	14.2	63.1	14.7
Wandsworth	35	7,631	129	137	266	1.6	1.52	104	6.8	10.2	69.0	14.0

14.1 *(continued)*

	Area (sq km)	Persons per sq km	Population (thousands)			Total population percentage change 1981-1996	Total period fertility rate (TPFR)[2]	Standardised mortality ratio (UK=100) (SMR)[3]	Percentage of population aged			
			Males	Females	Total				Under 5	5-15	16 up to pension age[4]	Pension age[4] or over
SOUTH EAST (GOR)	19,096	413	3,875	4,021	7,895	*9.0*	*1.69*	92	*6.3*	*13.9*	*61.3*	*18.6*
Berkshire	1,259	628	396	395	791	*13.9*	*1.70*	96	*6.8*	*14.4*	*64.3*	*14.5*
Bracknell Forest	109	1,006	56	54	110	*30.0*	*1.64*	103	*7.4*	*14.9*	*65.4*	*12.3*
Newbury	704	204	71	72	144	*17.2*	*1.65*	93	*6.3*	*14.9*	*64.0*	*14.7*
Reading	40	3,536	72	71	143	*3.9*	*1.71*	85	*6.9*	*13.4*	*64.6*	*15.1*
Slough	27	4,027	55	56	110	*13.2*	*1.87*	109	*8.0*	*15.0*	*63.4*	*13.6*
Windsor and Maidenhead	198	713	70	71	142	*4.5*	*1.51*	103	*6.0*	*13.4*	*63.6*	*17.1*
Wokingham	179	795	72	70	142	*21.7*	*1.87*	90	*6.6*	*14.9*	*65.0*	*13.4*
Milton Keynes UA	309	639	98	99	197	*56.5*	*1.77*	98	*7.5*	*16.3*	*64.7*	*11.5*
Buckinghamshire County	1,568	303	235	239	475	*6.8*	*1.74*	91	*6.5*	*14.3*	*63.2*	*16.0*
Aylesbury Vale	903	172	77	78	155	*15.5*	*1.82*	101	*6.9*	*14.7*	*64.0*	*14.4*
Chiltern	196	471	45	47	93	*2.1*	*1.62*	81	*5.6*	*14.4*	*61.7*	*18.3*
South Buckinghamshire	145	436	31	32	63	*1.1*	*1.62*	102	*6.1*	*13.6*	*61.5*	*18.8*
Wycombe	325	505	82	82	164	*4.3*	*1.75*	86	*6.7*	*14.1*	*64.1*	*15.1*
Former county of Buckinghamshire	1,877	358	334	338	672	*17.8*	*1.75*	93	*6.8*	*14.9*	*63.7*	*14.7*
Brighton and Hove UA	82	3,034	121	128	250	*5.2*	*1.38*	95	*5.4*	*11.5*	*62.9*	*20.2*
East Sussex County	1,713	283	228	257	485	*13.4*	*1.69*	88	*5.7*	*13.3*	*54.9*	*26.1*
Eastbourne	44	2,014	41	48	89	*14.8*	*1.37*	86	*5.4*	*11.6*	*54.4*	*28.6*
Hastings	30	2,760	39	43	82	*8.4*	*2.08*	103	*6.5*	*14.4*	*57.0*	*22.1*
Lewes	292	297	41	46	87	*10.0*	*1.92*	86	*5.7*	*13.7*	*54.5*	*26.2*
Rother	511	175	41	48	89	*16.9*	*1.62*	83	*5.2*	*12.5*	*50.5*	*31.8*
Wealden	836	165	66	72	138	*15.7*	*1.59*	86	*5.7*	*14.1*	*57.0*	*23.2*
Former county of East Sussex	1,795	409	349	386	735	*10.5*	*1.55*	90	*5.6*	*12.7*	*57.6*	*24.1*
Portsmouth UA	40	4,728	97	93	190	*-0.5*	*1.68*	100	*6.4*	*13.0*	*62.7*	*17.9*
Southampton UA	50	4,311	108	107	215	*2.4*	*1.63*	94	*6.4*	*13.4*	*62.5*	*17.6*
Hampshire County	3,689	331	600	622	1,222	*12.3*	*1.67*	91	*6.2*	*14.3*	*61.7*	*17.8*
Basingstoke and Deane	634	233	73	74	148	*12.1*	*1.80*	96	*7.1*	*14.6*	*64.2*	*14.1*
East Hampshire	515	215	54	57	111	*20.9*	*1.67*	92	*6.2*	*15.1*	*61.6*	*17.0*
Eastleigh	80	1,401	55	56	112	*20.3*	*1.69*	91	*6.6*	*14.6*	*62.9*	*15.9*
Fareham	74	1,397	50	53	104	*16.6*	*1.49*	80	*5.5*	*13.9*	*61.1*	*19.5*
Gosport	25	3,023	36	40	76	*-1.9*	*1.68*	105	*7.1*	*15.0*	*60.5*	*17.4*
Hart	215	399	44	42	86	*22.7*	*1.54*	84	*5.9*	*13.8*	*66.8*	*13.4*
Havant	55	2,120	57	61	117	*1.4*	*1.84*	95	*5.7*	*15.1*	*58.3*	*20.8*
New Forest	753	225	82	87	170	*16.5*	*1.61*	89	*5.6*	*12.9*	*57.2*	*24.3*
Rushmoor	39	2,197	43	43	86	*-1.4*	*1.80*	95	*7.6*	*14.2*	*65.0*	*13.2*
Test Valley	637	168	53	54	107	*14.3*	*1.57*	89	*6.0*	*14.7*	*62.8*	*16.5*
Winchester	661	160	52	54	106	*14.0*	*1.65*	85	*5.6*	*13.8*	*61.1*	*19.5*
Former county of Hampshire	3,779	431	805	822	1,627	*9.3*	*1.67*	92	*6.3*	*14.0*	*61.9*	*17.8*
Isle of Wight UA	380	328	60	65	125	*6.3*	*1.93*	93	*5.2*	*13.0*	*55.7*	*26.1*
Kent	3,735	417	762	796	1,557	*4.9*	*1.78*	97	*6.4*	*14.1*	*60.6*	*19.0*
Ashford	581	169	48	50	98	*12.6*	*1.77*	96	*6.5*	*14.4*	*60.7*	*18.5*
Canterbury	309	442	66	70	136	*11.7*	*1.56*	90	*5.3*	*13.1*	*58.7*	*23.0*
Dartford	73	1,152	42	42	84	*3.3*	*1.68*	110	*6.6*	*13.4*	*63.5*	*16.4*
Dover	315	341	52	55	107	*3.8*	*1.69*	95	*6.2*	*14.0*	*58.3*	*21.4*
Gillingham	32	2,927	47	48	95	*-1.7*	*1.78*	106	*6.6*	*15.8*	*62.8*	*14.8*
Gravesham	99	926	45	47	92	*-4.0*	*1.96*	95	*6.7*	*14.7*	*60.8*	*17.9*
Maidstone	393	358	69	71	141	*7.6*	*1.65*	93	*6.2*	*14.0*	*62.6*	*17.1*
Rochester-upon-Medway	160	905	71	73	144	*0.5*	*1.89*	107	*7.3*	*14.8*	*63.3*	*14.5*
Sevenoaks	368	300	54	56	110	*0.7*	*1.73*	88	*6.3*	*14.2*	*60.5*	*19.0*
Shepway	357	277	47	51	99	*14.6*	*1.56*	90	*6.1*	*13.2*	*58.0*	*22.7*
Swale	373	315	59	59	118	*6.8*	*2.03*	100	*6.5*	*14.8*	*61.3*	*17.4*
Thanet	103	1,215	60	66	126	*3.1*	*1.85*	104	*5.8*	*13.5*	*54.8*	*25.8*
Tonbridge and Malling	240	437	52	53	105	*7.3*	*1.82*	89	*6.8*	*14.1*	*62.4*	*16.6*
Tunbridge Wells	332	309	50	53	103	*4.2*	*1.98*	100	*6.1*	*14.1*	*60.5*	*19.4*
Oxfordshire	2,606	231	301	302	603	*11.3*	*1.58*	89	*6.5*	*14.1*	*63.3*	*16.0*
Cherwell	589	225	65	67	133	*21.5*	*1.56*	91	*7.3*	*15.4*	*63.0*	*14.3*
Oxford	46	3,012	69	68	137	*5.3*	*1.24*	89	*5.6*	*12.5*	*66.9*	*15.1*
South Oxfordshire	679	184	61	63	125	*6.4*	*1.81*	87	*6.8*	*14.6*	*61.6*	*17.0*
Vale of White Horse	579	194	57	56	113	*8.7*	*1.90*	88	*6.1*	*14.6*	*62.1*	*17.1*
West Oxfordshire	714	134	48	48	96	*17.5*	*1.72*	89	*6.8*	*13.6*	*62.4*	*17.2*

14.1 *(continued)*

	Area (sq km)	Persons per sq km	Population (thousands)			Total population percentage change 1981-1996	Total period fertility rate (TPFR)[2]	Standardised mortality ratio (UK=100) (SMR)[3]	Percentage of population aged			
			Males	Females	Total				Under 5	5-15	16 up to pension age[4]	Pension age[4] or over
Surrey	1,677	624	514	534	1,047	3.2	1.67	88	6.2	13.4	61.8	18.7
Elmbridge	97	1,289	60	64	125	10.7	1.66	87	6.4	13.5	62.1	18.0
Epsom and Ewell	34	2,032	34	35	69	-0.1	1.54	78	5.9	13.0	61.5	19.6
Guildford	271	460	62	63	125	-0.3	1.56	83	6.0	13.1	62.5	18.4
Mole Valley	258	307	39	41	79	2.4	1.82	84	5.7	12.3	60.1	21.9
Reigate and Banstead	129	924	59	61	119	2.0	1.78	98	6.3	13.3	61.3	19.1
Runnymede	78	975	38	38	76	4.4	1.55	85	6.2	12.3	62.4	19.2
Spelthorne	57	1,578	44	45	89	-3.9	1.72	91	6.1	12.3	62.3	19.3
Surrey Heath	95	867	41	42	82	8.4	1.66	93	6.8	14.8	64.3	14.2
Tandridge	250	311	37	40	78	-0.5	1.62	90	5.9	14.3	60.3	19.6
Waverley	345	331	55	59	114	1.8	1.81	84	5.9	14.0	59.7	20.4
Woking	64	1,426	45	46	91	10.6	1.70	96	6.8	13.9	63.4	15.9
West Sussex	1,988	371	354	384	737	10.7	1.67	90	5.8	13.2	57.9	23.1
Adur	42	1,409	28	31	59	0.6	1.75	92	5.8	13.0	56.2	25.0
Arun	221	625	66	72	138	16.4	1.66	91	5.1	11.8	53.8	29.3
Chichester	786	132	48	56	104	5.3	1.55	87	5.5	12.8	55.2	26.5
Crawley	44	2,113	46	47	93	13.6	1.69	89	7.2	14.1	62.4	16.3
Horsham	530	224	58	60	119	18.2	1.62	83	6.2	14.4	60.5	18.8
Mid Sussex	333	376	62	64	125	8.6	1.73	87	5.6	14.2	61.9	18.3
Worthing	32	3,055	46	53	99	7.3	1.65	97	5.5	12.0	55.0	27.5
SOUTH WEST	23,829	203	2,366	2,475	4,842	10.5	1.70	90	5.8	13.5	59.5	21.2
Bath and North East Somerset UA	351	471	80	84	165	2.0	1.59	88	5.4	12.7	60.7	21.2
Bristol UA	110	3,622	198	201	400	-0.4	1.62	90	6.4	13.4	62.5	17.7
North Somerset UA	375	497	90	95	185	13.8	1.72	91	5.4	13.5	59.4	21.7
South Gloucestershire UA	497	474	118	118	235	15.7	1.87	85	6.9	13.7	63.3	16.1
Former county of Avon	1,333	741	486	499	985	6.0	1.69	89	6.2	13.4	61.8	18.7
Cornwall and the Isles of Scilly	3,559	136	235	249	483	13.3	1.77	92	5.4	13.7	58.1	22.9
Caradon	664	120	39	41	80	17.7	1.76	83	5.4	14.2	59.2	21.2
Carrick	461	184	41	44	85	12.1	1.71	89	5.3	13.4	56.6	24.7
Kerrier	473	188	43	46	89	6.7	1.74	93	5.7	13.7	58.9	21.7
North Cornwall	1,190	66	38	41	79	21.5	1.68	94	5.7	13.6	57.8	23.0
Penwith	304	196	29	31	60	10.1	2.02	96	4.9	12.5	57.4	25.2
Restormel	452	198	44	46	89	13.9	1.80	100	5.3	14.0	58.6	22.1
Isles of Scilly	15	124	1	1	2	-2.9	..	84	5.1	17.9	54.0	23.0
Devon	6,703	158	512	547	1,059	9.7	1.68	89	5.6	13.4	58.4	22.7
East Devon	814	151	58	65	123	14.3	1.74	80	4.8	11.8	53.1	30.3
Exeter	47	2,291	53	55	108	7.1	1.73	93	5.8	13.1	62.5	18.7
Mid Devon	915	72	32	34	66	12.4	1.85	88	5.8	14.3	58.6	21.3
North Devon	1,086	79	42	44	86	10.2	1.92	93	5.6	13.2	58.2	22.9
Plymouth	80	3,210	126	130	256	1.0	1.54	100	6.0	14.2	61.8	18.0
South Hams	887	89	38	41	79	18.9	1.75	86	5.4	13.6	58.0	23.0
Teignbridge	674	173	56	60	117	21.9	1.72	85	5.5	12.9	56.8	24.8
Torbay	63	1,963	58	65	123	9.1	1.70	88	5.3	12.6	55.6	26.5
Torridge	979	56	26	28	54	11.9	1.85	90	5.5	14.8	56.7	23.0
West Devon	1,160	40	22	24	46	8.6	1.83	85	5.1	13.9	57.9	23.1
Bournemouth UA	46	3,481	76	84	161	12.1	1.45	91	5.3	11.2	58.1	25.4
Poole UA	65	2,150	67	72	139	15.7	1.61	87	6.0	13.2	58.7	22.1
Dorset County	2,542	150	185	197	382	14.1	1.67	82	5.1	13.0	56.4	25.5
Christchurch	50	857	20	23	43	12.9	1.75	75	4.8	10.9	51.1	33.2
East Dorset	354	231	40	42	82	18.7	1.53	75	4.4	12.2	56.1	27.3
North Dorset	609	96	29	30	58	18.8	1.72	77	5.3	14.2	58.0	22.5
Purbeck	404	112	22	23	45	12.0	1.63	78	5.4	13.1	58.6	22.8
West Dorset	1,082	84	43	47	90	12.9	1.72	85	5.1	13.1	54.8	27.0
Weymouth and Portland	42	1,505	31	32	63	8.3	1.76	102	5.9	13.9	59.8	20.4
Former county of Dorset	2,653	257	329	353	682	13.9	1.60	85	5.3	12.6	57.3	24.8

14.1 *(continued)*

	Area (sq km)	Persons per sq km	Population (thousands)			Total population percentage change 1981-1996	Total period fertility rate (TPFR)[2]	Standardised mortality ratio (UK=100) (SMR)[3]	Percentage of population aged			
			Males	Females	Total				Under 5	5-15	16 up to pension age[4]	Pension age[4] or over
Gloucestershire	2,653	210	275	281	556	*9.9*	*1.72*	92	*6.1*	*13.8*	*60.6*	*19.6*
Cheltenham	47	2,288	52	54	107	*3.8*	*1.58*	92	*5.7*	*12.9*	*61.2*	*20.3*
Cotswold	1,165	70	40	42	81	*15.8*	*1.57*	83	*5.7*	*13.3*	*59.2*	*21.7*
Forest of Dean	526	144	38	38	76	*3.7*	*1.99*	103	*5.6*	*13.5*	*60.9*	*20.0*
Gloucester	41	2,636	53	54	107	*6.6*	*1.87*	100	*7.4*	*14.9*	*60.8*	*17.0*
Stroud	461	234	53	55	108	*12.4*	*1.71*	91	*5.9*	*14.2*	*60.0*	*20.0*
Tewkesbury	414	187	39	38	77	*21.8*	*1.66*	82	*5.9*	*13.5*	*61.4*	*19.2*
Somerset	3,452	140	235	248	483	*12.1*	*1.72*	89	*5.8*	*14.0*	*58.2*	*22.0*
Mendip	739	133	48	50	98	*9.5*	*1.88*	96	*6.2*	*15.4*	*59.0*	*19.4*
Sedgemoor	564	180	50	52	102	*13.2*	*1.71*	91	*5.7*	*13.6*	*58.9*	*21.8*
South Somerset	959	157	74	77	151	*13.2*	*1.69*	88	*5.9*	*13.9*	*58.4*	*21.8*
Taunton Deane	462	214	48	51	99	*11.9*	*1.67*	86	*5.6*	*14.1*	*58.4*	*22.0*
West Somerset	727	45	15	17	33	*11.3*	*1.66*	82	*5.2*	*11.3*	*52.4*	*31.1*
Swindon UA	230	759	87	87	175	*15.2*	*1.84*	101	*6.8*	*14.6*	*62.6*	*16.0*
Wiltshire County	3,246	129	207	212	419	*12.1*	*1.76*	91	*6.4*	*14.1*	*61.1*	*18.5*
Kennet	957	79	37	38	75	*15.0*	*1.80*	83	*6.8*	*14.3*	*61.1*	*17.9*
North Wiltshire	768	159	61	61	122	*16.0*	*1.82*	89	*7.0*	*13.9*	*62.6*	*16.5*
Salisbury	1,004	112	55	58	113	*9.7*	*1.59*	92	*5.6*	*14.1*	*60.2*	*20.0*
West Wiltshire	517	211	54	55	109	*8.6*	*1.86*	97	*6.1*	*14.1*	*60.2*	*19.6*
Former county of Wiltshire	3,476	171	294	300	593	*13.0*	*1.78*	93	*6.5*	*14.3*	*61.5*	*17.7*

1 The table reflects the implementation of the local government re-organisation up to 1 April 1997. See Notes and Definitions.
2 The total period fertility rate (TPFR) is the average number of children which would be born to a woman if the current pattern of fertility persisted throughout her child-bearing years.
3 Adjusted for the age structure of the population. See Notes and Definitions to the Population chapter.
4 Pension age is 65 for males and 60 for females.

Source: Office for National Statistics

14.2 Vital and social statistics: by sub-region

	Live births[1] per 1,000 population		Deaths[1] per 1,000 population		Perinatal mortality rate[2,3]	Infant mortality rate[3,4]	Percent-age of live births under 2.5 kg	Percent-age of live births outside marriage	Children looked after by LAs per 1,000 population aged under 18
	1991	1996	1991	1996	1994-1996	1994-1996	1996	1996	1996[5]
United Kingdom	13.7	12.5	11.2	10.9	8.8	6.1	*7.2*	*36*	..
England	13.7	12.5	11.1	10.7	8.8	6.1	*7.3*	*36*	4.5
North East	13.4	11.6	12.2	11.7	9.6	6.4	*7.3*	*44*	5.1
Hartlepool UA	14.9	12.3	11.5	11.7	7.1	5.5	*7.4*	*52*	..
Middlesbrough UA	15.1	13.2	11.1	10.0	10.7	8.8	*7.6*	*52*	..
Redcar & Cleveland UA	14.0	12.2	10.9	11.1	6.7	5.3	*7.1*	*48*	..
Stockton-on-Tees UA	14.9	12.4	10.4	9.6	8.6	5.9	*7.3*	*42*	..
Former county of Cleveland	14.7	12.5	10.9	10.4	8.5	6.5	*7.3*	*48*	4.1
Durham#	13.0	11.3	12.4	12.0	8.9	5.5	*7.2*	*42*	4.5
Northumberland	11.8	10.7	12.6	12.6	10.8	7.6	*6.0*	*37*	4.0
Tyne & Wear	13.4	11.5	12.7	11.9	10.3	6.6	*7.7*	*46*	6.0
North West (GOR) and Merseyside	14.2	12.3	12.0	11.6	8.8	6.3	*7.6*	*42*	4.9
North West (GOR)	14.2	12.4	11.9	11.4	8.9	6.4	*7.6*	*40*	4.6
Cheshire	13.5	11.9	10.7	10.8	8.6	6.1	*6.5*	*34*	1.5
Cumbria	12.7	11.1	12.7	12.0	7.7	5.3	*7.1*	*36*	4.3
Greater Manchester	14.9	12.9	11.8	11.2	9.7	6.6	*8.1*	*43*	5.4
Lancashire	13.9	12.2	12.7	12.0	8.2	6.6	*7.5*	*39*	5.2
Merseyside	14.0	12.1	12.4	12.3	8.1	6.0	*7.9*	*50*	6.1
Yorkshire and the Humber	13.8	12.3	11.5	11.1	9.0	7.0	*7.4*	*38*	5.3
East Riding of Yorkshire UA	11.8	9.9	12.0	11.4	8.7	7.0	*6.8*	*33*	..
Kingston upon Hull UA	15.6	13.5	10.9	11.0	8.2	6.6	*8.0*	*55*	..
North East Lincolnshire UA	14.5	12.3	10.9	10.5	5.1	4.6	*6.8*	*49*	..
North Lincolnshire UA	13.0	11.4	11.2	10.7	9.8	7.8	*7.2*	*38*	..
Former county of Humberside	13.7	11.7	11.3	11.0	8.1	6.5	*7.3*	*45*	6.2
York UA	12.3	11.1	11.6	10.5	7.0	5.5	*6.6*	*33*	..
North Yorkshire County	11.7	11.2	12.4	12.0	6.6	5.0	*5.2*	*27*	..
Former county of North Yorkshire	11.8	11.2	12.2	11.6	6.7	5.1	*5.5*	*28*	2.9
South Yorkshire	13.7	12.1	11.7	11.4	9.8	8.0	*7.3*	*42*	4.8
West Yorkshire	14.5	13.1	11.2	10.6	9.5	7.3	*8.1*	*37*	5.8
East Midlands	13.4	11.9	10.9	10.6	8.8	6.3	*7.3*	*36*	4.0
Derbyshire#	13.4	11.9	11.6	11.0	7.6	5.5	*6.6*	*37*	4.9
Leicestershire#	13.7	12.2	10.0	9.7	9.7	6.5	*8.2*	*32*	2.9
Lincolnshire	11.7	10.9	11.8	12.1	9.2	6.4	*6.2*	*34*	3.8
Northamptonshire	14.1	12.4	10.3	10.0	8.3	7.0	*7.5*	*36*	4.2
Nottinghamshire	13.7	12.0	10.8	10.6	9.3	6.4	*7.6*	*41*	4.1
West Midlands	14.1	12.7	10.8	10.6	10.3	7.0	*8.1*	*37*	4.6
Hereford & Worcs.	12.6	11.6	10.7	10.9	9.3	5.5	*6.6*	*33*	4.1
Shropshire	13.3	12.1	10.4	10.4	8.6	5.1	*7.0*	*36*	3.9
Staffordshire#	13.2	11.6	10.7	10.5	9.3	6.7	*7.2*	*36*	3.7
Warwickshire	12.5	11.5	10.5	10.6	9.1	5.6	*6.3*	*31*	3.8
West Midlands (Met. county)	15.2	13.7	11.0	10.7	11.3	7.9	*9.2*	*38*	5.3
Eastern	13.3	12.2	10.3	10.2	7.6	5.3	*6.6*	*31*	3.6
Bedfordshire#	15.2	14.0	9.0	8.7	9.5	7.0	*7.3*	*30*	3.7
Cambridgeshire	13.6	12.1	9.2	9.3	6.9	5.2	*7.2*	*30*	4.7
Essex	13.3	12.1	10.6	10.7	7.5	4.7	*6.1*	*34*	3.8
Hertfordshire	13.6	13.0	9.5	9.1	7.8	4.9	*6.7*	*27*	2.8
Norfolk	11.6	10.8	12.1	11.8	7.4	5.9	*6.8*	*34*	3.7
Suffolk	12.8	11.5	11.2	11.1	7.3	4.9	*6.5*	*31*	2.9
London	15.4	14.9	10.0	9.3	9.6	6.3	*7.8*	*34*	5.7
South East (GOR)	13.0	12.1	10.8	10.6	7.6	5.0	*6.6*	*30*	3.8
Berkshire	14.3	13.6	8.5	8.5	6.9	4.9	*6.8*	*28*	3.7
Buckinghamshire#	14.3	13.2	8.4	8.9	8.4	5.5	*6.7*	*26*	3.3
East Sussex#	11.5	10.4	15.0	14.1	8.3	5.3	*6.7*	*38*	5.0
Hampshire#	13.1	12.0	10.0	10.0	7.7	5.1	*6.9*	*31*	2.8
Isle of Wight UA	10.6	10.6	15.5	15.1	7.4	6.4	*7.1*	*41*	5.2
Kent	13.4	12.3	11.2	11.2	7.9	5.1	*6.5*	*35*	..
Oxfordshire	13.7	12.1	8.8	8.8	6.6	3.8	*6.2*	*26*	3.5
Surrey	12.3	11.9	10.4	10.3	7.2	4.7	*5.9*	*23*	2.8
West Sussex	11.7	11.2	13.5	13.1	7.6	5.0	*6.4*	*29*	4.4

Regional Trends 33, © Crown copyright 1998

14.2 *(continued)*

	Live births[1] per 1,000 population		Deaths[1] per 1,000 population		Perinatal mortality rate[2,3]	Infant mortality rate[3,4]	Percentage of live births under 2.5 kg	Percentage of live births outside marriage	Children looked after by LAs per 1,000 population aged under 18
	1991	1996	1991	1996	1994-1996	1994-1996	1996	1996	1996[5]
South West	12.2	11.3	11.9	11.6	7.6	5.3	6.7	33	4.2
Bath and North East Somerset UA	11.1	10.6	11.4	11.5	8.3	5.7	6.0	31	..
Bristol UA	13.9	12.7	11.2	9.9	7.7	6.0	7.8	43	..
North Somerset UA	11.0	10.5	12.2	12.5	8.6	4.6	6.1	29	..
South Gloucestershire UA	13.9	13.8	8.4	8.1	6.3	5.0	7.0	26	..
Former county of Avon	12.9	12.2	10.8	10.2	4.8	5.4	7.0	34	4.8
Cornwall	11.5	10.5	12.9	12.7	9.0	5.1	6.7	37	4.2
Devon	11.8	10.8	12.9	12.6	7.2	5.6	6.8	36	5.2
Dorset#	11.1	10.3	13.7	13.3	7.2	5.3	6.5	31	3.4
Gloucestershire	12.6	11.6	10.8	10.9	8.5	5.3	6.5	31	3.2
Somerset	12.1	10.9	11.9	11.9	6.5	4.4	6.7	32	3.6
Wiltshire#	13.5	12.7	10.2	9.9	7.6	5.3	6.6	30	3.4
New local government structure with effect from 1 April 1997									
Former county of Durham									
Darlington UA	14.3	11.7	13.9	11.9	7.8	5.7	7.0	41	..
Durham County	12.8	11.2	12.1	12.0	9.3	5.8	7.2	42	..
Former county of Derbyshire									
Derby UA	15.4	12.8	11.8	10.5	8.8	7.6	7.1	40	..
Derbyshire County	12.8	11.6	11.6	11.2	7.2	4.9	6.4	35	..
Former county of Leicestershire									
Leicester UA	16.5	14.4	11.3	10.6	10.0	7.9	10.4	39	..
Rutland UA[3]	9.8	9.5	8.7	9.0	8.8	4.9	6.6	23	..
Leicestershire County	12.5	11.3	9.4	9.3	9.5	5.7	6.9	29	..
Former county of Staffordshire									
Stoke-on-Trent UA	14.3	12.4	12.1	11.3	11.2	7.7	8.0	44	..
Staffordshire County	12.9	11.4	10.3	10.2	8.7	6.4	6.9	34	..
Former county of Bedfordshire									
Luton UA	18.5	16.6	8.8	8.0	10.1	7.7	8.7	30	..
Bedfordshire County	13.7	12.7	9.1	9.0	9.2	6.7	6.4	29	..
Former county of Buckinghamshire									
Milton Keynes UA	17.1	14.8	7.2	7.0	8.8	6.9	6.7	36	..
Buckinghamshire County	13.3	12.6	8.8	8.9	8.2	4.9	6.7	22	..
Former county of East Sussex									
Brighton and Hove UA	12.1	11.2	13.9	12.6	8.7	5.1	6.7	42	..
East Sussex County	11.2	10.0	15.5	14.9	8.0	5.3	6.7	35	..
Former county of Hampshire									
Portsmouth UA	14.2	12.6	12.0	11.2	10.1	5.0	7.6	40	
Southampton UA	13.8	12.4	11.1	10.0	8.3	6.3	8.0	44	..
Hampshire County	12.7	11.9	9.5	9.8	7.1	4.9	6.6	27	..
Former county of Dorset									
Bournemouth UA	11.1	10.2	16.0	15.4	8.4	6.3	6.5	38	..
Poole UA	12.2	11.0	12.7	12.1	7.5	6.1	7.0	30	..
Dorset County	10.6	10.0	13.0	12.8	8.8	5.3	6.4	28	..
Former county of Wiltshire									
Swindon UA	15.1	13.9	9.5	9.3	6.4	4.1	7.2	35	..
Wiltshire County	12.8	12.3	10.5	10.2	8.2	6.0	6.4	27	..

New local government structure came into effect on 1 April 1997.
1 Births are on the basis of year of occurrence in England and Wales and year of registration in Scotland and Northern Ireland. Deaths relate to year of registration.
2 Still births and deaths of infants under 1 week of age per 1,000 live and still births.
3 The figure for Rutland UA should be treated with caution as the perinatal mortality rate and infant mortality rate were based on fewer than 20 deaths.
4 Deaths of infants under 1 year of age per 1,000 live births.
5 At 31 March. Under 18 mid-1995 population estimates used. In some cases figures are estimates which take account of missing or incomplete data.

Source: Office for National Statistics; Department of Health

14.3 Education and training: by sub-region

	Day nursery places per 1,000 population aged under 5 years[1] March 1996	Children under 5 in education[2] (percent-ages) Jan. 1997	Pupil/teacher ratio 1996/97 (numbers)		Pupils and students participating in post-compulsory education, (percentages) 1995/96[3]	Pupils in last year of compulsory schooling[4,5] 1995/96 with		Average A/AS level points score[5,6] 1995/96	Employees of working age receiving job-related training[7], 1996-97[8]
			Primary schools	Secondary schools		No graded results	5 or more A*-Cs at GCSE		
United Kingdom	..	59	22.8	16.2	78	7.1	43.2	16.7	14.5
England	..	60	23.4	16.7	77	7.5	41.7	16.8	14.7
North East	27.5	85	23.8	17.1	70	10.1	36.3	16.1	14.6
Hartlepool UA		99	25.2	17.1	..	12.0	31.9	15.2	..
Middlesbrough UA	..	96	23.7	16.2	..	16.3	26.9	14.6	..
Redcar & Cleveland UA	..	108	24.3	17.2	..	8.2	37.6	-	..
Stockton-on-Tees UA	..	98	24.2	17.1	..	9.8	37.2	18.7	18.7
Former county of Cleveland	17.6	..	..	..	71	11.3	33.9	17.4	16.3
Durham#	27.9	83	24.1	17.4	67	9.4	36.2	16.1	17.6
Northumberland	21.2	81	24.5	18.6	74	6.3	46.1	16.7	12.3
Tyne & Wear	34.2	80	23.2	16.6	68	10.8	34.9	15.5	12.7
North West (GOR) and Merseyside	..	69	23.9	16.6	74	8.4	41.0	18.3	14.2
North West (GOR)	71.6	67	24.0	16.7	74	7.6	42.2	18.9	14.3
Cheshire	69.6	59	23.8	17.0	82	4.8	49.3	19.5	13.7
Cumbria	49.7	69	23.4	16.9	76	6.7	44.2	18.4	17.1
Greater Manchester	63.6	74	23.9	16.5	72	9.0	38.9	18.4	13.8
Lancashire	95.5	58	24.4	16.7	74	7.3	42.6	19.0	14.6
Merseyside	..	77	23.4	16.3	74	11.7	36.3	16.7	14.0
Yorkshire and the Humber	44.8	71	24.1	17.2	74	9.8	37.1	18.1	15.6
East Riding of Yorkshire UA	..	61	25.5	17.0	..	5.9	43.6	17.6	15.0
Kingston upon Hull UA	..	74	25.5	18.2	..	16.3	22.8	20.0	14.2
North East Lincolnshire UA	..	66	25.0	17.9	..	10.2	32.4	14.1	..
North Lincolnshire UA	..	62	24.6	17.5	..	5.6	37.6	15.0	18.1
Former county of Humberside	28.0	..	..	..	72	9.6	34.4	17.0	15.8
York UA	..	59	24.3	16.3	..	7.4	47.7	23.3	..
North Yorkshire County	..	58	23.5	16.4	..	4.3	53.0	21.5	15.2
Former county of North Yorkshire	58.3	..	..	..	85	4.9	51.9	21.7	14.4
South Yorkshire	30.9	69	24.0	17.2	68	11.6	34.5	17.9	15.4
West Yorkshire	55.7	78	23.9	17.3	74	10.3	35.1	16.8	16.1
East Midlands	..	58	24.4	17.0	74	7.3	40.7	16.8	11.9
Derbyshire#	57.8	67	25.9	17.4	73	6.5	42.0	18.1	10.4
Leicestershire#	63.9	44	23.5	17.2	79	7.1	39.7	16.0	10.9
Lincolnshire	..	56	23.9	15.9	71	6.5	44.5	19.3	14.2
Northamptonshire	57.6	58	23.5	16.8	75	5.9	43.5	14.6	12.8
Nottinghamshire	56.0	64	24.8	17.3	74	9.5	36.4	16.2	12.5
West Midlands	..	66	23.6	16.9	76	8.2	39.3	16.7	13.8
Hereford & Worcs.	82.5	38	23.2	17.8	80	6.3	44.6	18.1	14.9
Shropshire	67.2	45	24.4	16.5	80	4.8	48.0	17.3	16.6
Staffordshire#	..	64	24.9	17.7	75	7.6	40.9	16.6	13.5
Warwickshire	63.4	59	24.5	17.4	81	6.6	43.7	16.5	14.3
West Midlands (Met. county)	..	77	23.1	16.3	74	9.7	35.3	16.2	13.0
Eastern	..	49	23.0	16.6	80	5.7	45.0	16.4	14.3
Bedfordshire#	38.3	56	23.3	17.8	80	5.6	42.7	17.3	16.6
Cambridgeshire	..	45	24.4	17.4	78	5.8	46.7	15.3	14.1
Essex	51.2	41	23.0	16.6	76	6.4	43.1	17.5	14.9
Hertfordshire	6.4	65	22.9	15.9	94	5.4	49.3	16.6	13.8
Norfolk	28.6	48	22.3	15.7	75	6.1	41.9	15.8	14.2
Suffolk	28.0	41	22.3	16.6	79	4.1	47.0	14.8	12.2
London	..	67	21.9	15.9	80	7.7	39.0	15.3	16.2

14.3 *(continued)*

| | Day nursery places per 1,000 population aged under 5 years[1] March 1996 | Children under 5 in education[2] (percentages) Jan. 1997 | Pupil/teacher ratio 1996/97 (numbers) | | Pupils and students participating in post-compulsory education, (percentages) 1995/96[3] | Pupils in last year of compulsory schooling[4,5] 1995/96 with | | Average A/AS level points score[5,6] 1995/96 | Employees of working age receiving job-related training[7], 1996-97[8] |
			Primary schools	Secondary schools		No graded results	5 or more A*-Cs at GCSE		
South East (GOR)	56.5	46	23.2	16.7	81	5.9	47.0	16.6	15.5
Berkshire	62.5	46	23.5	16.6	84	5.6	48.8	16.7	15.7
Buckinghamshire#	58.9	41	23.9	17.3	77	6.0	50.5	18.9	13.1
East Sussex#	73.1	54	22.8	16.2	80	6.6	43.3	15.2	21.0
Hampshire#	40.5	46	23.0	16.6	80	5.0	46.5	16.3	14.8
Isle of Wight	36.1	49	22.6	18.2	84	4.3	44.5	14.1	..
Kent	59.5	46	23.9	16.3	80	6.4	43.7	16.8	14.8
Oxfordshire	62.4	34	23.6	18.1	82	6.6	45.8	15.2	16.2
Surrey	67.1	58	22.3	16.9	82	5.8	50.5	16.0	16.6
West Sussex	43.5	36	22.7	16.8	82	5.6	50.6	15.3	14.6
South West	..	45	23.7	17.1	82	5.2	46.6	16.6	14.9
Bath and North East Somerset UA	..	54	22.4	16.6	..	4.5	47.4	15.8	..
Bristol UA	..	73	23.0	15.6	..	10.6	30.9	13.8	21.5
North Somerset UA	..	42	23.8	16.0	..	3.9	52.5	16.5	16.9
South Gloucestershire UA	..	51	24.2	16.7	..	4.9	44.7	15.2	16.8
Former county of Avon	57.3	..	..	..	81	6.5	42.4	15.6	18.3
Cornwall	31.0	51	23.7	17.4	81	3.7	46.9	15.3	13.0
Devon	30.3	36	24.1	17.1	78	5.4	44.2	16.5	12.3
Dorset#	54.9	43	24.6	17.7	86	5.6	49.3	18.0	13.8
Gloucestershire	..	41	23.6	17.3	85	5.2	50.2	17.3	13.3
Somerset	60.4	45	23.5	18.0	83	4.1	50.0	15.5	15.7
Wiltshire#	..	34	23.5	17.0	79	4.7	48.3	17.2	16.2

New local government structure came into effect on 1 April 1997.

1 Local authority provided and registered day nurseries only. A small number of places provided by facilities exempt from registration are excluded. Population data used are mid-1995 estimates.

2 Figures relate to all pupils as a percentage of the three and four year old population.

3 Pupils and students aged 16 in education as a percentage of the 16 year old population (ages measured at the beginning of the academic year).

4 Pupils in their last year of compulsory schooling as a percentage of the school population of the same age.

5 Figures relate to maintained schools only; hence they are not directly comparable with those in Tables 4.6, 16.3 and 17.3 which are for all schools.

6 Figure for United Kingdom relates to England and Wales average.

7 Males aged 16-64 and females aged 16-59. Job-related education or training received in the four weeks before interview. In some cases sample sizes are too small to provide reliable estimates.

8 Data relate to the period March 1996 to February 1997. Figure for United Kingdom relates to Great Britain.

Source: Department of Health; Department for Education and Employment

14.4 Housing and households: by local authority[1]

| | Housing starts 1996[2] (numbers) | | Stock of dwellings[3] 1996 (thousands) | Households 1996 | | | | | | Local authority tenants: average weekly unrebated rent per dwelling (£) April 1997[6] | Council Tax (£) April 1997[7] |
	Private enterprise	Housing associations local authorities etc		All households (thousands)	Average household size (thousands)	Lone parents[4] as a percentage of all households	One-person households as a percentage of all households	Households receiving Housing Benefit[5] as a percentage of all households			
UNITED KINGDOM	151,826	31,224	24,607	24,115.3	2.40	..	28.4	20.3		..	.
ENGLAND	121,127	22,461	20,516	20,206.6	2.39	5.6	28.8	19.6		41.18	688
NORTH EAST	5,606	954	1,097	1,080.9	2.38	6.5	29.6	26.6		34.17	782
Hartlepool UA	262	127	38	37.3	2.44	7.0	27.8	30.2		35.66	886
Middlesbrough UA	308	56	59	58.2	2.49	10.0	28.5	32.2		41.35	712
Redcar & Cleveland UA	266	76	59	57.5	2.40	6.4	28.0	23.3		37.87	942
Stockton-on-Tees UA	1,048	181	73	72.4	2.45	6.4	27.7	22.0		36.41	801
Former county of Cleveland	1,884	440	231	225.4	2.45	7.4	28.0	26.3		38.07	..
Darlington UA	349	38	43	42.0	2.36	5.6	30.3	19.0		34.36	598
Durham County	1,122	49	214	209.1	2.39	5.7	27.7	24.5		36.17	779
Chester-le-Street	200	6	23	23.6	2.36	4.4	27.0	19.5		32.70	706
Derwentside	141	15	37	36.4	2.38	6.2	28.2	26.3		38.32	796
Durham	293	6	35	35.9	2.47	5.3	27.3	19.2		36.59	726
Easington	140	0	41	39.1	2.41	6.3	28.4	31.9		37.68	813
Sedgefield	237	16	38	37.3	2.39	6.1	26.6	25.7		34.62	835
Teesdale	41	6	11	10.3	2.35	2.7	29.3	14.1		33.65	731
Wear Valley	70	0	27	26.6	2.34	6.3	27.8	25.3		35.62	791
Former county of Durham	1,471	87	257	251.1	2.39	5.7	28.1	23.6		35.96	..
Northumberland	679	43	134	126.7	2.38	4.5	27.8	19.0		31.89	736
Alnwick	104	7	14	13.0	2.35	4.5	26.4	17.6		32.73	734
Berwick-upon-Tweed	53	0	13	11.7	2.23	3.3	33.6	17.6		32.22	735
Blyth Valley	27	0	34	33.2	2.39	5.1	27.3	22.9		29.77	715
Castle Morpeth	215	0	20	19.6	2.40	3.7	26.6	13.5		34.01	738
Tynedale	136	15	25	23.5	2.41	4.1	28.4	13.0		37.26	733
Wansbeck	144	21	27	25.7	2.40	5.1	26.8	24.7		30.25	765
Tyne and Wear	1,315	377	486	477.7	2.33	7.0	31.6	30.4		32.55	791
Gateshead	175	60	88	86.3	2.31	6.3	31.5	29.9		32.69	863
Newcastle-upon-Tyne	227	44	122	120.6	2.31	7.8	34.8	33.4		35.89	831
North Tyneside	406	157	88	84.5	2.27	6.1	31.6	25.8		29.20	809
South Tyneside	111	56	67	66.5	2.32	7.6	32.2	31.9		28.83	763
Sunderland	396	60	120	119.8	2.43	7.1	28.3	30.1		33.41	704
NORTH WEST (GOR) & MERSEYSIDE	15,675	2,588	2,893	2,816.7	2.41	6.7	29.2	22.5		38.43	798
NORTH WEST (GOR)	12,642	1,666	2,285	2,242.5	2.40	6.2	29.0	20.6		37.44	766
Cheshire	3,096	140	404	398.7	2.43	5.1	26.7	15.4		33.82	710
Chester	346	18	51	49.9	2.35	5.2	30.1	16.0		35.70	704
Congleton	383	0	38	34.6	2.47	3.2	24.9	9.5		35.94	709
Crewe and Nantwich	366	0	45	46.3	2.44	4.7	26.4	13.9		35.58	704
Ellesmere Port and Neston	..	..	33	32.4	2.47	5.8	24.2	15.9		28.25	734
Halton	..	..	48	48.1	2.54	8.3	24.8	27.9		31.66	686
Macclesfield	513	31	66	63.8	2.35	4.0	27.9	10.1		37.32	704
Vale Royal	449	33	48	46.1	2.48	4.3	25.0	14.2		37.12	719
Warrington	713	58	77	77.5	2.41	5.4	27.5	15.7		31.48	722
Cumbria	1,001	130	217	205.6	2.34	4.1	29.3	16.3		38.14	759
Allerdale	175	30	42	39.7	2.36	3.8	30.1	19.1		38.84	748
Barrow-in-Furness	65	0	31	30.3	2.35	5.1	28.8	19.3		41.89	790
Carlisle	258	74	44	43.5	2.34	4.4	29.4	17.3		35.12	782
Copeland	87	14	30	29.0	2.41	5.3	27.6	20.7		35.21	753
Eden	198	0	21	20.1	2.37	2.9	27.0	10.0		53.08	747
South Lakeland	218	12	47	43.1	2.27	2.8	31.2	10.6		37.94	743
Greater Manchester	5,118	1,106	1,086	1,058.4	2.41	7.3	30.0	25.1		38.21	794
Bolton	..	..	111	108.3	2.43	6.0	28.9	21.5		32.65	787
Bury	290	79	75	74.3	2.41	5.3	28.1	15.0		36.94	711
Manchester	649	448	189	177.9	2.38	12.8	35.3	50.3		45.04	898
Oldham	498	111	91	90.0	2.42	7.2	29.1	22.2		33.24	818
Rochdale	426	64	87	83.9	2.45	7.5	29.1	22.5		35.96	770
Salford	666	37	102	96.2	2.35	8.1	33.2	32.6		39.13	874
Stockport	233	101	120	121.6	2.37	5.1	29.0	13.3		32.55	839
Tameside	281	50	93	90.5	2.42	6.1	27.7	20.1		37.11	815
Trafford	339	52	89	89.7	2.41	5.9	29.5	15.4		37.44	620
Wigan	1,044	0	128	126.0	2.44	5.3	26.5	18.9		31.80	748

14.4 *(continued)*

	Housing starts 1996[2] (numbers)		Stock of dwellings[3] 1996 (thousands)	Households 1996						Local authority tenants: average weekly unrebated rent per dwelling (£) April 1997[6]	Council Tax (£) April 1997[7]
	Private enterprise	Housing associations local authorities etc		All households (thousands)	Average household size (thousands)	Lone parents[4] as a percentage of all households	One-person households as a percentage of all households	Households receiving Housing Benefit[5] as a percentage of all households			
Lancashire	3,437	290	594	579.8	2.41	5.8	28.7	17.3	37.53	763
Blackburn	322	115	58	54.3	2.53	7.7	28.4	23.7	44.15	835
Blackpool	120	6	66	65.3	2.24	5.5	32.9	22.7	33.46	729
Burnley	290	0	39	36.7	2.42	7.9	28.3	21.5	38.34	791
Chorley	..	..	39	38.5	2.47	5.2	24.1	13.2	29.16	730
Fylde	354	28	33	32.2	2.24	3.4	31.3	10.2	32.59	734
Hyndburn	213	0	34	32.4	2.43	6.7	28.4	19.6	38.95	807
Lancaster	208	51	55	56.1	2.38	6.1	30.1	17.0	36.07	731
Pendle	108	0	37	34.5	2.43	6.0	30.1	16.4	36.49	803
Preston	358	21	55	54.0	2.44	6.9	31.7	21.8	39.61	784
Ribble Valley	221	0	22	20.4	2.48	3.3	27.0	7.4	33.17	746
Rossendale	69	25	28	26.3	2.43	5.9	27.3	19.1	36.54	815
South Ribble	339	17	42	41.0	2.49	4.8	23.5	9.3	.	730
West Lancashire	281	0	42	43.6	2.48	6.3	25.1	18.8	36.24	752
Wyre	209	27	44	44.4	2.31	4.0	29.4	9.9	.	739
MERSEYSIDE	3,033	922	610	574.2	2.43	8.5	29.7	29.9	42.01	930
Knowsley	559	80	61	58.7	2.61	12.8	24.5	39.1	44.32	864
Liverpool	..	..	202	190.2	2.42	10.3	32.9	40.5	41.12	1111
Sefton	..	..	118	116.8	2.42	6.1	29.4	19.5	39.26	821
St Helens	500	94	74	72.8	2.45	6.2	25.7	24.1	40.46	882
Wirral	357	196	139	135.8	2.39	7.2	29.7	22.9	45.13	858
YORKSHIRE AND THE HUMBER	12,422	1,893	2,099	2,076.6	2.39	5.6	28.8	20.8	32.36	710
East Riding of Yorkshire UA	..	..	129	126.3	2.41	3.7	25.7	11.8	33.14	782
Kingston upon Hull UA	545	126	112	110.0	2.40	7.6	32.0	34.0	32.17	683
North East Lincolnshire UA	35	32	67	64.9	2.41	6.8	26.9	20.2	33.27	788
North Lincolnshire UA	..	..	63	62.1	2.43	5.1	25.5	16.9	31.84	932
Former county of Humberside	2,126	188	372	363.2	2.41	5.7	27.8	20.9	32.45	..
York UA	743	25	73	73.7	2.33	4.8	29.7	15.3	39.68	605
North Yorkshire County	1,682	268	268	229.7	2.37	3.8	27.8	11.1	39.68	626
Craven	140	0	23	21.3	2.36	4.0	29.3	10.6	40.08	635
Hambleton	236	52	35	33.4	2.48	3.3	24.8	10.6	.	557
Harrogate	538	87	62	61.0	2.34	4.0	28.8	11.0	42.96	655
Richmondshire	91	25	19	18.5	2.43	3.8	25.6	10.7	38.36	628
Ryedale	184	24	23	20.5	2.35	2.1	26.9	11.2	.	659
Scarborough	228	26	50	46.7	2.25	4.8	31.3	18.6	38.90	616
Selby	265	54	30	28.3	2.48	3.2	24.1	12.1	37.44	632
Former county of North Yorkshire	2,425	293	316	303.4	2.36	4.0	28.2	12.1	39.68	..
South Yorkshire	2,719	292	541	542.1	2.38	5.5	28.4	24.6	30.21	716
Barnsley	572	5	94	92.3	2.43	5.3	25.5	24.3	29.62	674
Doncaster	818	117	120	118.9	2.42	5.9	26.1	22.0	30.36	655
Rotherham	646	69	104	104.4	2.43	5.4	26.1	22.6	27.38	715
Sheffield	683	101	224	226.5	2.32	5.5	31.8	27.0	31.57	767
West Yorkshire	4,684	1,037	868	867.8	2.40	6.1	29.6	21.5	32.95	713
Bradford	1,026	359	189	189.2	2.52	6.8	28.9	20.6	35.81	714
Calderdale	216	53	82	81.0	2.35	5.6	29.7	18.0	33.68	778
Kirklees	1,102	125	161	159.3	2.42	5.9	29.4	18.9	36.40	800
Leeds	1,571	443	303	307.4	2.34	6.3	31.4	23.6	31.07	674
Wakefield	769	57	132	130.9	2.40	5.0	26.8	23.2	31.66	650
EAST MIDLANDS	13,820	1,432	1,723	1,690.6	2.42	4.9	26.7	16.9	35.67	705
Derby UA	506	53	97	96.4	2.39	6.1	29.6	21.1	34.49	672
Derbyshire County	2,564	172	309	301.3	2.39	3.9	26.4	15.7	32.38	734
Amber Valley	..	..	50	48.0	2.38	3.4	25.9	13.5	36.73	732
Bolsover	307	0	31	29.0	2.43	3.8	24.5	21.7	29.40	767
Chesterfield	84	147	44	43.3	2.30	4.1	30.3	22.6	30.96	716
Derbyshire Dales	175	10	30	28.7	2.39	2.9	26.5	9.5	34.29	734
Erewash	456	10	45	44.6	2.37	4.9	26.9	15.5	31.28	724
High Peak	239	0	36	36.0	2.42	4.5	27.0	13.6	38.19	733
North East Derbyshire	169	4	41	41.1	2.39	3.9	25.1	15.7	29.40	758
South Derbyshire	614	0	32	30.7	2.50	3.8	23.4	12.2	34.45	719
Former county of Derbyshire	3,070	225	406	397.7	2.39	4.5	27.1	17.0	32.87	..

14.4 *(continued)*

| | Housing starts 1996[2] (numbers) | | Stock of dwellings[3] 1996 (thousands) | Households 1996 | | | | | Local authority tenants: average weekly unrebated rent per dwelling (£) April 1997[6] | Council Tax (£) April 1997[7] |
	Private enterprise	Housing associations local authorities etc		All households (thousands)	Average household size (thousands)	Lone parents[4] as a percentage of all households	One-person households as a percentage of all households	Households receiving Housing Benefit[5] as a percentage of all households		
Leicester UA	398	144	115	114.4	2.54	8.1	30.6	27.7	41.91	610
Rutland UA	72	4	13	13.7	2.49	5.2	23.4	9.5	43.44	793
Leicestershire County	2,236	182	240	238.7	2.48	3.6	24.4	9.4	34.74	704
Blaby	395	12	35	33.7	2.51	3.4	21.0	6.4	32.62	719
Charnwood	503	74	59	62.0	2.49	4.0	26.0	10.1	32.92	714
Harborough	417	29	29	29.3	2.49	3.0	24.5	8.1	40.83	700
Hinckley and Bosworth	319	12	40	40.0	2.42	3.2	25.0	9.2	36.71	674
Melton	..	..	19	18.9	2.43	3.5	24.7	10.5	33.65	702
North West Leicestershire	389	43	34	33.9	2.47	3.8	25.0	13.0	34.76	716
Oadby and Wigston	80	12	21	20.9	2.54	3.7	22.3	7.9	32.91	702
Former county of Leicestershire	2,706	330	368	366.8	2.50	5.0	26.3	15.1	38.66	..
Lincolnshire	2,950	150	268	256.9	2.36	4.1	26.4	15.5	34.78	658
Boston	237	18	24	22.8	2.34	3.8	27.2	18.5	34.62	661
East Lindsey	403	64	55	52.0	2.31	3.4	26.9	15.0	36.64	648
Lincoln	234	34	37	36.4	2.26	6.1	32.6	26.6	30.90	656
North Kesteven	715	30	37	35.4	2.38	3.6	22.6	10.7	34.72	664
South Holland	426	0	31	30.0	2.35	2.9	24.5	11.8	37.60	672
South Kesteven	654	0	50	49.0	2.43	4.6	25.3	13.4	36.92	642
West Lindsey	281	4	34	31.2	2.43	3.9	25.1	13.2	34.17	682
Northamptonshire	2,819	207	251	242.7	2.46	5.1	25.3	15.5	37.76	659
Corby	152	0	22	20.3	2.54	9.0	21.9	25.1	35.59	661
Daventry	338	46	27	26.0	2.48	3.3	23.1	11.1	36.68	638
East Northamptonshire	509	0	29	28.5	2.46	3.5	24.4	13.0	37.20	666
Kettering	346	44	34	32.8	2.43	4.4	26.0	14.5	36.82	664
Northampton	720	68	80	77.6	2.44	5.8	27.6	18.0	39.87	679
South Northamptonshire	514	23	29	29.7	2.50	3.1	23.1	9.0	42.14	685
Wellingborough	240	26	29	27.8	2.42	6.2	26.2	16.5	34.24	585
Nottinghamshire	2,156	414	431	426.4	2.39	5.7	27.6	20.0	35.37	769
Ashfield	220	63	46	44.5	2.42	4.5	25.7	17.9	35.85	762
Bassetlaw	376	26	44	43.6	2.40	4.1	25.2	17.7	37.31	760
Broxtowe	64	0	46	46.8	2.36	4.7	26.6	12.3	32.21	752
Gedling	202	48	47	46.6	2.38	3.6	26.4	10.7	32.19	747
Mansfield	239	19	43	41.5	2.42	5.6	25.8	21.8	41.39	758
Newark and Sherwood	258	0	43	42.5	2.43	4.5	25.2	16.1	35.21	808
Nottingham	272	149	118	118.5	2.36	9.3	31.9	33.0	34.20	809
Rushcliffe	525	109	41	42.5	2.39	3.8	26.7	9.0	36.10	714
WEST MIDLANDS	11,951	2,167	2,160	2,132.2	2.46	5.6	27.2	19.8	37.96	701
Hereford and Worcester	2,568	274	291	282.9	2.43	4.4	25.3	14.0	36.53	615
Bromsgrove	280	18	37	34.4	2.44	3.8	22.1	8.8	34.37	604
Hereford	27	20	21	20.2	2.39	6.4	28.5	22.9	34.78	607
Leominster	142	29	17	16.6	2.46	2.8	24.7	13.7	.	610
Malvern Hills	341	61	37	37.4	2.39	3.1	26.3	11.8	.	604
Redditch	170	75	31	30.3	2.53	6.4	22.9	19.8	37.93	647
South Herefordshire	280	16	23	22.3	2.43	3.0	25.2	11.0	37.61	611
Worcester	666	12	38	38.5	2.36	5.5	27.5	16.2	35.59	608
Wychavon	531	32	45	44.1	2.42	3.7	24.9	10.9	.	607
Wyre Forest	131	11	40	39.3	2.43	4.5	26.2	14.6	37.70	636
Shropshire	1,765	259	176	169.5	2.45	4.5	25.8	16.4	37.47	666
Bridgnorth	122	0	21	20.4	2.44	3.9	24.5	12.4	37.18	641
North Shropshire	155	13	23	21.5	2.46	2.4	25.3	13.6	33.29	673
Oswestry	119	23	15	14.5	2.36	3.7	28.7	16.1	34.16	661
Shrewsbury and Atcham	433	40	39	39.6	2.41	4.8	29.1	14.0	35.47	643
South Shropshire	110	75	17	16.7	2.39	3.0	24.9	12.7	.	647
The Wrekin	826	108	60	56.9	2.51	6.1	23.7	21.8	39.91	697

14.4   *(continued)*

	Housing starts 1996[2] (numbers)		Stock of dwellings[3] 1996 (thousands)	Households 1996					Local authority tenants: average weekly unrebated rent per dwelling (£) April 1997[6]	Council Tax (£) April 1997[7]
	Private enterprise	Housing associations local authorities etc		All households (thousands)	Average household size (thousands)	Lone parents[4] as a percentage of all households	One-person households as a percentage of all households	Households receiving Housing Benefit[5] as a percentage of all households		
Stoke-on-Trent UA	368	102	105	103.7	2.43	*5.5*	*28.1*	*22.3*	36.80	645
Staffordshire County	2,065	108	324	318.0	2.49	*4.0*	*23.8*	*13.1*	35.66	632
Cannock Chase	..	..	36	35.5	2.54	*4.9*	*22.1*	*18.2*	40.26	672
East Staffordshire	..	..	41	40.1	2.48	*3.5*	*25.1*	*13.9*	33.46	655
Lichfield	194	1	37	36.6	2.50	*3.4*	*21.7*	*10.6*	.	632
Newcastle-under-Lyme	246	6	50	49.7	2.44	*3.9*	*27.8*	*13.9*	30.74	641
South Staffordshire	206	49	41	41.6	2.46	*3.6*	*22.4*	*11.4*	.	566
Stafford	301	0	49	48.7	2.50	*3.8*	*24.2*	*11.6*	35.47	633
Staffordshire Moorlands	138	0	39	37.8	2.47	*3.2*	*23.4*	*8.4*	34.69	654
Tamworth	331	10	28	28.1	2.57	*6.1*	*21.5*	*19.1*	41.27	607
Former county of Staffordshire	2,433	210	429	421.8	2.47	*4.3*	*24.8*	*15.4*	36.09	..
Warwickshire	1,472	190	207	205.0	2.42	*4.3*	*26.3*	*13.3*	36.84	713
North Warwickshire	160	9	25	24.7	2.47	*4.1*	*25.2*	*14.0*	34.17	757
Nuneaton and Bedworth	285	34	48	47.5	2.48	*4.9*	*24.3*	*15.8*	35.55	746
Rugby	128	40	36	35.8	2.41	*4.9*	*26.2*	*13.2*	36.65	721
Stratford-on-Avon	486	65	47	46.2	2.38	*2.9*	*27.2*	*10.6*	.	682
Warwick	413	42	51	50.7	2.37	*4.7*	*28.0*	*13.3*	40.00	695
West Midlands (Met. County)	3,719	1,233	1,057	1,053.0	2.48	*6.8*	*29.1*	*24.9*	38.73	762
Birmingham	670	771	397	404.5	2.49	*8.3*	*31.8*	*27.5*	40.49	794
Coventry	457	38	124	123.9	2.44	*7.7*	*30.0*	*21.8*	37.12	839
Dudley	362	16	125	126.8	2.44	*4.2*	*26.0*	*18.8*	38.66	697
Sandwell	883	53	123	116.9	2.48	*5.7*	*28.7*	*30.9*	41.65	746
Solihull	379	61	81	81.8	2.48	*5.3*	*24.5*	*13.9*	40.57	661
Walsall	624	77	105	102.6	2.54	*5.3*	*25.2*	*23.9*	33.55	662
Wolverhampton	344	217	101	96.6	2.50	*7.1*	*28.9*	*29.2*	34.66	867
EASTERN	18,295	2,436	2,222	2,169.2	2.41	*4.4*	*26.9*	*15.4*	42.71	639
Luton UA	180	68	71	71.7	2.51	*6.3*	*27.0*	*18.6*	45.23	602
Bedfordshire County	1,185	343	149	149.2	2.43	*4.3*	*26.1*	*13.5*	43.68	764
Mid Bedfordshire	608	167	48	47.5	2.46	*3.1*	*24.7*	*10.1*	42.64	739
Bedford	366	173	57	56.8	2.39	*4.8*	*28.6*	*16.3*	35.99	762
South Bedfordshire	211	3	45	44.9	2.46	*4.8*	*24.4*	*13.4*	44.33	793
Former county of Bedfordshire	1,365	411	221	220.9	2.46	*4.9*	*26.4*	*15.1*	44.47	..
Cambridgeshire	3,006	324	283	286.8	2.42	*4.6*	*26.7*	*14.8*	42.09	590
Cambridge	271	39	42	49.8	2.28	*6.3*	*35.0*	*16.7*	41.77	634
East Cambridgeshire	460	110	28	27.4	2.45	*2.4*	*24.2*	*12.6*	.	570
Fenland	342	13	35	33.2	2.36	*3.1*	*26.3*	*15.9*	41.10	614
Huntingdonshire	810	78	62	60.7	2.48	*4.7*	*22.7*	*11.1*	40.66	579
Peterborough	409	6	67	64.9	2.42	*6.5*	*27.9*	*21.7*	42.13	611
South Cambridgeshire	714	78	50	50.8	2.49	*2.9*	*23.5*	*9.1*	44.57	549
Essex	4,872	886	665	650.5	2.41	*4.5*	*26.8*	*15.6*	44.22	645
Basildon	692	227	69	66.5	2.44	*5.5*	*25.9*	*20.7*	44.35	678
Braintree	882	114	52	51.6	2.42	*4.3*	*26.1*	*16.3*	42.39	639
Brentwood	64	80	29	29.0	2.43	*3.3*	*26.7*	*9.7*	49.01	631
Castle Point	121	0	35	33.9	2.49	*3.4*	*22.6*	*9.1*	53.27	668
Chelmsford	191	111	63	63.5	2.44	*3.7*	*25.7*	*11.2*	45.87	645
Colchester	469	47	63	61.8	2.44	*5.3*	*26.1*	*15.5*	43.53	636
Epping Forest	208	10	49	49.3	2.40	*3.7*	*26.5*	*13.6*	46.41	640
Harlow	434	92	31	30.1	2.42	*6.0*	*27.4*	*26.6*	41.72	705
Maldon	..	..	23	21.8	2.48	*3.1*	*24.9*	*12.6*	.	622
Rochford	348	15	31	30.4	2.49	*3.5*	*24.0*	*9.5*	43.70	648
Southend-on-Sea	46	38	73	75.1	2.25	*5.6*	*32.3*	*19.7*	45.99	617
Tendring	241	9	61	57.7	2.24	*3.3*	*32.0*	*14.3*	41.45	635
Thurrock	706	119	56	52.5	2.50	*5.7*	*23.6*	*19.6*	43.00	642
Uttlesford	196	24	28	27.4	2.48	*3.3*	*24.5*	*10.5*	46.27	639

14.4 *(continued)*

	Housing starts 1996[2] (numbers)		Stock of dwellings[3] 1996 (thousands)	Households 1996					Local authority tenants: average weekly unrebated rent per dwelling (£) April 1997[6]	Council Tax (£) April 1997[7]
	Private enterprise	Housing associations local authorities etc		All households (thousands)	Average household size (thousands)	Lone parents[4] as a percentage of all households	One-person households as a percentage of all households	Households receiving Housing Benefit[5] as a percentage of all households		
Hertfordshire	3,546	294	413	410.8	2.44	*4.3*	*26.8*	*14.6*	45.40	628
Broxbourne	356	16	33	32.5	2.50	*2.6*	*23.2*	*12.1*	52.99	591
Dacorum	230	15	55	55.7	2.40	*4.7*	*27.8*	*14.5*	42.62	599
East Hertfordshire	766	100	50	49.4	2.48	*3.0*	*25.1*	*10.7*	47.59	606
Hertsmere	154	91	37	37.7	2.46	*4.5*	*25.6*	*13.0*	42.93	619
North Hertfordshire	432	30	47	47.7	2.38	*3.9*	*28.4*	*16.0*	45.69	625
St Albans	312	29	51	52.1	2.44	*3.8*	*27.2*	*10.6*	48.17	634
Stevenage	398	9	32	30.7	2.48	*6.6*	*24.8*	*25.1*	46.49	655
Three Rivers	..	..	32	33.8	2.45	*3.8*	*26.2*	*12.1*	47.98	642
Watford	377	4	33	32.2	2.42	*5.9*	*29.7*	*17.5*	43.87	701
Welwyn Hatfield	161	0	40	38.9	2.43	*4.4*	*28.7*	*18.0*	41.23	648
Norfolk	3,189	346	349	327.9	2.33	*4.3*	*27.6*	*16.8*	36.98	620
Breckland	508	14	49	47.3	2.37	*4.0*	*25.5*	*13.1*	.	602
Broadland	938	72	49	46.0	2.43	*3.0*	*22.4*	*8.3*	.	602
Great Yarmouth	175	2	39	37.6	2.33	*5.0*	*29.2*	*23.5*	34.77	611
Kings Lynn and West Norfolk	630	106	62	54.8	2.35	*3.6*	*26.9*	*15.7*	36.22	620
North Norfolk	443	22	48	41.3	2.28	*3.4*	*29.2*	*14.4*	38.34	621
Norwich	68	130	56	56.8	2.19	*7.2*	*34.6*	*29.7*	36.96	664
South Norfolk	427	0	46	44.0	2.38	*3.5*	*24.4*	*11.1*	39.92	623
Suffolk	2,201	181	285	272.4	2.39	*4.1*	*26.8*	*15.8*	40.29	651
Babergh	259	52	34	32.7	2.39	*3.5*	*24.9*	*14.0*	43.81	652
Forest Heath	106	4	24	26.0	2.57	*5.3*	*24.2*	*10.4*	38.39	612
Ipswich	101	9	50	48.1	2.34	*5.9*	*30.0*	*23.1*	39.27	719
Mid Suffolk	467	6	34	32.5	2.44	*2.7*	*24.6*	*11.1*	42.03	651
St Edmundsbury	572	7	40	38.5	2.38	*3.5*	*24.8*	*14.3*	41.39	636
Suffolk Coastal	476	42	51	48.6	2.40	*2.9*	*27.5*	*12.0*	38.09	642
Waveney	220	61	49	46.0	2.30	*4.4*	*28.7*	*20.9*	37.78	623
LONDON	8,616	3,483	3,011	2,998.8	2.33	*7.5*	*33.4*	*26.1*	54.23	651
Barking and Dagenham	..	..	61	61.7	2.47	*7.1*	*29.2*	*29.8*	42.10	635
Barnet	468	129	126	127.9	2.46	*5.4*	*30.0*	*16.0*	52.60	665
Bexley	191	88	91	89.5	2.44	*4.7*	*25.7*	*13.8*	58.52	624
Brent	48	0	102	99.5	2.46	*9.3*	*30.8*	*33.1*	69.05	554
Bromley	171	39	127	125.3	2.33	*4.5*	*29.9*	*13.2*	42.72	581
Camden	189	131	88	86.7	2.08	*7.8*	*44.3*	*38.9*	59.69	800
City of London	231	0	3	2.8	1.70	*3.0*	*57.2*	*48.7*	55.82	475
City of Westminster	741	319	104	98.4	1.96	*5.4*	*48.6*	*25.1*	66.65	304
Croydon	168	306	134	137.0	2.41	*6.8*	*28.8*	*18.6*	62.78	625
Ealing	155	25	114	121.0	2.42	*6.7*	*32.3*	*23.0*	58.72	585
Enfield	325	6	112	106.3	2.45	*5.8*	*28.4*	*19.9*	52.79	638
Greenwich	585	173	90	87.8	2.39	*9.5*	*31.7*	*33.3*	51.14	821
Hackney	336	535	84	83.6	2.29	*12.4*	*36.7*	*50.9*	55.25	797
Hammersmith and Fulham	112	42	74	75.3	2.05	*8.5*	*41.2*	*31.1*	54.26	790
Haringey	82	155	91	94.7	2.26	*9.9*	*35.8*	*39.5*	56.02	827
Harrow	49	110	80	82.3	2.53	*4.6*	*26.6*	*13.9*	65.17	669
Havering	144	30	94	93.2	2.46	*4.4*	*25.6*	*12.9*	44.95	654
Hillingdon	..	..	98	100.4	2.44	*5.0*	*28.1*	*15.3*	64.20	627
Hounslow	383	9	87	83.2	2.44	*6.0*	*29.8*	*21.7*	50.81	691
Islington	..	..	78	79.7	2.17	*11.1*	*38.9*	*41.2*	57.16	879
Kensington and Chelsea	258	0	81	79.6	1.92	*6.7*	*48.5*	*22.4*	68.72	526
Kingston upon Thames	371	51	59	59.0	2.37	*4.1*	*31.8*	*12.4*	61.64	641
Lambeth	125	114	117	121.7	2.14	*12.9*	*37.6*	*34.0*	54.01	655
Lewisham	..	..	106	106.3	2.25	*11.0*	*32.9*	*35.2*	48.90	658
Merton	..	..	78	76.9	2.36	*5.6*	*29.9*	*16.3*	53.05	698
Newham	..	..	87	86.3	2.64	*10.5*	*29.8*	*47.4*	44.21	648
Redbridge	425	45	94	91.2	2.50	*4.6*	*28.9*	*16.1*	66.36	627
Richmond-upon-Thames	273	2	75	80.2	2.21	*4.1*	*36.1*	*11.9*	54.54	745
Southwark	..	..	112	103.1	2.21	*12.0*	*38.2*	*43.0*	50.56	748
Sutton	336	12	112	74.0	2.34	*5.0*	*30.2*	*14.7*	53.08	634
Tower Hamlets	..	..	72	71.3	2.44	*10.9*	*36.9*	*47.0*	49.21	646
Waltham Forest	185	430	93	92.7	2.36	*7.8*	*32.7*	*27.3*	49.36	827
Wandsworth	297	12	118	120.0	2.18	*7.7*	*35.7*	*23.8*	60.17	423

Regional Trends 33, © Crown copyright 1998

14.4 *(continued)*

	Housing starts 1996[2] (numbers)		Stock of dwellings[3] 1996 (thousands)	Households 1996					Local authority tenants: average weekly unrebated rent per dwelling (£) April 1997[6]	Council Tax (£) April 1997[7]
	Private enterprise	Housing associations local authorities etc		All households (thousands)	Average household size (thousands)	Lone parents[4] as a percentage of all households	One-person households as a percentage of all households	Households receiving Housing Benefit[5] as a percentage of all households		
SOUTH EAST (GOR)	20,549	4,920	3,245	3,229.5	2.40	4.3	27.5	0.0	47.04	640
Berkshire	1,893	211	302	316.1	2.47	4.5	26.0	13.0	51.09	641
Bracknell	529	5	42	43.4	2.50	4.9	24.1	12.9	45.02	584
Newbury	..	..	54	56.7	2.51	3.7	23.9	9.9	45.15	649
Reading	..	..	54	60.4	2.33	6.0	31.0	19.4	57.45	706
Slough	251	65	41	43.5	2.52	6.7	27.5	21.1	50.91	594
Windsor and Maidenhead	308	41	55	57.4	2.42	3.1	27.3	10.1	.	628
Wokingham	294	76	54	54.7	2.57	2.9	21.4	5.9	48.86	665
Milton Keynes UA	1,279	417	83	79.7	2.46	6.7	25.9	19.3	37.72	634
Buckinghamshire County	1,085	125	197	187.9	2.49	3.4	24.6	10.2	48.42	639
Aylesbury Vale	666	0	62	61.0	2.49	3.2	24.4	10.9	45.27	644
Chiltern	156	7	46	36.9	2.47	3.5	25.1	8.6	.	650
South Buckinghamshire	126	25	81	25.4	2.44	3.8	24.1	10.0	44.67	600
Wycombe	137	93	26	64.7	2.51	3.4	24.6	10.5	52.19	645
Former county of Buckinghamshire	2,364	542	280	267.6	2.48	4.4	25.0	12.9	43.24	..
Brighton and Hove UA	255	277	114	114.4	2.12	5.5	37.8	8.3	44.69	599
East Sussex County	1,053	509	218	209.1	2.26	4.3	31.7	0.0	46.10	691
Eastbourne	108	312	41	40.2	2.13	5.4	35.9	19.9	44.53	685
Hastings	..	..	39	35.7	2.22	6.4	35.0	28.6	.	704
Lewes	207	33	40	37.6	2.26	3.7	31.0	13.2	47.28	687
Rother	160	45	40	38.6	2.25	3.5	31.4	13.2	52.24	672
Wealden	463	59	59	57.1	2.38	3.2	27.4	8.7	41.62	704
Former county of East Sussex	1,308	786	333	323.5	2.21	4.7	33.9	0.0	45.43	..
Portsmouth UA	191	127	78	78.7	2.35	6.5	31.1	27.3	44.46	603
Southampton UA	458	16	88	90.1	2.35	6.2	31.4	24.6	40.66	603
Hampshire County	4,080	886	492	492.5	2.44	4.1	24.7	10.9	48.04	659
Basingstoke and Deane	287	222	58	58.9	2.49	4.3	23.3	12.5	.	644
East Hampshire	291	109	42	44.1	2.46	3.8	24.3	9.7	.	669
Eastleigh	417	201	45	45.1	2.46	4.0	22.9	10.9	62.30	675
Fareham	559	5	43	42.1	2.42	3.4	23.1	7.6	44.42	646
Gosport	60	88	32	31.4	2.39	6.9	25.7	16.4	50.14	658
Hart	294	32	32	33.5	2.50	3.2	21.7	6.1	63.74	653
Havant	208	105	49	47.7	2.43	5.1	25.3	9.2	.	665
New Forest	410	37	72	71.5	2.33	3.5	27.4	10.9	50.50	677
Rushmoor	266	63	33	33.7	2.44	4.9	24.4	13.2	.	651
Test Valley	917	0	43	42.8	2.46	3.9	24.1	11.1	47.45	637
Winchester	371	24	41	41.9	2.46	3.1	27.4	12.3	46.31	658
Former county of Hampshire	4,729	1,029	658	661.3	2.41	4.7	26.3	14.7	44.72	..
Isle of Wight UA	308	79	58	52.9	2.29	4.1	29.8	17.2	34.80	675
Kent	3,234	751	646	633.5	2.42	4.5	27.0	16.4	47.57	631
Ashford	346	29	39	39.8	2.43	4.5	26.1	14.8	50.04	626
Canterbury	459	14	54	55.8	2.38	4.4	29.3	15.4	48.11	637
Dartford	251	58	34	33.7	2.44	3.9	25.6	14.7	47.78	643
Dover	143	35	45	44.6	2.35	4.8	29.8	19.5	50.19	641
Gillingham	160	9	39	37.8	2.49	5.2	25.0	13.7	42.14	617
Gravesham	30	0	38	36.7	2.48	5.1	25.3	18.9	47.64	593
Maidstone	259	24	56	56.2	2.47	3.9	24.7	13.3	48.74	671
Rochester-upon-Medway	244	64	60	57.7	2.48	4.9	24.6	17.6	.	542
Sevenoaks	305	187	44	44.1	2.48	3.5	25.5	11.8	.	647
Shepway	183	18	44	42.4	2.28	5.4	31.3	18.6	43.57	659
Swale	235	91	48	46.8	2.48	4.5	23.9	18.0	35.04	616
Thanet	166	0	57	54.0	2.26	5.5	32.1	24.4	45.25	653
Tonbridge and Malling	318	10	42	41.5	2.50	3.7	23.7	12.7	.	645
Tunbridge Wells	135	212	42	42.3	2.37	3.2	29.9	14.0	.	633
Oxfordshire	1,790	818	232	236.7	2.50	4.5	25.8	12.9	45.89	635
Cherwell	497	38	50	52.0	2.52	5.0	23.5	11.5	44.91	617
Oxford	405	554	49	53.8	2.48	6.6	32.1	22.0	43.52	706
South Oxfordshire	448	135	51	48.7	2.52	3.7	24.5	10.1	52.68	641
Vale of White Horse	189	41	44	44.0	2.52	2.7	23.6	9.0	.	614
West Oxfordshire	251	50	38	38.2	2.46	3.8	24.3	9.9	44.33	593

14.4 (continued)

	Housing starts 1996[2] (numbers)		Stock of dwellings[3] 1996 (thousands)	Households 1996						Local authority tenants: average weekly unrebated rent per dwelling (£) April 1997[6]	Council Tax (£) April 1997[7]
	Private enterprise	Housing associations local authorities etc		All households (thousands)	Average household size (thousands)	Lone parents[4] as a percentage of all households	One-person households as a percentage of all households	Households receiving Housing Benefit[5] as a percentage of all households			
Surrey	2,489	244	427	425.2	2.41	3.4	27.2	10.1	51.75	627
Elmbridge	408	43	50	50.6	2.43	4.0	27.7	10.1	52.75	653
Epsom and Ewell	92	27	27	27.2	2.43	3.4	28.3	7.9	46.71	621
Guildford	301	0	50	50.3	2.41	3.8	27.3	12.0	55.21	636
Mole Valley	202	0	33	33.3	2.34	2.4	28.4	9.6	45.14	601
Reigate and Banstead	244	24	50	48.7	2.39	3.0	27.5	10.7	50.25	637
Runnymede	191	36	29	31.3	2.37	3.0	28.3	10.5	57.54	560
Spelthorne	64	26	39	37.8	2.34	3.0	27.6	10.6	.	631
Surrey Heath	302	48	31	32.2	2.52	3.9	22.1	6.9	.	621
Tandridge	273	39	31	30.6	2.46	2.8	26.8	8.5	44.73	634
Waverley	118	0	47	46.1	2.43	3.6	27.7	11.2	49.51	640
Woking	294	1	37	37.1	2.41	4.0	26.5	10.5	57.31	629
West Sussex	2,460	510	318	312.6	2.31	3.8	29.8	12.4	47.96	652
Adur	50	22	26	25.0	2.33	3.9	29.6	13.6	46.34	687
Arun	216	92	62	61.4	2.18	3.3	32.0	13.2	54.62	659
Chichester	345	144	47	44.3	2.28	3.6	30.1	12.5	44.49	639
Crawley	..	..	38	37.5	2.47	5.9	25.2	17.3	45.34	652
Horsham	596	166	49	48.8	2.40	3.0	27.1	9.9	54.57	641
Mid Sussex	554	29	52	50.9	2.41	3.4	27.0	9.2	.	651
Worthing	83	41	45	44.8	2.15	3.9	36.9	13.0	44.81	654
SOUTH WEST	14,193	2,588	2,064	2,012.2	2.36	4.4	28.2	0.0	41.45	667
Bath and North East Somerset UA	347	182	69	69.0	2.35	3.9	28.6	15.8	38.93	708
Bristol UA	..	..	166	169.7	2.32	6.4	31.9	22.6	38.65	915
North Somerset UA	82	51	77	94.2	2.47	3.9	23.9	11.8	49.19	625
South Gloucestershire UA	1,103	101	95	76.2	2.37	3.7	26.8	12.0	42.82	690
Former county of Avon	2,212	603	407	409.1	2.37	4.9	28.5	17.0	40.57	..
Cornwall and the Isles of Scilly	903	401	214	200.5	2.35	4.5	27.5	18.0	41.09	647
Caradon	182	0	35	32.9	2.39	4.4	25.0	15.3	40.49	644
Carrick	233	118	38	35.8	2.31	3.9	29.1	17.3	40.39	653
Kerrier	113	29	38	36.5	2.39	5.0	26.2	17.5	42.46	657
North Cornwall	174	111	35	32.6	2.36	4.3	27.2	18.2	40.96	659
Penwith	9	91	29	25.4	2.28	5.0	29.5	22.3	.	642
Restormel	..	..	38	36.6	2.37	4.4	28.3	18.5	41.33	626
Isles of Scilly	4	0	1	0.7	2.50	5.4	22.7	14.1	40.77	453
Devon	2,976	472	458	442.4	2.33	4.7	29.0	17.5	39.41	629
East Devon	549	27	55	53.6	2.23	3.6	30.6	11.3	37.43	607
Exeter	..	..	42	44.8	2.34	5.1	32.1	19.3	36.49	595
Mid Devon	332	39	28	27.2	2.40	3.4	26.8	14.5	39.77	640
North Devon	263	27	38	35.9	2.33	4.2	28.3	16.9	47.28	626
Plymouth	298	161	104	105.2	2.37	6.5	28.1	23.4	35.79	679
South Hams	243	62	38	32.9	2.35	3.2	27.1	14.0	47.78	622
Teignbridge	585	26	51	48.8	2.32	3.4	28.1	13.2	43.81	628
Torbay	221	58	56	52.9	2.24	5.7	32.1	20.8	43.77	601
Torridge	225	39	24	22.0	2.43	3.6	26.0	15.4	38.95	613
West Devon	84	33	20	19.1	2.36	3.6	27.4	12.9	44.19	640
Bournemouth UA	207	144	72	70.8	2.17	5.0	34.2	21.5	44.29	612
Poole UA	399	54	61	58.4	2.34	3.9	28.7	13.2	43.39	610
Dorset County	1,114	162	168	162.0	2.31	3.5	28.7	12.3	42.96	705
Christchurch	129	39	21	19.6	2.16	3.6	32.4	11.5	.	692
East Dorset	246	25	34	34.8	2.32	2.9	25.0	7.9	.	716
North Dorset	234	38	24	24.0	2.39	3.8	27.8	10.5	.	697
Purbeck	139	0	20	18.6	2.38	2.5	27.2	12.9	49.05	692
West Dorset	286	0	41	38.7	2.28	2.8	31.0	13.2	.	709
Weymouth and Portland	80	60	27	26.2	2.30	5.8	29.5	18.7	39.65	707
Former county of Dorset	1,720	360	301	291.2	2.28	4.0	30.1	14.7	43.57	..

14.4 *(continued)*

	Housing starts 1996[2] (numbers)		Stock of dwellings[3] 1996 (thousands)	Households 1996					Local authority tenants: average weekly unrebated rent per dwelling (£) April 1997[6]	Council Tax (£) April 1997[7]
	Private enterprise	Housing associations local authorities etc		All households (thousands)	Average household size (thousands)	Lone parents[4] as a percentage of all households	One-person households as a percentage of all households	Households receiving Housing Benefit[5] as a percentage of all households		
Gloucestershire	1,551	309	234	230.5	2.38	4.1	28.0	14.1	43.84	642
Cheltenham	157	28	47	46.7	2.23	5.2	34.5	15.7	46.07	637
Cotswold	132	56	35	33.9	2.38	3.0	27.4	12.0	.	638
Forest of Dean	377	37	32	30.5	2.45	2.9	24.8	13.8	40.37	666
Gloucester	479	85	44	43.7	2.41	5.8	27.6	18.1	44.95	628
Stroud	189	87	44	43.9	2.43	3.8	26.1	13.2	45.67	691
Tewkesbury	217	16	31	31.9	2.40	3.2	25.1	10.5	39.10	572
Somerset	1,273	129	202	199.3	2.38	3.9	27.8	16.1	42.44	658
Mendip	228	0	40	39.5	2.46	4.0	28.1	16.0	41.96	666
Sedgemoor	226	36	42	42.3	2.37	4.2	26.6	15.7	44.25	657
South Somerset	424	65	62	62.1	2.39	3.4	26.9	14.6	43.46	670
Taunton Deane	331	24	41	41.3	2.34	4.9	29.3	17.7	38.01	633
West Somerset	64	4	16	14.2	2.23	2.8	29.6	19.5	50.50	661
Swindon UA	893	26	46	71.9	2.41	5.0	25.5	15.2	37.35	606
Wiltshire County	1,940	221	200	167.5	2.45	3.8	24.6	13.3	49.97	650
Kennet	212	57	30	29.2	2.52	3.7	23.5	13.5	.	631
North Wiltshire	759	79	50	48.0	2.49	4.2	22.5	11.3	.	665
Salisbury	627	24	45	45.4	2.41	3.8	25.6	14.6	50.60	644
West Wiltshire	342	61	47	44.9	2.39	3.6	26.5	14.0	49.09	651
Former county of Wiltshire	2,833	247	246	239.4	2.43	4.2	24.9	13.9	43.29	..

1 The table reflects the implementation of the local government reorganisation up to 1 April 1997. See Notes and Definitions.
2 District figures do not always add to county totals; see Notes and Definitions.
3 The figures for housing stock at local authority level shown in this table are derived using different methods from the regional stock figures shown in Table 6.1. This has led to small discrepancies between the two sets of figures. The figures in Table 6.1 provide the definitive regional estimates.
4 Lone parents with dependent children only.
5 Figures relating to households receiving Housing Benefit are an average of three quarters - May, August and November 1996.
6 Some local authorities have no housing stock following large scale voluntary transfers to Housing Associations.
7 See Notes and Definitions.

Source: Department of the Environment, Transport and the Regions; Department of Social Security

14.5 Labour market statistics[1]: by sub-region

	In employment 1996-97[2]		ILO unemployment rate 1996-97[2] (percentages)	Average gross weekly full-time earnings[4], April 1997 (£)						
				Males			Females			All persons total
					10 per cent earned			10 per cent earned		
	Total[3] (thousands)	Manufacturing (percentages)		Total	Less than	More than	Total	Less than	More than	
United Kingdom	26,462	*19.1*	*8.0*	407.3	197.6	653.9	296.2	153.8	470.9	366.3
England	22,328	*19.3*	*7.7*	414.0	200.0	667.1	301.3	156.1	479.9	372.7
North East	1,069	*22.0*	*10.2*	360.1	184.3	557.2	269.0	143.3	431.2	327.6
Hartlepool UA	38	*28.7*	*..*	..	..	..	..	..	..	..
Middlesbrough UA	55	*21.2*	*12.5*	373.7	204.6	576.1	268.2	142.8	431.0	330.2
Redcar & Cleveland UA	61	*24.4*	*10.1*	406.7	201.4	571.1	..	..	..	372.8
Stockton-on-Tees UA	76	*22.5*	*9.8*	373.9	193.7	578.4	245.1	146.5	385.6	338.2
Former county of Cleveland	230	*23.7*	*10.4*	..	..	..	..	..	..	..
Durham#	260	*26.3*	*8.7*	..	..	..	..	..	..	..
Northumberland	136	*17.3*	*7.5*	332.2	177.5	507.4	266.1	140.0	417.5	304.4
Tyne & Wear	443	*20.1*	*11.7*	354.4	180.3	553.7	278.9	151.2	450.0	326.7
North West (GOR) and Merseyside	2,965	*22.0*	*7.9*	386.4	192.4	614.8	277.4	153.0	444.4	345.8
North West (GOR)	2,428	*23.1*	*7.0*	387.4	192.2	617.5	275.8	152.8	440.0	346.6
Cheshire	457	*22.8*	*6.1*	415.8	199.9	659.4	282.0	152.6	458.1	368.9
Cumbria	223	*22.9*	*7.3*	386.8	195.4	603.5	260.2	146.2	431.8	342.1
Greater Manchester	1,111	*22.5*	*7.9*	387.7	193.1	630.0	281.1	155.1	447.6	346.9
Lancashire	637	*24.5*	*6.1*	363.0	187.5	552.8	263.9	148.6	420.4	328.4
Merseyside	537	*17.0*	*11.8*	381.7	194.2	602.5	284.4	153.4	455.6	342.4
Yorkshire and the Humber	2,206	*21.9*	*8.5*	363.9	189.1	570.2	268.9	147.7	434.5	330.5
East Riding of Yorkshire UA	145	*20.5*	*6.8*	372.4	200.0	584.1	252.6	131.3	409.8	336.2
Kingston upon Hull UA	99	*23.9*	*12.9*	356.4	183.4	575.8	270.9	157.1	410.6	323.5
North East Lincolnshire UA	64	*30.4*	*13.1*	378.1	185.9	575.8	..	..	..	343.6
North Lincolnshire UA	81	*29.2*	*6.9*	396.7	216.9	602.8	237.4	149.7	400.6	351.3
Former county of Humberside	391	*24.7*	*9.5*	..	..	..	..	..	..	..
York UA	82	*13.5*	*..*	396.8	206.1	602.2	263.5	150.6	422.3	351.1
North Yorkshire County	254	*17.8*	*3.8*	351.8	175.4	579.3	243.1	131.8	409.3	315.9
Former county of North Yorkshire	336	*16.8*	*4.1*	..	..	..	..	..	..	..
South Yorkshire	525	*22.5*	*10.9*	358.9	191.3	555.5	263.6	147.0	423.7	325.7
West Yorkshire	953	*22.1*	*8.3*	363.3	190.7	566.4	279.6	152.7	448.4	332.7
East Midlands	1,933	*26.0*	*6.8*	369.2	195.0	567.4	260.3	143.8	416.3	332.9
Derbyshire#	449	*28.6*	*7.4*	..	..	..	..	..	..	..
Leicestershire#	457	*30.8*	*5.4*	..	..	..	..	..	..	..
Lincolnshire	290	*19.0*	*7.4*	350.9	187.8	547.8	254.3	132.0	434.5	317.7
Northamptonshire	296	*24.9*	*4.5*	384.7	210.7	581.7	265.8	153.3	393.5	344.1
Nottinghamshire	441	*23.5*	*8.7*	362.2	185.0	573.4	260.5	146.4	410.7	327.2
West Midlands	2,384	*27.4*	*7.9*	375.4	194.3	575.8	268.5	147.7	434.5	337.8
Hereford & Worcs.	348	*24.4*	*6.5*	350.1	190.8	546.6	266.7	150.3	432.3	320.1
Shropshire	190	*21.7*	*6.3*	349.0	180.0	542.1	238.7	132.0	391.6	311.1
Staffordshire#	509	*28.8*	*5.9*	..	..	..	..	..	..	..
Warwickshire	247	*25.6*	*5.4*	392.3	206.4	593.1	273.0	155.7	444.8	352.5
West Midlands (Met. county)	1,091	*29.1*	*10.1*	386.5	200.0	592.6	275.5	149.7	438.6	347.3
Eastern	2,539	*18.2*	*6.5*	399.5	204.2	638.2	295.9	159.8	465.1	362.4
Bedfordshire#	278	*22.3*	*7.4*	..	..	..	..	..	..	..
Cambridgeshire	339	*20.0*	*6.8*	402.9	207.0	657.9	299.3	162.3	468.3	365.1
Essex	735	*17.4*	*6.0*	397.5	200.6	636.5	299.3	161.2	470.4	362.3
Hertfordshire	519	*16.6*	*5.9*	447.0	220.0	728.1	320.5	173.7	494.2	399.9
Norfolk	358	*17.7*	*7.9*	354.9	188.4	566.2	269.6	148.8	433.9	325.6
Suffolk	310	*17.9*	*5.7*	364.7	196.0	580.6	263.2	149.4	426.8	329.5
London	3,151	*10.2*	*11.1*	541.3	230.0	932.8	386.3	199.9	592.6	480.1
South East (GOR)	3,841	*16.1*	*5.5*	428.3	203.8	696.3	306.5	164.4	478.9	382.5
Berkshire	408	*17.0*	*4.5*	482.1	223.2	808.1	334.1	178.9	518.2	425.5
Buckinghamshire#	347	*20.2*	*4.1*	..	..	..	..	..	..	..
East Sussex#	322	*11.9*	*8.1*	..	..	..	..	..	..	..
Hampshire#	773	*18.8*	*6.2*	..	..	..	..	..	..	..
Isle of Wight	48	*16.6*	*..*	340.6	178.9	487.4	..	..	..	304.2
Kent	744	*15.4*	*6.5*	387.8	196.7	603.7	287.8	149.4	460.4	350.4
Oxfordshire	316	*17.1*	*4.0*	416.2	209.5	671.8	302.0	166.1	448.0	372.0
Surrey	538	*12.6*	*4.1*	497.1	216.6	806.1	330.5	175.1	524.5	435.2
West Sussex	345	*14.7*	*5.0*	430.6	210.0	715.1	313.4	164.4	507.2	384.4

14.5 *(continued)*

	In employment 1996-97[2]		ILO unemploy-ment rate 1996-97[2] (percentages)	Average gross weekly full-time earnings[4], April 1997 (£)						
				Males			Females			All persons total
					10 per cent earned			10 per cent earned		
	Total[3] (thousands)	Manufacturing (percentages)		Total	Less than	More than	Total	Less than	More than	
South West	2,241	*16.8*	*6.3*	382.4	190.2	603.8	274.8	145.9	450.0	342.7
Bath and North East										
Somerset UA	79	*17.0*	*6.9*	361.5	193.0	597.9	..	..	..	342.4
Bristol UA	182	*14.9*	*8.4*	412.4	203.5	646.7	301.6	176.6	465.7	367.6
North Somerset UA	92	*14.6*	*..*	389.1	205.3	598.9	255.9	145.7	415.6	343.1
South Gloucestershire UA	123	*18.1*	*..*	422.2	220.0	672.3	287.8	152.3	471.2	385.3
Former county of Avon	475	*16.0*	*6.5*	..	..	..	..	..	..	..
Cornwall	203	*11.7*	*7.9*	315.2	167.0	503.1	240.6	129.0	406.1	284.5
Devon	443	*15.8*	*8.4*	344.2	176.6	565.8	260.1	141.6	434.5	312.7
Dorset#	296	*15.4*	*5.8*	..	..	..	..	..	..	..
Gloucestershire	273	*19.9*	*5.0*	404.3	203.3	634.8	273.0	154.0	434.5	357.7
Somerset	230	*19.0*	*5.3*	364.3	190.0	575.8	274.9	138.9	460.5	332.7
Wiltshire#	319	*19.6*	*3.9*	..	..	..	..	..	..	..
New local government Unitary authorities with effect from 1 April 1997										
Former county of Durham										
Darlington UA	46	*18.9*	*11.8*	..	..	..	..	..	..	325.3
Durham County	214	*27.8*	*8.0*	356.6	187.7	537.1	260.8	141.1	418.0	322.1
Former county of Derbyshire										
Derby UA	103	*27.6*	*8.8*	390.8	195.8	598.5	264.1	141.1	453.1	356.6
Derbyshire County	346	*28.9*	*6.9*	358.6	187.7	544.0	252.6	143.4	409.2	327.1
Former county of Leicestershire										
Leicester UA	120	*35.0*	*9.8*	358.1	202.0	537.1	263.8	149.9	415.5	320.9
Rutland UA	15	*..*	*..*	..	..	..	..	..	..	..
Leicestershire County	321	*29.5*	*3.7*	390.9	211.1	608.0	263.2	143.8	451.9	349.7
Former county of Staffordshire										
Stoke-on-Trent UA	114	*33.8*	*9.2*	329.0	176.6	517.5	243.2	148.5	358.7	297.4
Staffordshire County	395	*27.4*	*4.9*	371.5	192.5	575.6	265.2	140.0	471.6	334.4
Former county of Bedfordshire										
Luton UA	81	*28.7*	*12.1*	437.1	248.3	667.7	307.2	175.8	484.6	395.6
Bedfordshire County	197	*19.6*	*5.2*	394.3	215.0	603.6	302.3	156.6	478.6	360.2
Former county of Buckinghamshire										
Milton Keynes UA	105	*20.8*	*..*	435.3	216.8	691.0	314.6	179.0	522.0	389.9
Buckinghamshire County	242	*19.9*	*4.1*	450.7	194.0	815.7	317.2	163.2	502.9	401.9
Former county of East Sussex										
Brighton and Hove UA	114	*8.5*	*12.1*	366.4	191.4	547.0	298.1	172.7	452.5	335.9
East Sussex County	209	*13.7*	*5.8*	347.5	179.9	561.0	294.2	149.9	447.9	325.8
Former county of Hampshire										
Portsmouth UA	87	*20.1*	*10.6*	429.7	208.1	686.2	281.9	153.6	458.2	377.3
Southampton UA	94	*16.9*	*11.6*	408.9	200.4	618.8	293.1	166.8	452.8	365.1
Hampshire County	592	*18.9*	*4.6*	407.3	200.0	649.3	291.2	167.1	436.1	367.3
Former county of Dorset										
Bournemouth UA	66	*13.5*	*8.0*	..	..	..	..	..	..	314.0
Poole UA	61	*13.7*	*..*	407.5	205.7	643.8	287.5	163.8	437.6	360.4
Dorset County	169	*16.7*	*4.6*	355.4	186.9	570.5	264.0	140.0	447.2	323.1
Former county of Wiltshire										
Swindon UA	100	*25.8*	*..*	484.1	240.4	750.2	302.2	180.5	470.3	424.2
Wiltshire County	219	*16.8*	*4.2*	380.0	187.1	591.3	274.4	143.9	460.4	340.8

New local government structure came into effect on 1 April 1997.
1 See Notes and Definitions to the Labour market chapter. In some cases sample sizes are too small to provide reliable estimates.
2 Data are from the Labour Force Survey and relate to the period March 1996 to February 1997.
3 Includes those on government-supported employment and training programmes and unpaid family workers.
4 Earnings estimates have been derived from the New Earnings Survey and relate to full-time employees whose pay for the survey pay-period was not affected by absence.

Source: Office for National Statistics

14.6 Labour market[1], deprivation and economic statistics: by local authority[2]

| | Economically active[3] 1996-97 (percentages) | Claimant count January 1998 | | | Income Support bene-ficieries[5] Aug. 1996 (percentages) | Ranking from Index of Local Depriv-ation[6] 1998 | Businesses registered for VAT 1996 | | Stock of busin-esses end 1996 (numbers) |
		Total (thousands)	Of which females (percentages)	Of which long-term unemployed[4] (percentages)			Registration rates[7] (percentages)	Deregistration rates[7] (percentages)	
UNITED KINGDOM	78.6	1,479.3	23.2	26.9	..	.	11	10	1,611,300
ENGLAND	78.8	1,190.8	23.5	26.8	14	.	11	10	1,363,820
NORTH EAST	74.2	93.7	19.1	28.4	18	.	10	10	42,220
Hartlepool UA	73.5	4.6	17.8	30.9	21	37	8	12	1,220
Middlesbrough UA	69.9	7.6	17.3	30.9	22	24	10	10	1,895
Redcar & Cleveland UA	76.1	5.7	17.8	29.8	19	43	9	10	1,860
Stockton-on-Tees UA	78.4	7.7	19.3	30.4	17	49	10	11	2,830
Former county of Cleveland	74.8	25.6	18.1	30.5	19	.	10	11	7,795
Darlington UA	82.7	3.4	19.7	28.7	15	113	11	12	2,070
Durham County	75.1	13.7	20.4	23.8	15	.	9	10	8,685
Chester-le-Street	79.6	1.5	20.1	25.5	11	139	12	10	780
Derwentside	79.5	2.5	18.8	24.7	18	79	9	9	1,395
Durham	79.8	2.2	23.8	20.0	10	155	11	11	1,360
Easington	60.6	2.6	18.2	22.9	20	52	9	10	1,120
Sedgefield	74.5	2.3	21.6	20.8	15	108	9	10	1,495
Teesdale	80.4	0.5	28.0	28.0	11	193	5	8	1,145
Wear Valley	78.2	2.1	18.8	28.9	19	61	8	10	1,395
Former county of Durham	76.4	17.0	20.3	24.8	15	.	9	10	10,755
Northumberland	76.9	8.4	22.7	26.5	12	.	7	8	7,490
Alnwick	73.5	0.9	24.7	26.7	13	170	6	6	1,080
Berwick-upon-Tweed	86.0	0.8	25.4	11.4	10	152	5	6	1,090
Blyth Valley	75.3	2.4	23.0	25.4	15	94	9	13	975
Castle Morpeth	71.4	1.1	22.6	26.8	8	299	8	8	1,335
Tynedale	82.2	1.0	25.1	21.3	9	229	7	7	2,305
Wansbeck	76.0	2.3	19.5	34.9	16	58	10	11	705
Tyne and Wear	72.0	42.6	18.4	29.0	20	.	11	11	16,185
Gateshead	74.5	6.4	17.5	27.9	19	35	11	11	3,240
Newcastle-upon-Tyne	69.7	11.6	18.7	33.7	20	19	11	10	4,890
North Tyneside	76.0	6.9	19.2	27.2	18	62	11	12	2,685
South Tyneside	74.2	7.0	19.7	22.9	20	38	10	12	1,795
Sunderland	68.7	10.7	17.3	29.6	20	21	11	11	3,570
NORTH WEST (GOR) & MERSEYSIDE	75.7	181.3	21.4	25.3	17	.	10	10	157,655
NORTH WEST (GOR)	77.0	124.1	21.5	21.0	15	.	10	10	135,495
Cheshire	79.4	18.5	22.3	20.8	11	.	11	10	26,410
Chester	80.9	2.2	20.8	24.6	11	293	10	9	3,690
Congleton	86.5	1.0	25.9	17.1	8	271	9	9	2,785
Crewe and Nantwich	76.5	1.9	22.4	17.6	11	272	10	10	2,780
Ellesmere Port and Neston	76.2	1.8	21.5	21.2	13	126	11	10	1,370
Halton	72.8	4.5	22.0	25.7	20	34	11	11	1,820
Macclesfield	82.7	1.8	20.5	14.7	8	240	11	9	6,420
Vale Royal	79.3	1.9	23.7	18.7	11	132	11	9	3,220
Warrington	79.6	3.4	23.3	19.1	11	128	12	11	4,305
Cumbria	80.1	12.7	21.8	26.3	11	.	6	7	16,035
Allerdale	79.7	3.2	21.4	30.1	13	102	5	7	3,105
Barrow-in-Furness	74.0	2.3	17.6	27.3	17	55	7	10	1,060
Carlisle	81.9	2.5	23.8	22.0	11	140	6	8	2,935
Copeland	77.8	2.8	20.2	33.2	15	106	8	9	1,500
Eden	83.2	0.5	30.5	15.3	6	192	5	6	2,995
South Lakeland	83.8	1.3	26.4	13.4	7	310=	8	7	4,445
Greater Manchester	75.1	64.2	21.0	22.5	17	.	11	11	57,835
Bolton	75.9	5.5	19.2	13.3	16	47	10	11	5,635
Bury	80.6	2.7	22.7	11.4	14	116	11	12	4,185
Manchester	63.9	19.4	20.9	30.5	29	3	13	12	10,230
Oldham	76.2	5.0	21.7	18.6	17	33	10	10	4,450
Rochdale	79.2	5.8	20.8	22.5	19	29	10	10	4,260
Salford	70.3	5.6	18.8	20.4	20	23	11	11	4,475
Stockport	82.0	4.8	21.1	20.5	11	177	10	11	7,865
Tameside	77.5	4.7	22.4	20.0	16	53	11	11	4,595
Trafford	80.8	4.0	21.4	24.0	13	129	11	11	6,200
Wigan	73.6	6.8	22.3	18.1	14	85	11	11	5,945

14.6 *(continued)*

	Economically active[3] 1996-97 (percentages)	Claimant count January 1998			Income Support bene-ficiaries[5] Aug. 1996 (percentages)	Ranking from Index of Local Depriv-ation[6] 1998	Businesses registered for VAT 1996		Stock of busin-esses end 1996 (numbers)
		Total (thousands)	Of which females (percentages)	Of which long-term unemployed[4] (percentages)			Registration rates[7] (percentages)	Deregistration rates[7] (percentages)	
Lancashire	*77.7*	28.8	*21.8*	*15.6*	*14*	.	*10*	*10*	35,205
Blackburn	*73.0*	3.2	*19.5*	*13.9*	*19*	41	*10*	*11*	2,945
Blackpool	*75.6*	5.0	*20.7*	*12.3*	*18*	51	*10*	*12*	3,045
Burnley	*76.1*	1.4	*20.9*	*10.9*	*16*	65	*11*	*12*	1,815
Chorley	*78.5*	1.5	*23.8*	*13.4*	*10*	144	*11*	*10*	2,650
Fylde	*76.7*	0.6	*20.6*	*7.2*	*9*	199	*9*	*12*	1,900
Hyndburn	*76.2*	1.4	*22.1*	*13.2*	*14*	76	*9*	*11*	1,815
Lancaster	*73.6*	3.8	*22.9*	*23.7*	*13*	125	*8*	*9*	3,145
Pendle	*74.1*	1.5	*22.9*	*9.6*	*16*	99	*9*	*10*	2,155
Preston	*73.7*	3.4	*20.0*	*17.1*	*18*	68	*11*	*11*	3,245
Ribble Valley	*89.7*	0.4	*25.0*	*13.4*	*6*	310=	*9*	*9*	2,105
Rossendale	*85.0*	0.8	*23.8*	*8.9*	*14*	107	*10*	*10*	1,945
South Ribble	*83.9*	1.3	*27.7*	*11.3*	*9*	181	*12*	*10*	2,450
West Lancashire	*78.3*	2.8	*22.3*	*26.6*	*14*	160	*9*	*9*	3,030
Wyre	*85.3*	1.7	*21.9*	*13.3*	*11*	184	*8*	*9*	2,960
MERSEYSIDE	*70.8*	57.2	*21.1*	*34.6*	*23*	.	*13*	*11*	22,160
Knowsley	*65.4*	7.2	*20.4*	*35.3*	*32*	9	*12*	*12*	1,575
Liverpool	*66.1*	24.1	*20.7*	*39.5*	*29*	1	*12*	*11*	7,460
Sefton	*74.7*	5.2	*21.6*	*21.5*	*18*	54	*17*	*11*	5,360
St Helens	*73.0*	9.1	*21.4*	*32.9*	*18*	45	*11*	*11*	2,835
Wirral	*75.6*	11.6	*22.0*	*31.0*	*20*	44	*11*	*13*	4,925
YORKSHIRE AND THE HUMBER	*77.3*	146.3	*22.0*	*25.3*	*15*	.	*10*	*10*	118,155
East Riding of Yorkshire UA	*78.6*	7.0	*24.8*	*20.3*	*11*	275	*8*	*9*	9,310
Kingston upon Hull UA	*71.3*	12.4	*20.9*	*18.8*	*23*	26	*10*	*10*	4,365
North East Lincolnshire UA	*77.0*	6.7	*20.1*	*25.1*	*17*	73	*10*	*11*	3,250
North Lincolnshire UA	*86.1*	4.2	*22.4*	*23.9*	*13*	111	*9*	*9*	3,925
Former county of Humberside	*77.6*	30.4	*21.9*	*21.2*	*16*	.	*9*	*10*	20,850
York UA	*79.3*	3.6	*24.1*	*19.1*	*10*	310=	*9*	*10*	2,470
North Yorkshire County	*79.4*	9.7	*26.8*	*19.9*	*9*	.	*8*	*8*	24,045
Craven	*80.1*	0.6	*23.7*	*11.7*	*9*	230	*7*	*7*	2,695
Hambleton	*74.5*	1.2	*28.4*	*18.6*	*7*	310=	*6*	*7*	3,905
Harrogate	*83.0*	1.7	*27.0*	*15.2*	*8*	270	*11*	*9*	5,825
Richmondshire	*78.0*	0.6	*35.0*	*12.7*	*6*	310=	*7*	*6*	1,980
Ryedale	*81.6*	1.1	*28.6*	*19.5*	*7*	268	*6*	*6*	3,540
Scarborough	*75.1*	3.4	*25.8*	*22.8*	*14*	172	*8*	*9*	3,160
Selby	*82.9*	1.8	*25.8*	*23.0*	*9*	310=	*9*	*6*	2,940
Former county of North Yorkshire	*79.4*	13.2	*26.1*	*19.7*	*7*	.	*8*	*8*	26,515
South Yorkshire	*73.9*	45.8	*20.6*	*30.9*	*17*	.	*10*	*11*	22,955
Barnsley	*72.7*	6.9	*19.6*	*23.5*	*17*	42	*10*	*11*	3,750
Doncaster	*73.7*	10.6	*19.6*	*29.2*	*18*	39	*10*	*11*	4,985
Rotherham	*75.4*	9.2	*19.8*	*31.7*	*17*	50	*10*	*10*	4,165
Sheffield	*73.9*	19.0	*21.9*	*34.1*	*17*	25	*11*	*10*	10,050
West Yorkshire	*78.5*	57.0	*22.2*	*24.4*	*15*	.	*10*	*10*	47,835
Bradford	*75.4*	14.0	*22.7*	*23.4*	*18*	28	*11*	*10*	10,465
Calderdale	*82.3*	4.7	*22.7*	*24.0*	*15*	96	*10*	*9*	5,540
Kirklees	*79.2*	9.2	*23.2*	*18.0*	*14*	80	*10*	*10*	9,425
Leeds	*80.5*	20.4	*21.2*	*29.6*	*14*	56	*11*	*11*	16,330
Wakefield	*75.3*	8.7	*22.8*	*20.7*	*14*	74	*10*	*9*	6,075
EAST MIDLANDS	*80.0*	88.9	*23.8*	*22.6*	*12*	.	*10*	*10*	109,730
Derby UA	*78.6*	6.9	*22.2*	*25.0*	*16*	71	*13*	*12*	4,035
Derbyshire County	*81.4*	15.2	*22.6*	*22.4*	*11*	.	*9*	*9*	19,340
Amber Valley	*81.9*	2.1	*24.5*	*19.9*	*10*	158	*9*	*10*	3,035
Bolsover	*78.4*	1.9	*18.3*	*26.7*	*14*	86	*11*	*10*	1,240
Chesterfield	*79.5*	3.2	*21.2*	*26.2*	*15*	91	*11*	*10*	2,110
Derbyshire Dales	*82.6*	0.9	*26.1*	*15.5*	*7*	259	*7*	*8*	3,490
Erewash	*80.5*	2.3	*24.0*	*17.0*	*12*	137	*10*	*10*	2,395
High Peak	*84.8*	1.4	*23.0*	*21.2*	*9*	188	*9*	*8*	2,735
North East Derbyshire	*80.6*	2.2	*22.7*	*23.9*	*12*	141	*10*	*9*	2,425
South Derbyshire	*82.9*	1.4	*24.4*	*23.6*	*10*	264	*9*	*10*	1,910
Former county of Derbyshire	*80.7*	22.1	*22.5*	*23.2*	*12*	.	*10*	*10*	23,370

14.6 *(continued)*

	Economically active[3] 1996-97 (percentages)	Claimant count January 1998			Income Support bene-ficiaries[5] Aug. 1996 (percentages)	Ranking from Index of Local Depriv-ation[6] 1998	Businesses registered for VAT 1996		Stock of busin-esses end 1996 (numbers)
		Total (thousands)	Of which females (percentages)	Of which long-term unemployed[4] (percentages)			Registration rates[7] (percentages)	Deregistration rates[7] (percentages)	
Leicester UA	73.0	8.3	22.4	24.8	20	32	11	11	7,400
Rutland UA	80.9	0.2	26.9	6.9	5	310=	11	8	1,245
Leicestershire County	84.1	7.2	28.1	18.2	8	.	10	10	17,845
Blaby	86.7	0.9	29.6	19.5	8	308	10	10	2,265
Charnwood	82.1	2.2	28.1	19.3	8	310=	9	10	4,060
Harborough	82.1	0.5	26.8	11.8	7	310=	10	9	2,985
Hinckley and Bosworth	86.0	1.0	29.2	13.8	7	292	10	9	3,155
Melton	79.9	0.6	30.3	13.4	7	185	8	9	1,625
North West Leicestershire	86.8	1.4	25.5	24.4	9	161	10	11	2,495
Oadby and Wigston	84.2	0.7	28.2	16.9	8	235	11	11	1,265
Former county of Leicestershire	80.6	15.7	25.1	21.5	12	.	10	10	26,490
Lincolnshire	82.2	12.9	25.9	18.0	12	.	8	9	19,520
Boston	79.0	1.1	21.7	9.2	11	153	7	9	1,860
East Lindsey	81.4	3.3	27.5	12.4	14	166	7	9	4,425
Lincoln	75.2	3.2	20.8	27.0	18	46	11	10	1,675
North Kesteven	84.8	1.2	28.8	18.2	9	254	8	8	2,490
South Holland	85.8	0.8	32.5	13.6	9	253	7	9	2,825
South Kesteven	82.9	1.7	28.9	15.7	9	310=	9	11	3,685
West Lindsey	85.5	1.6	26.5	22.2	11	207	7	8	2,550
Northamptonshire	82.9	9.9	25.4	23.5	10	.	11	10	18,175
Corby	81.0	1.2	25.8	20.6	14	101	10	9	975
Daventry	87.2	0.8	29.9	14.7	7	310=	10	9	2,835
East Northamptonshire	81.4	0.9	26.6	15.8	8	300	10	10	2,300
Kettering	88.6	1.2	26.2	26.1	11	298	11	11	1,990
Northampton	80.0	4.0	24.1	28.1	13	169	12	10	4,585
South Northamptonshire	86.4	0.6	29.3	20.8	6	310=	11	10	3,035
Wellingborough	80.3	1.2	22.8	20.7	12	258	12	12	2,445
Nottinghamshire	75.7	28.3	22.6	24.6	14	.	11	12	22,180
Ashfield	75.5	3.1	21.4	26.4	14	93	10	12	1,940
Bassetlaw	76.0	3.0	22.9	27.3	13	123	10	9	2,660
Broxtowe	80.8	2.0	26.3	19.2	10	187	11	14	2,040
Gedling	81.3	2.2	25.2	22.0	9	175	11	14	2,230
Mansfield	77.0	3.0	21.0	21.3	14	67	11	12	1,720
Newark and Sherwood	75.8	2.1	23.2	20.1	11	159	10	10	2,950
Nottingham	68.5	11.4	21.6	26.6	22	16	12	12	5,960
Rushcliffe	81.6	1.4	24.9	24.1	8	274	9	11	2,685
WEST MIDLANDS	78.3	131.3	23.9	28.1	15	.	10	10	135,240
Hereford and Worcester	83.6	12.0	27.6	21.3	10	.	9	9	24,495
Bromsgrove	83.6	1.5	31.3	24.0	8	310=	10	11	2,705
Hereford[6]	82.5	1.2	24.5	14.5	12	..	9	10	1,270
Leominster[6]	84.1	0.7	26.7	19.9	9	..	6	7	2,530
Malvern Hills[6]	82.3	1.2	26.1	19.8	10	244	8	8	3,930
Redditch	82.4	1.8	29.1	30.0	12	151	10	8	1,990
South Herefordshire	82.1	0.8	32.1	14.9	9	.	7	8	2,740
Worcester	81.9	1.7	21.8	22.2	11	212	12	11	2,120
Wychavon	86.4	1.3	30.9	16.8	8	213	8	9	4,480
Wyre Forest	87.4	1.7	27.4	21.5	11	291	9	10	2,735
Shropshire	79.0	6.7	25.0	18.2	11	.	8	9	14,100
Bridgnorth	81.8	0.6	28.1	19.8	8	295	9	8	2,175
North Shropshire	78.6	0.6	28.0	15.6	10	286	5	7	2,415
Oswestry	70.6	0.8	28.4	24.7	12	273	7	9	1,250
Shrewsbury and Atcham	83.5	1.3	24.0	20.0	10	304	8	9	3,005
South Shropshire	81.1	0.6	25.1	19.9	8	211	7	7	2,135
The Wrekin	76.4	2.7	23.0	15.3	14	92	12	12	3,130

14.6 *(continued)*

| | Economically active[3] 1996-97 (percentages) | Claimant count January 1998 | | | Income Support bene-ficieries[5] Aug. 1996 (percentages) | Ranking from Index of Local Depriv-ation[6] 1998 | Businesses registered for VAT 1996 | | Stock of busin-esses end 1996 (numbers) |
		Total (thousands)	Of which females (percentages)	Of which long-term unemployed[4] (percentages)			Registration rates[7] (percentages)	Deregistration rates[7] (percentages)	
Stoke-on-Trent UA	77.1	6.1	22.1	17.2	16	48	10	10	4,580
Staffordshire County	80.9	13.9	26.5	19.2	10	.	10	9	21,550
Cannock Chase	75.8	2.0	26.7	21.7	12	118	10	10	2,260
East Staffordshire	77.4	2.3	24.4	20.5	11	182	10	10	3,015
Lichfield	83.0	1.4	29.5	17.2	8	283	10	10	2,925
Newcastle-under-Lyme	81.2	1.9	24.5	14.7	10	142	9	11	2,410
South Staffordshire	83.8	1.7	26.3	24.4	9	215	10	10	2,750
Stafford	84.9	1.7	26.0	19.5	8	210	11	9	3,495
Staffordshire Moorlands	79.1	1.4	30.6	15.0	9	200	7	8	3,195
Tamworth	80.2	1.5	26.1	19.1	13	164	11	8	1,500
Former county of Staffordshire	80.0	20.0	25.2	18.6	11	.	10	10	26,125
Warwickshire	82.8	7.6	25.3	23.1	10	.	10	10	15,925
North Warwickshire	79.6	0.9	28.0	18.1	9	114	9	10	1,965
Nuneaton and Bedworth	81.8	2.3	25.4	23.1	13	119	10	11	2,280
Rugby	85.9	1.4	26.0	24.1	10	310=	9	9	2,565
Stratford-on-Avon	82.9	1.2	26.9	24.3	7	204	9	9	5,095
Warwick	82.9	1.8	22.4	24.2	10	310=	12	10	4,020
West Midlands (Met. County)	75.1	85.1	22.9	32.6	19	.	11	11	54,595
Birmingham	73.6	39.4	22.5	35.8	23	5	11	10	20,865
Coventry	72.4	8.6	21.8	28.8	18	40	11	11	5,185
Dudley	83.1	7.1	24.0	27.9	14	110	10	11	7,420
Sandwell	73.2	9.9	23.8	30.6	21	7	10	11	6,210
Solihull	82.6	3.7	26.4	31.4	10	263	12	10	4,465
Walsall	72.5	8.5	23.3	33.0	18	31	10	10	5,640
Wolverhampton	72.8	8.0	21.5	27.2	20	27	11	12	4,810
EASTERN	81.4	94.8	25.0	24.8	11	.	10	10	158,035
Luton UA	78.0	4.9	23.3	31.7	16	72	12	12	3,795
Bedfordshire County	84.9	5.2	27.6	21.5	9	.	11	10	11,755
Mid Bedfordshire	86.1	1.1	31.5	13.3	7	305	11	10	4,355
Bedford	82.6	2.6	25.4	26.3	12	218	10	10	3,965
South Bedfordshire	86.6	1.4	28.6	18.7	9	189	10	10	3,435
Former county of Bedfordshire	82.6	10.0	25.5	26.4	11	.	11	10	15,545
Cambridgeshire	81.2	11.0	25.7	19.8	10	.	10	9	21,980
Cambridge	75.3	2.2	25.7	23.9	9	149	10	8	3,040
East Cambridgeshire	81.5	0.8	29.3	19.0	8	214	8	8	2,735
Fenland	79.1	1.7	25.0	20.7	13	133	8	9	2,660
Huntingdonshire	85.8	1.7	29.2	15.4	7	262	10	9	5,040
Peterborough	78.9	3.5	23.2	19.4	15	135	12	10	3,470
South Cambridgeshire	85.7	1.1	26.6	18.6	6	221	9	8	5,030
Essex	79.1	30.2	24.4	27.5	12	.	11	10	43,780
Basildon	76.8	3.4	24.9	25.3	15	131	12	11	3,915
Braintree	77.9	2.1	26.7	20.6	10	294	10	9	4,090
Brentwood	78.9	0.7	26.0	23.0	8	310=	12	11	2,380
Castle Point	77.6	1.5	25.3	28.6	13	173	11	11	2,130
Chelmsford	84.4	2.2	25.2	30.4	7	310=	11	9	4,280
Colchester	75.2	2.3	25.2	16.7	10	301	11	9	4,190
Epping Forest	81.5	1.8	27.9	24.5	9	150	11	10	4,025
Harlow	85.2	1.7	26.3	27.5	16	84	12	12	1,375
Maldon	85.3	0.8	23.8	34.3	9	202	9	8	2,300
Rochford	82.5	1.2	24.8	21.7	10	223	10	9	2,090
Southend-on-Sea	79.0	5.7	21.8	37.3	16	104	12	12	3,925
Tendring	73.9	3.1	21.7	23.0	15	134	9	10	3,065
Thurrock	76.7	3.1	22.9	30.6	14	95	13	10	2,565
Uttlesford	79.0	0.6	32.1	19.2	6	310=	10	9	3,445

14.6 *(continued)*

| | Economically active[3] 1996-97 (percentages) | Claimant count January 1998 | | | Income Support beneficieries[5] Aug. 1996 (percentages) | Ranking from Index of Local Deprivation[6] 1998 | Businesses registered for VAT 1996 | | Stock of businesses end 1996 (numbers) |
		Total (thousands)	Of which females (percentages)	Of which long-term unemployed[4] (percentages)			Registration rates[7] (percentages)	Deregistration rates[7] (percentages)	
Hertfordshire	84.1	11.9	24.7	20.7	9	.	12	10	33,625
Broxbourne	78.5	1.1	25.8	27.6	11	242	9	11	2,260
Dacorum	87.9	1.5	24.6	18.3	8	310=	11	9	4,620
East Hertfordshire	83.7	1.1	27.8	20.6	7	310=	11	9	4,885
Hertsmere	81.4	1.1	25.5	20.7	9	303	13	11	3,190
North Hertfordshire	85.2	1.5	24.3	18.7	9	310=	12	10	4,290
St Albans	86.3	1.1	24.4	13.2	7	302	13	10	4,830
Stevenage	86.2	1.6	24.4	19.6	13	157	14	12	1,580
Three Rivers	84.7	0.9	23.8	26.5	7	297	12	10	2,670
Watford	81.8	1.2	22.7	28.3	11	203	12	10	2,615
Welwyn Hatfield	82.2	0.9	24.4	14.9	9	310=	11	10	2,680
Norfolk	81.9	18.6	25.3	24.3	12	.	8	9	23,060
Breckland	84.6	1.9	28.0	18.4	10	276	8	9	3,500
Broadland	79.9	1.5	27.6	22.8	8	288	9	9	3,160
Great Yarmouth	78.4	4.1	25.9	27.1	16	82	9	11	2,275
Kings Lynn and West Norfolk	86.0	2.8	25.5	22.3	12	205	7	8	4,135
North Norfolk	79.9	2.0	25.8	20.4	12	248	7	9	3,165
Norwich	78.5	4.8	22.0	27.4	18	66	10	11	3,040
South Norfolk	84.7	1.6	27.7	24.9	8	310=	8	8	3,790
Suffolk	81.5	13.1	25.1	26.0	10	.	9	9	20,035
Babergh	85.4	1.2	25.7	24.0	10	310=	9	8	3,040
Forest Heath	85.4	0.7	23.7	24.3	7	257	11	11	1,950
Ipswich	80.7	3.1	20.2	29.1	15	89	13	11	2,355
Mid Suffolk	83.3	0.9	29.9	19.3	7	236	9	8	3,405
St Edmundsbury	87.4	1.4	28.5	20.8	9	309	9	9	3,035
Suffolk Coastal	76.8	1.8	26.6	19.8	8	241	9	9	3,580
Waveney	74.2	3.9	26.0	30.8	13	121	8	9	2,670
LONDON	76.9	236.6	26.1	33.1	19	.	14	11	252,405
Barking and Dagenham	77.2	4.0	23.7	24.5	21	15	13	16	2,200
Barnet	76.7	6.8	28.3	29.8	12	130	13	13	10,595
Bexley	82.4	4.6	27.8	30.3	12	148	12	10	4,465
Brent	75.4	11.3	25.8	35.1	25	20	14	12	7,685
Bromley	82.0	5.2	24.0	29.8	10	179	12	11	7,870
Camden	73.8	8.6	28.6	35.7	23	17	14	9	17,295
City of London	*	0.1	29.6	32.4	11	183	9	8	11,695
City of Westminster	69.1	6.0	29.6	32.0	16	57	15	10	34,295
Croydon	79.9	8.9	24.1	37.1	14	88	12	12	8,155
Ealing	72.5	8.0	26.0	29.8	18	36	15	11	8,535
Enfield	79.5	7.8	25.6	35.8	17	70	14	11	5,960
Greenwich	73.5	9.0	24.7	37.9	22	11	14	11	3,650
Hackney	64.6	13.6	26.5	35.6	35	4	18	14	6,230
Hammersmith and Fulham	76.2	6.7	28.0	40.6	21	18	15	11	6,995
Haringey	70.3	12.6	25.7	37.8	28	13	18	13	5,735
Harrow	79.7	3.8	28.8	29.6	12	145	13	13	6,100
Havering	81.7	3.5	24.0	22.9	11	143	12	10	5,170
Hillingdon	84.2	4.0	24.9	26.8	12	120	13	12	6,880
Hounslow	76.9	4.5	26.0	24.9	16	59	13	12	6,495
Islington	73.8	10.5	29.2	40.2	28	10	15	11	9,165
Kensington and Chelsea	73.1	4.7	32.7	40.2	14	63	15	10	9,960
Kingston upon Thames	85.8	2.1	28.7	25.3	9	220	13	11	4,620
Lambeth	81.4	14.7	26.9	36.9	26	12	16	10	6,075
Lewisham	79.7	11.5	24.4	40.3	24	14	15	12	4,090
Merton	81.9	3.9	26.3	31.8	12	122	13	11	5,010
Newham	66.2	11.0	23.5	24.5	33	2	15	13	3,625
Redbridge	77.8	5.8	27.4	23.4	15	90	14	13	5,115
Richmond-upon-Thames	81.2	2.4	27.5	29.6	7	156	13	10	7,585
Southwark	75.2	12.2	26.4	34.0	28	8	16	11	6,760
Sutton	84.4	2.6	23.8	26.8	10	284	12	9	4,695
Tower Hamlets	65.3	9.7	21.1	26.3	35	6	16	13	6,845
Waltham Forest	74.5	7.8	25.2	27.2	23	22	14	12	4,225
Wandsworth	81.1	8.6	26.6	33.5	16	30	15	9	8,640

Regional Trends 33, © Crown copyright 1998

14.6 *(continued)*

| | Economically active[3] 1996-97 (percentages) | Claimant count January 1998 | | | Income Support bene- ficiaries[5] Aug. 1996 (percentages) | Ranking from Index of Local Depriv- ation[6] 1998 | Businesses registered for VAT 1996 | | Stock of busin- esses end 1996 (numbers) |
		Total (thousands)	Of which females (percentages)	Of which long-term unemployed[4] (percentages)			Registration rates[7] (percentages)	Deregistration rates[7] (percentages)	
SOUTH EAST (GOR)	82.6	120.7	23.7	23.5	10	.	11	10	242,745
Berkshire	83.6	8.7	21.7	20.2	8	.	13	10	26,740
Bracknell	85.3	0.9	20.5	15.9	7	209	15	11	2,960
Newbury	87.5	1.0	23.6	13.6	6	227	11	9	5,810
Reading	80.9	2.3	20.8	18.8	12	112	13	12	3,790
Slough	82.2	2.4	21.0	24.6	15	100	13	12	2,785
Windsor and Maidenhead	83.6	1.4	23.9	26.5	6	217	12	10	6,340
Wokingham	82.3	0.8	22.0	12.3	4	310=	13	10	5,050
Milton Keynes UA	86.9	2.9	25.1	18.4	12	219	14	11	5,450
Buckinghamshire County	83.9	4.4	23.5	22.0	7	.	10	10	20,295
Aylesbury Vale	84.1	1.6	24.0	22.1	7	310=	11	9	5,860
Chiltern	82.9	0.6	25.0	19.2	6	310=	10	9	4,010
South Buckinghamshire	84.9	0.5	23.8	22.9	5	208	11	9	3,365
Wycombe	83.9	1.6	22.3	22.7	7	290	10	11	7,065
Former county of Buckinghamshire	84.8	7.3	24.1	20.6	8	.	11	10	25,740
Brighton and Hove UA	81.4	9.3	26.5	31.7	19	60	14	12	6,280
East Sussex County	80.7	8.7	23.0	24.0	11	.	10	10	14,395
Eastbourne	80.9	1.8	22.8	19.8	13	176	11	10	1,775
Hastings	77.8	3.0	21.0	27.8	19	81	10	11	1,710
Lewes	83.5	1.4	23.4	25.4	11	260	10	10	2,565
Rother	79.8	1.3	24.2	23.8	10	216	10	10	2,790
Wealden	81.0	1.1	26.6	18.8	7	225	10	9	5,545
Former county of East Sussex	80.9	17.9	24.8	28.0	14	.	11	11	20,670
Portsmouth UA	81.5	5.2	21.8	26.4	15	75	13	12	3,375
Southampton UA	78.3	6.1	19.0	26.7	16	78	13	10	4,150
Hampshire County	81.6	13.8	23.8	19.5	7	.	11	10	35,890
Basingstoke and Deane	84.7	1.4	24.9	21.1	7	310=	11	9	4,575
East Hampshire	81.4	1.1	22.3	21.5	7	251	10	9	4,235
Eastleigh	85.3	1.1	24.7	19.1	7	310=	11	9	2,860
Fareham	83.3	0.9	23.2	18.6	7	310=	11	12	2,630
Gosport	78.4	1.6	24.9	24.6	8	168	10	13	965
Hart	81.2	0.4	24.3	15.4	4	310=	12	10	3,030
Havant	76.6	2.5	20.1	20.8	13	165	13	11	2,355
New Forest	76.0	2.1	24.4	17.5	8	198	10	10	5,225
Rushmoor	85.5	0.9	25.2	15.4	8	255	12	12	2,130
Test Valley	83.7	0.9	27.1	15.6	6	310=	10	9	3,830
Winchester	82.1	0.9	26.2	18.8	6	228	11	9	4,060
Former county of Hampshire	81.1	25.2	22.2	22.7	10	.	11	10	43,415
Isle of Wight UA	77.0	5.0	25.9	28.8	14	98	9	10	3,110
Kent	82.3	34.9	23.5	25.1	12	.	11	11	40,305
Ashford	83.7	1.7	20.8	27.6	10	186	10	10	3,200
Canterbury	82.5	2.9	23.8	25.0	12	190	9	11	3,080
Dartford	82.2	1.9	23.6	28.0	11	154	12	10	1,980
Dover	77.2	3.1	20.2	29.2	13	103	12	12	2,160
Gillingham[6]	84.7	1.9	26.5	19.3	13	124	13	12	1,610
Gravesham	80.0	2.5	26.1	23.2	14	138	12	12	1,915
Maidstone	84.9	2.2	25.2	18.6	10	237	10	11	4,355
Rochester-upon-Medway[6]	79.8	3.9	24.5	20.0	14	124	14	12	3,085
Sevenoaks	82.9	1.4	26.9	25.4	8	180	10	10	4,260
Shepway	85.8	3.0	20.5	31.5	14	127	10	11	2,265
Swale	79.7	3.1	25.1	26.4	16	109	9	9	2,870
Thanet	77.1	4.7	21.3	30.4	20	64	11	12	2,140
Tonbridge and Malling	88.2	1.3	25.6	16.8	8	238	10	12	3,315
Tunbridge Wells	85.3	1.3	23.9	17.9	10	266	10	10	4,075
Oxfordshire	83.6	6.0	25.9	19.5	8	.	11	9	19,885
Cherwell	88.3	1.2	26.5	12.7	8	310=	11	10	4,285
Oxford	74.3	2.5	24.6	24.7	11	147	11	9	2,745
South Oxfordshire	86.4	1.0	26.7	20.7	6	191	11	10	5,425
Vale of White Horse	85.5	0.7	25.0	17.5	6	233	11	9	3,675
West Oxfordshire	84.9	0.6	29.5	13.5	6	282	10	10	3,750

14.6 *(continued)*

| | Economically active[3] 1996-97 (percentages) | Claimant count January 1998 | | | Income Support bene-ficiaries[5] Aug. 1996 (percentages) | Ranking from Index of Local Depriv-ation[6] 1998 | Businesses registered for VAT 1996 | | Stock of busin-esses end 1996 (numbers) |
		Total (thousands)	Of which females (percentages)	Of which long-term unemployed[4] (percentages)			Registration rates[7] (percentages)	Deregistration rates[7] (percentages)	
Surrey	83.4	8.0	24.6	19.1	7	.	12	10	40,820
Elmbridge	82.9	1.0	27.6	22.0	6	310=	12	11	5,260
Epsom and Ewell	89.3	0.6	23.3	18.0	6	310=	12	11	2,015
Guildford	82.6	1.0	25.4	19.8	7	239	12	10	4,720
Mole Valley	82.9	0.5	20.2	16.6	6	201	10	8	3,645
Reigate and Banstead	81.0	1.0	22.7	14.9	8	289	12	11	4,275
Runnymede	85.6	0.6	23.9	23.3	6	178	11	10	2,850
Spelthorne	85.2	0.8	25.0	25.4	7	307	13	10	3,405
Surrey Heath	87.3	0.5	26.3	11.6	5	310=	13	11	3,325
Tandridge	84.7	0.6	24.5	20.9	7	269	10	9	3,170
Waverley	78.8	0.8	24.9	18.4	6	310=	11	10	5,000
Woking	82.1	0.6	25.4	14.6	7	310=	13	11	3,155
West Sussex	83.4	7.6	24.2	18.3	9	.	11	11	22,055
Adur	79.7	0.7	28.1	20.7	11	306	12	11	1,345
Arun	87.7	1.5	22.9	12.5	10	243	11	11	3,510
Chichester	79.3	1.2	25.5	17.6	7	296	10	9	4,300
Crawley	79.4	1.3	23.1	20.9	10	245	12	12	1,950
Horsham	84.5	0.8	25.5	14.6	6	265	10	10	4,510
Mid Sussex	86.1	0.9	27.6	19.1	7	310=	11	11	4,285
Worthing	83.3	1.3	20.3	23.7	11	279	13	12	2,150
SOUTH WEST	80.9	97.2	25.4	22.6	11	.	9	9	147,635
Bath and North East Somerset U	83.2	2.5	26.3	17.2	10	278	11	9	5,185
Bristol UA	79.2	10.9	23.4	21.8	16	69	13	10	10,535
North Somerset UA	84.5	2.5	26.1	16.5	10	261	11	11	4,885
South Gloucestershire UA	85.2	2.5	25.9	16.9	8	287	11	11	5,650
Former county of Avon	82.3	18.5	24.5	19.8	12	.	12	10	26,255
Cornwall and the Isles of Scilly	76.8	15.5	28.7	20.4	14	.	7	8	16,475
Caradon	80.6	1.7	28.1	18.0	11	162	7	9	2,645
Carrick	78.1	2.7	26.2	19.8	14	117	9	9	3,005
Kerrier	71.1	3.0	26.5	26.8	15	87	7	9	2,545
North Cornwall	77.5	2.1	29.7	19.8	13	146	6	6	3,635
Penwith	72.8	2.8	31.3	21.6	18	77	6	9	1,895
Restormel	80.5	3.2	30.2	15.9	13	115	7	8	2,610
Isles of Scilly	..	-	42.4	9.1	-	267	..	3	150
Devon	77.7	26.6	25.1	24.2	13	.	8	9	32,390
East Devon	86.2	1.8	25.9	17.6	8	280	7	8	4,130
Exeter	74.4	2.7	25.1	26.0	13	171	11	11	2,395
Mid Devon	81.8	1.0	29.1	20.7	10	252	7	7	3,315
North Devon	77.1	2.1	26.7	19.8	14	226	7	8	3,565
Plymouth	71.2	8.8	23.1	27.8	15	83	12	13	3,550
South Hams	82.2	1.5	28.8	19.1	11	310=	8	8	3,535
Teignbridge	78.9	2.2	25.7	24.4	12	195=	9	9	3,815
Torbay	78.1	4.2	24.3	22.5	18	97	10	12	2,935
Torridge	77.7	1.5	27.6	26.6	14	167	6	7	2,695
West Devon	84.4	0.8	26.4	23.5	11	234	6	7	2,450
Bournemouth UA	77.6	4.3	21.3	30.0	16	105	12	13	4,045
Poole UA	80.6	2.2	21.3	24.4	10	281	12	12	3,630
Dorset County	80.1	5.1	25.4	19.5	9	.	9	9	12,500
Christchurch	87.7	0.6	21.3	19.2	9	310=	12	11	1,260
East Dorset	75.7	0.7	24.7	19.8	8	197	10	9	2,885
North Dorset	78.6	0.5	29.5	12.5	7	285	8	9	2,280
Purbeck	72.0	0.5	26.9	15.6	9	206	9	9	1,395
West Dorset	82.3	1.2	29.4	18.4	8	247	7	7	3,615
Weymouth and Portland	86.2	1.6	22.5	23.6	12	174	11	12	1,065
Former county of Dorset	79.6	11.5	23.1	24.3	11	.	10	10	20,170

14.6 *(continued)*

	Economically active[3] 1996-97 (percentages)	Claimant count January 1998			Income Support bene-ficieries[5] Aug. 1996 (percentages)	Ranking from Index of Local Depriv-ation[6] 1998	Businesses registered for VAT 1996		Stock of busin-esses end 1996 (numbers)
		Total (thousands)	Of which females (percentages)	Of which long-term unemployed[4] (percentages)			Registration rates[7] (percentages)	Deregistration rates[7] (percentages)	
Gloucestershire	82.8	9.0	24.8	26.5	10	.	10	9	18,315
Cheltenham	83.9	2.1	22.8	30.2	10	224	14	11	3,085
Cotswold	79.8	0.6	24.8	18.0	6	277	9	7	3,975
Forest of Dean	78.1	1.3	28.1	22.3	11	232	9	10	2,780
Gloucester	84.1	2.5	22.5	31.1	14	136	9	10	2,215
Stroud	83.2	1.5	27.4	22.5	9	310=	9	9	3,865
Tewkesbury	85.7	0.9	27.2	23.1	8	194	9	9	2,400
Somerset	82.2	8.5	25.3	24.1	11	.	8	8	16,775
Mendip	85.3	1.7	25.5	22.5	11	310=	8	9	3,740
Sedgemoor	79.8	2.1	24.1	22.8	12	246	8	9	3,405
South Somerset	81.4	1.9	25.9	26.3	14	249	7	8	5,160
Taunton Deane	83.4	1.9	23.5	26.6	8	256	9	8	3,105
West Somerset	80.0	0.9	30.2	19.6	10	163	6	8	1,365
Swindon UA	87.1	2.7	24.0	19.8	12	231	13	12	3,710
Wiltshire County	85.4	4.9	27.2	19.0	8	.	11	9	13,535
Kennet	83.9	0.8	30.2	16.8	7	310=	11	10	2,590
North Wiltshire	88.4	1.1	28.7	15.6	7	250	10	8	4,210
Salisbury	84.1	1.3	23.4	18.7	8	222	10	8	3,535
West Wiltshire	84.2	1.7	27.6	22.7	9	310=	11	10	3,200
Former county of Wiltshire	85.9	7.6	26.0	19.3	9	.	11	10	17,245

1 See Notes and Definitions to the Labour market chapter.

2 With the exception of the Index of Local Deprivation (see footnote 6 below), the table reflects the implementation of the local government reorganisation up to 1 April 1997. See Notes and Definitions.

3 Based on the population of working age. Data are from the Labour Force Survey and relate to the period March 1996 to February 1997.

4 Persons who have been claiming for more than 12 months as a percentage of all claimants.

5 Claimants and their partners aged 16 or over as a percentage of the population aged 16 or over. Data are from the Income Support Quarterly Statistical Enquiry.

6 The rankings for the Index of Local Deprivation relate to the local government structure/boundaries as at 1 April 1998. Within the county of Hereford and Worcester, a new Unitary Authority called Herefordshire, which subsumed Hereford and most of Leominster, was created for which the ILD ranking is 196. The Malvern Hills index ranking of 244 relates to the smaller geographic area post 1 April 1998. In Kent, the districts of Gillingham and Rochester-on-Medway were combined to form the Medway Towns UA which has an ILD ranking of 124. Hence this figure is shown against both former districts. See Notes and Definitions for details of the Index.

7 Registrations/deregistrations during 1996 as a percentage of the stock at the end of 1995.

Source: Office for National Statistics; Department of Social Security; Department of the Environment, Transport and the Regions; Department of Trade and Industry

14.7 Regional accounts: by county

| | Gross domestic product[1,2] | | | | Household income 1995 | | Disposable household income 1995 | |
| | 1991 | | 1995 | | | | | |
	£ million	£ per head index (UK=100)	£ million	£ per head index (UK=100)	£ million	£ per head index (UK=100)	£ million	£ per head index (UK=100)
United Kingdom	490,282	100.0	597,742	100.0	600,739	100.0	496,468	100.0
England	416,035	101.8	506,245	101.5	507,797	101.3	418,048	100.9
North East	18,815	85.2	22,621	85.1	23,106	86.5	19,519	88.4
Cleveland#	4,243	89.4	5,130	89.9	4,913	85.7	4,170	88.0
Durham#	4,009	78.0	4,862	78.4	5,400	86.7	4,574	88.9
Northumberland	1,952	75.1	2,549	81.3	3,207	101.8	2,670	102.6
Tyne & Wear	8,610	89.8	10,081	87.4	9,587	82.7	8,105	84.6
North West (GOR) and Merseyside	53,154	91.0	64,012	91.0	64,248	90.8	53,943	92.3
North West (GOR)	43,997	95.4	53,289	95.5	51,595	92.0	43,150	93.1
Cheshire	8,484	103.5	11,153	111.8	10,222	102.0	8,307	100.3
Cumbria	4,500	108.5	5,221	104.4	4,839	96.3	4,072	98.1
Greater Manchester	20,053	92.0	23,924	91.0	23,469	88.8	19,838	90.8
Lancashire	10,960	91.7	12,991	89.3	13,066	89.4	10,933	90.5
Merseyside	9,157	74.5	10,723	73.7	12,653	86.5	10,793	89.3
Yorkshire and the Humber	38,689	91.5	46,775	91.2	47,413	92.0	39,796	93.4
Humberside#	7,067	95.0	8,525	94.0	8,162	89.6	6,860	91.1
North Yorkshire#	6,172	101.2	7,484	100.4	8,326	111.2	7,019	113.4
South Yorkshire	8,936	80.9	10,064	75.7	11,294	84.5	9,573	86.7
West Yorkshire	16,514	93.4	20,703	96.4	19,631	90.9	16,344	91.6
East Midlands	33,386	97.5	40,377	96.0	40,063	94.8	33,156	94.9
Derbyshire#	7,237	90.5	8,796	90.0	8,932	91.0	7,461	91.9
Leicestershire#	7,902	104.2	9,960	105.8	9,062	95.8	7,332	93.8
Lincolnshire	4,584	91.5	5,683	91.1	6,335	101.0	5,399	104.2
Northamptonshire	5,110	102.7	6,377	104.3	6,143	100.0	4,976	98.0
Nottinghamshire	8,553	98.9	9,561	90.8	9,590	90.7	7,988	91.4
West Midlands	41,391	92.7	50,766	93.8	50,846	93.5	42,392	94.3
Hereford & Worcs.	5,011	86.2	6,820	96.3	7,238	101.7	5,944	101.1
Shropshire	3,146	90.1	4,126	96.3	4,305	100.0	3,540	99.5
Staffordshire#	7,478	84.0	8,846	82.1	10,240	94.6	8,479	94.7
Warwickshire	4,120	99.3	5,130	100.9	5,437	106.4	4,474	105.9
West Midlands (Met. county)	21,635	97.0	25,843	96.1	23,626	87.4	19,955	89.3
Eastern	42,124	96.4	51,381	95.8	57,748	107.2	47,249	106.1
Bedfordshire#	4,553	100.8	5,422	97.4	5,917	105.8	4,862	105.2
Cambridgeshire	6,134	108.1	8,232	116.3	7,566	106.4	6,205	105.6
Essex	10,971	83.6	13,769	85.6	17,415	107.7	14,151	105.9
Hertfordshire	8,835	105.4	10,413	101.0	12,578	121.3	10,018	116.9
Norfolk	6,123	95.1	7,002	88.9	7,763	98.1	6,486	99.1
Suffolk	5,507	99.3	6,544	97.7	6,509	96.7	5,527	99.3
London	83,795	143.4	99,854	139.7	85,019	118.4	68,031	114.6

14.7 *(continued)*

	Gross domestic product[1,2]				Household income 1995		Disposable household income 1995	
	1991		1995					
		£ per head index		£ per head index		£ per head index		£ per head index
	£ million	(UK=100)	£ million	(UK=100)	£ million	(UK=100)	£ million	(UK=100)
South East (GOR)	66,588	102.2	83,194	103.9	89,889	111.7	72,279	108.7
Berkshire	8,398	131.5	10,687	133.8	9,650	120.2	7,436	112.1
Buckinghamshire#	6,149	113.4	7,946	117.0	8,241	120.7	6,343	112.5
East Sussex#	4,625	76.2	5,634	75.6	7,863	105.0	6,603	106.6
Hampshire#	13,854	103.3	17,545	106.4	17,678	106.7	14,370	104.9
Isle of Wight	790	73.8	876	68.7	1,229	95.8	1,074	101.3
Kent	11,998	92.1	14,645	92.6	16,414	103.2	13,545	103.1
Oxfordshire	5,281	107.2	6,640	108.8	6,825	111.3	5,469	107.9
Surrey	9,572	109.2	11,536	108.3	13,642	127.4	10,532	119.0
West Sussex	5,921	98.0	7,684	103.0	8,347	111.3	6,908	111.5
South West	38,093	95.2	47,265	96.0	49,465	100.0	41,683	101.9
Avon#	8,668	105.9	10,600	105.8	9,716	96.5	8,075	97.0
Cornwall	2,886	71.8	3,625	73.6	4,601	93.0	4,010	98.1
Devon	7,628	86.6	9,496	87.9	10,318	95.1	8,831	98.5
Dorset#	5,203	92.9	6,248	90.3	7,084	101.8	5,990	104.2
Gloucestershire	4,673	102.1	5,872	104.2	5,943	104.9	4,942	105.5
Somerset	3,611	90.9	4,497	91.7	4,906	99.5	4,129	101.3
Wiltshire#	5,424	111.9	6,928	115.0	6,897	113.9	5,706	114.1

New local government structure came into effect on 1 April 1996 and 1 April 1997.

1 The GDP data in this table are consistent with the national figures published in the ONS' *United Kingdom National Accounts (Blue Book)1997.* Figures for the United Kingdom exclude the Continental Shelf which in 1995 was £10,348 million.

2 See Notes and Definitions to this table and to Chapter 12 .

Source: Office for National Statistics

15 Sub-regions of Wales

Unitary Authorities in Wales

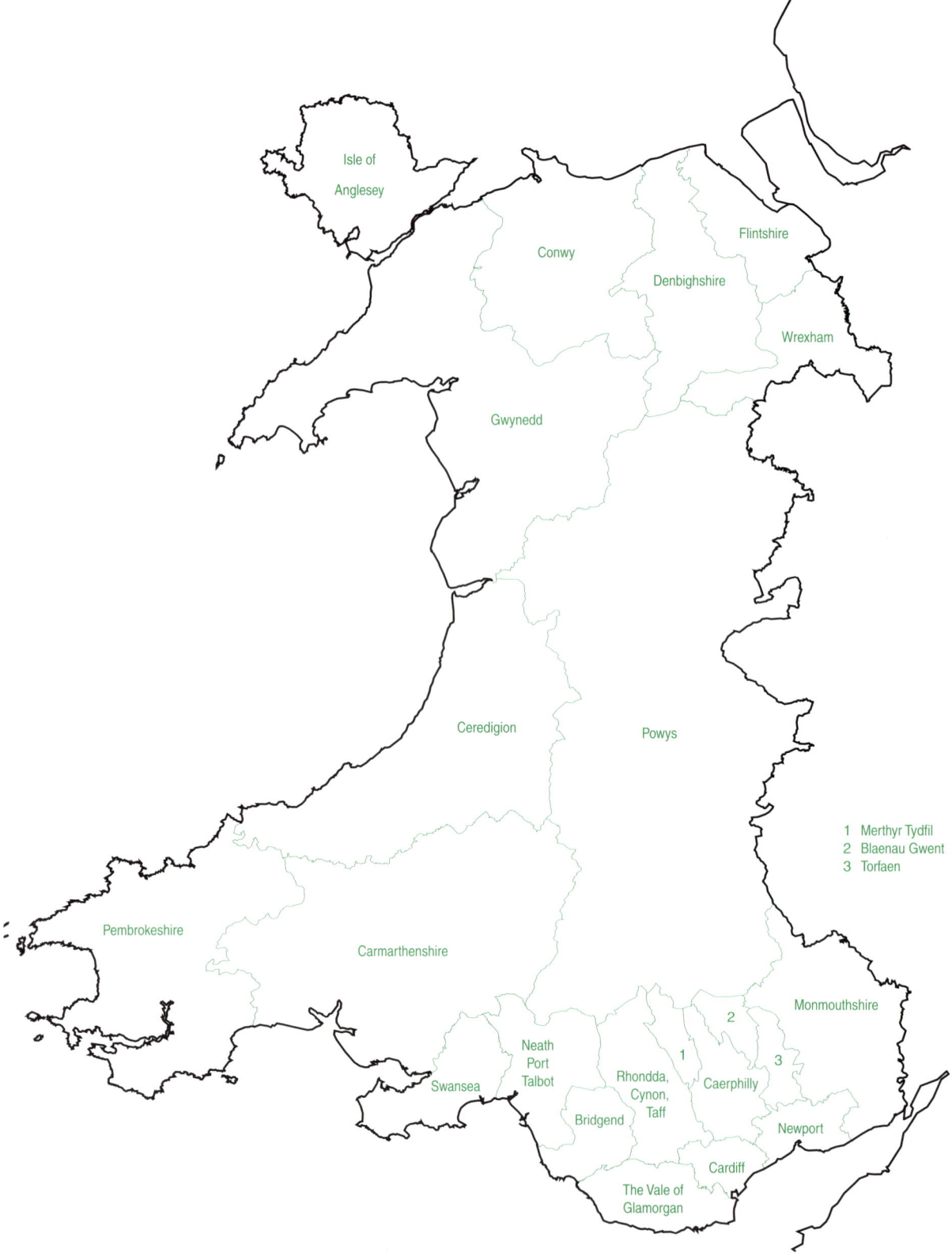

Isle of Anglesey

Conwy

Flintshire

Denbighshire

Wrexham

Gwynedd

Ceredigion

Powys

1 Merthyr Tydfil
2 Blaenau Gwent
3 Torfaen

Pembrokeshire

Carmarthenshire

Monmouthshire

Neath Port Talbot

Swansea

Rhondda, Cynon, Taff

2

1

Caerphilly

3

Bridgend

Newport

Cardiff

The Vale of Glamorgan

15.1 Area and population, 1996

	Area (sq km)	Persons per sq km	Population (thousands)			Total population percentage change 1981-1996	Total period fertility rate (TPFR)[1]	Standardised mortality ratio (UK=100) (SMR)[2]	Percentage of population aged			
			Males	Females	Total				Under 5	5-15	16 up to pension age[3]	Pension age[3] or over
United Kingdom	242,910	242	28,856	29,946	58,801	*4.3*	1.72	100	*6.4*	*14.2*	*61.3*	*18.1*
Wales	20,779	141	1,428	1,493	2,921	*3.8*	1.82	102	*6.1*	*14.5*	*59.5*	*19.9*
Isle of Anglesey	714	94	33	34	67	*-1.5*	2.03	97	*6.1*	*14.6*	*57.9*	*21.4*
Gwynedd	2,548	46	57	61	118	*5.3*	1.84	96	*5.8*	*13.7*	*58.5*	*22.0*
Conwy	1,130	98	53	58	111	*11.8*	1.85	89	*5.3*	*12.9*	*55.3*	*26.6*
Denbighshire	844	109	44	48	92	*6.4*	1.82	100	*6.1*	*13.5*	*56.6*	*23.7*
Flintshire	438	331	71	73	145	*4.6*	1.76	104	*6.3*	*14.3*	*62.1*	*17.3*
Wrexham	498	248	60	63	123	*3.4*	1.73	109	*5.9*	*14.8*	*60.4*	*18.8*
Powys	5,196	24	62	63	124	*10.9*	1.77	91	*5.6*	*13.8*	*58.7*	*21.9*
Ceredigion	1,795	39	34	35	70	*13.7*	1.50	87	*5.0*	*12.8*	*60.4*	*21.8*
Pembrokeshire	1,590	71	55	58	114	*5.8*	1.87	100	*5.9*	*14.8*	*58.3*	*21.0*
Carmarthenshire	2,395	71	82	87	169	*2.5*	1.88	105	*5.4*	*13.6*	*57.9*	*23.1*
Swansea	378	609	113	117	230	*0.4*	1.73	99	*5.7*	*13.9*	*59.8*	*20.5*
Neath Port Talbot	442	316	68	71	139	*-2.3*	1.89	107	*6.0*	*14.3*	*58.7*	*21.0*
Bridgend	246	529	63	67	130	*3.0*	1.86	103	*6.3*	*14.4*	*60.1*	*19.2*
The Vale of Glamorgan	335	356	58	61	119	*5.4*	1.93	97	*6.3*	*15.3*	*59.2*	*19.2*
Cardiff	140	2,250	155	160	315	*9.8*	1.70	95	*6.8*	*14.9*	*61.0*	*17.3*
Rhondda, Cynon, Taff	424	566	119	122	240	*0.7*	1.80	115	*6.1*	*15.0*	*60.7*	*18.2*
Merthyr Tydfil	111	523	28	30	58	*-4.0*	2.09	126	*6.8*	*16.2*	*58.4*	*18.6*
Caerphilly	278	608	83	86	169	*-1.5*	1.99	112	*6.7*	*15.6*	*60.1*	*17.6*
Blaenau Gwent	109	670	36	37	73	*-3.6*	1.85	116	*6.6*	*14.9*	*59.0*	*19.5*
Torfaen	126	718	44	46	90	*-0.2*	1.99	113	*6.8*	*15.0*	*59.7*	*18.5*
Monmouthshire	850	102	43	44	87	*13.4*	1.68	87	*5.6*	*14.1*	*60.3*	*20.1*
Newport	190	720	67	70	137	*3.3*	1.98	103	*6.7*	*15.5*	*59.1*	*18.7*

1 The total period fertility rate (TPFR) is the average number of children which would be born to a woman if the current pattern of fertility persisted throughout her child-bearing years.
2 Adjusted for the age structure of the population. See Notes and Definitions to the Population chapter.
3 Pension age is 65 for males and 60 for females.

Source: Office for National Statistics; Welsh Office

15.2 Vital and social statistics

	Live births[1] per 1,000 population		Deaths[1] per 1,000 population		Perinatal mortality rate[2] 1994-1996	Infant mortality rate[3] 1994-1996	Percentage of live births under 2.5 kg 1996	Percentage of live births outside marriage 1996	Children looked after by LAs per 1,000 population aged under 18 1996[4]
	1991	1996	1991	1996					
United Kingdom	13.7	12.5	11.2	10.9	8.8	6.1	*7.2*	*36*	..
Wales	13.2	11.9	11.8	11.9	8.2	5.9	*6.9*	*41*	4.4
Isle of Anglesey[2,3]	12.2	11.9	11.6	12.2	4.5	5.0	*5.8*	*37*	3.0
Gwynedd[3]	12.2	11.4	13.0	12.6	5.6	3.7	*6.5*	*40*	0.4
Conwy	11.8	11.0	15.6	15.0	7.3	6.2	*6.6*	*41*	2.1
Denbighshire[2,3]	12.6	11.2	13.9	14.8	5.8	3.9	*5.9*	*42*	2.8
Flintshire	13.4	12.1	10.5	10.6	8.3	5.7	*6.5*	*35*	2.2
Wrexham	13.1	11.8	11.2	12.1	7.9	8.8	*6.2*	*42*	3.9
Powys	12.0	10.8	12.4	11.7	9.6	5.4	*7.1*	*35*	2.4
Ceredigion[2,3]	10.8	8.8	12.6	11.4	7.6	5.6	*5.6*	*33*	2.9
Pembrokeshire	13.0	11.3	11.2	11.8	8.3	6.0	*7.3*	*38*	4.6
Carmarthenshire	11.3	11.3	13.1	14.1	9.8	7.2	*6.1*	*37*	4.5
Swansea	12.5	11.3	11.8	11.9	8.6	5.8	*5.5*	*42*	5.0
Neath Port Talbot	12.4	11.8	13.2	13.1	7.9	6.1	*8.3*	*44*	4.7
Bridgend	13.3	12.5	11.6	11.5	10.4	5.9	*5.7*	*41*	4.4
The Vale of Glamorgan	13.4	12.4	11.5	10.8	7.7	5.0	*6.7*	*43*	5.5
Cardiff	14.8	12.8	10.8	9.9	8.4	5.6	*8.1*	*41*	6.7
Rhondda, Cynon, Taff	13.4	12.2	11.6	12.0	8.5	5.6	*7.2*	*49*	4.9
Merthyr Tydfil	14.7	13.7	11.6	13.4	10.8	8.4	*8.2*	*52*	6.1
Caerphilly	14.2	13.1	10.0	11.2	7.8	6.5	*7.4*	*45*	3.5
Blaenau Gwent[3]	14.8	11.9	12.5	13.2	8.5	7.0	*9.0*	*52*	5.2
Torfaen	14.3	13.1	11.4	11.8	9.7	6.5	*7.2*	*38*	3.3
Monmouthshire[2,3]	11.8	10.8	11.1	10.6	5.0	4.7	*5.7*	*28*	2.1
Newport	12.4	13.2	10.6	11.0	7.8	4.6	*7.7*	*44*	9.0

1 Births are on the basis of year of occurrence in England and Wales and year of registration in Scotland and Northern Ireland. Deaths relate to year of registration.
2 Still births and deaths of infants under 1 week of age per 1,000 live and still births. Figures for some UAs should be treated with caution as the perinatal mortality rate was based on fewer than 20 deaths.
3 Deaths of infants under 1 year of age per 1,000 live births. Figures for some UAs should be treated with caution as the infant mortality rate was based on fewer than 20 deaths.
4 At 31 March 1996; 31 March 1995 for Powys, Cardiff and Torfaen. Under 18 mid-1995 population estimates used. In some cases figures are estimates which take account of missing or incomplete data.

Source: Office for National Statistics; Welsh Office

15.3 Education and training

	Day nursery places per 1,000 population aged under 5 years[1] March 1997	Children under 5 in education[2] (percent- ages) Jan. 1997	Pupil/teacher ratio 1996/97 (numbers)		Pupils in last year of compulsory schooling[3,4] 1995/96 with		Average A/AS level points score[4,5] 1995/96
			Primary schools	Secondary schools	No graded results	5 or more A*-Cs at GCSE	
United Kingdom	..	*59*	22.8	16.2	*7.1*	*43.2*	16.7
Wales	46.0	*76*	22.6	16.2	*10.6*	*40.8*	15.5
Isle of Anglesey	14.0	*58*	21.9	15.4	*8.2*	*43.9*	16.3
Gwynedd	45.4	*51*	21.0	14.5	*7.0*	*45.2*	15.4
Conwy	86.1	*71*	22.9	16.2	*6.5*	*43.9*	15.9
Denbighshire	126.1	*81*	23.9	16.2	*9.3*	*39.5*	15.9
Flintshire	78.9	*83*	25.1	16.5	*5.2*	*45.9*	15.1
Wrexham	75.8	*87*	23.8	16.6	*12.6*	*39.7*	13.9
Powys	56.5	*58*	21.0	14.6	*7.0*	*48.0*	16.5
Ceredigion	68.8	*65*	18.9	15.8	*5.9*	*51.5*	17.4
Pembrokeshire	30.3	*73*	20.8	15.8	*5.6*	*45.4*	16.8
Carmarthenshire	22.9	*75*	20.0	16.8	*8.8*	*47.5*	14.7
Swansea	44.7	*97*	21.6	16.1	*10.1*	*43.1*	16.3
Neath Port Talbot	19.8	*92*	20.6	16.1	*10.8*	*35.6*	14.5
Bridgend	32.5	*72*	24.7	16.5	*16.9*	*38.8*	14.8
The Vale of Glamorgan	52.5	*72*	22.4	16.4	*11.1*	*45.6*	17.3
Cardiff	70.9	*68*	22.8	16.6	*12.5*	*38.8*	16.7
Rhondda, Cynon, Taff	25.8	*87*	23.6	16.1	*12.5*	*36.3*	13.5
Merthyr Tydfil	23.3	*83*	23.4	15.6	*18.6*	*29.3*	13.6
Caerphilly	9.4	*73*	23.6	16.1	*14.3*	*33.8*	13.3
Blaenau Gwent	6.6	*72*	22.9	16.1	*15.1*	*28.4*	13.5
Torfaen	25.6	*71*	24.2	17.0	*9.1*	*38.4*	16.4
Monmouthshire	37.1	*57*	24.3	16.7	*7.3*	*46.9*	15.6
Newport	48.6	*79*	25.0	16.8	*10.8*	*37.8*	14.6

1 Local authority provided and registered day nurseries only. A small number of places provided by facilities exempt from registration are excluded. Population data used are mid-1996 estimates.
2 Figures relate to all pupils as a percentage of the three and four year old population.
3 Pupils in their last year of compulsory schooling as a percentage of the school population of the same age.
4 Figures relate to maintained schools only; hence they are not directly comparable with those in Tables 4.6, 16.3 and 17.3 which are for all schools.
5 Figure for United Kingdom relates to England and Wales average.

Source: Welsh Office

15.4 Housing

	Housing starts 1996[1] (numbers)		Stock of dwellings 1996 (thousands)	Local authority tenants: average weekly unrebated rent per dwelling (£) April 1997	Council Tax (£) April 1997[2]
	Private enterprise	Housing associations local authorities etc			
United Kingdom	151,826	31,224	24,607	..	.
Wales	5,311	1,655	1,233	38.0	496
Isle of Anglesey	50	0	31	35.2	424
Gwynedd	106	30	56	34.4	515
Conwy	171	63	51	35.6	403
Denbighshire	144	69	38	34.0	529
Flintshire	236	128	58	35.0	511
Wrexham	219	46	53	32.3	520
Powys	281	90	54	36.5	426
Ceredigion	70	32	30	39.5	562
Pembrokeshire	242	76	51	34.9	451
Carmarthenshire	264	26	74	36.2	557
Swansea	394	265	94	37.8	478
Neath Port Talbot	205	71	61	36.2	621
Bridgend	259	5	55	37.9	539
The Vale of Glamorgan	374	12	48	42.7	443
Cardiff	572	319	123	44.1	486
Rhondda, Cynon, Taff	416	49	101	37.0	560
Merthyr Tydfil	42	50	25	36.3	569
Caerphilly	590	133	69	39.9	519
Blaenau Gwent	64	44	32	37.9	492
Torfaen	88	50	38	43.7	483
Monmouthshire	265	49	34	41.7	403
Newport	259	48	57	41.4	413

1 April to December 1996 only.
2 See Notes and Definitions.

Source: Welsh Office

15.5 Labour market statistics[1]

	Economically active 1996-97[2,3] (percentages)	In employment 1996-97[3] Total[4] (thousands)	In employment 1996-97[3] Manufacturing (percentages)	ILO unemployment rate 1996-97[3] (percentages)	Claimant count January 1998 Total (thousands)	Claimant count January 1998 Of which females (percentage)	Claimant count January 1998 Of which long-term unemployed[5] (percentages)	Average gross weekly full-time earnings, all persons[6], April 1997 (£)
United Kingdom	78.6	26,462	19.1	8.0	1,479.3	23.2	26.2	366.3
Wales	74.7	1,220	21.4	8.1	76.5	22.1	24.4	330.1
Isle of Anglesey	69.4	22	..	..	2.6	22.6	37.4	..
Gwynedd	75.4	49	..	..	4.7	23.5	30.2	289.9
Conwy	74.5	42	..	..	2.9	23.5	23.4	284.1
Denbighshire	75.6	35	16.0	..	2.1	20.5	22.0	322.5
Flintshire	79.4	68	31.4	..	2.8	22.4	21.4	345.4
Wrexham	74.0	52	28.1	..	2.6	22.5	21.1	337.0
Powys	82.3	60	22.0	..	2.1	26.8	17.8	311.4
Ceredigion	78.9	30	..	..	1.6	26.0	22.0	..
Pembrokeshire	76.0	46	13.1	14.7	4.5	23.3	26.7	..
Carmarthenshire	75.0	65	17.3	11.8	4.0	21.6	27.2	310.1
Swansea	71.7	90	15.5	6.0	5.6	20.7	20.0	319.0
Neath Port Talbot	67.1	55	25.8	..	3.4	22.7	17.5	351.4
Bridgend	78.9	59	33.7	..	3.3	23.3	20.9	318.2
The Vale of Glamorgan	76.0	52	13.9	..	2.9	23.1	22.0	357.0
Cardiff	79.7	143	14.7	6.5	8.7	19.6	28.9	349.1
Rhondda, Cynon, Taff	69.4	95	30.7	10.1	6.3	20.4	23.4	314.3
Merthyr Tydfil	71.9	24	..	..	1.7	21.3	20.1	..
Caerphilly	67.6	64	32.0	8.7	4.4	22.0	21.3	312.4
Blaenau Gwent	66.8	27	42.2	..	2.4	20.3	32.5	309.7
Torfaen	81.4	43	29.3	..	2.1	22.3	18.9	330.4
Monmouthshire	77.7	39	19.6	..	1.5	27.7	22.2	310.8
Newport	75.3	59	26.7	10.4	4.2	21.9	26.6	336.4

1 See Notes and Definitions to the Labour market chapter. In some cases sample sizes are too small to provide reliable estimates.
2 Based on the population of working age.
3 Data are from the Labour Force Survey and relate to the period March 1996 to February 1997.
4 Includes those on government-supported employment and training programmes and unpaid family workers.
5 Persons who have been claiming for more than 12 months as a percentage of all claimants.
6 Earnings estimates have been derived from the New Earnings Survey and relate to full-time employees on adult rates whose pay for the survey pay-period was not affected by absence.

Source: Office for National Statistics

16 Sub-regions of Scotland

New Councils in Scotland

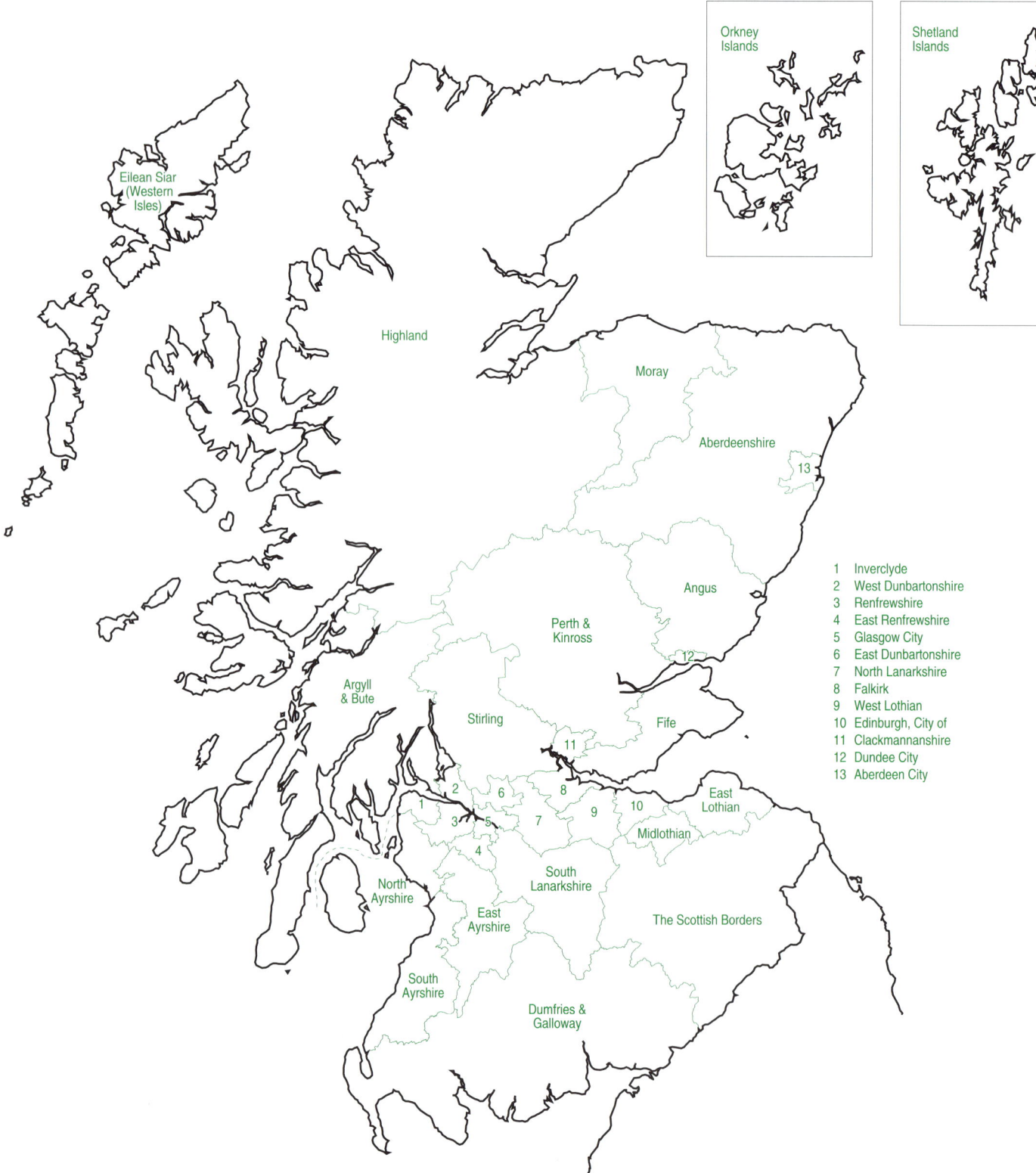

Orkney Islands

Shetland Islands

Eilean Siar (Western Isles)

Highland

Moray

Aberdeenshire

13

Angus

Perth & Kinross

12

1 Inverclyde
2 West Dunbartonshire
3 Renfrewshire
4 East Renfrewshire
5 Glasgow City
6 East Dunbartonshire
7 North Lanarkshire
8 Falkirk
9 West Lothian
10 Edinburgh, City of
11 Clackmannanshire
12 Dundee City
13 Aberdeen City

Argyll & Bute

Stirling

Fife

11

2   6   8
1   9   10   East Lothian
  3   5   7
    4   Midlothian

North Ayrshire

South Lanarkshire

East Ayrshire

The Scottish Borders

South Ayrshire

Dumfries & Galloway

Regional Trends 33, © Crown copyright 1998

16.1 Area and population, 1996

| | Area (sq km) | Persons per sq km | Population (thousands) | | | Total population percentage change 1981-1996 | Total period fertility rate (TPFR)[1] | Standardised mortality ratio (UK=100) (SMR)[2] | Percentage of population aged | | | |
			Males	Females	Total				Under 5	5-15	16 up to pension age[3]	Pension age[3] or over
United Kingdom	242,910	242	28,856	29,946	58,801	*4.3*	*1.72*	100	*6.4*	*14.2*	*61.3*	*18.1*
Scotland	78,133	66	2,486	2,642	5,128	*-1.0*	*1.56*	116	*6.1*	*13.9*	*63.1*	*17.8*
Aberdeen City	186	1,169	106	111	217	*2.2*	*1.35*	105	*5.8*	*12.3*	*65.8*	*17.1*
Aberdeenshire	6,318	36	113	114	227	*20.4*	*1.64*	97	*6.5*	*15.3*	*63.8*	*15.3*
Angus	2,181	51	54	57	111	*4.9*	*1.67*	113	*6.0*	*13.9*	*61.6*	*19.4*
Argyll and Bute	6,930	13	45	46	91	*-0.1*	*1.70*	109	*5.5*	*13.6*	*61.1*	*20.8*
Clackmannanshire	157	312	24	25	49	*1.2*	*1.76*	115	*6.6*	*14.6*	*63.0*	*16.7*
Dumfries and Galloway	6,439	23	72	76	148	*1.4*	*1.78*	107	*5.9*	*13.8*	*60.3*	*21.2*
Dundee City	65	2,306	72	79	150	*-11.4*	*1.57*	118	*5.9*	*13.3*	*62.0*	*19.9*
East Ayrshire	1,252	98	59	63	122	*-3.9*	*1.64*	114	*6.3*	*14.5*	*61.9*	*18.3*
East Dunbartonshire	172	645	54	57	111	*1.0*	*1.56*	102	*5.8*	*14.2*	*64.5*	*16.5*
East Lothian	678	130	43	45	88	*9.2*	*1.77*	112	*6.4*	*13.7*	*61.5*	*19.5*
East Renfrewshire	173	510	43	45	88	*9.8*	*1.67*	96	*6.2*	*14.6*	*63.0*	*17.1*
Edinburgh, City of	262	1,711	217	232	449	*0.6*	*1.34*	111	*5.7*	*11.6*	*65.8*	*17.9*
Eilean Siar (Western Isles)	3,134	9	14	15	29	*-8.5*	*1.65*	117	*5.5*	*15.1*	*59.8*	*20.7*
Falkirk	299	478	69	74	143	*-1.5*	*1.58*	121	*6.2*	*13.7*	*63.8*	*17.4*
Fife	1,323	264	169	180	349	*2.3*	*1.55*	109	*6.0*	*14.4*	*62.3*	*18.3*
Glasgow City	175	3,522	294	322	616	*-13.5*	*1.48*	137	*6.3*	*13.3*	*63.2*	*18.1*
Highland	25,784	8	102	106	209	*7.1*	*1.77*	109	*6.2*	*14.9*	*61.8*	*18.1*
Inverclyde	162	538	42	45	87	*-13.9*	*1.66*	138	*6.2*	*14.6*	*61.7*	*18.6*
Midlothian	356	225	39	41	80	*-4.2*	*1.61*	119	*6.1*	*14.3*	*64.2*	*16.4*
Moray	2,238	39	43	44	87	*3.6*	*1.76*	108	*6.6*	*14.6*	*61.8*	*18.0*
North Ayrshire	884	158	67	72	140	*1.6*	*1.63*	115	*6.2*	*15.0*	*62.2*	*17.6*
North Lanarkshire	474	688	158	168	326	*-4.6*	*1.66*	126	*6.4*	*14.9*	*63.8*	*15.9*
Orkney Islands	992	20	10	10	20	*3.2*	*1.78*	106	*6.0*	*15.3*	*61.2*	*18.5*
Perth and Kinross	5,311	25	64	69	133	*8.8*	*1.61*	103	*5.6*	*13.8*	*60.7*	*20.9*
Renfrewshire	261	683	86	92	179	*-3.5*	*1.59*	125	*6.3*	*14.1*	*63.7*	*17.0*
Scottish Borders, The	4,734	22	51	55	106	*4.8*	*1.67*	100	*5.8*	*13.3*	*60.2*	*21.8*
Shetland Islands	1,438	16	12	11	23	*-12.6*	*1.77*	117	*7.0*	*15.9*	*62.9*	*14.9*
South Ayrshire	1,202	95	55	60	115	*1.3*	*1.55*	105	*5.5*	*13.7*	*61.1*	*20.9*
South Lanarkshire	1,771	174	149	159	307	*-0.8*	*1.55*	125	*6.3*	*14.5*	*63.8*	*16.5*
Stirling	2,196	38	40	43	83	*3.1*	*1.55*	110	*5.7*	*13.6*	*63.8*	*17.9*
West Dunbartonshire	162	590	46	50	96	*-9.5*	*1.70*	130	*6.4*	*15.3*	*61.4*	*17.8*
West Lothian	425	355	74	77	151	*8.3*	*1.63*	126	*6.8*	*15.1*	*65.8*	*13.2*

1 The total period fertility rate (TPFR) is the average number of children which would be born to a woman if the current pattern of fertility persisted throughout her child-bearing years.

2 Adjusted for the age structure of the population. See Notes and Definitions to the Population chapter.

3 Pension age is 65 for males and 60 for females.

Source: Office for National Statistics; General Register Office for Scotland

16.2 Vital and social statistics

	Live births[1] per 1,000 population		Deaths[1] per 1,000 population		Perinatal mortality rate[2]	Infant mortality rate[3]	Percentage of live births outside marriage
	1991	1996	1991	1996	1994-1996	1994-1996	1996
United Kingdom	13.7	12.5	11.2	10.9	8.8	6.1	36
Scotland	13.1	11.6	12.0	11.8	9.3	6.2	36
Aberdeen City	12.5	11.0	10.8	10.4	7.7	5.7	35
Aberdeenshire	13.5	11.3	9.6	9.0	9.0	3.8	24
Angus[3]	12.3	11.0	12.9	13.2	5.6	3.2	33
Argyll and Bute	13.0	10.5	12.7	13.8	8.6	7.0	33
Clackmannanshire	13.7	12.3	10.1	11.3	10.4	6.3	40
Dumfries and Galloway	12.1	10.9	13.1	12.8	8.8	7.8	34
Dundee City	12.9	11.5	12.4	13.1	8.6	6.8	51
East Ayrshire[3]	13.9	11.4	11.9	11.6	12.3	6.5	40
East Dunbartonshire	12.4	10.5	8.7	9.2	8.1	7.2	19
East Lothian	13.1	12.3	12.6	12.6	7.6	5.2	29
East Renfrewshire	13.0	11.5	9.5	9.5	7.4	6.2	19
Edinburgh, City of	12.9	11.4	12.5	11.7	8.1	6.4	33
Eilean Siar (Western Isles)[2,3]	11.2	9.7	14.9	14.9	11.2	5.7	19
Falkirk	13.5	11.7	11.5	11.7	7.9	4.8	34
Fife	12.6	11.0	11.9	11.4	8.7	7.1	37
Glasgow, City of	14.3	12.5	14.4	14.0	11.1	6.9	49
Highland	13.0	11.4	11.5	11.4	8.3	6.5	34
Inverclyde	12.9	11.7	13.6	14.5	11.5	8.0	45
Midlothian	13.5	11.2	10.6	10.7	10.8	6.0	35
Moray	13.8	12.4	11.2	11.0	9.8	7.4	26
North Ayrshire[2,3]	13.9	11.3	11.7	11.8	11.6	6.9	42
North Lanarkshire	13.6	12.5	11.1	11.1	11.6	8.5	38
Orkney Islands	12.1	10.9	11.8	11.6	7.5	1.4	30
Perth and Kinross[3]	12.2	10.5	13.0	12.6	9.8	5.9	29
Renfrewshire[3]	12.6	11.9	11.5	11.6	8.0	4.5	39
Scottish Borders, The[3]	12.1	10.7	13.8	12.8	8.0	4.9	28
Shetland Islands[2,3]	14.4	11.7	10.4	10.9	9.9	6.5	28
South Ayrshire	10.8	10.1	13.3	12.7	6.2	4.3	33
South Lanarkshire	13.3	11.5	10.5	11.3	9.2	5.1	33
Stirling	11.9	11.1	11.8	11.8	7.7	4.9	33
West Dunbartonshire	13.1	12.5	12.5	12.7	11.7	8.7	42
West Lothian	14.3	13.1	9.2	9.5	8.7	4.6	33

1 Births are on the basis of year of occurrence in England and Wales and year of registration in Scotland and Northern Ireland. Deaths relate to year of registration.

2 Still births and deaths of infants under 1 week of age per 1,000 live and still births. Figures for some Council areas should be treated with caution as the perinatal mortality rate was based on fewer than 20 deaths.

3 Deaths of infants under 1 year of age per 1,000 live births. Figures for some Council areas should be treated with caution as the infant mortality rate was based on fewer than 20 deaths.

Source: Office for National Statistics; General Register Office for Scotland

16.3 Education and training

	Day nursery places per 1,000 population aged under 5 years[1] Nov. 1996	Children under 5 in education[2] (percentages) Jan. 1997	Pupil/teacher ratio 1996/97 (numbers)		Pupils and students participating in post-compulsory education, (percentages) 1995/96[3]	Pupils in last year of compulsory schooling[4,5] 1995/96 with		Employees of working age receiving job-related training[6] 1996-97[7]
			Primary schools	Secondary schools		No graded results	5 or more Grades 1-3 SCE Standard Grade (or equivalent)	
United Kingdom	..	59	22.8	16.2	78	7.4	45.5	14.5
Scotland	80.6	39	19.6	13.0	93	3.6	53.6	12.5
Aberdeen City	126.0	50	19.9	12.9	113	1.9	53.0	15.4
Aberdeenshire	34.4	34	18.6	13.8	81	9.2	58.2	11.4
Angus	70.2	38	19.1	13.0	89	..	62.0	..
Argyll and Bute	38.8	13	17.3	12.4	81	8.6	54.1	..
Clackmannanshire	90.9	47	21.2	13.4	78	..	63.6	..
Dumfries and Galloway	21.3	44	18.9	12.7	93	2.7	60.2	..
Dundee City	114.3	59	18.0	12.2	117	0.6	46.9	..
East Ayrshire	43.4	43	21.0	13.5	89	6.4	50.2	..
East Dunbartonshire	76.2	11	22.2	13.9	94	..	71.2	..
East Lothian	48.6	56	20.6	13.4	66	12.7	46.0	..
East Renfrewshire	146.0	33	22.3	14.0	91	..	78.8	..
Edinburgh, City of	132.3	50	20.7	13.4	109	2.3	56.7	14.7
Eilean Siar (Western Isles)	12.6	..	13.0	9.5	102	3.2	60.9	..
Falkirk	81.8	40	21.3	13.6	91	4.0	49.4	..
Fife	20.2	51	19.1	13.4	106	5.3	52.1	13.5
Glasgow City	99.8	53	19.3	12.4	88	12.7	41.9	15.3
Highland	41.5	19	17.3	11.8	94	..	60.0	..
Inverclyde	105.8	27	21.4	13.6	95	..	56.2	..
Midlothian	49.0	54	19.9	13.6	77	3.8	53.0	..
Moray	21.6	31	18.9	12.2	91	8.0	54.3	..
North Ayrshire	115.3	23	21.2	13.4	72	10.5	45.6	..
North Lanarkshire	64.4	25	20.2	13.4	94	2.3	47.5	11.8
Orkney Islands	31.8	52	15.1	10.9	97	-	69.3	..
Perth and Kinross	93.2	45	18.7	12.5	78	10.2	53.9	..
Renfrewshire	119.6	31	22.0	13.7	103	..	55.9	15.5
Scottish Borders, The	56.9	22	18.5	12.1	92	1.3	61.7	..
Shetland Islands	14.8	42	12.7	8.1	79	..	73.6	..
South Ayrshire	70.4	36	21.0	13.6	99	..	61.9	..
South Lanarkshire	103.9	15	20.7	13.7	92	3.6	51.5	13.7
Stirling	200.5	46	19.5	13.3	81	2.9	61.4	..
West Dunbartonshire	81.9	47	20.3	14.0	108	..	52.5	..
West Lothian	53.6	51	20.3	13.5	80	6.3	46.8	..

1 Social Work Provision only (local authority and registered); includes Day Nurseries, Children's Centres, Family Centres and Private Nursery Schools. Population data used mid-1996 estimates.

2 Figures relate to all pupils as a percentage of the three and four year old population.

3 In Scotland pupils in S5 at September 1995. The figure for the United Kingdom relates to 16 year olds in education at the beginning of the academic year. Some students in Scotland participate on short courses. They are counted for each course; hence there is double counting which results in some percentages being greater than 100.

4 Pupils in their last year of compulsory schooling as a percentage of the school population of the same age.

5 Figures relate to all schools; hence they are not directly comparable with those in Tables 14.3 and 15.3 which are for maintained schools only.

6 Males aged 16-64 and females aged 16-59. Job-related education or training received in the four weeks before interview. In some cases sample sizes are too small to provide reliable estimates.

7 Data relate to the period March 1996 to February 1997. Figure for United Kingdom relates to Great Britain.

Source: The Scottish Office Home Department; The Scottish Office Education and Industry Department; Department for Education and Employment

16.4 Housing and households

	Housing starts 1996 (numbers)		Stock of dwellings 1996 (thousands)[3]	Households 1996 (thousands)	Local authority tenants: average weekly unrebated rent per dwelling (£) April 1997	Council Tax (£) April 1997[4]
	Private enterprise[1]	Housing associations local authorities etc[2]				
United Kingdom	151,826	31,224	24,607	24,115.3	..	.
Scotland	15,759	4,768	2,232	2,136.2	33.6	783
Aberdeen City	1,142	136	100	96.8	27.5	712
Aberdeenshire	533	90	92	87.1	29.7	643
Angus	272	167	48	46.2	23.5	679
Argyll and Bute	300	266	43	37.7	35.0	801
Clackmannanshire	125	37	21	20.0	29.6	753
Dumfries and Galloway	388	159	66	62.3	32.7	714
Dundee City	182	151	72	67.5	36.8	920
East Ayrshire	262	30	51	50.1	26.9	779
East Dunbartonshire	236	6	42	41.3	29.6	771
East Lothian	469	165	38	36.3	28.8	724
East Renfrewshire	295	96	34	33.1	28.9	682
Edinburgh, City of	1,496	525	206	198.2	43.8	837
Eilean Siar (Western Isles)	75	10	13	11.6	36.5	599
Falkirk	651	66	61	59.1	29.8	680
Fife	202	251	152	145.6	30.3	747
Glasgow City	1,884	1,056	286	271.9	40.4	982
Highland	664	161	95	85.8	38.5	719
Inverclyde	291	126	39	38.0	34.6	831
Midlothian	362	61	32	30.8	25.2	858
Moray	327	0	37	34.9	28.0	652
North Ayrshire	344	157	60	57.7	30.2	718
North Lanarkshire	1,557	175	130	128.5	31.3	787
Orkney Islands	0	6	9	8.1	33.8	515
Perthshire and Kinross	448	147	59	55.0	28.2	732
Renfrewshire	732	66	77	75.1	32.5	783
Scottish Borders, The	245	98	49	44.9	29.7	612
Shetland Islands	131	21	10	8.9	36.1	486
South Ayrshire	182	80	49	47.6	30.7	765
South Lanarkshire	488	98	124	122.3	35.3	793
Stirling	341	66	34	33.1	33.6	776
West Dunbartonshire	193	139	42	40.4	33.4	978
West Lothian	942	156	61	60.3	28.3	792

1 Includes estimates for outstanding returns.
2 Based on incomplete returns.
3 Number of residential dwellings taken from the Council Tax Register.
4 See Notes and Definitions.

Source: The Scottish Office Development Department

16.5 Labour market statistics[1]

| | Economically active 1996-97[2,3] (percentages) | In employment 1996-97[3] | | ILO unemployment 1996-97[3] (percentages) | Claimant count January 1998 | | | Average gross weekly full-time earnings[6], all persons, April 1997 (£) |
		Total[4] (thousands)	Manufacturing (percentages)		Total (thousands)	Of which females (percentages)	Of which long-term unemployed[5] (percentages)	
United Kingdom	78.6	26,462	19.1	8.0	1,479.3	23.2	26.2	366.3
Scotland	77.1	2,277	17.1	8.7	152.2	22.0	22.4	336.8
Aberdeen City	82.4	113	14.3	4.9	3.6	21.0	17.6	404.8
Aberdeenshire	80.2	112	14.5	..	2.8	26.5	16.3	330.9
Angus	86.3	59	16.9	..	3.2	28.3	23.3	320.0
Argyll and Bute	80.4	41	..	11.9	2.9	27.1	22.8	305.2
Clackmannanshire	64.7	17	..	..	1.6	22.0	27.5	..
Dumfries and Galloway	79.0	67	17.7	..	4.4	24.3	23.4	300.2
Dundee City	72.2	60	14.6	9.3	6.2	21.2	26.3	327.4
East Ayrshire	75.2	50	23.1	14.2	4.5	20.5	28.9	307.6
East Dunbartonshire	81.1	53	..	..	2.2	23.2	17.3	329.2
East Lothian	80.3	41	..	..	1.7	20.5	16.3	310.3
East Renfrewshire	83.0	42	16.8	..	1.4	23.8	20.9	..
Edinburgh, City of	74.5	207	10.3	6.6	11.1	22.1	20.4	362.8
Eilean Siar (Western Isles)	83.8	15	..	..	1.4	19.9	23.8	..
Falkirk	77.6	66	23.4	..	4.5	21.5	19.9	335.6
Fife	77.9	147	21.7	9.3	11.1	22.5	22.7	325.2
Glasgow City	65.3	210	14.2	15.2	26.9	19.4	29.5	341.5
Highland	80.9	100	12.9	9.3	7.9	25.9	20.9	296.2
Inverclyde	80.2	39	26.5	..	2.5	18.5	12.7	323.4
Midlothian	84.8	39	..	..	1.6	19.4	13.7	309.0
Moray	86.4	43	14.3	..	2.2	27.2	15.4	285.0
North Ayrshire	73.5	58	27.4	9.1	5.1	23.7	19.2	317.8
North Lanarkshire	74.7	133	21.2	12.4	10.7	20.8	20.1	336.7
Orkney Islands	87.8	10	..	..	0.4	26.8	24.4	..
Perthshire and Kinross	86.6	66	11.3	..	2.8	23.0	17.8	..
Renfrewshire	78.5	80	20.1	11.3	5.5	20.5	23.3	336.1
Scottish Borders, The	80.6	49	20.6	..	2.1	23.7	12.3	303.5
Shetland Islands	84.8	11	..	..	0.4	23.2	14.2	..
South Ayrshire	79.2	48	22.9	10.3	3.6	23.6	23.4	346.2
South Lanarkshire	78.4	146	22.0	8.3	8.2	21.7	21.8	319.1
Stirling	77.2	37	..	..	2.1	23.0	19.5	346.6
West Dunbartonshire	71.5	36	..	13.6	4.2	19.3	27.3	319.0
West Lothian	82.2	78	32.6	..	3.5	21.2	10.2	335.5

1 See Notes and Definitions to the Labour market chapter. In some cases sample sizes are too small to provide reliable estimates.
2 Based on the population of working age.
3 Data are from the Labour Force Survey and relate to the period March 1996-February 1997.
4 Includes those on government-supported employment and training programmes and unpaid family workers.
5 Persons who have been claiming for more than 12 months as a percentage of all claimants.
6 Earnings estimates have been derived from the New Earnings Survey and relate to full-time employees on adult rates whose pay for the survey pay-period was not affected by absence.

Source: Office for National Statistics

17 Sub-regions of Northern Ireland

Boards in Northern Ireland

Health and Social Services Boards

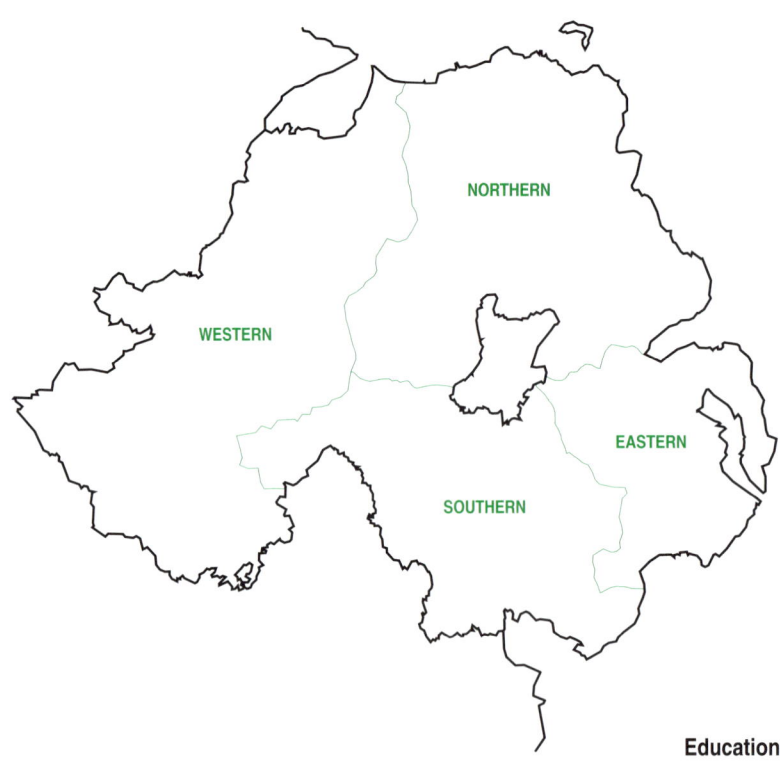

Education and Library Boards

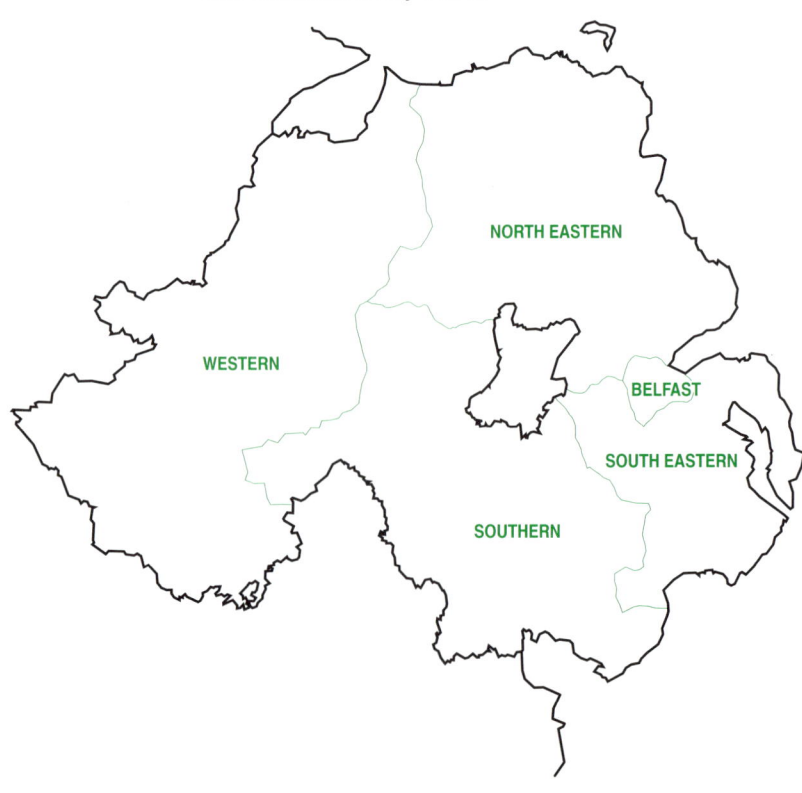

Regional Trends 33, © Crown copyright 1998

17.1 Area and population: by Board[1] and district, 1996

| | Area (sq km) | Persons per sq km | Population (thousands) | | | Total population percentage change 1981-1996 | Total period fertility rate (TPFR)[2] | Standardised mortality ratio (UK=100) (SMR)[3] | Percentage of population aged | | | |
			Males	Females	Total				Under 5	5-15	16 up to pension age[4]	Pension age[4] or over
United Kingdom	242,910	242	28,856	29,946	58,801	*4.3*	1.72	100	*6.4*	*14.2*	*61.3*	*18.1*
Northern Ireland	13,576	123	812	851	1,663	*8.2*	1.95	107	*7.5*	*17.5*	*60.0*	*15.0*
Eastern	1,751	384	323	350	673	*5.3*	1.79	104	*7.1*	*16.2*	*59.9*	*16.8*
Ards	380	177	..	..	68	*16.8*	..	..	..	..	..	..
Belfast	110	2,712	..	..	297	*-5.7*	..	..	..	..	..	..
Castlereagh	85	755	..	..	64	*5.8*	..	..	..	..	..	..
Down	649	95	..	..	61	*14.6*	..	..	..	..	..	..
Lisburn	447	243	..	..	108	*27.7*	..	..	..	..	..	..
North Down	81	919	..	..	74	*11.4*	..	..	..	..	..	..
Northern	4,093	101	204	212	415	*10.7*	1.87	106	*7.2*	*16.9*	*61.2*	*14.7*
Antrim	421	116	..	..	49	*7.0*	..	..	..	..	..	..
Ballymena	630	92	..	..	58	*6.0*	..	..	..	..	..	..
Ballymoney	416	60	..	..	25	*8.3*	..	..	..	..	..	..
Carrickfergus	81	438	..	..	35	*23.8*	..	..	..	..	..	..
Coleraine	486	112	..	..	55	*16.7*	..	..	..	..	..	..
Cookstown	514	62	..	..	32	*12.0*	..	..	..	..	..	..
Larne	337	90	..	..	30	*4.1*	..	..	..	..	..	..
Magherafelt	564	67	..	..	38	*15.0*	..	..	..	..	..	..
Moyle	494	30	..	..	15	*3.5*	..	..	..	..	..	..
Newtownabbey	151	525	..	..	79	*9.7*	..	..	..	..	..	..
Southern	3,075	98	149	152	300	*9.8*	2.24	106	*8.1*	*18.8*	*59.3*	*13.8*
Armagh	671	79	..	..	53	*7.7*	..	..	..	..	..	..
Banbridge	451	83	..	..	37	*24.7*	..	..	..	..	..	..
Craigavon	282	279	..	..	79	*7.1*	..	..	..	..	..	..
Dungannon	773	61	..	..	47	*7.1*	..	..	..	..	..	..
Newry and Mourne	898	94	..	..	85	*9.3*	..	..	..	..	..	..
Western	4,658	59	137	138	275	*9.9*	2.26	121	*8.3*	*20.0*	*59.4*	*12.3*
Derry	381	274	..	..	104	*16.3*	..	..	..	..	..	..
Fermanagh	1,699	33	..	..	55	*6.4*	..	..	..	..	..	..
Limavady	586	53	..	..	31	*14.7*	..	..	..	..	..	..
Omagh	1,130	42	..	..	47	*5.8*	..	..	..	..	..	..
Strabane	862	42	..	..	37	*0.8*	..	..	..	..	..	..

1 Health and Social Services Board areas.
2 The total period fertility rate (TPFR) is the average number of children which would be born to a woman if the current pattern of fertility persisted throughout her child-bearing years.
3 Adjusted for the age structure of the population. See Notes and Definitions to the Population chapter.
4 Pension age is 65 for males and 60 for females.

Source: Northern Ireland Statistics and Research Agency; Office for National Statistics

17.2 Vital and social statistics: by Board[1]

| | Live births[2] per 1,000 population | | Deaths[2] per 1,000 population | | Perinatal mortality rate[3] | Infant mortality rate[4] | Percentage of live births outside marriage | Children looked after by LAs per 1,000 pop. aged under 18 |
	1991	1996	1991	1996	1994-1996	1994-1996	1996	1996[5]
United Kingdom	13.7	12.5	11.2	10.9	8.8	6.1	*36*	..
Northern Ireland	16.4	14.8	9.4	9.1	9.8	6.7	*26*	4.5
Eastern	15.9	13.8	10.4	10.0	10.8	7.2	*31*	5.3
Northern	15.2	14.2	8.7	8.8	7.3	5.4	*24*	4.6
Southern	18.2	16.0	8.9	8.2	9.6	6.5	*18*	3.2
Western	17.9	16.8	8.7	8.4	9.5	6.1	*26*	4.1

1 Health and Social Services Board Areas.
2 Births are on the basis of year of occurrence in England and Wales and year of registration in Scotland and Northern Ireland. Deaths relate to year of registration.
3 Still births and deaths of infants under 1 week of age per 1,000 live and still births.
4 Deaths of infants under 1 year of age per 1,000 live births.
5 At 31 March. Data relate to children in care excluding children home on trial. Legislation in Northern Ireland relating to children in care is different from that in the rest of the United Kingdom. Figures are not directly comparable with similar data in the England and Wales chapters.

Source: Northern Ireland Statistics and Research Agency; Department of Health and Social Services, Northern Ireland

17.3 Education: by Board[1]

	Day nursery places per 1,000 population aged under 5 years[2] March 1996	Pupil/teacher ratio 1996/97 (numbers)		Pupils in last year of compulsory schooling[3,4] 1995/96 with	
		Primary schools	Secondary schools	No graded results	5 or more A*-Cs at GCSE
United Kingdom	..	22.8	16.2	7.4	45.5
Northern Ireland	27.2	19.8	14.5	4.6	51.6
Belfast	..	19.0	14.4	5.5	55.1
South Eastern[5]	37.6	20.7	14.8	4.1	48.0
Southern	20.4	19.4	14.6	4.9	52.6
North Eastern	27.9	20.5	14.4	3.5	50.7
Western	11.7	19.6	14.3	5.4	51.2

1 Education and Library Boards, except for day nursery information which refers to Health and Social Services Board Areas.
2 Local authority provided and registered day nurseries only. A small number of places provided by facilities exempt from registration are excluded. Population data used are mid-1995 estimates.
3 Pupils in their last year of compulsory schooling as a percentage of the school population of the same age.
4 Figures relate to all schools; hence they are not directly comparable with those in Tables 14.3 and 15.3 which are for maintained schools only.
5 South Eastern figure for day nursery places includes Belfast.

Source: Department of Health and Social Services, Northern Ireland; Department of Education, Northern Ireland

17.4 Labour market[1] and benefit statistics: by district

	Economically active 1996-97[2,3] (percentages)	Claimant count January 1998			Employees of working age receiving job-related training[5] 1996-97[3] (percentages)	Income Support bene-ficiaries[6] November 1997 (percentages)	Households receiving Housing Benefit at November 1997 as a percentage of all households[7]
		Total (thousands)	Of which females (percentages)	Of which long-term unemployed[4] (percentages)			
United Kingdom	78.6	14,793	23.2	26.9	..	..	..
Northern Ireland	71.9	598	20.4	44.9	10.2	14	27
Antrim	73.1	12	22.9	33.7	9.2	10	20
Ards	79.7	19	25.1	36.1	12.7	9	20
Armagh	73.2	18	22.9	43.8	13.1	12	19
Ballymena	78.5	15	23.7	38.4	9.3	10	17
Ballymoney	74.1	9	18.0	48.9	..	12	23
Banbridge	77.2	7	24.7	37.3	13.5	10	18
Belfast	66.4	137	18.4	44.8	9.7	18	32
Carrickfergus	79.1	10	26.2	39.2	15.9	9	21
Castlereagh	83.2	13	22.6	34.1	6.5	8	17
Coleraine	68.0	22	22.8	42.6	13.7	11	23
Cookstown	69.9	10	20.2	48.9	..	16	21
Craigavon	72.6	21	21.2	41.8	7.1	14	26
Derry	81.9	59	18.2	49.6	10.6	21	38
Down	70.4	22	23.8	38.7	..	11	19
Dungannon	70.0	19	22.3	50.7	..	16	21
Fermanagh	74.6	24	20.8	55.0	17.1	14	14
Larne	66.7	8	21.3	32.4	..	10	20
Limavady	73.7	13	14.5	47.8	10.4	13	25
Lisburn	65.3	28	22.1	40.9	7.3	11	24
Magherafelt	66.0	12	19.1	47.7	..	14	22
Moyle	70.4	8	16.9	47.7	..	14	24
Newry and Mourne	61.1	38	18.4	52.3	16.4	18	22
Newtonabbey	80.6	18	24.0	37.1	13.7	10	20
North Down	77.6	18	27.0	33.4	14.2	7	14
Omagh	70.1	20	20.3	56.6	..	15	19
Strabane	64.1	19	15.0	53.8	..	19	33

1 See Notes and Definitions to the Labour market chapter.
2 Economic activity rates based on the population of working age. Data are from the Labour Force Survey.
3 Relates to the period March 1996 to February 1997.
4 Persons who have been claiming for more than 12 months as a percentage of all claimants.
5 Males aged 16-64 and females aged 16-59. Job-related education or training received in the four weeks before interview. In some cases sample sizes are too small to provide reliable estimates.
6 Claimants and their partners aged 16 or over as a percentage of the population aged 16 or over.
7 Households for NI are taken from the 1991 Census. ten per cent of Housing Benefit claimants had missing postcodes and could not be allocated to a District Council.

Source: Office for National Statistics; Department of Economic Development & Department of Health and Social Services, Northern Ireland

Notes and Definitions

REGIONAL CLASSIFICATION

Government Office Regions within England

Most of the statistics in *Regional Trends* are on the basis of the Government Office Regions (GORs) of England, together with Wales Scotland and Northern Ireland. Although Merseyside currently has a Government Office of its own, for statistical purposes it has not been adopted as a region in its own right. Wherever possible, however, figures for the two components of the North West and Merseyside region are given separately. Maps of the GORs are on pages 13 to 25 and 165.

Standard Statistical Regions

Prior to the introduction of the GORs, regional statistics were presented on the basis of the Standard Statistical Regions (SSRs) of the United Kingdom. A few tables in *Regional Trends 33* continue to be presented on this classification. The SSRs are shown in a map on page 214 and their relationship to the GORs is given in a table on page 12.

Sub-regions of England

The implementation of local government reorganisation in England, which has taken place in four phases on 1 April in each year between 1995 and 1998, is summarised below. The reorganisation involves only the non-metropolitan counties. Unitary Authorities have replaced the two-tier system of County Councils and Local Authority District Councils in parts of some shire counties and in some instances across the whole county. The local government structure at 1 April 1997 is used in Chapter 14 and throughout the rest of the book unless otherwise specified. A map showing these boundaries is given on page 165.

Counties, Districts and Unitary Authorities in England

	Non-metropolitan areas			Metropolitan areas	
Year	Counties	Districts	Unitary Authorities	London boroughs	Metropolitan boroughs
1994	39	296	0	33	36
1995	38	294	1	33	36
1996	35	274	14	33	36
1997	36	260	27	33	36
1998	34	238	46	33	36

Unitary Authorities of Wales

On 1 April 1996, the 8 counties and 37 districts of Wales were replaced by 22 Unitary Authorities. A map is given on page 198. In Chapter 15, the Unitary Authorities are presented in the tables in geographical order from North to South.

New Councils of Scotland

On 1 April 1996, the 10 Local Authority regions and 56 districts of Scotland were replaced by 32 Unitary Councils. A map is given on page 204. In Chapter 16, the New Councils are presented in the tables in alphabetical order.

Northern Ireland

The 26 districts of Northern Ireland are listed in Chapter 17. For some topics, they have been grouped into either the five Education and Library Boards or the four Health and Social Services Boards. For the claimant unemployment rates in Map 5.24 the travel-to-work areas are used. The districts comprising the Education and Library Boards are as follows:

Board	Districts
Belfast	Belfast
South Eastern	Ards, Castlereagh, Down, Lisburn, North Down.
Southern	Armagh,Banbridge, Cookstown, Craigavon, Dungannon, Newry and Mourne.
North Eastern	Antrim, Ballymena, Ballymoney, Carrickfergus, Coleraine, Larne, Magherafelt, Moyle, Newtownabbey.
Western	Derry, Fermanagh, Limavady, Omagh, Strabane.

Health and Social Services Boards are as follows:

Northern	as North Eastern Education and Library Board but including Cookstown.
Eastern	as South Eastern Education and Library Board but including Belfast.
Southern	as Southern Education and Library Board but excluding Cookstown.
Western	as Western Education and Library Board.

Maps of the Boards are on page 210.

Standard Statistical Regions

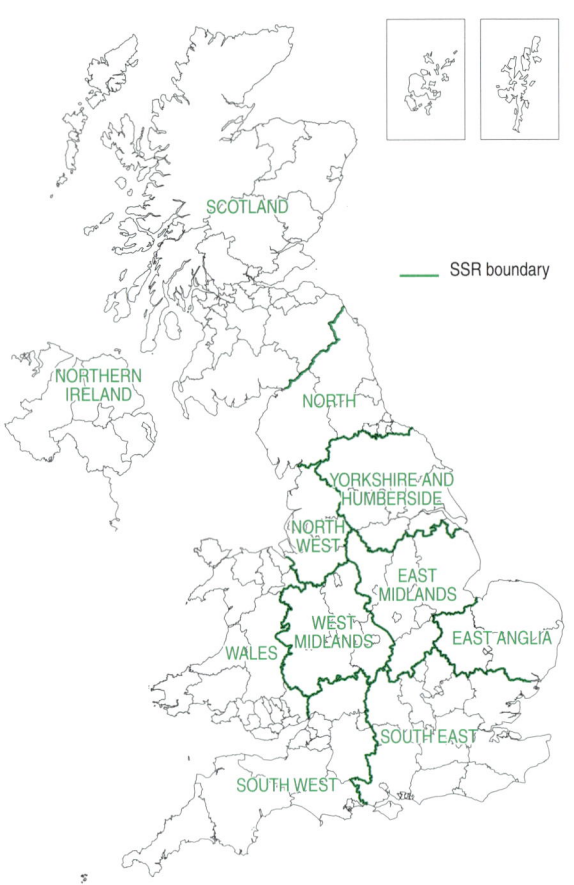

SSR boundary

SCOTLAND

NORTHERN IRELAND

NORTH

YORKSHIRE AND HUMBERSIDE

NORTH WEST

EAST MIDLANDS

WEST MIDLANDS

EAST ANGLIA

WALES

SOUTH EAST

SOUTH WEST

Environment Agency regions

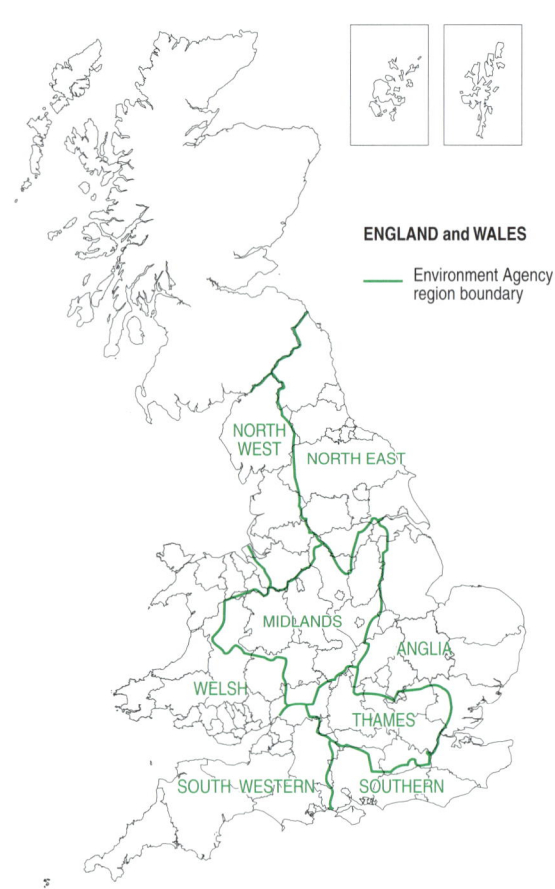

ENGLAND and WALES

Environment Agency region boundary

NORTH WEST

NORTH EAST

MIDLANDS

ANGLIA

WELSH

THAMES

SOUTH WESTERN

SOUTHERN

Regional Health Authority areas
(up to 31 March 1994)

ENGLAND and WALES

Health authority boundary

NORTHERN

YORKSHIRE

N WESTERN

MERSEY

TRENT

WEST MIDLANDS

EAST ANGLIA

WALES

NW THAMES

OXFORD

NE THAMES

SE THAMES

SOUTH WESTERN

WESSEX

SW THAMES

NHS Regional Office areas
(from April 1996)

ENGLAND and WALES

Health Authority boundary

NORTHERN & YORKSHIRE

NORTH WEST

TRENT

WEST MIDLANDS

WALES

ANGLIA & OXFORD

NORTH THAMES

SOUTH & WEST

SOUTH THAMES

Police Force areas

ENGLAND and WALES

— Police Force area boundary

Department of Trade and Industry regions

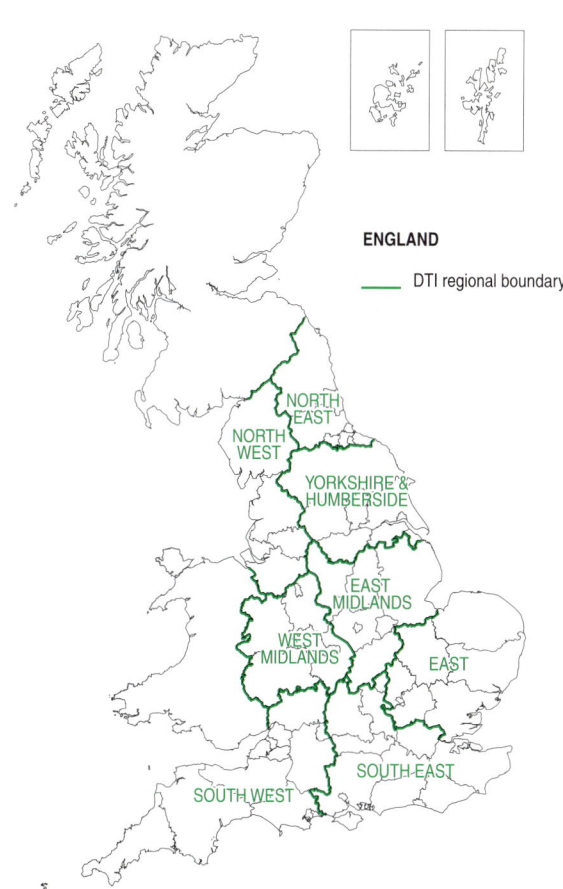

ENGLAND

— DTI regional boundary

Tourist Board regions

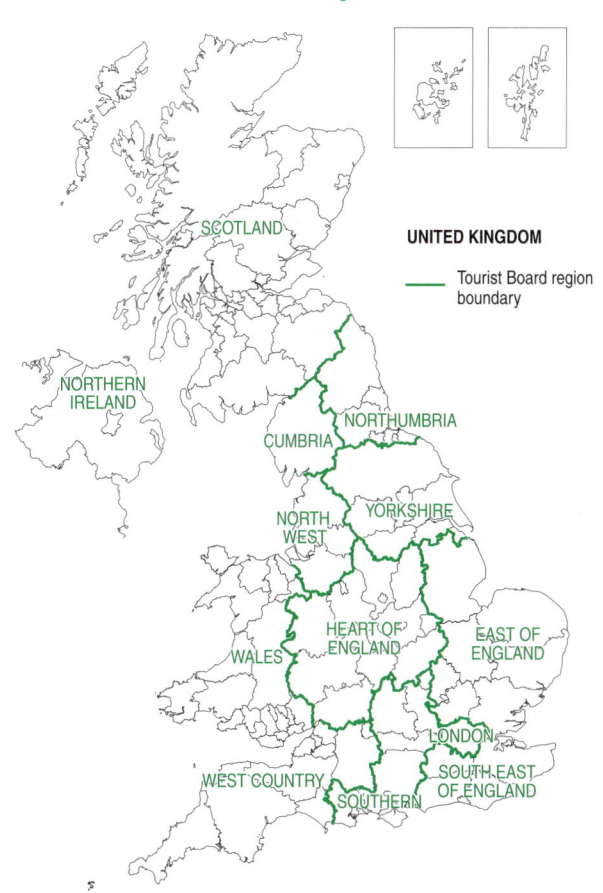

UNITED KINGDOM

— Tourist Board region boundary

Other Regional Classifications

Maps of non-standard regions used in *Regional Trends* are shown on pages 214 and 215.

The UK Continental Shelf is treated as a separate region in Tables 12.1, 12.3 and 12.10 (see Notes and Definitions to the Regional accounts chapter).

**CHAPTER 1:
REGIONAL PROFILES**

The Regional Profiles do not highlight much information from Chapter 7: Health due to the boundary differences between the GORs and the Regional Health Authority areas.

**CHAPTER 2:
EUROPEAN UNION
REGIONAL STATISTICS**

The data appearing in this section are based on information in the statistical database REGIO produced by the Statistical Office of the European Communities (EUROSTAT) which uses the Nomenclature of Territorial Units for Statistics (NUTS) classification.

NUTS provides a single, uniform breakdown of territorial units for producing regional statistics across the European Union. It has been used since 1988 in Community legislation for determining the distribution of the Structural Funds. The current NUTS nomenclature includes the main levels of spatial disaggregation used within the United Kingdom for statistical purposes.

NUTS-1 is equivalent to the Standard Statistical Regions (SSRs), which have been used widely for presenting regional statistics since the 1960s, for instance in *Regional Trends*. NUTS-2 level was devised purely for European purposes and comprises counties or groups of counties, but has been used very little for internal UK purposes. NUTS-3 and NUTS-4, equivalent to the two tiers of local government - counties and districts - have been used wherever lower level disaggregation is possible and required. NUTS-5, currently wards, have mainly been used as the building blocks for analysing Census data, and in particular for deriving travel-to-work areas.

In the light of local government reorganisation in England, Wales and Scotland and the change from the SSRs to the Government Office Regions as the primary classification for the presentation of regional statistics within England, the United Kingdom is seeking the agreement of Eurostat to the modification of the NUTS structure. Further details are available on request from the ONS. The presentation order for the English regions in the tables reflects the existing NUTS classification.

Table 2.3 Economic statistics

Employment statistics are derived from the annual Community Labour Force Survey (CLFS), which uses national Labour Force Survey (LFS) data although there may be minor differences in interpretation compared with the national LFS. Since the survey is conducted on a sample basis, results relating to small regions should be treated with caution. One of the main statistical objectives of the CLFS is to divide the population of working age into three groups: persons in employment, unemployed persons and inactive persons (those not classified as employed or unemployed). The groups are used to derive the following measures: activity rates - the labour force as a percentage of the population of working-age; employment/population ratios - persons in employment as a percentage of the population of working-age; and unemployment rates - unemployed persons as a percentage of the labour force.

The definitions of employment and unemployment used in the CLFS closely follow those adopted by the 13th International Conference of Labour Statisticians and promulgated by the International Labour Organisation (ILO) and are as follows (further detail is available in the EUROSTAT publication *Labour Force Survey, Methods and Definitions, 1992*):

Employment: the employed comprise all persons above a specified age who during a specified brief period either one week or one day were in the following categories:
a) paid employment - at work or with a job but not at work ie temporarily absent but in receipt of a wage or salary;
b) self-employment - at work ie persons who during the reference period performed some work for profit or family gain, in cash or kind, or with an enterprise but not at work ie temporarily absent. (An 'enterprise' may be a business enterprise, a farm or a service undertaking.)

Unemployment: the unemployed comprise all persons above a specified age who, during the reference period, were:
a) without work - ie were not in paid employment or self-employment;
b) currently available for work - ie were available for paid employment or self-employment during the reference period;
c) seeking work - ie had taken specific steps in a specified recent period to seek paid employment or self-employment.

The type of employment is classified by Economic activity in accordance with the General Classification of Economic Activities in the European Communities (NACE): Agriculture (NACE code O), Industry (NACE codes 1 to 5) and Services (NACE codes 6 to 9).

Long-term unemployment: persons who have been unemployed for 12 or more consecutive months.

Purchasing Power Standard: a unit of measurement which expresses an identical volume of goods and services for each country taking account of differences in price levels.

**Chart 7.13 Cancer:
Directly age-standardised
registration rates**

The directly age-standardised rates in each country and region of the United Kingdom have been calculated using the European standard population. This is done by multiplying the age specific incidence rates in each area by the number of people in the corresponding age groups in the standard population and summing to give the overall rate per 100,000 population. This gives comparable overall rates for areas which have different population structures. The standardised incidence of selected cancer sites in each area have been compared with the United Kingdom as a whole (expressed as the ratio of the rates multiplied by 100).

Directly age-standardised registration rates for the United Kingdom, 1992 are:

Selected sites	Males	Females
Lung	91.8	35.3
Colorectal	54.3	37.0
Breast	..	106.7
Prostate	54.6	.

**Tables 7.12 and 7.14
Age-adjusted mortality rates**

Mortality rates vary with age so the rates for different areas can be affected by the age structure of their populations. The figures in Tables 7.12 and 7.14 have been adjusted to take account of these differences in age structure. The rates have been standardised to the mid-1991 UK population for males and females separately: this means it is permissible to compare rates across areas for each gender, but not to compare male and female rates.

The causes of death included in Table 7.14 correspond to International Classification of Diseases (9th Revision) codes as follows: all circulatory diseases - 390-459; ischaemic heart disease - 410-414; cerebrovascular disease - 430-438; all respiratory diseases - 460-519; bronchitis et al - 490-493 +496; cancers (malignant neoplasms) - 140-208; all injuries and poisonings - 800-999; road traffic accidents - E810-E819; suicides and open verdicts -E950-E959 and E980-E989.

7.15 NHS hospital waiting lists

The waiting list figures are resident-based. That is, they are based on figures received from Health Authorities and not from Hospital Trusts where treatment is to be undertaken. For England, resident-based returns exclude all patients living outside England and all privately funded patients waiting for treatment in NHS hospitals. However, they do include NHS funded patients, living in England, who are waiting for treatment in Scotland, Wales and Northern Ireland, abroad, and at private hospitals, which are not included in the corresponding provider based returns.

Data for Scotland are derived from NHS Trusts returns and are collected for days waiting. Patients whose area of residence was outside Scotland or was not recorded are included; Scottish residents awaiting treatment outside Scotland are excluded. The figures exclude privately funded patients waiting for treatment in NHS hospitals in Scotland.

Figures for Northern Ireland are provider-based. They include all patients waiting for treatment at NI Trusts including private patients and patients from outside Northern Ireland.

Mean waiting time:

This is calculated approximately for any category as the total waiting times for patients still on the list for that category divided by the corresponding number of people waiting in that category.

Median waiting time:

The waiting time for the middle case of those still on the list when the cases are ranked by waiting time. The waiting time of 50 per cent of those patients will be less than the median length. This is a better indicator of the 'average' case since it is generally unaffected by abnormally long or short waiting times at the end of the distribution.

Table 7.16 Hospital activity

Data for England are based on Finished Consultant Episodes (FCEs). An FCE is a completed period of care of a patient using an NHS hospital bed, under one consultant within one health care provider (an NHS Trust or a Directly Managed Unit). If a patient is transferred from one consultant to another, even if this is within the same provider, the episode ends and another one begins. The transfer of a patient from one hospital to another with the same consultant and within the same provider does not end the episode. Data for Wales, Scotland and Northern Ireland are based on a system where transfers between consultants do not count as a discharge except in Scotland where figures include patients transferred from one consultant to another within the same hospital, provided there is a change of specialty. Transfers from one hospital to another, with the same consultant, however, count as a discharge. New-born babies are included for Northern Ireland but excluded for the other countries. Deaths are included in all four countries.

For Scotland figures include NHS beds/activity in Joint-User and Contractual Hospitals; these hospitals account for a relatively small proportion of total NHS activity. This is a change in presentation from previous years. In 1996-97 a change in recording practice was phased in across Scotland; in-patient and day case figures are equivalent to information presented for previous years. For out-patient data, the change in recording has meant a slight discontinuity with data for earlier years.

A day case is a person who comes for investigation, treatment or operation under clinical supervision on a planned non-resident basis, who occupies a bed for part or all of that day, and who returns home as planned the same day.

An out-patient is defined as a person attending a consultant's out-patients' department for treatment or advice. A new out-patient is one whose first attendance of a continuous series (or single attendance where relevant) at a clinical out-patient department for the same course of treatment falls within the period under review. Each out-patient attendance of a course or series is included in the year in which the attendance occurred. Persons attending more than one department are counted in each department.

Mean duration of stay: this is calculated for any category as the total bed-days for that category divided by the number of ordinary admissions (Finished Consultant Episodes in England and Northern Ireland) for that category. An ordinary admission is one where the patient is expected to remain in hospital for at least one night. For Scotland figures exclude learning disabilities.

Table 7.18 NHS Hospital and Community Health Service directly employed staff

General Medical Practitioners (ie family GPs), General Dental Practitioners, the staff employed by the practitioners, pharmacists in General Pharmaceutical Services and staff working in other contracted out services are not included in the figures.

Medical and dental staff included are those holding permanent paid (whole-time, part-time and part-time sessional) and/or honorary appointments in NHS hospitals and Community Health Services. Figures include clinical assistants and hospital practitioners. Occasional sessional staff in Community Health Medical and Dental Services for whom no whole-time equivalent is collected are not included. The whole-time equivalent of staff holding appointments with more than one region is included in the appropriate region.

Nursing, midwifery and health visiting staff excludes nurse teachers, nurses in training and students on '1992' courses. Scientific, therapeutic and technical staff comprises of Scientific and Professional and Technical staff. Administration and estates comprises of Administration and Clerical, Senior Managers and Works staff. Other staff comprises PAMs, Ancillary, Trades and Ambulance staff.

Table 7.19 General practitioners

The figures for General Medical Practitioners (GPs) relate to unrestricted principals. An unrestricted principal is a practitioner who provides the full range of general medical services but whose list is not limited to any particular group of persons. In a few cases, he/she may be relieved of the liability for emergency calls out-of-hours from patients other than his/her own. Doctors may also practice in the general medical services as restricted principals, assistants, associates or GP Registrars.

The figures for General Dental Practitioners include principals, assistants and vocational trainees in the General Dental Service. Salaried dentists are excluded. Neither the Hospital Dental Service nor the Community Dental Service are reflected.

CHAPTER 8: LIFESTYLES

Comparability of earnings statistics

Earnings statistics shown in this and the labour market sections are not comparable owing to differences in the coverage of the surveys, differences in classifying individuals to regions and different levels of reliability of the regional data. The bases of the surveys differ, in that the Survey of Personal Incomes is a sample of administrative records, the Family Expenditure Survey is a sample of households and the New Earnings Survey is a sample of employees. The administrative and household surveys are classified according to regions of residence while the surveys of employees and firms are classified according to the region of work place. The reliability depends partly upon the size of the sample and response rates. Different surveys will have their own sources of bias which will affect the reliability of their results.

Tables 8.1 and 8.2 Household income

The Family Expenditure Survey (FES) is a continuous, random sample survey of private households in the United Kingdom and collects information about incomes as well as detailed information on expenditure. All members of the household aged 16 or more keep individual diaries of all spending for a period of two weeks. In 1996-97, 6,415 households took part in the survey.

See the FES annual report, *Family Spending*, for a description of the concepts used and details of the definitions of expenditure and income.

Tables 8.3, 8.4, 8.7 and 8.13 Family Resources Survey (FRS)

The Family Resources Survey (FRS) is a continuous survey of over 25 thousand private households in Great Britain and is sponsored by the Department of Social Security. Results are based on unweighted survey data which are unadjusted for non response. The overall response rate was 69 per cent for 1996-97 but varied regionally. In common with other surveys, there is evidence to suggest some problems of misreporting certain types of benefit, such as the under-reporting of Income Support, where respondents have stated that all money received comes from a single benefit eg Retirement Pension or Unemployment Benefit.

Table 8.3 Measure of income

The measure of income used in compiling Table 8.3 is that used in the Department of Social Security's Households Below Average Income. The income of a household is the total income of all members of the household after the deduction of income tax, National Insurance contributions, contributions to occupational pension schemes, additional voluntary contributions to personal pensions, maintenance/child support payments and Council Tax. Income includes earnings from employment and self-employment, social security benefits including Housing Benefit, occupational and private pensions, investment income, maintenance payments, educational grants, scholarships and top-up loans and some in-kind benefits such as luncheon vouchers. Income is adjusted for household size and composition by means of the McClements equivalence scale (see below). This reflects the common sense notion that a household of five will need a higher income than a single person living alone to enjoy a comparable standard of living. The total equivalised income of a household is used to represent the income level of every individual in that household; all individuals are then ranked according to this level.

McClements equivalence scale

	Before housing costs
Household member:	
First adult (head)	0.61
Spouse of head	0.39
Other second adult	0.46
Third adult	0.42
Subsequent adults	0.36
Each dependent aged:	
0-1	0.09
2-4	0.18
5-7	0.21
8-10	0.23
11-12	0.25
13-15	0.27
16 or over	0.36

Table 8.5 and Chart 8.6 Survey of Personal Incomes

The Survey of Personal Incomes uses a sample of around 80 thousand cases drawn from all individuals for whom income tax records are held by the Inland Revenue: not all cases in the sample are taxpayers - about 6 per cent do not pay tax because the operation of personal allowances and reliefs removes them from liability. The data in Table 8.5 relate to individuals whose income over the year amounted to the threshold for operation of Pay-As-You-Earn (£3,525 in 1995-96) or more. Below this threshold, coverage of incomes is incomplete in tax records. A more complete description of the survey appears in *Inland Revenue Statistics*.

Table 8.5 Distribution of income liable to assessment for tax

The income shown is that which is liable to assessment in the tax year. In most cases, this is the amount earned or receivable in that year, but for business profits and professional earnings the assessments are normally based on the amount of income arising in the trading account ending in the previous year. Those types of income that were specifically exempt from tax eg certain social security benefits are excluded.

Incomes are allocated to regions according to the place of residence of the recipient, except for the self-employed, where allocation is according to the business address. For many self-employed people home address and business address are the same, and for the majority the region will correspond.

The table classifies incomes by range of total income. This is defined as gross income, whether earned or unearned, including estimates of employees' superannuation contributions, but after deducting employment expenses, losses, capital allowances, and any expenses allowable as a deduction from gross income from lettings or overseas investment income. Superannuation contributions have been estimated and distributed among earners in the Survey of Personal Incomes consistently with information about numbers contracted in or out of the State Earnings Related Pension Scheme and the proportion of their earnings contribution. The coverage of unearned income also includes estimates of that part of the investment income (whose liability to tax at basic rate has been satisfied at source) not known to tax offices.

Sampling errors need to be borne in mind when interpreting small differences in income distributions between regions.

Chart 8.6 Average total income and average income tax payable

Income tax is calculated as the liability for the income tax year, regardless of when the tax may have been paid or how it was collected.

The income tax liability shown here is calculated from the individual's total income, including tax credits on dividends, and interest received after the deduction of tax grossed up at the appropriate rate. Allowable reliefs etc, and personal allowances are deducted from total income in order to calculate the tax liability. However, relief given at source on mortgage interest is not deducted as it cannot be estimated with sufficient reliability at regional level.

The average of total incomes for males and females by Government Office Region are based on all individuals with total income in excess of the single person's allowance, which was £3,525 in 1995-96. This will include some individuals who are not liable to tax because of the operation of their personal allowances and reliefs. The average income tax payable for males and females by Government Office Region are based on those individuals who are liable to tax.

Table 8.7 Households in receipt of benefit

See notes on Family Resources Survey above.

Income Support is a non-contributory benefit payable to people working less than 16 hours a week, whose incomes are below the levels (called 'applicable amounts') laid down by Parliament. The applicable amounts generally consist of personal allowances for members of the family and premiums for families, lone parents, pensioners, the disabled and carers. Amounts for certain housing costs (mainly mortgage interest) are also included.

Housing Benefit is administered by local authorities. People are eligible only if they are liable to pay rent in respect of the dwelling they occupy as their home. Couples are treated as a single benefit unit. The amount of benefit depends on eligible rent, income, deductions in respect of any non-dependants and the applicable amount. 'Eligible rent' is the amount of a tenant's rental liability which can be met by Housing Benefit. Payments made by owner-occupiers do not count. Deductions are made for service charges in rent which relate to personal needs.

Council Tax Benefit is also administered by local authorities. Generally, it mirrors the Housing Benefit scheme in the calculation of the claimant's applicable amount, resources and deductions in respect of any non-dependants.

Unemployment Benefit (UB) was payable to those who were unemployed, available for, and actively seeking employment, satisfy conditions for the receipt of UB and were free from certain grounds for disallowance or disqualification. If National Insurance contribution conditions were satisfied in full, UB was normally payable at a standard rate with additional components for dependants. Jobseeker's Allowance (JSA) replaced Unemployment Benefit and Income Support for unemployed people on 7 October 1996. There are contribution-based and income-based routes of entry to JSA. Both types of JSA are included under the Unemployment Benefit/Jobseeker's Allowance column of the table.

Retirement Pensions are paid to men aged 65 or over and women aged 60 or over who have paid sufficient National Insurance contributions over their working life. A wife who cannot claim a pension in her own right may qualify on the basis of her husband's contributions. The table excludes non-contributory pensions which are paid to people aged 80 or over who did not qualify for the standard retirement pension, or whose pension was lower than the non-contributory rate.

Incapacity Benefit replaced Sickness and Invalidity Benefits from 13 April 1995. It is paid to people who are assessed as being incapable of work and who meet the contribution conditions. The figures do not include expenditure for Statutory Sick Pay (SSP).

Industrial injuries includes pensions, gratuities and sundry allowances for disablement and specified deaths arising from industrial causes.

Child Benefit is normally paid for children up to the age of 16. Benefit may continue up to age 19 for children in full-time education up to 'A' level standard. 16 and 17 year olds are also eligible for a short period after leaving school.

A brief description of the main features of the various benefits paid in Great Britain is set out in *Social Security Statistics* (published annually by TSO). Detailed information on benefits paid in Northern Ireland is contained in *Northern Ireland Annual Abstract of Statistics* and *Northern Ireland Social Security Statistics*.

Chart 8.8 Children's spending

For the first time in 1995-96, as part of the Family Expenditure Survey, children aged between 7 and 15 were asked to complete diaries of their daily expenditure. In the 1996-97 survey, 1,993 children from 1,286 households in Great Britain completed diaries over a two week period .

Expenditure covers anything children buy with their own money. The data in the chart do not therefore include money spent on children. They include money spent by children on school dinners, and on fares to and from school. However, money spent direct by the parent on these items is excluded. Spending by the child on behalf of the parent is also excluded, eg where the child is given money to buy a loaf of bread from the local shop.

Chart 8.9 Charitable giving

The figures relate to charitable donations and subscriptions (excluding entrance fees to bazaars, jumble sales, etc). This included animal charity, Big Issue (charity), blind box, cancer league, candles (church), carol singers, charity collection, church collection, donation to charity, Gold Heart (charity), Marie Curie Memorial Foundation, missionary box, Mothers Union collection, Poppy (charity), Red Cross donation, Rugby Life Line, Salvation Army, school fund, sponsor money, Sunday School collection.

Table 8.10 Household expenditure

This table contains results from the Family Expenditure Survey for 1996-97. Some details of the survey are given in the notes to Tables 8.1 and 8.2.

Expenditure excludes savings or investments (eg life assurance premiums), income tax payments, National Insurance contributions, housing benefit and mortgage and other payments for the purchase of, or major additions to, dwellings.

Housing expenditure of households living in owner-occupied dwellings consists of the payments by these households for Council Tax (rates in Northern Ireland), water, ground rent, etc, insurance of the structure and mortgage interest payments. Mortgage capital repayments and amounts paid for the outright purchase of the dwelling or for major structural alterations are not included as housing expenditure.

Estimates of household expenditure on a few items are below those which might be expected by comparison with other sources eg alcoholic drink, tobacco and, to a lesser extent, confectionery and ice cream.

Tables 8.11 and 8.12 National Food Survey

The National Food Survey (NFS) is a continuous sample survey in which about 7-8,000 households per year in GB keep a record of the type, quantity and costs of foods entering the home during a one week period. Nutritional intakes are estimated from the survey data. Recent developments include, from 1996, the participation in the survey of about 600 households in Northern Ireland (though figures quoted in this report and elsewhere still generally cover GB for the sake of continuity). From 1994, data are also available on food eaten out in Great Britain (but not Northern Ireland).

Detailed survey results and definitions are published by The Stationery Office in an annual report *National Food Survey*.

Table 8.16 Local voluntary work

The Survey of English Housing interviews one person in each household - almost always the household head or their partner. Therefore, for convenience, the respondents in Table 8.16 are referred to as 'householders'.

The table shows the proportions of householders who had been involved in some form of voluntary work to improve their local area or neighbourhood in the 12 months prior to the survey in 1996-97. This could include:
. improving local people's quality of life (eg being involved with cultural, sport or health activities);
. helping with activities for local children;
. improving the local environment;
. tackling crime and improving community safety (such as being involved with Neighbourhood Watch);
. involvement with local employment initiatives (eg helping the unemployed get back to work, such as unemployment worker centres or work placement groups);
. addressing local housing issues;
. improving local people education skills (eg as a school governor or involvement in PTA work, adult education or voluntary training scheme).

CHAPTER 9: CRIME AND JUSTICE

There are three main reasons why the recorded crime figures for Scotland and the notifiable offences figures for England and Wales and Northern Ireland cannot be compared. They are as follows:

(i)   Differences in legal systems. The legal system operating in Scotland differs from that in England and Wales and Northern Ireland.

(ii)   Differences in classification. The offences included within the recorded crime categories and the notifiable offence categories vary significantly. For example, simple possession of a controlled drug is **included** in the Scottish figures and in those for Northern Ireland but excluded from notifiable offences figures in England and Wales.

(iii) Counting rules. In Scotland **each** individual offence occurring within an incident is recorded whereas in England and Wales and Northern Ireland a principal offence rule is applied (in general) ie only the main offence is counted.

Tables 9.1, 9.3-9.7 and Map 9.9

The figures are compiled from police returns to the Home Office or directly from court computer systems, from police returns to The Scottish Office Home Department and from statistics supplied by the Royal Ulster Constabulary in Northern Ireland.

In England and Wales and Northern Ireland, indictable offences cover those offences which must or may be tried by jury in the Crown Court and include the more serious offences. Summary offences are those for which a defendant would normally be tried at a magistrates' court and are generally less serious - the majority of motoring offences fall into this category. In general in Northern Ireland non-indictable offences are dealt with at a magistrates' court. Some indictable offences can also be dealt with there.

In Scotland the term 'crimes' is generally used for the more serious criminal acts (roughly equivalent to indictable offences); the less serious are termed 'offences', although the term 'offence' is also used in relation to serious breaches of criminal law. The majority of cases are tried summarily (without a jury) in the Sheriff or District Court, while the more serious cases are tried in the Sheriff Court under solemn procedure (with a jury), or in the High Court. With effect from April 1996 (the date which the relevant section of the *Criminal Procedure (Scotland) Act 1995* came into force) 'offending while on bail' is no longer an offence in its own right and therefore does not appear in the recorded crime figures for Scotland. Thus, to facilitate across year comparisons, such offences have been removed from the historical recorded crime figures.

Cautions - if a person admits to committing an offence he may be given a formal police caution by, or on the instruction of, a senior police officer as an alternative to court proceedings. The figures exclude informal warnings given by the police, written warnings issued for motoring offences and warnings given by non-police bodies eg a department store in the case of shoplifting. Cautions by the police are not available in Scotland, but warnings may be given by the Procurator Fiscal.

Tables 9.2, 9.12 and 9.13 Crime Surveys

The British Crime Survey (BCS) was conducted by the Home Office in 1982, 1984, 1988, 1992, 1994 and 1996. Each survey measured crimes experienced in the previous year, including those not reported to the police. The survey also covers other matters of Home Office interest including fear of crime, contacts with the police, and drug use. The 1996 survey had a nationally representative sample of 16,300 people aged 16 and over in England and Wales. The sample was drawn from the Postcode Address File - a listing of all postal delivery points. The response rate was 83 per cent.

Scotland participated in sweeps of the British Crime Survey in 1982 and 1988 and ran its own Scottish Crime Surveys in 1993 and 1996 based on nationally representative samples of 5,000 respondents aged 16 or over interviewed in their homes. In addition 495 young people aged between 12 and 15 completed questionnaires in 1993 and 353 completed questionnaires in the 1996 survey. Addresses were randomly generated from the Postcode Address file in 1993 and 1996. Both the 1993 and 1996 surveys had response rates of 77 per cent.

The Northern Ireland Crime Survey was commissioned by the Northern Ireland Office in 1994. The survey was conducted throughout Northern Ireland and fieldwork took place between October 1994 and January 1995. Almost 3,000 people aged 16 years and above participated in the survey. They were sampled from the rating valuation list which is the most up-to-date listing of private households in Northern Ireland. The response rate was 72 per cent.

In each of the surveys, respondents answered questions about offences against their household (such as theft or damage of household property) and about offences against them personally (such as assault or robbery). However, none of the surveys provides a complete count of crime. Many offence types cannot be covered in a household survey (eg shoplifting, fraud or drug offences). Crime surveys are also prone to various forms of error, mainly to do with the difficulty of ensuring that samples are representative, the frailty of respondents' memories, their reticence to talk about their experiences as victims, and their failure to realise an incident is relevant to the survey.

Table 9.3 Clear-up rates

In England and Wales and Northern Ireland offences recorded by the police as having been cleared up include offences for which persons have been charged, summonsed or cautioned, those admitted and taken into consideration when persons are tried for other offences, and those admitted by prisoners who have been sentenced for other offences (except in Northern Ireland).

In Scotland a revised definition of cleared up came into effect from 1 April 1996. Under the revised definition a crime or offence is regarded as cleared up where there exists a sufficiency of evidence under Scots Law, to justify consideration of criminal proceedings not withstanding that a report is not submitted to the procurator fiscal because either:

i.   by standing agreement with the procurator fiscal, the police warn the accused due to the minor nature of the offence or

ii.   reporting is inappropriate due to the non age of the accused, death of the accused or other similar circumstances.

The clear-up rate is the ratio of offences cleared up in the year to offences recorded in the year. Some offences cleared up may relate to offences recorded in previous years. There is considerable variation between police forces in the emphasis placed on certain of the methods listed above and, as some methods are more resource intensive than others, this can have a significant effect on a force's overall clear-up rate.

Table 9.5 Seizure of controlled drugs

The figures in this table, which are compiled from returns to the Home Office, relate to seizures made by the police and officials of HM Customs and Excise, and to drugs controlled under the *Misuse of Drugs Act 1971*. The Act divides drugs into three categories according to their harmfulness. A full list of drugs in each category is given in Schedule 2 to the Misuse of *Drugs Act 1971*, as amended by Orders in Council.

Table 9.8 Persons found guilty of offences

The power to partly suspend certain sentences of imprisonment in England and Wales was abolished on 1 October 1992 following the implementation of Section 5 of the Criminal Justice *Act 1991*. As a result, the term 'suspended sentence' is known as 'fully suspended sentence' and 'immediate custody' includes unsuspended sentences of imprisonment and sentence to detention in a young offender institution. Fully and partly suspended sentences are not available to Scottish courts; partly suspended sentences are not available to courts in Northern Ireland.

Table 9.12 Community Attitudes Survey

The Community Attitudes Survey was commissioned in 1992 following a review of crime survey needs in Northern Ireland. Following the recommendation of the review, the Northern Ireland Statistics and Research Agency (NISRA) was commissioned to conduct a continuous survey of attitudes towards law and order named the Community Attitudes Survey. The survey was conducted by NISRA in 1992/93, 1993/94, 1994/95 and 1995/96. Each survey measured a broad range of attitudes towards crime, policing and the courts.

The 1995/96 survey was conducted throughout Northern Ireland and fieldwork took place between November 1995 and October 1996. Over 2,100 people aged 16 or over participated in the survey. The sample was drawn from the Valuation and Lands Agency list, the most up-to-date listing of private households in Northern Ireland. The response rate was 75 per cent.

CHAPTER 10: TRANSPORT

Table 10.3 Age of household cars

The main or only car available to the household applies to the vehicle with the greatest annual mileage. In the majority of cases this will be the newest car.

Table 10.4 Annual average daily flow

Traffic estimates are derived from roadside traffic counts and take two forms; occasional 12 hour counts at a large number of sites to estimate the absolute level of traffic (the 'rotating' census) and frequent counts at a small number of sites (the 'core census') to estimate changes in the amount of traffic.

Tables 10.4 and 10.5 Roads

Trunk roads: these are roads comprising the national network of through routes for which the Secretary of State for Transport, in England and the Secretaries of State for Wales and Scotland are the Highway Authorities.

Non-trunk roads: roads for which the local authorities (Unitary Authorities in Wales and Councils in Scotland) are Highway Authorities.

Principal roads: important regional or local roads for which local authorities are the Highway Authorities.

Major roads: motorways and A roads.

A Roads: trunk and principal roads (excluding motorways)

Minor roads: B,C and unclassified roads.

Built-up roads: all those having a speed limit of 40mph or less (irrespective of whether there are buildings or not).

Non built-up roads: all those with a speed limit in excess of 40 mph.

Tables 10.5-10.7 Road accidents/casualities

An accident is one involving personal injury occurring on the public highway (including footways) in which a road vehicle is involved and which becomes known to the police within 30 days. The vehicle need not be moving and it need not be in collision with anything.

Persons killed are those who sustained injuries which caused death less than 30 days after the incident.

A serious injury is one for which a person is detained in hospital as an in-patient, or any of the following injuries whether or not they are detained in hospital: fractures, concussion, internal injuries, crushing, severe cuts and lacerations, severe general shock requiring medical treatment, and injuries causing death 30 or more days after the accident.

There are many reasons why accident rates per head of population (for all roads) and per 100 million vehicle kilometres (for major roads) vary by region. They will be influenced by the mix of pedestrian and vehicle traffic within each region, which vary as a result of the considerable differences in vehicle ownership by region.

In addition, an area that 'imports' large numbers of visitors or commuters will have a relatively high proportion of accidents related to vehicles or drivers from outside the area. A rural area of low population density but high road mileage can be expected, other things being equal, to have lower than average accident rates.

The National Travel Survey (NTS) is the only comprehensive national source of travel information for Great Britain which links different kinds of travel with the characteristics of travellers and their families. Since July 1988, the NTS has been conducted on a small scale continuous basis. The last of the previous ad hoc surveys was carried out in 1985/86.

From about 3,300 households in Great Britain each year, every member provides personal information (eg age, gender, working status, driving licence, season ticket) and details of journeys carried out in a sample week, including purpose of journey, method of travel, time of day, length, duration, and cost of any tickets bought.

Travel included in the NTS covers all journeys by GB residents within Great Britain for personal reasons, including travel in the course of work. Travel information is recorded at two levels for multi-stage journeys: journey and stage.

A journey is defined as a one-way course of travel having a single main purpose. It is the basic unit of personal travel in the survey. A round trip is split into two journeys, with the first ending at a convenient point about half way round as a notional stopping point for the outward destination and return origin.

A stage is that portion of a journey defined by the use of a specific method of transport or of a specific ticket (a new stage being defined if either the mode or ticket changes).

The purpose of a journey is normally taken to be the activity at the destination, unless that destination is 'home' in which case the purpose is defined by the origin of the journey. The classification of journeys to 'work' are also dependent on the origin if the journey.

CHAPTER 11: ENVIRONMENT

The Environment Agency for England and Wales was formally created on 8 August 1995 by the *Environment Act 1995*. It took up its statutory duties on 1 April 1996.

The Agency brings together the functions previously carried out by the National Rivers Authority, Her Majesty's Inspectorate of Pollution, the waste regulatory functions of 83 local authorities and a small number of units from the then Department of the Environment dealing with the aspects of waste regulation and contaminated land. One of the key reasons for setting up the Agency was to promote a more coherent and integrated approach to environmental management.

The Agency's principal aim is to protect and improve the environment. Its business can be grouped under two broad headings: pollution prevention and control which includes regulating the disposal of controlled waste, protecting and improving the quality of rivers estuaries and coastal waters, and regulating major industrial processes, nuclear sites and premises authorised to dispose of radioactive waste; and, water management covering water resources, flood defence, fisheries, recreation, conservation and navigation.

The Agency has a budget of around £550 million per annum. About 30 per cent of this is allocated to the prevention and control of pollution; nearly 50 per cent is spent on flood defence, and the remaining 20 per cent on the Agency's other waste management functions.

The chemical quality of rivers and canal waters in the United Kingdom are monitored in a series of separate national surveys in England and Wales, Scotland and Northern Ireland. In England and Wales the National Rivers Authority (now superseded by the Environment Agency) developed and introduced the General Quality Assessment (GQA) Scheme to provide a rigorous and objective method for assessing the basic chemical quality of rivers and canals based on three determinands: dissolved oxygen, biochemical oxygen demand (BOD) and ammoniacal nitrogen. The GQA grades river stretches into six categories (A-F) of chemical quality and these in turn have been grouped into two broader groups - good/fair (classes A, B C and D) and poor/bad (classes E and F).

In Northern Ireland, the grading of the 1991 and 1995 surveys is also based on the GQA scheme. In Scotland, the chemical quality of rivers and canals is assessed using the following classes: unpolluted/fairly good, poor/grossly polluted. This system is not directly comparable with the GQA.

To provide a more comprehensive picture of the health of rivers and canals, biological testing has also been carried out. Biological grading is based on the monitoring of small animals (ie invertebrates) which live in or on the bed of the river. Research has shown that there is a relationship between species composition and water quality. Using a procedure known as the River Invertebrate Prediction and Classification System (RIVPACS), species groups recorded at a site were compared with those which would be expected to be present in the absence of pollution, allowing for the different environmental characteristics in different parts of the country. In England and Wales and Northern Ireland, two different summary statistics (known as ecological quality indices (EQI)) were calculated and the biological quality assigned to one of six bands (A-F) based on a combination of these two statistics. These six bands have been grouped into two broader groups - good/fair (classes A, B, C and D) and poor classes (E and F). In Scotland, a third EQI was also calculated and the grading system based on all three EQIs and river and canal waters classified as good/moderate or poor/very poor. The results for Scotland are not directly comparable with those of England and Wales and Northern Ireland.

Table 11.5 Water pollution incidents

The Environment Agency defines three categories of pollution incidents:

Category 1
A 'major' incident involving one or more of the following:

> a) potential or actual persistent effect on water quality or aquatic life;
> b) closure or portable water, industrial or agricultural abstraction necessary;
> c) extensive fish kill;
> d) excessive breaches or consent conditions;
> e) extensive remedial measures necessary;
> f) major effect or amenity value.

Category 2
A 'significant' pollution which involves one or more of the following:

> a) notification to abstractors necessary;
> b) significant fish kill
> c) measurable effect on invertebrate life:
> d) water unfit for stock;
> e) bed of watercourse contaminated;
> f) amenity value to the public, owners or user reduced by odour or appearance.

Category 3
'Minor suspected or probable ' pollution which, on investigation, proven unlikely to be capable of substantiation or to have no notable effect.

Map 11.8 Ground level ozone levels

Ground level ozone (O_3) occurs naturally but levels can be increased when nitrogen oxides and other pollutants react with strong sunlight. Episodes in which concentrations rise substantially above background levels occur in summer heat waves when there are long hours of bright sunlight, temperatures above 20°c, and little or no winds. At ground level O_3 can affect human health and can damage crops.

Map 11.9 Outdoor gamma-ray dose rates

Some of the naturally-occurring radionuclides in rocks, soils and building materials emit gamma rays. The gamma levels also contain a minor component from radionuclides on the ground which have arrived from washout by rain, etc and simple settling of fallout. The units used on this map are nSv $=10^{-6}$ millisieverts, the average annual dose from natural gamma radiation is estimated to be 0.35 millisieverts.

Table 11.12 Land changing to urban use

Land use refers to the main activity taking place on an area of land, eg agriculture, housing. Details of changes in land use are recorded for the Department of the Environment , Transport and the Regions by Ordnance Survey as part of its map revision programme. Under this programme, physical development (eg housing) tends to be recorded relatively sooner than changes between other uses (eg agriculture and forestry), some of which may not be recorded for some years. Hence the statistics are best suited to analyses of changes to urban uses and recycling of land already in urban uses.

Map 11.14 and Table 11.15 Designated Protected areas

National Parks, Areas of Outstanding Natural Beauty in England and Wales and Northern Ireland, Defined Heritage Coasts in England and Wales and National Scenic Areas in Scotland are the major areas designated by legislation to protect their landscape importance. Green Belts have been designated in England, Scotland and Northern Ireland to restrict the sprawl of built-up areas onto previously undeveloped land and to preserve the character of historic towns. Other areas, such as National Nature Reserves, Special Protection Areas, Marine Nature Reserves, are protected for their value as wildlife habitat, in particular for endangered species. Sites in the United Kingdom are protected by Sites of Special Scientific Interest (SSSI) status.

CHAPTER 12: REGIONAL ACCOUNTS

The sources and methodology used to compile the regional accounts are given in a booklet in the *Studies in Official Statistics series* (HMSO), No 31, *Regional Accounts*, and more recently in the Eurostat publication *Methods used to compile regional accounts*.

Tables 12.1, 12.3,12.4, Chart 12.2 and Map 12.5 Gross Domestic Product (GDP)

Regional estimates of GDP are compiled as the sum of factor incomes, ie incomes earned by residents, whether corporate or individual, from the production of goods and services. This approach breaks the total down into three components: income from employment; income from self-employment and gross trading profits; and rent (including the imputed charge for consumption of non-trading capital). Stock appreciation is deducted from the sum of total domestic income to give GDP. The figures for all regions are adjusted to sum to the national totals as published in *United Kingdom National Accounts 1997* (TSO).

In order to accommodate the offshore oil and gas extraction industry in the regional accounts, a region known as the Continental Shelf is included. GDP for this region includes only profits and stock appreciation related to the offshore activities of UK and foreign contractors. The allocation of income from employment is not altered by the Continental Shelf region since throughout the regional accounts this is altered according to the region of residence of the employee.

Table 12.7 Personal income

Total personal income is an estimate of the income of the personal sector including households, other individuals and non-profit making bodies serving persons. Total personal income includes the wages and salaries of employees plus employers' contributions; self-employment income; rent, dividends, and net interest received by the personal sector; National Insurance benefits and other current grants from general government; and the imputed charge for consumption of private non-profit making bodies. Figures are also shown of personal disposable income, which is the income remaining after deduction of taxes on income, National Insurance etc. contributions, the Community Charge or Council Tax and transfers abroad (net). The Community Charge was introduced in Scotland in April 1989 and in England and Wales in April 1990 and was superseded by the Council Tax in April 1993. However, Northern Ireland has retained domestic rates. Care should therefore be taken when making comparisons between the countries of the United Kingdom, or when comparing time series, since domestic rates are not deducted when calculating personal disposable income.

Tables 12.8 and 12.9 Consumers' expenditure

Consumers' expenditure measures expenditure by households and non-profit making bodies resident in a region. Estimates are based mainly on the Family Expenditure Survey and are subject to sampling error and should be used with caution.

Up-to-date information on the data can be obtained from *Economic Trends*, No 535 June 1998 (TSO).

CHAPTER 13: INDUSTRY AND AGRICULTURE

Maps 13.1, 13.3, 13.15 and 13.16

The industrial breakdown used is in accordance with the Standard Industrial Classification (SIC) Revised 1992. Agriculture, industry and services are broken down as follows:

AGRICULTURE:

Section A	Agriculture, hunting and forestry
Section B	Fishing

INDUSTRY:

Section C	Mining and quarrying
Section D	Manufacturing
Section E	Utilities
Section F	Construction

SERVICES:

Section G	Wholesale and retail trade; repair of motor vehicles, motorcycles and personal and household goods
Section H	Hotels and restaurants
Section I	Transport, storage and communications
Section J	Financial intermediation
Section K	Real estate, renting and business activities
Section L	Public administration and defence; compulsory social security
Section M	Education
Section N	Health and social work
Section O	Other community, social and persona; service activities

Tables 13.5 and 13.6 Annual Inquiry into Production

The Annual Inquiry into Production covers UK businesses engaged in the production and construction industries: Divisions 1-5 of the Standard Industrial Classification (SIC) Revised 1980 and Section C to F of the SIC Revised 1992. Regional information is available only for manufacturing industry: ie Divisions 2-4 of the SIC 1980 and Section D of the SIC 1992.

Businesses often conduct their activities at more than one address (local unit) but it is not usually possible for them to provide the full range of data for each. For this reason, data are usually collected at the enterprise level. Gross value added (GVA) is estimated for each local unit by apportioning the total GVA for the business in proportion to the total employment at each local unit using employment from the IDBR.

Gross value added (GVA) is defined as:

The value of total sales and work done, adjusted by any changes during the year in work in progress and goods on hand for sale

> *less:* the value of purchases, adjusted by any changes in the stocks of material, stores and fuel etc.
> *less:* payments for industrial services received
> *less:* net duties and levies etc.
> *less:* the cost of non-industrial services, rates and motor vehicle licences.

GVA per head is derived by dividing the estimated GVA by the total number of people employed. The data include estimates for businesses not responding, or not required to respond, to the inquiry.

Table 13.9 Government expenditure on regional preferential assistance to industry

The types of assistance included in Table 13.9 for Great Britain are: Regional Development Grants; Regional Selective Assistance; Regional Enterprise Grants; expenditure on Land and Factories by the English Industrial Estates Corporation (until 1993-94 after which this falls under the province of the Single Regeneration Budget), Scottish Enterprise, the Welsh Development Agency; and expenditure on Land and Factories and Grants by the Development Board for Rural Wales and Highlands and Islands Enterprise.

Northern Ireland has a different range of financial incentives available and so the figures have not been aggregated into a United Kingdom total. The items included are: Industrial Development Board grants and loans; expenditure on land and factories; Standard Capital Grants; and Local Enterprise Development Unit grants and loans.

All figures are gross and include payments to nationalised industries. GB payments relate only to projects situated in the Assisted Areas of Great Britain. A map showing the areas qualifying for preferential assistance to industry was included in *Regional Trends 31.*

Table 13.10 EU Structural Funds

Funds are allocated in the prices of the year of the European Commission (EC) decision. For the majority of the allocations shown in the table, this was 1994. Those that were allocated in the prices of later years have been deflated to 1994 using EC GDP deflators.

Regions may be eligible for funding in one of three categories. 'Objective 1' funds promote the development of regions which are lagging behind the rest of the EU. To be eligible regions need to have a per capita GDP of 75 per cent or less of the EU average, although there are some exceptions to this. In these areas, emphasis is placed on creating a sound infrastructure: modernising transport and communication links, improving energy and water supplies, encouraging research and development, providing training and helping small businesses.

Areas suffering from industrial decline may be designated 'Objective 2'. These areas need help adjusting their economies to new industrial activities; they have high unemployment rates, and a high but declining share of industrial activity. EU grants may be provided to help create jobs, encourage new businesses, renovate land and buildings, promote research and development, and foster links between universities and industry.

Rural areas where economic development needs to be encouraged may be designated 'Objective 5b'. In these areas the focus is on developing jobs outside agriculture in small businesses and tourism, and improvements to transport and basic services are promoted to prevent rural depopulation.

Grants under Objectives 1, 2 and 5b are disbursed under the terms of Single Programming Documents or their equivalents, which provide a strategic framework relevant to the region concerned. The other objectives under which grants are allocated (3, 4, 5a), which cover long-term unemployment, jobs for young people and modernisation of farms, are not defined geographically. In addition the Structural Funds provide support for Community-wide Initiatives. These Initiatives account for 9 per cent of the Structural Funds budget.

A map showing the areas qualifying for EU Structural Funds under Objectives 1,2 and 5b was included in *Regional Trends 31.*

Table 13.11 Business registrations and deregistrations

Annual estimates of registrations and deregistrations are compiled by the Department of Trade and Industry. They are based on VAT information which the Office for National Statistics (ONS) holds. The estimates are a good indicator of the pattern of business start-ups and closures, although they exclude firms not registered for VAT, either because their main activity is exempt from VAT, or because they have a turnover below the VAT threshold (£49,000 with effect from 1 December 1997) and have not registered voluntarily. Large rises in the VAT threshold in 1991 and 1993 affected the extent to which the VAT system covers the small business population. This means that the estimates are not entirely comparable before and after these years.

Tables 13.17-13.20 Agricultural census

The annual census encompasses the 234 thousand main agricultural holdings in the United Kingdom in 1996. Estimates for minor holdings are included in the national totals for England, Wales and Northern Ireland; estimates are not included for Scotland or the English regions. Generally, minor holdings are characterised by a small agricultural area, low economic activity and a small labour input.

Table 13.18 Less Favoured Areas	Land in the Less Favoured Areas is commonly infertile, unsuitable for cultivation and with limited potential which cannot be increased except at excessive cost. Such land is mainly suitable for extensive livestock farming.
Table 13.19 Areas and yields	The figures for specific crops relate to those in the ground on the date of the June census or for which the land is being prepared for sowing at that date. In England and Wales cereal production is estimated from sample surveys held in September, November and April; oilseed rape production is estimated from a sample survey held in August. In Scotland, cereals and oilseed rape yields are estimated by local office staff in mid-September, followed by sample surveys later in the year. The Department of Agriculture for Northern Ireland estimates cereal and oilseed rape yields from a stratified sample survey of 200 farms carried out in the autumn of each year.
CHAPTERS 14-17: SUB-REGIONAL STATISTICS	The statistics cover: Government Office Regions, counties and where available, districts/unitary authorities in England; unitary authorities in Wales; the new areas in Scotland; Health and Social Service Boards/Education and Library Boards/districts as available in Northern Ireland. They complement the data shown regionally in Chapters 3 to 13. A wide range of data are presented, covering population, vital statistics, education, housing and households, labour market, deprivation, economic statistics and regional accounts.
	In the local authority tables for England, where data can be easily combined, county, regional and national totals are given to make comparison easier. However, it is sometimes the case that different sources of data or methodologies are used when disaggregating data to lower and lower geographical levels, and therefore it is not necessarily the case that data in this chapter are strictly comparable with data in other chapters. These data identify local as well as regional trends and because of the level of disaggregation more caution in interpretation is neccessary.
	There are specific and known problems in comparing population, employment and unemployment data for small areas. For example, for the claimant count rate the numerator is residence-based while the denominator is largely workplace-based and this should be borne in mind when comparing claimant count rates for small areas.
	Allowing for the difficulties in interpreting such geographically disaggregated data, the figures in the relevant sub-regional tables can be used to give a broad picture of a particular district and how it compares with other districts.
	The tables are intended to take a reasonably broad sweep across a range of subjects. More detailed statistics on specific topics may be readily available. For example:
	Key population and vital statistics (local and health authority areas of England and Wales)
	Local Housing Statistics England and Wales (quarterly statistics by Local Authority area)
	Projections of Households in England to 2016 (statistics for counties, metropolitan districts and London boroughs)
	Labour Market Trends (unemployment by local authority districts and parliamentary constituency).
Tables 14.3-17.3 Education	Pupils in last year of compulsory schooling with no graded results are those who either did not attempt any GCSE, GSE, CSE or SCE examinations or did not achieve a sufficient standard to be awarded a grade.
Table 14.4 Housing starts	The housebuilding figures are compiled from data provided by local authorities and by the National House-Building Council. If a local authority has not sent back statistical returns for 1996, the table shows that the data are not available. The table also shows where there has been a partial local authority response for the year. County, regional and England figures, however, include estimated figures that allow for these missing data. It is inappropriate to derive figures for any missing authorities from these estimated totals.
Tables 14.4-16.4 Council Tax	Amounts shown for Council Tax are headline Council Tax for the area of each billing authority for B and D, 2 adults, before transitional relief and benefit. The ratios of other bands are: A 6/9, B 7/9, C 8/9, E 11/9, F 13/9, G 15/9 and F 18/9.
	Averages are calculated by dividing the sum of the tax requirement for each area by the tax base for the area. The taxbase is calculated by weighting each dwelling on the valuation list to take account of exemptions, discounts and disabled relief and the valuation band it falls into. It therefore represents the number of Band D equivalent (fully chargeable) dwellings.
Table 14.6 Index of Local Deprivation	The Department of Environment, Transport and the Regions has in association with the University of Manchester, produced a new index measuring relative multiple deprivation in the districts/UA's of England. The index combines a number of indicators chosen to cover a range of economic, social, housing and environmental concerns. It is presented in the table in the form of a ranking: the greater the overall level of deprivation, the higher the position in the ranking (where '1' is higher).

There were 12 indicators: the level of unemployment; the ratio of long-term to all unemployed; Income Support recipients; children in households receiving Income Support, non-income support recipients of Council Tax Benefit; standardised mortality ratios; low educational (GCSE) attainment; low educational participation of 17 year olds; home insurance weightings (as a proxy for crime); overcrowded housing; housing lacking basic amenities; and derelict land. Full details of the index can be found in the *1998 Index of Local Deprivation - Summary of Results* - Department of the Environment, Transport and the Regions 1998.

Table 14.7 Regional accounts

Gross Domestic Product (GDP) measures the value of production of goods and services within each county of England. It does not measure the income of a county for two reasons.

Firstly, GDP excludes transfer payments such as pensions, social security, dividends and interest, which are important sources of income for residents and vary considerably between counties. Secondly, county GDP is measured on a workplace basis which means that the income from employment of commuters is attriibuted to the counties where they work rather than to those where they reside.

Comparisons of GDP between areas are usually in terms of GDP per head. However, in calculating GDP per head at county level, workplace estimates of GDP are divided by resident population: this results in very high estimates of GDP per head in urban counties where many workers are commuters, and low estimates for surrounding counties where these commuters reside. Thus the figures should be treated with caution.

The sources and methods used to compile county GDP are similar to those used for regional GDP although a simpler approach is sometimes necessary. A description of the methods is given in *Economic Trends*, No. 411 January 1988 (HMSO).

Tables 15.1-15.5 and16.1-16.5 Unitary Authority/ New Council Statistics

The warnings given above on the local authority tables for England apply to these tables. Further Unitary Authority statistics can be found in:

Wales   *Digest of Welsh Local Area Statistics 1998* (Welsh Office);

Scotland   *The New Councils: Statistical Report* (The Stationery Office).

Index

Figures in the index refer to table or chart numbers, page numbers refer to maps. The Notes and Definitions are not indexed.

Regional Trends 33, © Crown copyright 1998

Social Trends 28

OFFICE FOR
**NATIONAL
STATISTICS**

Want to know how much our lives have changed over the years?

Social Trends 28 provides a comprehensive guide to UK society today, illustrating how our lives have changed over the years and also reflecting the realities of contempory lifestyles.

Social Trends is an invaluable resource for all involved in social policy, marketing, advertising, research, journalism and teaching, as well as anyone interested in how we live today.

Published *for*
Office *for* **National Statistics** *by* The Stationery Office
Price £39.50
ISBN 0-11-620987-9